airplanes

from the dawn of flight to the present day

airplanes

from the dawn of flight to the present day

by enzo angelucci

color illustrations and design by marco rota

McGraw-Hill Book Company

New York • St. Louis • San Francisco • Toronto

Originally published in Italian under the title
GLI AEROPLANI
Copyright © 1971 by Arnoldo Mondadori Editore,
Milan

Library of Congress Cataloging in Publication Data

Angelucci, Enzo.
    Airplanes from the dawn of flight to the present day.

    Translation of Gli aeroplani.
    Bibliography: p.
    1. Aeroplanes—History. I. Title.
TL670.3.A513   629.13'09'04   72-12755
ISBN 0-07-001807-3

First published in America by
McGraw-Hill Book Company, 1973

Printed and bound in Italy
by Arnoldo Mondadori Editore, Verona

CONTENTS

INTRODUCTION

On the morning of July 16, 1969, I was at Cape Kennedy watching the first launch carrying three astronauts destined to land on the moon. I had just begun work on this book and while watching the gigantic rocket which was to carry Apollo to its challenge with space, I thought of men like the Wright brothers, Saint-Exupéry, Mermoz and Lindbergh, and was reminded of the heroic years when aviation was just beginning. I asked myself how these men would have felt if they could have been there for this launch, the beginning of such a long, mysterious and incredible voyage. Hardly 32 years had passed since one of them, Charles Augustus Lindbergh, ventured into the unknown while the world held its breath, just as it was doing now for the adventure facing Neil Armstrong, Edwin Aldrin, Jr. and Michael Collins. In 1927, the obstacle to conquer was the Atlantic: in 1969, it was the great space between Earth and the moon.

If man ventures into space today, he owes it to the miraculous developments in technical aeronautics, but most of all to the passion, courage and sacrifice of the few thousand men who, in 60 years, have been able to take the heavier-than-air machine higher and faster and further and further until it has conquered the skies. This book, not so much "written" as "composed," like a mosaic of thousands of illustrations, bits of information and data, proposes to go back over the stages on the road to progress, examining the aircraft, which, along with their designers, builders and pilots, are part of aviation's past history and its present achievements. The aircraft studied here number close to 1000, but could have been more, many more, because even the prototypes, though generally unfamiliar, merit a nod of recognition. My desire to make this book a living history and not a cold catalogue has naturally limited my choices from this vast field. But I hope that because of the inevitable omissions I will not be accused of serious negligence. I have tried not to omit any aircraft considered of "consequence" by the large public of flight enthusiasts. I have given the essential information for each aircraft; the more technical data appears in the Appendix. I have tried to "see" the airplanes as they must have appeared in their own times and in their proper settings. For the Second World War I thought it appropriate to include a chronological appendix which will help to place the aircraft within the framework of historical events of which they were often the heroes. For those readers who wish to do further research on any specific topic, I have assembled a list of titles—each important in itself—in the Bibliography.

This book is dedicated to the pioneers of aviation, the designers and the builders, but above all, it is dedicated to pilots all over the world, of all times. The British scholar Sir Walter Alexander Raleigh said that the engine is the heart of the airplane but the pilot is its soul. My thanks go to those who in war and peace have given and continue to give the flying machine a soul and who give us a new sense of man's capacities each time they repeat the miracle of flight.

THE AUTHOR

FROM LEONARDO DA VINCI TO SAMUEL LANGLEY

It is impossible to say exactly when man's mind first conceived the urge to fly, the dream of moving through the air like birds. We can safely assume that the dream first took shape in the darkness of time, since even in ancient records and legends of the remote past there is always a god, hero or king able to fly, either because he himself has wings or because he is borne by giant birds or by winged horses.

In ancient times the ability to fly was an indisputable sign of power, of the supernatural. Even if man had mastered the earth, his natural element, and had successfully faced the challenge of the seas, the sky above him was still beyond his reach. It is thus no wonder that Greek mythology is filled with gods who fly; no wonder that Roman mythology has its Mercury; that even in the first works of art in which they are represented the angels have wings, although the Bible never specifically mentions this detail. Nor is it a surprise that legends, including those of the Chinese, Persians, Norsemen and Africans, all tell of men who fly, from Icarus to Simon Magus, from the Chinese Emperor Shun to the Persian King Kai Kawus, from the Norsemen Wieland the Smith to the African Kibaga.

For centuries flight was an unfulfilled dream. Then, some began to try. The legend of Daedalus and Icarus was brought to life again when more than one man began to think that a pair of wings attached to the body would be enough to sustain him in a jump from the top of a tower. A Saracen from Constantinople believed it. Around the year 1000 the English monk Oliver believed it. Five hundred years later, the Italian Giovanni Damiani believed it. The first two died trying. The third was crippled for life.

Putting aside the legends and the dedicated crackpots whom we have mentioned, we should observe that before man could fly a number of scientific principles and notions had to be discovered. Among these: that substances lighter than air tend to rise; that air exerts pressure against all surfaces; that for every action there is an equal and opposite reaction.

It seems that the first philosopher and sage to study flight was Archytas of Taranto in 400 B.C., who built a flying machine, possibly a kite. Whether he did or not, it is certain that the Chinese preceded him by at least two centuries. At any rate, no one took advantage of his experience. Another learned man, Roger Bacon, attacked the problem 900 years later; although he made no concrete contribution to the science of flight, he did predict man's success in a time of extreme skepticism.

Actually Leonardo, born in 1452 in Vinci near Florence, was the first to approach the

(continued on page 12)

Self-portrait of Leonardo (above) and (facing) several of his sketches: study of the wing, ornithopter, machine for vertical takeoff, study of the parachute.

10

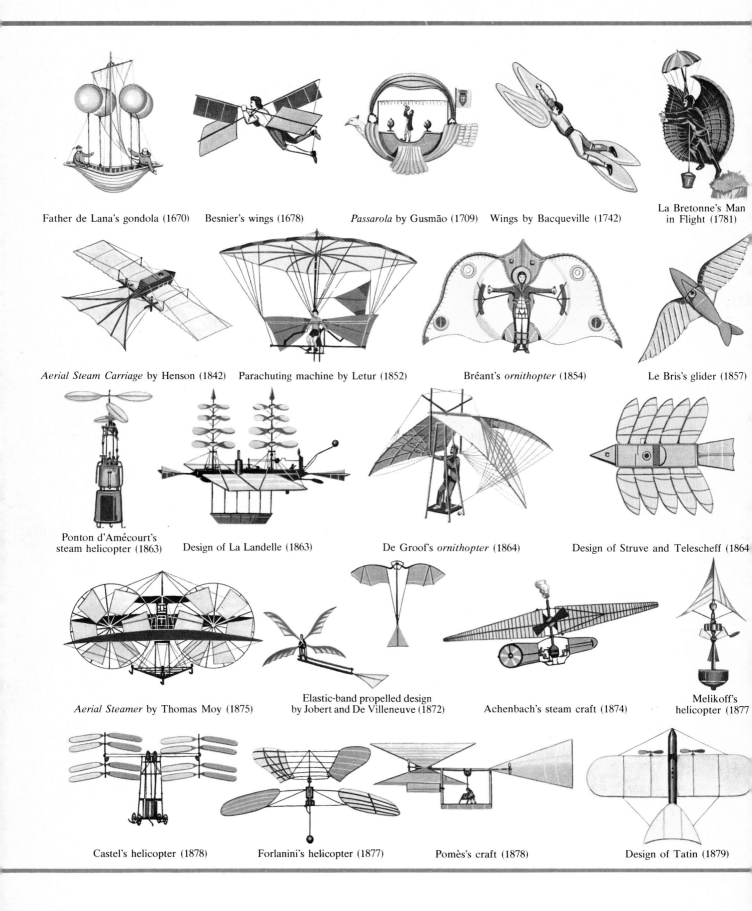

Father de Lana's gondola (1670)   Besnier's wings (1678)   *Passarola* by Gusmão (1709)   Wings by Bacqueville (1742)   La Bretonne's Man in Flight (1781)

Aerial Steam Carriage by Henson (1842)   Parachuting machine by Letur (1852)   Bréant's *ornithopter* (1854)   Le Bris's glider (1857)

Ponton d'Amécourt's steam helicopter (1863)   Design of La Landelle (1863)   De Groof's *ornithopter* (1864)   Design of Struve and Telescheff (1864)

Aerial Steamer by Thomas Moy (1875)   Elastic-band propelled design by Jobert and De Villeneuve (1872)   Achenbach's steam craft (1874)   Melikoff's helicopter (1877)

Castel's helicopter (1878)   Forlanini's helicopter (1877)   Pomès's craft (1878)   Design of Tatin (1879)

Gérard's craft (1784)

Degen's *ornithopter* (1809)

Du Temple's
steam craft (1857)

Bright's helicopter (1859)

Steam machine
by Smythies (1860)

Design of J. J. Boucart (1866)

Stringfellow's
steam triplane (1868)

Pomès and De la Pauze's
helicopter (1871)

Pénaud's monoplane (1876)

Dieuaide's machine (1877)

Dandrieux's *ornithopter* (1879)

T. Edison's flying ship (1880)

DREAMS AND VISIONS BETWEEN 1670 AND 1880

If the fruits of Leonardo's studies had not lain ignored in a drawer until quite recently, man's dream of flight might have been realized several centuries ago. But from the death of this great genius in 1519 until the first half of the last century, aeronautical progress was made in complete darkness, illuminated every now and then by some faint flashes of intuition or by some dedicated if naïve experiments.

In 1670 the Jesuit priest, Francesco de Lana, made an approximate determination of the weight of air at sea level, but he could never have succeeded in raising his ship using only four light copper spheres in which he had created a vacuum. Even if the Brazilian Jesuit Laurenço de Gusmão firmly believed in his *Passarola* (probably badly represented in the illustrations which have survived), he certainly never succeeded in building anything except a fragile glider. Although Bacqueville, Letur and De Groof were personally able to test their ornithopters (the last two died in the attempt), dozens of others never went beyond the drafting of plans for their fantastic and unrealizable projects. When men finally understood that muscle power alone was not enough to lift man off the ground and sustain him and his machine in flight no matter how light it was, they began to design for the use of the steam engine (Henson, Du Temple, Smythies, Stringfellow and others). But neither the steam engine (later used with some success in lighter-than-air flight) nor the gunpowder motor planned by Pomès and De la Pauze, could offer the correct solution for heavier-than-air flight because the weight of these engines was too great in proportion to the power created.

With these bold attempts, with the projects for vertical takeoff flight of Bright, d'Amécourt, Melikoff, Castel and Forlanini; with the dreams of La Landelle and Edison, the twentieth century dawned.

Mankind owes much to these scientists and dreamers of the last 4 centuries, for having continued to believe, in spite of their failures and disillusionments, that someday man would be able to fly; for having kept hope burning, sometimes at the price of their lives.

12

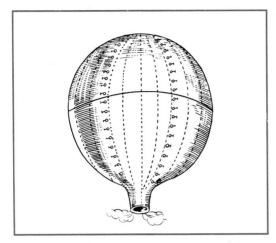

The hot-air balloon, created by Joseph and Étienne Montgolfier, which rose into the skies of Annonay, France, reached an altitude of about 6000 feet on June 4, 1783. It was the first lighter-than-air object to leave the ground.

The richly decorated *Montgolfière* which, on November 21, 1783, carried two men in flight for the first time: the Frenchmen François Pilâtre de Rozier and the Marquis d'Arlandes. The balloon flew for 35 minutes covering a distance of 5½ miles.

The *Charlière,* a hydrogen balloon which carried its inventor, J. A. C. Charles and the elder Robert brother from the Tuileries, in the heart of Paris, to Nesle about 37 miles away, on December 1, 1783. The balloon measured 27 feet, 6 inches in diameter.

problem on a scientific basis. In Milan in 1486 he began studying the wings of birds and 10 years later he drew plans for the first *orni-thopters,* machines with man-powered flapping wings. It was probably when he came to realize that man's muscle power alone was not enough to move the machine that he turned his attention to a helicopter—equipped with a helical screw-shaped spring-driven propeller—which might actually have been able to "penetrate the air" had it ever been built and tested. Leonardo also set forth the principle of the parachute, thus solving the problem of surface resistance and demonstrating his knowledge of many of the fundamental laws of physics and aerodynamics. He wrote over 5000 pages of notes, accompanied by hundreds of designs and drew plans for no less than 150 machines. At his death in 1519 this immense treasure fell into the hands of a friend who failed to recognize the extraordinary importance for humanity of Leonardo's discoveries. The papers came to light again only in the last century after the work of dozens of scholars had at last achieved the identical results. In the meantime, three centuries were lost.

Between 1519 and the middle of the 1800s, amid a host of dreamers and quacks *(pp. 10, 11),* some truly scientific minds distinguished themselves; Henry Cavendish, George Cayley and others, whose work was destined to make possible lighter-than-air and, later on, heavier-than-air flight. Still it was more through man's curiosity than scientific achievement that the miracle of flight was first realized. For centuries scholars and enthusiasts, watching fire, had seen smoke rising, never thinking that this simple phenomenon held the key to the initial solution to the problem of flight. In 1783 two Frenchmen, the brothers Joseph and Étiénne Montgolfier, owners of a paper factory in Annonay, near Lyon, responded to the clue. They thought that smoke was a "gas" and that if they could enclose it in a very light container, it would "take-off." They did not realize that smoke rises because it contains expanded warm air and is, therefore, lighter than the air of the atmosphere. But this detail didn't stop them: they conducted several successful experiments on small models, and on June 4, 1783, in the main square of Annonay where an immense fire had been lit, the first *Montgolfier* rose majestically toward the sky before an astonished and frightened crowd of peasants. Then, on November 21, 1783, with Louis XVI and Marie Antoinette looking on, for the first time man rose and floated in the air—aboard a wicker basket attached to a *Montgolfier.* The two men fortunate enough to have ventured into the air were François Pilâtre de

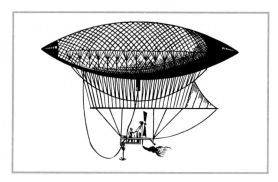

Henri Giffard's dirigible balloon, the first with mechanical propulsion (3-horsepower steam engine) which, on September 24, 1852, flew its inventor from the Paris Hippodrome to Trappes, about 17 miles away, at a speed of 5 miles per hour.

The *No. 9,* with a 3-horsepower Clement engine, one of the dirigibles built in Paris between 1898 and 1905 by the Brazilian Alberto Santos-Dumont, the first man to fly a heavier-than-air vehicle in Europe (1906).

Rozier and the Marquis d'Arlandes. Actually, 17 years earlier, science had already made a discovery which would have led to the same results. The English scientist Henry Cavendish isolated and described a gas which he called *inflammable air,* later called hydrogen by the French chemist Lavoisier in 1790.

Hydrogen, which is lighter than air, afforded an excellent substitute for warm air in the balloons. Jacques Alexandre César Charles, member of the French Academy of Science, used the gas in his *Charlière* which he launched on August 23 of that same fateful year, 1783.

The lighter-than-air men had triumphed: man was going to the clouds. The balloons—*Montgolfiers* and *Charlières*—multiplied both in number and in achievement. The Frenchman Jean-Pierre François Blanchard accompanied by the American John Jeffries, crossed the English Channel by balloon on January 7, 1785. In June of the same year Jean-François Pilâtre de Rozier died because he tried to combine hot air with hydrogen in a balloon. He had been the first to go up in a balloon and was the first to pay for such daring with his life. His death did not dampen the general enthusiasm and balloons even came to be used by the military, in the Napoleonic wars, the Franco-Prussian War of 1870—breaking the siege of Paris—and during the American Civil War as observers over enemy lines.

But in the long run, the shortcomings and limitations of the balloons became evident. Aboard them, man had risen into the air, floated on it, traveled in it; but he had not yet flown. Flight means dominating the wind, not being dominated by it. A dispute had arisen at the end of the 1700s between the partisans of lighter-than-air flight (already a reality) and the heavier-than-air school. The enthusiasts of the latter, who could not yet demonstrate their theory, claimed that the solution of their problems would assure mastery of the skies. The former, on the strength of their advantage, planned bigger and bigger balloons, with either rigid or flexible structures, gave them aerodynamic shapes, and built and equipped them with steering devices and steam engines capable of moving the rear propellers. In a word, they created the *dirigible.*

Their rivals did not give up. The success of the balloons proved to them that nothing was impossible. They drew new hope and a solid technical framework from the writings of Sir George Cayley. In 1804 Cayley wrote an unpublished *Essay upon the Mechanic Principles of Aerial Navigation.* In 1809 he wrote in *Nicholson's Journal of Philosophy* that the problem was to establish a flat surface of a given weight, pushed by a force sufficient to overcome the resistance of air, rear wings to

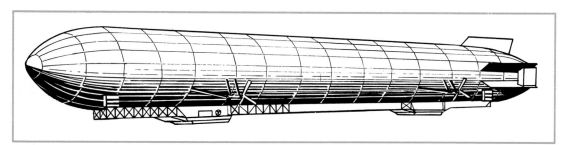

The 1900 *Zeppelin I.* Count Ferdinand von Zeppelin began constructing his revolutionary dirigibles with hard aluminum structures in 1900 on Lake Constance in Germany. On July 2, of the same year, the prototype *LZ-1,* flown by the count himself, made its first flight with 5 passengers aboard. The giants of the air built by the Prussian industrialist were widely used during World War I and later in civilian service until 1936. The *Zeppelin I* was 426 feet long, equipped with 4 Mercedes Daimler 85-horsepower motors.

The German engineer Otto Lilienthal with one of his gliders, ready to take off from a small hill. Author of the volume *Der Vogelflug als Grundlage der Fliegekunst (Bird-flight as the Basis of Aviation),* published in 1889, Lilienthal made more than 2000 glides in his monoplanes and biplanes between 1891 and 1896. He was planning to equip one of his crafts with a motor when, on August 9, 1896, he crashed from a height of 50 feet during a flight at Rhinow, and died the next day.

ensure lateral balance, an elevator to allow for take-off and landing, a steering device to provide for horizontal movement and motor-driven appurtenances equipped with propellers. It is clear from these words that Cayley had solved, at least theoretically, the major problems of flight. Shortly before his death in 1857, he stated the mathematical principles on which to base the flight of a heavier-than-air vehicle, established the fundamentals of aerodynamics, suggested the utility of bi-planes and triplanes in increasing lift without adding too much extra weight, and super-vised the construction of the first glider to carry a man in flight. Had a gas-powered engine existed in Cayley's day, it is probable that the first airplane would have been born in England.

Times change; increased communications —including journals and books—made the most important events accessible to all. In 1784, a book by the Swiss Jean Huber was published on bird flight. In 1810 a volume by the Englishman Thomas Walker appeared, entitled *Treatise Upon the Art of Flying by Mechanical Means.* In 1784 Thibaut de Saint-André, and in 1797 the Garnerin brothers contributed to advances in the parachute (in 1797 the full-size parachute was used success-fully) and also in 1797 Blanchard contributed to the structure and function of the propeller. In 1856 Le Bris presented information on the lift function of the wings. The British Aero-nautical Society was founded in 1866 and in 1868 the first World Aeronautical Exposi-tion was held in London. In 1863 Gabriel de la Landelle christened heavier-than-air flight *aviation* from the Latin *avis* (bird) and *actio* (action). Stringfellow, Du Temple, Penaud, Tatin, Maxim and Chanute are among those

who made important contributions in both scholarship and enthusiasm.

The inventor of the first airplane might have been Cayley, or perhaps Otto Lilienthal. A German engineer and inventor, Lilienthal made his debut in the aeronautical field in 1889, when he published a volume on *Bird Flight as the Basis of Aviation.* He applied his theories to the construction of numerous gliders (monoplanes, biplanes) which he personally "test flew," launching himself and the craft from a conical hill he had con-structed. The "test flights" were successful and after several hesitant hops, he was finally able to cover distances of over 800 feet, nota-ble if one considers that the glider had no thrust other than the inventor's running with it to launch it. Although initially convinced that the secret of flight was contained in moveable wing tips, like the wings of birds, Lilienthal later converted to the principle of the fixed wing and was planning to equip one of his crafts with an engine. Unfortunately on August 9, 1896, during one of his many flights at Rhinow, near Stöllen, he crashed from a height of 50 feet and died the next day.

Some maintain that the inventor of the first heavier-than-air vehicle to get off the ground was Clément Ader, an engineer from Tou-louse who, at the age of 49, built his first fly-ing machine, the *Eole,* which he tested in 1890, claiming the flight was crowned with success. The *Eole* actually lifted only a short distance from the ground. Heartened by the result, Ader had been substantially funded by the French government to research whether the craft could lift off the ground and cover a given distance, and he himself invested all he had in the construction of the *Avion III,* which he presented before the French War

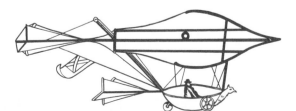

Sir George Cayley's glider. In 1852 Sir George had planned that his coachman fly it. The poor fellow quit his job, saying he was paid to drive, not to fly.

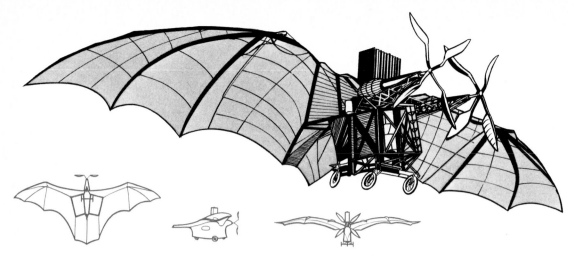

The French engineer Clément Ader's *Avion III* is the subject of controversy even today. According to some, on October 14, 1897, it lifted several feet off the ground at Satory, in the presence of War Ministry representatives, thus making it the first "heavier than air" to fly. At any rate, the contradictory eyewitness accounts tend more to deny rather than confirm Ader's claim. Others maintain that he achieved the feat earlier, on October 9, 1890, with his first craft, the *Éole,* three side views of which are shown here below the *Avion III.* The *Avion III* was equipped with two 20-horsepower steam engines.

Ministry on October 14, 1897. What happened on that foggy October day was that the plane did not fly a yard. After the experiment, the War Ministry abandoned Ader to his destiny. Among other factors the French engineer, like so many others, was betrayed by his engines, which were too heavy and too weak to lift the *Avion III* off the ground.

Six years later, newspapers all over the world loudly proclaimed the latest in a series of failures. On October 7, 1903, the hopes of Professor Samuel Pierpont Langley, of the Smithsonian Institution, and those of his pilot and engineer Charles M. Manly, crashed miserably into the waters of the Potomac River. A physicist and mathematician, Langley had devoted his attention to flight since 1890 and 6 years later succeeded in flying a small model. Sure that his theories were correct, he obtained government funds to build an aircraft of man-carrying scale. In 1901 he had successfully tested the second model, the first unmanned propeller craft driven by a

gas powered engine. Everything seemed to guarantee the success of a manned venture. The *Aerodrome,* as the craft had been christened, was to take off from a houseboat anchored in the river. On October 7, 1903, the experiment failed. The plane was repaired and retested on December 8, but again it crashed with a thud into the water and Langley's last hopes crashed with it.

The more than 100 journalists invited to witness the experiment wrote that if a man like Langley, strongly backed by the technical and financial support of the government of the United States, had failed, it meant that the problem of flying a heavier-than-air vehicle would not be solved for years to come. Little did they know that only 9 days later, on the sand dunes at the Kill Devil Hills near Kitty Hawk, two young bicycle builders without virtually any help and with just a few dollars to their name, launched a flight that would eventually silence the pessimists once and for all.

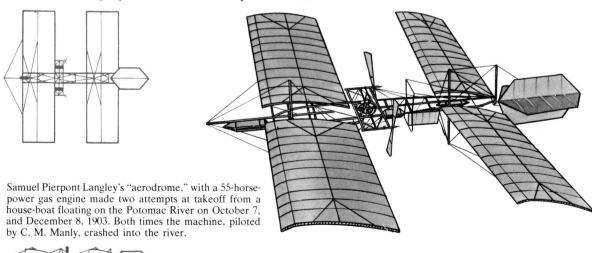

Samuel Pierpont Langley's "aerodrome," with a 55-horsepower gas engine made two attempts at takeoff from a house-boat floating on the Potomac River on October 7, and December 8, 1903. Both times the machine, piloted by C. M. Manly, crashed into the river.

16

FROM THE WRIGHT BROTHERS' FIRST FLIGHT TO 1914

In 1878 when the Protestant bishop Milton Wright chose a rudimentary model of a helicopter as a present for his young sons Wilbur, 11, and Orville, 7, he certainly never imagined that he was making history. With that toy, their passion for the problems of flight, which was to last for the rest of their lives, was born. During their school years and later as bicycle manufacturers in their hometown of Dayton, Ohio, the brothers also devoted time to their hobby of building kites.

They were already small businessmen, proud of their bicycle shop, when news reached them of the death of Otto Lilienthal. They had been following his achievements closely and decided at that point to devote even more of their time and money to their hobby. They contacted one of the most famous American civil engineers of the day, Octave Chanute, who in 1894 had published a basic text, *Progress in Flying Machines.* He had followed Lilienthal's studies more closely than anyone else in the United States. Chanute, then in his seventies, was generous with his advice to the two young men who, in October 1900, spent their vacation on the windy beaches of Kitty Hawk, North Carolina, to test their first 17-foot-span glider. Heartened by a series of successful results, the following year they went to a spot with an adequate sand hill, Kill Devil Hills (about 4 miles from Kitty Hawk), to test-fly gliders large enough to sustain man's weight. Chanute made his first of several visits to encourage them, but the tests went badly.

Although discouraged—Wilbur said, "Nobody will fly for a thousand years"—they did not give up. Quite the opposite: the brothers redoubled their efforts. By testing wing models in a primitive "wind tunnel," they made progress on the problem of the lift/drag characteristics of various wing shapes. This data enabled them to design wings and propellers that would yield the desired performance. In the meantime, they worked on the construction of a small, light, gas engine.

September of 1903 found them again at Kill Devil Hills. The new machine, christened *Flyer,* the trade name of their bicycle, was ready. It was made of wood and muslin, with a closely woven structure of cables and a tiny engine attached by simple bicycle chains to two rear propellers. Preparations for the tests had taken much time, and in a few days it would be Christmas. Finally, on December 17, everything was ready. It was 10:35 in the morning: five hardy souls were present besides the Wright brothers, braving an icy wind which blew at more than 20 miles per hour. They started the engine: the machine, vi-

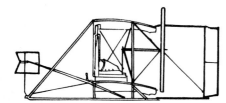

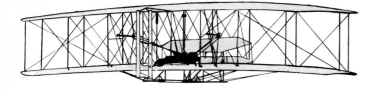

FLYER I (1903, USA). The first heavier-than-air vehicle to fly on its own engine power. On December 17, 1903, at 10:35 A.M. this wood and muslin craft, with a 4-cylinder engine, stayed in flight 12 seconds covering about 120 feet at Kill Devil Hills beach in North Carolina. Orville and his brother Wilbur, inventors and builders of the craft, took turns manning the controls. On the same day, with Wilbur flying it, the *Flyer I* made 3 other flights during one of which it flew 852 feet in 59 seconds. The effort, passion and sacrifice of the two men were justly rewarded.

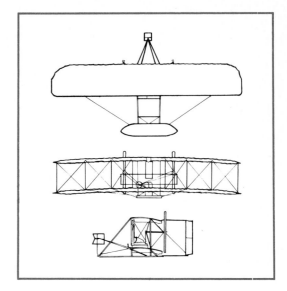

brating under the pull of the propellers, was held back by a restraining wire on a special wooden track they had constructed. At the word "go," the machine accelerated, shook, began to rise like a clumsy bird with huge white wings and hopped about 120 feet. Success. They tried again. Once, twice, three times . . . on the fourth try, the Flyer rose some feet off the ground and flew about 852 feet over the ground in 59 seconds, but with a 27 mile-per-hour headwind, this was the equivalent of a quarter of a mile through the air. The miracle had taken place: a heavier-than-air machine, powered only by its own engine, had lifted itself and its pilot off the ground, flown and landed safely. Wilbur's and Orville's joy at their success was dampened by the general incredulity. The world press commented doubtingly, if at all, on the event. A man had flown, but mankind still refused to believe it.

The Wright brothers were not ready to repeat the experiment immediately since the *Flyer* had been badly damaged and it would take a week or two to repair. But throughout the next year or so they made many more flights, and finally, in September 1905, the

Flyer III, a noticeably improved model, began a new series of tests which ended with a 38 minutes- and 3-seconds flight. The pilot had handled the craft at will, rising, dipping, turning right and left. *Flyer III* wasn't a glider with an engine, but an "airplane."

Inexplicably, this time as well, not much was written or heard of the event so that most of the world sincerely believed that the era of flight did not begin until November 12, 1906, in Bagatelle, a suburb of Paris. There, before thousands of people, the Brazilian Alberto Santos-Dumont flew his *14-bis* for some 721 feet at a height of about 20 feet. Santos-Dumont himself, whom the French nicknamed *Le Petit,* believed that he was the first man to fly. Nevertheless, a true gentleman, when he learned of the Wright brothers' earlier feats, he congratulated the American pioneers, settling for his place in history as the first man to have flown a heavier-than-air vehicle on the European continent.

The time was ripe for aviation: in 1904 Henri Deutsch de la Meurthe and Ernest Archdeacon offered a prize of 50,000 francs to the first man who could fly a heavier-than-air craft over a one-kilometer closed course.

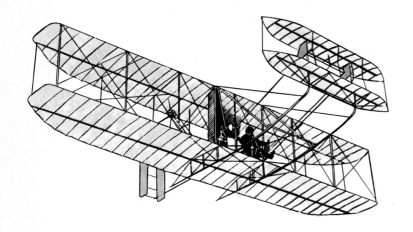

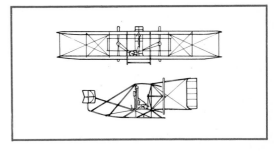

FLYER III (1905, USA). The Wright brothers' third craft may be considered the world's first practical "airplane" able to takeoff and change altitude and direction at the pilot's will. With Wilbur piloting, it covered a distance of 24½ miles in 38 minutes and 3 seconds on October 5, 1905, over Huffman Prairie, near Dayton, Ohio.

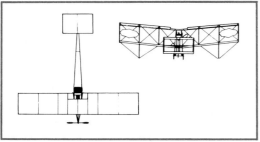

SANTOS-DUMONT 14-BIS (1906, F). The first heavier-than-air, engine-powered machine to fly in Europe, piloted by its inventor the Brazilian Alberto Santos-Dumont. In Bagatelle, on the outskirts of Paris, the aircraft "jumped" 23 feet during its first test on September 13, 1906. On October 23, the airplane flew 200 feet and on November 12, 722 feet in 21 seconds at an altitude of about 20 feet. The *14-bis*, built of bamboo and canvas with an *Antoinette* engine, was designed with the steering gear and the fuselage situated in front of the wings.

In 1905 the International Aeronautics Federation was founded and began to attend to the keeping of records. In the same year, the Aero Club of America was born. In 1903 Léon Levasseur, a civil engineer, and Jules Gastambide, a businessman, formed the first company to build an ultra-light engine (called the *Antoinette*) specially designed for the "flying machines." At this stage, only the aircraft themselves were lacking, but the wait for them was not long.

Alberto Santos-Dumont's success served to intensify the efforts of those who had for some time been trying to fly. On September 17, 1907, Louis Blériot flew his first tractor-propeller monoplane, the *Blériot VI,* for 603 feet. On November 9, Henri Farman flew 3380 feet for one minute, fourteen seconds in his *Voisin,* winning the Deutsch-Archdeacon prize. The following year Léon Delagrange, using a *Voisin,* completed the first flight in history that carried a passenger. Blériot, Farman and Delagrange became the idols of all Europe. Delagrange took his *Voisin* to other countries where larger and larger crowds greeted the news—man could fly! In Italy—in Rome, Milan and Turin—where

Delagrange toured in 1907, posters proclaimed his arrival with the words, "Delagrange will fly!" More than an advertising slogan, the words were an act of faith.

While some were already flying, others were busy with "their" airplanes, experimenting with different forms and systems, each convinced that his solution was the best. Several principles immediately established themselves: the aircraft would be a monoplane, biplane or at the most triplane; it would in most cases have only one propeller, pulling if situated in front of the craft and pushing if situated behind the wing structure.

In 1908 even the Wright brothers had their reward: the American Army requested a demonstration of their *Flyer,* and a French company paid $100,000 for the patents to construct the craft in Europe. Wilbur reached Paris, welcomed with esteem that more than made up for the previous indifference of the French. On August 8, in the Hunaudières Hippodrome near Le Mans, Wilbur flew for the first time in Europe, remaining airborne for 1 minute and 45 seconds, circling twice at a height of 33 feet. Repeating the demonstration in the days that followed, he progressive-

(continued on page 22)

VOISIN BIPLANE (1907, F). Built by the brothers Gabriel and Charles Voisin in their workshop in Billancourt, France, it was the first aircraft after the Wright brothers' *Flyer* to remain in flight for more than one minute. The event took place on November 9, 1907, when a *Voisin* piloted by Henri Farman flew 3380 feet in 1 minute and 14 seconds. It was one of the most successful of the pioneer aircraft, the first to fly in Italy (1907), Austria, Russia, Sweden (1908) and Argentina (1910).

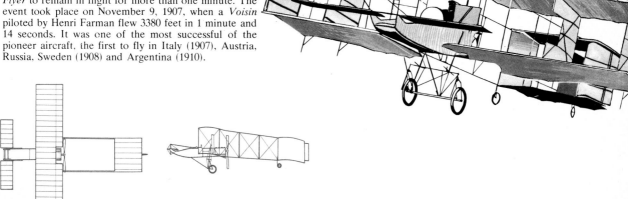

THE LEGENDARY FLYING MACHINES

After the success of the Wright brothers in 1903 in the United States and that of Santos-Dumont in 1906 in Europe, a noticeable revival of interest in heavier-than-air machines took place. History has not been able to record for us the names of all the scientists, engineers, mechanics and geniuses who put all they had into their efforts to build "their" aircraft. From 1904 to 1912, hundreds of prototypes appeared, most of which were left rotting on the fields. Among the most important of these flying machines was, for example, the *Ellehammer,* built by the Dane Jacob Christian Hansen Ellehammer, which rivals the *14-bis* of Santos-Dumont for the title of first plane to fly in Europe. On September 12, 1906, in fact, the plane "hopped" 140 feet. By the same token, Henri Fabre's *Hydravion* deserves its acknowledgement as the world's first seaplane. On March 29, 1910, it flew about 3.75 miles, making a perfect "splashdown." Other aircraft which should be mentioned are the *Dunne D-5,* the first "all wing" in the world built by John William Dunne; the *Muller* and the *Chiribiri,* among the first to be designed and built in Italy: the *Cody,* built by the American expatriot Samuel Franklin Cody who lived in Great Britain and was the first to fly in that country.

No concrete proofs exist that the *Givaudan,* with drum-shaped wings, the *Safety,* with looped wings, the *Edward,* with rhomboidal wings or the *Seddon,* resembling a science-fiction monster, ever got off the ground. Nevertheless, they did testify to the dedicated commitment to research and stood as objects of study and inspiration for all those men who held dear the problems of flight.

Those which definitely did "hop" were: Captain Dorand's *Aéroplane,* destined for military use; the *Koechlin-De Pischoff;* the *Cygnet II,* designed by the American Alexander Graham Bell (father of the telephone) and built by the Aerial Experiment Association, the society to which Glenn Curtiss belonged. It seems impossible that this strange craft, built like a honeycomb, was able to fly before crashing on frozen Lake Keuka, in New York State in 1909. And it never did fly!

Horatio Frederick Phillips' *Multiplane* flew only a short distance, but the studies he made on wing-surface curvature and later tried to test, became very important for the future. Nor did the young Rumanian engineer Henri Coanda's aircraft, which he presented at the second Salon de L'Aéronautique in Paris in 1910, ever fly, but its design somewhat anticipated the advent of the turbine engine. At least 25 years would pass before others would succeed where Coanda had failed, perhaps only because he had tried to anticipate progress.

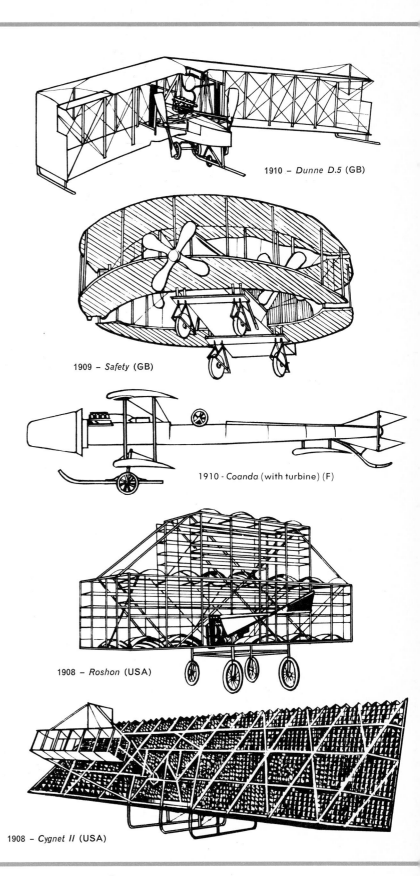

1910 – *Dunne D.5* (GB)

1909 – *Safety* (GB)

1910 - *Coanda* (with turbine) (F)

1908 – *Roshon* (USA)

1908 – *Cygnet II* (USA)

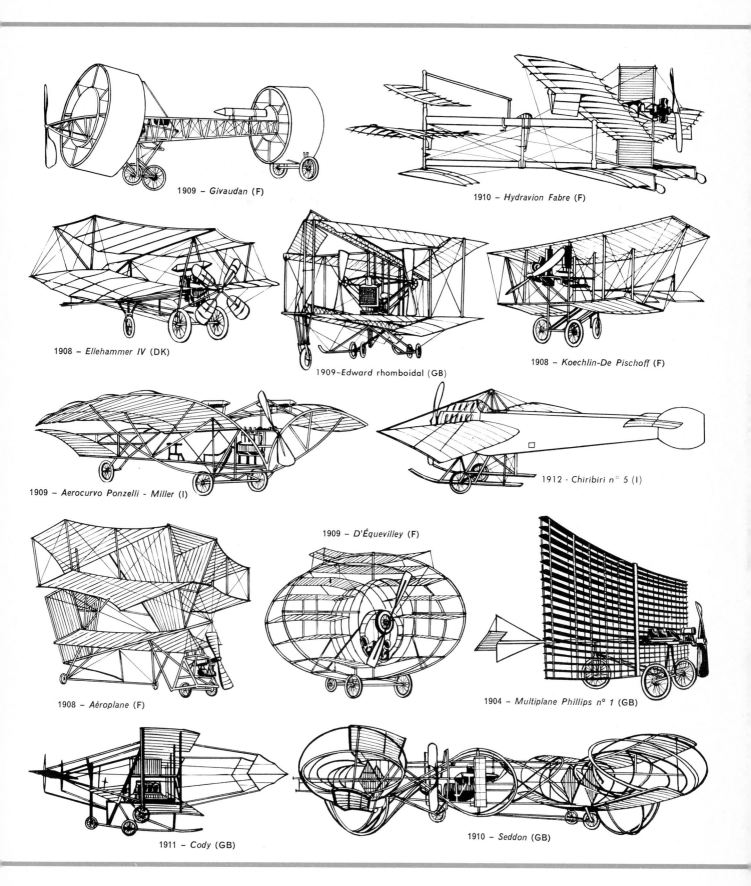

1909 – Givaudan (F)

1910 – Hydravion Fabre (F)

1908 – Ellehammer IV (DK)

1909 – Edward rhomboidal (GB)

1908 – Koechlin-De Pischoff (F)

1909 – Aerocurvo Ponzelli - Miller (I)

1912 - Chiribiri n° 5 (I)

1909 – D'Équevilley (F)

1908 – Aéroplane (F)

1904 – Multiplane Phillips n° 1 (GB)

1911 – Cody (GB)

1910 – Seddon (GB)

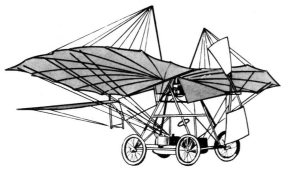

VUIA I BIS (1906, F). Designed by the Austrian Trajan Vuia, a naturalized Frenchman, the craft never showed its real ability, achieving only short flights. But it did suggest the principle of the tractor-propeller monoplane, later improved by Blériot. It was the first airplane with variable wing angle and the first to use pneumatic rather than solid rubber tires on landing gear.

GOUPY II (1909, F). Designed by Ambroise Goupy in collaboration with the Italian Mario Calderara (one of the Wright brothers' first students) the *Goupy II* with the *Breguet III*, was head of the large generation of tractor propellered biplanes. It was built in the Blériot factory and had a number of elements in common with the *Blériot XI* monoplane.

HENRI FARMAN III (1909, F). The structure of this craft was similar to the *Voisin*, in which Henri Farman had set numerous records in 1908. It was different, however, in that it was one of the first aircraft to be equipped with effective ailerons and a newly conceived skid-and-wheels landing gear. It was one of the main features of the Reims Air Meet.

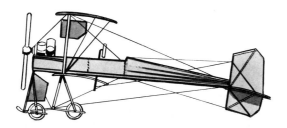

BREGUET III (1912, F). One of the first examples of the classic tractor-propeller biplane, most of its frame was canvas-covered iron instead of wood. It was christened *Tin Whistle* by the English army pilots. A large number of this aircraft was manufactured at the Breguet plant and was the mainstay, with the *Bleriot XI*, of the French and English air forces until 1914.

ly bettered his time until on September 21 he made a spectacular flight of one hour, 31 minutes and 25 seconds, leaving the European pioneers astounded.

1909 was one of the most important years in the history of aviation and witnessed two important events: the aerial crossing of the Channel and the Reims Air Meet. On October 5, 1908, the London newspaper the *Daily Mail* offered a prize of £1000 to the first pilot to cross the Channel aboard a "flying machine." If the promise of fame had not been enough, the prize money in itself would have been sufficient incentive to lure contestants. Hubert Latham, half-English, half-French, who had lived in France for many years, decided to participate. He bought one of the new *Antoinette* aircraft and on July 19, 1909, at 6:47 A.M., he took off from Sangatte, near Calais, for Dover. Thirty-three minutes later, the *Harpon,* a torpedo boat which was to follow the adventurous pilot's progress, sighted Latham in the waters about 11 miles off the coast of France. Engine trouble had forced him to ditch his plane. While Latham was preparing for a second try, Louis Blériot arrived at Les Baraques, not far from Sangatte, with his monoplane, the *XI*. Without worrying much about weather conditions, which were not exactly ideal, Blériot took off at 4:35 in the morning on July 25, and at 5 A.M. he sighted the white cliffs of Dover. He touched land (to put it mildly, for his landing was rather rough) at 5:12 at Dover Castle. In 37 minutes he had covered a distance of 23.5 miles; for the first time an airplane had crossed a body of water, the English Channel. Blériot won the *Daily Mail* prize and earned a triumphal welcome into London and the medal of the French Legion of Honor, awarded for the first time for accomplishment in aviation. Latham, in true sporting spirit, tried again on July 27, but again his aircraft failed him. It was unfortunate because the *Antoinette* was an excellent airplane which, in fact, was to prove herself to Latham several days later in Reims.

The consortium of wine producers of the Champagne region had organized the *Grande Semaine d'Aviation de la Champagne* (the Great Aviation Week of the Champagne region) under the auspices of the president of the French Republic, offering a rich purse to winners of the various events. The meet took place during the week of Sunday, August 22–Sunday, August 29 and was a memorable success: upon the same fields where Joan of Arc's forces had camped descended tens of thousands of people, among them kings and prime ministers. Even more astounding was the number of participants: a grand total of 38. They lined up around the field, in their ranks 3 *Farmans,* 7 *Voisins,* 3 *Wrights,* 3 *Antoin-*

DEMOISELLE *20* (1909, F). Made of bamboo and wood, light and manageable, built in about 15 copies, it was Santos-Dumont's first really successful aircraft. It was also the Brazilian pioneer's last design, for in 1910, ill with sclerosis, he abandoned the world of aviation at only 37 years of age.

ANTOINETTE IV (1908, F). Designed by Léon Levavasseur (creator of the famous *Antoinette* engine), it is closely identified with Hubert Latham who piloted the aircraft in two unlucky attempts to cross the Channel. Nevertheless, it proved to be one of the best airplanes at the Reims Air Meet.

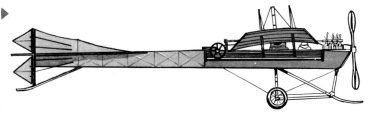

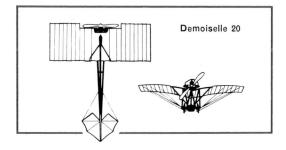

Demoiselle 20

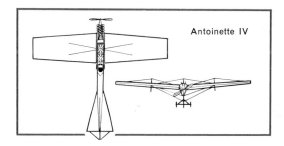

Antoinette IV

ettes, and 4 *Blériots,* models *XI, XII* and *XIII.*

The winner of the speed trials was an unknown name in Europe: one Glenn Curtiss, an American, flying his *Golden Flyer.* He was, however, by then well known in the States. A builder of motorcycles and a daring racing driver, in 1907 he had joined the Aerial Experiment Association, founded by Alexander Graham Bell, the inventor of the telephone. Curtiss had made his debut on the aeronautics scene in July of 1908 with an aircraft called the *June Bug* winning the trophy offered by the magazine *Scientific American.* At Reims, he presented an aircraft which his new company, Herring-Curtiss, had built. In the *Golden Flyer* he had created a plane superior not only to the Wrights' *Flyer,* which made a bad showing, but also to the *Blériot,* beaten in the Gordon Bennett Cup trials, and to the *Antoinette,* defeated in the Prix de Vitesse.

During the various trials at Reims, Henri Farman broke the time record, staying in flight for three hours, fifteen minutes, and won the "passenger prize" carrying 2 passengers for 10 minutes, 39 seconds. Latham, with his *Antoinette VII,* won the altitude prize, reaching 508½ feet. Blériot won for best time around the 6.2 mile runway, averaging the incredible speed of 47¾ miles per hour.

At Reims, aviation had been officially baptized; in Paris, some days later, it was presented to the general public at the first Salon de l'Aeronautique where the following aircraft, among others, were offered for sale: the *Wright,* for 30,000 francs; the *Antoinette* for 25,000; the *Farman* for 23,000; the *Voisin* for 12,000 the *Bleriot* for 10,000 and, finally, Santos-Dumont's very light *Demoiselle,* which, at 7500 francs, was intended to be the "budget" aircraft of the skies.

Aviators' meetings were repeated in all the major cities of Europe and the U.S. In September 1909, the elite of aviation came to Brescia in Italy where Glenn Curtiss won the Grand Prize, beating all the European contenders for 31.1 miles in 49 minutes and 24 seconds. Immediately after his victory, the American flyer returned to the U.S. to present his already famous aircraft before army and navy committees and to win the $10,000 prize offered by the newspaper the New York *World* for a 141-mile flight from Albany to New York City.

News of the meetings, prizes and various contests filled the newspaper pages, arousing the public's enthusiasm for the fledgling airplane. All of England cheered as Claude Grahame-White and Louis Paulhan battled for the 10,000 prize promised by the *Daily*

24

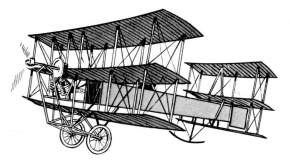
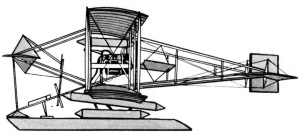

ROE II TRIPLANE (1909, GB). The first triplane to prove its usefulness, it was also the first completely English aircraft (in both design and engine) to fly (July 23, 1909), piloted by its inventor, Aliott Verdon Roe. In the course of one of its races it was nicknamed the *Yellow Peril* by the public, after the color of its oil-paper covering. Roe later abandoned the concept of the triplane to devote his efforts to the monoplane and biplane. He was one of the most successful English designers with his *Avro*'s (abbreviation of the initials of his name A. V. Roe).

CURTISS HYDRO-AEROPLANE (1911, USA). Glenn Curtiss' first seaplane was none other than his already proven *Golden Flyer* (p.25), with floats attached, one at the center of the fuselage and one at each of the wing tips. The first flight took place on January 26, 1911, after more than a year of tests, and 10 months after Fabre's successful attempt in France. Curtiss continued work on the seaplane and built several models which are still famous today. Already during the First World War the U.S. Navy used *Curtiss* seaplanes, such as the *H-12* and *N-9* (p.42).

Mail to the winner of the 198.8-mile race from London to Manchester. Grahame-White left first on April 23, 1910, flying a *Farman,* but was forced to stop after covering 84.4 miles. On the twenty-seventh, at 5:00 P.M.. Paulhan took off from London also piloting a *Farman* and, after an intermediate stop, reached Manchester in four hours and twelve minutes of effective flying time, winning the race.

But all the world grieved for the unlucky but courageous George Chavez, a Peruvian who had lived in France for several years. Chavez decided to attempt a crossing of the Alps in his *Blériot.* He took off on September 23, 1910, from Brig, disappeared into the clouds and next appeared over the landing field of Domodossola. He had done it! But during his landing his engine began to fail: the airplane crashed from a height of 32.8 feet, and Chavez lost his life.

Even though a heavy and sad price was paid in human life for aeronautical progress,

the number of lives lost, when considered in proportion to the fragility and imperfections of those first craft, was not really high. One death in 1908, 3 in 1909, 29 in 1910 and about 100 in 1911. (The last figure may seem unusually high unless one considers that in the same year 1350 aircraft had been built and 1,615,910 miles flown.)

What does seem like a bitter twist of fate is the number of pioneers who achieved dangerous and heralded feats, coming through them without a scratch, only to lose their lives in freak accidents. Thus Léon Delagrange, one of the first men to fly, died on January 4, 1910, while test flying his *Blériot.* Calbraith P. Rodgers, after having flown from New York City to Pasadena in a fragile *Wright Baby* (covering 3220 miles in 49 days, 68 stops, for a total of 82 hours and 4 minutes effective flying time, from September 17 to November 5, 1911) and surviving at least 20 accidents during that flight, died 4 months later during a short demonstration flight.

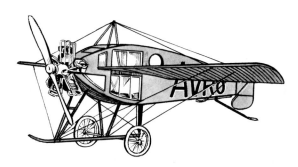

AVRO F (1912, GB). The first aircraft to fly a pilot in a glass cockpit (May 1, 1912) completely sheltering him from wind and bad weather.

DEPERDUSSIN RACER (1912, F). The first aircraft with aerodynamic lines, built for speed racing. It was the first to break the 200 kilometer (about 125 miles) speed record (September 29, 1913).

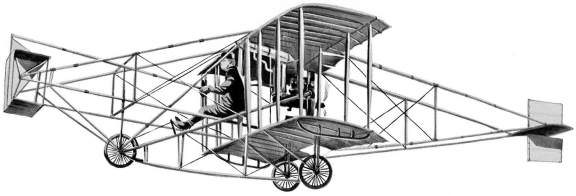

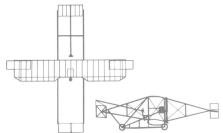

GOLDEN FLYER (1909, USA). This aircraft, designed and built by Glenn Curtiss, won two major victories in the great Air Meet at Reims. On August 28, flying an average of 47 miles per hour, it won the Gordon Bennett Aviation Cup, offered to the fastest airplane to cover 12.43 miles. On the twenty-ninth he won the Prix de Vitesse in an 18.64-mile race, at a speed of 52.63 miles per hour. Another *Golden Fl er* was the first to take-off from the deck of a ship, the *Birmingham,* at Hampton Roads, Virginia, on November 14, 1910, and to land on a specially built wood platform on the American cruiser *Pennsylvania,* in San Francisco Bay on January 18, 1911.

But aviation was already a proven fact and these dramatic incidents cound not dampen the enthusiasm of an ever-increasing number of people. By the end of 1912, flying licenses were held by 966 people in France, 382 in England, 355 in Germany, 193 in America, 186 in Italy, 162 in Russia and about 500 people in other countries of the world.

On September 23, 1913, Roland Garros flew the Mediterranean for the first time, making the 453.3-mile trip (310 of those over water) with his *Morane-Saulneir H* in 7 hours and 53 minutes, taking-off from Saint-Raphaël on the Cote d'Azur and landing in Bizerta, where he was given a triumphal welcome.

In the meantime, clouds gathered on the European horizon. Would the promising progress of aeronautics be brusquely interrupted by a war? It seemed so. Even though the new machines had been used in military action in 1911, in the Italo-Turkish War for reconnaissance flights in North Africa, few people believed they could be effectively used should a conflict break out in Europe.

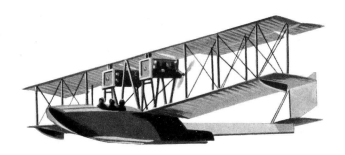

BENOIST XIV (1914, USA). This seaplane began the first regular passenger air service in the world. On January 1, 1914, air service was opened between St. Petersburg and Tampa, Florida, with a *Benoist XIV,* piloted by Tony Janus, capable of carrying two passengers. The almost 20-mile trip took about 20 minutes' flying time. The price of a ticket was $5.00 a person with baggage. Oddly enough passengers weighing over 200 pounds had to pay overweight! The St. Petersburg-Tampa Airboat Line offered regular service of 2 flights per day for about 4 months and carried in all 1200 paying passengers. About fifteen years were to go by before comparable service was offered again in that area.

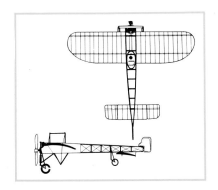

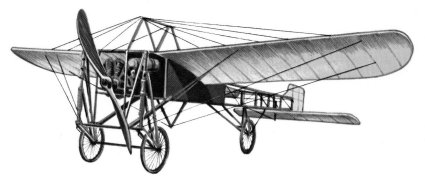

BLERIOT XI (1909, F) The first aircraft to cross the Channel, on July 25, 1909, with Louis Blériot piloting, and to cross the Alps on September 23, 1910, with George Chavez as pilot. According to some historians, the aircraft was designed by Raymond Saulnier and not by Bleriot. However, it was without doubt a leader on the aviation scene until 1913: first at Reims Air Meet for the fastest lap of 6.2 miles and second to the *Golden Flyer* for the Gordon Bennett Cup; first to be sold in quantity to the army in France and other countries, and, on October 22, 1911, was also first to take part in a wartime action: it was piloted by the Italian Capt. Carlo Piazza in Libya during the Italo-Turkish War.

RECORDS FROM 1906 TO 1914

Altitude

Date	Place	Name	Airplane	Engine	Height Feet
1908 13 XI	Issy (F)	Henri Farman	Voisin	40 hp Vivinus	82
1908 13 XI	Auvours (F)	Wilbur Wright	Wright	24 hp Wright	82
1908 18 XII	Auvours (F)	Wilbur Wright	Wright	24 hp Wright	360
1909 18 VII	Douai (F)	Louis Paulhan	Voisin	50 hp Gnome	492
1909 29 VIII	Reims (F)	Hubert Latham	Antoinette	50 hp Antoinette	508
1909 20 IX	Brescia (I)	Rougier	Voisin	50 hp E.N.V.	633
1909 18 X	Juvisy (F)	De Lambert	Wright	24 hp Wright	984
1909 1 XII	Chalons (F)	Hubert Latham	Antoinette	50 hp Antoinette	1436
1910 7 I	Chalons (F)	Hubert Latham	Antoinette	50 hp Antoinette	3444
1910 12 I	Los Angeles (USA)	Louis Paulhan	H. Farman	50 hp Gnome	4110
1910 14 VI	Indianapolis (USA)	Walter Brookins	Wright	40 hp Wright	4379
1910 7 VII	Reims (F)	Hubert Latham	Antoinette	50 hp Antoinette	4539
1910 10 VII	Atlantic City (USA)	Walter Brookins	Wright	40 hp Wright	6237
1910 11 VIII	Lanark (USA)	Armstrong Drexel	Blériot	50 hp Gnome	6603
1910 29 VIII	Le Havre (F)	Léon Morane	Blériot	50 hp Gnome	7042
1910 3 IX	Deauville (F)	Léon Morane	Blériot	50 hp Gnome	8469
1910 8 IX	Issy (F)	Geo Chavez	Blériot	50 hp Gnome	8484
1910 1 X	Mourmelon (F)	Jan Wijnmalen	H. Farman	50 hp Gnome	9118
1910 31 X	Belmont Park (USA)	Ralph Johnstone	Wright	60 hp Wright	9600
1910 9 XII	Pau (F)	Geo Legagneux	Blériot	50 hp Gnome	10,168
1911 9 VII	Buc (F)	Loridan	H. Farman	70 hp Gnome	10,496
1911 5 VIII	Étampes (F)	Cap. Félix	Blériot	70 hp Gnome	10,988
	Chicago (USA)	Lincoln Beachey	Curtiss	60 hp Curtiss	11,578
1911 4 IX	St-Malo (F)	Roland Garros	Blériot	70 hp Gnome	12,824
1911 6 IX	Dinard (F)	Roland Garros	Blériot	70 hp Gnome	16,269
1912 17 IX	Issy, Villalonblay (F)	Geo Legagneux	Morane	80 hp Gnome	18,050
1912 11 XII	Tunisi (TN)	Roland Garros	Morane	80 hp Gnome	18,400
1913 11 III	Buc (F)	Édouard Perreyon	Blériot	80 hp Gnome	19,290
1913 29 XII	St-Raphaël (F)	Geo Legagneux	Nieuport	60 hp Le Rhône	20,060
1914 9 VII	Johannisthal (D)	Gino Linnekogel	Rumpler	100 hp Mercedes	21,653
1914 14 VII	Lipsia (D)	Harry Oelerich	D.F.W.	100 hp Mercedes	25,725

Speed

Date	Place	Name	Airplane	Engine	Speed per hour
1908 21 IX	Auvours (F)	Wilbur Wright	Wright	24 hp Wright	27.2 mi
1909 31 V	Juvisy (F)	Léon Delagrange	Voisin	45 hp Antoinette	27.9
1909 3 IX	Juvisy (F)	Cap. Ferber	Voisin	45 hp Antoinette	29.7
1909 28 VIII	Reims (F)	Blériot	Blériot	60 hp E.N.V.	47.7
1910 29 X	Belmont Park (USA)	Alfred Leblanc	Blériot	100 hp Gnome	67.5
1911 1 VII	Eastchurch (GB)	C. Weymann	Nieuport	100 hp Gnome	70.5
1912 9 IX	Chicago (USA)	Jules Védrines	Deperdussin	100 hp Gnome	105
1913 29 IX	Reims (F)	Marcel Prévost	Deperdussin	160 hp Le Rhône	124.5

Duration

Date			Place	Name	Airplane	Engine	Time (h m s)		
1906	12	XI	Bagatelle (F)	Santos-Dumont	Santos-Dumont	50 hp Antoinette	0	0	21
1907	26	X	Issy (F)	Henri Farman	Voisin	40 hp Vivinus	0	0	52
1908	13	I	Issy (F)	Henri Farman	Voisin	50 hp Antoinette	0	1	28
1908	21	III	Issy (F)	Henri Farman	Voisin	50 hp Antoinette	0	3	39
1908	11	IV	Issy (F)	Léon Delagrange	Voisin	40 hp Vivinus	0	6	39
1908	30	V	Roma (I)	Léon Delagrange	Voisin	50 hp E.N.V.	0	15	26
1908	6	VII	Issy (F)	Henri Farman	Voisin	50 hp Antoinette	0	20	19
1908	6	IX	Issy (F)	Léon Delagrange	Voisin	40 hp Vivinus	0	29	53
1908	21	IX	Auvours (F)	Wilbur Wright	Wright	24 hp Wright	1	31	25
1908	18	XII	Auvours (F)	Wilbur Wright	Wright	24 hp Wright	1	54	53
1908	31	XII	Auvours (F)	Wilbur Wright	Wright	24 hp Wright	2	20	23
1909	27	VIII	Béthény (F)	Louis Paulhan	Voisin	50 hp Gnome	2	43	24
1909	27	VIII	Béthény (F)	Henri Farman	H. Farman	50 hp Gnome	3	4	56
1909	3	XI	Mourmelon (F)	Henri Farman	H. Farman	50 hp Gnome	4	17	53
1910	9	VII	Reims (F)	Labouchère	Antoinette	50 hp Antoinette	4	19	0
1910	10	VII	Reims (F)	Jan Olieslaegers	Blériot	50 hp Gnome	5	3	5
1910	28	X	Étampes (F)	Maurice Tabuteau	M. Farman	70 hp Renault	6	0	0
1910	18	XII	Étampes (F)	Henri Farman	H. Farman	50 hp Gnome	8	12	23
1911	1	IX	Buc (F)	Fourny	M. Farman	70 hp Renault	11	1	20
1912	11	IX	Buc (F)	Fourny	M. Farman	70 hp Renault	13	17	57
1914	4	II	Johannisthal (D)	Langer	L.F.G. Roland	100 hp Mercedes	14	7	0
1914	24	IV	Étampes (F)	Poulet	Caudron	50 hp Gnome	16	28	56
1914	24	VI	Johannisthal (D)	Basser	Rumpler	100 hp Mercedes	18	10	0
1914	28	VI	Johannisthal (D)	Landmann	Albatros	100 hp Mercedes	21	50	0
1914	10	VII	Johannisthal (D)	Boehm	Albatros	100 hp Mercedes	24	12	0

Distance

Date			Place	Name	Airplane	Engine	Distance
1906	14	IX	Bagatelle (F)	Santos-Dumont	Santos-Dumont	50 hp Antoinette	8.6 yd
1906	12	XI	Bagatelle (F)	Santos-Dumont	Santos-Dumont	50 hp Antoinette	244.4 yd
1907	26	X	Issy (F)	Henri Farman	Voisin	40 hp Vivinus	855.5 yd
1908	13	I	Issy (F)	Henri Farman	Voisin	50 hp Antoinette	0.625 mi
1908	21	III	Issy (F)	Henri Farman	Voisin	50 hp Antoinette	1.25
1908	11	IV	Issy (F)	Léon Delagrange	Voisin	40 hp Vivinus	2.50
1908	30	V	Roma (I)	Léon Delagrange	Voisin	50 hp E.N.V.	7.7
1908	6	IX	Issy (F)	Léon Delagrange	Voisin	40 hp Vivinus	15.3
1908	17	IX	Issy (F)	Léon Delagrange	Voisin	40 hp Vivinus	41.5
1908	21	IX	Auvours (F)	Wilbur Wright	Voisin	24 hp Wright	60.9
1908	18	XII	Auvours (F)	Wilbur Wright	Wright	24 hp Wright	62
1908	31	XII	Auvours (F)	Wilbur Wright	Wright	24 hp Wright	77.5
1909	26	VIII	Reims (F)	Henri Farman	H. Farman	50 hp Gnome	112
1909	3	XI	Mourmelon (F)	Henri Farman	H. Farman	50 hp Gnome	150
1910	10	VII	Reims (F)	Jan Olieslaegers	Blériot	50 hp Gnome	139.5
			Reims (F)	Jan Olieslaegers	Blériot	50 hp Gnome	245
1910	28	X	Étampes (F)	Maurice Tabuteau	M. Farman	70 hp Renault	290
1910	30	XII	Étampes (F)	Maurice Tabuteau	M. Farman	70 hp Renault	362.7
1911	16	VII	Kiewitt (D)	Jan Olieslaegers	Blériot	50 hp Gnome	393.7
1911	1	IX	Buc (F)	Fourny	M. Farman	70 hp Renault	448.3
1911	24	XII	Pau (F)	Gobé	Nieuport	70 hp Gnome	460
1912	11	IX	Étampes (F)	Fourny	M. Farman	70 hp Renault	633
1914	28	VI	Johannisthal (D)	Landmann	Albatros	100 hp Mercedes	1178

28

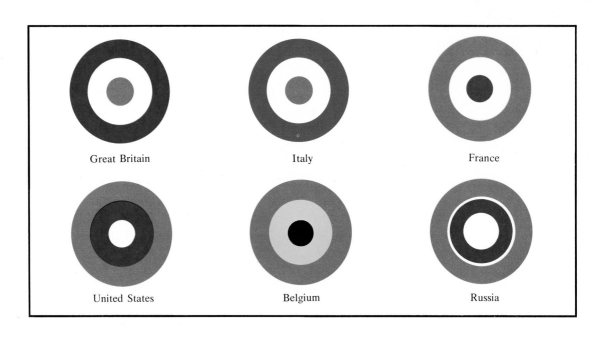

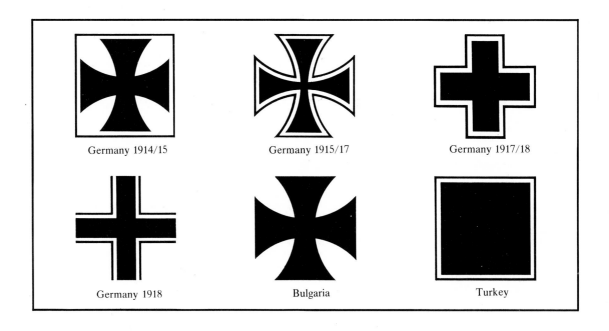

AIRCRAFT OF WORLD WAR I

At the outbreak of World War I, very few thought of the airplane as an instrument of war. Most limited its possible use to reconnaissance, as "eyes beyond enemy lines." On the other hand, in 1914 the standard military aircraft, unarmed, capable of speeds of between 50 and 75 miles per hour, with an operating ceiling of 10,000 feet, and with low range, was not suitable to more ambitious purposes. For this reason as well, the belligerent nations began operations with very few combat-ready aircraft.

Within a few months, facts made even the most skeptical change their minds. Those wood and canvas craft, without navigational instruments, piloted by courageous men (who didn't even have parachutes!), began to attract attention with a series of sensational actions. Then, in a short span of time, aviation left its adolescence and made itself felt in military terms as an important factor for victory. In a few years, the countries at war had built about 177,000 planes, a dizzying number when one remembers that from 1903 to August 1914 total world production was only slightly over 10,000 units. During the course of the War, the military airplane was slowly being transformed to meet new needs and duties; from the slow reconnaissance the one-seat fighter was born, armed first with a manual and later an automatic machine gun; light and heavy bombers were developed; the ground attack, the land reconnaissance, the reconnaissance seaplane and many other types came into being. In 1918 there were fighters armed with two machine guns and capable of reaching 125 miles per hour at a ceiling of 20,000 feet; bombers that carried up to 3300 pounds of bombs at 87-miles-per-hour speed, ceiling 15,000 feet with a range of over 300 miles! Very different specifications from those of the 1914 aircraft!

During the war, the first completely metal airplane was built, designed by Hugo Junkers. More powerful but proportionately lighter engines were created. The technical development which took place from 1914 to 1918 is almost incredible. In conclusion, the First World War, with all its griefs and horrors, was nevertheless a decisive factor in the definitive triumph of the "heavier-than-air." If this is true, it is due in part to the designer and technicians, but above all to the pilots who made the aircraft live and breathe. The aces and the other pilots alike, the pilots of the First World War, fully deserve even today that aura of admiration, romanticism and legendary fame which won them the title of "knights of the skies." Serving under different flags, they fought each other as true enemies, but they remained brothers, united by their mutual passion for flying.

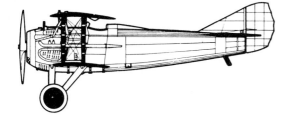

MAURICE FARMAN MF-11 (1914). Designed by Henri Farman's brother, it was the standard reconnaissance used by the Allies from the beginning of the War (in its MF-7 version) until the end of 1915. It was then used in pilot-training schools. The *MF-7* was christened "Longhorns" and the *MF-11* "Shorthorns," because of the shape and length of the landing skids.

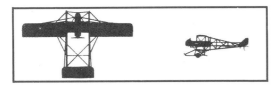

DORAND AR-1 (1917). A reconnaissance used with good results in 18 observation squadrons during the last months of the War on the French and Italian fronts. It was designed by Colonel Dorand (whose *DO-1* was already in use in 1914) and took its initials *AR* from *Section Technique de l'Aéronautique,* the French army factory which built it.

CAUDRON G-IV (1915). The losses suffered by a group of *G-IV*'s in a daylight bombing raid on the Rhineland in November 1915 made it advisable to relegate the aircraft to reconnaissance missions. It was used by the English and the Italians (especially in the Alps) as well as the French. The *G-IV* and the *Caudron R-11* (1918) were the only two-engine French aircraft in the War.

FRANCE

The French army built its first air units in 1910. At the beginning of World War I it could count on 24 squadrons with 160 aircraft of 14 different types *(Blériot, Voisin, Caudron)* and 15 dirigibles. The appearance of a German airplane in the skies over Paris and the progress of war operations convinced the War Ministry of the importance of strengthening its air power. The young French aeronautics industry, at that time the only one in the world, worked miracles, and in 1916 France had about 1500 aircraft; by the time of the Armistice, nearly 3000! Production had gone from 341 aircraft in 1914 to fifty times as many in 1918. In four years of war French factories produced 50,040 airplanes and 92,594 engines, meeting the needs of the nation and its allies. France was the first country to use aerial bombardment in the War, on August 14, 1914 (two *Voisins* bombed the *Zeppelin* base in Metz-Frascaty); it was the first country to down an enemy aircraft (an *Aviatik*), on October 5, 1914; the first (in 1915) to create Squadrons made up exclusively of bombers and fighters; the first to form an Aviation Ministry *(Sous-Secrétariat d'État de l'Aéronautique),* in 1915. It produced high quality aircraft, mainly fighters, such as the *Nieuport* and *Spad,* and could boast courageous and worthy pilots, among them 158 aces (pilots with a record of downing more than 5 enemy aircraft). The ace of the aces was Capt. René Fonck, who downed 75 enemies, followed by Capt. Georges Guynemer (54), Lt. Charles Nungesser (45) and Lt. Georges Madon (41), Lt. Maurice Boyan (35), Lt. Michel Coiffard (34). Fonck and many other French aces belonged to Fighter Group 12, which included the famous Stork Squadron. One of the first French aces to lose his life, on June 17, 1916, was Jean Navarre, nicknamed the "Verdun Sentinel," who had shot down 12 enemy aircraft.

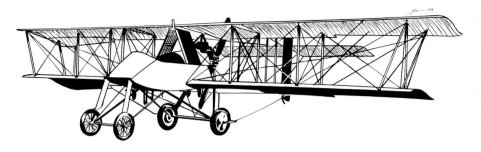

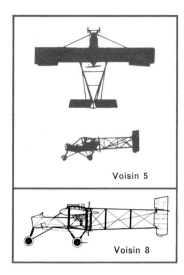

Voisin 5

Voisin 8

VOISIN 5 (1915). Standard allied bomber with steel frame and pusher propeller. It was to be used from 1914 to 1918 in different versions, from *1* to *10,* each with a more powerful engine to allow for higher speeds and larger bomb loads. Over 3500 were built, many of them in Italy. The first air duel of the War took place on October 5, 1914, near Reims between a *Voisin 1* and an *Aviatik* which was shot down. The *Voisin 5* was among the first to be used in night bombing and the first aircraft equipped with a 37- or 47-millimeter gun. The few aircraft of this type, called *avion-canon,* proved to be very efficient in ground strikes.

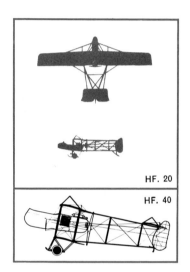

HF. 20

HF. 40

HENRI FARMAN HF-20 (1914). Designed by the famous French pioneer and built in the factory that Farman and his brother Maurice had opened, it was used in action from the first day of the War as a reconnaissance. Adopted by the French, Belgians, English, Russians and Rumanians, it was already outdated when it became operational. It was equipped with a machine gun for the observer, but not until the last months of 1915. The aircraft was gradually replaced by the *HF-40,* faster and aerodynamically better. The *HF-40* was used by 50 French squadrons until 1917. It was later replaced by the *AR-1.*

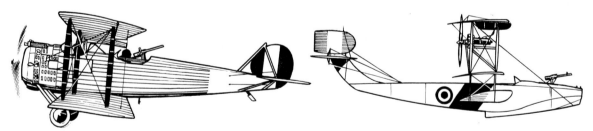

SALMSON 2 (1918). Built by Émile Salmson, (whose engines were famous as far back as 1917), it was the last and best of the French World War I reconnaissance aircraft. The *Salmson 2* was fast and well-armed and over 3200 were built. In April, 1918, The American W. P. Erwin, in a memorable air battle, downed 8 enemies with the front machine gun of his *Salmson 2.*

F.B.A. C (1915). The reconnaissance seaplane used in largest numbers during the War, built by the Franco-British Aviation of Paris, based on Levêque's design modified by Max Schreck. More than 980 of the perfected type *H* were built in Italy, with an Isotta-Fraschini 180-horsepower engine, and used by the Italian Navy.

The personal emblem of Capt. Georges Guynemer, the second-ranking French ace (54 victories).

32

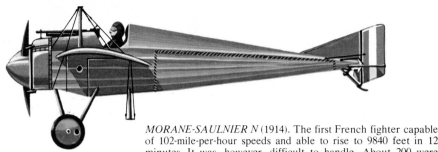

MORANE-SAULNIER N (1914). The first French fighter capable of 102-mile-per-hour speeds and able to rise to 9840 feet in 12 minutes. It was, however, difficult to handle. About 200 were built for France, Great Britain and Russia. It was the favorite aircraft of the French ace Jean Navarre and the Russian ace A. A. Kazakov. Thanks to the inventiveness of Roland Garros, in early 1915 it was the first Allied aircraft to be equipped with a forward-firing gun mounted behind the propeller.

NIEUPORT 11 BÉBÉ (1915). Developed from a racing aircraft designed by Gustave Delage for the Gordon Bennett Cup in 1914, it was the first Allied fighter able to match the *Fokker E.* It led the air battle at Verdun (February 1916) and was the aces' plane. Ball, Bishop, De Rose, Navarre, Nungesser and Baracca won many of their aerial duels with the small *Bébé*. It was the standard fighter used by the Italians until 1917 and by the Americans in the Lafayette Escadrille.

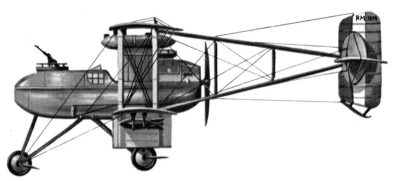

BREGUET-MICHELIN BrM-5 (1915). The first 100 *BrM-2* and *BrM-3* bombers were built at the (André and Édouard) Michelin brothers' factory and offered to the Aviation Militaire. Even the improved model, the *BrM-5*, was too slow for daylight bombing and beginning in late 1916 was used for night bombing. A Hotchkiss 37-millimeter gun as well as a machine gun was mounted on some of the last *BrM-5* models.

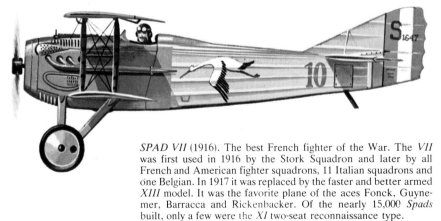

SPAD VII (1916). The best French fighter of the War. The *VII* was first used in 1916 by the Stork Squadron and later by all French and American fighter squadrons, 11 Italian squadrons and one Belgian. In 1917 it was replaced by the faster and better armed *XIII* model. It was the favorite plane of the aces Fonck, Guynemer, Barracca and Rickenbacker. Of the nearly 15,000 *Spads* built, only a few were the *XI* two-seat reconnaissance type.

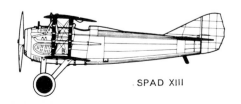
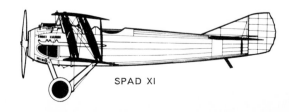

SPAD XIII   SPAD XI

HANRIOT HD-1 (1917). A fast and maneuverable fighter. Ready after the *Spad VII,* it was ignored by the French but used by the Belgians and Italians. In Italy, the Nieuport-Macchi factory built 831 aircraft of this model which replaced the *Nieuport* in the fighter Squadrons. Flying an *HD-1,* the Belgian ace Willy Coppens achieved most of his 37 victories.

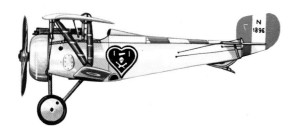

NIEUPORT 17 (1916). Larger than the *Bébé,* which it succeeded, equipped with a synchronized Vickers machine gun, it led all others in its field until the *Spad VII* appeared. It fought well against the *Fokker E,* the *Halberstadt D-II* and even the *Albatros D-I,* particularly during the battles of the Somme and Isonzo.

BREGUET Br-14B2 (1917). The bomber (the first aircraft of predominantly hard aluminum structure) with which 55 French bomber squadrons were outfitted during the last year of the war. As many as 5500 were built before 1918 and a total of 8000 by 1926. The *Br-14B2* illustrated here belonged to the 96th Squadron of the American Expeditionary Force.

From left to right and from top to bottom, the emblems of the squadrons: SPA 103, SPA 73, SPA 26, SPA 3, (the Stork Group), SPA 48, SPA 15, SPA 88, SPA 89, SPA 84, SPA 77, BR 11, BR 205, C 115, BR 127.

BRISTOL SCOUT D (1915). Derived from the *Baby Biplane* designed in 1913 by Frank Barnwell, the *C* and *D* models were used in almost all British squadrons as fast escorts. In March 1916, it was the first English aircraft with a synchronized machine gun to reach the front. It was used until autumn 1916 on all fronts.

B.E.12 (1916). Over 600 were built. The aircraft was evolved from the *B.E.2 (p.35)* to be the fighter capable to match the *Fokker*. Not very maneuverable, it was totally unsuccessful. First in combat on August 25, 1916, with the 21st Squadron, it was recalled to Great Britain in mid-September. A few *B.E. 12*'s were used as bombers in the Middle East.

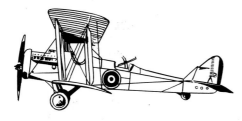

AIRCO D.H.4 (1917). Designed by Geoffrey de Havilland, it was considered the best single-engine bomber in the war. Over 6295 were built, 4846 of these in the U.S. It was used in 13 squadrons of the American Expeditionary Force. Flown in action from March 1917, it fought successfully on all fronts until the Armistice. In 1930 several *D.H.4*'s were still in use.

GREAT BRITAIN

In August 1914, the Royal Flying Corps had fewer than 60 aircraft and the Royal Navy Air Service about 100 aircraft and 7 dirigibles; of this extremely weak force, 73 aircraft (mainly *B.E.2c*'s and *Avro 504*'s divided into 4 squadrons) were sent to the French front. While, in the initial phase of the war, the French were counted on to provide planes, under the pressure of need, a new British aeronautics industry was born and developed rapidly, thanks to the availability of designers such as Geoffrey de Havilland (*Airco D.H.2, B.E.2c, Airco D.H.4* and *D.H.5*), Frank Barnwell (*Bristol Scout* and *F-2b*) and Herbert Smith (*Sopwith Triplane* and *Camel*) who gave Great Britain a high-quality fighter force. Subject to German bombardment (especially over London) Great Britain agreed with Russia and Italy on the importance of strategic bombing and produced extremely advanced heavy bombers such as the *Handley Page 0/400* and *V/1500*. From 1914 to 1918, British factories of Avro, Armstrong-Whitworth, Bristol, Handley Page, Short, Sopwith, Vickers and the Royal Aircraft Factory produced more than 40,000 aircraft, at peak production 3500 per month. In 1916 the Air Ministry was created and on April 1, 1917, the Royal Air Force was born joining into one independent unit the air power previously divided between the Royal Flying Corps and the Naval Air Service. As of the Armistice the R.A.F. had 1799 aircraft in service; during the conflict it fought valorously in the English skies, and on the Western, Italian, Macedonian, Aegean and Middle-Eastern fronts, producing 532 aces (at least 5 planes downed) among them Maj. Edward Mannock (73), the Canadians Lt. Col. Billy Bishop (72) and Raymond Collishaw (60), Maj. James McCudden (57) and ten other pilots each with a record of more than 40 aircraft downed. Incredibly, Mannock was blind in one eye!

AIRCO D.H.2 (1916). G. de Havilland's first design for Airco, considered the first English match for the *Fokker E.* In January 1916 it was assigned to the No. 24 Squadron, the first to be outfitted completely with one-seat fighters. Ace Maj. L. G. Hawker, commander of the 24th, flew a *D.H.2* when shot down by Von Richthofen (flying an *Albatros D 11*) November 23, 1916. Production continued until mid-1917.

F.E.2b (1915). This two-seat fighter was designed in 1913, ordered for mass production in 1914 and equipped combat units from June 1915. The 2190 built proved among the best of the English aircraft. The *F.E.2b* downed ace Max Immelmann, the "Eagle of Lille" (15 victories), on June 18, 1916, and ace Karl Schaefer (30 victories). From autumn 1917 it was used as a night bomber.

AIRCO D.H.5 (1917). This fighter remained on the front line only 8 months (May 1917 to January 1918) because it was unsuitable for high-altitude flights. Designed by De Havilland, it was not successful. Its unusual back-staggered wing allowed greater pilot visibility. The *D.H.5*'s of the 64th and 68th squadrons were used in ground strikes in the battle of Cambrai.

SOPWITH TRIPLANE (1917). Operational in February 1917, this fighter was immediately recognized as superior, and 14 German plants began to study the triplane concept. Canadian ace Raymond Collishaw downed 16 aircraft in 4 weeks flying a *Triplane,* and his squadron, the 10th Naval, counted another 61 victories in 2 months using only 5 aircraft. Only 144 *Triplanes* were built and the model was replaced by the *Camel.*

R.E.8 (1916). The standard English reconnaissance plane of the second half of the War. A total of 4077 were built and served in France, Italy and Palestine. In October 1918 the model outfitted 18 squadrons. Strong and relatively fast, it was sometimes used as a bomber. An *R.E.8* flew 147 missions and compiled 441 flight hours before being taken out of service.

B.E.2c (1915). Designed in 1911 by G. de Havilland and F. M. Green for the Royal Aircraft Factory, it was the first English aircraft to reach France with the 2nd and 4th squadrons at the outbreak of the War. Unarmed in the *a* and *b* models, it was widely used for reconnaissance and light bombing until May 1917. There were 3535 produced by 22 factories.

AVRO 504J (1914). Of these aircraft, 8340 were used from 1914 to 1933! On August 22, 1914, a *504A* was the first English aircraft to be shot down by the enemy. The first bombing of the *Zeppelin* base at Friedrichshafen was effected by 3 *504A*'s on November 12, 1914. Over 2267 *504J*'s were in use in flight-training schools by November 1918. Thousands of pilots, including the future King George VI, trained using the legendary *504.*

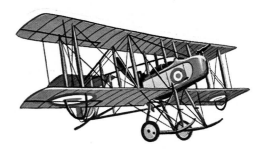

VICKERS F.B.5 (1914). The first aircraft designed to be armed with a machine gun was the *Destroyer,* presented by Vickers at the 1913 London Aero Show. Rechristened *F.B. (Fighting Biplane),* it was mass produced beginning in 1914 and in February 1915 outfitted the world's first fighter squadron, the 11th of the Royal Flying Corps. The *F.B.5* or *Gun-Bus* was operational until the summer of 1916.

SOPWITH F-1 CAMEL (1917). Descended from the *Pup* and the *Triplane,* it was one of the best fighters of the war and brought down the highest number of enemy aircraft (1294), among these the *Fokker Dr-I* flown by Von Richthofen. There were 5490 produced and flown in combat from July 1917 until the Armistice. Its record was particularly good in the battles of Ypres and Cambrai. The naval model was used on 43 British battleships.

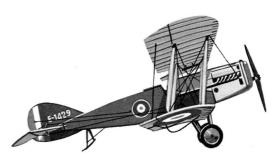

BRISTOL F-2B (1917). Two-seat fighter designed by F. Barnwell, who also designed the *Scout.* First used in action on March 8, 1917, after an unlucky debut it proved excellent. From June 20, 1917, until the following January the Canadians A. E. McKeever and L. F. Powell flying their *F-2B*'s shot down 30 enemy planes. Greatly feared by German aviation, 4470 *F-2B*'s were constructed. They remained in service until 1932.

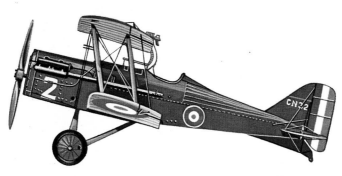

S.E.5a (1917). The best English fighter after the *Sopwith Camel,* it proved to be superior even to the French *Nieuport* and the *Spad.* It made its first flight on begun in January 1917 and ended after 5205 were completed. Used in action from spring 1917, it fought in 24 British, 2 American and 1 Australian squadron. It was the favorite of many aces, among them W. A. Bishop, J. T. B. McCudden and Edward Mannock, the British ace of aces. Mannock downed 73 enemy planes, 50 of these while at the controls of an *S.E.5a.*

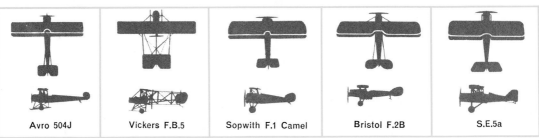

| Avro 504J | Vickers F.B.5 | Sopwith F.1 Camel | Bristol F.2B | S.E.5a |

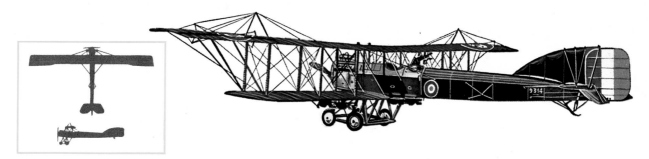

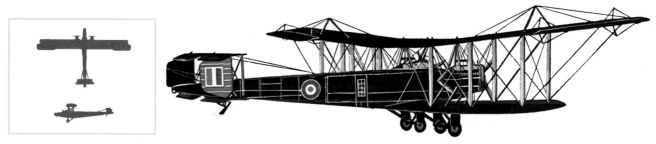

SHORT BOMBER (1916). Short (a firm specializing in seaplanes) built this bomber for the 1915 competition for bomber design sponsored by the Air Department of the British Admiralty. Eighty-three *Short Bombers* in all were built by 5 different factories. This model, which carried either four 250-pound or eight 112-pound bombs, had its trial by fire in the bombing of Ostend during the night of November 15, 1916. The operation, in which 4 *Bombers* participated, was the first of a series on the Ostend port and on the base at Zeebrugge. In April 1917 the *Short Bomber* was replaced by the *Handley Page 0/100.*

HANDLEY PAGE 0/400 (1916). The first real heavy night bomber, brought into being by the will of the British Admiralty. There were two types: *0/100* (46 aircraft built) and the more powerful version, the *0/400* (550 built). The former arrived in France in November 1916 and the latter followed in the spring of 1917. The *0/400* was used in night bombing on military objectives in German occupied zones until August 1918, when a series of actions was begun on the Saar- and the Rhineland, the heart of the German war industry. The *0/400* carried either twelve 112-pound bombs or one large 1650-pound bomb.

HANDLEY PAGE V/1500 (1918). The first British 4-engine aircraft, it was the largest plane of the First World War, the first true strategic bomber. Built on the orders of the Air Ministry, which planned to use it in action over Berlin, it never saw combat. Before the Armistice only three *V/1500*'s had been delivered to the fighting units. It could carry thirty 250-pound bombs or two gigantic 3300-pound bombs. It was the forerunner of the World War II *Halifax* and *Lancaster.*

BLACKBURN KANGAROO (1918). A heavy bomber which made its first flight in January 1918. Only 16 aircraft were ready in time to enter the action. Assigned to the No. 246 Squadron of the newly formed Royal Air Force, it made a notable showing in action against German submarines in the North Sea, sinking one in August 1918 and damaging four others. A few *Kangaroos*, modified for commercial use, were still flying in 1929.

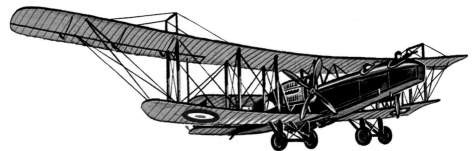

ILYA MOUROMETZ V (1915). The *Le Grand* was the world's first 4-engine aircraft. Designed by Igor Sikorsky and G. I. Lavrov, it flew on May 13, 1913, and the following February broke the "weight-altitude" record, carrying 16 passengers at 6500 feet. Ordered in mass production at the R.B.V.Z. factory in the spring of 1914, it was renamed the *Ilya Mourometz* after a legendary Russian hero. It first saw action during the War on February 15, 1915, bombing a target in East Prussia. In the *Eskadra Vordushnykh Korablei,* i.e. "Flying Ships Squadron," the *Ilya* completed more than 400 missions over Germany and Lithuania, losing only two aircraft! Eighty were built. They were armed with 7 machine guns and carried about 1150 pounds of bombs.

RUSSIA

Czarist Russia entered the War with extremely weak air power (fewer than 150 aircraft), almost exclusively *Farman*s, *Voisin*s, *Caudron*s and *Morane*s bought from France. It could, however, boast the first gigantic 4-engine bomber, the *Ilya Mourometz* designed by Igor Sikorsky (who was to play such a large part in the history of aviation after his move to the United States. With 80 of these 4-engine aircraft the world's first heavy bomber squadron was formed and set an incredible record—over 400 missions, with only two airplanes downed by the enemy. But Russian aviation industry could not make up for time lost before the War and thus it can be said to have been virtually nonexistent. It was limited to producing only a modest number of reconnaissance aircraft and the *Ilya.* The Revolution and the separate peace of Brest-Litovsk (March 3, 1918) sharply cut all projected plans for development. In spite of its numeric and qualitative inferiority in respect to the enemy, Czarist aviation fought well, and about 20 aces, first among them Capt. Alexander Kazakov (17 planes downed), Capt. P. V. d'Argueeff (15) and Lt. A. P. Seversky.

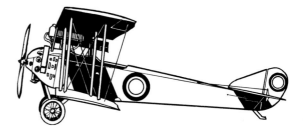

ANATRA DS (1916). A reconnaissance modeled after a captured *Aviatik,* it was built by the Anatra factory in Odessa which until then had built the *Voisin* under license. In service in the summer of 1916, it was put into full use a year later. An irremediable weakness in the wing structure made the *Anatra DS* particularly dangerous; consequently its production was limited.

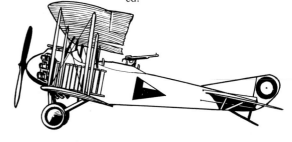

LEBED 12 (1916). This two-seater Russian reconnaissance produced under the direction of one of the pioneers of Czarist aviation, Vladimir A. Lebedev, also closely resembled a German plane: the *Albatros B-II.* The first version, *Lebed 11,* appeared in 1915 and only 10 were built. The definitive model, the *Lebed 12* made its first flight on December 28, 1915, but did not begin service until 10 months later because of continuing structural difficulties. The Imperial Air Service ordered 225 *Lebed 12*'s but only 214 were produced in time for use before the Armistice.

ITALY

The first nation to use an aircraft in wartime (1911) could count on only 89 airplanes when it entered the War on May 24, 1915, despite the fact that the experience on the French front should have signaled the need for air power. In 1915 the young Italian aeronautics industry had produced only 382 aircraft, all under French license. In the following three years, however, Ansaldo, Caproni, Macchi, Pomilio, SIA-Fiat and Savoia produced over 19,000 aircraft, some of which were of Italian design and among the best of their types, such as *S.V.A.* and the *Caproni*. On November 4, 1918, Italy had 1758 aircraft combat-ready, all nationally built. It is certain, nonetheless, that if Italy had not been able to buy fighters (*Hanriot HD-1, Nieuport, Spad VII*) from France, she could never have sustained aerial combat with the Austrian and German forces. But credit must go to Italy for having developed, second only to Russia, the first strategic bombers, excellent examples of which are the *Caproni Ca-3* and *Ca-4*. This development was made possible by the perseverance of Gen. Giulio Douhet (commander of the First Aviators' Battalion in 1911) who believed in the importance of a strong and uniform bombing force which could make heavy strikes on faraway objectives in enemy territory. In 1917 Douhet's ideas were put into effect with bombings on Lubiana, Pola and other important cities, using groups of as many as 130 aircraft. Twenty-eight gold medals and 1800 silver medals (Italy's highest honors) stand as proof of the valor and ability of the Italian aviators led by Maj. Francesco Baracca (34 planes downed). Among the other 42 aces were Lt. Silvio Scaroni (26), Lt. Col. Pier Ruggero Piccio (24), Lt. Flavio Torello Baracchini (21), Capt. Fulco Ruffo di Calabria (20). The Italians counted 763 aircraft downed against 166 of their own lost.

POMILIO PE (1917). The Pomilio brothers' fast reconnaissance was the most widely produced aircraft (1616) of Italian design of the War. It was the first used in action in March 1917 and one year later the *PE* outfitted 30 squadrons. It took part (with 112 aircraft) in the battle of Vittorio Veneto. In 1918 the Pomilio brothers emigrated to the U.S. where they designed two new aircraft for the U.S. Signal Corps.

FIAT R-2 (1917). When, in 1918, the Società Italiana Aviazione became Fiat Aviation, civil engineer Celestino Rosatelli redesigned the *SVA 7B*, first designed by U. Savoia and R. Verduzio. The new aircraft was called *R-2,* the first to bear the Fiat name. Only 129 were built before the Armistice but it remained the standard Italian reconnaissance until 1925.

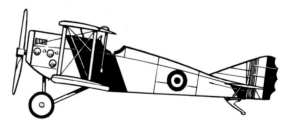

ANSALDO A-1 BALILLA (1917). Designed by G. Brezzi, it was the first Italian-designed fighter to be mass produced. Tested in November 1917, it was judged fast but poorly manageable by the aces Baracca, Piccio and Ruffo di Calabria. Called the *Balilla,* 150 were built but only two were used in action as escorts for a bomber unit over Pola in July 1918.

The emblems of the 82nd and 77th squadrons.

MACCHI M-5 (1917). A one seat fighter flying boat which could match the land-based fighter it was descended from, the *M-3*, Macchi's first original aircraft, designed by Calzavara and Buzio in 1913. About 200 *M-3*'s were used by the Navy at the beginning of the war; one of these broke the height record in 1916 in a 17,716-foot flight over Lake Varese. There were 350 *M-5*'s built and entered in service in 1917, with 5 naval squadrons in the Adriatic. Macchi had built the first flying boat (139 *L-1*'s copied from the Austrian *Lohner L-40*) for the Ministry of the Navy in 1914.

ANSALDO S.V.A. 5 (1917). The *S.V.A.* (by Savoia and Verduzio, designers, and Ansaldo) was the best reconnaissance–light bomber of the war. In all, 1248 were produced. It outfitted 6 squadrons beginning in February 1918 and remained in service until 1930. The aircraft achieved sensational feats such as L. Locatello's and A. Ferrarin's reconnaissance flight over Friedrichshafen (440 miles) and the incursion on Vienna (625 miles) carried out on August 9 by nine planes of the 87th Squadron, "la Serenissima." with the well-known Italian poet Gabriele D'Annunzio as a passenger. In February 1919 A. Ferrarin and Masiero, in *S.V.A.*'s, flew Rome–Tokyo (11,310 miles) in 109 hours' flying time.

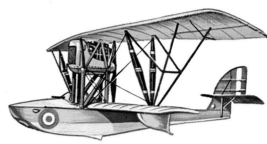

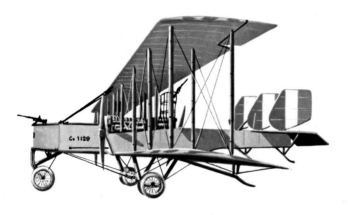

CAPRONI Ca-3 (1915). Besides Russia, Italy was the only power which believed in the usefulness of heavy strategic bombers as far back as the beginning of the War. The 3-engine *Caproni Ca-1* was already flying in 1914. The *Ca-2*, 167 of which were built equipped with Fiat engines, became operational in 1915. The *Ca-3*, identical to the *Ca-2* except for its Isotta-Fraschini engines, outfitted 12 squadrons of the Aeronautica Militare at the end of 1916. It had a 1000-pound-bomb capacity.

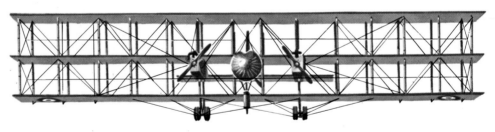

CAPRONI Ca-4 (1917). Basically very similar to the *Ca-3*, it was different in that it was a triplane and was larger. It never completely replaced the biplane, which remained in use until the end of the War, but was used with it, mostly in night bombing actions over Austria and the Adriatic coast. The *Ca-4*'s of the 181st and 182nd naval Squadrons were also used intensively in daylight bombing in the battle of Vittorio Veneto in October 1918. There were 41 *Caproni Ca-4*'s built. Their 3195-pound bomb capacity made them the most successful heavy bombers of the war.

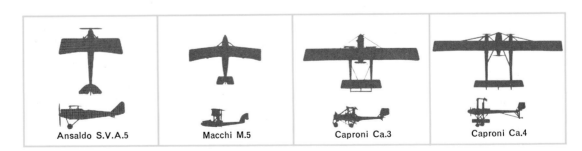

Ansaldo S.V.A.5 | Macchi M.5 | Caproni Ca.3 | Caproni Ca.4

Emblems (top to bottom and left to right): 70th Fighter Squadron ace Maj. Francesco Baracca (personal); 1st Reconnaissance Section; 80th Fighter Squadron; 81st Fighter Squadron.

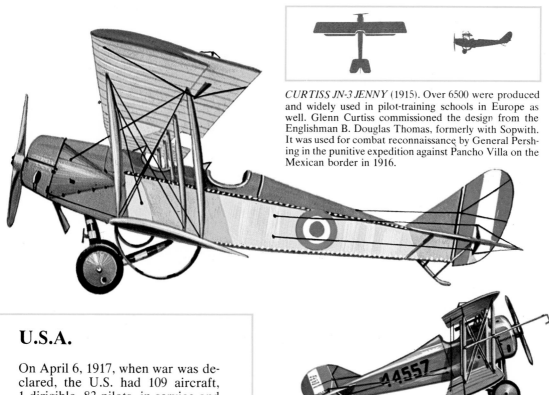

CURTISS JN-3 JENNY (1915). Over 6500 were produced and widely used in pilot-training schools in Europe as well. Glenn Curtiss commissioned the design from the Englishman B. Douglas Thomas, formerly with Sopwith. It was used for combat reconnaissance by General Pershing in the punitive expedition against Pancho Villa on the Mexican border in 1916.

U.S.A.

On April 6, 1917, when war was declared, the U.S. had 109 aircraft, 1 dirigible, 83 pilots in service and no aeronautic industry (64 airplanes were produced in 1916!). A sad count for the country which had invented the airplane. . . . What had taken place on the European fronts had not taught any lessons to the army officials in charge who were quite unprepared for war. Thus the American Expeditionary Force, on the orders of Col. William Mitchell, began operations in Europe in 1918, using French aircraft exclusively. American industries, developed in a rush, produced very few aircraft of their own design and many on license but too late for use in Europe. However, a large group of Americans had been fighting the Germans since 1916 when the Escadrille de Chasse 124, nicknamed *Lafayette,* made up of volunteers from the U.S., flying *Nieuports,* was formed. The 124th became the 103rd Pursuit Squadron of the A.E.F. in 1918. The A.E.F. boys brought down 781 enemy aircraft and had 88 aces, among them Capt. Edward V. Rickenbacker (26 planes downed), Lt. Frank Luke, Jr. (21) and Maj. Raoul Lufbery (17).

STANDARD E-1 (1917). Rejected as a fighter because of its low speed, 460 were ordered for advanced training. Only 168 *E-1*'s were produced before the Armistice. The Standard Aircraft Company of Elizabeth, New Jersey, produced European aircraft under license and in 1918 was the second largest aeronautics company in the U.S.

THOMAS-MORSE S-4 (1917). Designed by the same B. D. Thomas who had created the popular *Jenny,* it too proved inadequate as a fighter and 597 of the *S-4B* and *S-4C* models were produced for advanced training. At the end of the war, it was sold to a private owner as war surplus, and had its days of glory as a sports aircraft.

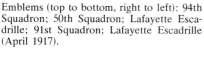

Emblems (top to bottom, right to left): 94th Squadron; 50th Squadron; Lafayette Escadrille; 91st Squadron; Lafayette Escadrille (April 1917).

42

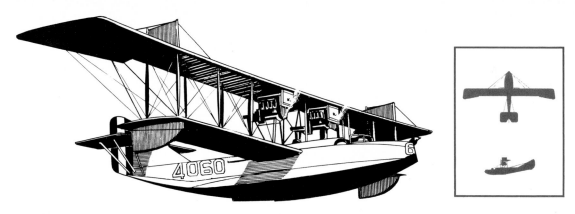

CURTISS H-12 (1917). Before the outbreak of hostilities in Europe, Glenn Curtiss, with the collaboration of the English Navy pilot John C. Porte, had been building a huge flying boat with which Rodman Wanamaker intended to attempt a transatlantic flight. When Great Britain entered the War, the aircraft was ceded to the Royal Navy. After testing it, the Navy ordered another 64 built, and these were delivered with the *H-4* name in mid-1915. The *H-12,* an ever more highly perfected model, was ordered by the U.S. Navy (which sent 50 to Europe) and by the British Admiralty, which received 71. The Royal Navy used them successfully against *Zeppelin*s and German submarines in the North Sea and the Channel. The *H-12* was the first U.S.-built aircraft to down an enemy airplane.

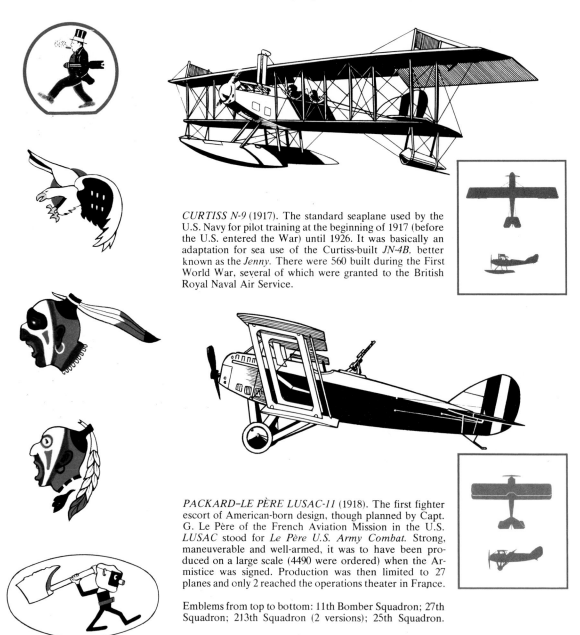

CURTISS N-9 (1917). The standard seaplane used by the U.S. Navy for pilot training at the beginning of 1917 (before the U.S. entered the War) until 1926. It was basically an adaptation for sea use of the Curtiss-built *JN-4B,* better known as the *Jenny.* There were 560 built during the First World War, several of which were granted to the British Royal Naval Air Service.

PACKARD–LE PÈRE LUSAC-11 (1918). The first fighter escort of American-born design, though planned by Capt. G. Le Père of the French Aviation Mission in the U.S. *LUSAC* stood for *Le Père U.S. Army Combat.* Strong, maneuverable and well-armed, it was to have been produced on a large scale (4490 were ordered) when the Armistice was signed. Production was then limited to 27 planes and only 2 reached the operations theater in France.

Emblems from top to bottom: 11th Bomber Squadron; 27th Squadron; 213th Squadron (2 versions); 25th Squadron.

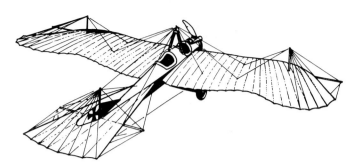

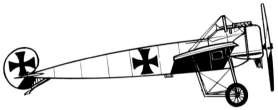

GERMANY AND THE CENTRAL POWERS

At the outbreak of the World War, Germany had the strongest military aviation force of the belligerents: about 300 aircraft and 6 dirigibles. The other Central Powers had 150 units. There were three factors in Germany's favor: the initial advantage; the luck of having designers of the caliber of the Dutchman Anthony Fokker, of Reinhold Platz (*Fokker Dr-I* and *D-VII*), R. Thelen and Schubert *(Albatros D),* Ernst Heinkel (*Albatros B* and *C, Hansa-Brandenburg D-I* and *W-12*), Hugo Junkers and many others; and high production capacity. Germany produced 4000 aircraft in 1915, 8000 in 1916 and 19,700 in 1917, for a grand total of nearly 48,000 during the course of the War. During the same period Austria-Hungary produced 5431 aircraft. Fokker's adaptation of synchronizing the firing of the machine gun with the revolutions of the propeller contributed much towards Germany's domination of the skies (with the *Fokker E*) until the middle of 1916, when the Allies were able to compete with the *Nieuport 11.* Air supremacy passed back and forth from Germany to the Allies, until 1918, when the Allies definitely gained the advantage. German air power, united under one independent command on October 8, 1916, remained a formidable challenge to its enemies.

Germany could boast the greatest ace of World War I, the legendary "Red Baron," Manfred von Richthofen (80 victories!) who, in his *Jagdgeschwader* or "circus," led many of the other 364 German aces. But the names of Max Immelmann (15), Ernst Udet (62), Erich Loewenhardt (53), Werner Voss (48), Oswald Boelcke (40) were certainly not any less known and respected. Among the Austrian pilots was the ace of aces Captain Godwin Brumowski with 40 enemy aircraft downed, followed by Lieutenant Julius Angi (32) and Lieutenant Frank Liuke-Crawford (30).

ETRICH A-II TAUBE (1910). Called the *Taube* ("dove" because of the shape of its wings), it was designed by the Austrian Igo Etrich in 1910, and became operational in 1915. On August 30, 1914, a *Taube,* piloted by Ferdinand von Hiddesen, dropped the five bombs, over 6.6 pounds each, on Paris. It was also the aircraft which trained all the best German aces.

FOKKER E-III (1915). Called *Scourge* by the Allies, it was the first German aircraft with a machine gun synchronized with the propeller. The first real fighter, it dominated until the advent of the *Nieuport* and the *F.E.2b* in January 1916. There were 450 produced. German ace Max Immelmann, the first to fly the *Fokker E-III* in action, was shot down in this aircraft by an *F.E.2b* on June 18, 1916.

AVIATIK B-II (1914). A reconnaissance widely used by the Germans and Austrians until 1916. The unarmed *B-1* version was used early in the war. From 1915, the spotter, seated in front of the pilot, was armed with a machine gun. Called *Gondola* by its crew because it rocked at the slightest turbulence, it was used in flight-training schools until 1917.

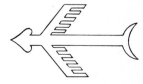

Emblems (top to bottom, right to left): Lt. Windisch, Jasta 66, on *Fokker D-VII;* Lt. Veltjens, Jasta 18, on *Albatros D-V;* Lt. Paul Baümer, Jasta 5, on *Albatros D-V.*

THE ALBATROS FAMILY

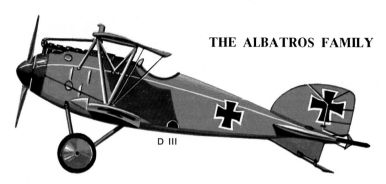

D III

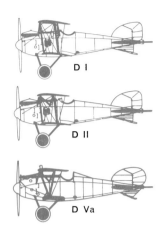

D I

D II

D Va

ALBATROS D (1916–1918). R. Thelen and Schubert, developing the designs of the 1914 *Albatros* racer, created the *D-I* in 1916, a fighter that was an equal match for the *D.H.2, B.E.2* and *Nieuport.* The ace Oswald Boelcke was among the first to fly the aircraft and was shot down in one on October 26, 1916. After about 40 *D-I's* came the *D-II,* offering better visibility to the pilot because of a new wing position. The *D-II's* began fighting in January 1917 with the new *Jastas* squadrons of one-seat fighters. The *D-III,* which incorporated several of the *Nieuport's* innovations, appeared in February 1917 and was the best of the lot, the leader until the appearance of the *Sopwith* and *Spad.* It won hundreds of aerial duels, many with Von Richthofen's Jasta II in the "Bloody April" of 1917. After about 800 *D-III's* were produced, the *D-V* followed, but never succeeded in matching its predecessor.

ALBATROS W-4 (1916). A sea-fighter directly descended from the *D-I,* it was to be used in defense of naval bases in Flanders (particularly Zeebrugge and Borkum) against frequent Allied incursions. First used in action in October 1916, it was adequate until the more powerful *Hansa-Brandenburg W-12* appeared in the summer of 1917. About 118 were produced and used in Aegean bases as well.

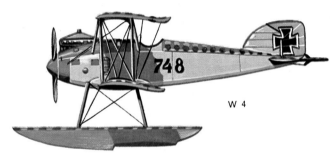

748

W 4

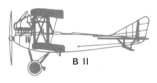

B II

ALBATROS B-II (1914). A two-seat reconnaissance designed by Ernst Heinkel, it was used during the entire course of the war and produced until 1917. It flew on all fronts until the end of 1915 when it was used in pilot-training schools, again proving its value. In the summer of 1914, a *B-II* piloted by Ernst von Lössl, set an altitude record of 14,760 feet.

ALBATROS C (1915–1917). The initial *C* identified armed reconnaissance planes in the German Air Force. The *C-I* was therefore an *Albatros B-II* with a more powerful engine and outfitted with a machine gun for the spotter. The ace O. Boelcke flew one for some time and Von Richthofen began his career in aviation as a spotter on a *C-I.* The *I* model became operational in the spring of 1915, followed by greater numbers of the *III* in 1916 with a new tail design. The *C-VII,* which began service at the front in 1917, was a completely new design for long-range reconnaissance. The last *Albatros C* was the *XII.* Three hundred of this model were flying when the Armistice was signed.

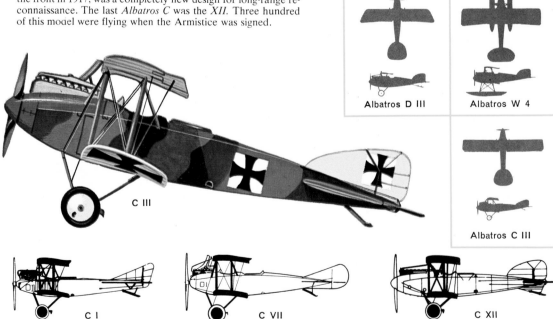

C III

Albatros D III

Albatros W 4

Albatros C III

C I

C VII

C XII

FOKKER Dr-I (1917). Designed by Reinhold Platz, it was the only German fighter triplane (*Dr.* stood for *Dreidecker,* or triplane). It was not a copy of the *Sopwith Triplane* and, in fact, proved to be a better aircraft. Because of an insoluble problem in the wing structure only slightly over 300 were built. It was finally replaced by the *Fokker D-VII.* The third *Dr-I* was delivered to Werner Voss on August 28, 1917, and the ace won over 20 duels with it by September 23, when it was shot down by an *S.E.5a.* The *Dr-I*'s fame was also closely linked to the *Richthofen Geschwader,* or "circus," and its legendary commander who, on April 21, 1918, was shot down while flying this type of aircraft.

RUMPLER C-I (1915). The reconnaissance *Rumpler B-I* was already in service at the beginning of the war and was replaced by the *C-I* in 1915. Initially the *C-I* had only one machine gun alongside the spotter, and later a second synchronized gun. It was produced by various factories until June 1917 and was used until the end of the War. In the spring of 1917, eight *C-I*'s adopted by General von Kress as spotter and liaison aircraft played an important role in the battle of Gaza.

L.V.G. C-I (1915). It was the first German reconnaissance (descended from the *B-I* in use in 1914) armed with a spotter's machine gun. On November 28, 1916, an *L.V.G. C-II* made a spectacular attack on London, dropping six 22-pound bombs on Victoria Station. Though it successfully completed the raid, the aircraft developed engine trouble on its return trip and was forced to land in Boulogne, where it fell into Allied hands. Designed by the Swiss Franz Schneider, a naturalized German, the *L.V.G. C-II* was one of the best German aircraft during the first two years of the War.

FOKKER D-VII (1918). The best German fighter, it was designed by R. Platz and won the contest sponsored by the War Ministry in 1918. It began flying in combat in April. By the Armistice, 48 Jastas were outfitted by more than 800 of the one thousand *D-VII*'s produced. The first unit to use them in battle was Von Richthofen's fighter group (Jastas 4, 6, 10 and 11) which was led by Hermann Goering after the death of the "Red Baron." In November 1918 Anthony Fokker moved to Holland bringing with him 400 engines and parts of 120 aircraft, thus violating the terms of the Armistice. The *D-VII,* therefore, remained in production for some years.

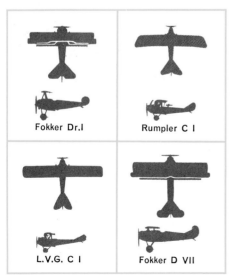

Fokker Dr.I

Rumpler C I

L.V.G. C I

Fokker D VII

Emblems (left to right): Captain Auffahrt, commander of the 29th Jasta on *Fokker D-VII;* ace Werner Voss, Jasta 5, on the *Albatros D-III.*

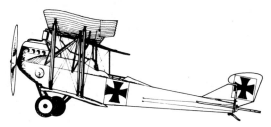

LOHNER C-I (1914). A two-seat Austrian reconnaissance plane manufactured by the Viennese industrialist Jakob Lohner, famous for his seaplanes. The *C-I* was an armed version of the *B-I* in use since 1914. It differed from the *B-I* in its longer fuselage. On February 14, 1916, several *Lohner C-I*'s took part in a bombing action (carried out basically as a show of force) over Milan.

LLOYD C-II (1915). An Austrian reconnaissance used throughout the War with the armed version type *C-II*. Beginning in 1915 it was widely used in combat on the Italian and Rumanian fronts. Nearly 500 were produced. During the summer of 1914 a *Lloyd C-I* piloted by Heinrich Bier with one passenger aboard, set an altitude record of 20,243 feet.

HANSA-BRANDENBURG D-I (1916). A one-seat fighter with the macabre nickname *Sarg,* or "coffin," it was designed in Germany by Ernst Heinkel for the Hansa-Brandenburg Co., owned by the Austrian Camillo Castiglione. It was produced exclusively for the Austro-Hungarian Air Force. Armed with one unsynchronized machine gun, its achievements were relatively modest.

AVIATIK D-I (1917). The first original Austrian fighter designed by Julius von Berg, chief designer for Aviatik, Austria, a branch of the German company. It replaced the *Hansa-Brandenburg D-I* and was used on the Russian, Italian and Baltic fronts. Production (over 700 planes) continued until the Armistice. It was the Austrians' best fighter.

HANNOVER CL-IIIa (1917). A two-seat escort and strike fighter designed by Hermann Dorner and the first original model built by Hannoversche Waggonfabrik. It first flew in combat in December 1917, with excellent results. Johann Bauer, later Hitler's personal pilot, shot down 9 enemy aircraft while at the controls of a *CL III.*

HALBERSTADT CL-II (1917). The first German *CL* (escort fighter and ground attack) had its first trial by fire on September 6, 1917, in the Battle of the Somme. It confirmed its worth the following November in the battle of Cambrai. The new *Schlachstaffeln,* or battle groups, created to operate as infantry support were outfitted with this model. Besides the machine guns, it could carry five 22-pound bombs.

Emblems (left to right): unidentified pilot; Joachim von Ziegesar, Jasta 15, on *Siemens D-III.*

PHÖNIX D-I (1917). A one-seat fighter used during the last months of the War. It was designed to substitute for the *Hansa-Brandenburg D-I,* from which it was basically developed. It began flying in the Austrian Air Force in February 1918, proving a worthy adversary for the Italian fighters. Too few were produced to restore to the Austrians the air dominance they had lost on the Italian front.

PFALZ D-III (1917). A one-seat fighter, it was the first original design by Rudolf Gehringer for the Pfalz Company. First used in September 1917, along with the *Albatros* and the *Fokker,* it was clearly inferior to them. The Allied pilots called it *Easy Meat.* At least 600 were built, 300 of which were still in action at the time of the Armistice.

L.F.G. ROLAND D-VIb (1918). A fighter derived from the two-seat *Roland C-II,* the War Ministry chose the *Fokker D-VII* over it. Still, since it was an excellent aircraft, a small number were ordered and reserved in case its more illustrious rival proved defective. It was first used in the spring of 1918 in the defense units at naval bases and airports.

JUNKERS CL-I (1918). Escort fighter and ground attack designed by Hugo Junkers, it was a metal structure completely covered by corrugated sheet-iron. It reached the front too late to prove its worth as an aircraft of its class. It made its first flight on May 4, 1918, and only 47 were delivered before the end of the War.

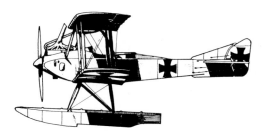

FRIEDRICHSHAFEN FF-33L (1916). Over 500 *FF-33*'s (the unarmed version) were built during the course of the War and used for reconnaissance. The *L* model was used as a naval fighter. It flew over the North Sea and the Channel from seaplane carriers. An *FF-33* was used on the auxiliary corsair cruiser the *Wolf* which sank 18 Allied ships in the Indian and Pacific oceans between 1916 and 1918.

HANSA-BRANDENBURG W-12 (1917). A two-seat naval fighter designed by Ernst Heinkel, 146 were produced and in use from the middle of 1917. Noticeably superior to the *FF-33L,* it proved to be an excellent aircraft. In the middle of 1918 it was replaced by the *W-19.* On December 17, 1917 Lieutenant Christiansen, flying a *W-12* downed the English dirigible the *C-27.*

Emblems (left to right): Captain Berthold on *Fokker D-VII;* Lieutenant Bertrass, Jasta 30, on *Albatros D-II.*

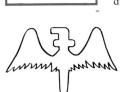

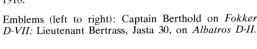

GOTHA G-VIII (1918). The *G* (*Grossflugzeug,* "large airplane") *VIII* was the last *Gotha* of World War I differing from its *G*-series predecessors by placing the propeller in the front rather than the rear of the craft. The *G-1* was designed for ground attack; the *G-II* and *G-III* in 1916 for bombing, with little success. The *G-IV* began to replace the *Zeppelin* dirigibles in daylight and night bombing attacks on London, and along with the *GV* dropped tons of explosives on the city beginning in April 1917. Although they caused little real damage, the *Gotha*s forced the English to recall home, for defense purposes, fighter squadrons that were being used at the front. The *Gotha G*'s were the best German strategic bombers of the War.

FRIEDRICHSHAFEN G-III (1917). A heavy bomber, it made its first flight in autumn, 1914. Only the prototype was produced without variations. The *G-II* (1916) still had too many weaknesses and only a few were built. The *G-III* became operational in February 1917, mostly over the Western front, in attacks on Paris, the rest of France and Belgium. It rarely participated in attacks on London. The *Friedrichshafen G,* with the *Gotha G,* outfitted the *Bombengeschwader,* German Air Force bomber groups. The Friedrichshafen Co., known for its seaplanes, was founded by Von Zeppelin, who was greatly interested in large aircraft as well as dirigibles.

ZEPPELIN R-VI (1917). The first *R* (*Riesenflugzeug,* or "gigantic airplane") designed by B. G. Klein and H. Hirth, under the supervision of Robert Bosch and Von Zeppelin himself, flew on April 11, 1915, and was followed by different prototypes of 4, 5 and even 6 engines, each representing an experiment of extraordinary interest. The only mass-produced *R* was the *VI* (18 produced in all) which made its first attack on London on September 17, 1917. An *R-VI,* on February 16, 1918, dropped the first 2200-pound bomb on England, hitting the Royal Hospital in Chelsea. The 501st Squadron, outfitted with *R-VI*s, made 11 attacks on London between December 18, 1917, and May 20, 1918, dropping 59,926 pounds of bombs on their target.

Emblems (left to right): Ritter von Schleich, Jasta 32; Lieutenant von Hantelmann, Jasta 15, on *Siemens Schuckert D-III.*

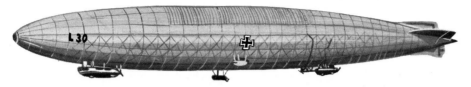

ZEPPELIN DIRIGIBLE (1915). On August 2, 1914, at the outbreak of World War I, Germany had 12 dirigibles, 6 of them *Zeppelins*, mostly for use in long-range bombing. On August 9, 1915, in fact, they flew their first mission over London. Although not as practical as the airplane, many others were in use before the end of the war. But put to the test they proved too vulnerable to the Allied fighter and basically more suitable as reconnaissance over the North Sea.

L.F.G. Roland C-II (1916). An armed reconnaissance designed by the engineer Tantzen and nicknamed the *Whale* or *Slug* by the English because of its shape, it was one of the most advanced designs of its time. It flew in action for the first time at Verdun and then over the Somme with excellent results. Three hundred were produced until the summer of 1917.

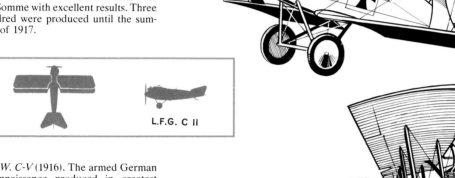

L.F.G. C II

D.F.W. C-V (1916). The armed German reconnaissance produced in greatest numbers during the War, it was certainly one of the best. Designed by Heinrich Oelerich, it became operational in the spring of 1916 and was in service until the Armistice, when 600 *D.F.W. C-V*'s were still flying. Its name is linked to the battle of Arras (April 1917).

A.E.G. G IV

D.F.W. C V

A.E.G. G-IV (1916). Designed as a long-range bomber though it was used for tactical bombing. The *G-I. G-II* and *G-III* types all appeared in 1915 but few were produced. The *G-IV* began flying in combat at the end of 1916 and immediately proved its effectiveness in the bombing of Bucharest in February 1917 and of Venice, Padua, Treviso and Verona in November 1917. Of the 400 *G-IV*'s built, almost all saw service in the *Kampfgeschwader der Obersten Heeresleitung* or *Kagohl* (Battle Squadrons of the Army High Command) and were used until the Armistice.

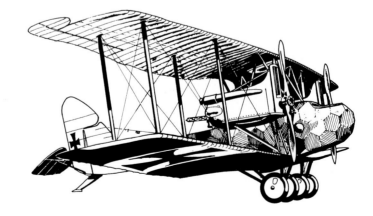

FROM 1918 TO LINDBERGH'S FLIGHT ACROSS THE ATLANTIC

During the last days of World War I, the skies of Europe were filled with thousands of aircraft, like hawks after prey. When the Armistice was declared they disappeared from the blue like a sudden migration. We rediscover them lying lifeless and abandoned on the flying fields. In the factories the buzz generated by feverish activity was replaced by the silence of inactivity caused by cancellations of all orders. Hundreds of flying fields went to seed and within a year were overgrown with tall grass and underbrush. Thousands of pilots returned to civilian life. No longer bound to their uniforms, they also no longer had a chance to fly. Though joy at a hard-won peace was great, confusion was rampant. If it were not for faith and strong will, aviation progress, which had taken giant steps forward in less than 20 years, would have come to a halt.

But fortunately, aviation had its prophets: builders like Curtiss, De Havilland, Caproni, Blériot, Farman, Fokker, Junkers, Dornier and many others, all of them "flight addicts" like those pilots who dared everything, even becoming acrobats of the skies, just to be able to keep the stick in their fists. These were the men who were to transform and develop the airplane as an instrument of peace.

The Germans, emerging from defeat, were the first to take the initiative. On February 5, three months after the Armistice was signed, the Deutsche Luft Reederei inaugurated the first European civil airline, flying the Berlin–Leipzig–Weimar route, with two *A.E.G.* aircraft *(p.54)*. Five other German companies were founded in the same year, opening the Berlin–Copenhagen, Dresden–Berlin, Munich–Berlin (via Frankfurt and Vienna) routes.

Also in 1919, the Lignes Aériennes Farman, the Compagnie Générale Transaériennes, the Compagnie des Messageries Aériennes, the Compagnie des Grands Exprès Aériens and many others were born in France, with service linking Paris to London, Brussels, Copenhagen and Casablanca. At the same time in Great Britain A. V. Roe and Company (Manchester–Southport–Blackpool), the Aircraft Transport and Travel (London–Paris, London–Amsterdam) and the Handley Page Air Transport began operating. On October 7, 1919, the Koninklijke Luchtvaart Maatschappij voos Nederland en Kolonien (KLM) was created. In 1920 the Syndicat National pour l'Étude des Transports Aériens (SNETA), which in 1923 became the Société Anonyme Belge d'Exploitation de la Navigation Aérienne (SABENA), was born.

In that same year in the United States,

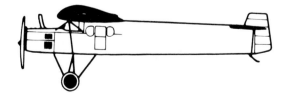

BREGUET 14T (1919, F). At least 200 ex-bombers of this type were used for the first French civilian air service by the Compagnie des Messageries Aériennes on their Paris–Lille–Brussels and Paris–London lines and by the Lignes Aériennes Latécoère on their Toulouse-Barcelona-Tangiers–Casablanca–Oran–Dakar lines for postal and sometimes passenger transport.

AIRCO D.H.4A (1919, GB). A modified cabin model of the famous *De Havilland* bomber, 7 were produced for Aircraft Transport and Travel Ltd. and for Handley Page Air Transport of London. On August 25, 1919, a *D.H.4A* inaugurated the English civilian air service with a flight from London to Paris. The cost of the ticket was 20 guineas.

Hubbard Air Transport Co., flying the Vancouver–Seattle line, was founded, as was the Aeromarine West Indies Airways, linking Key West and Havana. The Post Office Department opened an airmail line between New York City and Chicago with 17 war-surplus planes and 40 pilots, 31 of whom lost their lives in noble attempts to improve the line's efficiency and respect its timetables, regardless of atmospheric conditions: a high price to pay for progress.

The flowering of these airline companies did not mean a rapid or prosperous start for civil aviation. The major problems were a lack of suitable airplanes for passenger transport and the public's belief that flying was extremely dangerous, fit for reckless young men, but not appropriate for responsible businessmen, the only ones who were able to pay the price of a ticket merely to get them somewhere faster.

The airlines had a hard and troubled life. In Europe after a number of years, only those

airlines that were government financed could prosper: in Germany, Deutsche Lufthansa (1926), and in Great Britain, English Imperial Airways (1924), both of which had absorbed other minor companies; and KLM, the French Air Union, SABENA, the Ceskoslovenské Stàtni Aeroeinie (CSA), the Magyar Legiforgalmi (MALERT) and a few others.

The widely acclaimed aviation feats performed from 1919 on had a positive and decisive influence on the growth of civil aviation and were more convincing than any commercial advertising. May 6, 1919, witnessed the first transatlantic crossing, successfully completed in stages, by a *Navy Curtiss NC (p.53)* flying boat. Just over a month later the first nonstop transatlantic flight was made by John Alcock and Arthur Whitten Brown. The pilots won the £10,000 purse offered by the London *Daily Mail*. The crossing was made aboard a *Vickers-Vimy (p.53)*, a war-surplus plane. It was a great event, made even more exciting be-

CAPRONI C-60 TRANSAERO (1919, I). The largest flying ship built before 1920 was this gigantic multiwing seaplane designed by the engineer Caproni, creator of the World War I heavy bombers. This plane was to carry 100 passengers on transoceanic flights, but the engines of the time could not generate enough power for this giant. During its first flight attempt at Lake Maggiore it could not lift itself off the water and suffered heavy damage. The ambitious project was then abandoned.

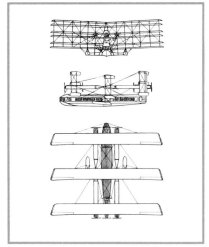

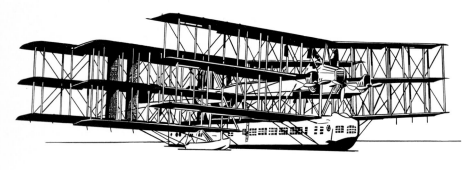

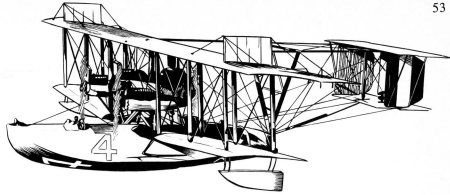

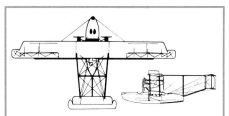

NAVY CURTISS NC (1919, USA). It was the first aircraft to fly the Atlantic in stages. The prototype of this large 4-engine flying boat, designed by G. Curtiss in collaboration with the U.S. Navy, made its first flight on October 4, 1918. On May 16, 1919, the *NC-1, NC-3* and *NC-4* led by Comdr. John H. Towers, left Trepassy Bay in Newfoundland, destination Europe. The first two aircraft were forced down, but the *NC-4* reached Plymouth, England, in triumph on May 31 after stops in the Azores and Lisbon. The flight from Trepassy Bay to the Azores (1392 miles covered in 15 hours and 18 minutes) set a record for the longest flight over water. Ten *NC*'s were built, at least two of which (*NC-5* and *NC-6*) were 3- rather than 4-engine models.

cause of the other attempts that were made.

For the English, the adventurous voyage of 4 Australians—Captain Ross Smith, his brother Keith and two other courageous companions—who flew from England to Australia, was particularly meaningful. Aboard a *Vickers-Vimy,* they reached Port Darwin after 27 days and 20 hours, crossing all of Europe and Asia. They thus won the £10,000 prize offered by the Australian government to anyone who would link London with the faraway Australian continent in less than 30 days flying an English-built plane.

Aviation achievements continued to hold a place of honor on the front pages of the newspapers. The round-trip crossing of the Atlantic by the English dirigible the *R-34* *(p.54),* champion of the lighter-than-air school, was less acclaimed than the voyage of two Italians, Arturo Ferrarin and Guido Masiero. Officers of the Aviazione Militare Italiana, they left Rome on February 14, 1920, flying an *S.V.A.,* and reached Tokyo, 11,250

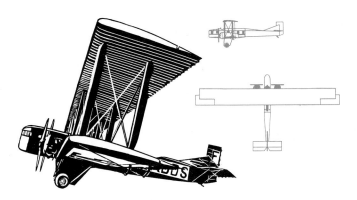

FARMAN F-60 GOLIATH (1919, F). Designed originally as a bomber, it was produced as a passenger liner and was not only one of the first, but also one of the most successful of its kind. No less than 60 aircraft of this type were built. On February 8, 1919, an *F-60* of the Farman Lines inaugurated the first passenger service between Paris and London. The *F-60* flew the Paris–London route for the Compagnie des Grands Exprès Aériens and the Paris–Brussels route for the Messageries Aeriennes. Beginning in 1921, the aircraft was used on the Paris–Amsterdam–Berlin line, it was adopted by many companies, among them SABENA and the Czech line, CSA. Several *F-60*'s were still flying in 1933.

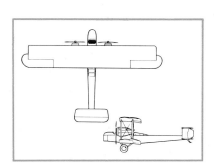

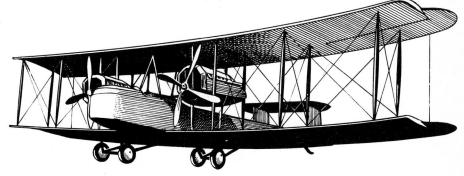

VICKERS-VIMY IV (1919, GB). The first aircraft to cross the Atlantic nonstop. In 1913, the London *Daily Mail* offered a £10,000 prize for a nonstop Atlantic crossing. At the end of World War I, the offer still held, and many contenders prepared to attempt the crossing with all types of aircraft imaginable, among these a *Handley Page* biplane, a *Curtiss Colossus* flying boat, a *Handley Page V/1500* and a *Sopwith Atlantic.* Nearly all chose to take off for Europe from Newfoundland in order to have the advantage of favorable winds. The winners were Capt. John Alcock and Lt. Arthur Whitten Brown, in a *Vimy IV,* a bomber which had never been flown in action during the war because it became operational too late. On June 14, 1919, the *Vimy IV* covered the 1890 miles between Newfoundland and Ireland in 16 hours and 27 minutes, at an average speed of 118 miles per hour.

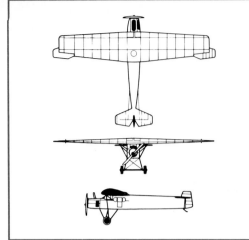

FOKKER F-III (1921, NL). This aircraft was developed from R. Platz's 1918 design to fill KLM's requirements and was very successful. About 60 *F-III*'s were used by various airlines on almost all major European routes. In 1931 at least 13 were still in service, 8 of these in Germany and 2 in Italy.

A.E.G. J-II (1919, D). This plane served the same purpose in Germany as the *Breguet 14T* and the *Airco D.H.4A* did in France and England. A modified version of the military aircraft, it began service in February 1919 with the newly founded Deutsche Luft Reederei and Deutsche Aero Lloyd. Only a few *J-II*'s were cabin models such as that illustrated here.

BLERIOT SPAD 46 (1921, F). In 1920 the *Spad 33,* a four-passenger plane, which in various versions remained in production until 1930, was born. The *Spad 46* was the second version and a few dozen were produced. These were used by the Cie des Messageries Aériennes, the Cie-Franco-Roumaine de Navigation Aérienne, SABENA and others.

miles away, after 109 hours' flying time, not without accidents and vicissitudes.

Alcock, Smith and Ferrarin had in mind the peacetime uses of flight, but the indomitable ex-commander of the aviation arm of the U.S. 1st Army in France in 1918, William Mitchell, could not help but think of war. Named Assistant Chief of the Army Air Service, that is, head of Military Aviation, he began a forceful campaign to convince the nation of the necessity of a strong air force which, according to him, would be the decisive element in future battles. Billy, as he was known to his pilots, insisted that the navy itself would take second place to the air force because of the vulnerability of vessels to air attack. He staged a spectacular practical demonstration to prove his point; on July 21, 1921, just outside Chesapeake Bay, eight *Martin MB* bombers *(p.61)* dropping 2000-pound bombs from a height of 2500 feet, sank the so-called invulnerable German battleship *Ostfriesland.* On previous days other types of aircraft had sunk a submarine, a destroyer and a light cruiser. The experiment made an enormous impression. It convinced the U.S. Navy to give the go-ahead for construction of

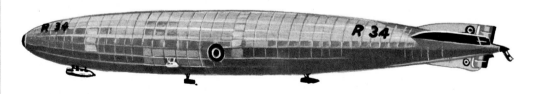

R-34 (1919, GB). The lighter-than-air men had a great triumph when a dirigible succeeded in crossing the Atlantic Ocean. On July 2, 1919, the R.A.F. *R-34* left Scotland and reached Mineola, Long Island, after about 110 hours' flying time. The return trip, with favorable winds, was made in only 80 hours!

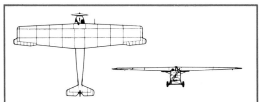

FOKKER T-2 (1921, NL). The first U.S. nonstop coast-to-coast flight, from Long Island, New York, to San Diego, California, was made in May 1923 by a *T-2*, a transport aircraft built in Holland and bought by the Air Service of the American Army. On May 2, Lt. Oakley Kelly and John Macready left the East Coast and reached California after 26 hours, 50 minutes and 38 seconds of flight, covering 2520 miles at an average of 94 miles per hour.

the first aircraft carriers; it pushed the American government to assign the status of Corps to the Air Service (Army Air Corps, 1926); it forced the military general staffs of all nations to review their strategy for future wars and to hold aviation in greater esteem. Still not happy with what he had accomplished, Billy kept on arguing, even with the President of the United States, so much that he was finally court-martialed for insubordination. The trial ended with a verdict of guilty and Mitchell resigned from the army. At the time few men believed he was right. Many years later, on December 7, 1941, with the destruction of the American fleet at Pearl Harbor from the air, the Japanese proved just how right he was.

While General Mitchell fought his personal battle in Washington, his pilots took it upon themselves to attract the public's attention. In May of 1923 an army *Fokker T-2* made the first nonstop flight across the U.S. from New York City to San Diego. In August 1923, Captain Lowell H. Smith and Lieutenant John P. Richter, aboard a quite outdated *D.H.4,* broke all flight-endurance records, remaining airborne 7 hours, 15 minutes and 14 seconds,

(continued on page 58)

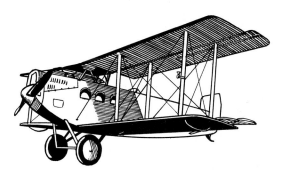

AERO A-10 (1924, CS). The first commercial aircraft (for 3 to 5 passengers) built in Czechoslovakia, it began service in 1924 flying the Prague-Brno-Bratislava line of the Ceskoslovenské Statni Aerolinie (CSA). Only 5 *A-10*'s were built. The Aero company also built several other types which were of interest in the following years.

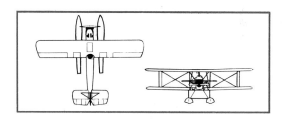

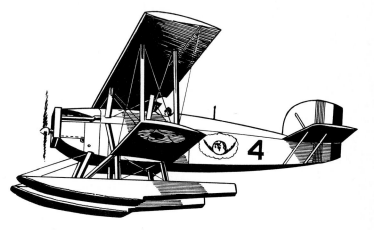

DOUGLAS DWC/0-5 WORLD CRUISER (1924, USA). The first aircraft to fly around the world. The *DWC* was not equipped with radio; it had regular undercarriage landing gear, which could be replaced by floats for marine flights. On April 6, 1924, four *DWC*'s, the *Chicago,* the *New Orleans,* the *Boston* and the *Seattle,* left the West Coast of the U.S., destination Japan. Only the *Chicago* and the *New Orleans,* flying over India, Persia, the Middle East, France, England, the Atlantic Ocean and Alaska, made it back to their Seattle base after a 28,000-mile flight. The flight took 175 days and 371 hours' flying time at an average speed of 74.5 miles per hour.

CIVIL AIRPLANES OF THE 1920s

At the end of the War the aeronautics industry entered a period of crisis which could be overcome only by making aircraft succeed as a means of civil transportation.

In 1919 the first airlines were born, using war-surplus planes such as the *Breguet 14T* and the *D.H.4A (p.52)*, the *A.E.G. J-II (p.54)* and the *Lévy-Lepen* flying boat. The latter opened the first air-line route in Equatorial Africa, flying between Kinshasa and Stanleyville in the Congo. At the same time, designers were studying aircraft for more functional, comfortable and safer passenger flying. The engineers G. Caproni, with his *Transaero (p.52)*, and Adolf Rohrbach, with the *Staaken 1000-PS*, had already designed their giants of the air, while Farman, Blériot, Junkers and Dornier worked on more modest but certainly more practical designs.

The French, first to arrive with the *Farman F-60 (p.53)* also designed the *Caudron C-61*, the *Blériot 135* and the *Lioré et Olivier 213*. These were used for the most part on the Paris–London line. But the French focused their attention on postal planes.

The English, after designing the *Handley Page W8B* in 1922, produced no other important planes until 1926, when the *D.H.66 Hercules* and the *A. W. Argosy (p.58)* appeared, expressly designed for Imperial Airways.

The Germans were even more active, despite the clause contained in the Armistice forbidding them to construct planes of over 60 horsepower faster than 106 miles per hour and with cargo capacity of over 1322 pounds. But Junkers and Dornier got around the clause by opening factories in Sweden, Russia and Italy. They created important aircraft such as the *Junkers F13* (forefather of the *G24*, the first 3-engine civil airplane of entirely metal construction with low wings) and the *Dornier Wal*, which remained in production until 1936. The industry was given much support by Deutsche Lufthansa, which used only national products (with the exception of a few *Fokkers*), such as the aircraft mentioned above, the small *Dornier*, the *Albatros L-73*, the *Focke-Wulf A-17a (p.59)* and the *Roland II*, direct descendant of the ill-fated *Staaken*.

In the field of passenger aircraft, Italy was relatively inactive during this time (the *Cant-10ter* was the first national flying boat to be used in service). The Czechs, Spanish and Russians were also relatively inactive. Only the Dutch, thanks to Fokker's genius, made outstanding contributions.

Up to 1927 the United States still had not created one important passenger plane. The industry devoted its efforts to mail planes, the *Douglas M-4* and the *Curtiss Falcon*, and to agricultural aircraft like the *Huff-Daland Petrel 31 Duster*. It seemed that once again, the U.S. would come in second to Europe in the race for aeronautical progress.

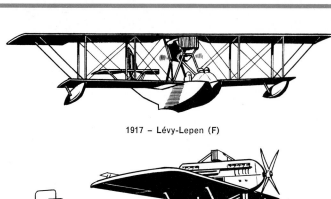

1917 – Lévy-Lepen (F)

1922 – Dornier Do J Wal (D)

1926 – Albatros L 73 (D)

1929 – Roland II (D)

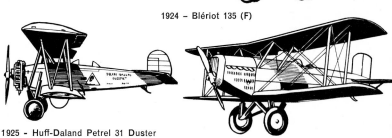

1924 – Blériot 135 (F)

1925 - Huff-Daland Petrel 31 Duster

1927 – Douglas M-4 (USA)

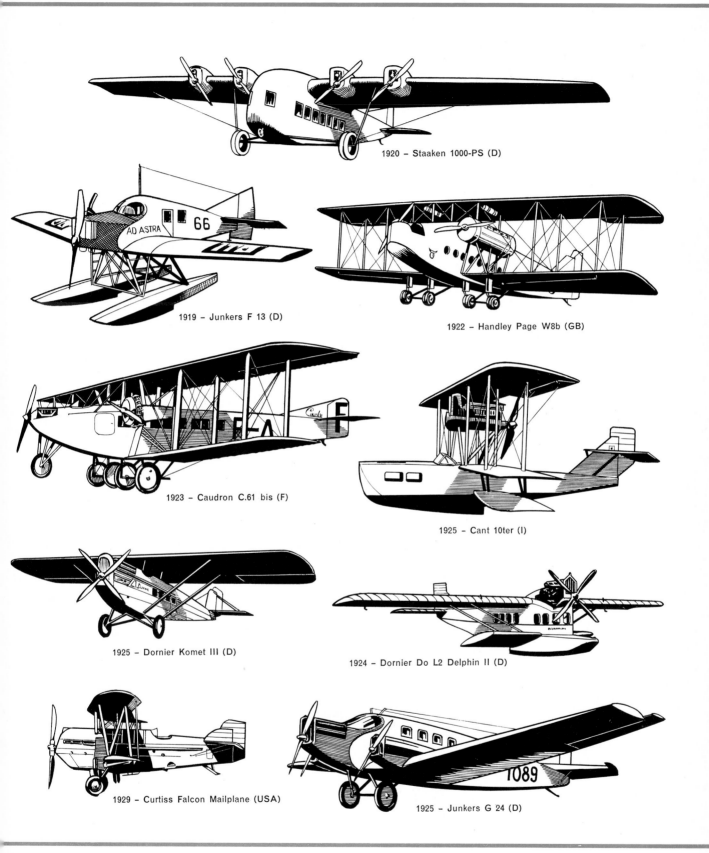

1920 – Staaken 1000-PS (D)

1919 – Junkers F 13 (D)

1922 – Handley Page W8b (GB)

1923 – Caudron C.61 bis (F)

1925 – Cant 10ter (I)

1925 – Dornier Komet III (D)

1924 – Dornier Do L2 Delphin II (D)

1929 – Curtiss Falcon Mailplane (USA)

1925 – Junkers G 24 (D)

DEH HAVILLAND D.H.66 HERCULES (1926, GB). Ordered by Imperial Airways, it began passenger, mail and cargo service on the Cairo-Karachi line on January 12, 1927. Although the route was mostly over the desert and the conditions extremely difficult, the *D.H.66* passed the test so brilliantly that it became a legend. Eleven were built. It was also used on the experimental Karachi–Melbourne, Australia, line.

FOKKER F-VIIa (1926, NL). Developed directly from the *F-VII* (one of which trailblazed the first Amsterdam-Djakarta, Indonesia, postal service for KLM in 1924), it was very popular and was used by at least a dozen European companies.

POTEZ 25A-2 (1925, F). Used mainly in South America by *Aeropostale* and *Aeroposta Argentina*. In July 1929, the famous French pilots Mermoz and Guillaumet inaugurated the Buenos Aires-Santiago de Chile mail service, flying a *25A-2* over the Andes Mountains.

refueling while in flight. In April 1924, four *Douglas DWC World Cruisers (p.55)* left the U. S. for the first round-the-world flight; and two of them brough the event to triumphant conclusion.

In the meantime, Great Britain, after the birth of Imperial Airways, was concerned with using the airplane as a means to reach the faraway corners of her empire. An exceptional pilot, Alan Cobham, flew from London to Rangoon, Burma, in 1924, and from London to Capetown, South Africa, in 1925 to explore routes which some years later would be regularly traveled by airline passengers. In April 1925, Francesco de Pinedo, accompanied by flight engineer Ernesto Campanelli, in an *S-16ter* flying boat *(p.60)* christened the *Gennariello* linked three continents in the longest flight completed up to that time: Rome–Australia–Japan–Rome; over 34,177 miles.

It seemed that nothing was impossible for

ARMSTRONG WHITWORTH ARGOSY I (1926, GB). One of the first multi-engine aircraft build on request for the newly founded Imperial Airways. It was widely used on the London–Paris and London to Basle, Salonika, Brussels and Cologne lines. Seven were built, each named for an English city. The *City of Coventry* was the last to retire from service in 1935.

DIRIGIBLE No. 1 NORGE (1926, I). Designed by Umberto Nobile, it flew over the North Pole under his command on May 12, 1926. Norway had bought the airship, which could hold 16 people, and entrusted the difficult mission to Roald Amundsen and Lincoln Ellsworth. The *Norge* flew more than 2200 miles nonstop over the ice, from Spitsbergen to Teller, Alaska, via the North Pole. On May 9, the Americans Richard E. Byrd and Floyd Bennett had been credited with the same feat with a 3-engine *Fokker,* the *Josephine Ford.*

the airplane, and men began to think of exploration of the North Pole. In 1926 two scientific expeditions were preparing simultaneously for just such a feat. One was American, under Commander Richard E. Byrd, the navigator during the 1919 *Navy Curtiss* transatlantic crossing. The other was Norwegian, led by the explorer Roald Amundsen. The Americans, with a 3-engine *Fokker* christened *Josephine Ford,* piloted by Floyd Bennett, have been credited with reaching their destination at 9:02 on May 9, 1926; the Norwegians, with the Italian-built dirigible the *Norge,* commanded by Colonel Umberto Nobile, followed three days later.

While Bennett and Nobile, with very little navigational equipment at their disposal, blazed a trail across a desert of ice, a young man of 23, Charles Augustus Lindbergh, was already dreaming about another great deed; a solitary, nonstop transatlantic flight from the U.S. to France. On May 22, 1919, just after

the end of the War, the American millionaire Raymond Orteig, owner of a chain of New York hotels, had offered a purse of $25,000 to the first man to fly the Atlantic nonstop from Paris or the French coast, to New York, or vice versa.

Lindbergh, with only $2000 to his name but with almost 2000 flying hours logged as a pilot, with mail-service and other flying feats behind him, decided to try his hand; the times seemed ripe for the attempt. By the end of 1926 other men were already far ahead of him in preparation. Among the more famous, the French ace René Fonck with his 3-engine *Sikorsky;* Byrd, the man who had flown the North Pole, with a 3-engine *Fokker;* Noel Davis and Stanton Wooster, American Navy *Keystone* officers, with a 3-engine *Pathfinder;* Charles Nungesser and Francois Coli, with a *Levasseur* christened *Oiseau Blanc*—the only contenders who planned to fly from France to the U.S. Compared to all these well-estab-

LIORÉ ET OLIVIER 213 (1927, F). An adaptation of the *LeO-20* bomber, it was one of the most deluxe planes of its time. It could carry 12 passengers and was furnished like a sumptuous dining room. Thirteen were built and used by Air Union, mostly on the London–Paris–Marseilles–Tunis line. When Air France was founded in 1933, eleven *213*'s were still in service.

FOCKE-WULF A-17a (1927, D). Built for Lufthansa, which had ordered 10, it remained in service until 1935 on the Berlin–Cologne and Cologne–Nuremburg lines. Nicknamed the *Möwe* or "seagull," because of its wing shape, it was the forefather of a long line of *Focke-Wulf* single-engine passenger aircraft.

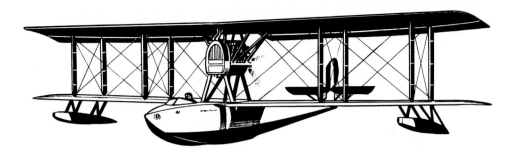

SAVOIA-MARCHETTI S-16ter (1923, I). In one of these flying boats, christened the *Gennariello,* Col. Francesco de Pinedo, with flight engineer Campanelli made the 34,175-mile flight Sesto Calende–Rome–Melbourne–Tokyo–Rome from April 20, to November 7, 1925. In 1924 an *S-16ter* set the flying-boat height record of 15,081 feet carrying a cargo of 1102 pounds. It was an exceptionally versatile aircraft and was used for endurance flights and attempts at record setting.

lished contestants, Lindbergh was definitely the dark-horse contender.

During Christmas of 1926, Lindbergh succeeded in convincing a group of St. Louis businessmen to put up some $10,000 for his flight; on February 23, 1927, he signed a contract with a small aviation firm, the Ryan factory, of San Diego, California, which agreed to supply him with a single-engine high-wing monoplane within 60 days for the sum of $10,580. During those 60 days, Lindbergh was never far from the hangar where "his" aircraft was being built. He helped to assemble each and every part; he advised, checked, rechecked and tested each phase. On the date it was due, the aircraft rolled out on the field for the first time.

On May 10, Lindbergh flew *The Spirit of St. Louis* in a nonstop flight, 14 hours and 25 minutes—a record in itself—from San Diego to St. Louis. His *Spirit of St. Louis* took its name from the city where he had financed his project. Two days later he was in New York getting ready for the rest of his journey. Lindbergh had chosen a single-engine plane for

this long and perilous flight; he felt that the greater the number of engines, the greater the danger of mechanical difficulties. The facts seemed to prove his point. Fonck's, Byrd's and Davis' and Wooster's attempts had failed because of engine trouble even before they had begun their crossings. Nungesser and Coli, who had left Paris on May 8, never reached the U.S. and were probably swallowed up by the Atlantic.

At 7:52 on May 20, 1927, his plane fueled almost beyond capacity, stripped of radio and parachute to save space and weight, and supplied with sandwiches and a thermos of hot coffee, Lindbergh took off from the long runway at Roosevelt Field which had been put a his disposal by his rival Richard Byrd in a gesture of good fellowship.

The young man did it! He was to land at Le Bourget 33½ hours after takeoff, covering 3648 miles at a speed of 117 miles per hour. With a shy, modest smile, he answered the delirious cheers of the crowd which carried him in triumph; basically Lindbergh considered himself a pilot, not a hero.

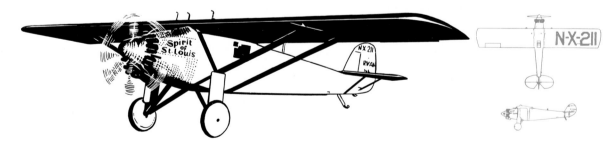

RYAN NYP "THE SPIRIT OF ST. LOUIS" (1927, USA). With this small aircraft, Charles Augustus Lindbergh made his solo nonstop Atlantic crossing, taking-off from Roosevelt Field, New York, and landing at Le Bourget, Paris. This single-engine monoplane made the 3600-mile trip in 33 hours and 30 minutes at an average speed of 117 miles per hour, leaving the U.S. at 7:52 on May 20, 1927, and arriving in France on the evening of the twenty-first, eagerly awaited by an enormous crowd which conferred triumphant honors on the daring young American pilot. The first nonstop flight connecting the U.S. and Continental Europe had finally been made.

CLASSIC MILITARY PLANES OF THE 1920s

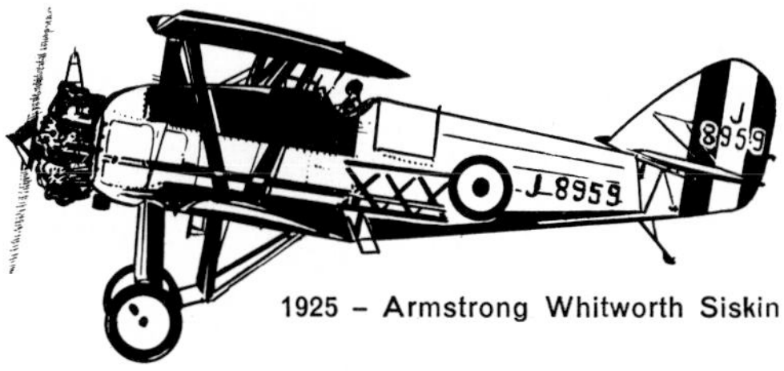

1925 – Armstrong Whitworth Siskin IIIA (GB)

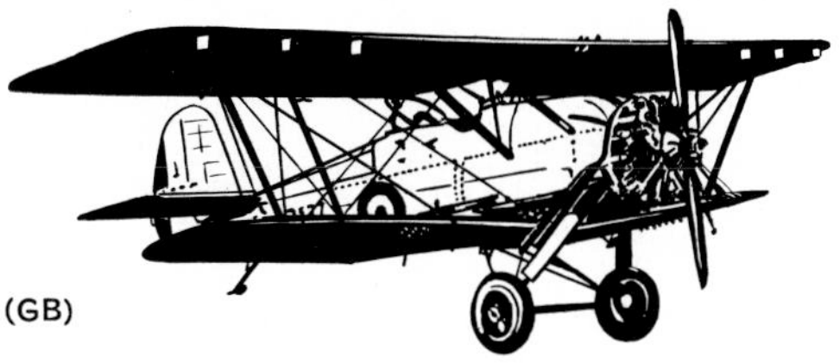

1927 – Armstrong Whitworth Atlas (GB)

1918 – Martin MB-I (USA)

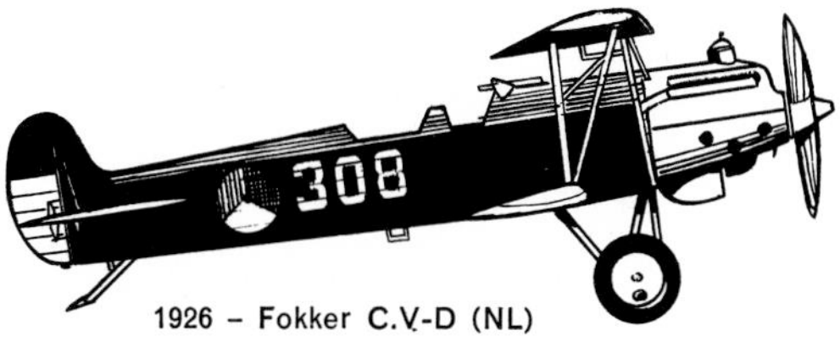

1926 – Fokker C.V-D (NL)

1927 – Nakajima Type 91 (J)

1926 – Vought 02U Corsair (USA)

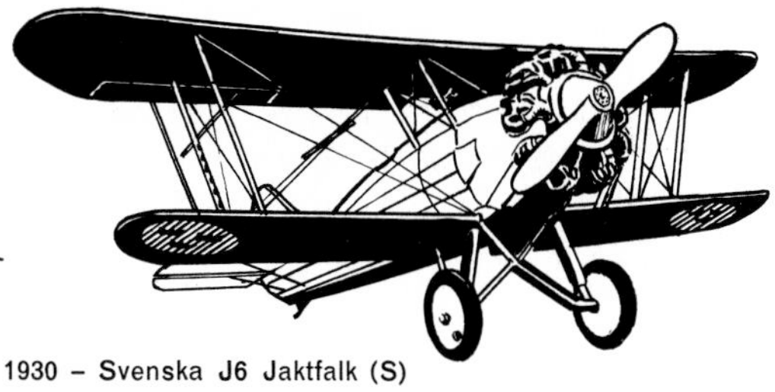

1930 – Svenska J6 Jaktfalk (S)

Although during the 1920s the aeronautics industry turned its attention mainly to civilian models, military aviation was not forgotten. Many military aircraft were developed, mostly fighters. These were important though not well known because they were never used in action.

Mention should be made of the first bomber of American design, the *Martin MB-1.* Fighters worthy of note were the *Armstrong Whitworth Siskin,* a standard R.A.F. model, the *Fokker C. V-D,* a direct descendant of the German World War I *Fokker,* used by Holland, Finland, Bolivia,

Chile, Japan, Switzerland, Denmark, Norway and other countries; the *Svenska Jaktfalk,* the first Swedish fighter used until 1940; and the first completely Japanese-designed *Nakajima 91.* Equally important are the *Armstrong Whitworth Atlas,* standard English reconnaissance aircraft, and the U.S. Navy reconnaissance *Vought O2U,* the first to be called *Corsair.* Only toward the middle of the 1920s did the military aviation heads feel it necessary to replace obsolete equipment which dated back to World War I with more up-to-date models.

SPORTING EVENTS FROM 1909 TO 1939

Even in the very first pages of aviation history, many prizes and sporting events are mentioned. Undeniably the large sums of money offered by newspapers and individual patrons to those who took giant steps forward on the road to aeronautical progress were a great inducement to builders and pilots during the difficult pioneering years.

Alberto Santos-Dumont won the prize offered by Ernest Archdeacon to the first man in Europe to fly a heavier-than-air vehicle; Henri Farman won the 50,000-franc prize offered by Henri Deutsch de la Meurthe and Archdeacon to the first man to fly one kilometer in a closed circuit; Louis Blériot won the *Daily Mail's* £1000 prize for the first airplane crossing of the Channel. It is virtually impossible to list all the prizes offered from 1905 on for aviation feats, to stimulate the pioneers, creativeness, talent and courage. In France aline, in 1908, the purses offered totaled more than 700,000 francs, a great deal of money in those days, when a *Vosin* cost close to 15,000 francs.

The sporting events which took place from 1909 until 1938 are worthy of discussion, since they had a decisive effect on aeronautical development. The "Grande Semaine d'Aviation de la Champagne" (Great Aviation Week of the Champagne Region), or the "Reims Meet," of 1909 (see p.22) was the first large aircraft meeting in history. It was on this occasion that the first speed race for the Gordon Bennet Aviation Cup was held. This cup was to be assigned to the nation which won the competition three times. James Gordon Bennett, Jr., publisher of the *New York Herald,* had offered two cups in the past: one for 2 yearly automobile races and one for a contest between balloons which was not awarded until 1935. An examination of the speeds reached in the 6 Gordon Bennett aviation races shows how much and how quickly progress had been made: in 1909 Glenn Curtiss won at Reims with an average speed of 47.65 miles per hour. In 1913, Maurice Prévost won in a *Deperdussin* at 124.50 miles per hour! After the interruption of the War, Sadi-Lecointe won the cup for France with a third victory at 168.50 miles per hour.

During the celebration dinner for the 1912 Gordon Bennett race, another patron, the Frenchman Jacques Schneider, announced that he was offering a trophy which would bear his name. It soon proved to be the most important international sporting event, pitting Frenchmen, Englishmen, Italians and Americans against one another in increasingly faster seaplanes and flying boats. The struggle for possession of the trophy continued from 1913

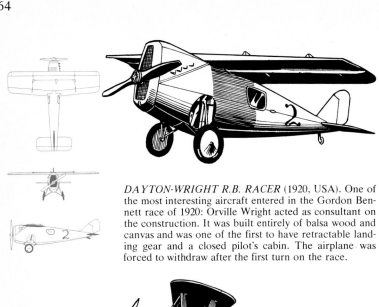

DAYTON-WRIGHT R.B. RACER (1920, USA). One of the most interesting aircraft entered in the Gordon Bennett race of 1920: Orville Wright acted as consultant on the construction. It was built entirely of balsa wood and canvas and was one of the first to have retractable landing gear and a closed pilot's cabin. The airplane was forced to withdraw after the first turn on the race.

VERVILLE-PACKARD R-1 (1920, USA). Winner of the 1920 Pulitzer Trophy, with an average speed of 156.5 miles per hour, it was criticized for its weight (2485 pounds), considered far too heavy for a single-seat racing aircraft. It won over its 37 competitors, beating a *Thomas Morse* and an *S.V.A.* (which came in second and third respectively) by a wide margin.

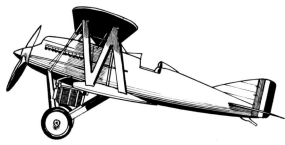

NAVY CURTISS R-1 (1921, USA). Winner of the 1921 Pulitzer Trophy, it was considered the most aerodynamically advanced aircraft ever built. Piloted by Bert Acosta, it won with an average speed of 176.7 miles per hour, beating a *Curtiss-Cox*, two *Thomas Morse*s, an *Ansaldo Balilla* and an *S.V.A.*

to 1931 (see p.66) and had a significant influence on the development of technical aeronautics. From the Schneider races the fastest piston-motor seaplane of all times, the *Macchi-Castoldi MC-72,* was born. Piloted by Francesco Agello, it set a speed record of 441 miles per hour. From the Schneider races, which Great Britain finally won in 1931, the English and the Italians gained precious experience in high-speed flights and developed some very important aircraft and engines. Some even say that the English owe their victory in World War II to Schneider. Even if the statement is exaggerated it is true that the best English fighter of the War, the *Spitfire,* was a direct descendant of the *Supermarine* which won the trophy in '27, '29 and '31.

While the Schneider trophy and many other national and Continental sporting events attracted the attention of the Europeans, in the United States, beginning in 1920, over 100,000 people gathered together for one week of the year, flocking to the airfield where the National Air Races were being held. What began as aviators' rallies became large festivals with acrobatic and formation flights and parachute jumps. They took on great technical importance when the Pulitzer Trophy was initiated and offered in an international speed race.

With the approval of the government and above all of General William Mitchell, the Pulitzer brothers, Ralph, Joseph and Herbert, publishers of the dailies, the New York *World* and the St. Louis *Post-Dispatch,* offered the trophy and substantial rewards to stimulate construction of prototypes whose performance would help in designing new fighter aircraft. Although an "international" event, the contestants were mostly Americans. The average winning speeds increased from 156.50 miles per hour in 1920 to 248.99 miles per hour in 1925.

CURTISS-COX CACTUS KITTEN (1921, USA). Commissioned by S. E. J. Cox and built by the Curtiss company, it was the only triplane to take part in these sporting events. After the 1921 Pulitzer race, in which it placed second, the aircraft was "sold" by Cox to the U.S. Navy for the token sum of one dollar.

ARMY CURTISS R-6 (1922, USA). Designed by Curtiss on commission for the Air Service, it is still considered by many romantics "the most beautiful aircraft ever built." It won the 1922 Pulitzer Trophy with an average speed of 205.8 miles per hour, followed by its twin ship and two *Navy Curtiss R-2*'s, which placed third and fourth.

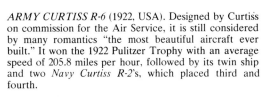

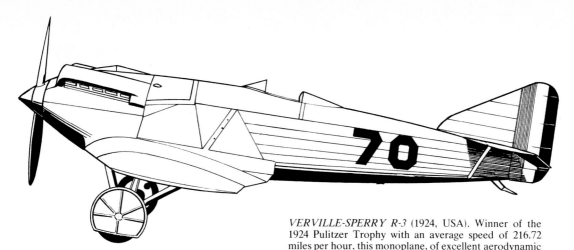

VERVILLE-SPERRY R-3 (1924, USA). Winner of the 1924 Pulitzer Trophy with an average speed of 216.72 miles per hour, this monoplane, of excellent aerodynamic line, had already participated in the two previous Pulitzer races. Despite proof of its capabilities, it was never considered by the Air Service for possible conversion and use as a fighter.

In 1925 when General Mitchell was court-martialled, the Pulitzer Trophy was withdrawn. Army and naval aviation, lacking both incentive and funds, no longer focused on experimental racing planes and in the succeeding years made a poor showing in the National Air Races. The press protested against this short-sighted policy in 1929 when a young civilian, Douglas Davis, in an aircraft which he had built with limited means, soundly beat the official army and navy entries flying the best fighters at their disposal.

The sporting events which took place in the United States during the last half of the 1920s and during the 1930s demonstrated three things: that the public's interest in aeronautics was very high; that the authorities were dangerously neglecting this area; and that the nation had an inexhaustible reserve of great designers and extraordinary pilots.

In 1930, Charles E. Thompson, a Cleveland industrialist, offered a new speed trophy. Once

(continued on page 68)

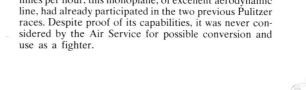

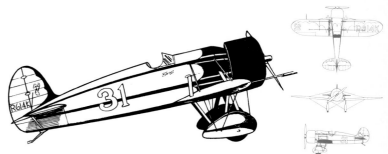

TRAVEL AIR "R" MYSTERY SHIP (1929, USA). It won the 1929 National Air Races with an average speed of 194.9 miles per hour, after having completed the first circuit at 208.69 miles per hour. This airplane was the first with an air-cooled radial engine to reach this speed. The following year it placed second in the Thompson Trophy with an average speed of 199.8 miles per hour.

LAIRD SUPER-SOLUTION (1931, USA). Piloted by Jimmy Doolittle, it won the 1931 Bendix Trophy, covering the 2043-mile distance between Burbank, California, and Cleveland, Ohio, in the record time of 9 hours, 10 minutes and 21 seconds, averaging 223.04 miles per hour. The *Laird* soundly beat two *Lockheed Orions* in their first national debut in sports competition.

SEVERSKY SEV-S2 (1937, USA). Designed by one of the Czarist fighter aces of World War I who had emigrated to the U.S., the *SEV-S2* (piloted by Frank Fuller, Jr.) won the 1937 Bendix Trophy race, which again covered the Burbank–Cleveland route, in 7 hours, 54 minutes, 26 seconds, averaging 258.24 miles per hour. The *SEV-S2* also won the 1938 (Jacqueline Cochran, 249.74 miles per hour) and 1939 (Frank Fuller, Jr., 282.09 miles per hour) races. This racing plane was virtually identical to the *Seversky P-35* fighter plane which was briefly used in action in the Philippines at the time of the Japanese attack.

P.63—The Gordon Bennett Cup; p.64, bottom left—the Pulitzer Trophy; facing—the Thompson Trophy.

THE JACQUES SCHNEIDER CUP

When the French industrialist Jacques Schneider announced the Coupe d'Aviation Maritime on December 5, 1912, very few imagined the importance it was to eventually assume. To promote seaplane and flying-boat development, Schneider offered an impressive trophy to be awarded to the nation which won the race three times out of a series of five. The first Schneider race began inconspicuously in 1913 with 3 Frenchmen and one American competing, all 4 flying French planes *(Deperdussin, Morane-Saulnier, Nieuport)* converted for marine use by the application of floats. The race was won by the Frenchman Maurice Prévost (p.69). Prévost, through an error on the part of the judges, was assigned an average speed of 45.75 miles per hour instead of his correct time of 60 miles per hour. It was the only French victory in the Schneider Cup's history. In fact, as early as 1914 an Englishman, flying a *Sopwith Tabloid,* beat their embattled French competitors, thus gaining the first international acknowledgment of an English-built aircraft.

Understandably, the War interrupted the yearly cup event, which was held again in England in 1919, with the victory going to the Italian Guido Janello flying a *Savoia.* However, the winner was not officially recognized because of alleged irregularities due to fog. The Italians won again in 1920 and 1921, thanks to inadequate preparation on the part of their competitors. A third Italian victory in the 1922 race held in Naples would have won them the Cup, but the English, victors that year with a *Supermarine Sea Lion II,* reopened the competition.

The Americans were official entries in 1923 and 1925 (in 1924 the race was not run), routing all other contenders. But in 1926 in Norfolk, Virginia, Mario de Bernardi's *Macchi M-39* stopped them. Disillusioned, the U.S.A. withdrew from all future Schneider races, citing economic reasons. It was a mistake for which the Americans paid dearly, for the studies and plans drawn up for the Schneider were to prove of great importance. For example, the *Spitfire,* star of the Battle of Britain, was in fact a descendant of the *Supermarine S-5, S-6* and *S-6B* which, with its three consecutive victories in 1927, 1929 and 1931, decisively won the Cup for Great Britain. Italy could not keep pace with Great Britain: the fastest piston-engine seaplane of all, the *Macchi-Castoldi MC-72,* was not ready until 1932. In 1934 it broke all seaplane speed records at 441 miles per hour.

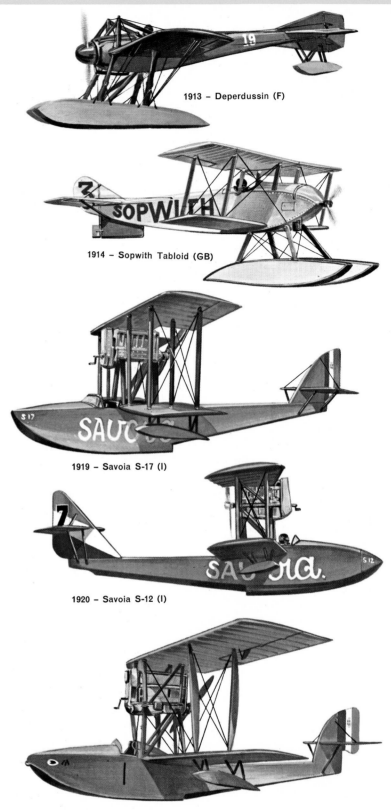

1913 – Deperdussin (F)

1914 – Sopwith Tabloid (GB)

1919 – Savoia S-17 (I)

1920 – Savoia S-12 (I)

1921 – Macchi M-7 (I)

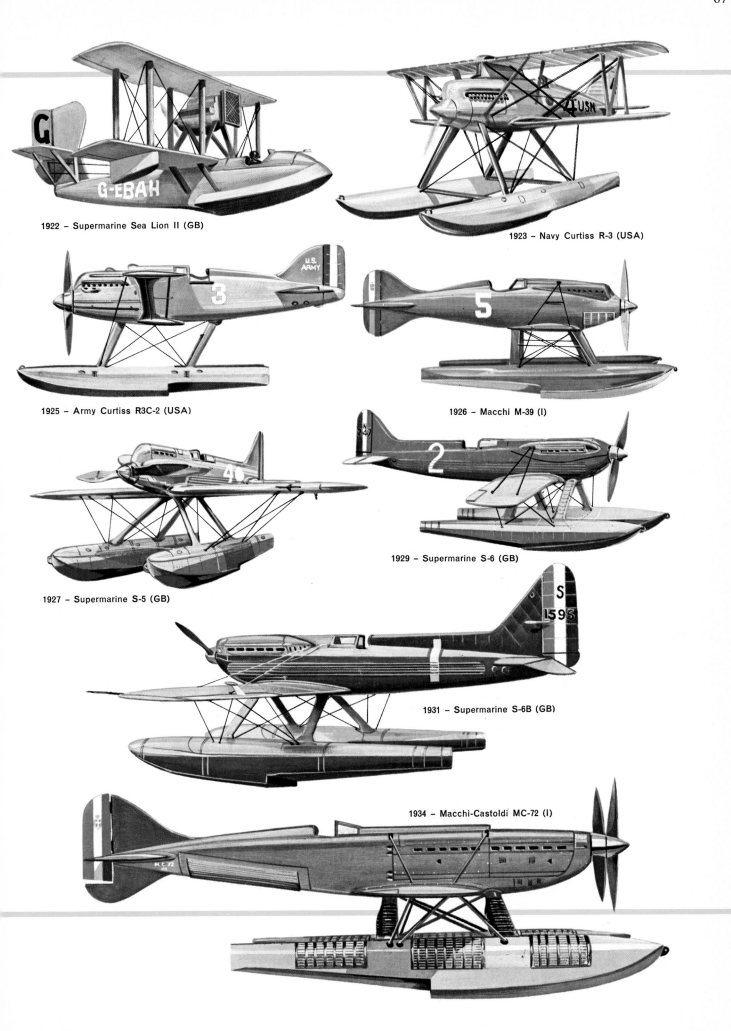

1922 – Supermarine Sea Lion II (GB)

1923 – Navy Curtiss R-3 (USA)

1925 – Army Curtiss R3C-2 (USA)

1926 – Macchi M-39 (I)

1927 – Supermarine S-5 (GB)

1929 – Supermarine S-6 (GB)

1931 – Supermarine S-6B (GB)

1934 – Macchi-Castoldi MC-72 (I)

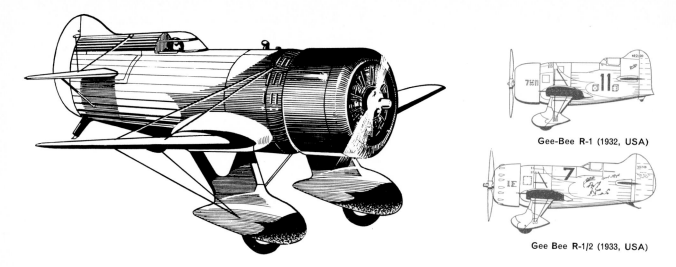

Gee-Bee R-1 (1932, USA)

Gee Bee R-1/2 (1933, USA)

GEE-BEE MODEL Z SUPER SPORTSTER (1931, USA). Robert Hall's original and distinctive model took such a high toll of lives that it must be considered "cursed." Lowell Bayles won the Thompson Trophy in 1931 piloting the *Z* model at an average speed of 236.24 miles per hour. On December 5 of that year, while attempting to set a record, he lost his life in the same aircraft. Jimmy Doolittle won the Thompson in 1932 at 252.68 miles per hour in the *R-1* but Russell Boardman died flying the same plane in the 1933 Bendix race. In the same year the *Model Y* crashed, killing Florence Klingensmith. The *R1/2* crashed just after takeoff for the 1935 Bendix race with Cecil Allen aboard. The *Gee-Bee:* a great plane to forget . . .

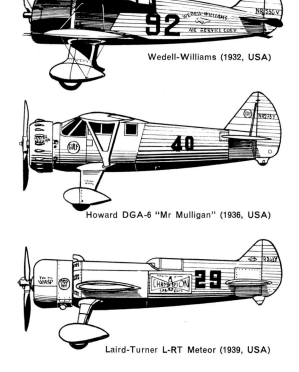

Wedell-Williams (1932, USA)

Howard DGA-6 "Mr Mulligan" (1936, USA)

Laird-Turner L-RT Meteor (1939, USA)

Three leaders in American aviation races during the 1930s: the *Wedell-Williams* which won the Thompson in 1933 and 1934, and the Bendix Trophy of 1932, 1933 and 1934; the *Howard "Mr. Mulligan,"* winner of two 1935 trophies, the Thompson and the Bendix; and finally the *Laird-Turner* which brought its pilot, Roscoe Turner, victories in the 1938 and 1939 Thompson, with average speeds of close to 282 miles per hour.

again, it was an international competition, but European participation was very limited. Only in 1936 did a Frenchman, Michel Detroyat, in a *Caudron C-460,* win the trophy and other events, reminding Americans that technical progress in Europe had not come to a halt. The Thompson Trophy Race was run from 1930 to 1939 and the average speeds rose from 201.91 miles per hour to 283.42 miles per hour.

Another memorable trophy was that offered in 1931 by Vincent Bendix, president of the Bendix Aviation Corporation, for a cross-country flight from Burbank, California, to Cleveland, Ohio. The race was run regularly until 1939 and speeds ranged from 223.04 miles per hour to 282.09 miles per hour. The airplanes which participated in these races were the most interesting of all. The *Lairds,* the *Gee-Bees* and the *Wedell-Williamses* were products of accurate and ingenious research. The pilots, stars of the races, still hold a fascination which time cannot erase, men and women like Bert Acosta, Jimmy Doolittle (the man who later led the daring bombing raid over Tokyo on April 18, 1942), James Wedell, Roscoe Turner, Frank Fuller, Jr., Michel Detroyat, Amelia Earhart, Jacqueline Cochran and Louise Thaden. Great pilots and great sportsmen, they carried the bright flame handed down by the Curtisses, the Blériots and the Grahame-Whites and were, in turn, to pass it on to the young of the new generation. But for several years these young people had no time to think of sports; they were called to fight a war which for the most part was to be won in the skies.

WINNERS OF THE MAJOR COMPETITIONS

Year	Pilot	Airplane	Nationality	Speed mph	km/h

THE GORDON BENNETT CUP

Year	Pilot	Airplane	Nationality	mph	km/h
1909	Glenn Curtiss	Curtiss Golden Flyer	USA	47.65	76,68
1910	Claude Grahame-White	Blériot XI Bis	GB	61.00	98,16
1911	Charles T. Weymann	Nieuport	USA	78.00	125,52
1912	Jules Védrines	Deperdussin	F	105.50	168,97
1913	Maurice Prévost	Deperdussin	F	124.50	200,35
1920	Sadi-Lecointe	Nieuport	F	168.50	271,16

THE SCHNEIDER CUP

Year	Pilot	Airplane	Nationality	mph	km/h
1913	Maurice Prévost	Deperdussin	F	45.75	73,62
1914	Howard Pixton	Sopwith Tabloid	GB	86.75	139,60
1920	Luigi Bologna	Savoia S-12	I	107.20	172,51
1921	Giovanni de Briganti	Macchi M-7	I	117.86	189,67
1922	Henry C. Baird	Supermarine Sea Lion II	GB	145.70	234,47
1923	David Rittenhouse	Navy Curtiss R-3	USA	177.38	285,45
1925	James Doolittle	Army Curtiss R3C-2	USA	232.57	374,27
1926	Mario de Bernardi	Macchi M-39	I	246.49	396,68
1927	Sidney N. Webster	Supermarine S-5	GB	281.65	453,25
1929	H. R. Waghorn	Supermarine S-6	GB	328.63	528,86
1931	John H. Boothman	Supermarine S-6B	GB	340.08	547,23

THE PULITZER TROPHY

Year	Pilot	Airplane	Nationality	mph	km/h
1920	Corliss Mosely	Verville-Packard R 1	USA	156.50	251,85
1921	Bert Acosta	Navy Curtiss R-1	USA	176.70	284,36
1922	R. L. Maughan	Army Curtiss R-6	USA	205.80	331,19
1923	Alford Williams	Navy Curtiss R2C-1	USA	243.67	392,13
1924	H. H. Mills	Verville-Sperry R-3	USA	216.72	348,76
1925	Cyrus Bettis	Army Curtiss R3C-1	USA	248.98	400,68

THE THOMPSON TROPHY

Year	Pilot	Airplane	Nationality	mph	km/h
1930	Charles Holman	Laird Solution	USA	201.91	324,93
1931	Lowell Bayles	Gee-Bee Super Sportster	USA	236.24	380,17
1932	James Doolittle	Gee-Bee Super Sportster R-1	USA	252.68	406,74
1933	James Wedell	Wedell-Williams	USA	237.95	382,93
1934	Roscoe Turner	Wedell-Williams	USA	248.13	399,31
1935	Harold Neumann	Howard "Mr Mulligan"	USA	220.19	354,35
1936	Michel Detroyat	Caudron C-460	F	264.26	425,27
1937	Rudy Kling	Folkerts KF-1 Jupiter	USA	256.91	413,44
1938	Roscoe Turner	Laird-Turner L-RT	USA	283.42	456,10
1939	Roscoe Turner	Laird-Turner L-RT	USA	282.53	454,68

THE BENDIX TROPHY

Year	Pilot	Airplane	Nationality	mph	km/h
1931	James Doolittle	Laird Super-Solution	USA	223.04	358,93
1932	James Haizlip	Wedell-Williams	USA	245.00	394,27
1933	Roscoe Turner	Wedell-Williams	USA	214.78	345,64
1934	Douglas Davis	Wedell-Williams	USA	216.24	347,99
1935	Ben Howard	Howard "Mr Mulligan"	USA	238.70	384,14
1936	Louise Thaden	Beechcraft C-17R	USA	165.34	266,08
1937	Frank Fuller Jr	Seversky SEV-S2	USA	258.24	415,58
1938	Jacqueline Cochran	Seversky SEV-S2	USA	249.74	401,91
1939	Frank Fuller Jr	Seversky SEV-S2	USA	282.09	453,98

KONINKLIJKE LUCHTVAART
MAATSCHAPPIJ
KLM
H-
Fokker
HNKLM
H
JAN WIJGA
De Vliegende Hollander
Eéns LEGENDE - thans WERKELIJKHEID

FROM 1927 TO 1940: THE GOLDEN AGE OF THE FLYING BOATS

1927 went down in the history of aviation as "the year of Lindbergh." No one would ever dream of questioning the importance of the achievement itself, nor the worthwhile repercussions for aviation of the extraordinary publicity which surrounded the event. But the objective historian cannot and should not ignore the innumerable other achievements which although less celebrated were certainly not less technically important. They also contributed significantly toward convincing the world that not even the oceans could stop the aircraft.

While Paris heaped laurels on the "Lone Eagle," New York was welcoming the pilots Francesco de Pinedo and Carlo del Prete with enthusiasm. With Zacchetti, their flight engineer, they had reached New York aboard a *Savoia-Marchetti S-55 (p.72)* christened the *Santa Maria.* Leaving Sesto Calende, on February 13, they had flown the south Atlantic, touching Rio de Janeiro, Buenos Aires and Asunción before reaching New York. Upon their arrival in Rome on June 16, they had successfully completed a 29,180-mile cruise making 51 stops, for a total of 193 hours' flying time.

In less than a year after the fateful May 1927 Lindbergh flight, more than 31 aircraft were still trying to repeat the young man's achievement. Only 10 succeeded. In the attempt, 20 courageous pilots lost their lives. On June 4, Clarence D. Chamberlin and Charles A. Levine on board a *Bellanca W.B.2* called the *Columbia,* made a 3850-mile flight nonstop from New York to a spot 117 miles from Berlin (they had not been able to land at Berlin because of thick fog). On June 29, Richard E. Byrd, who has been credited with flying over the North Pole, and the pilots Bert Acosta and Bernt Balchen, in a *Fokker C-2* christened *America (p.72),* flew from New York to the coast of Normandy. They were unable to reach Paris because of adverse weather conditions. On April 13 of the following year, Hermann Köhl, James Fitzmaurice and Günther von Hünefeld, flying a *Junkers W-33* called the *Bremen (p. 80)* made the first Atlantic crossing from east to west, reaching Labrador via Ireland. On June 17, 1928, Amelia Earhart became the first woman to successfully fly the Atlantic nonstop from Newfoundland to Wales in a *Fokker* with Wilmer Stulz and Louis Gordon. Finally, on September 2, 1930, Dieudonné Costes, the pilot and Maurice Bellonte, the navigator, on board a *Breguet XIX Super TR, Point d'Interrogation (p.72),* duplicated Lindbergh's trip flying in the opposite direction. They reached New York from Paris in 37 hours and 18 minutes flying time.

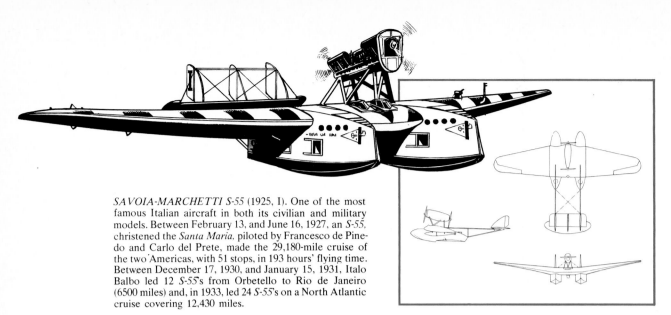

SAVOIA-MARCHETTI S-55 (1925, I). One of the most famous Italian aircraft in both its civilian and military models. Between February 13, and June 16, 1927, an *S-55,* christened the *Santa Maria,* piloted by Francesco de Pinedo and Carlo del Prete, made the 29,180-mile cruise of the two Americas, with 51 stops, in 193 hours' flying time. Between December 17, 1930, and January 15, 1931, Italo Balbo led 12 *S-55*'s from Orbetello to Rio de Janeiro (6500 miles) and, in 1933, led 24 *S-55*'s on a North Atlantic cruise covering 12,430 miles.

LOCKHEED VEGA MODEL 1 (1928, USA). The first highly successful Lockheed passenger aircraft. With the later *Vega* model, Wiley Post and Harold Gatty left New York on June 23, 1931, destination Berlin, and they made an around the world flight in 8 days, 15 hours and 51 minutes.

BREGUET XIX SUPER TR "POINT D'INTERROGA-TION" (1929, F). Piloted by Capt. Dieudonné Costes, with Maurice Bellonte as navigator, it duplicated Lindbergh's feat flying in the opposite direction, i.e., from Le Bourget, Paris, to Curtiss Field, New York, on September 2, 1930. The nonstop flight lasted 37 hours, 18 minutes.

In the meantime, the Pacific barrier was crossed: on June 28–29, 1927, Lieutenants Albert Hegenberger and Lester Maitland, flying a 3-engine *Fokker* christened *Bird of Paradise,* completed the first nonstop flight from Oakland, California, to Honolulu in the Hawaiian Islands in 25 hours and 50 minutes. Between May 31 and June 10, 1928, the Australians Charles Kingsford-Smith and C. P. T. Ulm, with the Americans Harry W. Lyons and J. W. Warner, flying a *Fokker F-VIIb-3m (p.72),* united the North American continent with Australia for the first time by air. The trip was made from Oakland to Brisbane via Hawaii and the Fiji Islands.

All of these long flights had been made with regular land planes. Many who made the attempt perished in the deep waters of the oceans. So it was only logical, especially with a view to future passenger traffic, to think that the flying boats would be more suitable for these crossings. Should engine trouble or other difficulties develop, the flying boat could always attempt a landing and float until help arrived. Another point in favor of the flying boat was that it was easier to spot a stretch of sea, river or lake in areas still virgni to aviation than it would be to spot a large

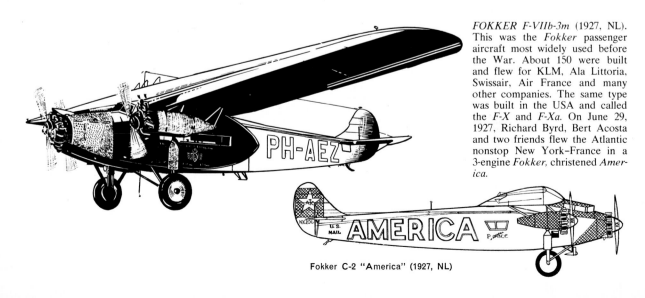

FOKKER F-VIIb-3m (1927, NL). This was the *Fokker* passenger aircraft most widely used before the War. About 150 were built and flew for KLM, Ala Littoria, Swissair, Air France and many other companies. The same type was built in the USA and called the *F-X* and *F-Xa.* On June 29, 1927, Richard Byrd, Bert Acosta and two friends flew the Atlantic nonstop New York–France in a 3-engine *Fokker,* christened *America.*

Fokker C-2 "America" (1927, NL)

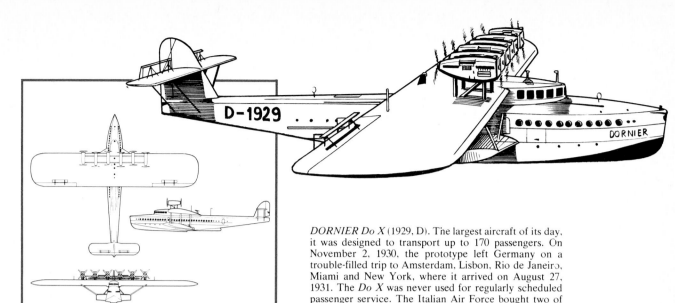

DORNIER Do X (1929, D). The largest aircraft of its day, it was designed to transport up to 170 passengers. On November 2, 1930, the prototype left Germany on a trouble-filled trip to Amsterdam, Lisbon, Rio de Janeiro, Miami and New York, where it arrived on August 27, 1931. The *Do X* was never used for regularly scheduled passenger service. The Italian Air Force bought two of these models, which were not, however, very successful.

enough clearing of open land to permit safe landing and takeoff. And so the golden age of the flying boats began...

At the same time, land planes were accomplishing miracles, as when, in July 1928 one of these, the small two-seat *Savoia Marchetti S-64 (p.75)* with Arturo Ferrarin and Carlo del Prete on board, made a nonstop flight from Guidonia, Italy, to Touros, Brazil, covering 4460 miles in 47 hours and 55 minutes.

At the time the public was still convinced that such feats were the province of exceptional pilots aboard experimental planes. It was Italian aviation that showed the world that good, mass-produced aircraft, entrusted to capable pilots, could duplicate the achievements of the pioneers. On December 17, 1930, 12 *Savoia-Marchetti S-55's (p. 72)*, under the command of General Italo Balbo, Aviation Minister, assisted by General Umberto Balle and Umberto Maddalena, left Orbetello near Rome in formation. On January 15, 1931, ten of them reached Rio de Janeiro after having flown 6500 miles with stops at Cartagena, Kenitra, Villa Cisneros, Bolama, Porto Natal and Bahia. The second Atlantic cruise made by Balbo and his *S-55* was even more sensa-

tional: on July 1, 1933, twenty-five flying boats took off from Orbetello and reached Chicago and New York, welcomed by delirious crowds after having stopped in Amsterdam, Londonderry, Reykjavik, Cartwright, Shediac and Montreal. For the return trip to Rome, where they arrived on August 12, the *S-55's* followed the southern route via the Azores and Lisbon, completing the 12,430-mile flight in formation.

These group flights were of undeniable psychological importance for public opinion, which was now ready to believe that aviation had "grown up." People no longer considered it so extraordinary or as the special preserve of courageous, if reckless, daredevils. The airplane was becoming a familiar means of transportation, although still far more expensive and dangerous than the ship, train or automobile.

1927 (the year of Lindbergh and those who followed him) brought about a great change in the history of civil aviation. It can be said that until then, passenger transportation in the United States had been practically nonexistent (see American Civil Aircraft of the 1930s, *p.78)*. In 1929, the Transcontinental Air Transport, also called the *Lindbergh Line,*

FORD TRI-MOTOR "TIN GOOSE" (1929, USA). Affectionately nicknamed the "tin goose," it was among Ford's few attempts in the field of aviation. The aircraft was widely used by American companies. On November 28, 1929, Richard Byrd and Bernt Balchen, on board a *Ford Tri-motor,* flew over the South Pole for the first time. Byrd's plane was equipped with skids.

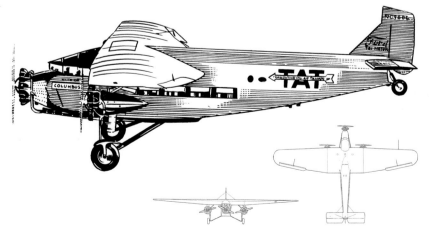

74

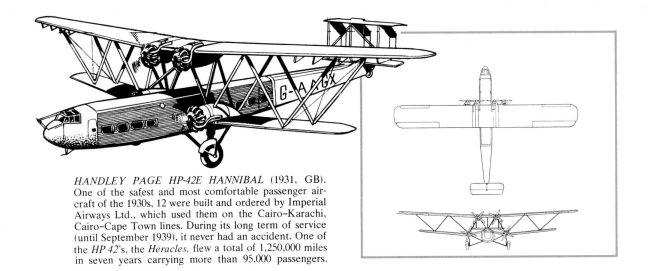

HANDLEY PAGE HP-42E HANNIBAL (1931, GB). One of the safest and most comfortable passenger aircraft of the 1930s, 12 were built and ordered by Imperial Airways Ltd., which used them on the Cairo–Karachi, Cairo–Cape Town lines. During its long term of service (until September 1939), it never had an accident. One of the *HP 42*'s, the *Heracles,* flew a total of 1,250,000 miles in seven years carrying more than 95,000 passengers.

had inaugurated service between New York and Los Angeles, with some stretches by train, for the price of $351.94 per person. In 1930, the United States had three gigantic airlines, United Airlines, American Airways and TWA (Transcontinental Western Air, which resulted from the merger of TAT and Western Air Express), as well as Pan American Airways (concentrating mostly on Caribbean and South American traffic) and dozens of smaller lines.

In Europe, passenger transport began immediately after the War, but it wasn't until 1927 that the surest and fastest development took place (see European Civil Aircraft of the 1930s, *p.81*). It would take thousands of pages to sketch even a brief history of civil transportation and, for those who wish to learn more about the subject, we recommend *A History of the World's Airlines* by R. E. G. Davies, *European Transport Aircraft* and

Annals of the British and Commonwealth Air Transport, both by John Stroud. But it is impossible to overemphasize the extent to which the birth and development of civil aviation was more than a technical, industrial or commercial fact. It was perhaps, above all, a romantic reality. One example is enough: in 1918, a Frenchman, Pierre Latécoère, began to plan the opening of an airmail service between France and South America. It was his dream to have the mail reach its destination within 4–5 days instead of the usual 60. On December 24, 1918, the first experimental flight aimed at crossing the first natural barrier along the route was made. The barrier was the Pyrenees, and service between Toulouse and Barcelona began. In 1919 the route reached Alicante, then Rabat and Casablanca. Latécoère was joined in his venture by pilots whose names have become legends: Daurat, Vachet, Ville, Guillaumet, Saint-

CONSOLIDATED COMMODORE (1929, USA). With 12 huge flying boats (each with a passenger capacity of 18) of this type, the NYRBA (New York, Rio and Buenos Aires Air Line, Inc.) opened its service between the U.S. and South America in 1929. In 1930, the NYRBA was absorbed by Pan American Airways which improved and extended service on the Miami–Buenos Aires route touching 15 nations along the over 9000-mile stretch.

LATÉCOÈRE 28 III (1930, F). Built in both land and sea models for Aeropostale's passenger and mail service. When the experimental Toulouse–Rio de Janeiro mail line was opened, Jean Mermoz, flying a *Laté* seaplane made the Saint-Louis, Senegal–Natal, Brazil trip in 21 hours. The *Laté 28* set 9 world records for speed, endurance and distance.

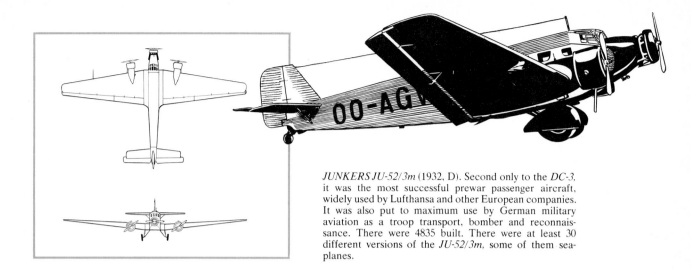

JUNKERS JU-52/3m (1932, D). Second only to the *DC-3*, it was the most successful prewar passenger aircraft, widely used by Lufthansa and other European companies. It was also put to maximum use by German military aviation as a troop transport, bomber and reconnaissance. There were 4835 built. There were at least 30 different versions of the *JU-52/3m*, some of them seaplanes.

Exupéry (whose splendid book *Night Flight* is still considered a classic) and Jean Mermoz. The latter was to write of the mail route: "... it is alive; it is alive with all that we have given of ourselves. When it was born, we were 18 young men who had vowed with all our souls that it would succeed. Today, only four of the original 18 are still alive. Those who have died, died at their posts, fighting so that the line would live...." These words were written in 1934. Mermoz himself was to die "fighting": on December 7, 1936, his *Latécoere 300 "Croix du Sud"(p.82)* lost all radio contact only four hours after taking off from Dakar headed for Natal, Brazil. The plane was never found. It was Mermoz's twenty-fourth flight over the south Atlantic: he had flown the ocean with a small *Latécoère 28 (p.74)*, with the splendid *Couzinet 70 "Arc-en-Ciel" (p.75)*, and was one of the original pioneers. He had been a symbol— now he was a legend. It was thanks only to

him and to men like him that Latécoère's dream became a reality. In 1925, the route had reached Dakar. This meant that Mermoz, Saint-Exupéry and other pilots had had to cross the African desert aboard the fragile *Breguet XIV*, risking death, in case of a crash landing, either as a result of thirst or torture at the hands of the nomad tribes who still considered the airplane the devil's machine. Between Dakar and South America lay the Atlantic. While waiting for the planes to be ready for this great jump, the Latécoère company, which became Aéropostale in 1924, opened its first lines in South America with the help of the Argentine pilot, Almonacid. The routes ran from Buenos Aires to Rio de Janeiro, and from Rio to Natal, the point in South America closest to the African continent. In 1929, Mermoz made the test flight from Buenos Aires to Santiago de Chile, flying over the Andes. On July 14 of the same

SAVOIA-MARCHETTI S-64 (1930, I). In May 1928, Arturo Ferrarin and Carlo del Prete, flying an *S-64*, set a world distance record, flying 4764 miles in 58 hours and 34 minutes in a closed circuit. Between July 3 and 5 of the same year, the two pilots made the 4466.5-mile nonstop crossing from Italy to Brazil in 47 hours and 55 minutes, breaking the straight-line flight record.

COUZINET 70 "ARC-EN-CIEL" (1929, F). Designed by René Couzinet, its purpose was to cover the transatlantic stretches of Aéropostale's France–South America line. The first flight (Saint-Louis, Senegal–Natal, Brazil) was flown on January 16, 1933, in 14 hours and 37 minutes. The pilot was Jean Mermoz. After this flight, the plane was modified and did not re-enter service on the transoceanic route until 1934.

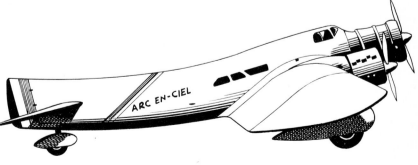

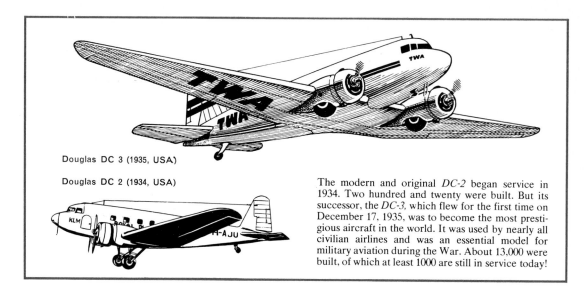

Douglas DC 3 (1935, USA)

Douglas DC 2 (1934, USA)

The modern and original *DC-2* began service in 1934. Two hundred and twenty were built. But its successor, the *DC-3,* which flew for the first time on December 17, 1935, was to become the most prestigious aircraft in the world. It was used by nearly all civilian airlines and was an essential model for military aviation during the War. About 13,000 were built, of which at least 1000 are still in service today!

year, Mermoz and Guillaumet inaugurated the route with the *Potez 25.* Guillaumet flew the route more than 400 times, earning the name "Angel of the Cordillera."

At the time, mail delivery took 2 days between Toulouse and Dakar, 4 to cross the Atlantic on fast ships and 2 from Natal, Brazil, to Buenos Aires or Santiago de Chile. Finally, on May 12, 1930, Jean Mermoz, with a flight engineer and a radio operator, aboard a single-engine *Latécoère 28* seaplane, crossed the south Atlantic for the first time, flying from Saint-Louis in Senegal to Natal, Brazil, for the postal service. A letter mailed in Toulouse reached Santiago in just 109 hours!

The line continued to give as regular service as possible, using different types of aircraft (see "Flying Boats of the 1930s," *p.82),* but it took an enormous toll in human life and in money. The adventures of Aéropostale, later absorbed by Air France, are an example of the high cost paid for the development and

progress of civilian aviation. The other large companies which planned to open intercontinental passenger service had an equally difficult and adventurous history. One of the pioneers (the Dutch KLM airlines founded in 1919) on September 12, 1929, accomplished the impressive feat of opening the first regular Amsterdam–Jakarta (8970 miles) service, flying nationally-built 3-engine *Fokkers.* The route, which had weekly service by 1930, filled the need for a quick connection between the mother country, Holland, and her Indonesian colony.

A similar need motivated Britain's Imperial Airways' opening its Middle East, Far East and African routes. The government-sponsored company was founded in 1924 with the consolidation of four minor companies. In 1939 it became BOAC. The opening of the Bassorah–Cairo (1927), Bassorah–Karachi (1929), London–Cape Town and London–Calcutta–Rangoon–Singapore (1933) lines

SAVOIA-MARCHETTI S-73 (1935, I). More than 40 civilian *S-73*'s were successfully used by SABENA, Ala Littoria and Avio Linee Italiane. On the Brussels–Belgian Congo line, the *S-73* reduced effective flying time from 53 to 44 hours. The Italian companies used it on major European and North African routes. It proved to be extraordinarily efficient on the Rome–Mogadiscio–Addis Ababa line. Some *S-73*'s were built on license in Belgium by SABCA. During World War II, the Italian Air Force used it as a transport. Many *S-81*'s, the bomber model, were built.

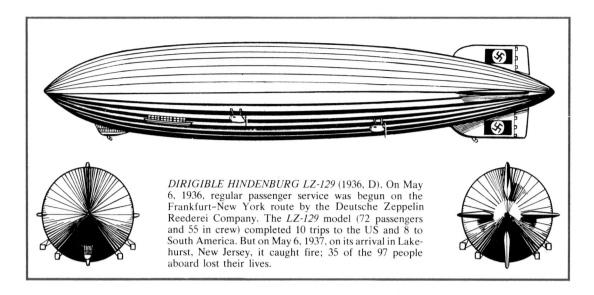

DIRIGIBLE HINDENBURG LZ-129 (1936, D). On May 6, 1936, regular passenger service was begun on the Frankfurt–New York route by the Deutsche Zeppelin Reederei Company. The *LZ-129* model (72 passengers and 55 in crew) completed 10 trips to the US and 8 to South America. But on May 6, 1937, on its arrival in Lakehurst, New Jersey, it caught fire; 35 of the 97 people aboard lost their lives.

was a tremendously difficult enterprise. When service was begun on the 12,645-mile London–Brisbane (Australia) line on April 13, 1935, it was a victory not only for Imperial Airways, but also for all of civil aviation. While Far East routes had been pioneered by a French company as well (which in 1931 had opened the Marseilles–Damascus–Saigon line), the African routes were flown by SABENA. By 1920 SABENA already had a line in the Congo and in the middle of the '30s opened the first regular service between Brussels and Léopoldville. The limits of the peace treaty did not stop German Lufthansa's notable expansion of its European network. Lufthansa also competed with the French in the attempt to open mail service to South America. German prestige suffered a harsh blow after the tragic accident of the *Hindenburg LZ-129* dirigible. In 1936, the airship had successfully completed about 20 transatlantic trips carrying about 50 passengers per trip.

DE HAVILLAND D.H.86 (1934, GB). Designed on commission for the Australian government for the Singapore–Australia line, 62 remained in service for over 10 years, mostly on the Far East and Africa routes.

LOCKHEED 10A ELECTRA (1935, USA). One of the best American passenger planes of the 1930s, and the first all-metal aircraft produced in the United States. The *10A Electra* was used by many American companies, principally by Braniff airlines. It was later replaced by the more spacious *DC-3*.

(continued on page 86)

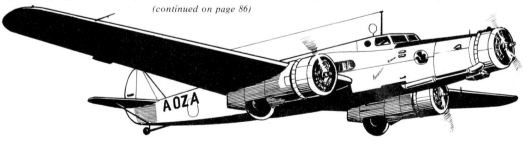

DEWOITINE D-338 (1935, F). The plane was developed from the *D-332* which Maurice Noguès had test flown to Saigon on December 22, 1933, to study the possibility of opening a new passenger line using the new plane. The *D-338* flew for the first time in 1935. Thirty-one were built for Air France, which used them on the Paris–Marseilles–Cannes, Paris–Damascus–Hanoi, Paris–Dakar and Paris–Hong Kong lines. Only nine of the *D-338*'s survived the War and re-entered service on the Paris–Nice line. This sleek and elegant craft proved to be one of the best prewar French passenger planes.

AMERICAN CIVIL AIRCRAFT OF THE 1930s

In Europe, air passenger transportation had been developing slowly since 1919; in the U.S. the pattern was different. The first real passenger airlines did not come into being until 1926. It is therefore only logical that at the end of the 1920s the U.S. found itself trailing European industry in the field of air transportation. But in 1927 two factors changed the picture and promoted the founding of large companies (such as United, TWA, American and Eastern): the government's decision to use private contractors for postal transport (indirect financing) and Lindbergh's flight, which, by arousing the entire country, inspired faith among potential passengers. The figures speak for themselves: in 1928, 60,000 Americans traveled by air; 165,000 in 1929; and over 500,000 in 1930. It took time for industry to adapt to the new situation. At the end of the 1920s mostly postal aircraft were produced, such as the *Boeing Model 40A* (used on the Chicago–San Francisco line since 1928), and the *Boeing Monomail*, the first American transport with retractable landing gear; or the maximum-10-passenger planes like the Stinson Detroiter with which the Tulsa–Oklahoma route was opened by Paul Braniff, the *Stinson Tri-motor* used by Boston Maine Airways (which later became Northeast Airlines), the Travel Air A6000A, flown by NAT on the Chicago–Kansas City route and the *Fairchild FC-2W* which was quite popular in the U.S. and Canada. On the main routes, with the heaviest passenger traffic, the best aircraft of the time were the *Boeing Model 80A*, the *Ford Tri-motor (p. 73)*, and the *Curtiss Condor*, the last American passenger biplane preferred by American and Eastern Airlines. The great *Fokker F-32*, the first American commercial 4-engine land plane, with 32 seats, arrived in 1930, too far ahead of its time; it was often forced to fly half empty and proved to be a financial disaster. So the American companies preferred to continue to use what they already had at their disposal, putting in service small new planes such as the *Consolidated Fleetster*, the *Northrop Delta*, the *Lockheed Orion*, while awaiting the arrival of passenger aircraft of the next generation, which would come along soon enough. In fact, in 1932 the first modern passenger aircraft appeared, the *Boeing 247*, which, available exclusively to United Airlines, made the company a success. TWA, in turn, commissioned a similar plane from Douglas which first built the *DC-2* and then the legendary *DC-3 (p. 76)*.

On the eve of World War II, of the 322 planes in service for the major U.S. companies, 260 were *DC-3*'s, 8 *DC-2*'s, 10 *Lockheed Lodestars*, 16 *Lockheed Electra*'s *(p. 77)* and 25 *Boeing 247*'s. And the products of American industry, even those in the civil-aviation sector, began to be exported; the U.S. had not only made up for lost time in respect to Europe, but had taken a decisive lead.

1929 – Stinson Detroiter SM-1F (USA)

1931 – Boeing Monomail Model 221A (USA)

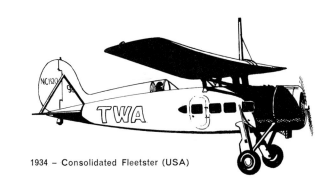

1934 – Consolidated Fleetster (USA)

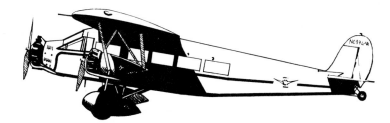

1931 – Stinson Tri-motor SM-6000 (USA)

1934 – Northrop Delta (USA)

1929 – Travel Air Model A-6000A (USA)

1930 – Curtiss Condor (USA)

1930 – Fokker F 32 (USA)

1928 – Boeing Model 40A (USA)

1928 – Fairchild FC-2W (USA)

1928 – Boeing 80A (USA)

1932 – Lockheed Orion (USA)

1932 – Boeing Model 247 (USA)

1937 – Lockheed Model 14 (USA)

1940 – Lockheed Lodestar (USA)

From left to right, emblems of American airlines during the twenties and thirties: American Airlines, National Air Transport, Transcontinental Air Transport, Transcontinental and Western Air, Boeing Air Transport, United Airlines.

1928 – Farman F 180 (F)

1928 – Farman F 190 (F)

1930 – Farman F 300 (F)

1935 – Potez 62 (F)

1932 – Savoia Marchetti SM 71 (I)

1932 – Ant-9-M-17 (SU)

1928 – Junkers Ju W-33 Bremen (D)

1933 – Heinkel He 70 (D)

1934 – Bloch 120 (F)

1934 – Fokker F.XXXVI (NL)

1937 – De Havilland D.H.91 Albatros (GB)

1935 – Junkers Ju 86 (D)

![Junkers G.38]
1929 – Junkers G.38 (D)

1932 – Wibault 283 T (F)

1932 – Armstrong Whitworth A.W.15 Atalanta (GB)

1934 – Savoia Marchetti SM 74 (I)

1938 – Armstrong Whitworth A.W.27 Ensign (GB)

EUROPEAN CIVIL AVIATION OF THE 1930s

Lindbergh's flight gave a new thrust to commercial airlines in Europe as well. Many of these, in 1919 and 1920, were born of the aeronautic industry's own initiative. By the beginning of the 1930s they were no longer directly linked to industry; since the European airlines were mostly government-financed, they had to chose nationally-built aircraft to outfit their fleets. And thus in all of the major European countries "tailor-made" aircraft were created to meet the specific needs of national companies. In France the Farman company was particularly active. Three prototypes of the *F-180,* christened *Oiseau Bleu,* a 2-engine biplane with unique characteristics, were built and used on the Paris–London line. The *F-300* was used on the routes with Germany and Finland, and the *F-190* (a four-passenger model), over 100 of which were built, was in service on less important internal routes. The 3-engine low-wing *Wibault 283 T* was Air France's most widely used plane in 1935. For the Far East and the colonial routes the 2-engine *Potez 62* and the 3-engine *Bloch 120,* both of them monoplanes famed for their safety and durability, were created. In 1928 Germany offered proof of its ambitious plans with the *Junkers JU-W-33 "Bremen,"* which repeated Lindbergh's flight in the opposite direction. The following year the giant *Junkers G-38* (2 were built) appeared, a 4-engine 34-passenger aircraft with its cabins located at the point where the wings joined the fuselage. The *Heinkel HE-70* was Germany's answer to the *Lockheed Orion (p.79)* the first European high-speed transport for 4 passengers. The extremely advanced *Junkers JU-86* was among the first European civil aircrafts to make an important dent in export markets. In the meantime the *Junkers JU-52/3M (p.75)* was carrying most of Lufthansa's passenger load....

On the other hand, the Dutch *Fokker* had lost ground in comparison to the previous decade; its *F-XXXVI* appeared, a 4-engine aircraft which might have had a future if the *DC-2 (p.76)* had not made its debut and found one of its first buyers in KLM. In Italy, Savoia-Marchetti in 1932 presented its first multi-engine aircraft, the *SM-71,* followed by the *SM-74,* assigned to the Rome–Paris line. The most widely seen Russian passenger plane of the prewar years was the *ANT 9-M-17,* which in its many versions was basic equipment for Aeroflot beginning in 1932. British industry found itself playing a leading role with aircraft of notable importance thanks to the needs of Imperial Airways. The *Handley Page HP-42F Hannibal (p.74)* was followed by the 1932 *A.W. 15 Atalanta* and in 1937 by 2 splendid planes: the *D.H. 91 Albatros* with perfect aerodynamic lines and the *A.W.27 Ensign,* the largest British civilian passenger aircraft of the prewar years.

FLYING BOATS OF THE 1930s

As intercontinental routes opened, more and more flights over long stretches of ocean were required. One of the main reasons for the development of the flying ships during the 1930s is the fact that, in case of damage, a craft which could land and rest on water was considered safer than a land plane. Furthermore, the sea, rivers and lakes offered convenient and economical bases. True to its tradition, France was an active innovator: for the Mediterranean it created the *Cams 53-1* (4 passengers) and the *Breguet 530 Saigon,* developed from the English *Short Calcutta;* for postal service on the south Atlantic (France's real objective) 3 huge flying boats were created, the postal *Latécoère 300 "Croix du Sud"* (the ship that Jean Mermoz was piloting when he disappeared on December 7, 1936); the *Bleriot 5190* (which in 1934 made 22 trips between Africa and Brazil) and the *Latécoère 521,* which might have had a future but for the advent of the War. These three ships were added to the 3-engine *Couzinet 70 (p.75)* and the small seaplane *Latecoère 28 III (p.74),* already part of France's postal fleet. The English contribution was equally important; routes for Africa and the Orient meant crossing the Mediterranean and the job was done by the *Short Calcutta* and the *Short S-17 Kent,* previous to the appearance of the *Short S-23 "C" (p.85).* With mail service to the U.S. in mind, *Short* created the first "composite plane" in the world: the *Mayo Composite.* This was made up of 2 flying ships of different sizes, one on top of the other, which upon take-off became a multiengine biplane; once airborne the smaller seaplane, loaded to full capacity, detached itself and proceeded toward its destination while the larger flying boat returned to base. The principle has been renewed in our time with designs for the lunar shuttle *(p.213).* On July 21, 1938, the *Mayo* first tested its mettle; the *S-20,* lifted to its cruising altitude by the *S-21,* reached Montreal, Canada, in 20 hours and 20 minutes after taking off from Ireland (2929 miles). The experiments were interrupted by the War. Italy built at least five flying boats of consequence: the famous *S-55 (p.72);* the *Cant 22 R-1;* the *SM-66;* the *MC-94;* and the *MC-100,* all used on national or Mediterranean routes. Germany built the *Super Wal,* the second generation of the famous *Dornier Do J (p.56),* also built in Italy and Spain, and the *Dornier Do X (p.73)* and the mail plane *HA 139B (p.85).* The U.S. serviced the Great Lakes and the nearby Caribbean routes with the *S-38* and South American routes with the *Consolidated Commodore (p.74),* the *S-42* and the *S-43.* But the Pacific and Atlantic oceans were definitively conquered with the *China Clipper* and the *Yankee Clipper (p.85),* which marked a historic turning point in the development of civil aviation.

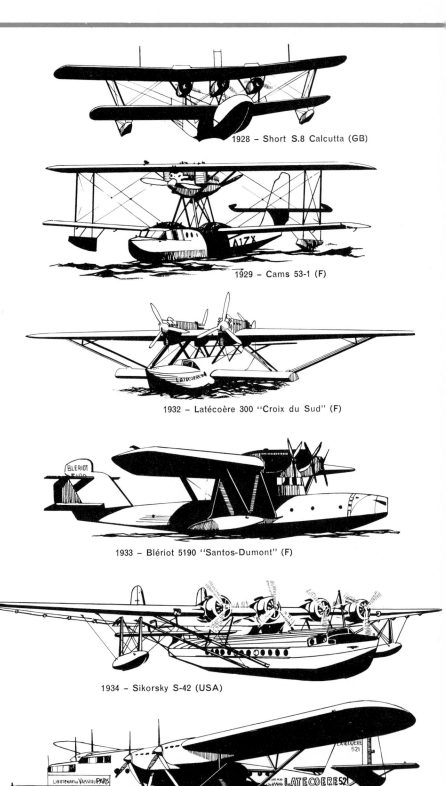

1928 – Short S.8 Calcutta (GB)

1929 – Cams 53-1 (F)

1932 – Latécoère 300 "Croix du Sud" (F)

1933 – Blériot 5190 "Santos-Dumont" (F)

1934 – Sikorsky S-42 (USA)

1935 – Latécoère 521 "Lieutenant de Vaisseau Paris" (F)

1928 – Sikorsky S-38 (USA)

1928 – Cant 22 R.1 (I)

1934 – Breguet 530 Saigon (F)

1931 – Short S 17 Kent (GB)

1932 – Savoia Marchetti SM 66 (I)

1929 – Dornier Do R4 Super Wal II (D)

1936 – Macchi MC 94 (I)

1932 – Sikorsky S-43 (USA)

1938 – Macchi MC 100 (I)

1937 – Short S 21 Maja-Short S 20 Mercury (GB)

CLASSIC MILITARY AIRCRAFT OF THE 1930s

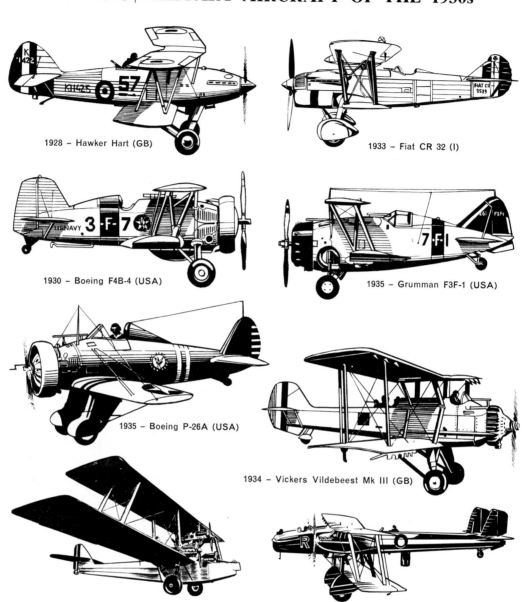

1928 – Hawker Hart (GB)

1933 – Fiat CR 32 (I)

1930 – Boeing F4B-4 (USA)

1935 – Grumman F3F-1 (USA)

1935 – Boeing P-26A (USA)

1934 – Vickers Vildebeest Mk III (GB)

1929 – Caproni Ca 90 (I)

1930 – Handley Page Heyford (GB)

Among the military aircraft born in the early 1930s (and already obsolete by the outbreak of World War II), those that should be mentioned as true aviation classics are: the *Hawker Hart* and the *Vickers Vildebeest,* respectively a light bomber and standard R.A.F. torpedo bomber up to 1938; the *Handley Page Heyford,* the last English heavy bomber biplane retired from the front line squadrons in 1937; the *Fiat CR-32,* considered the best fighter of the early 1930s, exported to many countries and victorious pro-tagonist in the furious duels with the Russian *Polikarpov I-16's (p.111)* during the Spanish Civil War; the 6-engine *Caproni Ca-90,* the largest bomber built before 1929 and never mass produced; the American aircraft carrier-borne fighters *F4B* and *F3F* (the latter was nicknamed the *Flying Barrel*), excellent planes ultimately replaced in 1940; and finally, the first entirely metal monoplane of the U.S. Army Air Corps, the *P-26A,* nicknamed the *Peashooter* by its pilots.

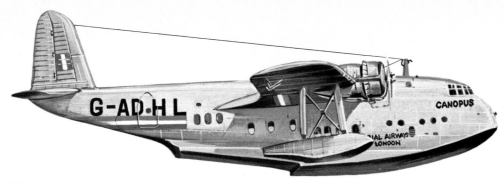

SHORT S-23 "C" (1936, GB). Forty-four of these enormous flying boats were built for Imperial Airways and gave excellent service beginning in 1937. In 1938 the *Empire Boats,* as they had been christened, made 7 flights a week to Egypt, 4 to India, 3 to Oriental Africa, 2 to South Africa, Malaysia, Hong Kong and Australia. On July 5, 1937, the *S-23 Caledonia* tried out its transatlantic airmail service between Shannon and Botwood, completing the crossing in 15 hours and 3 minutes. Regular service between Great Britain and the U.S. was inaugurated on August 8, 1939, and discontinued after only 8 voyages because of the outbreak of the War.

MARTIN 130 CHINA CLIPPER (1934, USA). It was built on order for Pan American, with a range sufficient to cross the 2386 miles of ocean between California and the Hawaiian Islands. On November 22, 1935, the *China Clipper* made the inaugural postal flight from San Francisco to Manila in the Philippines, via Hawaii–Midway–Wake and Guam in six days with 60 hours' effective flying time. Passenger service was begun on October 21, 1936; in April 1937 the route was extended as far as Hong Kong using a jointly owned China National Aviation Corp/Pan American aircraft. The doors of China had finally been opened!

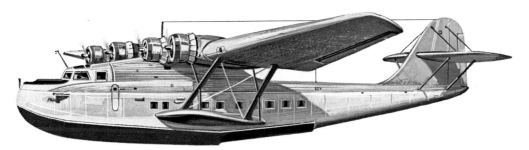

BOEING 314 YANKEE CLIPPER (1938, USA). With a *314,* Pan American, on May 20, 1938, opened the first nonstop airmail service on the North Atlantic, flying New York–Lisbon–Marseilles in 29 hours. On June 24, the New York–Newfoundland–Southampton route was inaugurated, and on July 8, passenger service was begun on both lines with biweekly flights. Because of the war, little notice was taken of the event. The 12 *Yankee Clippers* which were built (9 for Pan Am, 2 for the English government and 1 for the U.S. government) could carry 74 passengers and were used on the Atlantic and Pacific routes throughout the entire War.

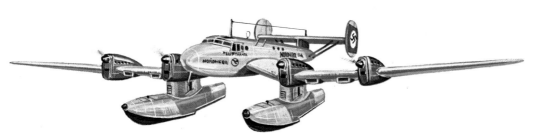

BLOHM AND VOSS HA-139B (1937, D). To experiment with mail service over the Atlantic, Lufthansa ordered three of these huge 4-engine seaplanes, built to be launched by catapult and able to take off even on very rough seas. The first 2 *HA-139*'s were delivered to the company in March 1937 and were used on board tenders on the Azore Islands–New York run. The experiments continued from August 15, to November 30, 1937, and from July 21, to October 19, 1938. The aircraft were also used on the line's Bathurst, West Africa–Recife, South America, route. When the war broke out, the three *HA-139*'s were requisitioned by the Luftwaffe.

ANT 20-Bis (1939, USSR). The *Ant 20,* which had flown for the first time on May 19, 1934, called the *Maxim Gorky,* was an enormous 8-engine aircraft that was destroyed in an air collision in 1935. The *Ant 20-Bis,* built with money collected by public subscription, was basically similar to its predecessor, with the exception of an improved line and only 6 engines. It seems that only one was built, carrying 64 passengers, and was used on the Moscow–Mineral'nye Vody line in 1940.

ANT 14 (1931, USSR). Designed, as was the *Ant 20,* by Andrei Nikolaevich Tupolev, it was ready for mass production at the very time that the Soviet government decided to give priority to single, or at most, 2-engine military aircraft. The *Ant 14* was used on scientific expeditions in Siberia and the Arctic.

ANT 25 (1935, USSR). Designed by Tupolev in 1932, on July 13, 1937, it flew Moscow–San Jacinto, California, nonstop, flying over the North Pole and all of the United States, and set a new straight-line distance record of 6295 miles.

NARDI FN-305D (1937, I). This aircraft set many records. On March 7, 1939, flown by Leonardo Bonzi and Giovanni Zappetta, it concluded a 2812-mile nonstop flight Rome–Addis Ababa in 18 hours and 49 minutes, flying an average speed of 150 miles per hour.

DE HAVILLAND D.H.88 COMET (1934, GB). Three were built for the England–Melbourne race which began on October 20, 1934. A *D.H.88* piloted by C. W. A. Scott and Tom Campbell Black, won the race in 70 hours and 54 minutes, beating a KLM *Douglas DC-2.*

On May 6, 1937, upon its arrival at Lakehurst, New Jersey, it inexplicably caught fire. Thirty-five of the 97 people aboard perished in the explosion. It was the last in a series of accidents that had also been suffered by French and American dirigibles and meant the irrevocable downfall of the lighter-than-air craft.

Italy had its first airlines in 1926, made up of national aircraft and Italian built *Dornier Wals.* The routes covered by the Italian companies went from 2898 miles in 1927 to 24,780 miles in 1938. Before the outbreak of World War II. LATI joined Ala Littoria (then the largest Italian company) for South American service.

Coming back to the U.S. (where we mentioned that the largest companies were formed during the 1930s, we see the emergence of literally the first modern transport aircraft. In 1928, the *Lockheed Vega (p.72)* appeared, a good example of how American industry was making up for lost time compared to European industry (the U.S. had begun passenger transportation rather late—toward the middle of the 1920s). in 1933, the *Boeing 247 (p.79)* appeared. This all-metal, 10-passenger aircraft was much faster, more comfortable and safer than the *Curtiss Condor (p.79)* and the 3-engine *Fokker* and *Ford (pp.72,73)* which had until then been the nucleus of the American companies' fleets. But Boeing had a substantial interest in United Airlines and refused to accept a large order for *247*s from TWA. TWA was forced to order a similar, if not better, airplane from Douglas Aircraft. The proto-

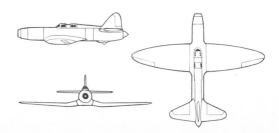

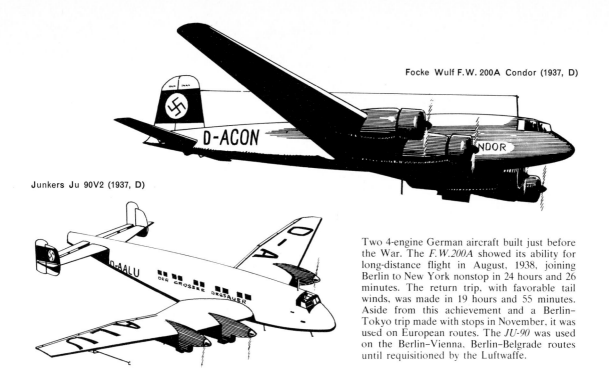

Focke Wulf F.W. 200A Condor (1937, D)

Junkers Ju 90V2 (1937, D)

Two 4-engine German aircraft built just before the War. The *F.W.200A* showed its ability for long-distance flight in August, 1938, joining Berlin to New York nonstop in 24 hours and 26 minutes. The return trip, with favorable tail winds, was made in 19 hours and 55 minutes. Aside from this achievement and a Berlin–Tokyo trip made with stops in November, it was used on European routes. The *JU-90* was used on the Berlin–Vienna, Berlin–Belgrade routes until requisitioned by the Luftwaffe.

type *DC-1* flew in 1933 and TWA approved it so wholeheartedly that it ordered 25. After some minor changes, these 25 began service as *DC-2*'s. This aircraft immediately proved its superiority to its nearest competitor, and it did it also in the sports world in the 1934 England-Australia Air Race. The race was won by one of the three *De Havilland D.H.88 Comets (p.86)* which had been designed and built especially for the competition. But second—and a very close second at that—was a *DC-2* flying for KLM. The *Boeing 247*, in the hands of the famous and experienced competition pilot Roscoe Turner, came in third. The race was resounding proof that the time had come when mass-produced aircraft flying long distances could hold their own against experimental and sports planes.

The *DC-2* was too small for coast-to-coast U.S. flights. On June 26, 1936, the first *DC-3* began service; it was to become the most successful passenger aircraft in the history of aviation. Of the approximately 13,000 *DC-3*'s produced between 1936 and 1946, at least 1000 are still flying today. No aircraft has ever been safer or more economically functional, both for peace and wartime use.

While the *DC-3* was impressing itself on the American and international markets for internal flights, Pan American, anxious to open its transoceanic routes, ordered the construction of the *Martin 130 China Clipper* and the *Boeing 314 Yankee Clipper (p.85)*. These two flying boats finally made passenger service on the Atlantic and Pacific oceans possible.

On November 22, 1935, airmail service between the United States and the Philippines was begun. It was transformed into passenger service on October 21, 1936. On May 20, 1938, the first regular airmail service over the North Atlantic from New York to Marseilles, with an intermediate stop at Lisbon, was inaugurated; it became a passenger route on June 24. Of the contenders in the fierce competition between Imperial Airways, Lufthansa and Pan American for the North Atlantic route, the Americans were taking a definite lead. They soon found themselves alone, for England and Germany were beginning to devote their attention to impending war.

Just eleven years after Lindbergh's flight, the Atlantic became a commercial route. It was an extremely important and exciting matter but somehow it was almost overlooked. The front pages of newspapers were devoting all their space to political events. Once again, civil aviation had to move aside and make way for military aviation. The Italians' war with Ethiopia in 1935, the 1936 Spanish Civil War, the Sino-Japanese War of 1937 and the Russo-Finnish War of 1939 were mere scuffles in comparison to the coming holocaust which was to involve almost all nations of the world.

All that had been discovered for peace was now to be used for war. Most civilian aircraft were requisitioned by military aviation to transport troops, munitions, refugees from battle zones, and the wounded. Pilots, until now the peaceful ambassadors of progress, traded their air-line uniforms for air-force uniforms.

CAMPINI N-1 (1940, I). It is considered the world's first jet aircraft by virtue of its completing a trip of more than 311 miles. On August 28, 1940, in fact, flown by Mario de Bernardi, it linked Milan to Rome, flying at a speed of 280 miles per hour.

88

United Kingdom

Australia

New Zealand

South Africa

France

Belgium

Holland

Norway

Denmark

Greece

Czechoslovakia

Bulgaria

Yugoslavia

Poland

United States to 1942

United States

Brazil

Soviet Union

Germany

Croatia

Slovakia

Rumania

Hungary

Italy

Italy

Italy

Soc. Rep. Italy

Japan

AIRCRAFT OF WORLD WAR II

The leading role that aviation played in the 1939–1945 war is unquestioned. Control of the skies meant the possibility for victory for both land and naval forces on the European and Pacific fronts. At the beginning of the War, German aviation allowed Hitler's armed divisions to wage the "lightning war" in Poland, to swiftly occupy Norway and Denmark and to forge the path for the army in the Low Countries, Belgium and France. On the other hand, because of the British Air Force, which met and exhausted the Luftwaffe in the Battle of Britain, the specter of invasion was driven from the island. The Normandy landing would have been inconceivable if the Allies had not had complete control of the air, and Germany would certainly have been able to hold out longer had it not been literally buried under a 1,211,620-ton carpet of bombs. Perhaps the U.S. would never have entered the War if the Japanese air attack on Pearl Harbor had not taken place; certainly the War in the Pacific theater could never have been won without four great naval air battles which followed one upon the other; Japan would never have been forced to surrender even before an American set foot on Japanese territory without the *B-29* bombing first, and then the dropping of the two atomic bombs.

About 675,000 aircraft were used during the War, 475,000 of these by the Allies, and the rest by Germany, Japan and Italy. These figures speak for themselves, but their significance in the history of military aviation should be taken into consideration. First of all, it meant the end of the biplane as both fighter and bomber and the decline of canvas planes which were replaced by those of all-metal construction. It meant the triumph of heavy strategic bombers and definitively affirmed the use of aircraft as a "weapon" aboard ship, making aircraft carriers the most efficient means of naval warfare and once and for all signaling the demise of the battleship. It meant the birth of night fighters equipped with radar and, even more important, the birth of the jet-powered aircraft, opening a new chapter in the history of technical aeronautics. It meant the beginning of large-scale air transport of millions of men and cargo from the U.S. to Europe and the Pacific, leading the way for commercial traffic. Leaving aside all other considerations, World War II meant the beginning of the atomic era, with the discovery and use of a weapon aboard an aircraft which astounded the world with its power to destroy. This event, particularly, would change the strategy of the major nations of the world, pressing them to seek for a new balance of power as security for peace.

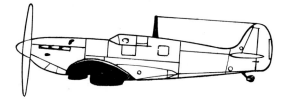

FRANCE

The nation which, during World War I, had best understood the importance of aviation as an instrument of war and which had been one of the strongest in air power found itself completely unprepared when the new war broke out. Its leaders not only underestimated Germany's power for rearmament despite the Versailles Treaty, but also had invested enormous sums of money on grandiose defensive measures such as the Maginot Line, without giving the necessary attention to air power. It wasn't until 1936 that the Armée de l'Air was born, the same year that 70 percent of the French aeronautical industry was nationalized. At last, it was deemed necessary to strenghten the air force, and great quantities of aircraft were ordered, both from French and American factories. But it was too late. On September 3, 1939, France entered the war with only 3600 aircraft, including those in its faraway colonies. On French territory only 510 fighters, 440 of these modern, were in flying condition; 500 reconnaissance planes were ready, only 51 of recent construction; 390 bombers were available, all obsolete. On June 20, 1940, France signed an armistice. Whatever men and materials were left in the nonoccupied territories were used to form the Vichy government's air force. Many pilots chose freedom and continued to fight for their country in the Free French Air Force founded by General de Gaulle and based in England. Among these young men was one who had begun combat as a sergeant and who was to become major and the ace of the French aces: Pierre Clostermann, with 33 victories. Beginning in March 1943, a fighter group composed of French pilots, called *Normandie,* operated in Russia with the First Soviet Armed Air Division; four of their officers, all with more than 10 planes downed to their credit, were declared Heroes of the Soviet Union.

BLOCH 210 (1934). The first low-wing French monoplane medium bomber with retractable landing gear, it was already completely obsolete by the time World War II broke out. Outfitting six bomber squadrons, it carried out a few night bombing raids on the Rhineland, Belgium and occupied France before it was relegated to use in flight-training schools.

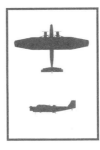

FARMAN F-222 (1936). A heavy 4-engine bomber already outdated in 1939. It was used as a reconnaissance and for propaganda flights over Germany and Czecholsovakia, dropping leaflets instead of bombs. After the Franco-German armistice (June 20, 1940), the air force of the Vichy government adopted it as a transport.

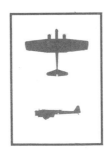

AMIOT 143 (1934). Born as a night bomber and reconnaissance aircraft, it entered service in 1935. By 1939 it could no longer compete with the more modern planes of the Luftwaffe. On May 14, 1940, twelve *Amiot 143*'s took off for a daylight raid against the Germans on the bridges of Sedan in France. Only one of the 12 made it back to base. Thereafter, it was used as a transport.

From left to right, bottom to top, the following insignia: Groupe de Chasse (Fighter Group) I/3—2nd Squadron GC II/4—4th Sq.; GC II/8—4th Sq.; GC II/7—4th Sq.; GC II/2—3rd Sq.; GC II/1—4th Sq.; GC II/3—3rd Sq.

BREGUET 691 (1939). Designed just before the War as a multi-purpose plane (the *B-2* as light bomber, the *AB-2* as dive bomber, the *A-3* as reconnaissance and the *C-3* as fighter). Numerically, not enough were produced in time to make a strong showing in action, but on the few occasions in which it did see action it proved to be a high-quality plane.

LATÉCOÈRE 298 (1936). A torpedo bomber and reconnaissance aircraft. There were 200 produced and they outfitted 5 naval squadrons in 1940. At the height of the German offensive it was also used in overland bombings on Boulogne. The *298*'s bombed Genoa many times and often attacked Italian ships in the Mediterranean.

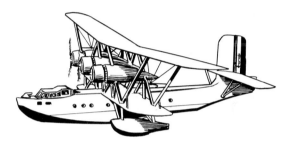

LIORÉ ET OLIVIER LEO 451 (1937). The only French medium bomber of modern design, only a few were produced. It was first flown in action on May 11, 1940, with the I/12 and II/12th *Groupes de Bombardement.* The plane was also used in bombing actions over occupied France, Northern Italy, Bavaria and Sicily.

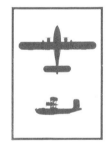

BREGUET 521 BIZERTE (1935). A navy reconnaissance flying boat based on the English *Short Calcutta.* In September 1939, it outfitted 5 navy squadrons and proved quite useful in patrolling the Atlantic and Mediterranean. After the Armistice the surplus *521*'s were used by the Luftwaffe for naval rescue and emergency missions.

BLOCH 174 (1939). Produced too late for wide use in action, this light bomber-reconnaissance was perhaps one of the best French aircraft of the War, capable of giving the Germans a run for their money. The first *Bloch 174* was flown in action on March 29, 1940, by Captain Antoine de Saint-Éxupéry, pioneer of French civil aviation and famous writer.

CAUDRON C-714 (1939). A light bomber, based on the 1935 *C-710* racer. Production was begun during the summer of 1939 but the Armée de l'Air did not consider it a good plane and ordered very few. The aircraft, however, was basic equipment for the I/145 Fighter Group made up of Polish pilots, refugees in France following the German occupation of their country.

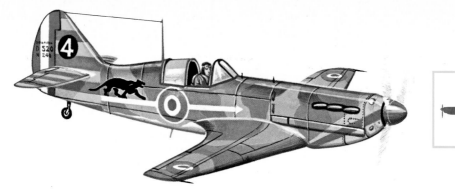

DEWOITINE D-520 (1939). The best French fighter of World War II. About 900 were built, many during the German occupation. It made its first flight in October 1938, and larger orders were put in by the air force (2200) and the navy (130). But in May 1940 only 36 *D-520*'s were in service. It proved to be excellent in combat against German fighters and bombers and, before the Armistice, scored 114 hits against only 54 losses. The positive features of the plane induced the Germans to continue its production and the *D-520*'s were used by the Luftwaffe, the Aeronautica Militare Italiana, the Bulgarian and Rumanian air forces and by the Free French units after the Allied invasion of the Continent.

BLOCH MB-152 (1938). Developed from the small, mediocre *MB-151* fighter (only 140 were built before 1939), production was begun during the last months of 1938. Of the 482 *MB-152*'s which came off the assembly line, fewer than 150 were used in action. Their performance was not outstanding. Many *MB-152*'s remained in service in the Vichy government's *Escadrilles de Chasse*. An attempt at equipping them with auxiliary tanks to permit their transfer to North Africa was discovered and squelched by the German authorities. Further development of the *MB-151* (that is, the *MB-155* and *MB-157*) took place too late to reach the stage of normal production because of the German occupation and the Armistice.

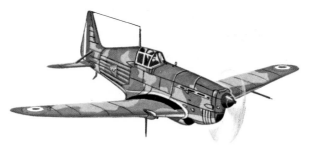

MORANE-SAULNIER M.S.406 (1938). The fighter which outfitted French fighter squadrons in greatest number at the outbreak of World War II. Four fighter squadrons, made up of 3 groups with 25 planes each, were in fact outfitted with the *M.S.406*. The 1037 which were built posed a real threat to the German *Bf-109*'s. Twelve *M.S.406*'s were also used in action in the Far East. Ordered by the Chinese government and requisitioned by the French Colonial Administration before delivery, they formed the nucleus of the 2/595th Squadron of Bach-Mai in Indochina. After the French surrender, many *M.S.406*'s were used by the Vichy Air Force. Others were given to Finland by the Germans who had already bought 30 by 1940.

POTEZ 63.11 (1938). The *Potez 630* was a multi-purpose plane designed in 1935. A total of 1250 (the *630* fighter, the *633* ground attack and the *63.11* reconnaissance) were built. The most important was the *63.11*, of which 748 were built and delivered to the *Groupes Aériens d'Observation*. Though it was an excellent reconnaissance aircraft, it totally depended on fighter protection, which was not always available when needed. For this reason the *63.11* accounted for more losses than any other French aircraft. Unlikely though it may seem, it was also used for ground attack in June 1940 against the Italian Army in Libya and Sardinia. Many of these planes were captured by the Luftwaffe, which used them in pilot-training schools.

From top to bottom, the following insignia: Groupe de Chasse (Fighter Group) I/4—2nd Squadron; GC III/6—5th Sq.; GC III/6—6th Sq.; GC II/1—4th Sq.

GREAT BRITAIN

In spite of Great Britain's concern for commercial and military aviation in the 1920s and 1930s, in September 1939 they had only about 1000 fighters combat-ready and equally few bombers. But designers had already planned such modern and excellent planes as the *Hurricane,* the *Spitfire* and the *Wellington,* and industry worked at top speed to produce them: from the 4000 aircraft built in 1938, the number rose to 7000 in 1939; 15,000 in 1940; 20,100 in 1941; 23,671 in 1942; 23,263 in 1943; 29,220 in 1944. But England's fate was decided before its aircraft industry reached its full production potential: shortly after Dunkirk (August 8, 1940), Germany began a full-force air attack to break Great Britain's resistance to invasion. In the "Battle of Britain," 3550 German aircraft (2000 bombers—600 of which were dive bombers—along with 1250 fighters and 300 reconnaissance planes) met less than 1000 *Hurricanes* and *Spitfires.* The battle raged until October 31 and the Luftwaffe was the loser, with 1733 aircraft downed against 915 English planes lost. Plans to invade the British Isles were indefinitely postponed. Britain owed much to its fighter force and to its excellent pilots who came from all the nations of the Commonwealth: the ace of aces, the South African Maj. Saint John Pattle (41 victories); the English Capt. James E. Johnson (38); the Australian Capt. Clive R. Caldwell (28); the Canadian Maj. George F. Beurling (31); the Irish Col. Brendan E. Finucane (32); the New Zealander Lt. Col. Colin F. Gray (27). But the part the bombers played in winning the war is equally important. In 687,462 missions on all fronts, they dropped 1,103,913 tons of bombs, more than 645,922 tons of which fell on German territory. When the 4-engine strategic bombers began operating, another deadly weapon was added.

DE HAVILLAND TIGER MOTH II (1932). One of the most famous training planes in the world, it was used in service by the R.A.F. for over 15 years. In 1939 more than 1000 were already flying. During the War more than 6954 were produced in countries of the British Empire. Practically all British pilots learned to fly on the old, faithful *Tiger Moth.*

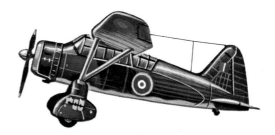

WESTLAND LYSANDER Mk. I (1938). Known affectionately as the *Lizzie* by her pilots, she marvelously filled her role as observer and army liaison until 1942. Widely used in France (the last British plane to leave Dunkirk), Egypt and Greece, 1368 were produced.

GLOSTER GLADIATOR (1937). The last British fighter biplane, about 260 were produced and entered service in 1937. Although outdated, they took part in the defense of France with the 607th and 615th squadrons, and in the Battle of Britain with the 247th. Three *Gladiators* christened *Faith, Hope* and *Charity* were outstanding in the June 1940 defense of Malta.

AIRSPEED OXFORD Mk.I (1937). The R.A.F.'s first advanced-training-model, twin-engine monoplane. The incredible number of 8751 were built and used from 1937 until 1954. The *Mk.I* was used in machine-gun and bomber training, the *Mk.II* in navigation and communications training and the *Mk.III* in ambulance and light transport.

AVRO ANSON Mk.I (1936). Also known as *Faithful Annie*. It set many records: the first monoplane and the first plane with retractable landing gear to enter service in the R.A.F. (1936); it stayed in service over 20 years, until 1942, as a reconnaissance plane and later as a trainer. There were 11,020 built, 2882 of them in Canada.

FAIREY FIREFLY F.R.I (1943). Carrier-borne fighter *(F.I)* and reconnaissance *(F.R.I)*, it began service in October 1943 with the 1770th Squadron on the *Indefatigable*. In July 1944, several *Fireflies* of the same unit cornered the battleship *Tirpitz* and helped sink it. About 840 *Fireflies* were also used effectively in the Pacific.

FAIREY FULMAR Mk.II (1940). The first carrier-borne fighter of the British Navy equipped with 8 machine guns, it began service in 1940 with the 806th Squadron on the aircraft carrier *Illustrious* stationed in the Mediterranean. It first flew in action against the Italian Air Force units. Six hundred were built, equipped 14 squadrons and remained in service until 1945. The *Seafire* took its place.

HAWKER TEMPEST Mk.V (1944). A total of 805 of these fighter bombers were built and began serving in action in January 1944 with the 3rd Squadron of the R.A.F. Because of its speed, it was used to intercept German *V.1* flying bombs, destroying 638 between June and September 1944. It also fought successfully against the new *Me-262* jet fighters, bringing down 20 of them.

HAWKER TYPHOON Mk.IB (1941). There were 3330 built as fighters and nicknamed "Tiffy." But the aircraft proved to be one of the best ground-attack fighters of the war, destroying airports, trains and tanks with astounding accuracy. On D-Day, June 6, 1944, 26 *Typhoon* squadrons played a decisive role during the invasion.

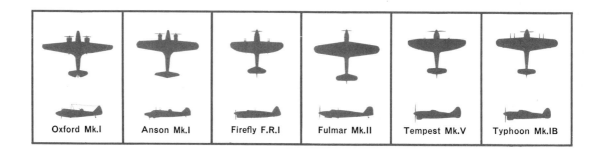

Oxford Mk.I — Anson Mk.I — Firefly F.R.I — Fulmar Mk.II — Tempest Mk.V — Typhoon Mk.IB

SUPERMARINE SEAFIRE F. Mk.III (1942). The *III* was the best carrier-borne fighter of the *Spitfire* family and was in service until 1952. The *Seafires* were extremely effective during the Allied landing at Salerno on September 9, 1943. They provided the main air support for the troops during the landing on that occasion and also during the invasion of France.

BLACKBURN ROC (1940). Carrier-borne fighter. Only 136 were built. It was the first English plane to be equipped with a revolving hydraulic machine-gun turret. It was first used on the carriers in February 1940, but did not prove very successful. It was replaced only a few months later by the *Fairey Fulmar*, certainly a more effective aircraft.

BOULTON PAUL DEFIANT Mk.I (1940). First British fighter without front armament, equipped with 4 machine guns on the revolving turret like the *Roc*. From its first flight in action at Dunkirk and the first phases of the Battle of Britain, it was clearly a failure. Equipped with radar, it was used with modest results as a night fighter. About 1064 were produced.

BRISTOL BEAUFORT Mk.I (1939). Typical bomber-torpedo-reconnaissance of the Coastal Command between 1940 and 1943, it was used a great deal (1120 were produced) on the English Channel, the Atlantic, the North Sea and the Mediterranean. The *Beaufort*s took part in the February 1942 attempt to prevent the *Gneisenau*, *Scharnhorst* and *Prinz Eugen* from leaving the English Channel.

FAIREY BARRACUDA Mk.II (1943). First all-metal torpedo and dive bomber to be used on British aircraft carriers, it saw action for the first time at Salerno in 1943. It was a great success during the April 3, 1944, attack on the *Tirpitz*, carried out by 44 planes of the *HMS Victorious* and *Furious*. A total of 2582 *Barracuda*s were built.

BRISTOL BEAUFIGHTER Mk.X (1940). In 1940–1941, the first British long-range night fighter able to successfully use its radar to intercept German bombers before they reached England. A total of 5962 units were produced. It was also an excellent anti-sub fighter *(Mk.X)* and was flown on all fronts, including the Pacific. The Japanese called it *Whispering Death*.

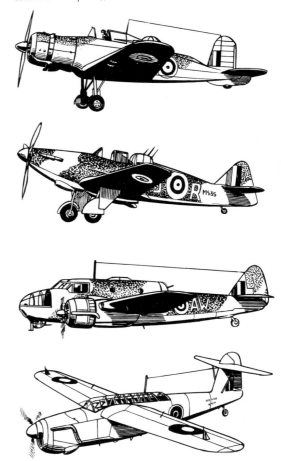

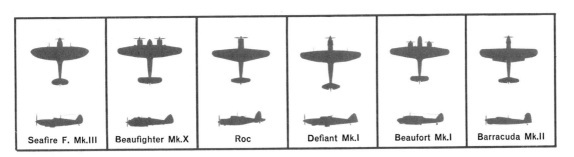

| Seafire F. Mk.III | Beaufighter Mk.X | Roc | Defiant Mk.I | Beaufort Mk.I | Barracuda Mk.II |

Spitfire Mk.V

SUPERMARINE SPITFIRE (1938). The most widely produced (20,351 in about 40 versions) British aircraft and the only Allied fighter to remain in production throughout the War. It was designed in 1936 by Reginald J. Mitchell, who also created the *Supermarine S-6 (p.67).* It began service in August 1938 *(Mk.I).* When war was declared there were 9 *Spitfire* squadrons and 19 when the Battle of Britain began on August 12, 1940. During the battle—that is, until October 31—a daily average of 957 *Spitfires* saw action, as compared to 1326 *Hurricanes*. The *Spitfire's* influence was enormous in helping England win the battle and stop the invasion. Among the best versions were: the *Mk.V* (1941), the most widely used; the *Mk.XII* (1943), the first with the *Griffon* engine; the *Mk.XVI* (1943), ground attack; and the *Mk.XIX* (1944), the fastest of the unarmed models used for reconnaissance and photography.

Spitfire Mk.IA

Spitfire Mk.XII

Spitfire Mk.XVI

Spitfire Mk.XIX

HAWKER HURRICANE Mk.I (1937). Designed in 1934 by Sidney Camm, it was the R.A.F.'s first monoplane fighter and the first faster than 300 miles per hour (480 kilometers). The first *Hurricanes* were delivered to the 111th Squadron in December 1937 and by September 1939 equipped 18 squadrons. Several of these were immediately sent to France. Over half the German planes downed during the first year of the War were hit by the *Hurricanes*. The heaviest part of the fighting during the Battle of Britain was played by the 32 available *Hurricane* squadrons. Their job was to attack German bombers, leaving the honor of confronting the Luftwaffe's fighters to the faster *Spitfires.* A total of 14,533 *Hurricanes* were produced in the *Mk.I* (1937), *MK.II* (1941) and *Mk.IV* (1943) versions. These were outstanding on all fronts, even ground attacks. In 1941 several *Mk.I*'s were modified for catapult launching. They were known as *Hurricats.* In 1942, the *Sea Hurricane* catapult and carrier-borne versions appeared. Also, 2952 *Hurricanes* were supplied to Russia during the first years of the War and also proved to be very efficient on that front.

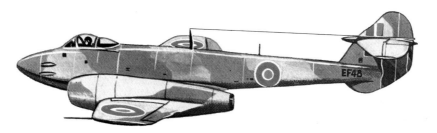

Spitfire Mk.V

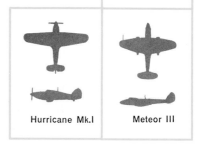

Hurricane Mk.I   Meteor III

GLOSTER METEOR III (1944). The first British jet fighter and the only Allied jet to enter action before the end of the War. The aircraft, designed by W. G. Carter, made its first flight on March 5, 1943. The first 7 of these 20 *Meteor I*'s ordered were assigned to the 616th Squadron during the first part of July 1944 and on the twenty-seventh of July were tested against the German *V-1* flying bombs over the Channel with good results. The more improved *Meteor III*'s (a total of 280 were produced) began outfitting squadrons in January 1945. They left Brussels airport for their first mission in action on April 16, 1945. Their task was to intercept the German *Me-262* jet fighters. But the encounter never took place and the War ended without the *Meteor* ever having been put to the test.

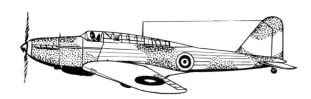

FAIREY BATTLE Mk.I (1937). A light bomber already outdated in 1939, it was replaced by September 1940. With the 226th Squadron, it was the first British plane to reach France at the beginning of the War and it fought bravely although it suffered heavy losses. Of the 2419 *Battle*s produced, the surviving planes were assigned to flight schools in 1941.

FAIREY SWORDFISH Mk.I (1937). In 1939 this carrier-borne torpedo bomber biplane still outfitted 13 squadrons. In all, 2391 were produced. In November 1940, they did an outstanding job during the attack on the Italian fleet at Taranto; in 1941 in the battle of Cape Matapan; and in 1942 they helped sink the German *Bismarck*. A good record for an obsolete aircraft.

BRISTOL BLENHEIM Mk.I (1937). The patrol bomber used by the R.A.F. since 1937; with 1007 planes it outfitted most bomber squadrons at the outbreak of the War (total produced were 4422). It operated on all fronts but even the improved *Mk.IV* and *Mk.IF* night-fighter versions were, at best, mediocre.

FAIREY SEAFOX (1937). The last British light seaplane designed for catapult launch, it fulfilled its reconnaissance tasks notably. Two *Seafox*es outfitted the cruiser *Ajax* and played a decisive role in the fight against the German battleship *Admiral Graf Spee* in December 1939. There were 64 built and used until 1943.

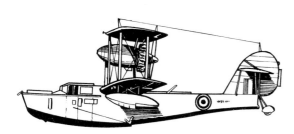

SUPERMARINE WALRUS II (1936). A catapult reconnaissance flying boat which was produced from 1936 until 1944 (740 were built). Besides being employed in its primary role, it was widely used in sea rescue and other missions, even bomber missions. On November 18, 1940, for example, a *Walrus* stationed on the cruiser *Dorsetshire* bombed zones in Italian Somaliland.

SHORT SUNDERLAND Mk.V (1938). Developed from the commercial flying boat the *Short S-2B* "C" *(p.85)*, about 700 were built between 1937 and 1945 in five successive series. Called the *Stachelschwein* or "porcupine" by the Germans because it was so exceptionally well armed for defense, it was priceless in navy reconnaissance, antisubmarine warfare and emergency transport.

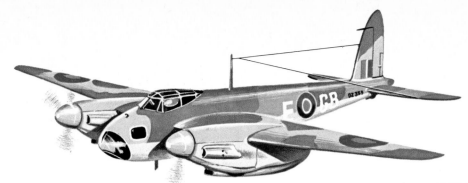

DE HAVILLAND B-IV MOSQUITO (1941). One of the most versatile aircraft of World War II. It was the fastest light bomber of the War. As a long-range day and night fighter, it distinguished itself with the downing of over 600 planes and just as many German flying bombs. As a photo-reconnaissance aircraft it was unequaled, flying faster and higher than all its possible interceptors. The prototype was first flown in November 1940, but the first *B-IV's* (bombers), *N.F. Mk.II's* (night fighters) and *P.R. Mk.I's* photo-reconnaissance) didn't enter service until 1942. The day and night *F.B. Mk.VI* fighter-bomber series (the most important) joined the squadrons in 1943. Before the end of the War, 6710 *Mosquito*es were built. Total production was 7781. Its continuous and effective night-shattering attacks on Northern Italy made it ironically "popular" with the Italians.

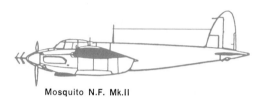

Mosquito N.F. Mk.II

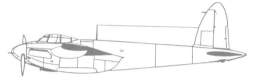

Mosquito F.B. Mk.VI

HANDLEY PAGE HAMPDEN (1939). A medium bomber (which made its first flight on June 21, 1936), its job along with the *Wellington* and the *Whitley*, was to bear the weight of the operations assigned to the bomber command during the first 2 years of the War. On September 3, 1939, a total of 10 squadrons were outfitted with *Hampdens* used in daylight bombings. They suffered heavy losses and soon proved to be insufficient for defense. Assigned to night bombings, the aircraft had its moments of glory taking part on August 25, 1940, in the first bombing of Berlin and later in the first massive (1000 bombers) raid over Cologne. It was replaced in the front lines in September 1942 and was reassigned to the coastal command, where it was used as a mine-layer and torpedo bomber. The *Hampdens,* which also operated from Russian bases, totaled 1430.

SHORT STIRLING III (1940). The first World War II British 4-engine bomber, it began service in August 1940 and was used in action for the first time in February 1941. In this aircraft as well as in others, defense armament proved insufficient to stand up to the highly efficient German fighters. For this reason, it was reassigned to night bombing duty in 1942. The *Stirling,* 2375 of which were produced, sadly ended its career as an improvised troop transport and "motherplane" for large gliders.

Whitley Mk.V

VICKERS WELLINGTON III (1938). Medium bomber used by the R.A.F. beginning in 1938. The 11,461 produced, in about 12 series, were the strong men of the bomber command until 1945 when the 4-engine heavy bombers arrived. Several of the 169 *Wimpey*s (as they were affectionately nicknamed) in service on September 3, 1939, entered in action the next day, with a few *Blenheim*s, effecting the first bombing raid of the war on Brunsbuttel. Assigned to night bombing on December 18, 1939, they were widely used. In the first major bombing over Cologne, on May 30, 1942, of 1000 aircraft involved, 599 were *Wellington*s. Used at El Alamein, in Greece and in the Far East, they completed one of their last missions over Treviso in March 1945.

Wellington III

ARMSTRONG WHITWORTH WHITLEY Mk.V (1937). The "senior" British twin-engine medium bomber in service at the outbreak of the War (with 207 operating aircraft), it was immediately used for night bombings. One of the first planes to bomb Germany, it was also the first Allied aircraft to hit Italian soil. In fact on June 11, 1940, *Whitley*s of the 10th, 51st, 77th, 88th, and 102nd squadrons reached Turin and Genoa. About 2900 *Whitley*s took part in action. After the bombing of Ostend during the night of April 29, 1942, they were moved from bomber command to the coastal command.

AVRO LANCASTER (1942). The best and most famous British 4-engine bomber. It was created in 1941 as a result of the failure of the twin-engine *Avro Manchester*. It was first used in action on March 2, 1942, and was a brilliant success all through the War. In all, 7366 made 156,000 missions. dropping 608,612 tons of bombs (among these several 2200-pound "Grand Slams"). Among its many sensational raids were the assault on the Moehne and Eder dams on May 17, 1943. and the sinking of the *Tirpitz* on November 12, 1944. In early 1945 more than 1000 *Lancaster*s outfitted 56 squadrons.

HANDLEY PAGE HALIFAX Mk.III (1940). It entered service 3 months after the *Stirling* and became deservedly famous, only slightly less so than the *Lancaster*. It made its first raid on March 11, 1941, on Le Havre and its last on April 25, 1945, giving excellent service to the bomber command during the 4 years: 75,532 missions, 227, 610 tons of bombs dropped on enemy objectives. Although mostly used on the Continent, it also saw action in the Middle East and was the only British 4-engine plane used for this task. There were 6176 produced in about 10 series, and the last of its kind were not retired until 1952. A *Halifax*, christened *Friday the Thirteenth* by its pilot, made 128 raids before being put out of commission.

Lancaster

Halifax Mk.III

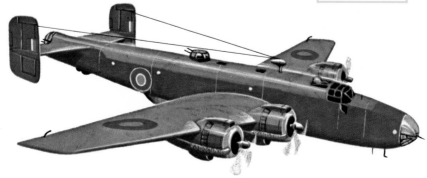

100

U.S.A.

At dawn on December 7, 1941, 423 planes left 6 Japanese aircraft carriers to attack the American fleet docked at Pearl Harbor in the Hawaiian Islands: the United States of America was at war. For many years, the Americans had sympathetically watched the British and French fighting in Europe, hoping not to become involved in the conflict. In fact, in 1938 only 1800 military planes were produced in the United States; and 2195 in 1939; 6028 in 1940; 19,445 in 1941. Most of these went to Great Britain. But once hit, the American colossus awoke: in 1942, 47,675 aircraft were produced; 85,433 in 1943; 95,272 in 1944, at the rate of one plane every 6 minutes! From January 1, 1942, to December 31, 1945, total American production was 275,245 aircraft and 733,760 aeronautical engines! In December 1941 the American air force was relatively small. In July 1944, the U.S. boasted the strongest air force of all times: 79,908 aircraft and 2 million men. The contribution of the U.S.A.A.F. to the war in Europe was immediate and generous: hundreds of thousands of fighter missions, a loss of about 3000 fighters, over 481,000 bombing missions, 982,728 tons of explosives dropped and a loss of 6524 bombers. But the major thrust was in the Pacific, where aside from front-line operations, the air forces of the American Army and Navy transported 1,300,000 men and 1,155,000 tons of materials from the United States to the Japanese Theater of Operations. In 1944, the bombing of Japan began with terrifying results: just one attack on Tokyo alone destroyed a vast area of the city. Among the American aces, we should remember Maj. Richard I. Bong (40 victories), Maj. T. B. McGuire (38), Capt. D. McCampbell (34), Col. F. S. Gabreski (31). The War ended in August 1945 when two atom bombs fell on Hiroshima and Nagasaki, each flown by a *B-29*, the most modern and powerful American bombers of World War II.

RYAN PT-20 (1940). A mainstay in pilot-training schools, it was descended from the *PT-16*. Along with its successors, the *PT-21* and the *PT-22*, it gave excellent service during the first years of the war. A total of about 1250 *PT-16*, *PT-20*, *PT-21* and *PT-22* aircraft were built before 1942, when production ceased. Several of these aircraft were exported to the Dutch Indies, Guatemala, Honduras and Mexico

VULTEE BT-13A VALIANT (1940). Standard training aircraft during the War, over 11,000 were produced, most for the U.S.A.A.F. At the end of the War, many *BT-13*'s and *BT-15*'s were sold as war-surplus aircraft to air forces of Latin America and were, for many years, the "first wings" for aspiring pilots.

NORTH AMERICAN AT-6G TEXAN/HARVARD (1940). Incredible as it may seem, several *AT-6*'s of the more than 15,000 built are still in service as advanced-training aircraft in some air forces. At least 5000 *Harvard AT-6*'s were used by the R.A.F. Several were employed as observers during the Korean War, which began in 1950 and in which the United States Air Force formed a part of the United Nations Expeditionary Force.

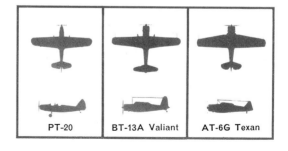

PT-20 | BT-13A Valiant | AT-6G Texan

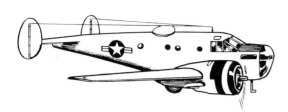

BEECH AT-11 (1940). A training aircraft for bombardiers and machine gunners, it was derived from the 6-passenger *C-45* light transport. The *AT-11*'s were easily recognizable because of their extreme front gun turret. Most of the crews of the *Flying Fortress*es were trained aboard the 1582 *AT-11*'s produced.

CESSNA UC-78 BOBCAT (1941). Twin-engine civilian aircraft built just before the War. It was known as the *T-50* and was at first chosen by the army and navy as a training aircraft *(AT-17)* and later as a 4-passenger light transport. In this capacity (3000 were built) it was widely used both in the U.S. and in Europe.

BELL P-63A Kingcobra (1943). Of all the 3303 fighters of this type built until 1945, more than 2000 were supplied to Russia and about 300 to the Free French Air Force. The *P-63*, descended from the *P-39*, flew for the first time on December 7, 1942. The U.S.A.A.F. did not consider it as a good aircraft and used it only as target.

REPUBLIC P-43 LANCER (1940). A fighter and reconnaissance aircraft descended from the *Seversky P-35*, only a limited number (272) were built, and they were not very successful. It is memorable, nevertheless, because of the 108 *P-43*'s supplied by the U.S. to China. These aircraft fought courageously against the best Japanese fighters of the time, winning many victories.

DOUGLAS A-20G HAVOC (1941). A ground-attack bomber, it was the first aircraft of the U.S.A.A.F. to see action in Europe—on July 4, 1942. It was also built in night-fighter *(P-70)* and training versions. Production was interrupted in 1944 after the 7385th aircraft had been built. The most widely used model was the *A-20G*, supplied to Russia in large numbers.

NORTHROP P-61 BLACK WIDOW (1943). Bizarrely nicknamed the *Black Widow* after the ruthless spider found in certain parts of America, it was the first U.S.-designed night fighter. It didn't begin service until the middle of 1944—in time to make a good showing both in Europe and the Pacific. Just over 500 of these aircraft were enough to make its reputation as a "killer." The radar in its spacious "nose" was developed on a basically British plan by scientists at the famous Massachusetts Institute of Technology.

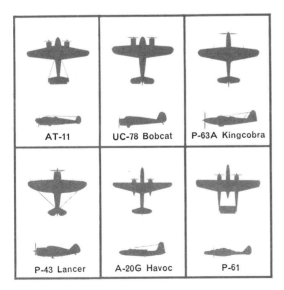

BELL P-39Q AIRACOBRA (1941). The world's first fighter with 3-wheel carriage and engine placed behind the pilot to leave more room for the cannon in the propeller-boss. It flew for the first time on April 6, 1939. It was ordered by the French and British before the Americans; after Pearl Harbor, with the *P-40*, it bore the burden of the Pacific and European theaters until the end of 1943. As many as 9558 were built (more than 5000 supplied to Russia). It was also an outstanding ground-attack fighter, especially good against tanks.

CURTISS P-40N WARHAWK (1941). Though not an extremely high-quality fighter, it flew on all fronts during the War and was particularly outstanding in the Pacific. Production (which totaled 13,733 in all) was initially slated for France, Russia and Great Britain as well as for the U.S.A.A.F. In Britain, the aircraft was first named *Tomahawk* and then *Kittyhawk*. In its *F* and later series (of which the 5200 *N*'s were most important), the *P-40*'s American name, *Warhawk*, was coined. The fighter was famous in China even before the U.S. entered the War. There a group of American volunteer pilots called the "Flying Tigers," led by Gen. Claire Chennault, won 286 victories against 26 losses with the *P-40*.

REPUBLIC P-47 THUNDERBOLT (1943). Considered one of the best American fighters and fighter bombers of the War. It was designed after the U.S. entered the War. Entering action on April 8, 1943, as an escort to the *B-17*'s of the 8th Air Force in the skies of Europe, it began service immediately thereafter in the Pacific. Produced until December 1945 (15,579 were built), it was used by the R.A.F. (590), and the Russian and Free French air forces. The plane flew for the U.S. Air National Guard until 1950.

LOCKHEED P-38E LIGHTNING (1941). The fighter which brought down more Japanese planes than any other American aircraft. It was used in all theaters of the War and was christened *Der Gabelschwanz* or "fork-tailed devil" by the Germans. Production was begun in 1940 and 9923 were built before 1945. The aircraft was also a reconnaissance (*F-4* and *F-5*), a fighter bomber (*F* and *L Droop Snoot,* the latter equipped with radar for bomb drops even with overcast skies), and night fighter *(M)*. In April 1943, the *P-38G*'s of the 339th Guadalcanal Squadron shot down the aircraft carrying Admiral Yamamoto, mastermind of the Japanese attack on Pearl Harbor.

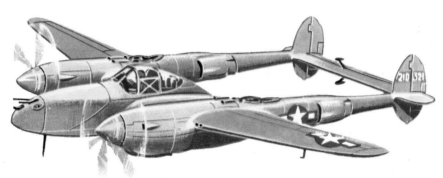

P-38F

P-38L Droop Snoot

P-38M

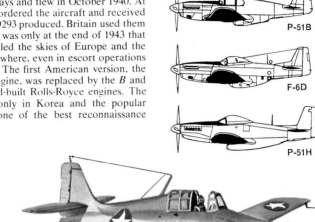

NORTH AMERICAN P-51D MUSTANG (1942). One of the best fighters of the War, it was designed in April 1940 on the request of the R.A.F. The prototype was built in the record time of 117 days and flew in October 1940. At first, only Great Britain ordered the aircraft and received the first 670 of the total 9293 produced. Britain used them in action in July 1942. It was only at the end of 1943 that U.S.A.A.F. *Mustang*s filled the skies of Europe and the Pacific, appearing everywhere, even in escort operations over Berlin and Tokyo. The first American version, the *P-51*, with an Allison engine, was replaced by the *B* and *D* versions with Packard-built Rolls-Royce engines. The *H* version saw action only in Korea and the popular *F-6D* was considered one of the best reconnaissance aircraft.

GRUMMAN F4F-4 WILDCAT (1940). Grumman's first monoplane. On December 7, 1941, it was the standard navy fighter stationed on aircraft carriers and bore the brunt of the air war in the Pacific until 1943. About 8000 were produced. They were also used by the British Royal Navy, under the name *Martlet*. Although inferior to the Japanese *Zero*, the *Wildcat* had a good record: 6.9 victories for each *F4F* shot down.

CHANCE-VOUGHT F4U-1 CORSAIR (1943). One of the best carrier-borne fighters, it stayed in production until 1952 (a total of 12,681 were built in different versions) and in service until 1965. It was one of the last piston-engine fighters. *Whistling Death*, as it was called by the Japanese, won more than 2000 victories before 1945. It was also put to excellent use later during the Korean War.

GRUMMAN F6F-3 HELLCAT (1942). A larger, heavier and more powerful direct descendant of the *Wildcat*. Production was begun during the last months of 1942 and continued until November 1945, for a total of 12,275 aircraft delivered to American and British naval aviation. Used by the British Fleet Air Arm as far back as July 1943, it made its U.S. combat debut from the aircraft carrier *Yorktown* on August 31, 1943, in the battle for Marcus Island. In June 1944, during the battle of the Philippine Sea, the *Hellcat*'s power was felt. Before the end of the conflict the *F6F*, operating from American aircraft carriers, downed 4947 Japanese aircraft. In service even after 1945, several *Hellcat*s saw action in Korea, operating from the carrier *Boxer*.

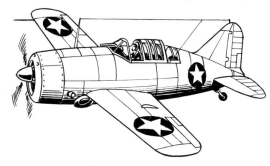

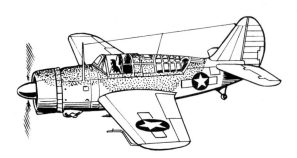

BREWSTER F2A-3 BUFFALO (1938). The first monoplane carrier-borne fighter of the U.S. Navy. In service from 1939, it proved to be a mediocre aircraft. Less than 500 were produced, more than 300 of these were turned over to Finland, the R.A.F., the British Navy and Dutch Indies aviation. Some *Buffalo*s took part in the battle of Midway, with disastrous results.

CURTISS SB2C-4 HELLDIVER (1943). A carrier-borne dive bomber, it joined the *Dauntless* during the height of the war in the Pacific. From its first day in action (at Rabaul, November 11, 1943) until 1945 it successfully took part in all the most important naval air battles. Many of the 7200 *Helldiver*s built stayed in service until 1950.

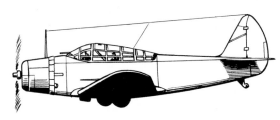

GRUMMAN TBF-1 AVENGER (1942). An excellent carrier-borne torpedo bomber which stayed in service until 1954, even though its first mission, on June 4, 1942, was disillusioning. On that day at Midway, 5 of the 6 *Avenger*s which took off from the decks of the *Hornet* never returned to base. Of the 9836 *Avenger*s produced, more than 1000 went to the British Royal Navy.

DOUGLAS TBD-1 DEVASTATOR (1936). A carrier-borne torpedo bomber which began service in 1937. During the first months of the War it outfitted 4 squadrons which fought courageously in the Marshall and Gilbert islands. At Midway, however, the *VT-8* squadron was completely destroyed by the Japanese *Zero*s. In all, 129 *TBD*'s were built.

DOUGLAS SBD-5 DAUNTLESS (1941). A carrier-borne bomber and reconnaissance, it was already outdated at the beginning of the War, but for lack of a valid replacement, was profitably used by the U.S. Navy which ordered 5936 before July 1944. At Midway the *SBD Dauntless*es were the aircraft that sank the Japanese carriers *Akagi*, *Kaga* and *Soryu* and damaged the *Hiryu!*

VOUGHT SB2U-3 VINDICATOR (1937). A carrier-borne reconnaissance and bomber. The U.S. Navy ordered only 169 which in 1940 outfitted 5 squadrons on the *Lexington*, *Saratoga*, *Ranger* and *Wasp*. Its performance in action was quite mediocre and after its unfortunate participation in the battle of Midway, it was retired before the end of 1942.

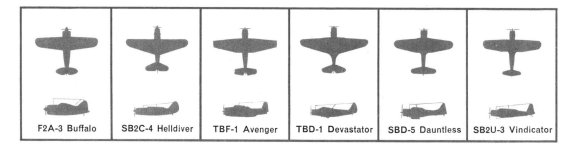

| F2A-3 Buffalo | SB2C-4 Helldiver | TBF-1 Avenger | TBD-1 Devastator | SBD-5 Dauntless | SB2U-3 Vindicator |

LOCKHEED C-60A LODESTAR (1941). The civilian 17-passenger *Lockheed Lodestar Model 18 (p.79)* caught the attention of military aviation, which ordered 3 as early as May 1940. When war broke out, the U.S.A.A.F. not only requisitioned the available private airships for adaptation for military use, but also ordered 325 *Lodestar*s for paratrooper transport. Beside their basic role, these aircraft, among the fastest of their type, carried out a great number of other duties, from evacuation of wounded to emergency supply transports, etc. Several *Lodestar*s also went to the R.A.F.

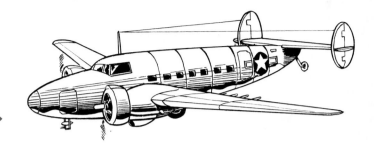

VULTEE A-35 VENGEANCE (1942). Designed in 1940 on request of the R.A.F., which urgently needed a dive bomber. The aircraft flew for the first time in July 1941 and was produced until May 1944 (1900 aircraft of which 1200 went to England). The *Vengeance*, flown by the R.A.F. for the most part in Burma, was never considered a very good plane, although it was used until 1945.

MARTIN B-26G MARAUDER (1942). A medium bomber known in the early stages of its career as the *Widow Maker*. It later proved to be one of the safest planes of its type. It began flying in April 1942 on the Pacific front attacking New Guinea. It took part in the battle of Midway, and bombed Japanese ships in the Aleutians from bases in Alaska. In November 1942 it began operations in North Africa and was very active in the skies over Europe between 1943 and 1945. There were 5157 *Marauders* produced in different series.

MARTIN A-30 IV BALTIMORE (1941). This medium bomber never flew for the U.S.A.A.F. The R.A.F., which hurried the aircraft's design in 1940, retired the entire lot of 1575 A-30's built before 1944. The A-30's were used in the Mediterranean theater. After the Armistice with Italy of September 8, 1943, an entire wing of Italian Air Force was outfitted by *Baltimores* and operated alongside the Allies until 1945.

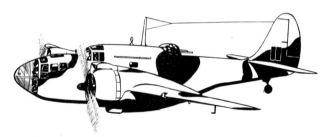

DOUGLAS A-26B INVADER (1944). A light bomber and ground-attack plane. More than 2446 would have been produced if the aircraft had not made its appearance at what was virtually the end of World War II. It entered in service in Europe in 1944 and in the Pacific zones in 1945, demonstrating its excellent quality which was later confirmed during the Korean War. It was retired in 1961, but some *Invaders* were recommissioned for service in Vietnam. Evidently, 25 years after its birth, the *Invader* is still an excellent aircraft.

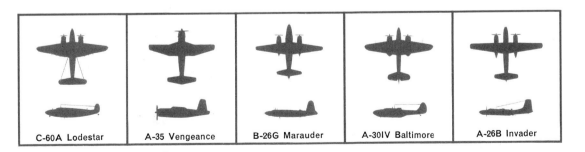

| C-60A Lodestar | A-35 Vengeance | B-26G Marauder | A-30IV Baltimore | A-26B Invader |

NORTH AMERICAN B-25J MITCHELL (1941). One of the best light bombers of World War II. It was named after General Billy Mitchell (*pp.41* and *54*) who, as far back as 1920, had the foresight to urge the U.S. to build a stronger and better-prepared air force. On the day that Pearl Harbor was attacked, only 40 *B-25*'s were in service, but before the end of the War more than 11,000 were operating on all fronts in almost all Allied air forces, achieving extraordinary feats. One of these was the bombing of Tokyo on April 18, 1942, by 16 *B-25 Mitchell*s which took off from the carrier *Hornet* commanded by the ex–sports pilot Jimmy Doolittle. After completing the mission the aircraft landed in China.

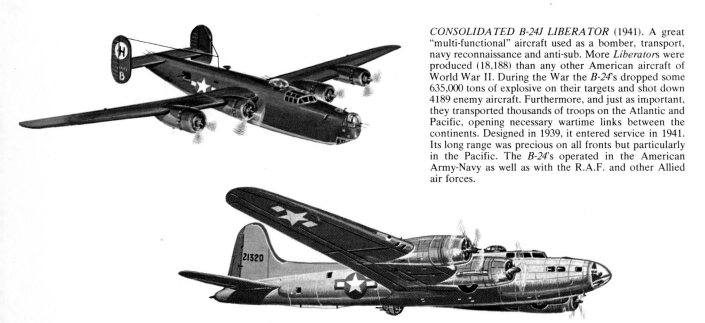

CONSOLIDATED B-24J LIBERATOR (1941). A great "multi-functional" aircraft used as a bomber, transport, navy reconnaissance and anti-sub. More *Liberator*s were produced (18,188) than any other American aircraft of World War II. During the War the *B-24*'s dropped some 635,000 tons of explosive on their targets and shot down 4189 enemy aircraft. Furthermore, and just as important, they transported thousands of troops on the Atlantic and Pacific, opening necessary wartime links between the continents. Designed in 1939, it entered service in 1941. Its long range was precious on all fronts but particularly in the Pacific. The *B-24*'s operated in the American Army-Navy as well as with the R.A.F. and other Allied air forces.

BOEING B-17F FLYING FORTRESS (1941). A bomber designed in 1934, it made its first flight on July 28, 1935, but wasn't ready for delivery until March 1940. The Japanese attack at Pearl Harbor (December 7, 1941) and on the Philippine airports (December 8) destroyed most of the *B-17*'s then in service. The few surviving *Flying Fortress*es flew the first American offensive of the War on December 10, bombing Japanese ships. Maximum production ensued and the *B-17*'s were ready to begin daylight bombing in Europe on August 12, 1942. There was continued bombing until 1945. As many as 12,731 *Flying Fortress*es were built.

BOEING B-29A SUPERFORTRESS (1943). A long-range heavy bomber, it was the first with a pressurized cabin. It flew for the first time on September 21, 1942. The Americans decided not to use the aircraft in Europe, and immediately the *B-29*'s were sent directly to the Pacific, where, beginning on June 15, 1944, they bombed objectives in Japan. They hit Tokyo for the first time on November 24. On August 6, 1945, a *B-29* (of the 393rd Squadron) named the *Enola Gay*, commanded by Col. Paul Tibbetts, dropped the first A-bomb on Hiroshima. On August 9, another *B-29*, *Bock's Car*, dropped the second atomic bomb on Nagasaki, forcing Japan to accept surrender terms on August 15. In all, 3970 *Superfortress*es were produced.

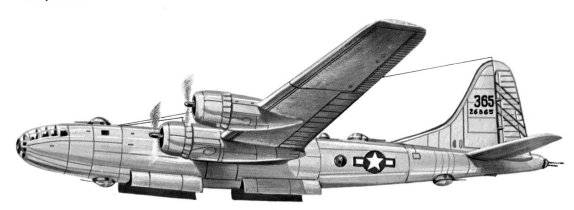

B-25J Mitchell

B-24J Liberator

B-17F Flying Fortress

B-29A Superfortress

C-53 Skytrooper

C-46 Commando

A-29 Hudson

PBY-5 Catalina

DOUGLAS C-53 SKYTROOPER (1941). In October 1941 the *C-53* better known by its civilian name, the *DC-3 (p.76)* began service for the American air force. In different versions (among these the *C-47 Skytrain*) 10,123 planes of this type were received by the U.S. Army and Navy, which made intense and invaluable use of them to transport troops, and paratroopers and materiél. More than 1200 of these aircraft (called *Dakota*s) went to the R.A.F. Eisenhower said that four things had helped the U.S. win the War: the bazooka, the jeep, the A-bomb and…the *DC-3*'s.

CURTISS C-46 COMMANDO (1943). Developed in March 1940 as a 36-passenger civilian aircraft, it was immediately adopted by the U.S.A.A.F. which ordered over 2900 more during the course of the War. Like the more famous *C-53*, it was used on all fronts, but especially in the Far East to transport troops, paratroopers, and materiels. The *C-46*'s "built" the famous air-bridge across the Himalayas to transport supplies from India into China after the fall of Burma. Some *C-46*'s have recently been recommissioned for use in Vietnam.

LOCKHEED A-29 HUDSON (1939). A Navy bomber and reconnaissance, it was the military version of the *Model 14 (p.79)*. More than 2000 *Hudsons* served in the squadrons of the British Coastal Command. One of them was the first Allied plane to down a German plane. At least 650 others were used by the U.S. Army and Navy. A *Hudson* was the first American aircraft to sink a German submarine. Production was stopped in 1943.

CONSOLIDATED PBY-5 CATALINA (1936). This flying boat was the most widely produced (3290 in the U.S. and Canada and several hundred more on license in the U.S.S.R.) and most popular of World War II. In service for the U.S. Navy from 1936, it was also much used by the British, Canadians, Australians and the Dutch in the East Indies. It was present on all seas as reconnaissance, bomber, anti-sub, transport and navy rescue. An amphibian version of the *Cat,* as it was affectionately nicknamed, was also built.

During World War II, American aircraft carried no squadron insignia on their cockpits to avoid enemy detection. Some planes did, however, carry designs drawn by their crews, for example, that which appeared on a *B-24* of the 93rd Group in Britain in 1942.

"THAR SHE BLOWS"

PIPER L-4 GRASSHOPPER (1941). An artillery observer and liaison aircraft. More than 5500 were used on all fronts. It was flown in action for the first time in 1943 during the Allied landings in North Africa.

STINSON L-5 SENTINEL(1941). Military version of the civilian *Stinson 105 Voyager,* it proved to be an excellent liaison plane. More than 3000 were produced and the *Sentinel* was used during the Korean War as well as World War II.

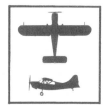

LOCKHEED PV-2 HARPOON (1944). A Navy reconnaissance plane developed from the *PV-1 Ventura,* another military version of the 1940 *Model 18 Lodestar,* a civilian aircraft. The 535 *Harpoon*s performed so well that they stayed in service for many years after 1945.

MARTIN PBM-3D MARINER (1941). A Navy reconnaissance and transport plane. About 1000 were produced between 1940 and 1947 in different versions, the last equipped with anti-sub radar. The *Mariner*s were used by the American Coast Guard.

CONSOLIDATED PB2Y-3R CORONADO (1940). A long-range Navy reconnaissance and transport aircraft, it flew for the first time on December 17, 1937, and began service in 1941. Of a total 216 *Coronado*s built, in various versions, 10 went to the Royal Navy which used them with great success for urgent transport of basic wartime cargos across the Atlantic. The *Coronado*s of the U.S. Navy, on the other hand, had an uneventful career which ended before 1945.

AMERICAN AIRCRAFT CODES OF WORLD WAR II

ARMY AIRCRAFT		OA	Amphibian observer	G	One-engine transport
		P	Fighter	H	Helicopter
A	Light bomber	PT	Primary trainer	J	General utility
AT	Advanced trainer	R	Rotating wing	L	Glider
B	Bomber (medium or heavy)	TG	Training glider	N	Training
BT	Basic trainer	UC	Utility transport	O	Observer
C	Transport			P	Reconnaissance
CG	Transport glider		NAVY AIRCRAFT	R	Multiengine transport
F	Reconnaissance			S	Scout
L	Liaison	B	Bomber	T	Torpedo bomber
O	Observer	F	Fighter		

U.S.S.R.

On February 22, 1935, the Air Force Chief of Staff, General Chripin, declared that the U.S.S.R. decided to create the largest air fleet in the world. During the Spanish Civil War, many Russian aircraft participated on the Republican side. This confirmed that the programs outlined were actually being implemented. Although the actual statistics of the Soviet Air Force were, and still are, a jealously guarded military secret, in the summer of 1941 when Germany invaded Russia, no one would have thought that only 3500 Luftwaffe aircraft would be sufficient to defeat the enemy's air resistance in just a few days. Thus, it was necessary that first Great Britain and later the U.S. furnish the Red Air Force with about 25,000 aircraft, 10,000 of these fighters. At the same time, national production was greatly accelerated, turning out 8000 aircraft in 1942; 18,000 in 1943; 30,000 in 1944; and 25,000 in 1945. As the Russian units were progressively strengthened and outfitted with excellent attack aircraft, and the weakened Luftwaffe was being recalled to other fronts, Soviet aviation began to win back the skies in November 1942 during the Battle of Stalingrad. The Russian fighter pilot with most victories was Colonel Ivan N. Kozhedub (62), followed by Aleksandr Pokrychkrin (59), and Captain Goulayev (53). Over 5000 women served as pilots in the Soviet Air Force, and several of them became fighter aces—for example Lt. Lilya Litvak (7 victories) and Lt. Katya Budanova (6). The lack of worthy transport planes hindered Russia from putting her parachute and air-transported troops to full use, just as the almost total absence of heavy bombers at the beginning of the War was a weak point which made the Russian Army pay dearly in its valorous attempt to stem the German tide.

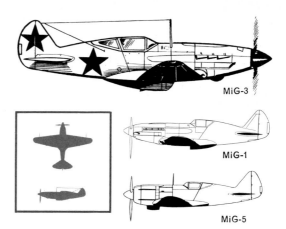

MiG-3

MiG-1

MiG-5

MIKOYAN-GUREVICH MIG (1940). The *MIG-1* fighter, which first flew in March 1940, was the beginning of a cooperative effort on the part of two aeronautical designers, Artem I. Mikoyan and Mikhail I. Gurevich, who designed and produced the prototype in less than 3 months. About 2100 *MIG-1*'s were built before 1941, when the improved *MIG-3* model replaced it. The *MIG-3* earned its creators the Stalin Prize. In a short time several thousand were in service. Nevertheless, even the *MIG-3*'s were no match for the German fighters and the plane soon was shifted to reconnaissance duties. In 1943, the *MIG-5* appeared, based on its predecessor but with a new engine. Production was interrupted almost immediately for the high priority *Lavochkin La-5*, which was considered a better fighter.

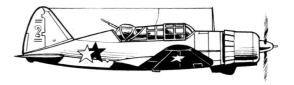

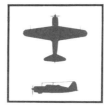

SUKHOI Su-2 (1940). A light bomber designed by Pavel Sukhoi in 1937 and initially called the *BB-1*. Many were in service when the Germans attacked and they were easy prey for the German fighters, so much so that they were retired from the front lines in 1942.

RUSSIAN AIRCRAFT CODES

Until the end of 1940, Russian aircraft codes indicated the aircraft's function: *ARK*, arctic service; *BB*, short-range bomber; *DB*, long-range bomber; *SB*, medium bomber; *TB*, heavy bomber; *I*, fighter; *KOR*, Carrier-based aircraft; *PS*, transport; *U*, trainer; *UT*, trainer.
Beginning in 1941, they indicated the name of the designer: *ANT*, A. N. Tupolev; *Il*, S. V. Ilyushin; *La*, S. A. Lavochkin; *LaGG*, Lavochkin, Gorbunov and Gudkov; *MIG*, A. I. Mikoyan and M. I. Gurevich; *Pe*, V. Petlyakov; *Po*, N. Polikarpov; *Su*, P. Sukhoi; *Tu*, A. N. Tupolev; *Yak*, A. S. Yakovlev.

La-5

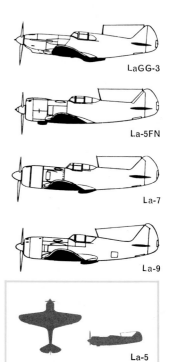

LaGG-3

La-5FN

La-7

La-9

La-5

LAVOCHKIN La (1941). In 1938 Semyon A. Lavochkin, with the help of the engineers Gorbunov and Gudkov, designed a fighter called the *I-22* which in its successive versions proved one of the best Russian planes of the War. It entered production as the *LaGG-1*. After a few of them had been built, the craft was transformed into the *LaGG-3;* although built of wood and canvas, it was extremely sturdy. At mid-1942, during the Battle of Stalingrad, the *La-5* appeared in the skies. For this last model, Lavochkin was awarded the title of Hero of Soviet Labor. More than 15,000 units of the *La-5,* and the improved *La-5FN, La-7* and *La-9* versions were built. The *La* was widely used as a fighter bomber and ground-attack plane, as well as fighter.

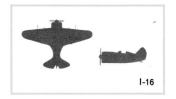

I-16

POLIKARPOV I-16 TYPE 24 (1934). A fighter and fighter bomber designed by Nikolai N. Polikarpov, it made its first flight on December 31, 1933, and was completely outdated by the time war broke out between Germany and the Soviet Union. It had been the first single-engine, low-wing fighter with retractable landing gear to be used in service in military aviation, but even the improvements made on the later types were not sufficient to prevent its becoming antiquated. It had its days of glory during the Spanish Civil War, where it was known as *Rata,* and in the Finnish-Russian War, during the German invasion it fought well and was used as a ground-attack plane before it was replaced by more modern aircraft in 1943. About 20,000 *I-16*'s were built between 1934 and 1942.

Yak-9

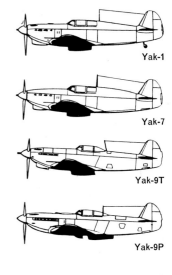

Yak-1

Yak-7

Yak-9T

Yak-9P

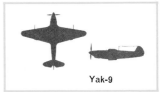

Yak-9

YAKOVLEV Yak (1940). The prototype of the *I-26* fighter, then the *Yak-1,* first flew in 1940 and won the Order of Stalin for its designer Alexander S. Yakovlev. After a few *Yak-1*'s were built, several thousand *Yak-7*'s followed and, by the end of 1941, outfitted many fighter squadrons. In October 1942, during the siege of Stalingrad, the *Yak-9* appeared in the skies of the city. It was developed from its predecessor and was for many years the "typical" fighter of Soviet aviation. The *Yak-9T* was the last version and was hardly used during World War II, but it was basic equipment for the North Korean Air Force during the war with South Korea. Over 30,000 *Yaks* were produced in all. In 1944, a just-liberated squadron of Russian-piloted *Yak-9*'s based in Southern Italy flew support missions for the partisan formations in Yugoslavia.

ILYUSHIN Il-2 SHTURMOVIK (1941). Considered the best antitank and ground-attack aircraft of the War by many, it began service during the summer of 1941 in its first one-seat version. It showed its exceptional ability immediately, being very effective against tanks, convoys and trains. But it had poor rear defense. In 1942, the two-seat version equipped with rear machine gun was ready. At least 35,000 units were produced. In December 1941, Stalin said of the Il-2: "It is as essential for the Red Army as oxygen and bread . . ."

POLIKARPOV I-15 (1933). Even more outdated than its "younger brother" the I-16, this fighter too, which had had its moments of glory in 1935 (breaking the world altitude record of 47,818 feet) and later during the Spanish Civil War and the Finnish-Russian War, proved definitely inferior when the Germans invaded Russia. The few I-15's still in service attempted, nevertheless, to confront the German fighters and paid dearly for their daring. Less than a month after the fighting had begun, not one I-15 was in flying condition in the squadrons.

PETLYAKOV Pe-2 (1941). Designed in 1938 by V. M. Petlyakov as a two-engine, high-altitude fighter, it was transformed into a light bomber, ground-attack, reconnaissance and night bomber. All in all, it was one of the most versatile Soviet aircraft of the War. In service from 1941, in its later versions, which had more powerful engines, it was able to hold a slight speed advantage over the German fighters. The Pe-2 along with the Il-2 were the cutting edges of the Soviet Air Force Tactical Bomb Command.

ILYUSHIN Il-4 (1940). The basic design of this bomber went back to 1936 (DB-3); in 1938 extensive improvements were carried out and the DB-3F was born. It later took on the new name of Il-4. It was the "standard" medium bomber of Soviet aviation during World War II and was also used by the navy, sometimes even as a torpedo bomber. Navy Il-4's were the aircraft which succeeded in bombing Berlin on August 8, 1941. The mission was extremely important in terms of propaganda if not strategically. The Il-4 remained in production from 1939 to 1944. The exact figures are unknown, but it is certain that over 5000 units reached bomber squadrons from the beginning of the German invasion.

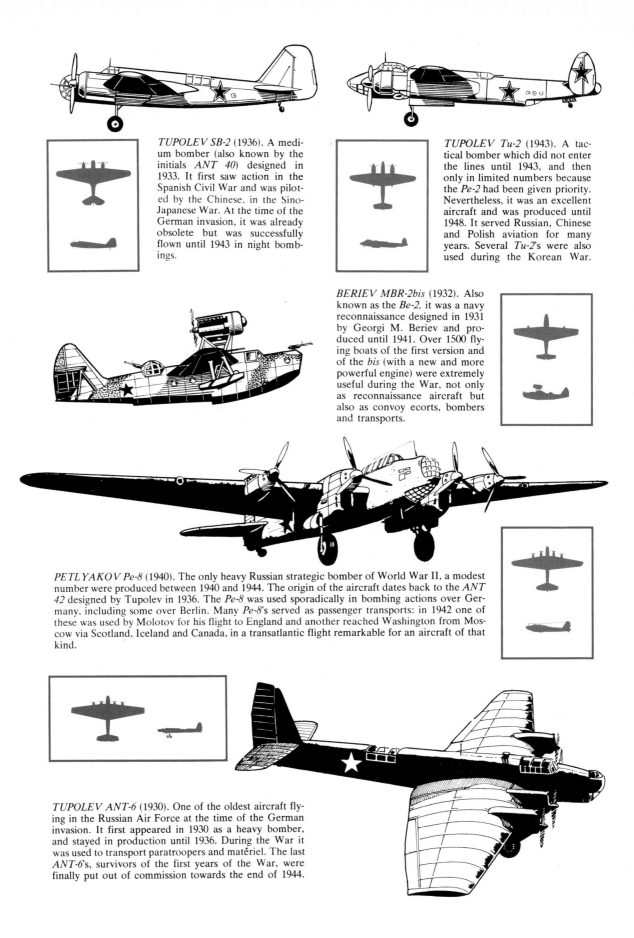

TUPOLEV SB-2 (1936). A medium bomber (also known by the initials *ANT 40*) designed in 1933. It first saw action in the Spanish Civil War and was piloted by the Chinese, in the Sino-Japanese War. At the time of the German invasion, it was already obsolete but was successfully flown until 1943 in night bombings.

TUPOLEV Tu-2 (1943). A tactical bomber which did not enter the lines until 1943, and then only in limited numbers because the *Pe-2* had been given priority. Nevertheless, it was an excellent aircraft and was produced until 1948. It served Russian, Chinese and Polish aviation for many years. Several *Tu-2*'s were also used during the Korean War.

BERIEV MBR-2bis (1932). Also known as the *Be-2,* it was a navy reconnaissance designed in 1931 by Georgi M. Beriev and produced until 1941. Over 1500 flying boats of the first version and of the *bis* (with a new and more powerful engine) were extremely useful during the War, not only as reconnaissance aircraft but also as convoy ecorts, bombers and transports.

PETLYAKOV Pe-8 (1940). The only heavy Russian strategic bomber of World War II, a modest number were produced between 1940 and 1944. The origin of the aircraft dates back to the *ANT 42* designed by Tupolev in 1936. The *Pe-8* was used sporadically in bombing actions over Germany, including some over Berlin. Many *Pe-8*'s served as passenger transports: in 1942 one of these was used by Molotov for his flight to England and another reached Washington from Moscow via Scotland, Iceland and Canada, in a transatlantic flight remarkable for an aircraft of that kind.

TUPOLEV ANT-6 (1930). One of the oldest aircraft flying in the Russian Air Force at the time of the German invasion. It first appeared in 1930 as a heavy bomber, and stayed in production until 1936. During the War it was used to transport paratroopers and matériel. The last *ANT-6*'s, survivors of the first years of the War, were finally put out of commission towards the end of 1944.

GERMANY

In defiance of the Versailles Treaty, the new Luftwaffe officially re-emerged on March 1, 1935, though by the end of that year, it already boasted more than 1000 combat-ready aircraft. As early as 1933, production had begun in secret. The Civil War in Spain gave Germany, which sided with the Nationalists, an opportunity to test men and fighting methods via its Condor Legion, against a weak enemy. When Poland was invaded on September 1, 1939, and war declared by Britain and France 2 days later, the Luftwaffe had 4800 aircraft, including 1750 medium bombers and dive bombers and 1200 fighters. German aviation proved virtually invincible in the "lightning war" against Poland, Norway, Denmark, Holland, Belgium and France. But its shortcomings became clear during the Battle of Britain: perhaps chiefly because of lack of heavy strategic bombers capable of self-defense; furthermore, aircraft like the *Stuka* proved disastrously vulnerable. The Luftwaffe continued to fight in the Mediterranean, North Africa, the Balkans and in Russia, and German industry achieved astonishing production feats. In all, 120,000 planes were produced: 8300 in 1939; 10,800 in 1940; 11,800 in 1941; 15,600 in 1942; 25,550 in 1943; 39,800 in 1944; and 8000 until May 1945. German aces compiled hundreds of victories partly because, unlike their Allied counterparts, they did not alternate tours of duty with rest periods. The ace of aces, of the entire War, was German Maj. Erich Hartmann (claiming 352 victories), followed by an impressive number of other German pilots with more than 100 victories each, including Gerhard Barkhorn (301), Günther Rall (275), Otto Kittel (267) and Walter Nowotny (258). The Luftwaffe began to decline early in 1944. Even the incredible jet aircraft—about a thousand strong—introduced as a last resort were powerless to change the course of a war that was already lost.

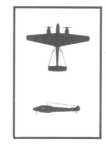

MESSERSCHMITT *Bf-110C* (1939). A long-range fighter, in production from 1938 until the end of 1944 (about 6100 units produced). It first saw action in 1939 against the Polish *P.Z.L. P-11 (p.131)*, then participated, though with little success, in the Battle of Britain, losing over 200 aircraft. However it proved to be a good night fighter and ground-attack plane.

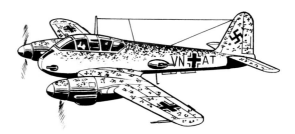

MESSERSCHMITT Me-410 A-1 HORNISSE (1943). A fighter bomber which was to replace the *Bf-110* but which proved a failure even in its first version, the 1942 *Me-210*. In service from 1943, a total of 1160 were produced, not including about 100 units built by Donau in Budapest, Hungary, for the Luftwaffe.

ARADO AR-240 (1942). A long-range fighter designed in 1938. It was never produced in large numbers because of a series of structural defects. Some were used on the Russian front and a few on the Italian front. The *AR-440* as well, derived from its predecessor, was never ordered in quantity, although it was a higher quality aircraft.

Insignia from left to right: III/KG 51 Edelweiss; 9/ZG 26 Horst Wessel. The key to some Luftwaffe codes is the following: *KG*, Bomber Group; *ZG*, long-range Fighter Group; *JG*, Fighter Wing; *NAGr*, Tactical Reconnaissance Wing; *KGzbV*, special-task Bomber Group; *Kü FL Gr*, Coastal Group.

FOCKE-WULF Fw-190 D9 (1941). Considered the best German fighter of World War II, the *Fw-190,* designed by Kurt Tank, flew for the first time on June 1, 1939, and immediately demonstrated its excellence. Mass production was begun in 1940 and continued until Germany fell. There were 13,367 fighter interceptors in different versions and 6634 fighter bombers delivered to combat units. First used in action in August 1941, over England, with the *JG-26* piloted by the fighter ace Adolf Galland, it proved a worthy match even for the latest versions of the *Spitfire*s. During the four years of the War in which it was the stronghold of the German fighter command, it was outstanding on all fronts, from Africa to Russia. In its *D* version (the most numerous) its job was to carry the burden as Germany's ultimate defense against Allied bombings.

MESSERSCHMITT Me-163B KOMET (1944). The first and only rocket-propulsion fighter of World War II. It first appeared against a formation of *B-17*'s on July 28, 1944, and before the end of the War was to score many victories. Its flying time was barely 10 minutes, but it could gain 6.215 miles' altitude in 2 minutes and 30 seconds! It was an extremely dangerous aircraft and of the nearly 350 *Me-163B*'s received by flight groups I/JG 400 and the 2/JG 400, more exploded during landing than were shot down by Allied fighters or defensive bomber weapons.

MESSERSCHMITT Me-262A STURMVOGEL (1944). The first jet-engine fighter and fighter bomber in the world to be used in action, it flew for the first time on July 18, 1942. However the *Me-262*'s were not ready for combat units until two years later. In July 1944, a *Mosquito* was attacked by the *Me-262* jet fighter, making it the first aircraft to be attacked by a jet. If the *Me-262* had reached the front one year earlier, it would have gravely menaced Allied air power. But because of its late appearance, it had no serious effect on the course of operations. Of the 1433 *Me-262*'s produced, only ¼ were used in combat.

HEINKEL He-162A SALAMANDER (1945). The prototype of this jet fighter, also known as the *Volksjäger,* "peoples fighter," was designed and built in the record time of only 69 days! Heinkel engineers began studying the project on September 8, 1944, and the aircraft made its first flight on December 6. Mass production was begun on January 1, 1945. Before the end of the War only 116 *He-162*'s came off the assembly line, and the very few that were flown in combat were piloted by veterans of the *JG-84.*

MESSERSCHMITT Bf-109E (1938). Designed by Willi Messerschmitt in 1935, the *Bf-109,* which was produced in greater number than any other aircraft in World War II (over 35,000), was first flown in combat in Spain in its *B* and *C* versions. On November 11, 1937, a *Bf-109* broke the world speed record, flying at 379.38 miles per hour. In 1939 the Germans considered it the best fighter in the world and it was standard equipment, in the *E* version, of the Jagdgeschwader. During the first months of the War, it was unrivaled in Czechoslovakia, Poland and France. However, it met a dangerous adversary in the *Spitfire* during the Battle of Britain and had its first reversals. Of the 1733 planes which the Luftwaffe lost (against 915 lost by the R.A.F.) 610 were *Bf-109*'s. It was transformed into a defensive fighter in the *F* model. In 1942 the *G, Gustav,* model appeared and stayed in service until 1945. Of its many versions, the *T* was one of the most interesting. It had been designed for aircraft carriers, which however Germany was never able to use in action. The *Bf-109* flew for the first three years of the war at all times and . . . everywhere. But even later, coupled with the better equipped *Fw-190,* it gave invaluable service straight up until the last day of a war in which it played a leading role.

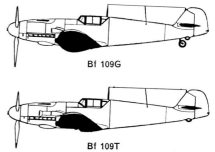

Bf 109G

Bf 109T

Me 163B Komet

Me 262A Sturmvogel

He 162A Salamander

Bf 109E

Ju 87B Stuka

He 111-H

Ju 88A

JUNKERS Ju-87B STUKA (1938). The "standard" German dive bomber in 1939, it had its days of glory in the opening months of the War, operating quite efficiently during the campaigns against Poland, France and the Low Countries. Its drawbacks (vulnerability and lack of speed) were evident during the Battle of Britain when it met a defense composed of fast and modern fighters. Forty-one *Ju 87*'s were lost during the first 6 days of the battle. Nevertheless, it was used in Libya, the Mediterranean (where it damaged the carrier *Illustrious* and sank the cruiser *Southampton*) in the Balkans, over Crete and finally in Russia. Production continued until 1944, and at least 5700 were produced in at least 10 different versions.

HEINKEL He-111-H (1936). A medium bomber (in the *B* version) which began service in the Luftwaffe in 1936. It was tested successfully during the Spanish Civil War in Germany's Condor Legion. Its *H* version was one of the main participants in the Battle of Britain. A major error was made in insisting that the aircraft could hold its own without an escort as it had in Spain and Poland. This miscalculation may have cost Germany victory in the British skies. After the heavy losses suffered, the *He-111* was used in night bombing and, with moderate success, as a torpedo bomber. Production was stopped in 1944 after more than 7000 units had been turned out.

JUNKERS Ju-88A (1939). Created in 1936 as a medium bomber, the *Ju-88* proved to be one of the most versatile aircraft of the War, outstanding as a dive bomber, ground-attack plane, torpedo bomber, reconnaissance, long-range fighter and night fighter. From September 1939 until the first months of 1945, 10,774 bombers came off the assembly line in about 20 versions, as well as about 6150 fighters, for a grand total of more than 16,000 units. As bomber it was particularly effective in the Battle of Britain, in Africa and in convoy attack in the Mediterranean, North Sea and the Atlantic. In 1943 the *Ju-188* was developed from the *Ju-88* and about 1000 were produced.

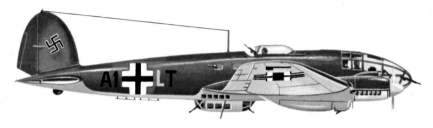

Ju 88A-15

Ju 188E-1

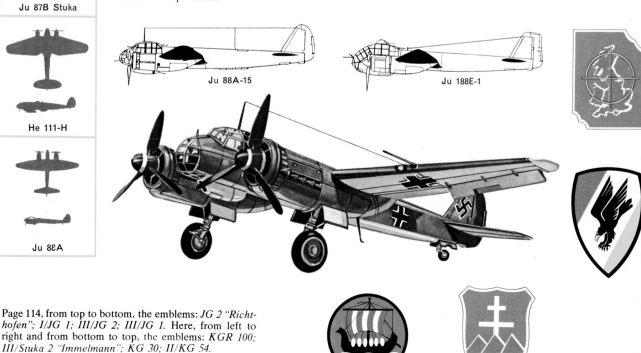

Page 114, from top to bottom, the emblems: *JG 2 "Richthofen"; I/JG 1; III/JG 2; III/JG 1.* Here, from left to right and from bottom to top, the emblems: *KGR 100; III/Stuka 2 "Immelmann"; KG 30; II/KG 54.*

HEINKEL He-177 (1942). The only German heavy bomber, it earned the sinister nickname the *Flaming Coffin* because of its poor performance. In spite of a series of fatal accidents which befell the prototypes, the aircraft went into production even though the problems had not been solved. About 1000 *He-177*'s entered service but were never outstanding.

HEINKEL He-219A-5 UHU (1942). Developed as an interceptor, it was produced as a night fighter equipped with radar. During one of its first missions on June 11, 1943, an *He-219* piloted by the ace Major Streib shot down 5 R.A.F. bombers. In spite of its high quality it was largely ignored by the Luftwaffe, which was supplied with less than 300.

HENSCHEL Hs-123A-1 (1935). A dive bomber and the last German biplane, first flown in combat during the Spanish Civil War, it was outdated by 1939 and production was stopped in 1940. No longer used in its primary role, because of the advent of the *Ju-87,* it had its second youth on the Russian front operating as an antitank aircraft.

DORNIER Do-17E-1 (1937). Nicknamed the *Flying Pencil* because of its long thin shape, 370 of this medium bomber, tested in Spain, were in commission at the beginning of the War. It was one of the first to fly in action in Poland and took part, with two squadrons, in the Battle of Britain. It was retired from operational units in mid-1943.

DORNIER Do-217E-2 (1940). A medium bomber derived from the *Do-17,* it was used for the first time in combat at the beginning of 1942 over England and in convoy attacks in the North Sea. Several of the 1730 *Do-217*'s produced were night fighters. On September 9, 1943, a group of *Do-217*'s hit the Italian battleships *Roma* and *Italia.*

ARADO Ar-234B-2 BLITZ (1944). The world's first jet-engine bomber, it flew for the first time in 1943 and became operational at the end of 1944. The few units which joined the II/KG 76 Group (of the 210 built) were very active on the famous Remagen bridge on the Rhine until fuel supplies ran out.

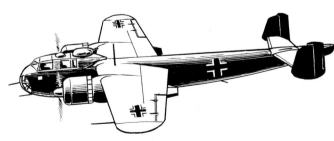

From left to right, the emblems: 7/JG 153; 8/KG 153; 9/KG 153; NAGr 3; 4 H/21; School B 1; 1/KGzbV 1; III/KGzbV 1

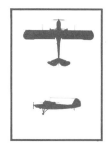

FIESELER Fi-156C-2 STORCH (1938). Throughout the War 2549 *Storch* (storks), were invaluable to the German Army on all fronts as observers, liaison and ambulances. On September 12, 1943, Otto Skorzeny flying a *Storch* freed Mussolini, who was being held prisoner atop the Gran Sasso mountain at a height of almost 10,000 feet.

JUNKERS Ju-52/3m g5e (1933). Born as a passenger aircraft *(p. 75)* it was used as a heavy bomber during the 1930s. It became one of the best transport aircraft of the War and was especially useful as a paratroop carrier. The more than 3500 *Ju-52/3m*'s which entered service (several in seaplane models) operated in all war zones.

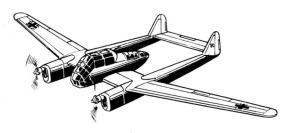

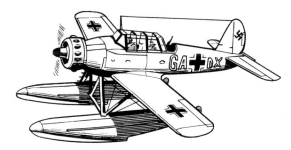

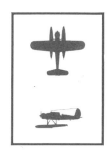

FOCKE-WULF Fw-189A-2 (1940). A reconnaissance produced between 1939 and 1944 (846 in total, part of which were built in Czechoslovakia), its greatest defect was its inability to defend itself against enemy fighters. Used intensively on the Russian front, it gradually passed to the second line and, from the spring of 1944, to training schools.

ARADO Ar-196A-3 (1939). A naval catapult reconnaissance aircraft standard for the German Navy, it was seen for the first time during the attack on the battleship *Admiral Graf Spee*. Of the *Ar-196*'s, 401 operated not only from large battleships but also from coastal bases, particularly in Norway, Denmark, France, Crete and Germany.

HEINKEL He-115B-1 (1939). About 400 of this maritime reconnaissance seaplane were produced and used also in anti-sub warfare and as mine-layers. It was outstanding during the occupation of Norway when 6 Norwegian *He-115*'s, bought in 1939, served their country equally well. Also later, and until 1943, the *He-115B*'s operated from Norwegian bases.

DORNIER Do-18G-1 (1936). A reconnaissance flying boat derived from the famous invincible *Wal (pp. 56 and 83)*, it became operational during the summer of 1936. In the first year of the War it operated in the North Sea and the Baltic Sea. Production was interrupted in the summer of 1940 after about 160 units had been produced. The *Do-18* ended its career as a maritime rescue aircraft.

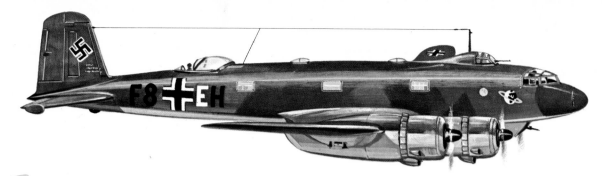

FOCKE-WULF.Fw-200C-3 CONDOR (1939). Designed as a civil aircraft *(p.87)*, when World War II broke out it was adapted as long-range maritime reconnaissance and was extremely useful in intercepting convoys headed for England and Russia in the I/KG 40 Squadron. It transmitted signals to submarines marauding in the area. However, when fighters began to be available as escorts for the convoys, the *Fw-200* returned to its original duties as a transport. Eighteen *Condors* of the KGzbV 200 formed an actual air bridge to supply German forces in Stalingrad before their defeat in that city.

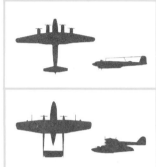

BLOHM & VOSS Bv-138C-1 (1940). A maritime reconnaissance flying boat which made its first flight on July 15, 1937, and began combat action in November 1940 with the 1/Kü Fl Gr 506 and 2/Kü Fl Gr 906 groups from a base in France. It was very successful in sighting convoys in the Atlantic Ocean, the Baltic Sea and the Arctic Ocean. Of about 270 *Bv-138*'s produced, 70 were adapted for catapult launch.

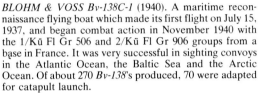

BLOHM & VOSS Bv-222C WIKING (1940). Fourteen (including the prototype) of these gigantic 6-engine flying boats (the largest of World War II) were used as troop and material transports. The *Bv-222* had been designed by Lufthansa for passenger service on the Atlantic route and flew for the first time on September 7, 1940. The prototype became militarily operational in September 1941 in a series of flights from Hamburg to Derna, Libya, via Athens, carrying emergency supplies to Rommel's Afrikakorps. Two or three more *Bv-222*'s were used in the Mediterranean, where the remaining units were based at Biscarosse, France.

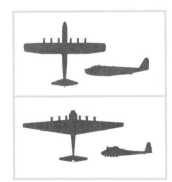

MESSERSCHMITT Me-323E GIGANT (1942). Originally designed as a glider (it required a 3 *Bf-110* to lift it off the ground), it became one of the largest transport aircraft of the War when, in April 1941. it was equipped with 6 engines. The first *Me-323*'s operated in November 1942 between Sicily and Tunisia. They were later used in Russia as well. In all, 198 were produced.

Top to bottom, the emblems: I/KG 40; 2/Kü Fl Gr 406; 2/Kü Fl Gr 306.

ITALY

In the years preceding World War II, the Regia Aeronautica was used extensively in Ethiopia and in Spain, where it fought for the Nationalists. When Mussolini entered the War on June 10, 1940, the R.A. was anything but ready. Only 1796 aircraft in all were in service (783 medium bombers, 594 fighters and 419 reconnaissance planes), with a reserve of scarcely 554 aircraft scattered over the peninsula and African territories. Furthermore, having forgotten General Douhet's theories and the efficiency of his heavy bombers in World War I, Italy had a predominantly defensive air force, without strategic bombers, without aircraft carriers (though it did have territories across the Mediterranean and had to exert control over that sea), without long-range escort aircraft. In the fighter sections, there were more *CR-42* biplanes than modern *G-50*'s or *MC-200* monoplanes. The scarcity of raw materials and the lack of adequate engines impeded industry's output: only 3257 aircraft were produced in 1940; 3503 in 1941, 2813 in 1942 and, finally, 1930 just before the Armistice in 1943. In all, Italy had only 13,853 aircraft and it is incredible that with such scant resources the R.A. was able to operate in the Mediterranean and in Africa, the Balkans, the Aegean and Russia. Despite air inferiority Italian pilots fought courageously. Maj. Adriano Visconti (26 victories), the Italian ace of aces, distinguished himself. On September 8, 1943, the R.A. had only 670 combat-ready aircraft. Those based in the south of the peninsula were absorbed by the new Aviazione Militare, which fought with the Allies until 1945, when the Allies resupplied them. The planes based in the north operated under German command.

REGGIANE Re-2001 FALCO II (1942). A fighter of excellent quality, only 252 were produced because of engine shortages. It first saw combat with the 2nd Fighter Group over Malta in May 1942. Over Northern Italy, 114 *Re-2001*'s were used as night fighters. After September 8, 1943, many operated with the R.S.I. air force.

MACCHI MC-202 FOLGORE (1941). One of the best Italian fighters, considered better than the *Hurricane*s and *Curtiss P-40*'s, its worst enemy was the scarcity of the Daimler-Benz engines built by Alfa-Romeo. Nevertheless, about 1500 *MC-202*'s operated on all fronts from Libya (with the 1st Wing) to Russia, in the skies over the Mediterranean and Italy.

FIAT G-55 CENTAURO (1943). Perhaps the best Italian fighter of the War, it had just gone into production and only a few units had reached the 53rd Wing and the 353rd Squadron when Italy signed the Armistice. It remained in production even after September 8, 1943 (about 105 were built in all), operating in the Repubblica Sociale Italiana's Air Force.

From left to right and from bottom to top, the emblems: 150th Fighter Group; 3rd Fighter Wing; 160th Fighter Group; 51st Fighter Wing; 153rd Fighter Group; 152nd Fighter Group.

120

BREDA Ba-65 (1936). A light bomber which had its days of glory during the 1930s, when it was exported to Hungary, Paraguay and Portugal. It flew in action in Ethiopia and during the Spanish Civil War. On June 10, 1940, 154 very outdated *Ba-65*'s were still in service with the 5th Stormo d'Assalto and other units. They operated in North Africa and the Balkans.

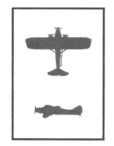

CAPRONI Ca-133 (1935). A completely obsolete bomber dating back to Italy's conquest of Ethiopia, it was nevertheless still in service in 1940: 183 *Ca-133*'s were flying in the East African Italian Air Force and about 70 in Libya. Many were destroyed by ground bombings during the first months of the War, and all had virtually disappeared before 1941.

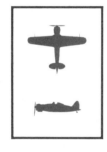

MACCHI MC-200 SAETTA (1937). This aircraft and the *Fiat CR-42* were the typical fighter planes of the Aeronautica Militare and in 1940 outfitted three fighter groups with 156 planes. Until the end of 1942, when it was relegated to bomber-escort missions, it was extremely effective over Malta, in Greece, in Yugoslavia, In Libya and, with the 22nd Group, in Russia. About 1000 were produced.

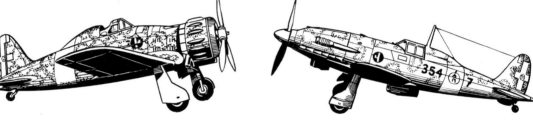

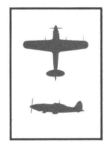

MACCHI MC-205 VELTRO (1943). According to American aviation experts, this fighter plane was an equal match for the *P-51D Mustang.* It began combat duty on July 8, 1943, over Pantelleria on the eve of the Allied landing in Sicily. On September 8 only 66 *MC-205*'s had reached fighting units. Total production was 262.

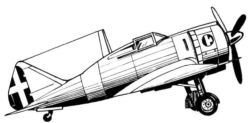

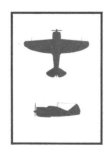

REGGIANE Re-2000 III FALCO I (1940). Presented for consideration to the Aeronautica Militare at the same time as the *MC-200* fighter, it was not accepted and was made available for export. Sweden ordered 60 and Hungary produced the aircraft under license. The Italian Navy did, however, order 36 *Re-2000 III*'s, the model adapted for catapult launch.

REGGIANE Re-2002 ARIETE (1942). The fighter bomber derived from the *Re-2001,* 218 were built. It began flying in 1942 and was used in action by the 5th and 50th Stormi d'Assalto during the Allied landing in Sicily. After the Armistice several *Re-2002*'s were used by the Luftwaffe and several by the Regia Aeronautica which operated with the Allies in Southern Italy.

From left to right, the emblems: 1st Fighter Wing; 370th Fighter Squadron; 8th Fighter Group; 162nd Fighter Squadron; 2nd Fighter Group; 6th Fighter Stormo.

REGGIANE Re-2005 SAGIT-TARIO (1943). At the Armistice only 48 of these fighters, the best produced by Reggiane, had been assigned to the 22nd Fighter Group, responsible for the defense of Rome and Naples, and to the 262nd Squadron which took them into action during the Allied landing in Sicily. Only a few more *Re-2005*'s were built for the Repubblica Sociale Italiana.

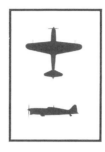

S.A.I. 207 (1943). During test flights this fighter could reach 590-miles-per-hour dive speed! The Aeronautica Militare ordered 2000 and the *S.A.I. 207* went into production. Before September 8, 1943, a grand total of only 13 planes had come off the assembly line. Three of these reached the 3rd Wing in Rome in July.

FIAT CR-42 FALCO (1939). The last in a series of famous biplane fighters, it was exported to Sweden, Hungary and Belgium. In 1940 it was outdated. However, 300 *CR-42*'s outfitted fighter squadrons, followed by 1481 more. The *Fiat CR-42*'s were incredibly versatile and served as everything: fighter interceptors, escort planes, bombers and night fighters, over Libya, the Mediterranean and Italian territory.

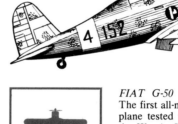

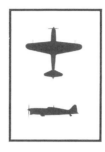

FIAT G-50 FRECCIA (1937). The first all-metal Italian fighter plane tested with fair results in the War in Spain, it was in the second rank of importance, below the *MC-200* and even the *CR-42*. In June 1940 only two wings, the 51st and 52nd, were outfitted with *G-50*'s. About 670 were built and operated in Libya, Belgium, the Aegean Sea, Greece and the Balkans.

I.M.A.M. Ro-37 (1935). The typical R.A. reconnaissance plane during the Spanish Civil War, it was exported to Afghanistan, Ecuador, Hungary and Uruguay between 1936 and 1938 and was completely outdated in 1940. There were 283 *Ro-37*'s in service. Although slow and vulnerable, they were used in North Africa, the Balkans, in Italian East Africa. They stayed in service until July 1943!

CAPRONI Ca-311M (1940). A light bomber and reconnaissance plane. Many versions were built though they were not widely used. The first dated back to 1936 (*Ca-309 Ghibli*). The *Ca-311M*'s operated in Russia with the 61st and 71st Aerial Observation groups, in Yugoslavia and in North Africa. They were destined to replace the *Ro-37*.

SAVOIA-MARCHETTI SM-79II SPARVIERO (1936). Nicknamed the *Hunchback* or the *Damned Hunchback*, it was the mainstay of the Italian bomber force in 1940 (of 975 bombers, 504 were *SM-79*'s). First used in action in Spain, where it was very successful, in 1937 three *SM-79*'s of the *Sorci Verdi* (Green Mice) Squadron won the Istres–Damascus–Paris race. Considered the best torpedo bomber of the War by many, this version was outstanding in the Mediterranean; as a bomber, reconnaissance and transport, it was very successful over Malta, in Libya anf in the Balkans.

FIAT BR-20M CICOGNA (1936). In the fall of 1940, 75 light bombers of this type were sent to Brussels as Italian support for the Battle of Britain, but three months later, after a few daytime raids and two night actions which were not very successful, it was transferred to the Greek front. In spite of its structural weaknesses, it was also used in Russia and in the Balkans. Total production in different versions never even reached 700. Only 67 were still in use when the Armistice was signed. In 1938 the Japanese government had bought 75 *Cicogne* for use in China, to replace the old *Mitsubishi Ki-1*.

CANT Z-1007bis ALCIONE (1940). Designed by one of the foremost Italian designers, Filippo Zappata, this all-wood-and-canvas medium bomber was, along with the *SM-79*, the typical aircraft of World War II Italian bomber squadrons. Production began in 1939 and by June 1940, 87 units were combat-ready in the *Z-1007* and *Z-1007bis* versions outfitting the 16th and 47th bomber wings. Its worst drawback was the scarcity of its defense armament, but in all other respects it proved to be an excellent bomber, operating in the Mediterranean (as a torpedo bomber as well), in North Africa and, briefly, in, Russia.

PIAGGIO P-108B (1942). The only Italian 4-engine heavy bomber of the War, it flew for the first time in 1939. During the test flight of a prototype, Bruno Mussolini, the Fascist dictator's son, was killed. An extremely advanced aircraft from a technical point of view, many considered it superior to its counterpart, the American *B-17*. Only a few *P-108B*'s were used in combat from 1942 with the 274th Long-Range Bomber Squadron in actions over Gibraltar, in North Africa and against convoys in the Mediterranean. Only 55 were produced, of which only 3 could fly on September 8, 1943.

Top to bottom, left to right, the emblems: 15th Bomber Stormo; 193rd Bomber Squadron; 1st Bomber Squadron; 22nd Fighter Group; 59th Night-Bomber Squadron; 36th Torpedo Bomber Wing.

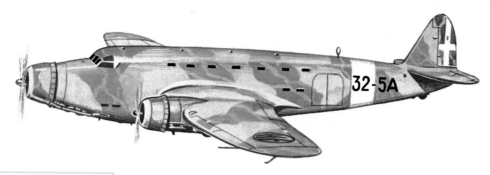

SAVOIA-MARCHETTI SM-82 CANGURO (1939). The largest Italian transport aircraft of the War and one of the best. It flew for the first time in 1938. Twelve *SM-82*'s were combat-ready in 1940 in the 149th Transport Group. In 1941 the *SM-82*'s supplied arms, men and matériel to Italian West Africa, and among them they also carried no fewer than 50 *CR-42* fighters. The *SM-82* was also used as a heavy bomber on many Mediterranean targets, including Palestine and Alexandria, Egypt.

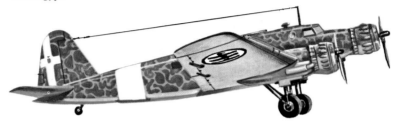

FIAT G-12T (1941). Designed in 1939 as a 14-passenger aircraft for Central European routes, it was soon modified for use as a troop (22 men and their equipment) and matériel transport. The prototype of this version flew for the first time in May 1941. It outfitted squadrons beginning in 1942 and was used in North Africa and in metropolitan territory. Many versions were built, among them a long-range civilian model, the *G.12LGA,* for use on South American routes. The aircraft stayed in production even after the War.

CANT Z-501 GABBIANO (1935). A maritime reconnaissance flying boat which made its debut in July 1935 setting a world's record for flying-boat distance, going from Monfalcone, Italy, to Berbera, British Somalia (3080 miles). Called the *Mammaiuto* ("Mamma help me") it was combat-ready in 1940 with 202 units. Although slow and inadequately armed it achieved miracles until the end of the war.

CANT Z-506B AIRONE (1940). Originally designed by the engineer Zappata as a civilian transport, it was the best Italian seaplane of the war: torpedo bomber, bomber and reconnaissance. In 1940, ninety-five *Z-506B*'s outfitted two navy bomber wings and three reconnaissance squadrons. It was widely used in combat until the end of 1941 and took part in the Battle of Punta Stilo; in 1942 it was used for reconnaissance. On September 8, 1943, twenty-eight *Z-506*'s were in Southern Italy: they operated in the Seaplane Group with the Allies for rescue at sea and later, until 1959, with the Centro di Soccorso Aereo (Aerial Rescue Center) of Vigna di Valle, near Rome.

CANT Z-511 (1943). Several sources affirm that this 4-engine seaplane was to transport a group of navy frogmen, with their underwater assault equipment (the famous "pigs"), to the vicinity of the mouth of the Hudson to attack the port of New York. Two *Z-511*'s were built and first flew in 1943. They were destroyed by Allied bombings before they could carry out their mission. ▼

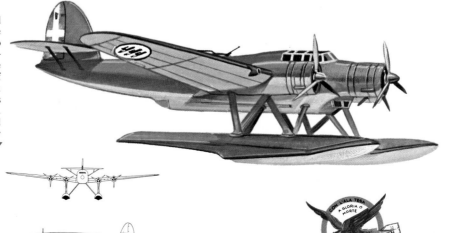

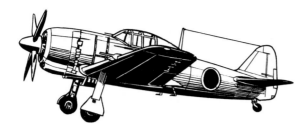

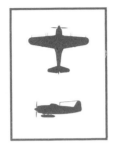

KAWANISHI N1K2-J (1942). Allied code name: *George.* A navy fighter, one of the best ever built up to that time, it began service in 1945 with only 428 units. The *N1K1-J,* its forefather, began operations at the beginning of 1944 and was outstanding in the defense of Okinawa and later in the suicide attacks on American ships.

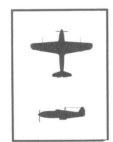

KAWASAKI Ki-61-II (1942). Allied code name: *Tony.* An Army fighter mistakenly considered a version of the German *Bf-109.* Before production was stopped in 1945, 2753 were turned out. Beginning in 1943, the aircraft was to be found on all fronts of the Pacific; it played an important role in defending national territory against American bombing attacks in the first months of 1945.

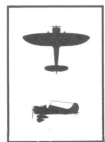

MITSUBISHI A5M4 (1937). Allied code name: *Claude.* The first monoplane deck fighter of the Japanese Navy. The aircraft was designed in 1935 and baptized in action during the war with China. At the end of 1941 only a few of the 882 *A5M*'s built were still in combat units on the carriers *Ryujo, Zuiho* and *Hosho.* These aircraft were decommissioned in 1942 without having had a chance to meet the enemy.

JAPAN

Toward the end of 1941, no military aeronautics expert would have suspected that Japan had assembled an air and naval force so numerically strong and so good in quality. In fact, until dawn of December 7, 1941, at Pearl Harbor, and the sinking 3 days later of 2 British battleships in the Gulf of Siam by 2 long-range land bombers, the world thought that Japan's force consisted of antiquated copies of other nations' aircraft. The Japanese armed forces had been reorganized in 1936; by 1938 more than 20 factories were producing aircraft of national design, some of them excellent, such as the *Zero.* By December 1941 Japan had 3525 aircraft combat-ready against 1290 Allied craft in the area. Thanks to its air supremacy, in just a few months Japan became the lord of the Pacific, but four great naval air battles (Coral Sea, May 7–8, 1942; Midway, June 3–6, 1942; Marianas, June 18–20, Leyte, October 23–26, 1944) reversed the situation. In them, Japan lost 12 aircraft carriers (against 3 American) and thereby lost supremacy in the skies. Allied forces inexorably reoccupied island after island, base after base, and by 1944 were ready to launch their final attack. More than 2000 *kamikaze* suicide pilots sacrificed their lives in a hopeless attempt to stop the enemy; only about 300 hit their targets with their aircraft, sinking 35 American ships and damaging 288. Meantime, *B-29*'s dropped 147,000 tons of bombs on Japan. The aces Shoichi Sougita (120 victories), Hiroyoshi Nashizawa (103), Saburo Sakai (64) and many others were helpless to stop them. The American bombings, culminating in the atom bombing of Hiroshima and Nagasaki, won the War against a country which had produced in 4 years more than 65,000 aircraft and which, at the time of surrender, still had 9,000 aircraft combat-ready and 2 million soldiers.

Left to right, the emblems: 19th Chutai Reconnaissance *(Ki-46);* 19th Sentai Fighters, 1st Chutai *(Ki-46);* 63rd Sentai Fighter, 2nd Chutai *(Ki-43);* 4th Sentai Fighter, 2nd Chutai *(Ki-45);* 5th Sentai Fighter *(Ki-45);* 25th Chutai Fighter *(Ki-45).*

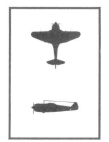

NAKAJIMA Ki-44II (1942). Allied code name: *Tojo.* A high-altitude Army interceptor-fighter which flew for the first time in August 1940, but which did not go into production (1225 units) until 1941. It proved to be an excellent and valuable aircraft against bombers headed for Japanese territory. On February 19, 1945, twelve *Ki-44*'s bore down on 120 *Superfortress*es and brought down 10 of them!

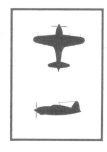

MITSUBISHI J2M3 (1942). Allied code name: *Jack.* Another navy interceptor-fighter, it began service in December 1943 and never made itself felt because of continuous engine trouble. Only about 500 were produced, even though the last version, the *J2M5* was finally a great aircraft. But it was too late for large-scale production.

NAKAJIMA J1N1-C (1942). Allied code name: *Irving.* Designed in 1938 as a fighter escort it began service in the navy air force in 1943 in the Solomon Islands as a reconnaissance. Many of the 479 *J1N1*'s were built in the night-fighter *S* version. These had some success in the first period of their operational career against *B-24*'s

KAWASAKI Ki-100 (1945). Allied code name: *Tony.* Perhaps the army's best high-altitude fighter-interceptor, it was developed too late to be operationally effective. The first *Ki-100*'s (the *Ki-61*'s fuselage adapted for the new engine) did not fly until the beginning of 1945. Only 384 were built but were nevertheless able to demonstrate their unusual qualities.

MITSUBISHI Ki-51 (1939). Allied code name: *Sonia.* An army tactical and dive bomber produced from 1939 to July 1945 (2385 were produced) it began flying in combat in China and was later used on all fronts. The pilots held it in great esteem. In 1945 many *Ki-51*'s were used by the *kamikaze* in suicide missions.

AICHI E13A1 (1940). Allied code name: *Jake.* A reconnaissance seaplane for catapult use which played an important part in all major actions of the War, from Pearl Harbor to the battles of the Coral Sea, Midway and the Solomons. A total of 1418 (more than any other seaplane of the Japanese Navy) entered service between 1938 and 1945.

MITSUBISHI A6M3 ZERO (1939). Allied code name: *Zeke*. The most widely produced (10,449 units) Japanese aircraft and one of the most famous of World War II. The first carrier-borne fighter equal, if not superior, in performance to ground fighters of the time, it was designed by Hiro Horikoshi. It flew for the first time on April 1, 1939. The *Zero* was a successful match for the American fighters at the beginning of its career, i.e., in China, attacking the "Flying Tigers'" *P-40*'s led by General Chennault. The successive versions were progressively improved and the aircraft was used in all navy air battles and in all the navy's major actions in the Pacific theater. The aircraft was without doubt superb at the time of the attack on Pearl Harbor, where it acted as a bomber escort, but lost its supremacy during the first months of 1943. It proudly ended its career with the construction of 465 special *kamikaze* versions for as many courageous though rash heroes.

NAKAJIMA Ki-27 (1937). Allied code name: *Nate.* The first Japanese low-wing monoplane fighter; it was standard equipment for the army squadrons from 1938 to 1942, beginning its career with the Russo-Japanese incident in Manchuria (against the *I-15* and *I-16*) and, in China, proving to be an excellent aircraft. Its production (3399 units) was discontinued in August 1940, but during the first months of the War it operated in many zones including the Philippines and Burma.

NAKAJIMA Ki-43-II (1940). Allied code name: *Oscar.* It succeeded the *Ki-27* as the standard army fighter. The 5919 built were used from the first to the last day of the War. The aircraft was particularly active at the beginning of the War in Malaya, Java and Sumatra and later in the battle for the Leyte Islands and in the defense of the Kuril Islands. It was last flown in suicide missions and, most unsuitably, in attempts at intercepting American bombers.

KAWASAKI Ki-45 KAIc (1942). Allied code name: *Nick.* Escort fighter, night fighter, ground-attack plane and "anti-ship," it was heavily used on all fronts from the moment it began flying in the army air force until the moment of the Japanese surrender. Many of the 1701 which were built were the night-fighter version. Outfitting the 10th Division assigned to defend Tokyo, it had its moment of glory during the last months of the War.

NAKAJIMA Ki-84 (1943). Allied code name: *Frank.* An extremely versatile army aircraft used intensively during the last year of the War as a night fighter, dive bomber, ground-attack plane and fighter-interceptor, it was a formidable opponent even for the excellent American fighters of 1945. As many as 3514 *Ki-84*'s were produced in 14 months. In July 1945 they replaced *Ki-45*'s in the difficult and valued assignment of defending the skies of the capital.

| A6M3 ZERO | Ki-27 | Ki-43-II | Ki-45 KAIc | Ki-84 |

From left to right and bottom to top, the emblems: 102nd Sentai Fighter, 2nd Chutai *(Ki-84);* 47th Sentai Fighter, 1st Chutai *(Ki-84);* 55th Chutai Reconnaissance *(Ki-46);* 18th Chutai Reconnaissance *(Ki-46);* 17th Sentai Fighter *(Ki-61);* 16th Chutai Reconnaissance *(Ki-46);* 81st Sentai Fighter, 3rd Chutai *(Ki-46);* 246th Sentai Fighter, 2nd Chutai *(Ki-27).*

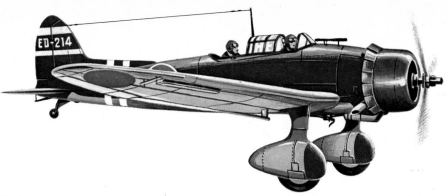

AICHI D3A1 (1941). Allied code name: *Val.* The first heavy wave of attack on Pearl Harbor on December 7, 1941, was made up of 126 of these *D3A1* carrier-borne dive bombers. In April 1942 they sank the English aircraft carrier *Hermes* and the cruisers *Cornwall* and *Dorsetshire.* The 1495 *D3A*'s sank more enemy ships than any other dive bomber of the War.

YOKOSUKA D4Y2 (1942). Allied code name: *Judy.* A carrier-borne dive bomber replacing the *D3A,* it was first used in combat at Midway. Not one of the 141 *D4Y*'s fighting in the Marianas was able to hit a single U.S. ship. Of the 2038 *D4Y*'s produced many were later used as reconnaissance. On August 15, 1945, Admiral Ugaki led 11 *D4Y*'s in a last suicide attack on Okinawa.

MITSUBISHI Ki-46-II (1941). Allied code name: *Dinah.* The best high-altitude long-range reconnaissance aircraft used by the Japanese Army during the War. Aerodynamically perfect, it was faster than any Allied fighter until 1944 and may be considered one of the greatest Japanese aircraft ever. The 1742 units which were built served from July 1941 until the end of the War.

MITSUBISHI G4M1 (1941). Allied code name: *Betty.* The most widely produced (2446) and most famous medium bomber of the navy, it served throughout the conflict. The first version, the *G4M1,* was so vulnerable that it was nicknamed *Flying Lighter* by American fighter pilots; in 1943 it began service as a transport, while the *G4M2*'s and *G4M2a*'s, more protected versions, continued bombing operations. Some *G4M2*'s were modified in order to be able to transport the Ohkas, the flying suicide bombs *(p.129).* On August 19, 1945, the Japanese delegation arrived at Ie Shima on board two *G4M1*'s to negotiate the surrender.

128

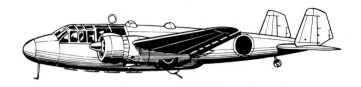

MITSUBISHI G3M1 (1940). Allied code name: *Nell.* A long-range medium bomber, predecessor of the *G4M,* it was the mainstay of the ground-based navy bomber squadrons in December 1941. There were 1048 built and they served until 1945. Its last months of service were as a transport. The most sensational action of the *G3M* was the sinking of the British battleships *Prince of Wales* and *Repulse* on December 10, 1941.

MITSUBISHI Ki-21-Ia (1940). Allied code name: *Sally.* Standard heavy bomber of the army in December 1941, 2064 of them were produced up to September 1944, although even in 1943 it had began to show signs of being outdated (it was designed in 1936). At the beginning of the War it was very effective in operations in Hong Kong, the Philippines, the East Indies, Malaya and wherever the Japanese Army reached.

MITSUBISHI Ki-67 (1944). Allied code name: *Peggy.* An army heavy and torpedo bomber which was to replace the *Ki-21,* it wasn't combat-ready until the summer of 1944 and only 698 were produced. In its one year of service, however, it proved to be the best Japanese bomber of the War, in particular in actions over Iwo Jima, the Marianas and at the American landing at Okinawa.

NAKAJIMA Ki-49-II (1942). Allied code name: *Helen.* An army heavy bomber (the first with a tail gun turret) it had its baptism by fire on February 19, 1942, during the bombing of Port Darwin, Australia, from bases in New Guinea. Only 819 *Ki-49*'s were built and, although active in Burma and in the Philippines, they never completely replaced the old *Ki-27*'s. During the battle of Leyte they suffered heavy losses and were decommissioned.

KAWASAKI Ki-48 (1940). Allied code name: *Lily.* An army light bomber which entered combat action in 1940 in China, where, in the absence of enemy fighter planes, it could operate quite effectively. But results were quite different later, when it had to confront the Allies who had finally reached a state of preparedness in both attack and defense. The aircraft was insufficiently armed and was easy prey for the American fighters. Production was interrupted in October 1944, after 1408 had been built.

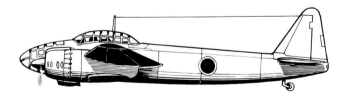

YOKOSUKA P1Y1 (1943). Allied code name: *Frances.* Some ground-based navy units received this light bomber in the spring of 1944. Although it was a good aircraft it never made itself 100-percent felt. The night-fighter version (96 of the total 1098), equipped with radar, was so involved and time-consuming to get ready that it was not operational before the end of the War.

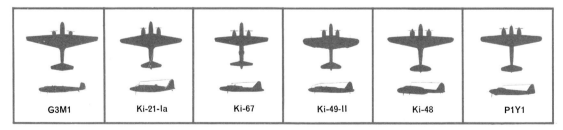

G3M1 | Ki-21-Ia | Ki-67 | Ki-49-II | Ki-48 | P1Y1

From left to right, the emblems: 74th Sentai Bomber, 2nd Chutai *(Ki-49);* Hamamatsu Bomber School *(Ki-21);* 8th Sentai Bomber, 2nd Chutai *(Ki-48).*
On page 129, from top to bottom, the emblems: 39th Chutai Fighter School *(Ki-43);* 38th Chutai Reconnaissance *(Ki-46).*

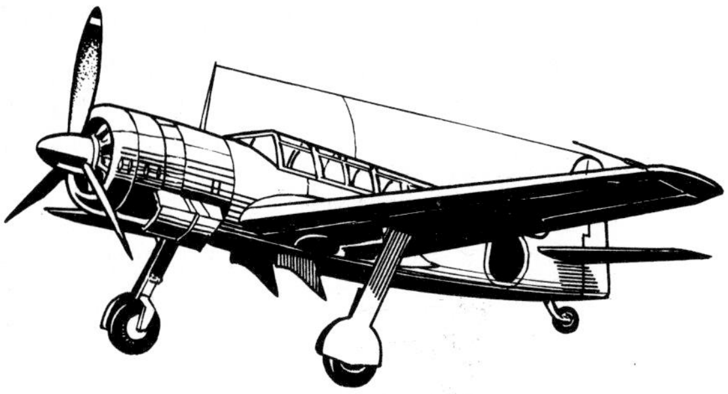

NAKAJIMA C6N1 (1943). Allied code name: *Myrt.* A carrier-borne fast reconnaissance; 463 were produced but did not appear at the front until June 1944 during the Allied landing at the Marianas. Its excellent qualities, most notable of which was its speed, led to its being considered for torpedo-bomber and night-fighter versions, but these models never became operative.

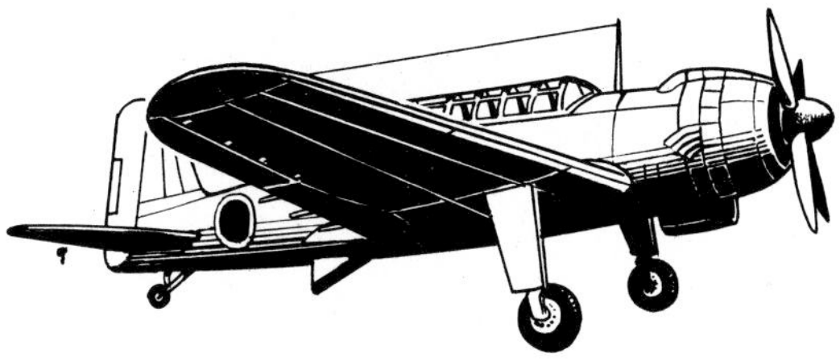

NAKAJIMA B6N2 (1943). Allied code name: *Jill.* From December 1943 this carrier-borne torpedo bomber, created to replace the *B5N,* gave excellent results operating against the American fleet in the Marshalls, Marianas and the Solomons, at Iwo Jima and finally in 1945, just a few months before the end of the War, at Okinawa. A total of 1268 *B6N*'s were produced.

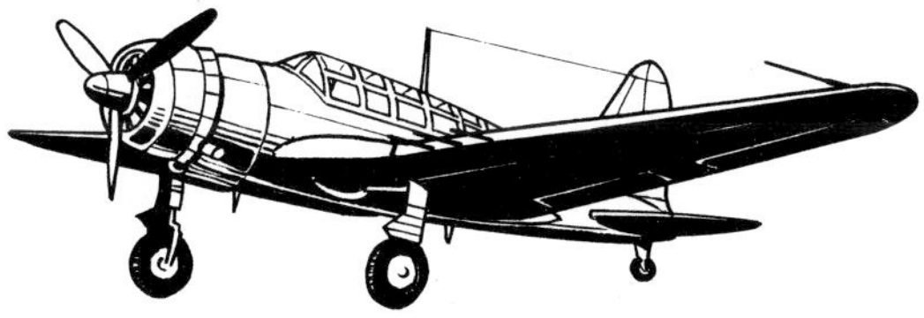

NAKAJIMA B5N2 (1937). Allied code name: *Kate.* The attack wave at Pearl Harbor was made up of 144 of these torpedo bombers. Needless to say, they were quite efficient. During the first 2 years of the war the 1149 *B5N*'s produced and stationed on aircraft carriers scored many other victories, among these the sinking of the carriers *Lexington, Yorktown* and *Hornet.*

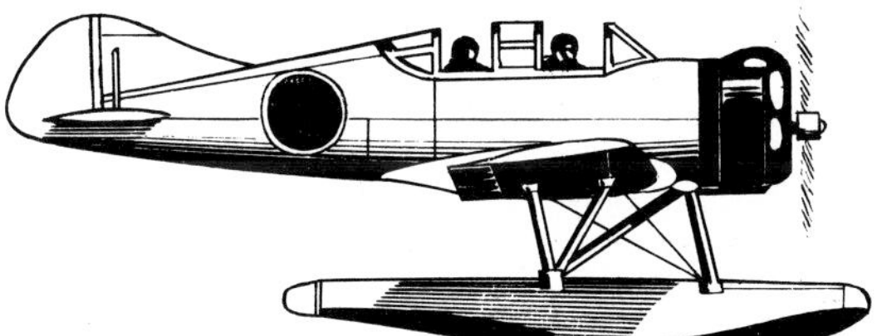

YOKOSUKA E14Y1 (1941). Allied code name: *Glen.* A reconnaissance seaplane designed to be embarked on oceanic submarines, it held the dubious distinction of being the only enemy plane to bomb the U.S. In fact in 1942 an *E14Y* left the *I-25* submarine and, piloted by Lieutenant Fujita, dropped four 167.5-pound phosphorus bombs on the woody coasts of Oregon.

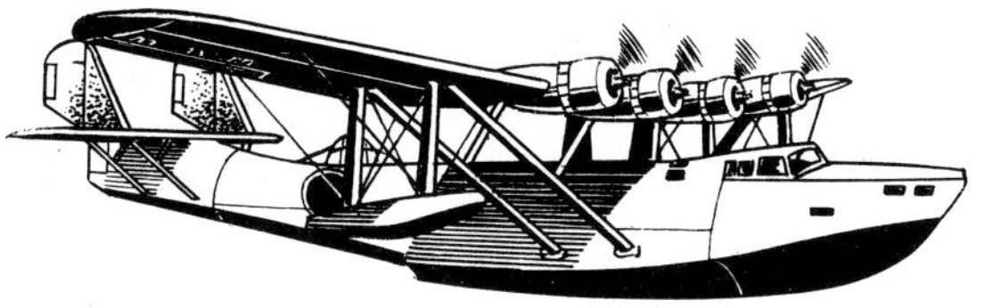

KAWANISHI H6K4 (1937). Allied code name: *Mavis.* A long-range navy reconnaissance flying boat sometimes used as a bomber and transport, it flew for the first time in 1936. Altogether, 215 were produced in different versions, and remained in service from 1938 to 1943 when they were replaced by the more modern and better-armed *H8K.*

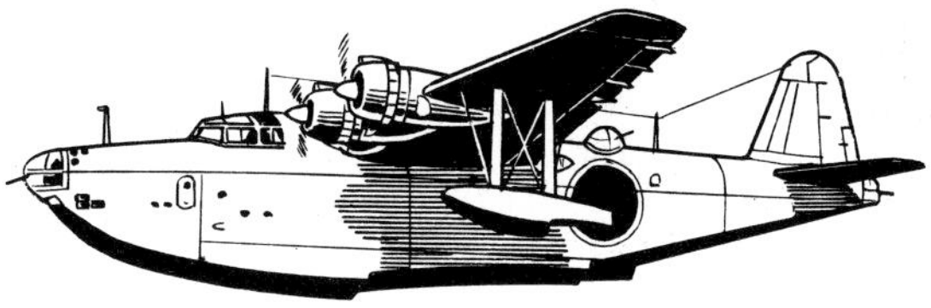

KAWANISHI H8K2 (1942). Allied code name: *Emily.* Though planned as a long-range reconnaissance, this flying boat was also used as a bomber. On March 5, 1942, three *H8K*'s bombed the island of Oahu in Hawaii, not being able to hit Pearl Harbor because of poor visibility. Of the 167 *H8K*'s, 36 were built to carry 64 passengers and supplies.

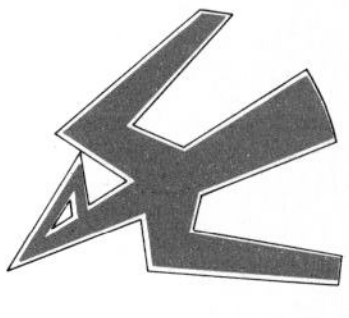

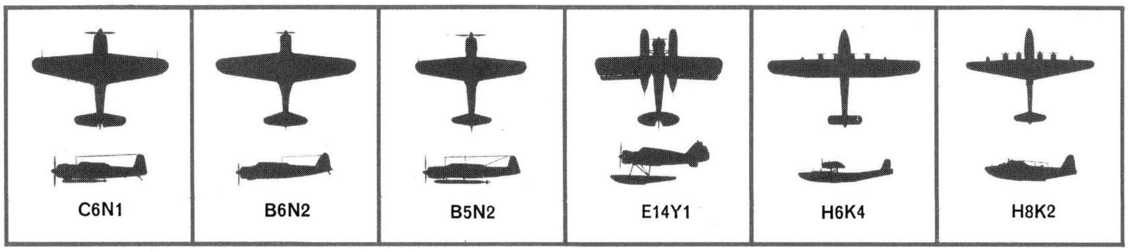
C6N1
B6N2
B5N2
E14Y1
H6K4
H8K2

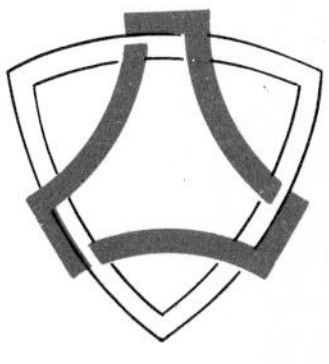

YOKOSUKA MXY7 OHKA 22 (1944). Allied code name: *Baka.* Designed in 1944 this suicide air bomb equipped with a jet engine was carried near its target by a *G4M2e.* Detaching itself from the vector, the craft, piloted by a *kamikaze* (divine wind) pilot, came direct at its target. A total of 852 *Ohkas* were produced in 5 different versions.

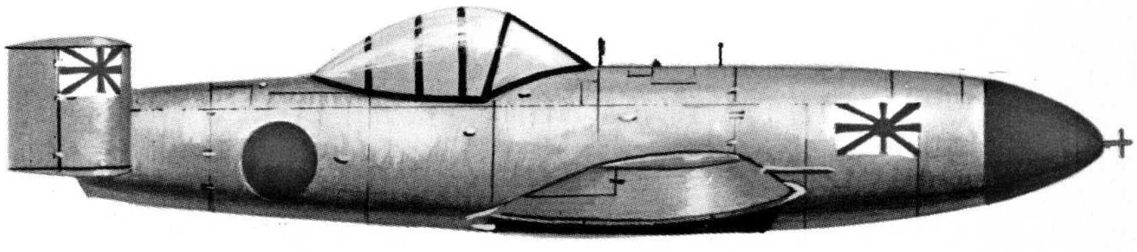

AVIA B-534 (1936, Czechoslovakia). At the time of the Nazi occupation this was the "standard" Czech fighter and 445 were in service. Several *B-534*'s outfitted three squadrons of the new Slovak Air Force and were used in July 1941 in the Russian campaign in the Kiev area. But many pilots defected to the Russians with their aircraft.

LETOV S-328 (1933, Czechoslovakia). A reconnaissance and light bomber designed in 1933, it was confiscated by the Luftwaffe during the occupation and assigned to pilot schools. However, few *S 328*'s operated against the Russians in the Slovak and Bulgarian air forces. In 1944 three *S 328*'s were captured by the partisans and used against the Germans.

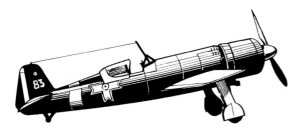

I.A.R. 80 (1941, Rumania). The only World War II fighter built by the Rumanians, it flew for the first time in 1938, and production was begun in 1941. Beginning in 1942 it flew with the fighter squadrons assigned to national defense. During the first months of 1944 at least 120 *I.A.R. 80*'s fought at the airports of the cities attacked by the Russians.

AUSTRALIA
CZECHOSLOVAKIA
HOLLAND
POLAND
RUMANIA

In the panorama of World War II planes, Australia presents a unique case. With the immense and understandable problems she had in receiving supplies of fighters from Great Britain, and with the Japanese at her doorstep, she improvised an aeronautics industry that produced in just a few weeks the prototype of a fighter of which 250 were eventually built. The situation in Czechoslovakia was quite different. It had a long tradition in aeronautics; its aircraft, outdated but still in condition for flight, never really had a chance to prove themselves. The history of Dutch aviation offered a warning: the *Fokker D-XX1* and *G-1* were doubtlessly worthy matches for any enemy aircraft and they proved it, but because of government hesitation only a limited number of aircraft were combatready—too few to offer their courageous and resolute pilots much hope of winning. The situation in Rumania was surprising. It was a nation which, before the War, had no flourishing aeronautics industry and which, just at the moment of being occupied by and allied to Germany, succeeded in producing a respectable, though not excellent fighter. What happened in Poland was pathetic. Just a few years before the invasion, the nation had succeeded in creating a real aeronautics industry, which found a hearty welcome even in foreign markets. But it was not able to keep pace with aeronautical progress, especially German progress. The *P.Z.L. P-11*'s, the pride of Poland, which shot down 126 German aircraft before they themselves were *all* destroyed—similar to the tragic and romantic image of the Polish cavalry divisions hopelessly launching a last charge against the armored waves of German tanks.

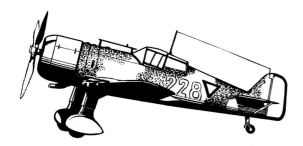

FOKKER D-XXI (1936, Holland). Even before the Dutch themselves, the Finns, Danes and Spanish Republicans ordered the fighter, which was designed in 1936. Only 39 *D-XXI*'s were combat-ready when the Germans invaded Holland and they fought courageously and well before succumbing to the enemy's massive and crushing attack.

FOKKER G-1A (1938, Holland). In 1938 the government ordered 36 of these superfighters and confiscated several *G-1*'s built for the Spanish Republican government. On May 10, 1940, when the Germans attacked, only 33 were in service. Many of them were destroyed on the ground; others faced and fought the enemy until they were *all* shot down.

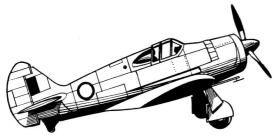

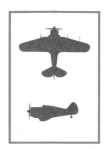

CA-12 BOOMERANG (1943, Australia). Faced with the scarcity of American and English fighters to oppose the Japanese who were advancing dangerously, Australia designed and built the *CA-12* prototype in 4 weeks. The aircraft went into production immediately. There were 250 built and they were a priceless help as backups for the Australian troops in New Guinea.

P.Z.L. P-11c (1933, Poland). At the time of the German attack, 125 of this very outdated aircraft (designed in 1930!) made up the full strength of the Polish fighter plane force. The 12 squadrons outfitted with *P-11*'s held off the more powerful enemy for 17 days, bringing down 126 enemy aircraft. Only 7 *P-11*'s were left when Poland surrendered to the Germans.

P.Z.L. P-24f (1934, Poland). Basically similar to the *P-11*, it was never used by the Polish Air Force but was quite successful as an export model. Large numbers were ordered by Turkey, Rumania, Bulgaria and Greece. Four Greek squadrons outfitted with *P-24*'s fought Italian Air Force units in November 1940.

P.Z.L. P-37B Los (1939, Poland). One of the best examples of Polish aviation industry this bomber flew for the first time in June 1936, exciting great interest. In September 1939 only 36 *Los* were operative and outdid themselves in the fight against the advancing German troops. Some *Los* were used by the Rumanian Air Force against the Russians.

THE POSTWAR YEARS: THE WORLD ENTERS THE JET ERA

In 1938, the year before the outbreak of World War II, all the world's commercial airlines flew a total of 2.5 million passengers, a large number if compared to the half million flown in 1929, but very few if we consider the number of companies and the extension of their routes, reaching across the Atlantic and Pacific oceans. Actually, flying was still an unusual experience; there was still some hesitation—we might even call it fear—on the part of the great mass of potential passengers about using this new means of transportation.

But the War changed many things: if the First World War was followed by the birth of civil aviation, the Second World War led to its explosion. Between 1939 and 1945, aircraft were in the public eye every day and even the man on the street was forced to recognize their decisive effect in many battles and the fact that the outcome of the War was being decided by airpower. Millions of young men in uniform had had a chance to get to know the airplane firsthand. Many times it had been their best friend or worst enemy. Furthermore, hundreds of thousands of these young men had flown for the first time, either being transported from one European or Mediterranean base to another or even at times flying over the Atlantic or Pacific. When these young men returned to civilian life, they no longer hesitated about using the aircraft for business or pleasure trips.

Other elements which favored the rapid expansion of commercial aviation after the War were the availability of incomparably more planes perfected than in the 1930s: the widespread existence of many larger and better equipped airports which had been created by military aviation and which were to be found all over the world; the greater safety offered by improved navigational systems using instruments such as radar; more highly skilled pilots who had had the opportunity to gain priceless practical experience during hundreds of flight hours served in all atmospheric conditions while encountering thousands of difficulties. It was natural that the best post-World War II civilian aircraft were American. Air transportation had been one of the fundamental aims which American industry had been called upon to fill, while European industry had had to concentrate its energies on military aircraft desperately needed on the front lines. In comparison with the rushed British and French experiments *(p.138),* the U.S.A. offered at least three great planes: the forever tried-and-true *Douglas DC-3 (p.76)* for short and medium distances, which had proved to be one of the safest and most useful aircraft of all times; the *Douglas DC-4,* known during the War as

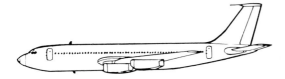

134

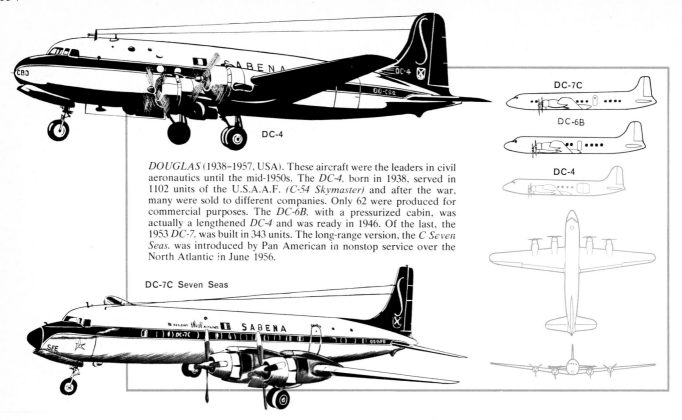

DC-4

DC-7C

DC-6B

DC-4

DOUGLAS (1938–1957, USA). These aircraft were the leaders in civil
aeronautics until the mid-1950s. The *DC-4*, born in 1938, served in
1102 units of the U.S.A.A.F. *(C-54 Skymaster)* and after the war,
many were sold to different companies. Only 62 were produced for
commercial purposes. The *DC-6B*, with a pressurized cabin, was
actually a lengthened *DC-4* and was ready in 1946. Of the last, the
1953 *DC-7*, was built in 343 units. The long-range version, the *C Seven
Seas*, was introduced by Pan American in nonstop service over the
North Atlantic in June 1956.

DC-7C Seven Seas

the *C-54*, and the *Lockheed Constellation
(p.135)*, widely used for transatlantic flights,
so much so that they clearly demonstrated the
impracticability and high cost of the prewar
flying boats, sounding their death knell.

Several statistics regarding passenger
traffic in the immediate postwar years are
indicative of the new thrust in civil aviation;
in 1945, a worldwide total of 9 million passengers flew; the number reached 18 million
in 1946 (doubling in one year), 21 million in
1947 and 24 million in 1948, 10 times the 1938
total on the eve of the War!

Obviously this growth phenomenon was
evident in the U.S. earlier than in any other
part of the globe. In 1940, before the Americans were drawn into the worldwide cata-
clysm, 2,900,000 passengers had already flown
on national airlines: the 2600-mile New York–
Los Angeles route was serviced mostly by
DC-3's and the flight lasted about sixteen to
twenty hours. After the War, the picture
changed radically. On February 15, 1946,
TWA began flying the *Constellation* on this

same route, while its rivals flew *DC-4*'s.
Flight time was reduced to about 10 hours.
In 1950, passenger traffic on U.S. domestic
routes reached 17 million, 6 times what it was
in 1943. By 1946, not only did the large and
famous companies such as TWA, American,
Eastern, United and Braniff multiply their
services opening routes and new stops, but
also many minor companies began to expand
for so-called local traffic. Several of these
companies are still flying today, for example,
Piedmont Airlines, Robinson Airlines (today
Mohawk), All American Airways (today
Allegheny Airlines) and Ozark Airlines. In
1958, just prior to the introduction in America
of jet passenger travel, the American commercial fleet totaled 1946 aircraft, 998 of
these built by Douglas (319 *DC-3*'s!) in comparison with the total U.S. commercial fleet
of 322 aircraft in 1942, most of them *DC-3*'s
(260) and *DC-2*'s (8).

Another phenomenon in the immediate
postwar period was the birth of the first "cargo only" lines which set up regular services

BOEING 307 STRATOLINER (1939, USA). Only 10 of this commercial aircraft had been built when the War broke out.
It was directly descended from the original design of the *B-17* bomber *(p.106)*, and used its engines, wings and tail. The
first passenger aircraft with a pressurized cabin, it made its inaugural flight on July 8, 1940, on the New York–Los Angeles
TWA line. Five *Stratoliners* were used by Pan American on its South American routes to replace the flying boats until,
at the end of 1941, they were finally requisitioned along with TWA's *Stratoliners* by U.S.A.A.F., which used them for
transport of military passengers throughout the duration of the War.

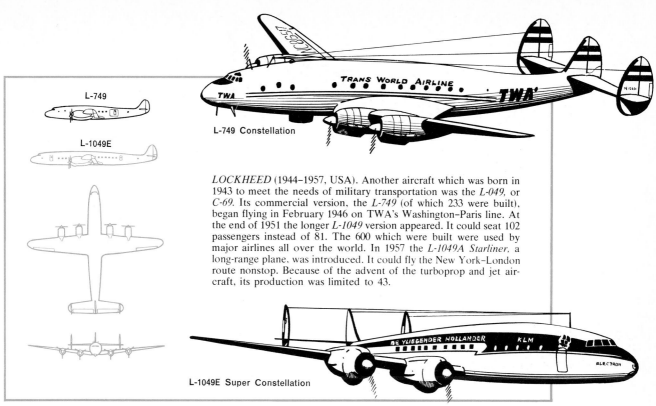

L-749

L-1049E

L-749 Constellation

LOCKHEED (1944–1957, USA). Another aircraft which was born in 1943 to meet the needs of military transportation was the *L-049*, or *C-69*. Its commercial version, the *L-749* (of which 233 were built), began flying in February 1946 on TWA's Washington–Paris line. At the end of 1951 the longer *L-1049* version appeared. It could seat 102 passengers instead of 81. The 600 which were built were used by major airlines all over the world. In 1957 the *L-1049A Starliner*, a long-range plane, was introduced. It could fly the New York–London route nonstop. Because of the advent of the turboprop and jet aircraft, its production was limited to 43.

L-1049E Super Constellation

only for freight transport. The first chronologically, and still one of the most important today, was the "Flying Tiger Line," made up of survivors of General Chennault's Flying Tigers who had earned such fame and glory in China. The possibility of buying up war-surplus planes like the *C-47's (p.107),* that is *DC-3's,* or the *C 54's,* that is *DC-4's,* at ridiculously low prices convinced several to start their own companies, but many of these enterprises failed; only 3 or 4 of the best were able to survive, but that was enough to fill the demands of the new market.

In the U.S., ten years after the end of the War, the curtain went up on the first act of the revolution in civil transportation; in 1955 the major American companies decided to refurbish their relatively young and still not entirely paid-for fleets, ordering the first jet-engine aircraft. United and Eastern ordered the new *DC-8's* from Douglas; American Airlines ordered the *707* from Boeing; TWA the *Convair 880* and the *Boeing 707.* Commercial aviation was about to enter the jet era.

To complete the picture of the American postwar situation, it is necessary to take a look at international traffic. Until 1941, the only American company authorized to service foreign countries was Pan Am, which practically had a monopoly. The situation was understandable and perhaps even necessary then because the volume of traffic was not great enough to warrant competition, which would have been perilous if not fatal for all operators. By 1945, the situation had changed drastically and the American authorities allowed many other companies to extend their routes beyond national borders. For European traffic, TWA and American Overseas Airlines (besides Pan Am) received the go-ahead; North West Airlines for Japan and the Pacific; Braniff International for Latin America; and National Airlines for the Caribbean. The U.S. felt ready to extend widely its influential air traffic throughout the rest of the world. It was a cruel challenge to Europe, still busy nursing its deep wounds.

At the end of the War, every country in

BOEING 377 STRATOCRUISER (1948, USA). The civilian version of the military *C-97* transport, of which 888 were produced. It was descended from the Superfortress *B-29 (p.106)* and had a two-level cabin. On the lower level were several seats, a bar, a cargo compartment. On the upper level were 55 seats. Of the 55 *377's* built, Pan American used 28; Northwest Airlines, 10; United Airlines 7; and BOAC, 10, which it kept on its North American line until 1958. Even this aircraft, which was extremely comfortable for its passengers, would have been more of a success if the turboprops and the jets (in particular the *707*) had not been introduced into the market.

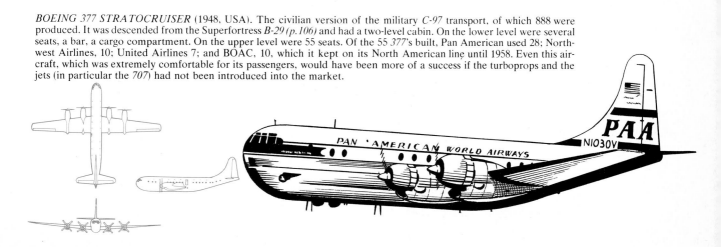

136

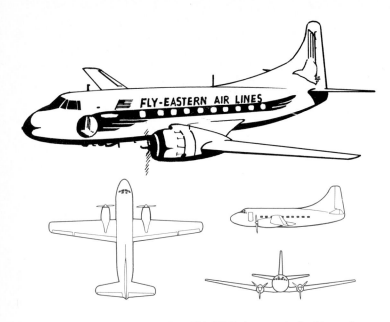

MARTIN 4-0-4 (1951, USA). A pressurized cabin version of the 2-0-2, it carried 42 passengers and entered service in November 1947 with Northwest Airlines and LAN of Chile. Its builders hoped that it would replace the DC-3, but it was not a success. Some in-flight accidents of the 2-0-2 decided the fate of its successor, the 4-0-4, only 104 units of which were ever produced.

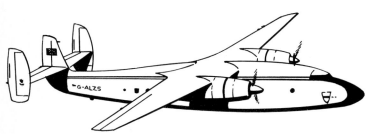

AIRSPEED A.S. 57 AMBASSADOR (1952, GB). The last British short-range passenger plane with piston engines, it had a pressurized cabin and was, from 1952 to 1958, BEA's standard passenger plane. Only twenty were built, apart from two prototypes. Even after BEA took it out of service it continued to enjoy great popularity with smaller companies.

Europe clearly saw the need to revitalize airlines as soon as possible and to reshape the close national and continental communications which had been lost. This restoration turned out to be incredibly swift and successful.

On August 1, 1946, there was formed, as an offshoot of British Overseas Airways Corporation (BOAC), a company which devoted itself completely and solely to European traffic: the British European Airways (BEA) established on modern concepts and with up-to-date goals, this airline was the first in Europe to benefit from the fact that its potential rivals (France, Germany and Italy) found themselves in far worse condition.

Air France also made an extremely rapid comeback: even before the company had been officially established on a new basis (September 1, 1948, Compagnie Nationale Air France), the Société Nationale Air France began service on January 1, 1946, replacing French military aviation on the Paris–London route and reopening routes which had been flown for years before the War. First with the *Corse, Bretagne, Languedoc (pp. 138, 139),* then with the *DC-4* and the *Constellation,* it quickly showed that it had caught up with its old rival, British civil aviation, not only on the Paris–London route, but also on the rest of the European routes.

KLM, SABENA and Swissair made equally fast comebacks. The Spanish line Iberia took advantage of the favorable situation: though short of aircraft and finances to renew its fleet, it too flew the European routes.

What happened in Italy can be termed incredible, considering the high toll the country had paid for her role in the War. In 1946, just a few months after war operations ceased on national territory, there were 7 airlines:

CONVAIR (1948–1965, USA). Another contender for the DC-3's vacated role as short and medium distance transport, it appeared, equipped with pressurized cabin, in its first series, the CV-240, in 1948. There were 176 civilian and 395 military Convairs of this type produced and it was followed in 1952 by the CV-340 (209 civilian and 108 military units produced). This airplane, with its lengthened cockpit, was adopted by many companies, including European ones. In 1956 the 56 passenger CV-440 Metropolitan appeared. When turboprop engines were introduced, many Convairs were modified and equipped with new engines: the CV-580, the CV-600, and the CV-640 are the remodelled versions of the earlier Convairs and are still being used by some smaller companies.

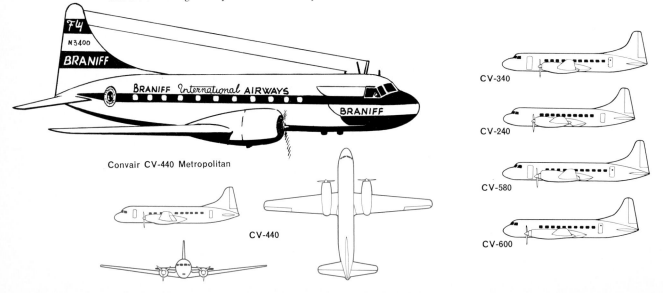

Convair CV-440 Metropolitan

CV-440

CV-340

CV-240

CV-580

CV-600

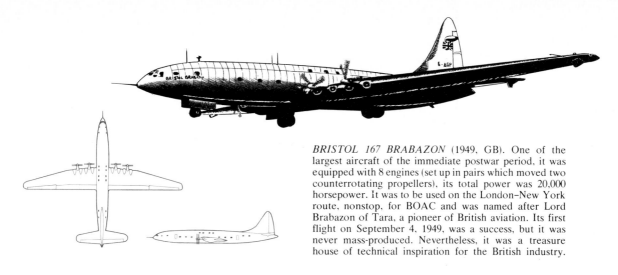

BRISTOL 167 BRABAZON (1949, GB). One of the largest aircraft of the immediate postwar period, it was equipped with 8 engines (set up in pairs which moved two counterrotating propellers), its total power was 20,000 horsepower. It was to be used on the London–New York route, nonstop, for BOAC and was named after Lord Brabazon of Tara, a pioneer of British aviation. Its first flight on September 4, 1949, was a success, but it was never mass-produced. Nevertheless, it was a treasure house of technical inspiration for the British industry.

the Aerolinee Italiane Internazionali (Alitalia) founded with a 30 percent BEA investment; the Linee Aeree Italiane (LAI) with a 40 percent TWA interest; the Società Italiana Servizi Aerei (SISA); the Società Transadriatica di Navigazione Aerea (Transadriatica); the Airone; the Salpanavi; and, finally, the Teseo. The most modern aircraft were the new but already outdated SM-95's, the G 112's, the war-surplus DC-3's and the Lancasterians. Even though Teseo and Salpanavi closed down in 1947 and SISA, Transadriatica and Airone were forced in 1949 to consolidate under the name Avio Linee Italiane-Flotte Riunite to survive, what is clear is that the will to resume full operation and the total desire for rebirth were so strong that right after the War Italy staked out a claim for the important position that Italian civil aviation was later to hold. In 1952, Avio Linee Italiane was absorbed by LAI, which itself merged at the end of 1957 with Alitalia, which is now the national Italian airline. In fact, 1957 BEA and TWA's last holdings in the Italian com-

panies came to an end. Besides opening the national lines, the various Italian companies immediately made every effort to regain routes which had been theirs before the War. Even today, it is still considered a small miracle that on May 26, 1947, Alitalia was able to inaugurate service to South America.

But the major European companies aimed immediately to inaugurate routes to North America, the fond dream of the 1930s. Other than the American companies (Pan Am, TWA and American Overseas Airways), the first European company to begin regular service to the U.S., flying modified B-17 bombers, was Svensk Interkontinental Lufttrafic (SILA). The initial flight was made on June 27, 1945. This company was the forerunner of the Scandinavian Airline System (SAS), which today holds an important place in European and intercontinental traffic. SAS was founded on July 31, 1946, when SILA, the Swedish international line, merged with Det Danske Luftfartselskab of Denmark and Det Norske Luftfartselkap of Nor-

SARO SR-45 PRINCESS (1952, GB). Instead of "Princess," this giant should have been named "Queen," the last queen of the flying boats. Its design was initially conceived during the War, in 1943, but the prototype did not make its first flight until August 19, 1952, when many other aircraft—such as the Boeing 377 Stratocruiser and the Lockheed Constellation were already successfully flying the North Atlantic over the very routes which were perfectly suited to the SR-45. Equipped with ten engines, its total power was 37,800 horsepower. It was unique in its class, but was never used commercially. It was sold as scrap in 1967 after a long wait for a fame it never won.

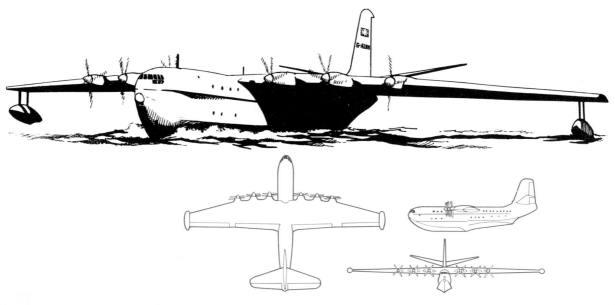

CIVIL AIRCRAFT OF THE 1950s

At the end of the War the American aviation industry held an advantage over the European, because one of its jobs had been to supply Allied airforces with good transport aircraft. The *DC-4 (p.134),* the *377 Stratocruiser,* the *Constellation (p.135)* were created during the period when British industry devoted itself full-time to the construction of military aircraft and most of the European countries were feverishly engaged in war production. Thus, the first British commercial planes after 1945 were direct descendants of the bombers. On long-distance routes, the *Avro York*—which utilized the wings and the tail of the *Lancaster (p.99)*—and the *Lancasterian* (adapted military aircraft) were used. The few original designs for transatlantic routes proved to be economically impractical, such as the *Avro 688 Tudor 4 (p.139),* the *Bristol Brabazon* and the *Saro Princess (p.137):* even BOAC wound up using American aircraft until the appearance of the *De Havilland Comet (p.140).*

On the other hand, British industry quickly caught up, by producing aircraft for short-range routes such as the *Vickers Viking,* the *Airspeed Ambassador (p.136)* used by BEA and, finally, with the world's first turboprop, the *Vickers Viscount (p.140),* later used by dozens of companies. The next two turboprops, the *Britannia* and the *Vanguard* were excellent aircraft, but were never as successful as the *Viscount,* because they were being pushed aside by the arrival of the jets. However, Canadair developed several versions of the *Britannia,* such as the *CL-44,* which is still quite popular.

Just after the War, the Italians began the hard job of rebuilding their commercial network with two aircraft, the *SM-95* and the *G.212,* both based on obsolete concepts and designs made during the War. They later bought planes from foreign markets.

The French also had a difficult time: apart from the small *Corse* and *Bretagne,* which were short-distance planes designed during the War, they only had two fairly successful commercial aircraft: the *Languedoc* (about 100 produced, 60 for export) and the *Breguet 763 Provence,* with two decks. This latter aircraft began its 10 years of service on the France–North African routes in 1953. The *SE-2010 Armagnac,* designed for long-distance flights, was turned down by Air France which preferred the more thoroughly tested and proved American aircraft.

In 1950, Sweden built its first passenger plane, the *Scandia.* The only commercial aircraft of any consequence built by the Russians was a gigantic turboprop, the *Rossiya,* which was derived from the *Tu-20* bomber *(p.160).* It was used mostly in domestic routes.

The least successful American aircraft of the period was the *Lockheed Electra* (only 170 were built). It was the first and only turboprop passenger aircraft built by the U.S. and its fate was sealed by a pair of fatal accidents and by the arrival of the revolutionary jets.

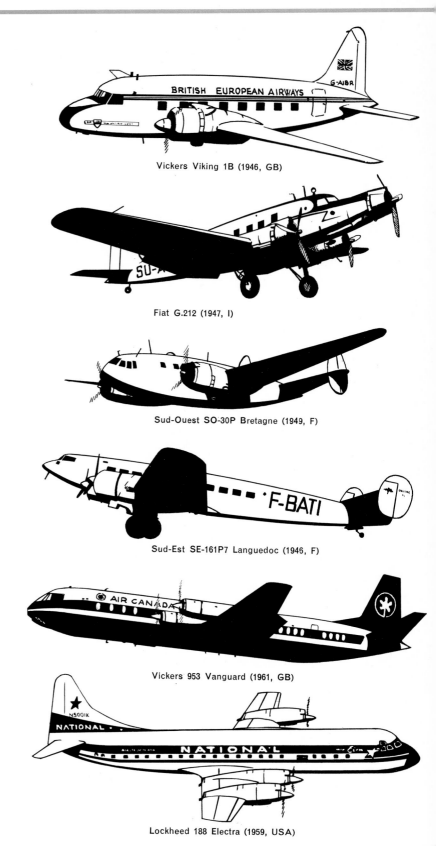

Vickers Viking 1B (1946, GB)

Fiat G.212 (1947, I)

Sud-Ouest SO-30P Bretagne (1949, F)

Sud-Est SE-161P7 Languedoc (1946, F)

Vickers 953 Vanguard (1961, GB)

Lockheed 188 Electra (1959, USA)

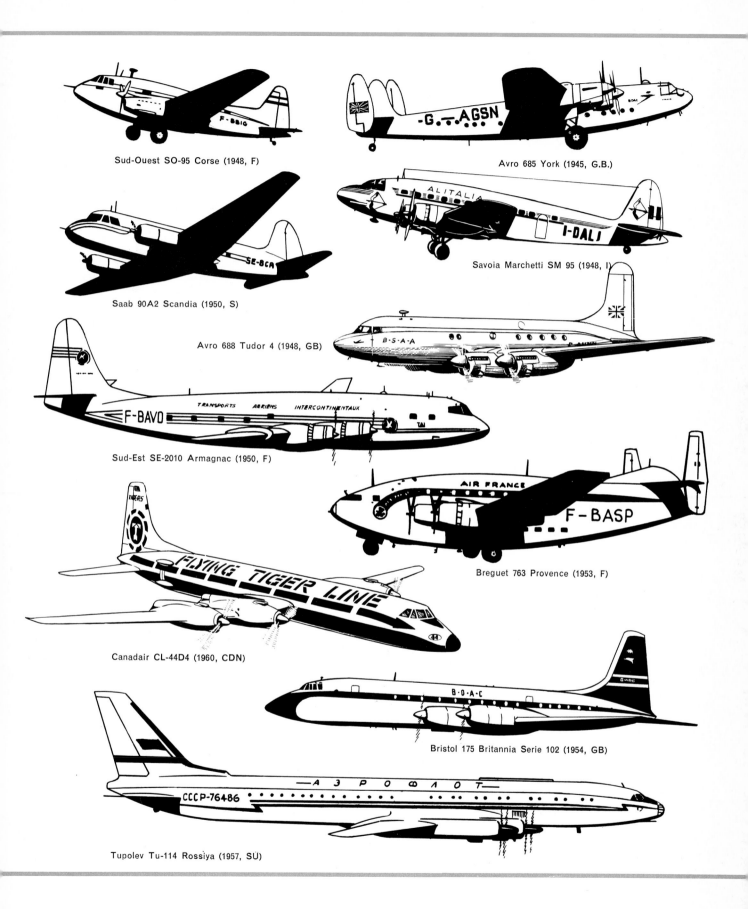

Sud-Ouest SO-95 Corse (1948, F)

Avro 685 York (1945, G.B.)

Saab 90A2 Scandia (1950, S)

Savoia Marchetti SM 95 (1948, I)

Avro 688 Tudor 4 (1948, GB)

Sud-Est SE-2010 Armagnac (1950, F)

Breguet 763 Provence (1953, F)

Canadair CL-44D4 (1960, CDN)

Bristol 175 Britannia Serie 102 (1954, GB)

Tupolev Tu-114 Rossïya (1957, SU)

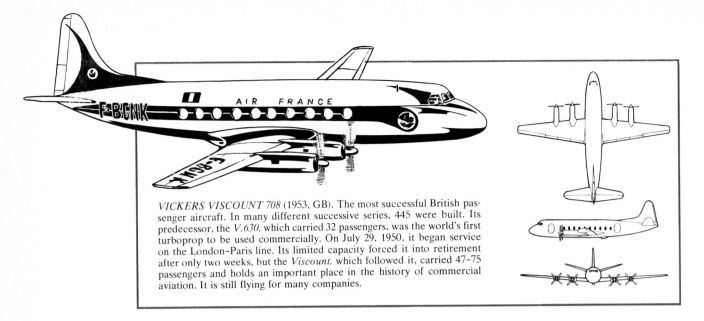

VICKERS VISCOUNT 708 (1953, GB). The most successful British passenger aircraft. In many different successive series, 445 were built. Its predecessor, the *V.630,* which carried 32 passengers, was the world's first turboprop to be used commercially. On July 29, 1950, it began service on the London–Paris line. Its limited capacity forced it into retirement after only two weeks, but the *Viscount,* which followed it, carried 47–75 passengers and holds an important place in the history of commercial aviation. It is still flying for many companies.

way. Three small countries chose to form a successful conglomerate to ensure air service capable of matching those of larger, though not necessarily wealthier, nations.

In 1946, KLM began air service to the U.S. on May 21; Air France began on June 24; BOAC on July 1; SAS on September 16. On June 4, 1947, it was SABENA's turn; on August 25, 1948, Loftleidir; on July 4, 1949, Swissair and, finally, on July 13, 1950, the Italian airline LAI. The European airlines had met the American challenge for air traffic over the North Atlantic.

An unusual fact worthy of note is that Great Britain's BOAC, which had run regular service across the Atlantic for the armed forces during the War, began commercial service on that route later than Dutch KLM and Air France, as a result of the difficult reorganization process BOAC pioneers in commercial aviation underwent after the War. But the time was not wasted. There were many problems. The company, which numbered aircraft of all types in its fleet, was now committed to purchasing British-produced planes exclusively. It had to overhaul and reopen routes connecting Great Britain to the remnants of a far-flung though virtually non-existent Empire, the countries of which still had strong ties to the United Kingdom. But the company succeeded brilliantly in overcoming its many obstacles. At a certain point it was, of course, necessary to use *DC-4's, Constellations, Stratocruisers (p. 135)* and *707's (p.141).* But the national resources were wisely exploited in also using the *Yorks,* the *Britannias (p.139)* and most of all the *De Havilland Comets.*

Between 1948 and 1970, traffic over the North Atlantic increased from 250,000 passengers to over 7,200,000. Needless to say, the companies which were among the first to get the biggest piece of the pie were best equipped to meet future problems. One of the last major companies to begin flying the North Atlantic routes was Lufthansa, which began service on June 8, 1955, with such energy and aggressiveness that in spite of its late arrival on the scene, it won a good share of the transatlantic passenger market.

DE HAVILLAND DH 106 COMET 1 (1952, GB). On May 2, 1952, BOAC inaugurated the first jet passenger service in the world with a *Comet 1* flying the London–Johannesburg route. The same year, the aircraft was assigned the London–Ceylon and London–Singapore routes, cutting flying time almost in half. Commercial aviation had entered the jet age. A couple of fatal accidents suffered by the *Comets* in 1954 nevertheless marked their retirement. In 1958 a new version, the *Comet 4,* appeared; 74 were built and it is still used today by several companies.

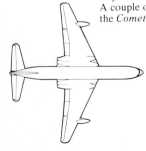

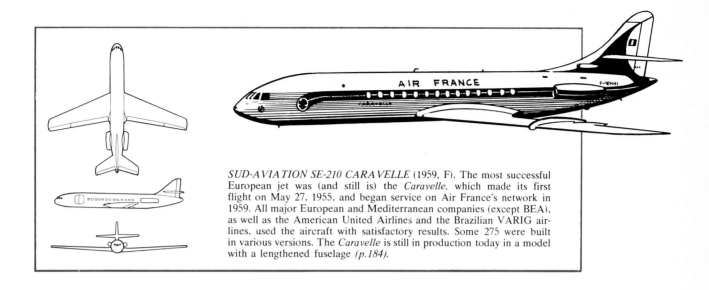

SUD-AVIATION SE-210 CARAVELLE (1959, F). The most successful European jet was (and still is) the *Caravelle,* which made its first flight on May 27, 1955, and began service on Air France's network in 1959. All major European and Mediterranean companies (except BEA), as well as the American United Airlines and the Brazilian VARIG airlines, used the aircraft with satisfactory results. Some 275 were built in various versions. The *Caravelle* is still in production today in a model with a lengthened fuselage *(p.184).*

Deutsche Luft-Hansa, which was quite famous before the War, died on April 21, 1945, when its last flight left Berlin, then partially in Russian hands. Eight years were to pass before the company could rise from the ashes, first as Lufttag in Cologne, and finally, as Lufthansa on August 6, 1954. Outfitted right from the beginning with the most modern aircraft, *Convair 340's (p.136)* for European traffic and *Lockheed Super Constellations (p.135)* for intercontinental flights, within a few short years Lufthansa regained its well-deserved fame and is now among the first European companies, challenging the supremacy of BEA and Air France.

The history of postwar civil aviation in the U.S. and the European countries is easily reconstructed through company records, official international statistics and purchase records for new aircraft. But digging out records and statistics to trace the history of commercial aviation in the Soviet Union is a well-nigh impossible task. The development of Aeroflot (the Russian airline) is enormously important if we consider that in 1959 (one

of the few reliable statistics available) 20 million passengers flew in Russia. When the War ended, the aeronautics industry in the Soviet Union continued producing military aircraft, and we can thus deduce that until the advent of the jet plane at the end of the 1950s, the growing needs of domestic traffic were satisfied by *Li-2's (DC-3's* built on license in Russia) and its improved versions, the *Il-12* and *Il-14's,* and by the immense passenger aircraft the *Tu-114 (p.139),* evolved from a bomber model. Aeroflot did not begin to extend its routes beyond national borders to India, several African countries and Europe until many years after the War. But, however, the size of the traffic is such that it must be ranked among the first in the category of civil transport.

Unfortunately, it is impossible to follow the fortunes of other airlines created and developed after the War, such as TAP, the Portuguese line; Finnair, the Finnish line; JAT, the Yugoslav line; or of those South American lines with previous experience such as VARIG, in Brazil; Aerolineas Argentinas;

(continued on page 144)

BOEING 707-121 (1958, USA). The prototype of one of the most successful passenger aircraft of all times, the *707* made its first flight on July 15, 1954. On October 26, 1958, Pan American was the first to use it nonstop across the Atlantic to Europe (aided by the favorable winds on flights from west to east) and a stopover on its return trip. In the same year, it was put into service on a transcontinental North American route by American Airlines, which had ordered 25. This 4-engine jet was to become one of the pillars of commercial aviation during the 1960s and is still being produced *(p.178).*

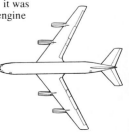

Dassault MD-450 Ouragan (1950, F)

Mikoyan-Gurevich MiG-15 (1948, SU)

Grumman F9F Panther (1949, USA)

Saab J 29F (1951, S)

Northrop F-89D Scorpion (1950, USA)

Douglas F4D Skyray (1956, USA)

Vought F7U Cutlass (1950, USA)

Gloster Javelin F(AW) Mk 9 (1952, GB)

McDonnell F3H-2 Demon (1956, USA)

Grumman F9F-6 Cougar (1952, USA)

Supermarine Scimitar (1958, GB)

Sud-Ouest SO-4050 Vautour (1958, F)

Lockheed U-2 (1956, USA)

North American F-100F Super Sabre (1954, USA)

Douglas C-124C Globemaster II (1950, USA)

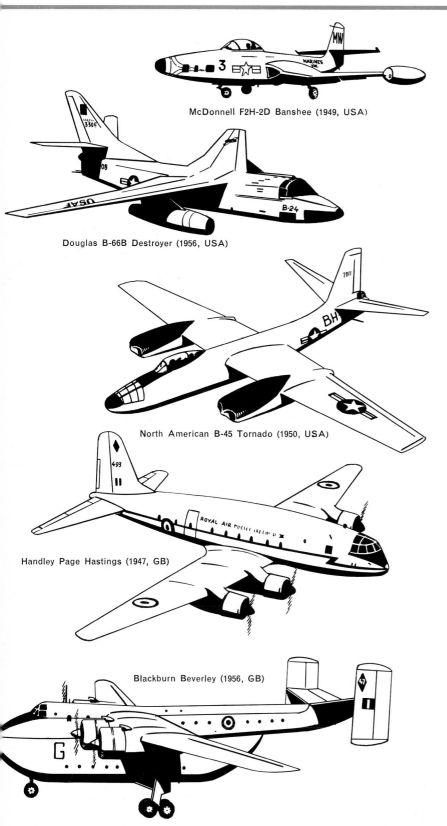

McDonnell F2H-2D Banshee (1949, USA)

Douglas B-66B Destroyer (1956, USA)

North American B-45 Tornado (1950, USA)

Handley Page Hastings (1947, GB)

Blackburn Beverley (1956, GB)

MILITARY AIRCRAFT OF THE 1950s

With the exception of the few aircraft presented on pages 158 and 167, the military planes which entered service during the 1950s have already passed into history. Here are some of the most important examples of the military production following the end of the War. It was characterized by the use of the new jet engines, and not for transport aircraft alone.

The *MIG-15* was the first Soviet jet fighter with back-swept wings to be mass-produced. Outstanding during the Korean War, it was used for a long time in several airforces of the iron-curtain countries until the more sophisticated *MIG-17 (p.147)* did arrive.

The many American aircraft give us a good idea of the power of the U.S. in the transition phase between piston engines and the more modern jets. In 1945–1946, the U.S. Navy ordered 3 carrier-borne fighters, the *F9F Panther* (the first Navy aircraft to enter combat in Korea), the *F2H Banshee* (also used in combat) and the *F7U Cutlass,* whose original design was based on studies carried out by German Arado technicians before 1945. The second generation of carrier jet fighters is made up of *F9F-6 Cougars,* a swept-wing version of the already quite successful *Panther,* the *F4D Skyray,* the first U.S. Navy aircraft with a delta wing, and finally the *McDonnell F3H Demon,* which was used until 1965 and was the predecessor of today's famous *McDonnell Douglas F-4 Phantom II (p.154).* Among the United States Air Force aircraft, other than the *P-80* and the *F-86 Sabre (pp. 146, 147),* 2 fighters are notable, the *F-89D Scorpion,* a two-seater, the first all-weather interceptor, in production until 1956, and the valorous *F-100F Super Sabre,* the first mass-produced jet to reach supersonic speed in horizontal flight; among the bombers, notable were the first 4-engine jet, the *B-45 Tornado,* used in Korea, and the *B-66B Destroyer,* which was the backbone of the Strategic Air Command until replaced by the B-47 *(p.145).* Nor should we forget the *Lockheed U-2,* the famous long-range high-altitude reconnaissance spy aircraft. On May 1, 1960, one of these planes crashed on Russian territory and helped increase the severe tension between Russia and the U.S. Finally, the *C-124C Globemaster II* should be mentioned as an example of the thoroughness with which the U.S. built its long-range transport aircraft.

French production is represented by the *MD-450 Ouragan* and by the *Vautour* fighter bomber used by the Armée de l'Air (until replaced by the *Mystère* and the *Mirage*) which have been in the news fairly recently because of the excellent use made of them by the Israeli pilots; British production is typified by the *Javelin* fighter, the first delta-winged 2-jet engine aircraft in the world, by the carrier-borne fighter *Supermarine Scimitar* and by the *Beverly* and *Hastings,* two military transports, the latter known in its commercial version as the *Hermes.* The parade is closed by the *Tunnan,* or barrel, *J-29F,* forefather of a generation of Swedish-designed fighter aircraft of great interest.

144

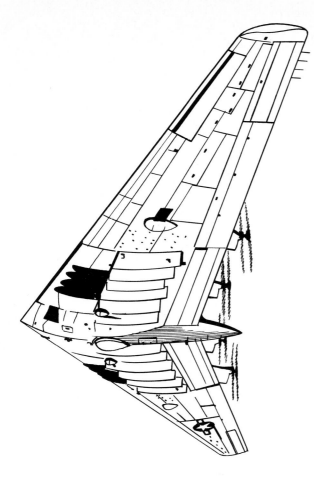

NORTHROP XB-35 FLYING WING (1947, USA). The first "flying wing," as this aircraft without tail or fuselage was called, flew for the first time on June 25, 1946. It was the *N9M*, an experimental prototype only a third the size of what was to be the *XB-35*. The results of the tests were excellent and three prototypes of the giant all-wing bomber, whose design had begun in 1941, flew the following year. Nevertheless, technical problems discouraged mass-production of the *XB-35*, armed with 20 machine guns and able to transport 4400 pounds of bombs. Later 2 of the 3 prototypes were equipped with jet engines *(YB-49),* but this experiment was not followed up.

or Chile's LAN. We must settle for emphasizing that they too contributed substantially to the quick increase of passenger-flight statistics. This data, more than anything else, bears witness to what we called at the beginning of the chapter the explosion in commercial aviation.

Between 1950 and 1965 the number of passengers flown on airlines of member-nations of the International Air Transport Association and the International Civil Aviation Organization (thus excluding traffic on Aeroflot and Communist Chinese lines) was as follows: 1950, 31 million; 1955, 68 million; 1960, 106 million; 1965, 177 million. For the following years, including approximate data for Russian traffic, the figures are as follows: 1966, 247 million; 1967, 288 million; 1968, 323 million; 1969, 358 million; 1970, 386 million. It should be kept in mind that in 1970, North Atlantic traffic alone numbered 7,200,-466 passengers flown, in descending order, by Pan American, TWA, BOAC, Air France, Lufthansa, Air Canada, Alitalia, KLM, SAS and 12 other companies. According to the predictions of experts, by 1980, just a few short years from now, a total of 1.2 billion people a year will travel by plane.

We should also note that the number of airplane accidents has progressively declined, so that flying is today one of the safest means of transportation. In 1950, the number of passengers killed in air accidents was 551; 407 in 1955; 873 in 1960; 684 in 1965; 1,123 in 1969—out of a total of 358 million passengers! Just the thought of the highway victims on a Sunday in August is enough to persuade one to go by plane rather than by car.

Civil aviation, too, officially entered the jet

CONVAIR B-36D (1946, USA). The largest bomber ever built was designed in 1941, and a prototype was ordered a few days before Pearl Harbor. The aircraft (without the 4 jet engines which were added to later models from the *D* version on) flew for the first time on August 8, 1946. Because it went into production just after the War and coincided with the appearance of bombers completely equipped with jet engines, its production was limited to 246 units. These formidable strategic bombers, of indubitable quality in spite of their unusual design, were in service until May 1958. In the final period of their existence, they were used for atomic experiments.

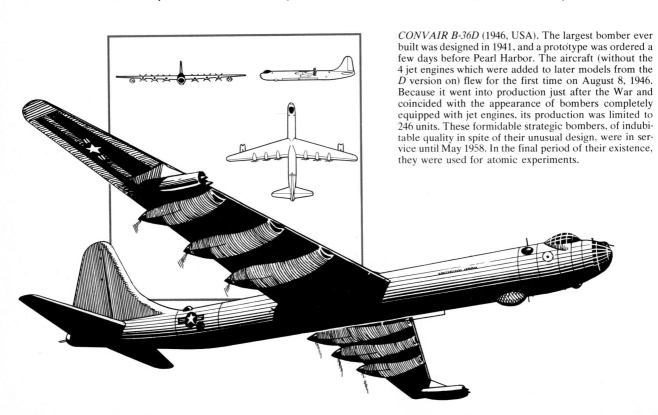

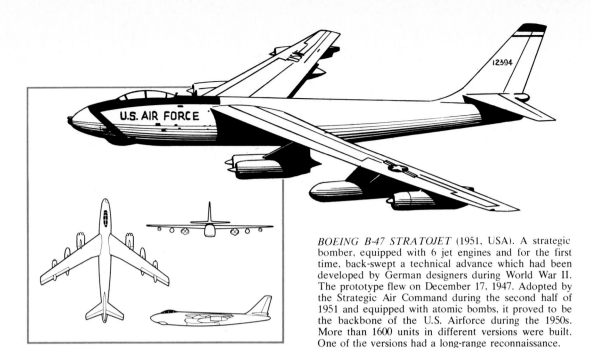

BOEING B-47 STRATOJET (1951, USA). A strategic bomber, equipped with 6 jet engines and for the first time, back-swept a technical advance which had been developed by German designers during World War II. The prototype flew on December 17, 1947. Adopted by the Strategic Air Command during the second half of 1951 and equipped with atomic bombs, it proved to be the backbone of the U.S. Airforce during the 1950s. More than 1600 units in different versions were built. One of the versions had a long-range reconnaissance.

age, though later than military aviation. On May 2, 1952, BOAC began flying the *DH-106 Comet 1 (p.140),* the world's first commercial jet plane, on its London–Johannesburg, South Africa, route. Six years were to pass before an American commercial jet, the *Boeing 707,* began passenger service, and 7 years before the French *Caravelle (p.141)* made its debut on short-distance flights. But English industry was not able to profit from its great advantage. The *DH-106*'s limited range did not permit its use on the most profitable North Atlantic routes and two fatal accidents on January 10 and April 8, 1954, caused by what is technically known as "metal fatigue," nipped any similar aircraft in the bud. Britain did, however, score a point with the creation of the

Vickers Viscount (p.140), the world's first turboprop and clearly the most successful. Unlike planes with piston engines, these planes had turbines, directly attached to the propellers. The *Viscount,* which was the first English passenger plane to be exported to the U.S. and which was widely used by the major European companies, was followed by two more turboprops, the *Britannia (p.139)* and the *Vanguard (p. 138),* both excellent aircraft. But because they arrived on the scene just as the airlines had begun planning to convert to jet aircraft, they. were not very successful. The only American turboprop, the *Lockheed Electra (p.138),* suffered more or less the same fate.

It was the beginning of the jet age; in just a

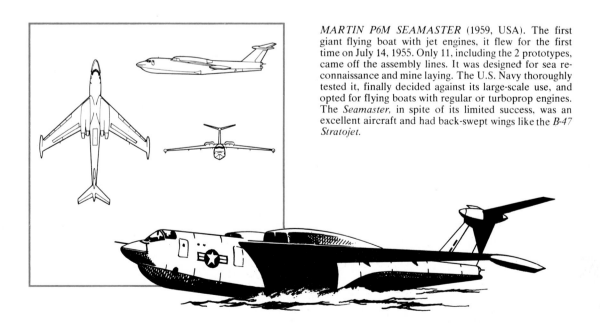

MARTIN P6M SEAMASTER (1959, USA). The first giant flying boat with jet engines, it flew for the first time on July 14, 1955. Only 11, including the 2 prototypes, came off the assembly lines. It was designed for sea reconnaissance and mine laying. The U.S. Navy thoroughly tested it, finally decided against its large-scale use, and opted for flying boats with regular or turboprop engines. The *Seamaster,* in spite of its limited success, was an excellent aircraft and had back-swept wings like the *B-47 Stratojet.*

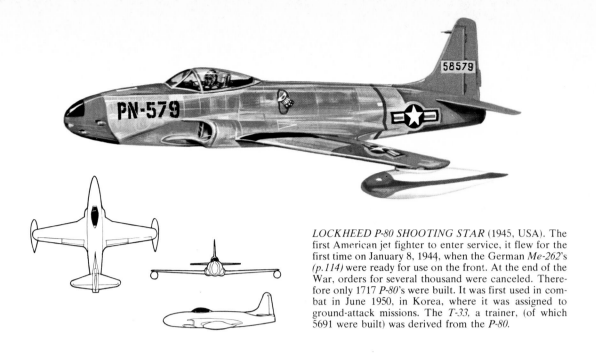

LOCKHEED P-80 SHOOTING STAR (1945, USA). The first American jet fighter to enter service, it flew for the first time on January 8, 1944, when the German *Me-262*'s *(p.114)* were ready for use on the front. At the end of the War, orders for several thousand were canceled. Therefore only 1717 *P-80*'s were built. It was first used in combat in June 1950, in Korea, where it was assigned to ground-attack missions. The *T-33,* a trainer, (of which 5691 were built) was derived from the *P-80.*

few years the *Comet 4,* the first version of the *Boeing 707,* and the *Caravelle* were joined by the *Douglas DC-8,* the *Convair 880,* the *Hawker Siddeley Trident,* the *BAC-111* and many other aircraft still flying for the major airlines. These will be taken up in the chapter "Civil Aviation Today." Going on to a brief review of military aviation, we should immediately mention that the end of World War II did not bring a period of inactivity or status quo as did the end of World War I. Quite the opposite, for the end of the War came just as the first jet planes appeared (the German *Me-262,* the English *Meteor,* the American *Bell P-59 Airacomet*) and the new technical development had to be carefully studied. American, British and Russian occupation forces in Germany came into possession of some very interesting and advanced plans in the field of jet propulsion, rocket propulsion and aerodynamics. As a result, blueprints and designs multiplied, contributing to the creation of a noticeable number of new aircraft in America, a few but high quality air-

craft in Great Britain, and lastly, in Russia, the *MiG-15,* forefather of a famous generation of jet fighters.

Furthermore, the political events did not encourage complete disarmament and in fact, immediately after the War, dangerous tension grew up between the U.S. and Russia, tension which ultimately led to the "Cold War." One of the first manifestations of this painful tension was the unilateral Russian decision of May 22, 1948, to cut off access to Berlin. When the War had ended, Berlin, an island in the heart of Soviet-occupied Germany, was governed by the American, British, French and Russian military authorities. With the Soviet decision to blockade Berlin, 2 million citizens of the city faced the threat of starvation. The only possible way of supplying the city was by air, through three "air corridors" which linked the one-time German capital to the rest of the Western world. And thus the Berlin Airlift was born. Until February, 1949, when the Russians reopened the city, Berlin was *completely* supplied by the airlift.

DE HAVILLAND VAMPIRE FB 5 (1946, GB). The second British jet fighter after the *Meteor (p.96),* it became operative in 1946 after the end of World War II, and was one of the standard aircraft of the R.A.F. fighter squadrons for many years. About 2000 units, including the fighter-bomber versions, were produced. It was put to limited use in combat in Malaya in 1950 in the fight against the terrorists. In July 1948, 6 *Vampires* of the 54th Squadron made their famous crossing of the Atlantic, reaching the U.S. from England with refueling stopovers in Iceland, Greenland and Labrador.

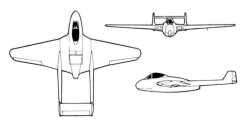

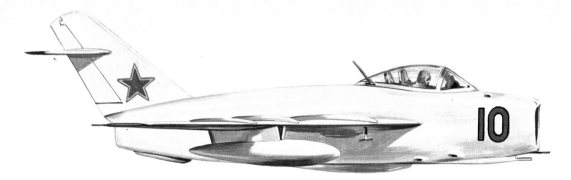

MIKOYAN-GUREVICH MIG-17 (1954, SU). NATO code name *Fresco-A*, this fighter, a direct descendant of the *MIG-15*, which had fought in the skies over Korea, was one of the most popular aircraft of the iron-curtain countries during the 1950s. It served in 21 air forces other than the Russian, including those of Albania, Iraq, North Korea, North Vietnam and even Morocco. It was built on license in the People's Republic of China, Czechoslovakia and Poland, and is still used in the air forces of many smaller countries.

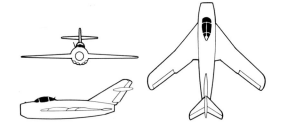

American transport aircraft (about 400 *Globemasters* and as many *C-54*'s) and English transports (*York* and *Lancaster*) made a total of 277,728 flights, reaching Berlin day and night through all kinds of weather, every three minutes, carrying a total of 2,326,205 tons of basic provisions, from flour to coal, from salt to medicines.

Another example of the turbulent state of affairs began on June 25, 1950, when, in faraway Korea a new war broke out. In 1945, after liberation from the Japanese, Korea was divided into two parts: the Northern zone, under a Communist regime, and the South, under a democratic government. When the North attacked the South, the U.N. came to its defense, but the U.S. bore the major burden of the conflict. In Korea too, aviation played a decisive role, and for the first time jet planes like the *P-80*'s, the *F9F Panthers*, the *F2H Banshees (p.142)*, the *F-86 Sabres*, the *F-84 Thunderjets (p.158)* and the *B-45 Tornado* bombers *(p.143)* flew side by side with *Mustang P-51*'s and *B-29* bombers. In Korea, the first air duels between jet aircraft

took place and the *MiG-15*'s demonstrated that Russia had lost no time preparing a modern if not revolutionary air fleet. A cease fire was signed on July 27, 1953, and the truce left the *status quo ante*. Peace talks were hastened by two heavy bombings carried out by 59 *F-84*'s on the dams of Toksan (May 13) and 90 *F-84*'s (May 16, 1953) on the Chasan dams. They were the first large group bombings carried out by jets.

Though peace returned to that corner of the world, the sky was still covered with dark clouds: the world was haunted by the possibility of another world war as soon as the Russians, catching up to the Americans, began testing atomic and nuclear bombs. The specter of nuclear war hung heavily on the horizon of international politics. The incredibly rapid development of missiles offered new perspectives; perhaps someday they would replace piloted aircraft. Perhaps . . . someday. . . . But meanwhile ready means of defense and counterattack were necessary, and the aircraft which make up today's military airforces came into existence.

NORTH AMERICAN F-86 SABRE (1949, USA). The first American fighter with swept wings, it flew for the first time on October 1, 1947, and had its baptism by fire in Korea in December 1950, where it fared better than the *P-80* against the Russian *MIG-15*'s. This outstanding aircraft became the standard fighter in the air forces of about 30 countries, European, South American and Asian. It was also built in Canada, Australia, Japan and Italy by Fiat. It was produced in many versions. Production was stopped at the end of the 1950s after about 5800 units had been delivered to Fighter Squadrons of half the world's air forces.

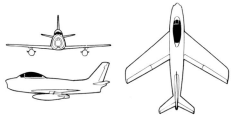

MILITARY AVIATION: TODAY

The echoes of the last explosion of World War II had not yet died down when the world was again thrown into the fear of a new conflict, more dramatic and perhaps more decisive for mankind. The victors were still shaking hands and congratulating one another when new interests and suspicions kindled the fires of counterinterests and differences to the point of polarizing most of mankind on opposite tension-charged sides. At the end of 1945 two distinct power blocks began to emerge, one dominated by the United States and the other by the Soviet Union. Nations which had been leaders on the world's scene, such as Great Britain, France, Germany, Italy and Japan, found themselves relegated to secondary roles, totally incapable of making their influence felt after a war which, whether they won or lost, had reduced them to disastrous circumstances. In the Far East the newly emerging People's Republic of China, although then part of the Soviet bloc and a member of the Communist International, was for many years more and more isolationist, afflicted by great internal strife. Within a short time the United States and Russia became arbiters of peace and war and were the only powers that continued to consider military aviation of fundamental importance in the event of total war. And it was probably the fear of a final irreparable holocaust, an apocalyptic nuclear war, which helped avoid war in Berlin in 1948 and in Cuba in 1962 and the various other small fires lit continually during the last 30 years.

Absurd as it may seem, the arms race (begun by the 2 superpowers 20-odd years ago and which only now seems to be slowing down with the Soviet-American SALT talks) has probably been the guarantor of peace. In the past, the power of the armed forces, the existence of new armaments or instruments of war were closely guarded state secrets; today information is more generally available. Even Russia, which is by no means as open a society as the U.S., allows the world to know a great deal about its might. This is so because world peace is dependent on a balance of power and the certainty that even the nation that attacks first will not survive. In the arms race in the last few years 2 important factors have been of major importance and both influence the structure and the very essence of military aviation: the development of an atomic deterrent and of missile power. World War II ended when the United States dropped the first 2 atom bombs, which had been developed in the Los Alamos laboratories by a group of scientists of many nationalities. Peace did not prompt abandoning the study of nuclear fission as an instrument of

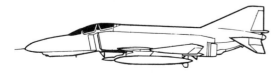

(continued on page 152)

MILITARY AVIATION INSIGNIA OF ALL COUNTRIES

Norway Sweden Finland U.S.S.R. Eire Great Britain Denmark

Holland Belgium Fed. Rep. of Germany Dem. Rep. of Germany Poland Czechoslovakia France

Switzerland Austria Hungary Bulgaria Portugal Spain Italy

Yugoslavia Albania Romania Greece Turkey Morocco Tunisia

Algeria Libia United Arab Rep. Sudan Mauritania Senegal

Ivory Coast Guinea Upper Volta Ghana Togoland Dahomey Niger

Nigeria Cameroons Ethiopia Somalia Congo Uganda Kenya

Tanzania Zambia Rhodesia Madagascar South Africa Australia New Zealand

Canada

 United States of America

 Mexico

 Guatemala

 Cuba

 Dominican Rep.

 Haiti

 Honduras

 El Salvador

 Nicaragua

 Colombia

Venezuela

 Ecuador

 Peru

 Bolivia

 Brazil

 Paraguay

 Uruguay

 Chile

 Argentina

 Lebanon

 Israel

 Syria

 Jordan

 Iraq

 Saudi Arabia

 Masqat & Oman

 Bahrain

 Kuwait

 Yemen

 Iran

 Afghanistan

 Pakistan

 India

 Nepal

 Ceylon

 People's Rep. of China

 Burma

 Malaysia

 South Vietnam

 Thailand

 Cambodia

 Laos

 Indonesia

Philippines

 South Korea

 North Korea

 Mongolia

 Japan

 Nationalist China

 United Nations

152

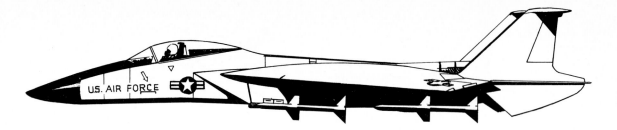

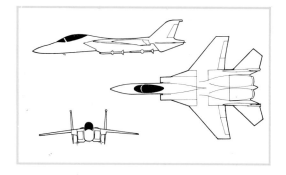

MCDONNELL DOUGLAS F-15 (1973, USA). It will be the new American Air Force air-superiority fighter at the end of the 1970s. The contract with Douglas for the building of 20 prototypes for a total of well over a billion dollars was signed in 1969; the first *F-15* flew in 1972. If the prototypes should prove successful, the new aircraft will go into mass-production and each one will cost about $8 million. The *F-15* is a one-seat fighter with fixed wing and with advanced electronic equipment for all-weather interception which can reach a speed close to Mach 3. Estimated production is 700 units.

war, but had the effect of multiplying the experts' efforts and of increased contacts among Russian, British and French scientific teams.

A few years later, in 1949, the Russians also had their atomic deterrent and became the equal of the United States with the discovery of the H-, or Hydrogen, bomb (1952), which, although much smaller in size than the bombs used on Hiroshima and Nagasaki, was much more powerful. Today only one medium-size atomic charge can equal the destruction wreaked by all the bombs dropped on Europe during World War II. In 1961, for example, the Soviet Union tested a 50-megaton bomb, equal to 50 million tons of explosive. A 100-megaton charge (which apparently exists!) exploding at low altitude would provoke a shock wave which could completely destroy an area of 2600 square kilometers. Thus, as far back as the 1950s nuclear war became a tragic possibility, with bombs far more

powerful and manageable than the atom bombs of 1945; the only remaining problem was how to carry the bombs to their objectives. Two choices seemed possible: an aircraft or a missile.

At the same time that nuclear weapons were being studied, the U.S. and the U.S.S.R. were proceeding with the development of a pilotless craft, propelled by rockets or jets, which could be launched at its target on a fixed trajectory or guided from the ground. The World War II German flying bombs, the V-1 and V-2, were virtually the first missiles in history. In 1950 the U.S. and the U.S.S.R. succeeded, more or less at the same time, in developing the first ICBM *(Intercontinental Ballistic Missile)*, whose trajectory could leave the Earth's atmosphere. ICBM's (several of which have been used to launch artificial satellites into orbit and to carry the capsules of the Gemini, Apollo, Vostok and Soyuz projects into space) were supposed to

GRUMMAN F-14B (1972, USA). A new U.S. Navy carrier-borne fighter which, beginning in 1973, should replace the *Phantoms* and which is expected to be greatly superior to the latter. Maximum foreseen speed: over Mach 2, which should be reached after about 2 minutes of flight. Among its main attributes should be its easy handling, a decisive factor in close-range combat. The *F-B*'s tasks will be to escort Navy forces, to protect carrier-borne aircraft and possibly to serve on ground-attack missions.

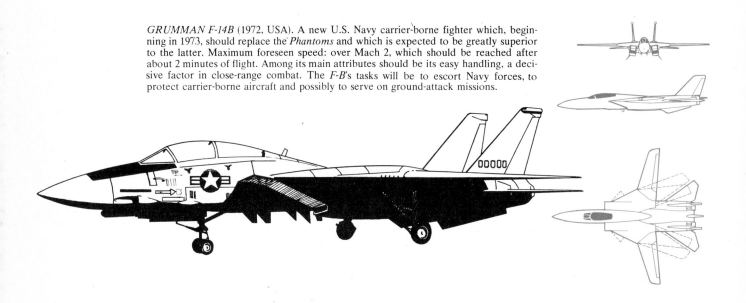

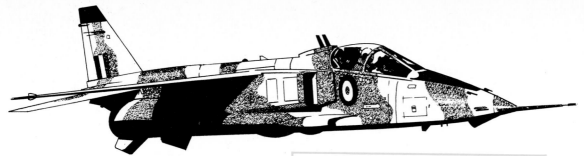

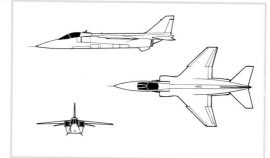

SEPECAT JAGUAR A (1970, F/GB). In 1966 the Breguet Aviation and the British Aircraft Corporation founded a company called Sepecat for the building of the *Jaguar*, designed for the R.A.F. and the Armée de l'Air in fighter-attack versions (*A*, French, and *S*, British), carrier-borne fighter-attack *(M)* and a two-seat advanced trainer (*B*, British and *E*, French). The *Jaguar*, based on a Breguet original design, is already in production. It can reach Mach 2 and can transport missiles, rockets or bombs for a total of 9920 pounds. It is also equipped with 2.30 millimeter guns.

have been the ideal vehicle for transporting deadly atomic charges to their objective. Many believed that the death knell had sounded both for bombers (whose function theoretically could be completely replaced by the missiles) and for fighters (which, since there would be no more bombers to attack while defending national territory, would be, in effect, obsolete).

But the situation was not so clean-cut; for example, the aircraft which was to have been the American strategic bomber of the 1970s, the *B-70 Valkyrie (p.211),* was never mass-produced because it was considered too expensive and, for all practical purposes, useless. Many experts believed that, at least for some time to come, the missiles could not totally replace tactical bombers: it was thus that the mixed marriage of missile and aircraft took place—the basic concept of military aviation of our times.

First of all, the surface-to-air missile has

been tied to the free-falling bomb used in the past. The former can be launched many kilometers away from its objective. It can carry either a conventional or an atomic charge. as in the case of the *Hound Dog,* with which the outdated American Strategic Air Command *B-52H*'s are equipped at present. The air-to-air missiles, terrifying weapons, have joined the small cannons of the past (though much improved upon, a 30 millimeter, such as the American *Vulcan,* the British *Aden* and the French *DEFA*) in air warfare. There are many types of air-to-air missiles differentiated by the kind of system which guides them to their objective: some, such as the American *Sidewinder* and the British *Firestreak,* are attracted by the infrared rays in the exhaust jet of enemy aircraft; others, such as the American Navy's *Sparrow,* are guided by radar; others, by radio or electromagnetic impulses. Improved upon greatly over the years, several air-to-air missiles today are

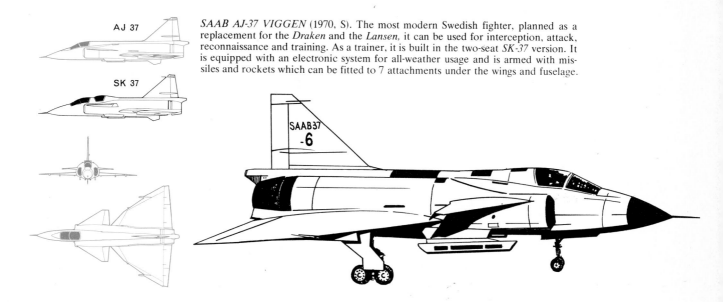

SAAB AJ-37 VIGGEN (1970, S). The most modern Swedish fighter, planned as a replacement for the *Draken* and the *Lansen,* it can be used for interception, attack, reconnaissance and training. As a trainer, it is built in the two-seat *SK-37* version. It is equipped with an electronic system for all-weather usage and is armed with missiles and rockets which can be fitted to 7 attachments under the wings and fuselage.

154

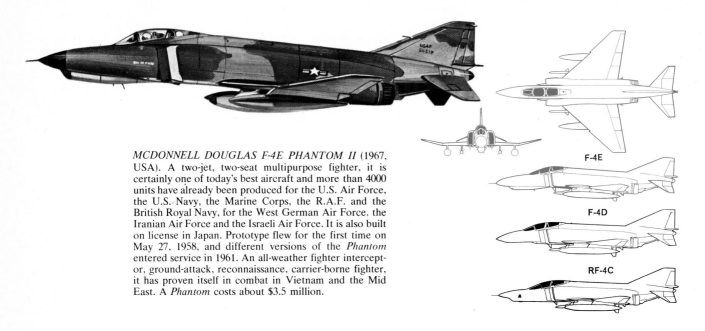

MCDONNELL DOUGLAS F-4E PHANTOM II (1967, USA). A two-jet, two-seat multipurpose fighter, it is certainly one of today's best aircraft and more than 4000 units have already been produced for the U.S. Air Force, the U.S. Navy, the Marine Corps, the R.A.F. and the British Royal Navy, for the West German Air Force. the Iranian Air Force and the Israeli Air Force. It is also built on license in Japan. Prototype flew for the first time on May 27, 1958, and different versions of the *Phantom* entered service in 1961. An all-weather fighter intercept-or, ground-attack, reconnaissance, carrier-borne fighter, it has proven itself in combat in Vietnam and the Mid East. A *Phantom* costs about $3.5 million.

F-4E

F-4D

RF-4C

theoretically able to reach an objective flying at a different altitude from the missile's launch vehicle.

Today the missile is the aircraft's best weapon and its most dangerous enemy. In fact air-to-air missiles have been joined by an- tiaircraft surface-to-air missiles. More than twenty have been produced and are part of the standard equipment of armies the world over.

Theoretically, if missiles, all missiles, could meet expectations, military aviation would be doomed. If an antimissile defense system had not been already conjured up, with the aid of

electronic equipment and other gear, every duel in the sky would end with the shooting down of one or perhaps both contenders. And if the threat of the antiaircraft missiles had not been deterred in some way, it would not be possible to penetrate enemy territory.

During the last few years, in spite of mis- sile development, many of the originally enthusiastic opinions about the new weapons are being slowly reconsidered because of the evolution of defense systems. Today a front- line military aircraft is equipped with highly specialized electronic gear which sometimes makes up $\frac{1}{3}$ of its total cost and is so compli-

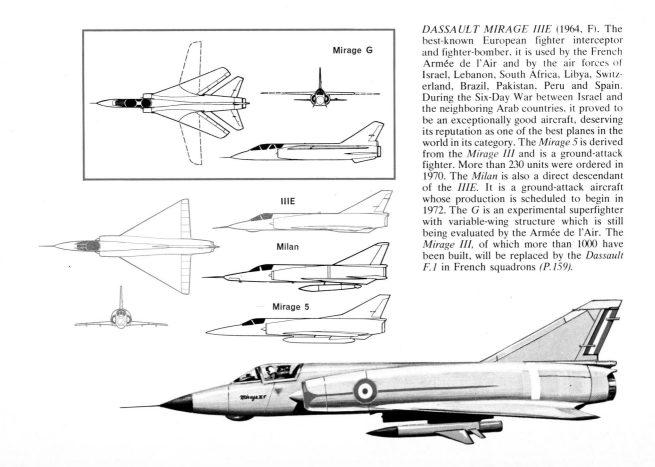

Mirage G

IIIE

Milan

Mirage 5

DASSAULT MIRAGE IIIE (1964, F). The best-known European fighter interceptor and fighter-bomber, it is used by the French Armée de l'Air and by the air forces of Israel, Lebanon, South Africa, Libya, Switz-erland, Brazil, Pakistan, Peru and Spain. During the Six-Day War between Israel and the neighboring Arab countries, it proved to be an exceptionally good aircraft, deserving its reputation as one of the best planes in the world in its category. The *Mirage 5* is derived from the *Mirage III* and is a ground-attack fighter. More than 230 units were ordered in 1970. The *Milan* is also a direct descendant of the *IIIE.* It is a ground-attack aircraft whose production is scheduled to begin in 1972. The *G* is an experimental superfighter with variable-wing structure which is still being evaluated by the Armée de l'Air. The *Mirage III,* of which more than 1000 have been built, will be replaced by the *Dassault F.1* in French squadrons *(P.159).*

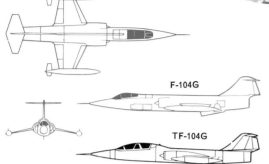

F-104G

TF-104G

LOCKHEED F-104G STARFIGHTER (1960, USA). The first *Starfighter* flew on February 7, 1954. Since then 2000 *F-104*'s have come off the assembly lines of Lockheed, Canadair, Fiat, Mitsubishi, and West German, Belgian and Dutch factories; they are being used by almost all nations in the West. Built in fighter, fighter-bomber, reconnaissance and trainer *(TF-104G)* versions, it can reach a speed over Mach 2.2 and can carry missiles, rockets and bombs weighing about 4000 pounds.

cated that it requires one man's complete attention. The seat that in the past was reserved for the gunner, had been taken over by the *Defense System Operator* in the American Air Force or by the *Air Electronics Officer* in the R.A.F.

The estimate of the efficiency of surface-to-air missiles which reached its apex when a *U-2 (p.142),* piloted by Capt. Francis Gary Powers, was shot down from an altitude of 65,600 feet into Russia, is slowly being seen in proper proportion after combat experiences in Vietnam, Israel and Egypt.

In conclusion, missiles are new and very

MIKOYAN-GUREVICH MIG-23 "FOXBAT" (1965, USSR). Seen for the first time in April, 1965, this all-weather fighter has set a new world's speed record flying at over Mach 3 (1441.5 miles per hour; 2320 kilometers per hour). Designed for high-altitude interception, it should be equipped with at least 10 missiles, but no precise information on this aircraft is available. To date, it has been used only by the Soviet Air Force and is believed to be its best fighter aircraft.

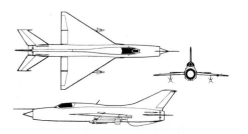

MIKOYAN-GUREVICH MIG-21PF "FISHBED D" (1960, USSR). The *MIG-21* in its many versions is one of the best-known and most widely used and most successful fighters. It is used by the air forces of more than 20 countries besides that of the Soviet Union, among them Egypt, Iraq, Algeria, Cuba and North Vietnam. It is a "pure" fighter interceptor, that is, not suitable for other missions such as attack. In Vietnam it has proved capable of matching the more costly *Phantoms.* The *PF,* all-weather version, has also been used by several of the Warsaw Pact nations in addition to the Soviet Union.

SUKHOI Su-9 "FISHPOT" (1957, USSR). It was born at the same time as the *MIG-21* but is bigger and heavier and should, even today, be the principal weapon of the Aviasiya Protivovozdushnoi Oborony Strany, the Soviet metropolitan defense system. A one-seat all-weather fighter, it is equipped with air-to-air missiles and its maximum speed is close to Mach 2. It is not known whether this aircraft is still in production and there is no proof that it has been sold to satellite-country air forces. It was last seen officially at the Domodedovo air parade in 1967.

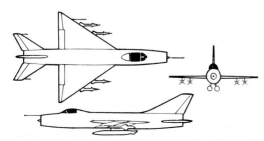

156

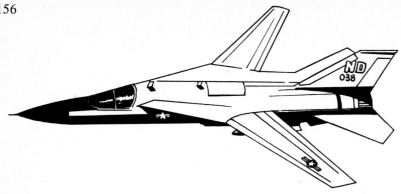

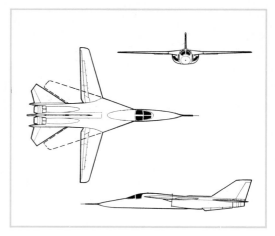

GENERAL DYNAMICS F-111A (1968, USA). One of the most talked about aircraft of our day, it is the first plane with variable wings to enter service in the U.S. Air Force. The fighter-bomber versions *A, E,* and *F,* were built for the Air Force, the *B* version for the Navy. The *FB-111A* is the strategic bomber and the *RF-111A* is the reconnaissance model. In March 1968, 5 *F-111A*'s made a disastrous debut in Vietnam, losing 2 aircraft in 5 days. Both the U.S. Navy and Australia have canceled their orders.

VFW-FOKKER VAK 191B (1971, G). An experimental prototype of a VTOL fighter-reconnaissance aircraft, it flew for the first time in 1971. The original design was developed by the VFW-Fokker in collaboration with Fiat, but in 1968 the Italian company decided to back out of the project. It is probable that the West German Defense Ministry will decide not to order the aircraft, preferring the *MRCA Panavia,* which is already in an advanced design stage.

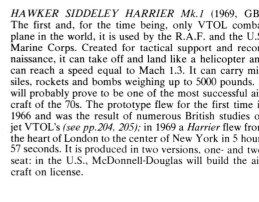

dangerous weapons which can be very useful to an air force. Nevertheless it must never be believed that they can substitute for an air force and must not become the device that condemns air forces to doom.

The Americans themselves are reviewing their basic concept of air power and are attempting to make up for time lost in hesitation and uncertainty, perhaps purposely fostered by Mr. Khrushchev. Khrushchev stated many times that Russian missile power was not only the strongest in the world but also the only means of defense and offense in the Soviet Union. Later it became known that while concentrating on the development of missiles, Russia had not by any means been ignoring her air force. This may be seen in the fact that today the Soviet Union can boast

YAKOVLEV VTOL "FREEHAND" (1967, USSR). This Russian subsonic fighter was seen for the first time at the Domodedovo air parade in July 1967 and at that time was certainly only an experimental prototype. It took off vertically and flew horizontally at an altitude of about 164 feet. It has not been possible to find out whether it has gone into regular mass-production or whether some other unspecified model has been chosen in its stead.

HAWKER SIDDELEY HARRIER Mk.1 (1969, GB). The first and, for the time being, only VTOL combat plane in the world, it is used by the R.A.F. and the U.S. Marine Corps. Created for tactical support and reconnaissance, it can take off and land like a helicopter and can reach a speed equal to Mach 1.3. It can carry missiles, rockets and bombs weighing up to 5000 pounds. It will probably prove to be one of the most successful aircraft of the 70s. The prototype flew for the first time in 1966 and was the result of numerous British studies on jet VTOL's *(see pp.204, 205);* in 1969 a *Harrier* flew from the heart of London to the center of New York in 5 hours 57 seconds. It is produced in two versions, one- and two-seat: in the U.S., McDonnell-Douglas will build the aircraft on license.

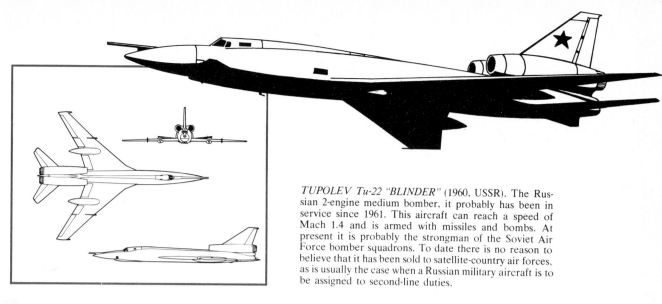

TUPOLEV Tu-22 "BLINDER" (1960, USSR). The Russian 2-engine medium bomber, it probably has been in service since 1961. This aircraft can reach a speed of Mach 1.4 and is armed with missiles and bombs. At present it is probably the strongman of the Soviet Air Force bomber squadrons. To date there is no reason to believe that it has been sold to satellite-country air forces, as is usually the case when a Russian military aircraft is to be assigned to second-line duties.

a certain aerial supremacy, with the only operative fighter aircraft ever to reach the speed of Mach 3, the *MiG-23 "Foxbat" (p.155),* and other attack aircraft which are certainly more advanced than their American counterparts. The U.S. seems intent on re-establishing an equilibrium with the strategic bomber *B-1 (p.161),* the USAF's *F-15* and the U.S. Navy's *F-14 (p.152).*

The return to the piloted strategic bomber is perhaps the most sensational of recent American decisions. The American Secretary of Defense Melvin Laird spoke with great enthusiasm of the substitute for the now-obsolete *B-52,* guaranteeing that it will have a better chance of survival under attack; will have higher penetration speed at low altitudes, and will be able to fly below radar

defense systems; it will also have a greater cargo capacity than its predecessor although it is smaller and lighter. The project, which is being carried out by North American Rockwell, represents more than a billion dollar investment. The aircraft should be able to transport up to 24 new SRAM's *(Short-range Attack Missile)* atomic surface-to-air missiles, which can be launched at a distance of 100 miles from their targets. The Americans are returning to the concept of insuring a new and flexible means of retaliation. The present system is made up of atomic submarines with their 656 *Polaris* missiles, soon to be replaced by the more powerful *Poseidons.* In the event of total war, after the initial missile attack and immediate or almost instantaneous counterattack, the possibility of relying on a vehi-

(continued on page 168)

BOEING B-52H (1956, USA). Although by now even its most recent versions are considered obsolete, it is the standard aircraft of the Strategic Air Command squadrons and will remain such for some time, possibly until it is replaced by the *B-1,* the planning of which has only just begun. A classic A-bomb carrier, it has proved to be of little use as a conventional bomber in Vietnam. Propelled by 8 turbofans, its range is over 10,000 miles!

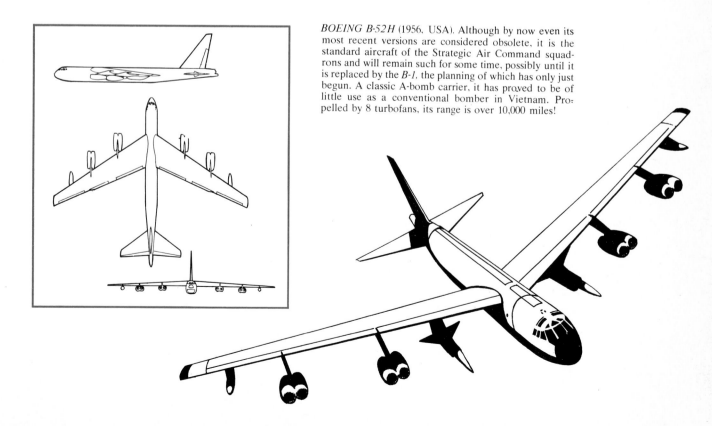

THE FIGHTERS

Among the many tasks of fighter planes in a modern air force, two are the most important: to insure superiority in air battles and to intercept enemy aircraft before they reach national territory.

Until a few years ago the same aircraft carried out both tasks. Clearly, for the first task, it was necessary to have exceptional planes with great absolute and climbing speeds extremely maneuverable at any altitude. With the appearance of the *MIG-23 "Foxbat" (p.155),* the only aircraft of its kind currently in service, the United States felt obliged to decide to acquire new superfighters, the Air Force's *F-15* and the Navy's *F-14 (p.152),* which are now in the development stage. The intention is to replace the famous *F-4E Phantom II (p.154),* a multipurpose fighter and one of the best in the Western world today and, perhaps later, the *F-106A, F-101B* and the *F-102,* which are at this time outfitting squadrons of the Air Defense Command. Modern fighter interceptors are the *Saab AJ-37 (p.153),* designed to replace the *Draken* for the Swedish Air Force, the *Mirage F-1* which will take the place of the very successful *Mirage III (p.154),* the Russian *Yak-28P,* the *Su-11,* and the *Tu-28P.* Still in use, although their days are numbered, are the Russian *MIG-21's,* flying in the air forces of more than 20 Soviet-bloc countries; the *Su-9 (p.155)* the standard all-weather fighter interceptor of Soviet defense Air Forces; the *Lightning,* the standard R.A.F. fighter. Aircraft like the *Lockheed F-104G (p.155),* which is the strong point of the air forces of 15 countries, including the major countries of Western Europe (except for France and Great Britain, which furnish their fighter squadrons with nationally built aircraft) are fast becoming obsolete.

While waiting for the European *MRCA (Multi Role Combat Aircraft)* and the *Panavia 200 (p.170),* which is scheduled to enter service not before the end of the 1970s, it is likely that many airforces will have to make other purchases in the U.S.A. Their most probably choice will be the *Northrop P-530 Cobra* which has been recently offered on the market. It could have a success equal to the unsophisticated *Northop F-5 Freedom Fighter* which was expressly built for export and which is presently serving in the airforces of 15 different countries. Incredible technical progress has been made in the last few years in the field of carrier-borne fighters, so much so that today a Navy aircraft can compare in performance with a ground aircraft. And in at least one case the same aircraft has been called upon to carry out both roles: the *Phantom II,* standard fighter of the U.S. Navy today, as well as the *Crusader,* whose production came to a halt in 1965.

Even the British Royal Navy will gradually replace its *Sea Vixens* with *Phantoms,* while the *Jaguar (p.153),* which is soon to be mass-produced, will shortly replace the *Étendard* currently in use on French aircraft carriers.

U.S.A.

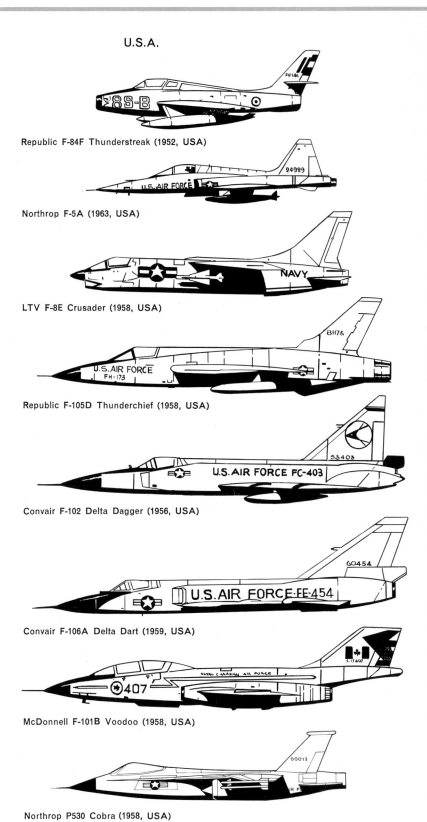

Republic F-84F Thunderstreak (1952, USA)

Northrop F-5A (1963, USA)

LTV F-8E Crusader (1958, USA)

Republic F-105D Thunderchief (1958, USA)

Convair F-102 Delta Dagger (1956, USA)

Convair F-106A Delta Dart (1959, USA)

McDonnell F-101B Voodoo (1958, USA)

Northrop P530 Cobra (1958, USA)

GREAT BRITAIN

BAC Lithning F. Mk.6 (1960, GB)

Hawker Siddeley Sea Vixen F.A.W.2 (1964, GB)

FRANCE

Dassault Super-Mistère B2 (1956, F)

Dassault Étendard IV M (1962, F)

Dassault Mirage F1 (1970, F)

EGYPT

Helwan HA-300 (1967, RAU)

INDIA

HAL HF-24 Marut (1964, IND)

U.S.S.R.

Mikoyan-Gurevich MiG-19 "Farmer-C" (1955, SU)

Mikoyan-Gurevich MiG-21F "Fishbed-C" (1958, SU)

Mikoyan-Gurevich MiG-21FL (1960, IND)

Yakovlev Yak-28P "Firebar" (1967, SU)

Sukhoi Su-11 "Flagon-A" (1967, SU)

Tupolev Tu-28P "Fiddler" (1961, SU)

SWEDEN

Saab J 35F Draken (1958, S)

160

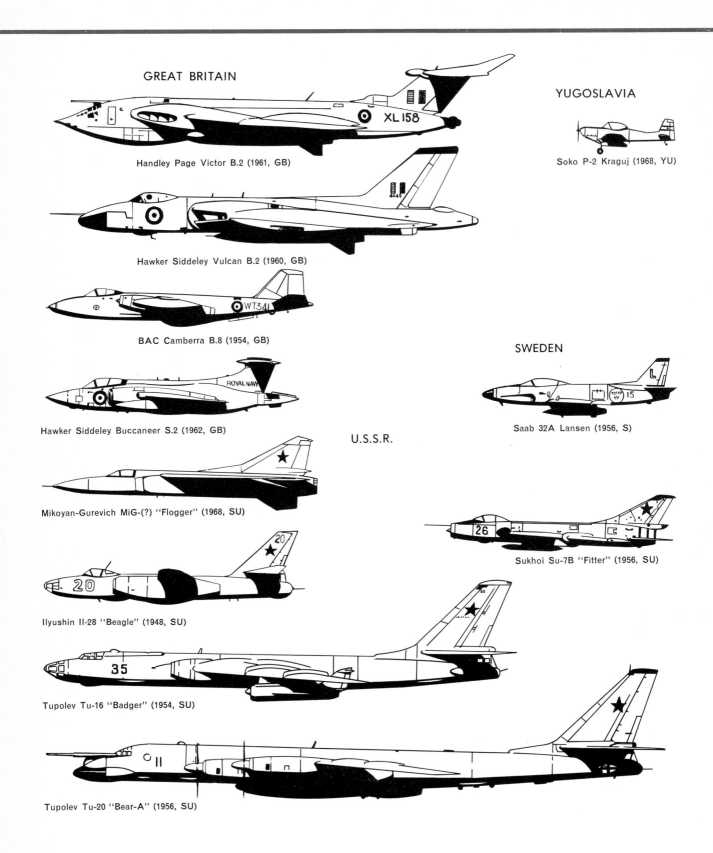

GREAT BRITAIN

Handley Page Victor B.2 (1961, GB)

Hawker Siddeley Vulcan B.2 (1960, GB)

BAC Camberra B.8 (1954, GB)

Hawker Siddeley Buccaneer S.2 (1962, GB)

Mikoyan-Gurevich MiG-(?) ''Flogger'' (1968, SU)

Ilyushin Il-28 ''Beagle'' (1948, SU)

Tupolev Tu-16 ''Badger'' (1954, SU)

Tupolev Tu-20 ''Bear-A'' (1956, SU)

U.S.S.R.

YUGOSLAVIA

Soko P-2 Kraguj (1968, YU)

SWEDEN

Saab 32A Lansen (1956, S)

Sukhoi Su-7B ''Fitter'' (1956, SU)

FRANCE

Dassault Mirage IVA (1964, F)

North American OV-10A Bronco (1967, USA)

North American T-28D (1967, USA)

McDonnell Douglas A-4F Skyhawk (1956, USA)

Cessna A-37B (1966, USA)

U.S.A.

LTV A-7B Corsair II (1966, USA)

Grumman A-6A Intruder (1963, USA)

North American Rockwell B-1 (1976, USA)

Convair B-58A Hustler (1959, USA)

BOMBER AND STRIKE AIRCRAFT

The concept of the World War II bomber, which was supposed to be able to fly fast and at high altitudes for long distances, and which could flee from fighters or defend itself with weapons on board has disappeared, now almost totally replaced by the Intercontinental Ballistic Missile.

Closest to this old concept is the strategic bomber, such as the *B-52 (p.157), B-58A Hustler, Handley Page Victor, Hawker Siddeley Vulcan, Tu-20, Tu-16,* and *Tu-22,* all or almost all of which have been relegated to the reserves, such as the *Hustler,* or are about to face a similar fate. Exemplifying the design of the strategic long-range bomber currently considered desirable is the *B-1,* now in process of being turned into a reality in the U.S. It is a rather small 4-engine jet, lighter and easier to handle than its predecessors and capable of transporting a heavier load of atomic weapons. It is also equipped with variable wings which allow it to fly both slowly at a low altitude and at over Mach 2 at high altitude. The first attempt at manufacturing this kind of aircraft, the *F-111A, B,* etc., was a failure. It is now up to the *B-1* to realize the potential of aircraft equipped with this kind of wing.

Aircraft built for tactical bombing are no longer even designated as tactical bombers but are called "strike" aircraft. Their task is to penetrate enemy territory, flying below radar's protective screen to reach their objective such as an airport, a military target, or a logistic strong-hold no farther than 500 miles from the base. The tactical bomber must be equipped with all-weather electronic equipment, its speed must be supersonic even at low altitude and it must be equipped with armament (such as air-to-air missiles and cannon) which enables it to defend itself. The European *Jaguar (p.153)* is supposed be such an aircraft, as well as the *Mirage IVA* (already surpassed by the *Milan,* |*p.154*| and the *G,* also built by Dassault). The best of these at present are the British *Buccaneer;* the American *A-4F Skyhawk,* the *A-7B Corsair II* and the *A-6A Intruder;* the Italian *Fiat G.91 (p.168);* the Russian *MiG "Flogger"* and the *Il-28 "Beagle."*

As a result of the Vietnam experience there came into existence COIN (i.e., "counterinsurgency") craft such as the American *OV-10A, Bronco,* the *T-28D,* or the Yugoslav *Kraguj,* which are relatively slow aircraft and are not actually equipped to face enemy attack in the skies, but which provide ground-troop support with their great fire power.

A new category of tactical-attack aircraft emerges with the first operative VTOL craft in the world, the *Hawker Siddeley Harrier (p.156);* aircraft with the same revolutionary characteristics will shortly be built in other countries, first among them the U.S.S.R.

RECONNAISSANCE AND ANTI-SUB

With the advent of artificial satellites—which, continuously revolving around the Earth, keep every corner of the globe under constant observation—the reconnaissance developments of the 1940s have virtually disappeared from use. The American *Lockheed SR-71A (p. 169)*, the slow but silent *Lockheed YO-3A (p.169)* which is still in the experimental stage, the Russian *Mandrake*, whose characteristics are little known, may be considered the last of these reconnaissance aircraft. Strategic reconnaissance flights to monitor an attack would be entrusted to the same type of aircraft that do the actual bombings, but these craft would be equipped with cameras and other instruments instead of bombs. On the other hand, sea reconnaissance has become much more important than in the past. Now the oceans are crossed by formidable atomic submarines equipped with nuclear warhead missiles.

There are two kinds of sea reconnaissance: one set up to take-off from a land base; the other, from an aircraft carrier. The first, for sea scanning not too distant from the coast with the most efficient sonar and radar equipment, etc., is a job for aircraft with a 12- to 16-hour range, such as the *Lockheed P-2H Neptune*, the *P-3C Orion*, the Japanese *Kawasaki P-2J* and the brand new *PS-1*, the English *Nimrod* (which is replacing the *Shackleton*), the French *Atlantic*, the Russian *Be-10* and *Mya-4*, and the Canadian *P-107 Argus*.

If the first type of sea reconnaissance is important, the second is absolutely vital for Naval forces at sea, made up of attack aircraft-carriers or anti-submarine carriers. Danger for these convoys can come equally from the sky or the sea. In order to be ready to face danger from the sky, the American, French and British carriers (which are truly air bases in the seas, equipped with attack aircraft and defense fighters and carrying nuclear weapons) build a radar umbrella, in effect, with aircraft such as the *Vigilante*, the *Grumman E-2B Hawkeye (p.169)*, the now old *E-1B Tracer*, the English *Gannet*, and the French *Alizé*. All these aircraft are capable of sighting attacking supersonic planes in enough time for the fighters to take off and face the enemy. To escape or to fight danger from the sea, carriers can rely on aircraft such as the *Tracker*, the *Albatros* and the very new *Lockheed S-3A*, as well as the extremely useful and precious anti-sub helicopters, all equipped with automatically aimed torpedos which are much more effective and lethal than the older depth charges.

There are very few examples of aircraft built for tactical battlefield observation, such as the *OV-1B Mohawk*. Usually the reconnaissance versions of the fighters themselves or reassigned attack aircraft are used for tactical reconnaissance.

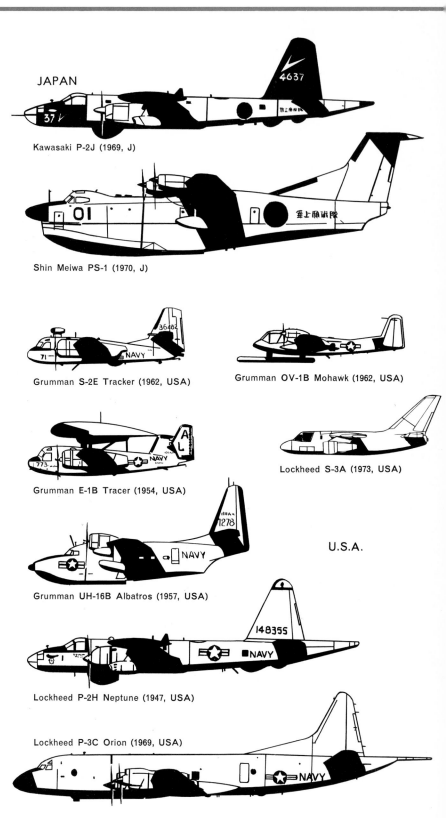

JAPAN

Kawasaki P-2J (1969, J)

Shin Meiwa PS-1 (1970, J)

Grumman S-2E Tracker (1962, USA)

Grumman OV-1B Mohawk (1962, USA)

Grumman E-1B Tracer (1954, USA)

Lockheed S-3A (1973, USA)

Grumman UH-16B Albatros (1957, USA)

U.S.A.

Lockheed P-2H Neptune (1947, USA)

Lockheed P-3C Orion (1969, USA)

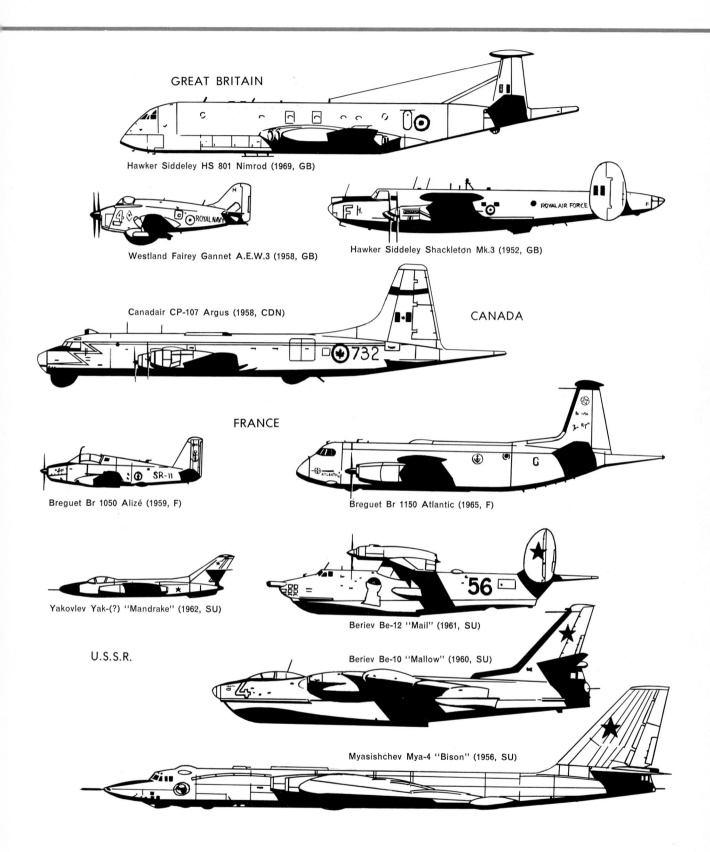

GREAT BRITAIN

Hawker Siddeley HS 801 Nimrod (1969, GB)

Westland Fairey Gannet A.E.W.3 (1958, GB)

Hawker Siddeley Shackleton Mk.3 (1952, GB)

Canadair CP-107 Argus (1958, CDN)

CANADA

FRANCE

Breguet Br 1050 Alizé (1959, F)

Breguet Br 1150 Atlantic (1965, F)

Yakovlev Yak-(?) "Mandrake" (1962, SU)

Beriev Be-12 "Mail" (1961, SU)

Beriev Be-10 "Mallow" (1960, SU)

U.S.S.R.

Myasishchev Mya-4 "Bison" (1956, SU)

164

U.S.S.R.

Sukhoi Su-7UTI "Moujik" (1966, SU)

Mikoyan-Gurevich MiG-21UTI "Mongol" (1956, SU)

Antonov An-14 "Clod" (1965, SU)

Yakovlev Yak-12M (1946, SU)

Antonov An-2P "Colt" (1948, SU)

U.S.A.

Cessna T-41A (1965, USA)

North American T-2 Buckeye (1965, USA)

Northrop T-38A Talon (1961, USA)

GREAT BRITAIN

Hawker Siddeley Gnat T.1 (1962, GB)

Hawker Siddeley Hunter T.7 (1957, GB)

BAC Jet Provost T.5 (1969, GB)

CANADA

INDIA

De Havilland DHC-1 Chipmunk (1946, CDN)

Canadair CT-114 Tutor (1962, CDN)

De Havilland DHC-2 Beaver (1948, CDN)

HAL HJT-6 Mk.II Kiran (1968, IND)

ITALY

Piaggio P-149D (1955, I)

Piaggio-Douglas PD-808 (1964, I)

Aerfer-Aermacchi AM-3C (1970, I)

FRANCE

Aérospatiale CM 170 Super Magister (1962, F)

Morane-Saulnier MS 760 Paris (1958, F)

Nord 3202 (1959, F)

Holste MH-1521M Broussard (1953, F)

BRAZIL

ARGENTINA

Neiva Regente C-42 (1965, BR)

IA 50 Guarani II (1963, RA)

Dinfia IA 35 Huanquero (1954, RA)

Mikoyan-Gurevich MiG-15UTI "Midget" (1950, SU)

Yakovlev Yak-18A (1947, SU)

CZECHOSLOVAKIA

Aero L-29 Delfin "Maya" (1962, CS)

Aero L-39 (1971, CS)

Cessna O-2A (1966, USA)

Helio U-10 Super Courier (1959, USA)

Beagle Basset CC Mk.1 (1964, GB)

JAPAN

Fuji T1A (1959, J)

Mitsubishi MU-2S (1964, J)

YUGOSLAVIA

Aero 3 (1958, YU)

Soko G2-A Galeb (1963, YU)

SWEDEN

Saab SK 60 (1965, S)

SPAIN

Hispano HA-200E Super Saeta (1960, E)

FRANCE-GERMANY OCC

Dassault-Breguet-Dornier "Alpha Jet" (1973, F/D)

GERMANY OCC

Dornier Do 27A (1956, D)

TRAINING AND UTILITY AIRCRAFT

Military training of a supersonic pilot today costs from a minimum of $50,000 to a maximum of $100,000.

Aside from this heavy initial investment, we should remember that pilots are in charge of an aircraft which in itself is worth several million dollars. This means that inadequate training may not only cost the life of one or more men (as in 1971, when an insufficiently trained Japanese trainee pilot caused his fighter to collide with a commercial airliner), but also a substantial financial loss. We must also bear in mind that flying one of the modern air-superiority fighters not only requires a decisive and quick-thinking pilot at the controls, but one with thorough knowledge of the aircraft and its hundreds of complicated mechanisms so that the human and mechanical elements are virtually fused. Therefore the problem of basic, primary and advanced pilot training is far more complicated than in the past. A few years ago it was generally believed that the trainee should begin his course by flying an aircraft equipped with jet engines; more recent opinion believes the young trainee should begin flying on piston-engine planes which are far less costly to purchase and to operate. Only those who show real ability to become supersonic pilots go on to jets while the others are trained to fly transport aircraft, helicopters, etc., depending on their inclination and aptitude. This is why modern air forces use many different types of aircraft—props and jets, depending on the needs of the country. Furthermore, in the matter of training aircraft each country that depends on foreign aircraft industries such as Brazil, Yugoslavia and Czechoslovakia tries to become self-sufficient by producing its own planes. Countries with important aircraft industries, such as Great Britain, France and Italy have become competitors with the powerful American aeronautics industry, with aircraft like the *Jet Provost,* the *Super Magister,* the *Macchi MB-326.* Collaboration among nations, as in the case of the new Franco-German *Alpha Jet,* may also be able to guarantee that, from its inception, a project will recover its initial investment.

In the field of liaison aircraft, light transports and "utility planes," where electronics are not so vital, medium and small national industries are proud of finally being able to provide some of their own craft to the airforces of their own countries.

STRATEGIC AND TACTICAL TRANSPORTS

If by strategical transport aircraft we mean craft that are capable of moving troops and equipment to meet the optimum of a nation's offensive and defensive capacities, it is immediately clear that the U.S. and the Soviet Union are the only world powers that have need of long-range transports. If the scope of action is limited, the range required is also limited, and smaller aircraft will satisfy the needs of the military. Because of their military needs, the world's two major aeronautical powers require the *Galaxy C-5A (p.171)*, the *C-133B Cargomaster*, the *Lockheed C-141A Starlifter*, the *An-22 (p.171)*, the *An-12* and the quite recent *Ilyushin Il-76* a four-jet transport similar to the American *Starlifter*, displayed for the first time at the Air Paris Show in 1971. For similar reasons, Great Britain, France, Italy and Germany desire strategic transports such as the British *Short Belfast*, the *Lockheed C-130 Hercules* (American) or the *Transall C-160* of French-German manufacture. The Russians clearly demonstrated the effectiveness and usefulness of their strategic air transport during the 1968 events in Czechoslovakia, when a large part of Soviet intervention was undertaken with the use of an improvised and efficient airlift. The Americans, on the other hand, have been equally efficient in organizing air lifts to supply their troops in Vietnam and in transferring, as a display of might, entire divisions between the U.S. and Europe within 24 hours. Another kind of air lift, and equally important, is the tactical or assault air lift which can carry men and matériel and equipment as close to the operating theaters as possible, even when these areas are under enemy fire. Obviously under such conditions, proper asphalt runways would not be available or, if available, would be exposed to damage or destruction by enemy attacks. That is why aircraft assigned this task must be able to take-off or land on any kind of terrain. The preferable aircraft for this purpose are STOL's (Short Takeoff and Landing), which can take advantage of any open landing area available. The problem could be even more definitively solved by using VTOL's now being designed: the *Bell X-222A* or the *Canadair CL-84-1 (p. 207)*.

For the time being, most such operations are carried out by medium and heavy helicopters which bear the greater burden of these operations, alongside such aircraft as the *Caribou*, the *Buffalo*, the *Noratlas* and the old *Provider* and *Flying Boxcar*, all of which may soon be joined by the *Fiat G222* and the *Namc XC-1A*. Though all these craft are faster and larger than helicopters, they are not as adaptable to landing and takeoff.

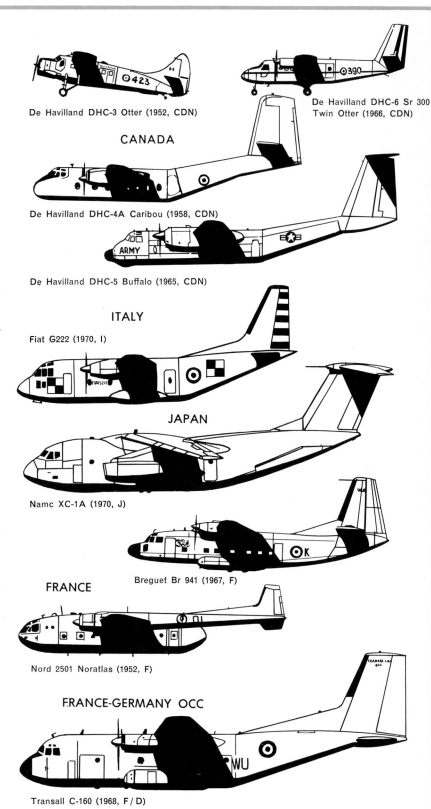

De Havilland DHC-3 Otter (1952, CDN)

De Havilland DHC-6 Sr 300 Twin Otter (1966, CDN)

CANADA

De Havilland DHC-4A Caribou (1958, CDN)

De Havilland DHC-5 Buffalo (1965, CDN)

ITALY

Fiat G222 (1970, I)

JAPAN

Namc XC-1A (1970, J)

Breguet Br 941 (1967, F)

FRANCE

Nord 2501 Noratlas (1952, F)

FRANCE-GERMANY OCC

Transall C-160 (1968, F / D)

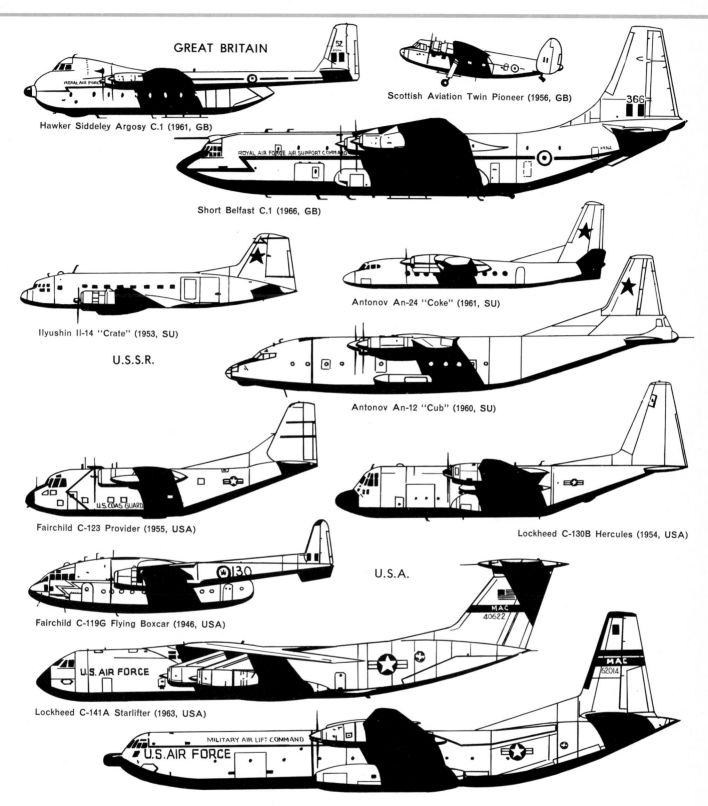

GREAT BRITAIN

Hawker Siddeley Argosy C.1 (1961, GB)

Scottish Aviation Twin Pioneer (1956, GB)

Short Belfast C.1 (1966, GB)

Ilyushin Il-14 "Crate" (1953, SU)

U.S.S.R.

Antonov An-24 "Coke" (1961, SU)

Antonov An-12 "Cub" (1960, SU)

Fairchild C-123 Provider (1955, USA)

Lockheed C-130B Hercules (1954, USA)

Fairchild C-119G Flying Boxcar (1946, USA)

U.S.A.

Lockheed C-141A Starlifter (1963, USA)

McDonnell Douglas C-133B Cargomaster (1957, USA)

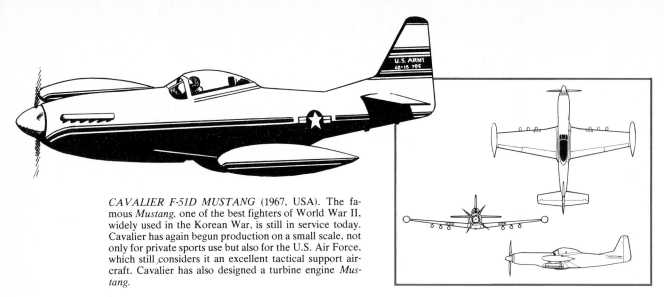

CAVALIER F-51D MUSTANG (1967, USA). The famous *Mustang,* one of the best fighters of World War II, widely used in the Korean War, is still in service today. Cavalier has again begun production on a small scale, not only for private sports use but also for the U.S. Air Force, which still considers it an excellent tactical support aircraft. Cavalier has also designed a turbine engine *Mustang.*

cle driven by man, and thus able to choose an objective still not hit, thereby initiating a second wave, is once more being given serious consideration. If only 10 percent of the attacking bombers were able to cross the defense lines and carry out the task of destruction and death, they could be decisive for victory but would, at any rate, be catastrophic for both winners and losers.

But the *B-1* may also be very useful in the unhappy event of a localized conventional war as a tactical bomber, with far better results than have been obtained with the *B-52* in Vietnam.

On the other hand, the *F-14* and the *F-15* (for the Army and Navy respectively) should equalize the fighter-plane situation for air-superiority—that is, control of the skies—in order to prevent enemy aircraft from crossing territorial borders. They are the typical examples, at least on paper, of today's best fighters:

horizontal and vertical speed in flight, ease of handling at every altitude, weapon capacity and range are all important components of an equation not easy to solve. Their electronic equipment will be the most sophisticated of its kind and will constitute about 50 percent of the aircraft's total cost. The electronic, all-weather automatic pilot drives the aircraft in any visibility and atmospheric condition; other electronic gear serves to aim the missiles at objectives both in the air and on the ground; electronic gear also provides the aircraft's defense against oncoming missiles. In the case of a plane which flies at Mach 3, about 2175 miles per hour, or about 0.6214 miles per second, it is clear that the pilot must have split-second reaction time. Piloting the plane and simultaneously attending to attack and defense would be impossible if the man at the controls could not avail himself of as automatic an aircraft as can be produced.

FIAT G.91Y (1968, I). Developed from the single jet *G.91,* built in 1960, the *G.91Y* is equipped with 2 jet engines. It is a tactical bomber and reconnaissance plane used by the Italian Air Force. Its speed is subsonic but it can take off from nonasphalted runways and can carry weapons weighing about 4000 pounds. Its predecessor, the single jet *G.91R,* is still in service in the Italian, German, Greek, Turkish and Portuguese air forces.

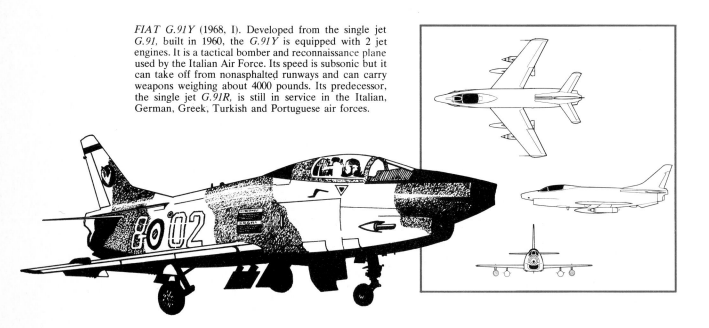

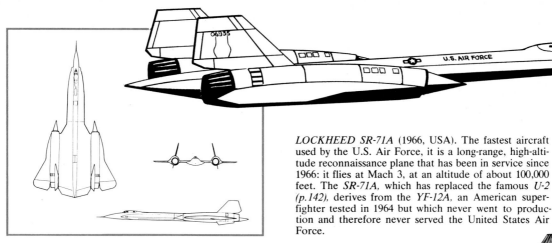

LOCKHEED SR-71A (1966, USA). The fastest aircraft used by the U.S. Air Force, it is a long-range, high-altitude reconnaissance plane that has been in service since 1966: it flies at Mach 3, at an altitude of about 100,000 feet. The *SR-71A*, which has replaced the famous *U-2 (p.142)*, derives from the *YF-12A*, an American super-fighter tested in 1964 but which never went to production and therefore never served the United States Air Force.

One of the major French aviation magazines, *L'Aviation*, recently stated, "In all fields of military aviation an effort must be made to define the most efficient partnership possible, a true marriage between the airplane, the engine which is its soul, the crew which serves it and the electronic equipment which assists it." This is, in short, the problem at the base of designs for today's new military aircraft. Naturally, the means at each nation's disposal must be taken into account. It is clear that the U.S. and the Soviet Union have far greater wealth and resources to solve these problems than France, Great Britain or other European countries—not only because of U.S. and U.S.S.R. financial power, but also because of their stimulus to achieve far more ambitious objectives. Furthermore, the U.S. and Russia are the official suppliers of military aircraft to almost all other nations, depending on their spheres of influence. The only other countries

LOCKHEED YO-3A (1971, USA). The quietest reconnaissance or spy aircraft in the world, it was developed from the design of a well-tested glider, the *YO-3A*, with a small 210 horsepower piston engine. It reaches a designated area, shuts off the engine and glides silently over the danger zone.

NORTH AMERICAN RA-5C VIGILANTE (1958, USA). A carrier-borne aircraft capable of speeds over Mach 2. It is fairly long-range and has been built in a nuclear bomber model and, far more important, tactical reconnaissance models. In service on American aircraft carriers since 1962, the *Vigilante* is still in production.

GRUMMAN E-2B HAWKEYE (1961, USA). It is outfitted with the most modern and complex radar equipment ever mounted on a carrier-borne aircraft. The *E-2B* can follow its carrier from the air in any weather and can detect approaching enemy planes, even supersonics, in ample time for defense fighters to take-off.

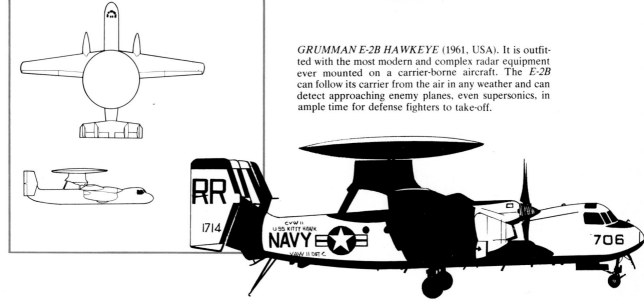

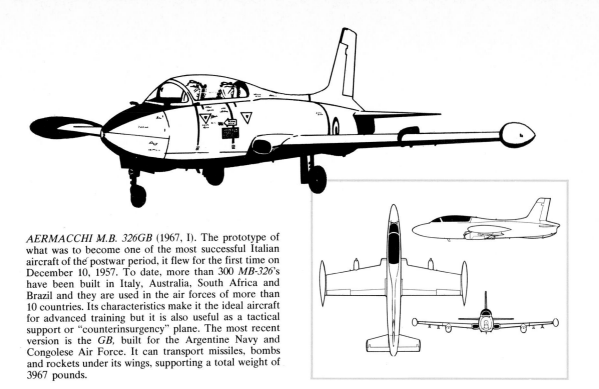

AERMACCHI M.B. 326GB (1967, I). The prototype of what was to become one of the most successful Italian aircraft of the postwar period, it flew for the first time on December 10, 1957. To date, more than 300 *MB-326*'s have been built in Italy, Australia, South Africa and Brazil and they are used in the air forces of more than 10 countries. Its characteristics make it the ideal aircraft for advanced training but it is also useful as a tactical support or "counterinsurgency" plane. The most recent version is the *GB,* built for the Argentine Navy and Congolese Air Force. It can transport missiles, bombs and rockets under its wings, supporting a total weight of 3967 pounds.

which build and export military aircraft today are Great Britain, France, Italy and Sweden, but not the "super sophisticated" crafts produced by American and Russian "air-superiority."

Between pages 158–167, in the pictorial review of military aircraft in service today, we briefly examine different types and it is evident that the two giant powers can offer a vast, almost-limitless range of choices. It is only in the last few years that European countries cooperating together have been able to provide some of their own aircraft without turning to American industry which, with an eye towards export, also designs less-sophisticated and less-costly planes in comparison to those produced for the USAF, as for example the *Lockheed F-104* and *Northrop F-5* already several years old, and the present *Northrop P-530 Cobra.* The only solution for

the Western European countries nowadays is to work in consortium. As far as countries in the Soviet bloc are concerned, they have no choice but to accept what Moscow offers them. It would be useful to briefly survey the actual sizes of some of today's air forces to have a more accurate idea of the situation. The U.S. can not only count on about 1100 Intercontinental Ballistic Missiles and 656 submarine-borne atomic missiles, which make up the first-attack or retaliatory atomic forces, but also on about 20,000 USAF, Army, Navy, and Marine first-line aircraft. Russia must have about 1400 ICBM's and between 15,000 and 16,000 aircraft combat-ready. The number of aircraft which make up first-line units in other Western European countries are approximately: 800 in Great Britain, 1000 in West Germany, 750 in France, 425 in Italy, 120 in Denmark, 120 in Norway, 650 in Swe-

PANAVIA 200 PANTHER (1973, D/GB/I). Also known as the European *MRCA (Multirole Combat Aircraft),* it represents one of the most important international projects of its kind: the German Messerschmitt-Bölkow-Blohm, the British Aircraft Corporation and the Italian Fiat companies are involved. The first flights of the *Panavia* prototypes should take place in 1973; the *100* version is a one-seat attack and reconnaissance plane; the *200* is a two-seat trainer.

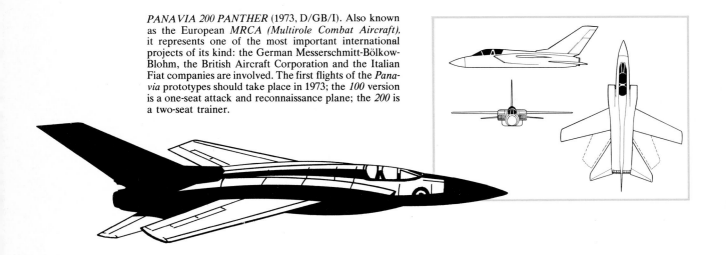

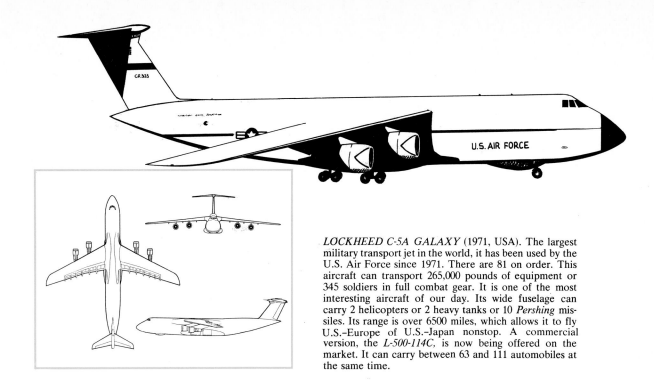

LOCKHEED C-5A GALAXY (1971, USA). The largest military transport jet in the world, it has been used by the U.S. Air Force since 1971. There are 81 on order. This aircraft can transport 265,000 pounds of equipment or 345 soldiers in full combat gear. It is one of the most interesting aircraft of our day. Its wide fuselage can carry 2 helicopters or 2 heavy tanks or 10 *Pershing* missiles. Its range is over 6500 miles, which allows it to fly U.S.–Europe of U.S.–Japan nonstop. A commercial version, the *L-500-114C,* is now being offered on the market. It can carry between 63 and 111 automobiles at the same time.

den, 45 in Finland, 210 in Belgium, 135 in Holland, 200 in Greece, 310 in Turkey, 220 in Spain, 150 in Portugal, 315 in Switzerland, 340 in Yugoslavia, 70 in Albania and 13 in Austria.

Air-combat forces in Warsaw Pact countries are approximately the following: Bulgaria 290, Czechoslovakia 620, East Germany 275, Hungary 150, Poland 750.

And, finally, some other countries: Canada 280, Israel 330, United Arab Republic 415, Algeria 170, Iran 175, Iraq 230, Jordan 38, Lebanon 24, Syria 210, Japan 450, South Africa 240. Little is known about Red China's air force, but it is estimated that it has a force of about 3000 aircraft. From the survey above, which is obviously based on estimates and is by necessity incomplete, it is evident that the U.S. and Russia must be considered unique and apart: they are the only two countries

which have an intercontinental missile force; which need a strategic air force; which, due to their political commitments (one as leader of the free world, the other as leader of the Soviet bloc), must constantly strive to maintain their equilibrium in the delicate balance of power which up to now has been able to ensure peace.

As far as the aeronautics field is concerned, the era of the two superpowers, ushered in at the end of World War II, is by no means over and a change in the situation is not yet in sight unless, in the near future, China should truly attain a position as an international power, a position it seems she desires to obtain. Nevertheless, it is doubtful that she would be able to reach, even in the field of aviation, the quantitative and qualitative front positions presently held, all but unassailably, by the U.S. and the Soviet Union.

ANTONOV An-22 "COCK" (1967, USSR). Seen for the first time in 1969 at the Paris Air Exhibition, it is still the largest Russian transport aircraft. It is equipped with 4 turboprop engines and can transport about 176,000 pounds of cargo. The aircraft, which is long-range, is also used by Aeroflot.

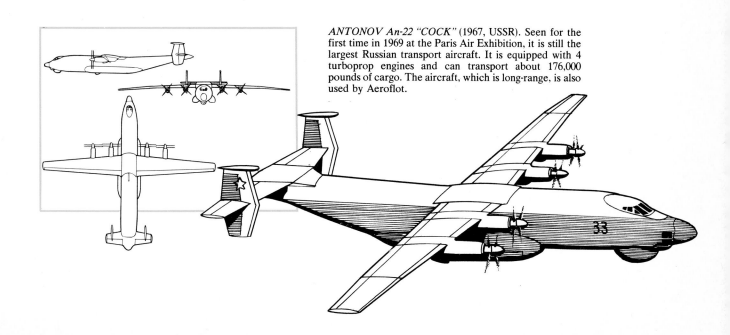

CIVIL AVIATION: TODAY

To the outsider, the field of civil aviation today must seem flourishing. Masses of people, in increasing numbers, use the airplane as a means of transportation as well as for the fun of it. Airports are always crowded and pulsate with frenetic activity; planes arriving and departing in every direction. Air travel has become not only easier but more comfortable than it was just a few short years ago. Take, for example, the new *Jumbos,* which have favorably impressed the public. Logically, we can speculate that the new giants of the air, the *Boeing 747*'s, have been adopted by so many companies because it was more economical and probably necessary to do so. To further confirm the outsider's opinion of the flourishing condition of commercial aviation, newspapers constantly report on the experimental flights of the first two supersonics (or *SST*'s) created for passenger transportation, the Anglo-French *Concorde* and the Russian *Tu-144.* French President Pompidou had the pleasure of making a preview flight on a *Concorde,* broadcasting from the plane's radio an enthusiastic affirmation of the results of the joint effort of the Anglo-French technicians. In the near future, passengers may be able to fly *SST*'s London to New York in 3 hours, thus bringing the world even closer together.

The rosy picture as seen by the man on the street is unfortunately further from the truth than one would imagine. Civil aviation and the aeronautics industry to which it is linked are passing through their most difficult times in many years.

Airlines are in difficult straits because they have had to invest substantial capital in new and larger aircraft without enjoying adequate passenger reservations to fill the seats on these new planes. Also, the progressive increase in maintenance costs has not been met either by a comparable increase in turnover or in air fares. The ever-growing competition among the airlines, especially on the more profitable routes, and the special "charter" flights have also contributed to the problem.

The market is dangerously saturated with aircraft which industry has been able to sell on wide markets. Generally the major airlines today own recently built units which can be profitably used for years to come and the troubled times do not encourage further heavy investment. Even the airports are in a state of crisis because such a large number of them are not able to adequately handle present-day needs (and therefore will be even less adequate for tomorrow's traffic) and have no room to expand in their present locations.

(continued on page 176)

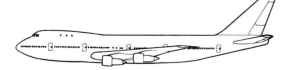

THE INSIGNIA OF THE MAJOR AIRLINE COMPANIES OF THE WORLD

Aer Lingus

Aeroflot

Air France

Alitalia

Austrian Airlines

ATI Aero Trasporti Italiani

BEA British European Airways

Finnair O/Y

Icelandair

Iberia

JAT Jugoslovenski Aerotransport

KLM Koninklijke Luchtvaart Maatschappij NV

LOT Polskie Linie Lotnicze

Swissair

TAP Transportes Aereos Portugueses

UTA Union de Transports Aériens

Air Canada

AA American Airlines

Braniff International

The Flying Tiger Line

Mohawk Airlines

National Airlines

New York Airways

Northwest Airlines

Pan American World Airways

AVIANCA Aerovias Nacionales de Colombia

BWIA British West Indian Airways

Servicos Aeros Cruzeiro do Sul

Empresa Consolidada Cubana de Aviacion

VARIG Empresa de Viacao Aerea Rio Grandense

LADECO Linea Aerea del Cobre

Air Congo

Air-Guinée

Air Malawi

Air Mali

COMAIR Commercial Airways

Ghana Airways

Libyan Arab Airlines

Nigeria Airways

SAA South African Airways

Sudan Airways

Suidwes Lugdiens

ALIA Royal Jordanian Airlines

CAL China Airlines

CAAC Civil Aviation Administration of China

EL AL Israel Airlines

Garuda Indonesia Airways

Indian Airlines

PAL Philippine Air Lines

SDI Saudi Arabian Airlines

Syrian Arab Airlines

THY Turk Hava Yollari

TMA Trans-Mediterranean Airways

Air New Zealand

BOAC British Overseas Airways Corp.

Balkan Bulgarian Air Transport

BUA British United Airways

CSA Ceskoslovenske Aerolinie

Cyprus Airways

Lúfthansa

MALEV Mayar Légiköz-lekédesi Vallalat

Malta Airways

Olympic Airways

SABENA
Sabena

SAS Scandinavian Airlines System

CP Air

CHA Chicago Helicopter Airways

Continental Air Lines

DELTA
AIR LINES
Delta Air Lines

Eastern Air Lines

EPA Eastern Provincial Airways

Quebecair

Seaboard World Airlines

TWA Transworld Airlines

UNITED
United Air Lines

Aerolineas Argentinas

Aeronaves de Mexico

Linea Aerea Nacional de Chile

VASP
VASP Viacao Aerea Sao Paulo

VIASA Venezolana Internacional de Aviacion

Air Afrique

Air Algérie

DETA Direccao de Exploracao dos Transportes Aéreos

DTA-Angola Airlines

EAA East African Airways

Ethiopian Airlines

Tunis Air

United Arab Airlines

Zambia Airways

Air Ceylon

Air-India

Air Vietnam

Iran Air

Iraqi Airways

JAL
Japan Air Lines

Kuwait Airways

Middle East Airlines Airliban

PIA
PIA Pakistan International Airlines

Ansett Airlines of Australia

NAC
NAC New Zealand National Airways

Qantas Airways

TAA
TAA Trans-Australia Airlines

IATA
IATA International Air Transport Association

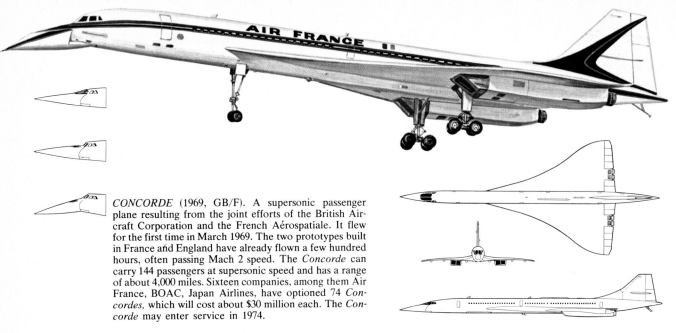

CONCORDE (1969, GB/F). A supersonic passenger plane resulting from the joint efforts of the British Aircraft Corporation and the French Aérospatiale. It flew for the first time in March 1969. The two prototypes built in France and England have already flown a few hundred hours, often passing Mach 2 speed. The *Concorde* can carry 144 passengers at supersonic speed and has a range of about 4,000 miles. Sixteen companies, among them Air France, BOAC, Japan Airlines, have optioned 74 *Concordes,* which will cost about $30 million each. The *Concorde* may enter service in 1974.

The problem of the commercial supersonic arises in the midst of a situation which in itself is problematic. Yet the advent of the supersonic is so important and pressing that it must be examined closely.

Ever since the introduction of jet engines in civil aviation, it was thought that a passenger supersonic was the inevitable next step. Supersonic flight was already an established fact in military aviation and it was taken for granted that in today's frenetic world civil aviation too would feel the same need for it. American industry, leader of the international commercial air travel market since the end of the War (90 percent of the jets in service today in the Western world are U.S. built), and fully satisfied with the good business it did selling existing long- and medium-range models, was reluctant to rush into change. French and British industry, on the other hand, aimed at being the first to market

a supersonic passenger aircraft in order to earn for themselves a share of the American world market. Private financing would have been totally insufficient to carry out such a project and therefore the French and British governments, on November 29, 1962, signed an agreement for a joint effort to manufacture the *Concorde,* leaving its realization to the British Aircraft Corporation and the state-owned French industry now known as Aerospatiale. The construction of the prototypes, one in England and one in France, began in February 1965: the *Concorde 001* flew for the first time on March 2, 1969, the *002* on April 9 of the same year. By now the two aircraft have successfully flown many hundreds of hours, reaching the maximum expected speed of about Mach 2.2. Many small technical problems are still to be resolved, but the *Concorde,* this giant which to date has cost about $1.78 billion could shortly be mass-

The silhouettes of the *Concorde* (red), the *Tupolev Tu-144* (black) and the American *Boeing SST* (blue). Note the similarity of design and size between the first 2, which carry, respectively, 144 and 121 passengers. The *SST* was to carry more than double that number of passengers on distances 1½ times longer than those foreseen for European aircraft.

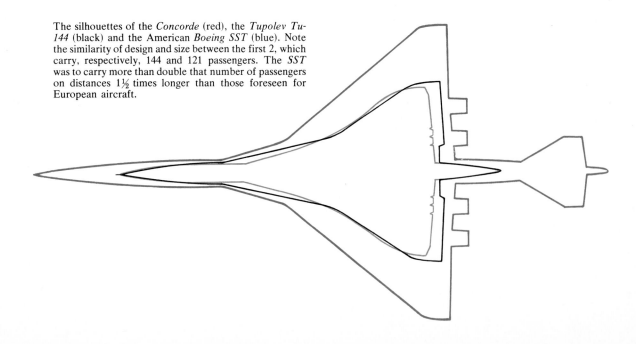

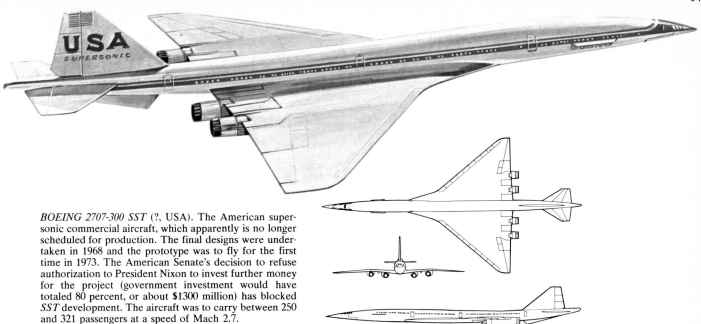

BOEING 2707-300 SST (?, USA). The American supersonic commercial aircraft, which apparently is no longer scheduled for production. The final designs were undertaken in 1968 and the prototype was to fly for the first time in 1973. The American Senate's decision to refuse authorization to President Nixon to invest further money for the project (government investment would have totaled 80 percent, or about $1300 million) has blocked *SST* development. The aircraft was to carry between 250 and 321 passengers at a speed of Mach 2.7.

produced and enter service around 1975.

Nevertheless, even before the *Concorde 001* took off from French soil, another civilian supersonic had earned the title of "first": the Russian *Tu-144,* designed by a group of technicians headed by Andrei Nikolaevich Tupolev. It flew for the first time on December 31, 1968. Since U.S.-Russian tension has been easing since 1965, the Soviet aeronautics industry could realistically plan on entering the international aviation market sooner or later. A civilian supersonic would be the obvious choice, especially as there would be no competition from the U.S. in this field. The Russian state-controlled aviation industry had no problem as far as capital investment was concerned, because the enterprise would be a great propaganda "plus" and it also knew that a certain number of aircraft would, at any rate, be absorbed by Aeroflot, also under state ownership. Thus today the

Tu-144 is also flying. Displayed for the first time at the Paris Air Exhibition, it is probably just about ready to reach the assembly lines.

The United States has been the last to act in the field of commercial supersonics. When, nonetheless, government and industry realized that the English and French on the one hand and the Russians on the other were in earnest, they gave the go-ahead to a project which, though it would reach the market some years later, would be much more economical and advanced. The American aircraft would have been able to transport more than double the number of passengers and to fly at higher speeds and for longer distances than the European model. The American choice proved to be a good one, for when on December 31, 1966, the American government approved the *Boeing 2707-300 SST* project, the company received over 122 options from 26 airlines, among these TWA, Pan

TUPOLEV Tu-144 "CHARGER" (1968, USSR). This Russian supersonic passenger aircraft flew for the first time on December 31, 1968, earlier than the *Concorde*. In May 1969 during one of its test flights it flew over Mach 2. Its normal cruising speed, with 121 passengers aboard, should be about Mach 2.3. The *Tu-144* should be ready to enter service for Aeroflot about the end of 1974. Today, with the American project seemingly blocked, Soviet aeronautic industries hope to furnish an alternative and a rival for the *Concorde* on the international market. The *Tu-144* should cost $5 million less than the Anglo-French supersonic.

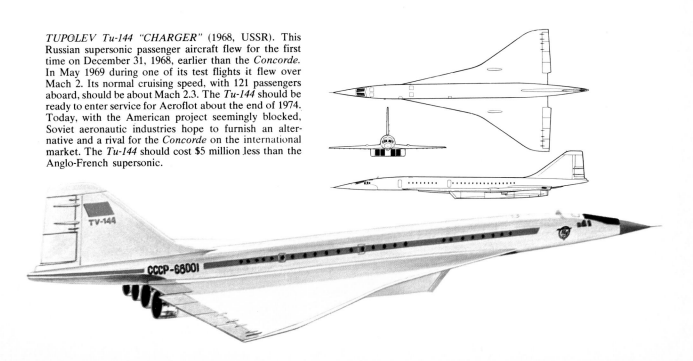

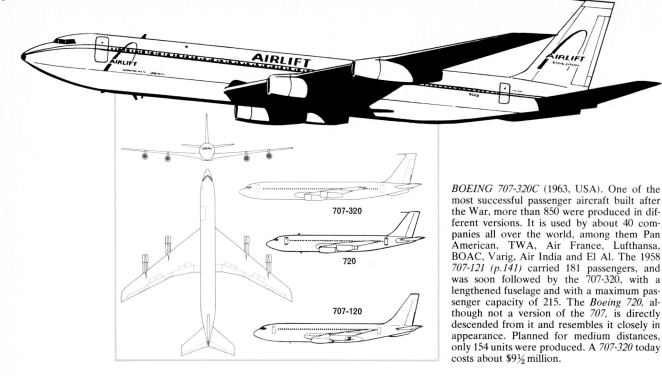

BOEING 707-320C (1963, USA). One of the most successful passenger aircraft built after the War, more than 850 were produced in different versions. It is used by about 40 companies all over the world, among them Pan American, TWA, Air France, Lufthansa, BOAC, Varig, Air India and El Al. The 1958 *707-121 (p.141)* carried 181 passengers, and was soon followed by the 707-320, with a lengthened fuselage and with a maximum passenger capacity of 215. The *Boeing 720,* although not a version of the *707,* is directly descended from it and resembles it closely in appearance. Planned for medium distances, only 154 units were produced. A *707-320* today costs about $9½ million.

American, American Airlines, Alitalia, Air France, BOAC and KLM. These 122 options, put in five years before the actual flight of the prototype, are quite substantial in number, especially in comparison to the 74 for the *Concorde,* which should become operative a few years earlier and which are far less costly. The price is $21 million, compared to $35 million for the American *SST.*

Therefore, in spite of the delay, the Americans should have again been able to guarantee their supremacy in the field of civil aviation. The total investment for building the two prototypes would have reached over $1.5 billion, $1.285 billion of which would have been provided by the U.S. government. Plans

proceeded swiftly and the two prototypes, which were to make their first flights in 1973, were about to enter the construction phase when, on March 24, 1971, the U.S. Senate rejected, by 51 to 46, President Nixon's proposal to award Boeing the $300 million needed for 1971–72. This was the death rattle for the American supersonic, for it proved impossible to find the necessary funding from private sources. Unless the policy changes in the future, the American *SST* will not be built.

The U.S. Senate's decision signaled the end of a fierce battle which had divided public opinion and politicians for many months. Senator Henry M. Jackson, who had led sup-

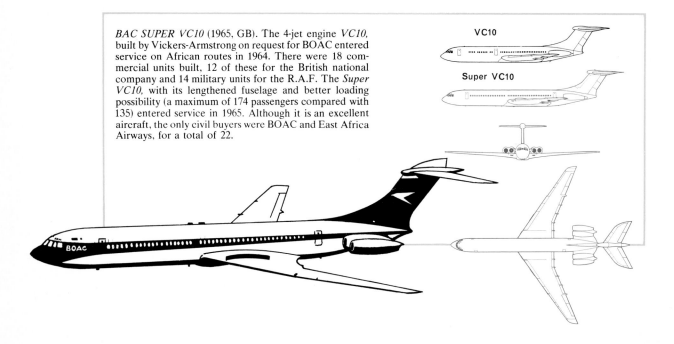

BAC SUPER VC10 (1965, GB). The 4-jet engine *VC10,* built by Vickers-Armstrong on request for BOAC entered service on African routes in 1964. There were 18 commercial units built, 12 of these for the British national company and 14 military units for the R.A.F. The *Super VC10,* with its lengthened fuselage and better loading possibility (a maximum of 174 passengers compared with 135) entered service in 1965. Although it is an excellent aircraft, the only civil buyers were BOAC and East Africa Airways, for a total of 22.

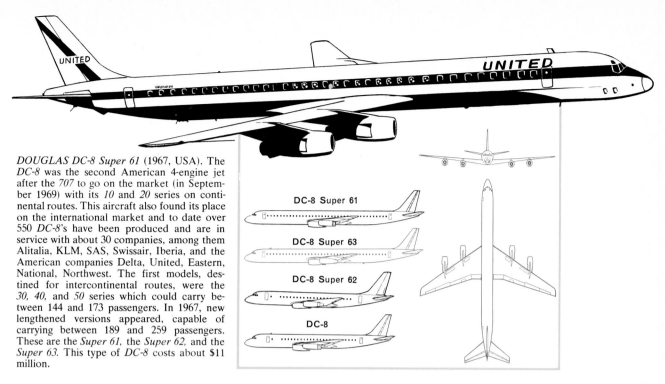

DOUGLAS DC-8 Super 61 (1967, USA). The *DC-8* was the second American 4-engine jet after the *707* to go on the market (in September 1969) with its *10* and *20* series on continental routes. This aircraft also found its place on the international market and to date over 550 *DC-8*'s have been produced and are in service with about 30 companies, among them Alitalia, KLM, SAS, Swissair, Iberia, and the American companies Delta, United, Eastern, National, Northwest. The first models, destined for intercontinental routes, were the *30, 40,* and *50* series which could carry between 144 and 173 passengers. In 1967, new lengthened versions appeared, capable of carrying between 189 and 259 passengers. These are the *Super 61,* the *Super 62,* and the *Super 63.* This type of *DC-8* costs about $11 million.

port for the project, commented on the defeat by saying he believed in good conscience that it was a vote against science and technology. His opponents, on the other hand, applauded the decision, stating that finally the United States had showed good sense by refusing to squander public funds which the nation could use for more urgent matters and had avoided in the name of so-called "progress" further damage to mankind from ultrasonic *"boom"* and air pollution from the exhaust fumes of the powerful supersonic engines.

The opponents of the *SST* insist they are trying to preserve the atmosphere not only by stopping production of an unnecessary plane

that would burden the American taxpayer but also by forbidding supersonic aircraft, regardless of their origin, to fly at supersonic speed over American territory or to land at American airports because the noise level would be greater than what are considered acceptable limits and because of atmospheric pollution. This position appears in a proposed law now on its way to being approved by various state legislatures. This action could condemn not only the American supersonic (which seems almost certain) but also the European supersonic.

Obviously, the most interesting and profitable route for the major airlines is the North Atlantic, and severe restrictions on use of

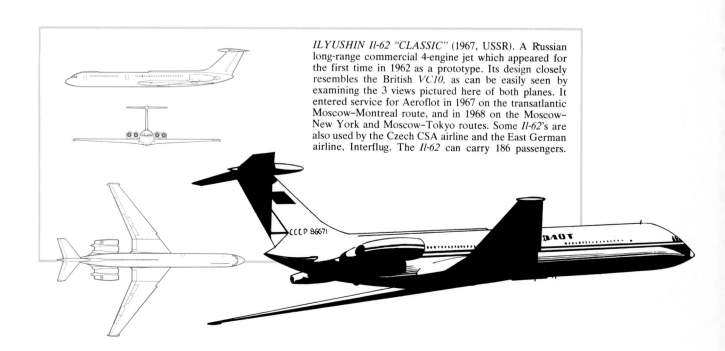

ILYUSHIN Il-62 "CLASSIC" (1967, USSR). A Russian long-range commercial 4-engine jet which appeared for the first time in 1962 as a prototype. Its design closely resembles the British *VC10,* as can be easily seen by examining the 3 views pictured here of both planes. It entered service for Aeroflot in 1967 on the transatlantic Moscow–Montreal route, and in 1968 on the Moscow–New York and Moscow–Tokyo routes. Some *Il-62*'s are also used by the Czech CSA airline and the East German airline, Interflug. The *Il-62* can carry 186 passengers.

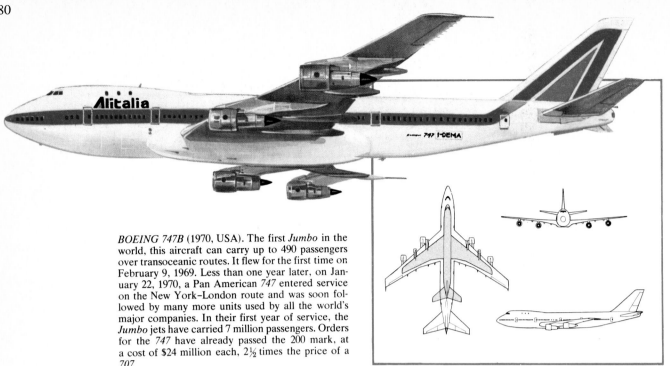

BOEING 747B (1970, USA). The first *Jumbo* in the world, this aircraft can carry up to 490 passengers over transoceanic routes. It flew for the first time on February 9, 1969. Less than one year later, on January 22, 1970, a Pan American *747* entered service on the New York–London route and was soon followed by many more units used by all the world's major companies. In their first year of service, the *Jumbo* jets have carried 7 million passengers. Orders for the *747* have already passed the 200 mark, at a cost of $24 million each, $2\frac{1}{2}$ times the price of a *707*.

American airports might conceivably convince these companies not to order the *Concorde*.

Aside from the high-minded and perhaps justified declarations of the environmentalists, undoubtedly the supersonic does present a number of problems, as its advocates themselves have realized: the noise level at take-off and landing; the "boom," which is the sound produced by an aircraft flying over the sound barrier (if the plane flies at an altitude of 65,600 feet, the boom can be heard for a ground radius of between 31 and 62 miles), and, last but not least, air pollution caused by the engines' exhaust fumes.

Technicians point out that the airport noise created by a supersonic is no greater than that of a *DC-8* and that the boom could be avoided by using supersonic speed only over the ocean. This would mean that the supersonic would at times fly at subsonic speed; notwithstanding, it would still be useful and economical since it is faster than today's aircraft. As far as air pollution is concerned, defenders of the supersonic insist that the situation would not worsen since the engines could be equipped with filters, although this will diminish engine power and increase production and maintenance costs.

The issue is still open and it is still too early to say who will have the last word and whether there will be a long wait before we enter the age of passenger supersonics.

Quite possibly the first, and perhaps the

LOCKHEED L-1011 TRISTAR (1971, USA). Lockheed's return to the construction of passenger aircraft with this large-capacity 3-engine jet has been made difficult by the financial difficulties of Rolls-Royce, which produced the engines. Today the problem seems to have been ameliorated and 175 *Tristar*s have been ordered by Eastern, Delta, Northwest, TWA and other American companies. These *Tristar*s will probably become formidable rivals of the *747*'s. The aircraft costs about $18 million, and can carry up to 345 passengers across the U.S.

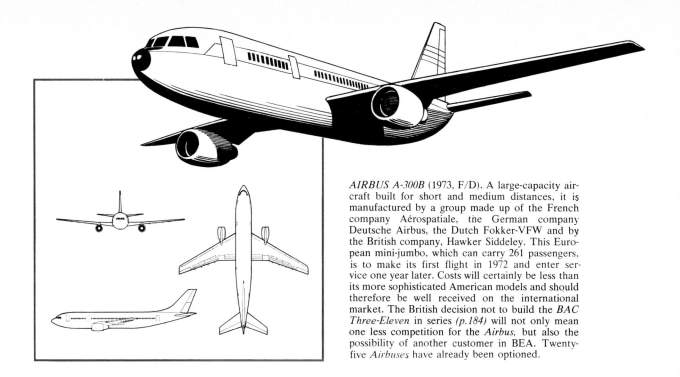

AIRBUS A-300B (1973, F/D). A large-capacity air-craft built for short and medium distances, it is manufactured by a group made up of the French company Aérospatiale, the German company Deutsche Airbus, the Dutch Fokker-VFW and by the British company, Hawker Siddeley. This European mini-jumbo, which can carry 261 passengers, is to make its first flight in 1972 and enter service one year later. Costs will certainly be less than its more sophisticated American models and should therefore be well received on the international market. The British decision not to build the *BAC Three-Eleven in series (p.184)* will not only mean one less competition for the *Airbus,* but also the possibility of another customer in BEA. Twenty-five *Airbuses* have already been optioned.

only, supersonic to enter service will be the Russian one, because of the previously mentioned political reasons and because of the fact that once in service on the Moscow–Tokyo route the aircraft will by flying over practically deserted areas while reducing flight time from 10 to 4 hours—an important advantage. Passenger traffic on this route, however, is so sparse that it is in no way comparable to North Atlantic traffic.

It is very hard to say whether or not the airlines regret not being able to use the supersonic too quickly, As far as the U.S. is concerned, as soon as one of the larger airlines purchased the supersonic, all the other companies would automatically have to follow suit. By the same token, if any one com-

pany should purchase the supersonic for its North Atlantic route, even with a fare increase, all other airlines would have to do so too, so as not to yield an edge in competition which has become even keener in the last few years. But would the airlines have the capital to enlarge their present fleets with the new aircraft?

As previously mentioned, 1970—in spite of the 386 million passengers flown (including the Soviet Union) in comparison to 358 million in 1969—was one of the blackest years in civil aviation. For the first time in a long while, 6 of the major American internal and international route carriers such as United Airlines, TWA, Braniff, National Airlines, Northeast Airlines, and Pan American, have

DOUGLAS DC-10 (1971, USA). It is considered the *Tristar*'s great rival. Like the *Tristar* it is a 3-engine jet, can carry 345 passengers and costs $18 million. Furthermore, it carries the name of Douglas, a definite guarantee of experience in the field of passenger planes. The first version, the *Sr-10,* is for short- and medium-distance flights. The second, the *Sr-20,* is built for intercontinental traffic. The *DC-10,* which has already entered service, has been ordered in over 200 units by American Airlines, National, Northwest, Alitalia, KLM, SAS, Swissair and numerous other companies.

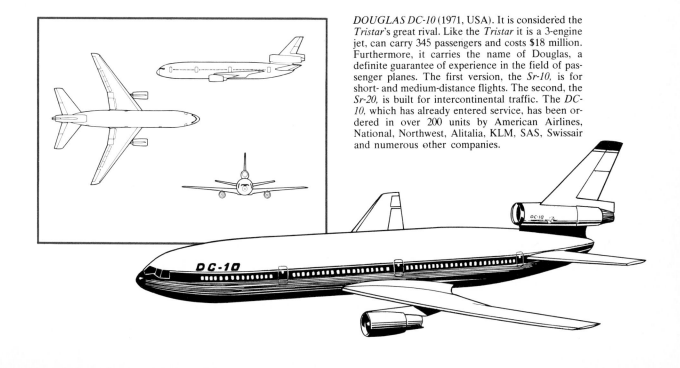

lost substantial sums of money, a total of $192.5 million. Other American companies have shown a general over-all decrease in profits, as have BEA and BOAC and many other European companies.

The advent of the *747,* the first of the new *Jumbo* generation with a large passenger capacity, has revolutionized the market and is partially responsible for the present financial state of affairs, along with the world's generally troubled economic situation. It can be stated as a fact that the over 1000 airlines in existence today would prefer not to repeat the year 1970, particularly those 104 companies which serve international routes and which belong to I.A.T.A. (International Air Transport Association).

I.A.T.A. was created after the Second World War as a free association of airlines whose aim was to promote, in its words, safe, regular and economical air transportation to benefit all people, to encourage air commerce and to study its related problems; to find means of cooperation between airlines directly or indirectly involved with international air transport; to cooperate with the International Civil Aviation Organization and other international organizations.

The international goals of the International Civil Aviation Organization (I.C.A.O.) must also be mentioned. I.C.A.O. is one of the United Nations Agencies whose goal is to promote the safe and orderly development of international civil, commercial and private aviation by establishing equal conditions for all member nations; to set international standards for the safety, dependability and regularity of aircraft navigation; to encourage the economic development of aviation; to reduce and simplify customs, immigration, currency exchange and sanitary procedures at international airports and, finally, to promote the continuous evolution of international aeronautic regulations and laws. It was only on October 15, 1970, that the U.S.S.R. decided to become a member of I.C.A.O., joining the other 120 member nations (but not including the People's Republic of China). This was an extremely important decision, which forced Aeroflot and the entire Soviet civil aviation system to follow the norms and regulations already in force and rigidly respected by most of the nations of the world. It should be remembered that Aeroflot not only manages passenger airlines (on a 372,000-mile network, one quarter of the world's international routes), but has numerous other duties, such as land cultivation, aerial surveillance for fire prevention in over 700 million hectares of forest land, civilian air rescue, etc. Its membership in I.C.A.O. will facilitate agreements between airlines of different nations and the Russian government for opening new routes and for the concession of transit and stopover privileges on Soviet territory in exchange for such rights for Aeroflot.

Soviet membership in I.A.T.A. is not held to be as urgent as its membership in I.C.A.O., at least not until it obtains routes which directly compete with those of the present members. One of the major problems which

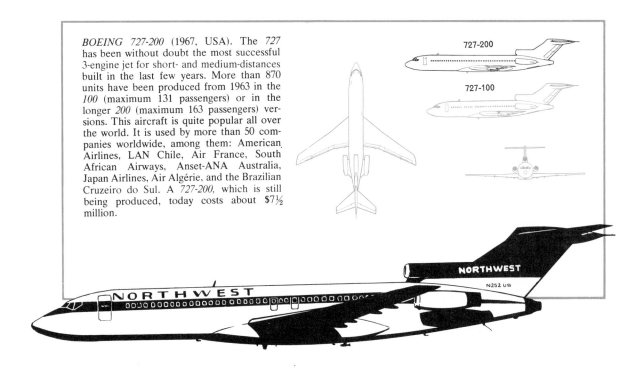

BOEING 727-200 (1967, USA). The *727* has been without doubt the most successful 3-engine jet for short- and medium-distances built in the last few years. More than 870 units have been produced from 1963 in the *100* (maximum 131 passengers) or in the longer *200* (maximum 163 passengers) versions. This aircraft is quite popular all over the world. It is used by more than 50 companies worldwide, among them: American Airlines, LAN Chile, Air France, South African Airways, Anset-ANA Australia, Japan Airlines, Air Algérie, and the Brazilian Cruzeiro do Sul. A *727-200,* which is still being produced, today costs about $7½ million.

727-200

727-100

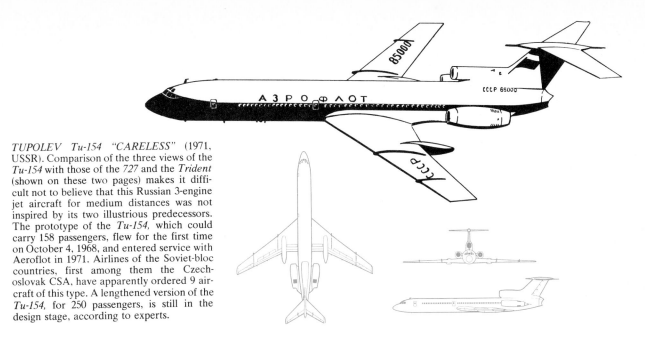

TUPOLEV Tu-154 "CARELESS" (1971, USSR). Comparison of the three views of the *Tu-154* with those of the *727* and the *Trident* (shown on these two pages) makes it difficult not to believe that this Russian 3-engine jet aircraft for medium distances was not inspired by its two illustrious predecessors. The prototype of the *Tu-154,* which could carry 158 passengers, flew for the first time on October 4, 1968, and entered service with Aeroflot in 1971. Airlines of the Soviet-bloc countries, first among them the Czechoslovak CSA, have apparently ordered 9 aircraft of this type. A lengthened version of the *Tu-154,* for 250 passengers, is still in the design stage, according to experts.

must be solved within I.A.T.A. itself is establishing unanimously approved air fares, which will then supposedly guarantee that the member nations will honor the established fares. Naturally each company's interests differ according to size, nationality and whether the stock is government or privately owned. To date, a compromise acceptable to all has somehow always been found within I.A.T.A.

The question at issue now, for example, is: since most airlines are equipped with aircraft of greater seating capacity, would it be advisable to reduce air fares in order to increase passenger volume or would it be better to retain present fares even if insufficient to cover

the increased maintenance and operating costs? Some have even suggested a fare increase in order to balance the higher operating costs. It is generally felt that in spite of the many problems and opposition, fares will shortly be reduced, especially on the North Atlantic route. As a matter of fact, the cost of a ticket on the North Atlantic route has progressivly decreased as seating capacity has increased, flight time has been shortened, and aircraft have enlarged their cargo capacity.

In 1946 a *Douglas DC-4* (80 passengers) flew Rome to New York at 225 miles per hour cruising speed, completing the flight in 17 hours flying time with two stopovers; in 1951 a *Super Constellation* (99 passengers) flying at

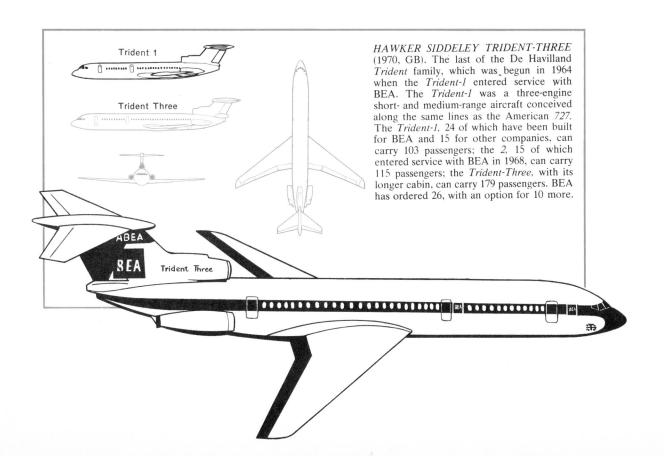

Trident 1

Trident Three

HAWKER SIDDELEY TRIDENT-THREE (1970, GB). The last of the De Havilland *Trident* family, which was begun in 1964 when the *Trident-1* entered service with BEA. The *Trident-1* was a three-engine short- and medium-range aircraft conceived along the same lines as the American *727.* The *Trident-1,* 24 of which have been built for BEA and 15 for other companies, can carry 103 passengers; the *2,* 15 of which entered service with BEA in 1968, can carry 115 passengers; the *Trident-Three,* with its longer cabin, can carry 179 passengers. BEA has ordered 26, with an option for 10 more.

184

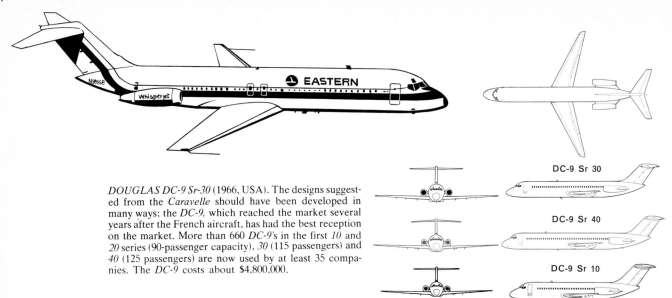

DOUGLAS DC-9 Sr-30 (1966, USA). The designs suggested from the *Caravelle* should have been developed in many ways; the *DC-9,* which reached the market several years after the French aircraft, has had the best reception on the market. More than 660 *DC-9's* in the first *10* and *20* series (90-passenger capacity), *30* (115 passengers) and *40* (125 passengers) are now used by at least 35 companies. The *DC-9* costs about $4,800,000.

DC-9 Sr 30

DC-9 Sr 40

DC-9 Sr 10

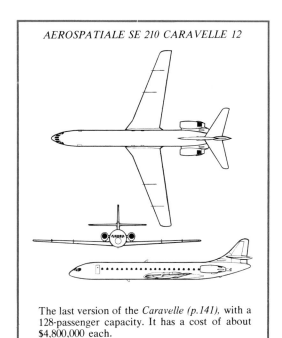

AEROSPATIALE SE 210 CARAVELLE 12

The last version of the *Caravelle (p.141),* with a 128-passenger capacity. It has a cost of about $4,800,000 each.

340 miles per hour completed the same flight in 11½ hours with one stopover; in 1961 a *Douglas DC-8* (150 passengers) flying at 590 miles per hour made the flight nonstop in 7 hours; and in 1971 a *Boeing 747* (400 passengers) flying at 680 miles per hour made it nonstop in 6½ hours. Obviously air transportation has changed to the extent of allowing for cheaper fares which, as long as there is a reasonable number of passengers, will mean profit for the airlines in spite of the increase in investment and operating costs.

One reason some companies have been willing to reduce fares as much as possible is the competition offered for some years now by charter flights. Of course charter companies, which fly only if the aircraft is full—that is, with the guarantee that expenses will be met and a profit made on each trip—can offer lower fares than companies which run regular schedules and must therefore see to it that a *DC-8* takes off on a scheduled transatlantic flight although there may be few-

BAC ONE-ELEVEN Sr 200 (1965, GB). One of the most successful English jets. Mainly for the international market, 200 units were built. The *One-Eleven,* in fact, was not immediately used by BEA and the most important initial buyers were American Airlines (30 aircraft), Braniff International Airways (14), Mohawk Airlines (18). The British flag company has bought only 18 *One-Eleven's* from the *500* series, which with a lengthened fuselage, can carry 119 passengers instead of 89. The *Three-Eleven,* designed for 220 passengers, apparently will not be mass-produced.

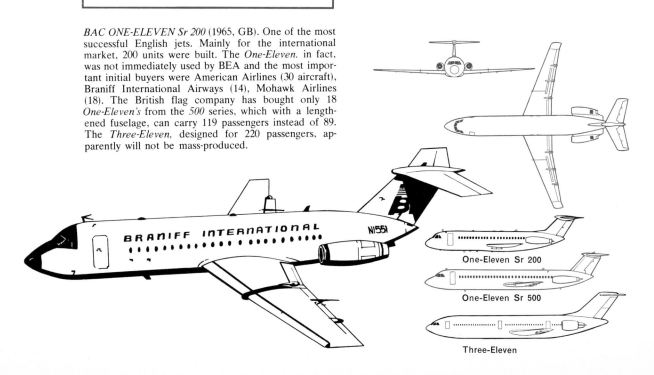

One-Eleven Sr 200

One-Eleven Sr 500

Three-Eleven

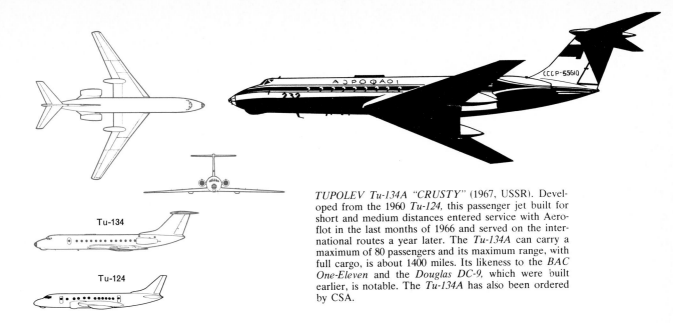

TUPOLEV Tu-134A "CRUSTY" (1967, USSR). Developed from the 1960 *Tu-124,* this passenger jet built for short and medium distances entered service with Aeroflot in the last months of 1966 and served on the international routes a year later. The *Tu-134A* can carry a maximum of 80 passengers and its maximum range, with full cargo, is about 1400 miles. Its likeness to the *BAC One-Eleven* and the *Douglas DC-9,* which were built earlier, is notable. The *Tu-134A* has also been ordered by CSA.

Tu-134

Tu-124

er than 10 passengers aboard. For passengers who travel for business, or even for the tourist who can afford it, regular airlines offer, among other advantages, regular flights, but the disadvantage of the uncertainty of charter flights is overlooked by many tourists because of the charter's lower fares.

This is why I.A.T.A. members are trying to set up a program of advantageous tourist rates (14 to 21 days, for passengers under 26 years of age) which will enable them to compete with the charters which, in turn, must meet international standards that guarantee passenger safety. In other words, when aircraft used on charter flights are no longer new, which is ever more often the case, they must meet the standards of all I.C.A.O. and other regulatory agencies anyway.

In 1970, jet planes used by civil airlines the world over, except for Aeroflot and the People's Republic of China lines, totaled about 4000 while turboprops numbered at least 2000. The major airlines have fleets made

(continued on page 188)

DASSAULT MERCURE

A short-distance mini-jumbo, with 155-passenger capacity, it should enter service in 1973.

BOEING 737-200 (1967, USA). A 2-engine jet which can carry 115 passengers (the *100* series) or 125 passengers, built for short distances and designed by Boeing in 1965. For reasons of economy, many components of the *Boeing 727 (p.182)* were utilized for this model as well. It began service in 1967 and more than 280 *737's* have already been delivered to at least 30 companies which include Lufthansa (22), Piedmont Airlines (12), United Airlines (75), Western Airlines (30) and many other minor companies such as Air California, Malaya-Singapore Airlines, etc. A *737* costs about $4,800,000.

737-100

737-200

AIR CALIFORNIA

MINOR CIVIL AIRCRAFT AND "EXECUTIVE" JETS

In this survey we present aircraft that are still in service but close to being dropped by the large airline companies: the short-range airmobiles which complement the large airplanes, and those which constitute the standard equipment of lesser compaines' fleets; and lastly, the jet-engine planes used by business executives, the "businessmen's jets."

The *Convair 990 Coronados* belong to the first group. A few of these were built and were used in Europe only by Swissair. Others of the first type: Aeroflot's *Ilyushin Il-18E* and the *Handley Page Herald* of which only a few were produced and which was beaten in the market place by the *Fokker F.27 (p.188)*.

The third group includes the *Mystère 20,* the *HS-125,* the *North American Rockwell Sabreliner,* the *Grumman Gulfstream II (p.192, 193),* the *Lockheed 1329 Jetstar* (the only 4-engine executive jet), the brand new *HFB-320 Hansa,* the *IAI Commodore* (new version of the *Aero Commander Jet Commander* of the 1965 built now in Israel), the *Learjet 24D,* (one of the less-expensive models), the *Cessna 500 Citation* and the *Aérospatiale SN 600 Corvette.* The last 2 have only recently appeared on the market.

Among the executive jets, that is, those used by large companies for their executives and technicians, are the *Handley Page Jetstream* and the *Yak-40.* The latter, upon its debut, caused a slight sensation, but like the *Fokker F.28* and the *VFW-614,* it is actually more suited for regular short-distance airline traffic.

All the other aircraft presented here are ideal for use by so-called "third-level carriers," which schedule connecting flights between small cities and the nearest airports that service major airlines. Usually they make trips of under 100 miles, and their seating capacity is necessarily limited. In the last few years these small companies have multiplied, growing from 12 with 70 aircraft in 1964 to over 350 with 2000 planes today. Most are to be found in the U.S. where, of the 9000 airports operating today, only 500 service the larger airline companies.

Today the aeronautics industry is creating aircraft expressly to meet the needs of these companies. Such planes include the *Swearingen Metro,* the *Short Skyvan,* the *Beechcraft 99A* or the *Britten-Norman Islander (p.190).* The Canadian *DHC-7* deserves special mention for its silent engines and its takeoff and short-landing features. It may prove to be the first of a new generation of aircraft for short-range traffic between cities equipped with new and special airports, created in an attempt to reduce travel time and offer some relief to the main airports from the crisis of overcrowding.

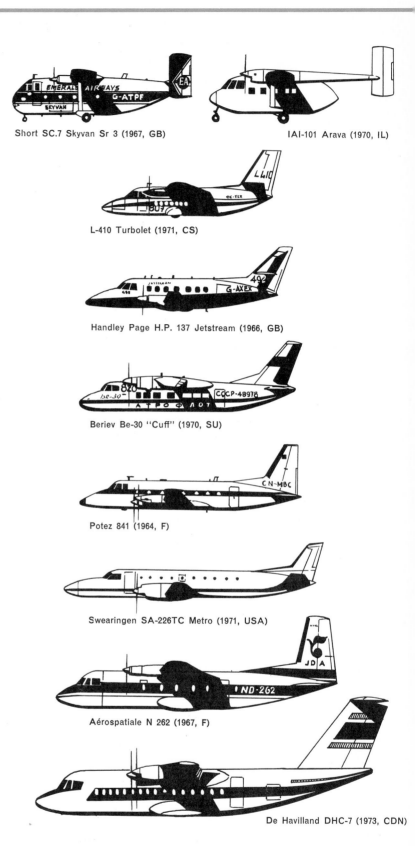

Short SC.7 Skyvan Sr 3 (1967, GB)

IAI-101 Arava (1970, IL)

L-410 Turbolet (1971, CS)

Handley Page H.P. 137 Jetstream (1966, GB)

Beriev Be-30 "Cuff" (1970, SU)

Potez 841 (1964, F)

Swearingen SA-226TC Metro (1971, USA)

Aérospatiale N 262 (1967, F)

De Havilland DHC-7 (1973, CDN)

Yakovlev Yak-40 "Codling" (1967, SU)

VF W-Fokker VFW 614 (1973, D)

Fokker F-28 Mk 1000 Fellowship (1969, NL)

Hawker Siddeley 748 Sr 1 (1962, GB)

Handley Page H.P.R. 7 Herald (1960, GB)

Ilyushin Il-18E "Coot" (1959, SU)

Lockheed 1329 Jetstar (1961, USA)

MBB HFB 320 Hansa (1966, D)

IAI Commodore Jet 1123 (1971, IL)

Learjet 24D (1966, USA)

Cessna 500 Citation (1971, USA)

Aérospatiale SN 600 Corvette (1971, F)

Convair 990 Coronado (1960, USA)

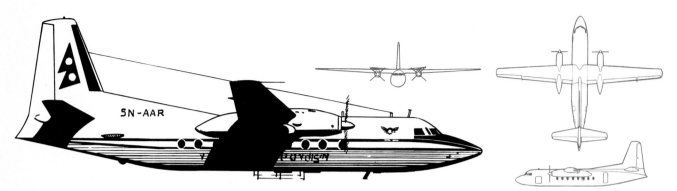

FOKKER F.27 FRIENDSHIP (1958, NL). Over 70 companies all over the world use the F.27, a passenger turboprop which has been in production since 1958 and which is certainly one of the most successful of its kind. Economical and safe, it can carry a maximum of 52 passengers in its most recent versions. It has proven unrivaled and invaluable on short-distance routes, over which the DC-3 had reigned supreme at the end of the War. Over 500 F.17's have come off the as sembly line. They cost about $1,400,000.

up exclusively of jets even for short and medium distances.

More than ⅓ of the 4000 jets are 4-engine aircraft used in long-distance flights: *Boeing 707*'s (over 700), *Douglas DC-8*'s (about 600), *BAC VC10*'s and *Super VC10*'s and about 200 brand new *Boeing 747*'s. The first *747* entered service on January 21, 1970, and was soon followed by others. In the first 12 months of flight, *Jumbos,* which have been purchased by all major airlines, broke all records by completing 30,000 scheduled flights and transporting 7 million passengers with no accidents of any consequence. In the near future more *747*'s, *707*'s and *DC-8*'s in the new stretched versions will enter service on long-distance routes.

There are also about 1000 3-jet aircraft, mainly *Boeing 727*'s (over 750) used on medi-

um-distance flights. Nevertheless an increase in the number of 3-engine jet planes, of the new *Jumbo* type, is foreseen. They will include such aircraft as the *Douglas DC-10* and the *Lockheed L-1011 Tristar.* The *Lockheed L-1011 Tristar* has endured so many setbacks and delivery is so late that some of the 174 orders placed since the project was announced have already been canceled. The principal reason for the delay has been the bankruptcy of the Rolls-Royce company which was to furnish the new *RB 211* engines, followed by subsequent subsidies from the British Government. The contract for these engines quoted a price of $575,000 each, a price which proved to be far below their actual cost. The contract has been modified, but the situation is still fluid. The *DC-10* will probably benefit from the situation,

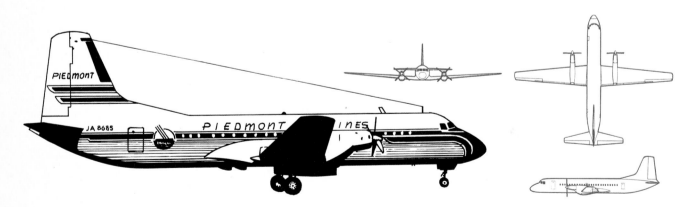

NAMC YS-11 Sr-200 (1964, J). The first Japanese passenger aircraft to be exported, it has been adopted by Piedmont Airlines in the U.S., by Cruzeiro do Sul in Brazil, and by Olympic Airways in Greece, as well as by many other companies. This turboprop, 200 units of which have been produced, flew for the first time in 1962 and entered service for All Nippon Airways in 1964. In 1970 the NAMC presented a new all cargo version requested by the Japanese Military Air Force.

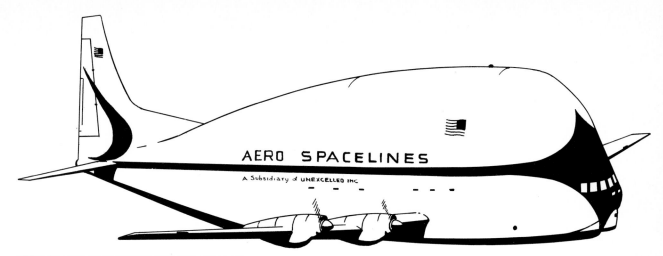

AERO SPACELINES GUPPY-201 (1971, USA). The most recent of the new enormous aircraft built to carry special cargoes, it was built utilizing the bottom part of the fuselage, the wings and tail of the *B-377* and parts of other planes. In order to load and carry cargo, the front of the plane opens 110 degrees. At present it transports sections of *DC-10's* fuselage, measuring about 20 feet in diameter from the Convair factory in San Diego to McDonnell-Douglas in Long Beach, California.

attracting buyers which might have purchased a *Tristar.*

The remaining jets are short-distance 2-engine craft: the *Douglas DC-9* (over 650), the *Aérospatiale Caravelle* (about 250), the *BAC One-Eleven* (less than 200), the *Boeing 737* (less than 300), etc.

The future evidently belongs to these aircraft, which will be joined by the *Airbus 300* and the *Dassault Mercure.* The giant planes will predominate: *747, DC-10, Tristar, Airbus 300,* which offer greater transport capacity than the jet aircraft of what might be called the "first generation." This should allow not only for more economical transportation, but also in the immediate future for a reduction in the overwhelmingly stepped-up number of takeoffs and landings at major airports that are such a safety hazard now.

In fact, if greater-capacity aircraft are not adopted to meet the anticipated and hoped-for increase in passenger travel, the number of flights will have to be multiplied. This would bring an already precarious situation of air traffic and airport control to a head, causing a long-term crisis. Airports, though they have continuously enlarged and expanded during the last few years, no longer have the physical space to accommodate new runways and further improvements. The larger aircraft have necessitated longer runways; the greater number of passengers carried by one plane requires changes in the airport's physical layout, from customs areas to the waiting rooms, from the baggage loading and unloading facilities to facilities such as bars, restaurants, etc. For better or for worse, this has been as true in New York as in Rome, in

(continued on page 192)

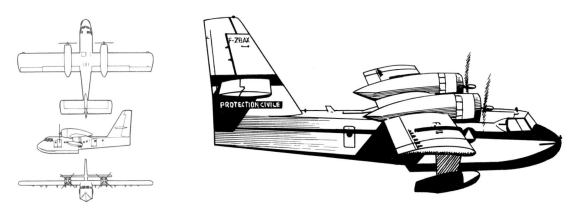

CANADAIR CL-215 (1969, CDN). An interesting amphibian 2-engine aircraft which can be put to many uses and which has become quite successful, mainly as a fire-fighting plane. The province of Quebec has already ordered 15 *CL-215's* to be used to fight forest fires; 10 have been ordered by the French Protection Civile which uses them along the French Riviera to fight fires. The Canadair *CL-215* can also be used as a cargo or passenger aircraft and can carry as many as 19 people.

Moravan Zlin Z526F (1947, CS)

Robin DR 221 Dauphin (1967, F)

SAN Jodel D.140E Mousquetaire IV (1958, F)

Socata MS 893 Rallye Commodore (1961, F)

Socata ST 60 Rallye 7-300 (1970, F)

Dornier Do 28 D-1 Skyservant (1967, D)

Piaggio P. 166C (1958, I)

Pilatus PC-6 Porter (1960, CH)

Britten-Norman BN-2A Islander (1967, GB)

Beechcraft B55 Baron (1960, USA)

Beechcraft A60 Duke (1968, USA)

Beechcraft B80 Queen Air (1962, USA)

Beechcraft B90 King Air (1966, USA)

Beechcraft 99A Airliner (1968, USA)

Cessna T210 Turbo-System Centurion (1966, USA)

Cessna 207 Skywagon (1970, USA)

Cessna 414 (1970, USA)

Aero Commander Hawk Commander (1966, USA)

Piper PA-23-250 Aztec D (1961, USA)

Piper PA-32-260 Cherokee Six C (1965, USA)

Piper PA-31-300 Navajo (1967, USA)

Wassmer WA-51 Pacific (1971, F)

Ambrosini NF 15 (1969, I)

SIAI-Marchetti S.208 (1968, I)

SIAI-Marchetti S.210 (1971, I)

MFI-15A (1970, S)

Mooney Mark 22 (1967, USA)

Beechcraft Bonanza A36 (1968, USA)

Beechcraft Musketeer Super R (1962, USA)

Cessna A-150K Aerobat (1958, USA)

Cessna T310Q Skynight (1957, USA)

Aero Commander Lark Commander (1968, USA)

Piper PA-18 Super Cub 150 (1951, USA)

Piper Turbo Comanche C (1970, USA)

Piper PA-39 Twin Comanche C / R (1970, USA)

GENERAL AVIATION

Most of the aircraft flying today are not, as one might think, military planes nor commercial planes in service with an airline; actually they are general aviation crafts such as those presented on these pages, very small or relatively large, owned by private individuals, air clubs, business or industrial organizations. Not counting Russian contributions, of which little or nothing is known regarding quantity, the aircraft of so-called "general aviation" today number over 200,000, a good 80 percent of which are to be found in the U.S., 10 percent in Europe and the rest on other continents. The small training aircraft of the past have been joined today by larger 4-, 5- and 10-passenger craft which, especially in the U.S., are often used like the automobile, for short-distance business and tourist trips. The aeronautical industry all over the world offers everything and for almost all pocketbooks: from the small 1-engine two-seat model at about $5000, such as the *Cessna 1-150K Aerobat*, to the $15,000 five-seat *SIAI-Marchetti S.208;* from the 2-engine eight-seat *Piper PA-31-300* at $95,000 to the $450,000 2-engine 11-passenger turboprop *Hawk Commander.*

The range extends from $5000 models to a grand maximum of $3.5 million, for the *Grumman Gulfstream (p.193)* which can carry up to 19 passengers on intercontinental flights and is equipped with two Rolls-Royce jet engines. In the U.S., excluding 1970 which, because of the general economic crisis, registered a temporary decline, the development of light aviation has been continuous and strong. Much of this results from the fact that there are over 9000 airports available in the U.S. and general aviation is more widely subscribed to than in Europe. In addition to the scarcity of European airports and the insufficient equipment in most of those airports that do exist, there are also problems of national borders, customs and red tape. A businessman wishing to pilot his own small single-engine plane from Stuttgart, West Germany to Verona, Italy (flying time 2½ hours with his slow craft), must, upon entering Italian air space, land in Bolzano and telephone for a customs man to stamp his papers before proceeding with his trip. Once in Verona (population 260,000), he lands at the airport where, unfortunately, they have no facilities for refueling his aircraft. Under these conditions, general aviation in Europe will have to wait a long time before catching up to the U.S. Perhaps a united Europe will soon become a reality, so that even a small aircraft will enjoy full rights of citizenship and will no longer be considered a Cinderella.

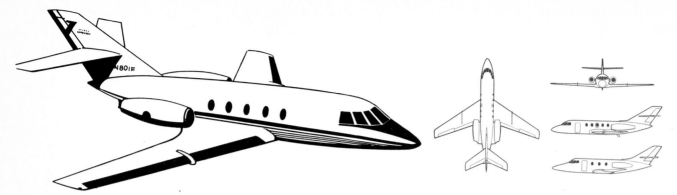

DASSAULT MYSTÈRE 20/Falcon 20 (1964, F). This elegant 2-engine executive jet can carry between 8 and 10 passengers. It comes off the assembly line of the same factory that produces the well-known *Mirage*. The prototype flew in May 1963, the same year that Pan Am's Private Aircraft Division gave a firm order for 54 units, thereby assuring the plane's immediate success. Known in the U.S. as the *Fan Jet Falcon,* more than 280 *Mystère 20*'s have been produced to date and production is continuing. In 1970 the *Falcon 10,* a smaller version for 7 passengers, appeared for the first time.

London as in Paris, in Chicago as in Tokyo. To ask these airports to sustain a doubling of the traffic load within the next 3 years would be unrealistic. And so, for the time being, the use of *Jumbo*'s on long-, medium- and short-distance flights may be a temporary solution, until the future seems clearer. One thing is certain: with or without the commercial supersonic, by 1980 the present airports will no longer be sufficient to withstand the estimated doubled traffic. Many possible solutions are under consideration: the first calls for the construction of new airports. It may be the most difficult to carry out: is sufficiently large space available close enough to cities but where air traffic will not disturb the residential population? On the other hand, moving too far outside city limits would run the risk that the time needed to get to and from the airports and the city would become greater than the actual flying time, unless city-to-airport-to-city traffic could be handled by fast and above all capacious helicopters, more suitable and more economical than those

presently in use *(see pp. 206, 207)*. Another solution might be to reroute all short- and medium-flight traffic away from the present airports to other airports closer to the city. This solution would become even more feasible if those new airports were used to accommodate only STOL (Short Takeoff and Landing) aircraft, which need only very short runways. The third solution to the problem of airport space, though not to that of noise, calls for the construction of enormous floating platforms on water surfaces (seas or lakes) near cities. Many large cities—New York, Rome, London, Amsterdam, Chicago, San Francisco, Los Angeles, Rio, Buenos Aires, Tokyo, and others—could adopt such a plan.

Obviously, on consideration of the problems mentioned in this brief review, it seems clear that civil aviation cannot afford to rest on its laurels. It must still solve the problem of blind landings under conditions of poor visibility, particularly fog; the problem of air pollution caused by the engines' exhaust fumes; the problem of noise. The answers are

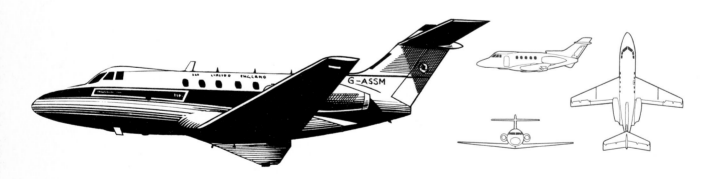

HAWKER SIDDELEY 125 (1964, GB). Also known by its original name, *De Havilland 125,* it is the British entry in the *executive* jet field. It flew for the first time in 1962 and since 1964, 250 *Hawker Siddeley 125*'s have been produced, 20 of which were for the R.A.F. Air Navigation School. The *125* can carry 7 passengers plus the pilot and co-pilot. It costs about $1,200,000 whereas the *Mystere* and the North American *Sabreliner 60* cost about $1,450,000. In the U.S., the *125* is sold under the name of *Beechcraft Hawker 125* by Beech Aircraft Corporation.

NORTH AMERICAN ROCKWELL SABRELINER Sr 60 (1961, USA). Born as a training and light-transport aircraft, it flew for the first time in 1958. Having had quite a number of units delivered to the U.S. Air Force and the U.S. Navy, it was presented on the executive market with considerable success. Better equipped than its rivals, it is also more expensive. Nevertheless, more than 150 units have been sold to private owners. There is also a smaller version, the *Sr 40,* and it is now being produced in the *Sr 70* version with a slightly more spacious cabin.

readily available, but care must be taken that the necessary expense will not prove too costly for the airlines to bear, since they are already in serious financial trouble. Lastly, one problem which will never be entirely solved, though it is well under control, is that of air-traffic safety, a basic concern of all civil-aviation authorities.

Nowadays one accident, albeit minor and without damage to human life or to property, occurs every 100,000 flights. According to a special report published in a journal, one passenger must fly for 28 years, making 100,000 flights, before there is a statistical probability that he will be involved in an accident. The data is more than reassuring but still not overly comforting, as no data can be which involves danger to human life.

That is why a commercial aircraft must prove that it fully meets all safety requirements before the official international organizations will grant it a certificate of approval. This is also why the standards which regulate passenger-plane traffic are so precise and

inflexible, even to specifying the number of landings which a landing tire can make before it must be changed regardless of the fact that it may still be in perfect condition.

Then, too, special attention must be paid to air-traffic control. As vast as the sky is, it is becoming increasingly overcrowded, particularly near large cities. The airlines are assigned actual "streets" or lanes at specified positions and altitudes. But there are also aircraft which belong to what is termed "general aviation," including private executive aircraft, planes of air clubs, agricultural spraying planes, etc. At the end of 1970 there were about 200,000 of these all over the world, the great majority of them in the U.S. It is easy to understand the tremendous responsibility placed on the shoulders of air-traffic control stations, with their enormous radar screens, which have, through split-second timing, often avoided tragedy.

Civil aviation today, with all its problems, is clearly fully responsible and ready to assume the heavy burdens of the future.

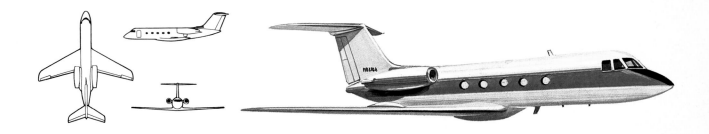

GRUMMAN GULFSTREAM II (1966, USA). The largest, most luxurious and most expensive executive-type plane on the market today, it can carry up to 19 passengers and offers the comforts of large commercial passenger aircraft. It was put on the market in 1966 and was well received. Over 80 *Gulfstream II*'s have already come off the assembly lines of Grumman factories in Long Island. It costs about $3,500,000, which is about the price of the *Fokker F-28* (65 passengers).

THE LONG ROAD TOWARDS VERTICAL TAKEOFF AND LANDING

"I find that if this instrument, shaped like a screw, is well made, that is to say, of linen, and its holes filled with starch, and if it is turned quickly, the said screw becomes female in the air and rises upwards." Thus wrote Leonardo da Vinci in 1493 about his vertical takeoff machine *(p.8)*. This genius, with his extraordinary intuition, had envisioned what were to become the basic principles of the modern helicopter but, just as in the case of the airplane, more than 4 centuries were to pass before a machine built along those principles was to rise a few inches off the ground.

In 1843 Sir George Cayley, unaware of Leonardo's studies, designed a machine which was to rise vertically, stay in the air and move according to the pilot's commands. *(Drawing on facing page.)* But for lack of a proper engine, the project was never carried out.

In 1877, Enrico Forlanini built a small helicopter model equipped with a tiny steam engine which lifted itself off the ground a few feet *(drawing on bottom left)*. But this model was not developed either, because the power was too weak to lift the heavy steam engine. When this experiment took place, man had already learned to fly with balloons but strove for a machine which could take-off, land or remain stationary in the air according to the pilot's wishes and not be subject to the whims of the wind. The object was to create a vehicle with an optimal thrust upwards. Today we speak of "Vertical Takeoff and Landing" (VTOL). Practically all those who dealt with this problem felt that the solution lay in large rotating propellers moved by an adequately powerful engine.

While the Wright brothers in the United States were studying what was to become the heaviest fixed-wing craft to fly, Louis Bréguet, in Europe, invented a craft with rotating wings which was built in collaboration with Charles Richet. In 1907 the *Gyroplane No. 1*, steadied by poles, took off vertically to an altitude of 4.11 feet. This was the first VTOL victory. Even the machines which were built the following year, the *No. 2* and the *No. 2bis* offered no solution to the many problems related to this type of craft, that of stability among the most outstanding. For this reason, Bréguet decided to devote his attention to fixed-wing crafts.

The young Russian student Igor Sikorsky, who in 1909 built, in Moscow, a helicopter which, because of lack of engine power (a small 25-horsepower Anzani) never left the ground, had come to the same conclusion. He was the man who later was to design and build the first 4-engine aircraft in the world *(p.38)* and several of the best flying boats

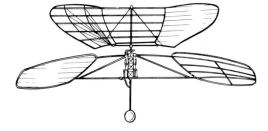

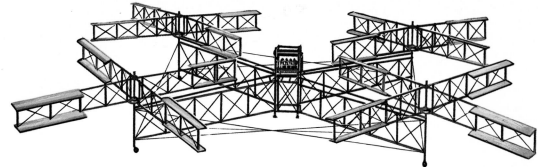

GYROPLANE No. 1 (1907, F). While the Wright brothers were successfully testing their fixed-wing aircraft, Louis Brè-quet, with the collaboration of Professor Charles Richet, was involved in the study of a machine with rotating wings. The *Gyroplane No. 1* lifted a few feet off the ground in 1907, as did the *No. 2* and the *No. 2bis,* both equipped with 2 rather than 4 rotors, in 1908–1909. But the engines available were inadequate and Brequet chose to devote his time to airplane design.

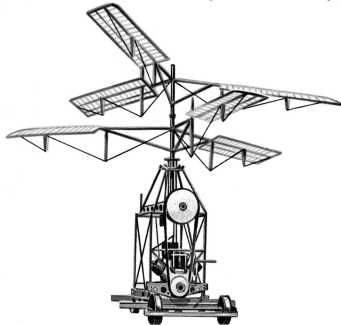

SIKORSKY I HELICOPTER (1909, R). The young student Igor Sikorsky brought home to Russia an Anzani engine from a trip to Paris. He used the engine in the prototype of his first helicopter, which never left the ground. He did not return to studying vertical takeoff until 1939.

ever developed. After these accomplishments, he again (this time successfully), returned to the rotating wing. And Paul Cornu, a mechanic born in Lisieux, France, who had made great progress on November 13, 1907, with his strange and fragile flying machines, later abandoned all further attempts. The fragility of the model, the continual breakdowns, the instability of the craft as soon as it got off the ground, all got the better of his great passion.

The vehicle built by Ellehammer—who in the preceding years had built several fixed-wing prototypes—was interesting because for the first time it introduced the concept of the "compound" or convertible, a model equipped with both propeller and rotors. The Danish pioneer carried out his experiments between 1912 and 1916, when he finally gave up for good.

The First World War interrupted helicopter study, and the decisive role of the airplane seemed a permanent setback for further helicopter experiments. Only a few, persevered—for example, the Frenchman Étienne Oemichen and the Spanish Marquis Raul Pateras Pescara. The former was able to ac-

CORNU'S HELICOPTER (1907, F). On November 13, 1907, Paul Cornu, a mechanic from Lisieux, had the satisfaction of watching his flying machine (he was aboard) rise a foot off the ground for about 20 seconds. But the model was too fragile and could not at the time be improved or developed practically.

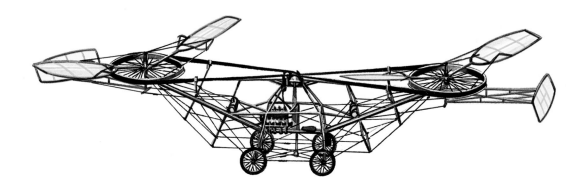

complish a vertical takeoff and a flight of a few hundred yards on May 24, 1924; the latter, in the same year, obtained even better results with a machine equipped with counterrotating coaxial rotators. It was not until 1930 that an Italian helicopter, designed by D'Ascanio and piloted by Marinello Nelli, beat the distance record established in 1924 by Pescara: from 2415 feet, the distance increased to 3535 feet! Nelli again beat the helicopter altitude record by rising 59 feet off the ground. The road towards VTOL was still long and difficult.

Ever since 1923 there was talk of the autogiro which the Spaniard Juan de la Cierva y Codornia had begun testing in 1920. Actually, it was not a VTOL craft, but rather, what is known today as a STOL (Short TakeOff and Landing). The autogiro was an airplane in all respects, equipped with a 3-blade free rotor, that is not connected to the engine. When the plane gathered speed on the runway, the blades began rotating, providing an added aerofoil. Takeoff could thus be achieved on a much shorter runway than was needed for the traditional aircraft, but the autogiro could neither take-off nor land vertically. Nor could it stay suspended in the air, since speed, no matter how little, was indispensable to keeping the blades rotating. The idea for this "windmill" came to de la Cierva when, still a very young man, he saw the prototype of his marvelous 3-engine aircraft, the first in Spanish aviation, crash because of a slow landing speed. He thought that if his planes were equipped with a rotor, they would be able to land gently even in case of engine trouble with the aid of the self-rotating blades. His concept was not entirely mistaken and the autogiros, perfected in subsequent years in Great Britain, the U.S. and Japan, were to have their moments of glory, such as

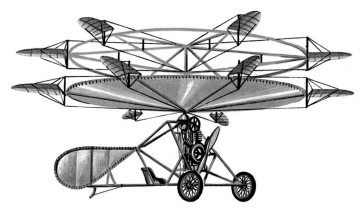

ELLEHAMMER'S HELICOPTER (1912, DK). The Dane Ellehammer, pioneer of flight, had already tested fixed-wing craft *(p.21)* and wanted to break into the helicopter field with this prototype, which was equipped with two co-axial rotors and which did rise a few inches off the ground before it was abandoned by its inventor in 1916.

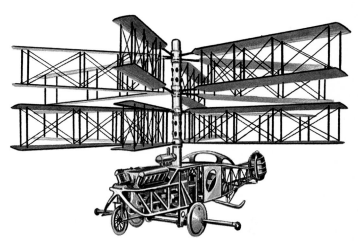

PESCARA NO. 2 (1924, E). The Spanish Marquis Raul Pateras Pescara began studying the helicopter in 1921, but it was not until 3 years later, in France, that he succeeded in making his *No.2* actually fly. A third craft, the *No. 3,* was ready when Juan de la Cierva's autogiro had already superseded it as a result of its practicality and brilliant technical advances.

OEMICHEN No. 2 (1922, F). An engineer at the Peugeot Automobile factory, Etienne Oemichen began building 2 vertical takeoff machines in 1919. After many previous attempts, Oemichen finally succeeded in getting his second craft off the ground and flying for about 262.0 feet on November 11, 1922; on May 24, 1924, he flew over 1 kilometer. Oemichen continued his studies on helicopters until World War II broke out.

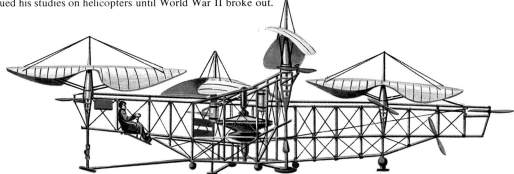

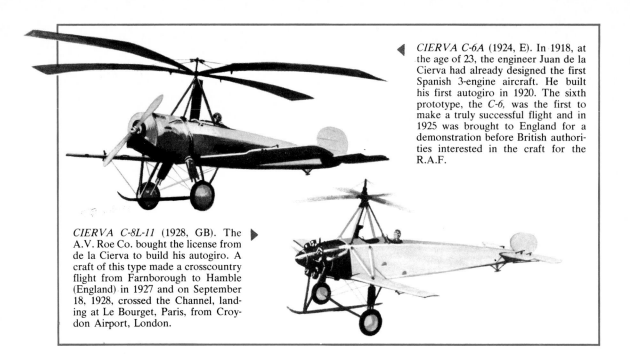

CIERVA C-6A (1924, E). In 1918, at the age of 23, the engineer Juan de la Cierva had already designed the first Spanish 3-engine aircraft. He built his first autogiro in 1920. The sixth prototype, the *C-6,* was the first to make a truly successful flight and in 1925 was brought to England for a demonstration before British authorities interested in the craft for the R.A.F.

CIERVA C-8L-11 (1928, GB). The A.V. Roe Co. bought the license from de la Cierva to build his autogiro. A craft of this type made a crosscountry flight from Farnborough to Hamble (England) in 1927 and on September 18, 1928, crossed the Channel, landing at Le Bourget, Paris, from Croydon Airport, London.

when the *C-8L-11* crossed the Channel for the first time, flying London to Paris; the *Kellett KD-1A,* which on July 6, 1939, inaugurated mail service from the roof of the Philadelphia post office to nearby Camden airport; the *Ka-1,* built in over 240 units by Kayaba and used by the Japanese Navy during the first phase of World War II.

The limited use of the autogiro, its inability to take-off vertically, contributed to a revival of interest in a craft with VTOL characteristics. The first of many to return to his old studies was Louis Bréguet who, in 1931, with René Dorand, began building the *Gyroplane Laboratoire.* In November 1936 his efforts were rewarded in a fantastic 27.3-mile closed-circuit flight. The helicopter was not an impossible dream after all. Heinrich Karl Johann Focke, a German engineer who had been an aeronautical designer since World War I, had the same idea. In 1924 he had founded the Focke-Wulf Flugzeugbau A.G.; in 1931 he left

the company and founded a new one for research on vertical takeoff and landing, the Focke-Achgelis GmbH. A VTOL craft came out of this small workshop in 1936; it was the *FA-61,* which made quite an impression on public opinion with its spectacular feats such as its flight in a large, closed area (to demonstrate its absolute controllability) and the 67.7-mile Bremen-Berlin flight in October 1937. The *FA-61* was followed by a larger craft, the *FA-223,* which could carry 6 passengers and which could have been very helpful to the German armed forces. But, among other reasons, because of the skepticism of the High Command and the heavy bombing of the aircraft factories where it was produced, only about 20 *FA-223*'s reached combat units, where they were hardly used.

The situation in the U.S. was quite different after Igor Sikorsky, technical manager of the Vought Sikorsky Division of the United Aircraft Corporation, again began to devote

GYROPLANE LABORATOIRE (1936, F). Louis Bréguet began studying vertical flight again in 1931, in collaboration with René Dorand. The craft, called the *Gyroplane* after the 1907 model, was very functional and set several records, among these closed-circuit distance (27.28 miles, November 21, 1936), and height (518.24 feet September 26, 1936). The tests continued during the War until the craft was unfortunately destroyed. In 1946, however, Bréguet built another helicopter.

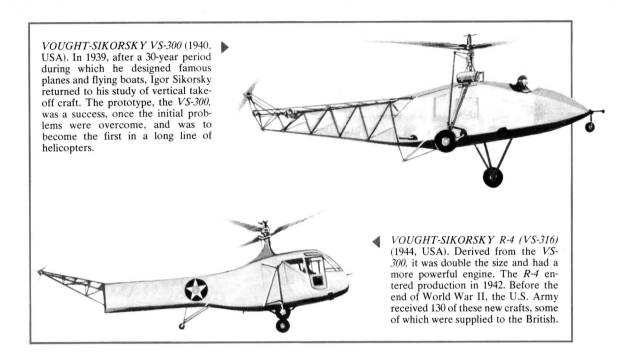

VOUGHT-SIKORSKY VS-300 (1940, USA). In 1939, after a 30-year period during which he designed famous planes and flying boats, Igor Sikorsky returned to his study of vertical take-off craft. The prototype, the *VS-300*, was a success, once the initial problems were overcome, and was to become the first in a long line of helicopters.

VOUGHT-SIKORSKY R-4 (VS-316) (1944, USA). Derived from the *VS-300*, it was double the size and had a more powerful engine. The *R-4* entered production in 1942. Before the end of World War II, the U.S. Army received 130 of these new crafts, some of which were supplied to the British.

his attention to the study of helicopters in 1939. With the full endorsement of the military authorities, he tested his *VS-300* in May 1940. The craft was equipped with a main rotor and a smaller one vertically mounted on the extremity of the tail to correct and balance the torsion effect caused by the rotation of the large blades. This principle was later applied universally to all helicopters equipped with only one large rotator. Twelve months after its first hesitant hop, the *VS-300* broke all flight-duration records, remaining aloft for 1 hour 32 minutes 26 seconds. It can therefore be stated that the modern helicopter was born with the success of the *VS-300*. In 1943 the first *VS-316*'s came off the Sikorsky assembly lines and were renamed the *R-4*'s by the American Air Force. Shortly later, they became operative in England.

Before the end of the War, 130 *R-4*'s entered combat and proved to be safe, reliable and extremely useful. Although no one had

yet thought of using them for such feats, on April 23, 1944, an *R-4* successfully rescued a pilot who had crashed over enemy territory. The helicopter had proved itself, and at the end of the War, particularly in the U.S., the number of firms manufacturing them increased. Here are some data on the production of military helicopters up to 1953: 22 in 1943; 144 in 1944; 275 in 1945; 44 in 1946; 57 in 1947; 153 in 1948; 73 in 1949; 60 in 1950; 360 in 1951; 983 in 1952; 943 in 1953. The reason for the sharp increase in production in those last two years was the fact that these new VTOL crafts had finally achieved full efficiency and had demonstrated their effectiveness during the Korean War. Marine Corps and Air Force helicopters reached the front within a month after hostilities began and were assigned to reconnaissance duties. Within a month, although small and not entirely suitable for transporting the wounded, they proved extremely helpful in evacuation

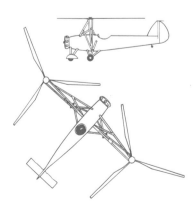

FOCKE FA-61 (1936, D). Having experimented with and tested the autogiro, Heinrich K. J. Focke, in 1936, built his first helicopter, which was certainly one of the most advanced. Its achievements, including a Bremen–Berlin flight, were exalted by Nazi propaganda and had vast international repercussions. Although it was an excellent machine, only about 20 *FA-223*'s, a later 6-passenger model, were delivered to the Luftwaffe during the War.

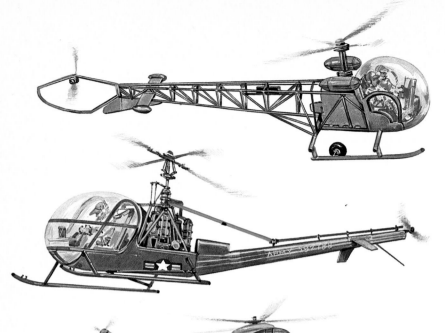

BELL 47G-2 (1946, USA). The first helicopter in the world to obtain a civilian license, it was seen for the first time in 1946 in its original version. Still in production today, it is built in the U.S. and on license in other countries. Over 5000 have been built and used for commercial and military purposes in almost all nations of the Western world.

HILLER H-23D RAVEN (1946, USA). Used in action for the first time during the Korean War, it was improved during the course of the years until its production was stopped in 1967 after 2000 units had been delivered to both military and civilian operators in more than 10 countries, not counting the many delivered to the U.S. Army and Navy.

SIKORSKY CH-37A (S-56) (1955, USA). One of the first attack-transport helicopters used by the Marines. It could carry 33 men in full combat gear and a 105 millimeter cannon or 3 jeeps. It has been in production since 1960; 156 units have been built, 94 for the Army and about 10, with special radar, for the U.S. Navy.

and emergency transport of wounded from combat and surrounding zones. At the end of the War, it was estimated that no less than 15,000 men had been carried to safety by the few helicopters used; more than 3000 wounded owed their lives to the rapidity with which the helicopter was able to carry them to medical aid. Also during the Korean War, the helicopter confirmed not only its ability as a rescue craft, but also its usefulness in low-altitude reconnaissance. In addition, it was ideal for rapid movement on the battlefield, a rapidity previously unheard of.

When the American troops found themselves involved in the new war in Vietnam, they already had at their disposal a series of helicopters equipped for all uses: reconnaissance, rescue, troop-and-matériel transport, escort and attack. The UH-1 *Iroquois* and the *CH-47C Chinook* were widely used in action

SIKORSKY UH-34D (S-58) (1955, USA). Used as an anti-sub by the U.S. Navy and Italian Navy, by the U.S. Marine Corps and Army, by the German, French and Italian armies and by the armed forces of many other countries as a transport, it is one of the most successful heavy helicopters. More than 1800 units were produced. It is still used for space-capsule recovery.

SIKORSKY HH-3E (S-61) (1961, USA). Known to the soldiers in Vietnam as the *Jolly Green Giant,* it is used by the Aerospace Rescue and Recovery Service to rescue pilots who have fallen over enemy territory and for evacuating the wounded. It can hold up to 30 men and has also been built in another version for the Navy *(Sea King).* It is also built on license in Canada, Italy, England and Japan and has been widely used commercially by many airlines, among them BEA, KLM and JAL.

BELL AH-1J SEACOBRA (1967, USA). A well-armed and fast helicopter used as escort for larger and slower transport helicopters, it was built to answer the needs that emerged during the war in Vietnam. In service since November 1967 on the front lines, a few hundred units have been ordered and it has proven satisfactory both for the Army and the Marine Corps. It is the first combat helicopter in the world.

LOCKHEED AH-56A CHEYENNE (1967, USA). Destined to replace the *Seacobra*, it is considered the most perfect helicopter of our times for combat. Equipped with a machine gun and small cannon, it can carry 2000 pounds of weapons, such as missiles, rockets and bombs, and is a formidable war machine. About a dozen *AH-56A*'s are under evaluation by the U.S. Army.

in a war which had no real front and which was fought under unusual conditions on a terrain of rice paddies and dense jungle. Thanks to these craft, the Airmobile First Cavalry Division, an entire division equipped with 428 helicopters, was able to intervene with unforeseen swiftness in the most widely dispersed enemy areas, making rapid strikes and returning within 12 to 14 hours.

The necessity of providing adequate protection for heavy-transport helicopters during the delicate phase of landing men and equipment in full battle stimulated the development of fast and long-range helicopters, heavily armed with machine guns, rockets, missiles and even napalm bombs. These craft could also be used to deter the enemy and hold him under constant fire. The most recent of such attack helicopters is the *AH-56A Cheyenne*, which is still being tested by American mili-

tary authorities. During this war, the crane helicopters, which can hook, lift and transport even the heaviest loads such as smaller helicopters, damaged aircraft lost over enemy lines, tanks, cannons and special containers for men and equipment, played a very important role.

But after the Korean War the helicopter's qualities were no longer considered sufficient. True, it can take-off and land vertically, but it is too slow and from this point of view cannot be compared to the airplane. This is why since 1952 studies have been underway to develop a new "generation" of VTOL's able to combine the qualities of both the helicopter and the airplane (*see* "VTOL: Yesterday's Experiments for Tomorrow's Craft," *p.204*).

Production in the last few years has reached new highs: in 1966, for example, the U.S.

BOEING-VERTOL CH-47C CHINOOK (1964, USA). This helicopter can transport cargo similar to that of a *C-47 (p. 107)* or the military version of the *DC-3*. It was delivered to the American Army in 1964 and has been irreplaceable ever since in Vietnam. When we think that it can transport an entire artillery section (2 cannons, men and munitions), we can understand why it was a formidable tactical weapon in guerrilla warfare. The civilian version, the *Model 107*, has also been very successful and has been adopted by several companies, including Pan American.

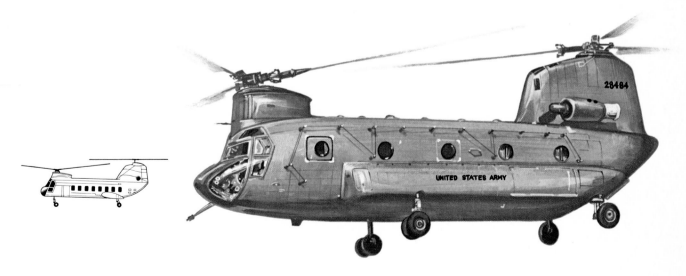

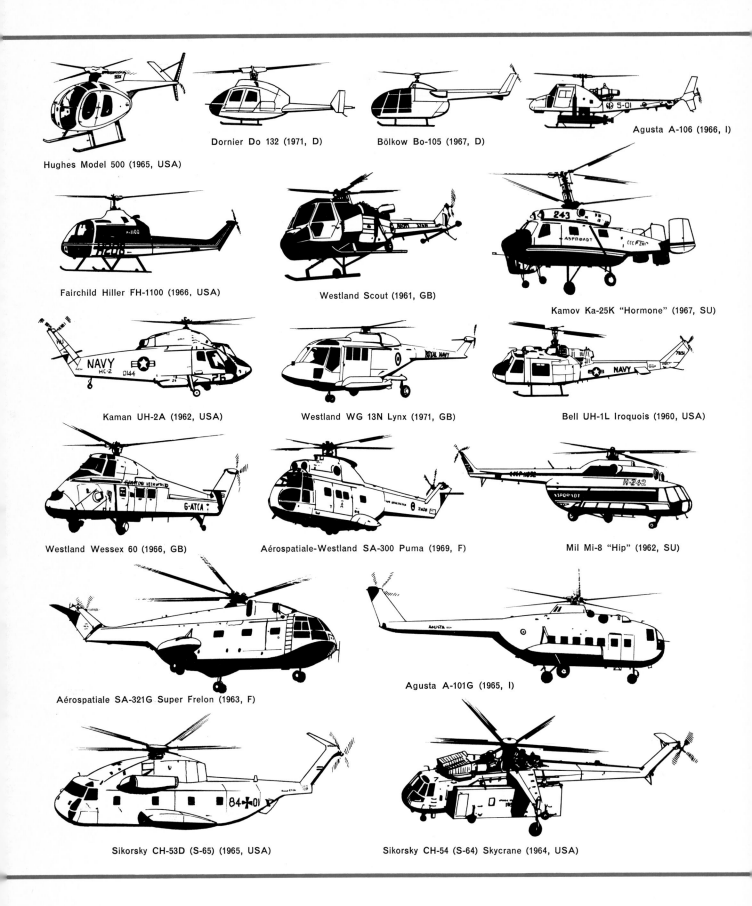

Hughes Model 500 (1965, USA)

Dornier Do 132 (1971, D)

Bölkow Bo-105 (1967, D)

Agusta A-106 (1966, I)

Fairchild Hiller FH-1100 (1966, USA)

Westland Scout (1961, GB)

Kamov Ka-25K "Hormone" (1967, SU)

Kaman UH-2A (1962, USA)

Westland WG 13N Lynx (1971, GB)

Bell UH-1L Iroquois (1960, USA)

Westland Wessex 60 (1966, GB)

Aérospatiale-Westland SA-300 Puma (1969, F)

Mil Mi-8 "Hip" (1962, SU)

Aérospatiale SA-321G Super Frelon (1963, F)

Agusta A-101G (1965, I)

Sikorsky CH-53D (S-65) (1965, USA)

Sikorsky CH-54 (S-64) Skycrane (1964, USA)

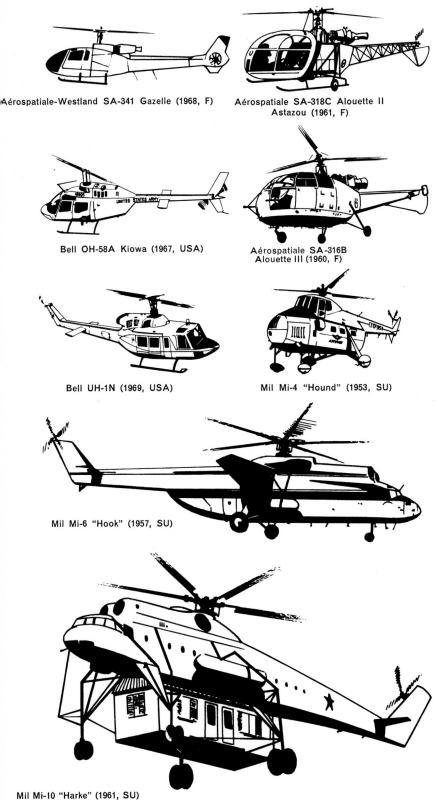

Aérospatiale-Westland SA-341 Gazelle (1968, F)

Aérospatiale SA-318C Alouette II Astazou (1961, F)

Bell OH-58A Kiowa (1967, USA)

Aérospatiale SA-316B Alouette III (1960, F)

Bell UH-1N (1969, USA)

Mil Mi-4 "Hound" (1953, SU)

Mil Mi-6 "Hook" (1957, SU)

Mil Mi-10 "Harke" (1961, SU)

HELICOPTERS: TODAY

The United States holds a prominent position in the manufacturing of helicopters today. The heavy use of helicopters in the Vietnam war has brought about the manufacture of new and improved types. The U.S. has manufactured at least 8 important models of helicopters other than the *Bell 47G,* the *Sikorsky S-58,* the *S-61 (p.200),* the *Seacobra* and the *Chinook (p.201).* Bell still produces the *HU-1L Iroquois,* a very successful all-purpose craft; the *OH-58A Kiowa,* the reconnaissance model of the *Model 206A Jetranger;* the *UH-1N* one of the most modern twin-turbo engines, developed from the Iroquois. Sikorsky produces the *S-65* troop transport, also purchased by West Germany and Israel, and the *Skycrane,* which rescued more than 400 airplanes during the Vietnam war as well as helicopters damaged over enemy lines. More than 1450 *Model 500*'s have come off the Hughes assembly lines, many of these in the Army reconnaissance versions *(OH-6A);* the *Kaman UH-2A,* used mainly by the Navy, and the *Fairchild Hiller FH-1100,* in both civilian and military versions, round out the picture.

The Soviet Union presumably is still producing the *Ka-25K,* used both by the Navy and by Aeroflot. This craft was designed by Nikolai I. Kamov. At least 5 helicopters designed by Mikhail L. Mil have also been built; the *Mi-4,* a few thousand of which have been built in both civilian and military versions; the *Mi-6,* which can carry 65 passengers, and was the largest helicopter in the world at the time it entered service; the *Mi-8,* used both by the Army and Aeroflot for transport; the *Mi-10,* the Russian skycrane, huge and powerful; the *Mi-12,* not shown here, a large 4-engine turbo craft which was first seen by the Western world at the Paris Aeronautical Show in 1971.

France has built the most successful helicopters in Western Europe; a new version of the *Alouette II,* 2000 units of which have been sold to 45 countries, is still in production, while mass-production of the *Gazelle* has begun, a craft designed to take the place of the *Alouette.* Deliveries of over 850 *Alouette III*'s (6 passengers) to 57 countries, as well as the *Super Frelon* and 163 new *Pumas,* are still being made.

The major British helicopter manufacturer, Westland, produces the *Scout* for the Army; the *Wessex 60,* a civilian version of the *Sikorsky S-58;* and the brand new *WG-13N Lynx,* the anti-sub, for the Royal Navy. In Italy, Agusta, which also produces helicopters under Bell license, has produced the *A-106* for the Italian Navy and the large *A-101G* for the Air Force. A civilian version of the latter is being planned. Finally, Germany has reentered the field of vertical flight in which she was a pioneer during the 1930s, with the *Bo-105* and the *Do-132.*

VTOL: YESTERDAY'S EXPERIMENTS FOR TOMORROW'S CRAFTS

The helicopter has been increasingly improved during the last 15 years. The piston engine has been replaced by the turbo engine, which is lighter and more powerful; new kinds of rotors have afforded better handling and speed. The helicopter still has one basic defect: the rotors which enable it to take-off vertically will not allow it to fly over certain speeds. The limit is 300 miles per hour, no matter how powerful the engines.

The need for a craft which combines the qualities of the VTOL helicopter with the speed of the airplane has since 1950 encouraged a wide range of studies and designs of experimental prototypes.

Initially it was believed that a solution was to be found in the *compound,* or convertible, a helicopter also equipped with propellers, whose engine could move either the rotors during takeoff or the propellers in horizontal flight. The *McDonnell XV-1* and the *Fairey Rotodyne* are good examples of the compound. The basic drawback is, as in other cases, the rotor which, even when operating in autorotation, still hinders speed, aggravated by the extra wing weight during takeoff. For these reasons the compound has proved unsatisfactory and economically unsound. Another attempt, later abandoned, was the vertiplane *(Convair XFY-1, Lockheed XFV-1, Ryan X-13),* a plane equipped with large propellers and a jet engine, thanks to which it was to take-off vertically and later assume a horizontal position upon reaching a given altitude. But in this case, too, tests were not successful.

The third solution is the *tilt-prop* or *tilt-wing* plane with propellers or wings at a 90-degree angle which can assume a vertical position at takeoff or landing and a horizontal position during flight. Examples of this type of craft are the *Bell XV-3,* the *N-500,* the *X-22A (p.207)* with rotating engines; examples of planes with rotating wings are the *Vertol VZ-2A,* the *X-18,* the *XC-142,* the *Canadair CL-84-1 (p.207).* Some practical results will probably be achieved when the last two models go into production.

The fourth and last alternative uses a jet engine: when the jet flow is aimed downwards, the necessary thrust for vertical takeoff is obtained. In flight, the jet is turned towards the rear to obtain horizontal thrust. In some cases two independent jets have been proposed to serve two different functions. After the first attempts *(Rolls-Royce TMR, C-450, Bell ATV),* new and more advanced prototypes were developed, such as the *Short SC-1,* the *X-14.* the *D-188A,* the *Balzac,* the *Ryan XV-5B,* the *Dormier 31E3 (p.207).* At least one of these planes is already fully operative, the *Hawker Harrier (p.156)* and will soon be followed by others. It is the designers' first tangible reward in their attempt to replace today's slow but excellent helicopter with a fast VTOL airplane.

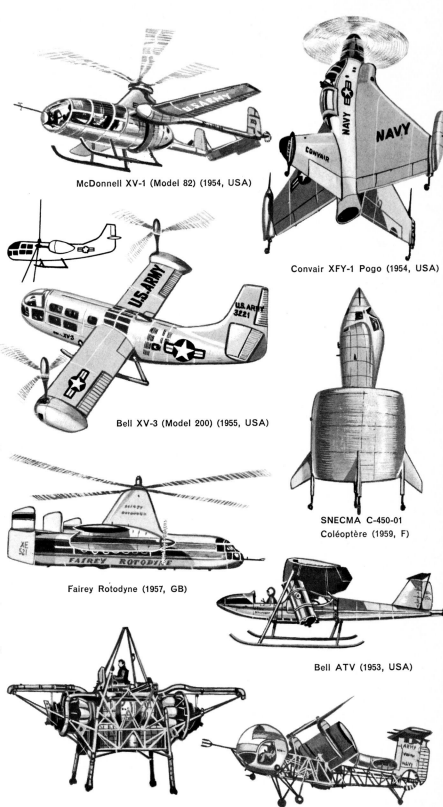

McDonnell XV-1 (Model 82) (1954, USA)

Convair XFY-1 Pogo (1954, USA)

Bell XV-3 (Model 200) (1955, USA)

SNECMA C-450-01 Coléoptère (1959, F)

Fairey Rotodyne (1957, GB)

Bell ATV (1953, USA)

Rolls-Royce TMR Flying Bedstead (1953, GB)

Vertol VZ-2A (Model 76) (1957, USA)

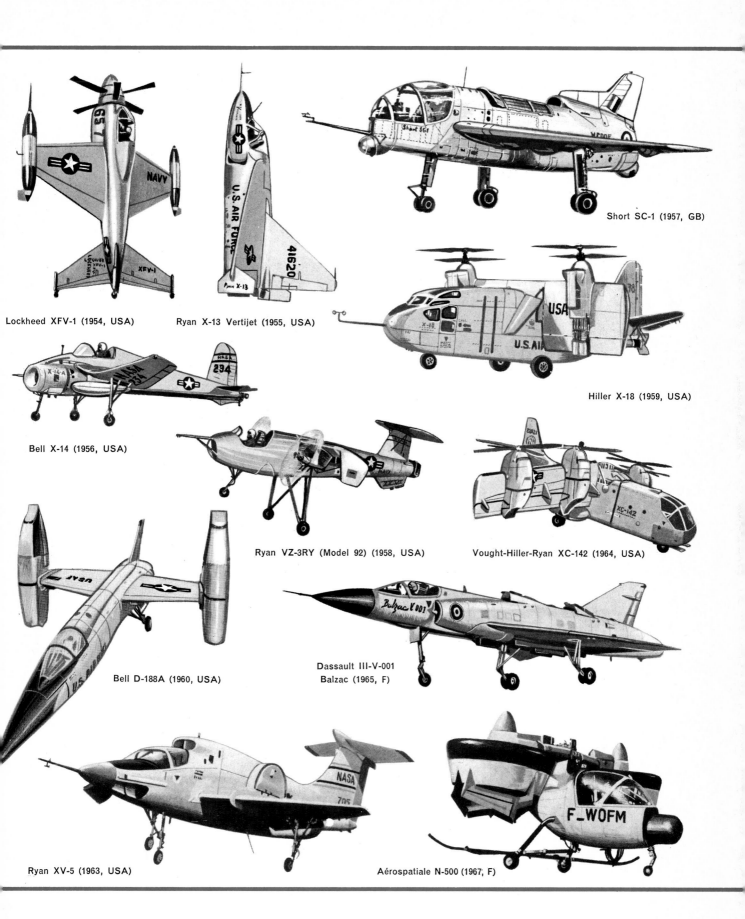

Lockheed XFV-1 (1954, USA)

Ryan X-13 Vertijet (1955, USA)

Short SC-1 (1957, GB)

Bell X-14 (1956, USA)

Hiller X-18 (1959, USA)

Ryan VZ-3RY (Model 92) (1958, USA)

Vought-Hiller-Ryan XC-142 (1964, USA)

Bell D-188A (1960, USA)

Dassault III-V-001
Balzac (1965, F)

Ryan XV-5 (1963, USA)

Aérospatiale N-500 (1967, F)

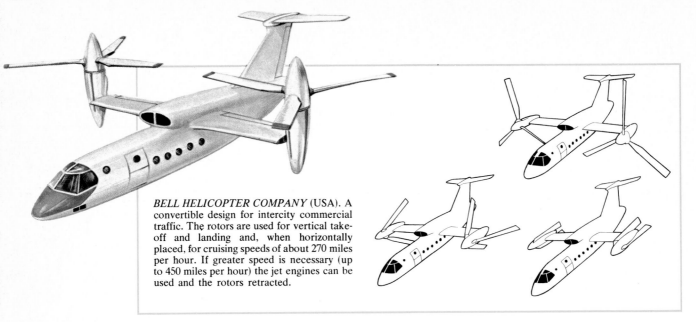

BELL HELICOPTER COMPANY (USA). A convertible design for intercity commercial traffic. The rotors are used for vertical take-off and landing and, when horizontally placed, for cruising speeds of about 270 miles per hour. If greater speed is necessary (up to 450 miles per hour) the jet engines can be used and the rotors retracted.

built 2825 helicopters. Only 583 of these were for commercial use. In 1967, 2903 were built, 455 for commercial use; the data for the following years has not been released to the public for reasons connected with the Vietnam war. It may be assumed that at least an equal number have been built in different countries, mainly Russia, thus bringing the total number of helicopters produced to a surprisingly high figure, especially if one considers that the helicopter is less than 30 years old (see "Helicopters: Today," p.203).

Although the VTOL vehicle has been accepted by military authorities, this does not hold true for civilian use. At first it was believed that it could become an extraordinary means of passenger transportation for short distances, since it could operate from small heliports located on the roofs of buildings. Initially the small transport capacity of existing vehicles did not allow for such experiments. But helicopters were used successfully,

for emergency operations, by the police, Red Cross and other public agencies.

The first helicopter passenger service was inaugurated in the U.S. at the beginning of the 1960s in Chicago, Los Angeles, San Francisco and New York, and generally adopted the *Boeing Vertol Model 107*, which carried 25 passengers. The helicopter routes generally connected the downtown areas of different cities with the airports or vice versa. In New York for example, the helicopter left the roof of the Pan Am skyscraper on Park Avenue in the heart of the city and reached Kennedy Airport, several miles away, in 10 minutes, an improvement on the hour or so taxi run. Nevertheless, none of the companies that tried the venture had an easy time, to such an extent that some have been obliged to drop the service, either because of financial difficulties or because local authorities denied them permission to use city bases as a result of noise disturbance caused by the rotors, the

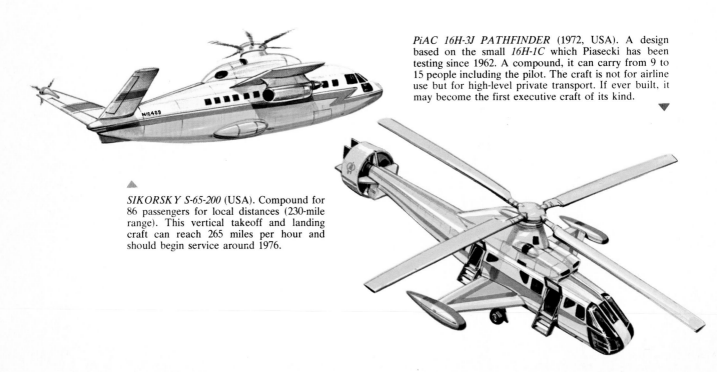

PiAC 16H-3J PATHFINDER (1972, USA). A design based on the small 16H-1C which Piasecki has been testing since 1962. A compound, it can carry from 9 to 15 people including the pilot. The craft is not for airline use but for high-level private transport. If ever built, it may become the first executive craft of its kind.

▼

SIKORSKY S-65-200 (USA). Compound for 86 passengers for local distances (230-mile range). This vertical takeoff and landing craft can reach 265 miles per hour and should begin service around 1976.

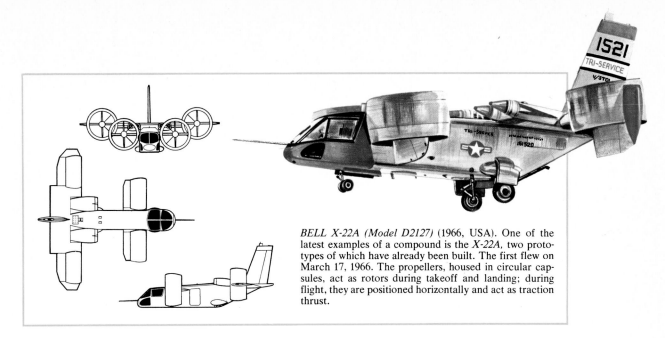

BELL X-22A (Model D2127) (1966, USA). One of the latest examples of a compound is the *X-22A*, two prototypes of which have already been built. The first flew on March 17, 1966. The propellers, housed in circular capsules, act as rotors during takeoff and landing; during flight, they are positioned horizontally and act as traction thrust.

danger of an accident in densely populated urban areas and air pollution in already polluted metropolitan areas.

From a financial viewpoint, the helicopter obviously costs more than surface transportation and over short distances passengers are reluctant to spend double the usual amount to save several minutes. Furthermore, commercial helicopters cannot fly except when visibility is perfect. The inability to guarantee regular helicopter transportation to potential passengers who might therefore miss a flight has been detrimental. As a result civilian helicopters have not met with much success, although they are used in some countries mostly by large companies like BEA, KLM, and SABENA, which can sustain the costs of nonprofitable operations for the sake of integrating and perfecting their network of services.

The problem of traffic in large airports is becoming more dramatic day by day, and

not only on the ground. There is also the problem that the highways of the sky are overcrowded with traffic. A solution might be found in replacing aircraft used for short distances with craft that do not need runways and can utilize other means to reach the city. New installations, such as heliports, would be required, as well as systems for controlling traffic quite different from those in existence; most of all, larger, faster, more economical VTOL crafts than those in use today would be needed. That is why some of the craft illustrated on the preceding page have become particularly important, such as the *S-65-200,* which can carry 86 passengers at a speed of 248.5 miles and which would resolve many problems such as that of the very congested air route between New York and Chicago. It is expected that a "second generation" of commercial VTOL transportation craft will have a greater chance of success than the "first."

DORNIER DO 31E3 (1967, D). Equipped with main jets for propulsion in horizontal flight and supplementary jets for vertical takeoff and landing, the prototypes of this model have made a good impression. Among other feats, it made a round-trip flight from Munich to Paris. The *DO-31E* is also being evaluated by NASA experts. ▼

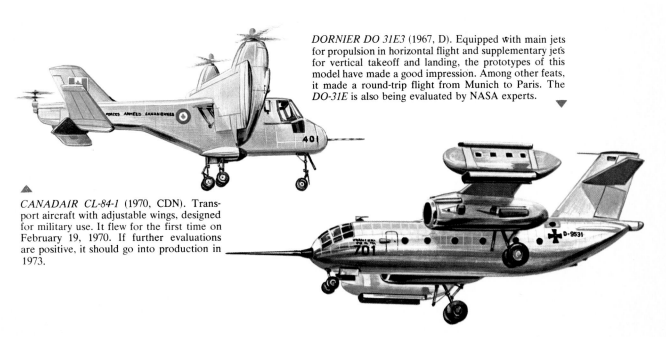

CANADAIR CL-84-1 (1970, CDN). Transport aircraft with adjustable wings, designed for military use. It flew for the first time on February 19, 1970. If further evaluations are positive, it should go into production in 1973.

FROM THE X-1 TO THE "SPACE SHUTTLE"

World War II had not yet ended when the U.S.A.A.F. and the National Advisory Committee for Aeronautics (N.A.C.A.) decided jointly to promote and finance the design and construction of the first aircraft able to break the sound barrier.

Thus a scientific program was begun which, in less than 25 years, was to bring man to break, first, the sound barrier, then the heat barrier and finally to navigate in space and set foot on the Earth's natural satellite, the moon.

When an object moves in the atmosphere, the molecules of air are shifted to make room for it; when the object's speed is greater than the speed of sound (760 miles per hour at sea level with temperature at 75 degrees Fahrenheit) these molecules do not have enough time to move, and create what is called "the sound barrier." If the object—an aircraft for example, is forceful enough to push away the compressed molecules, it passes at "supersonic" speed, provoking a sonic sound, similar to a clap of thunder, called *boom* or *bang* which can be heard for a radius of about 60 miles. As supersonic speed increases, heat caused by the friction generated by the structure against the atmosphere increases until it reaches the "heat barrier." At 1472 degrees Fahrenheit, the resistance of even the best steel is so lowered that the plane can disintegrate. This is what happens to meteors. To cross the heat barrier, special metals and alloys are needed. In 1945 these did not exist.

Thanks to the development of the *X*'s, progress taken has made such leaps forward that it has brought man to the exploration of space.

The *X-1* was ordered in February 1945. At that time the only object that had crossed the sound barrier was the bullet, and for this reason the *X-1* was given the same shape. It was originally supposed to probe the possibilities of supersonic speeds for aircraft. It made its first engineless gliderlike flight in January 1946 after being carried up by a *B-29*. Equipped with an extremely short-range rocket engine, piloted by Capt. Charles "Chuck" Yeager, it crossed the sound barrier for the first time on October 14, reaching 964 miles per hour, and, some days later, set an altitude record at 70,119 feet.

The *X-1* experiments continued for years and on December 12, 1953, aboard the *X-1A* the same Yeager reached 1612 miles per hour, the speed at Mach 2.42 (supersonic speed is measured in Machs, named after the Austrian physicist Ernst Mach who defined it in 1900. Mach 1 means the speed of sound; Mach 2, double that, and so on).

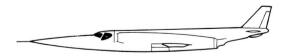

BELL X-1 (1946, USA). On October 14, 1947, Capt. "Chuck" Yeager of the U.S.A.A.F. on board an *X-1,* became the first man to break the sound barrier, that is, to fly at a speed of over Mach 1. Six *X-1's* were built, the first few without engines. They were carried to their altitude by a *Flying Superfortress B-29* and glided to a landing on the sand runway of Muroc Air Base in the California desert. Later equipped with rocket engines, they were flying at ultrasonic speeds in 1947. In 1953 an *X-1A* reached Mach 2.42 and in 1954 an altitude of about 98,400 feet. The *X-1's* were tested until 1956.

BELL X-2 (1953, USA). An experimental aircraft designed in an attempt to reach speeds near Mach 3, it made its first flight without engines in 1952, brought to its altitude by a *B-50* bomber. Equipped with a Curtiss-Wright engine, on September 27, 1956, piloted by Capt. Milburn G. Apt, it reached Mach 3.2, a record which stood until 1961. During the attempt, the *X-2* however, crashed against the "heat barrier" and its pilot was killed.

While the *X-1* supplied a harvest of precious data, other experimental craft were also ordered by the U.S.A.A.F. and N.A.C.A.: the *X-2* for Mach-3 speeds; the *X-3* to study ultrasonic speeds in jet- instead of rocket-engine aircraft; the *X-5* to test the use of variable wings. The order in which these prototypes became actual test flights does not follow their numerical project number. In fact the *X-5* flew for the first time on June 20, 1951, while the *X-2* made its first flight in June 1952 and the *X-3* in October of the same year.

The *X-5,* whose design was based on a study done by Messerschmitt technicians during the War, was tested until 1955 and was a source of very important information for the design of the *F-111 (p.156)* and of the very recent *F-14 (p.152).* The *X-2* made an inauspicious debut: during its first flight with the engines working, on May 12, 1953, it exploded in the air, killing the test pilot, Skip Ziegler. The second prototype reached a height of

BELL X-5 (1951, USA). Based on the German design for the *Messerschmitt P. 1101,* which fell into American hands at the end of the War. The *X-5* was the world's first aircraft with variable-angle wings. One of the two prototypes ordered by the U.S.A.A.F. flew for the first time on June 20, 1951, piloted by Skip Ziegler. Unfortunately the plane crashed on October 31, 1953 and the pilot, Maj. Raymond P. Popson was killed. Nevertheless, the second *X-5* continued flying for several years. The wings of the *X-5* could change in flight from a 20-degree to a 60-degree angle. The American aircraft currently in production with variable wings have all been designed on the basis of experience with the *X-5's.*

DOUGLAS X-3 STILETTO (1952, USA). The supersonic speeds of the *X-1* and *X-2* were obtained with rocket engines which, because they consumed great amounts of fuel, could only fly for a few minutes. The *X-3* had been designed to attempt to reach speeds near Mach 3 using 2 turbojets. At first the aircraft was equipped with two 7000-pound thrust engines which were later replaced by two 4200-pound engines. The plane flew for the first time on October 20, 1952, and was used in more than 20 experimental flights by N.A.C.A. pilots until May 1956. Of the 3 *X-3* prototypes ordered, only one was completed.

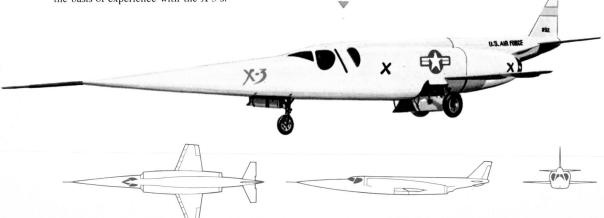

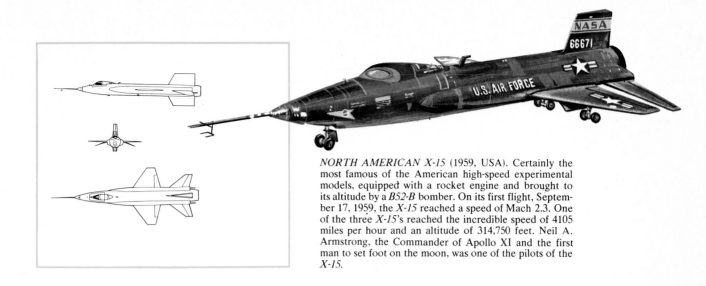

NORTH AMERICAN X-15 (1959, USA). Certainly the most famous of the American high-speed experimental models, equipped with a rocket engine and brought to its altitude by a *B52-B* bomber. On its first flight, September 17, 1959, the *X-15* reached a speed of Mach 2.3. One of the three *X-15*'s reached the incredible speed of 4105 miles per hour and an altitude of 314,750 feet. Neil A. Armstrong, the Commander of Apollo XI and the first man to set foot on the moon, was one of the pilots of the *X-15*.

126,000 feet on September 7, 1956, but on the twenty-seventh of the the same month, at a speed of Mach 3.2, as it broke the heat barrier, the plane exploded and the pilot, Capt. Milburn Apt, was killed.

The *X-3* with its marvelous aerodynamic stiletto design, built of a titanium alloy expressly to cross the heat barrier, never succeeded in reaching supersonic speeds, mostly because of inadequate engine power. But many successive planes owe something to it, among these the *Lockheed F-104 (p.155)* and the legendary *X-15,* which used the same wing design.

Among the more ambitious research programs, we should consider that of the *X-15,* designed to fly at Mach 6 at the incredible altitude of 262,000 feet. The aircraft was built of Inconel X Nickel to resist temperatures of about 1100 degrees Fahrenheit; 3 prototypes were ordered from North American in September 1955, jointly financed by N.A.C.A.

and the U.S. Army and Navy. While waiting for its 60,000-pound rocket engine, built by Reaction Motors, the first *X-15* was equipped with other engines and on its first flight on September 17, 1959, as it left the *B-52* which had carried it to its altitude, it passed Mach 2.3. Tests of the 3 *X-15*'s are not only quite celebrated, it would take a separate volume to describe the enthusiasm and surprise they aroused. On August 5, 1960, Joe Walker flew an *X-15* at 2194 miles per hour; on November 9, 1961, another *X-15* reached 4093 miles per hour! On July 17, 1962, an *X-15* reached an altitude of 313,918 feet and on August of the following year climbed over 354,108 feet (62 miles!). With these experiments N.A.C.A. became N.A.S.A. (National Aeronautics and Space Administration), and undertook the study of the first American space program. Three of the *X-15* pilots later became part of the first group of American astronauts—Joe Walker, Bob White and Neil Armstrong.

NORTH AMERICAN XB-70A VALKYRIE (1964, USA). Designed for the Strategic Air Command as a supersonic bomber to replace the *B-52,* it never became operative. Its construction as a bomber was never approved and it was transformed, in two prototypes, into an experimental plane for speed near Mach 3. One of the two *XB-70*'s exploded during a test flight, killing the entire test-flight crew aboard. Nevertheless, the experience gained and the insights provided by the gigantic aircraft proved to be invaluable to the study of the commercial American supersonic.

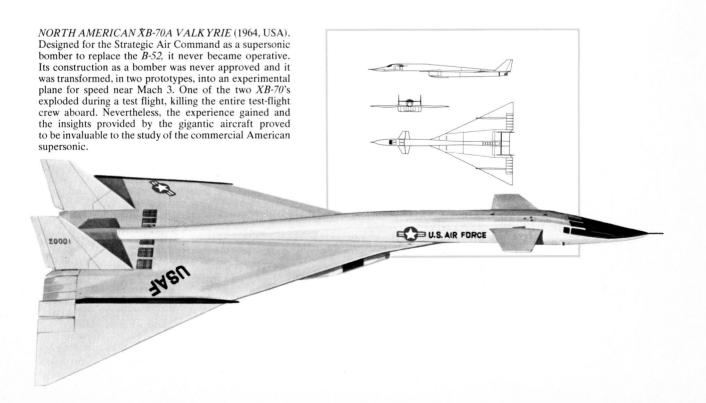

212

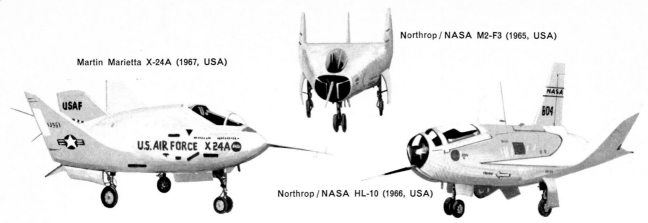

Martin Marietta X-24A (1967, USA)

Northrop / NASA M2-F3 (1965, USA)

Northrop / NASA HL-10 (1966, USA)

Called "lifting body" because they derive their lift from their own shape, they are wingless craft which are used experimentally for studying the orbiter (facing page). At present the craft is brought to its altitude attached to the wings of a B-52, and has already made numerous landings. The close resemblance between the orbiters and the Martin or the 2 Northrops is evident. By using the space-shuttle system, N.A.S.A. technicians hope to solve a double problem: recovery of the craft and its consequent availability for reuse. The economic advantage is obvious, but the orbiter regular landing would also resolve the problematic splashdown reentry of the capsule and the problems associated with "fishing" it out of the ocean.

The last was to become the first human being to set foot on the moon!

We need not dwell on the many other X's which preceded and followed the X-15; it is enough to say that today's most advanced military and commerical craft are a result of their developments. Scientific research in America, Russia, England and France has, in the last few years, amply proved that the enormous sums invested have thoroughly paid off. Nor is it necessary to note here all the milestones on the road to the conquest of space, milestones developed and realized by the genius of aeronautical technicians. For the space capsules, from the Gemini to the Apollo projects, to the Russian capsules, from the *Vostok* to the *Soyuz*, cannot really be called airplanes: they are actually spaceships. Rather we should note how, in the near future, even the space airmobiles will be linked with the airplane. These spacecraft will leave the ground with vertical takeoff and they will be able to land at the pilot's command, on a runway similar to those presently used in large airports.

After the triumph of the Apollo space

program, which enabled man to explore the moon, N.A.S.A. has planned to launch space stations in orbit. These will be true scientific space laboratories which should serve as bases for further exploration of the moon, the surrounding space, and at a future date, Mars. From an engineering point of view, the space station is a large capsule weighing about 50 tons, measuring 32.80 feet in diameter and 49.20 feet in length, divided into 4 floors where men can live relatively comfortably while rotating around the Earth in a 230 to 342-mile orbit. The inhabitants of a space station (which is being studied by technicians at McDonnel Douglas Astronautics and North American Rockwell) would have 90-day tours of duty and would be constantly supplied with food, technical instruments, etc., by a "space shuttle."

On February 18, 1970, N.A.S.A. asked the American aerospace industry for "proposals" for this new type of spaceship. It should be able to: carry about 24,000 pounds of useful cargo; be reusable; reenter the atmosphere with less deceleration and less heat exposure than the present capsules; and land

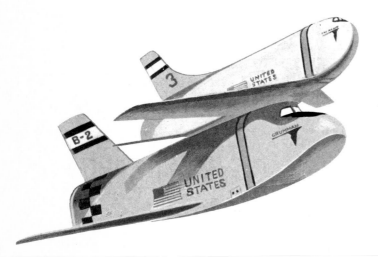

On March 2, 1970, Grumman, at the head of a large consortium made up of General Electric, Northrop and Eastern Airlines, announced its intention to bid on N.A.S.A.'s February 18 decision to initiate a project for the building of a space shuttle. The drawing here illustrates how the project could take shape. It shows a "booster" or vertical launch rocket plane whose task would be to bring the smaller spaceship orbiter into orbit. The orbiter would then complete the space mission. Both booster and orbiter would then reenter the atmosphere at a 60-degree angle, headed for the original launch pad and landing on a runway no longer than that necessary for a supersonic.

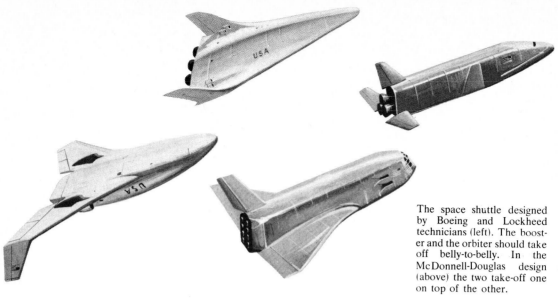

The space shuttle designed by Boeing and Lockheed technicians (left). The booster and the orbiter should take off belly-to-belly. In the McDonnell-Douglas design (above) the two take-off one on top of the other.

on permanent runways. Its long-run objective is obviously not only to make space transportation more economical than it is at present (for example, only the capsule from the Apollo project is salvageable though not reusable and the ship's reentry and splashdown entails a very costly recovery operation), but also to permit scientists who are no longer young or as physically fit as the present astronauts to travel into and study space. Three consortiums have made presentations of their projects: the group made up of Grumman—General Electric, Northrop, Eastern Airlines; the group formed by Boeing—Lockheed, TWA; and finally McDonnel Douglas—Martin Marietta, TRW, Pan American Airlines. All 3 based their projects on 2 main elements: a "booster" or elevator whose only task is to carry into orbit the "orbiter," a "spaceship" able to stay in space for 7 days before returning to Earth on its own. Propulsion would be supplied by rocket engines fueled by an oxygen—hydrogen high-pressure liquid. The ships would carry a 2-man crew each and between 10 and 12 people or supplies or parts for enlarging the space stations.

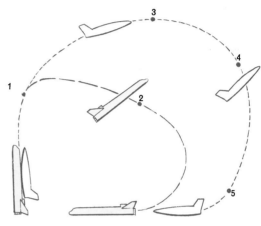

Above, a design of the space shuttle's operation: the booster bumps the orbiter to a 31-mile altitude, (1) detaches and reenters base, (2) the orbiter makes its space trip, (3) reenters the atmosphere and begins losing speed at altitude 76 miles, (4) passes to subsonic speed at altitude 55,760 feet, (5) and lands with a speed of 186 miles per hour. Below, North American Rockwell's design for orbiter (2 versions, A & B) and booster (C). The draftsmen present 2 alternative solutions.

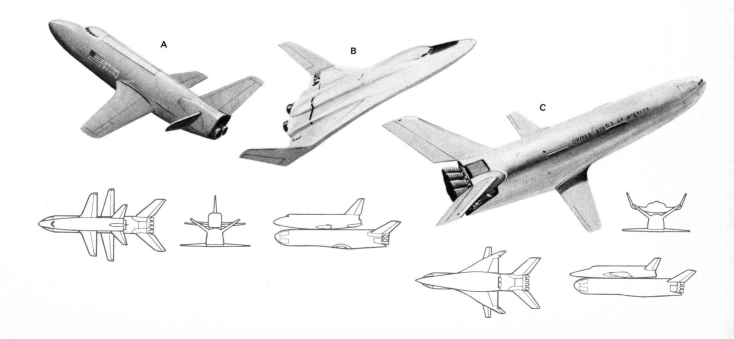

The orbiters would also be very useful for recovery and repair of artificial weather satellites, communications and controlling air-traffic satellites in space, etc. Before April 1970, 4396 "objects" had been launched into space, and 1859 of these are still circling around the Earth.

As part of the studies for "soft" reentry of the booster and orbiter into the Earth's atmosphere and their landing, "lifting bodies" such as the *Martin Marietta X-24A,* the *Northrop M2-F3* and the *Northrop HL-10* have been tested. The results have thus far been positive and it is understandable that the orbiters proposed by all these consortiums closely resemble these experimental prototypes, though they are of course much larger.

N.A.S.A. has roughly scheduled the launching of the first space stations into orbit by Saturn rockets for 1978. These stations would be serviced by the space shuttle. Recently the U.S. government has severely cut N.A.S.A.'s budget for space research. However to date there has been no official announcement that the program has been definitively canceled; we can therefore presume only that it will be delayed. When we consider that about $8 billion will be necessary to carry out the program, it begins to appear doubtful that such a sum will ever be made available to science. But the same doubts arose when it became known that the Apollo project would take millions of dollars. No one believed it would ever come about; very few thought it possible. And yet man has gone to the moon.

Today the idea of space stations, of spaceships which keep them in constant contact with Earth, of explorations of Mars may seem unrealistic. But as one of the very first pioneers, Giulio Douhet, said, "In aviation, 10 years is an eternity." Who knows whether in 10 years what we now consider science fiction may not become reality.

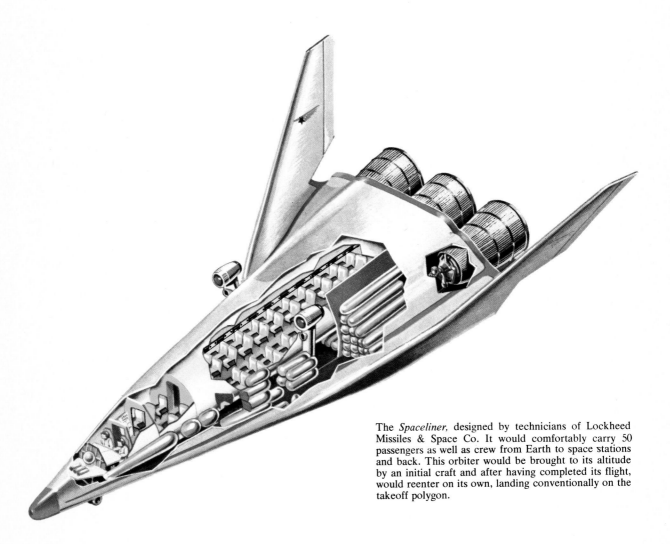

The *Spaceliner,* designed by technicians of Lockheed Missiles & Space Co. It would comfortably carry 50 passengers as well as crew from Earth to space stations and back. This orbiter would be brought to its altitude by an initial craft and after having completed its flight, would reenter on its own, landing conventionally on the takeoff polygon.

Color Drawings and Art Supervision:
MARCO ROTA

Jacket Design:

Albert Squillace

Black Drawings:

Ercole Arseni, Genni Buccheri, Gino Marchesi, Romano Peirano.

Production Supervision:

Giovanni Adamoli

Production Assistants:

Gian Franco Adamoli, Gian Alberto Bedendo, Laura Brancato, Daniele Casartelli, Gabriella Formigari, Nadia Morini, Mirka Soltoggio, Roberto Voltolina.

Research Assistants:

Lisa Goldberg, Anita Ladden, Giuliana Nannicini, Sisto Schultze.

Design:

Giuseppe Ricci and Ufficio Grafico Officine Grafiche Arnoldo Mondadori, Verona.

Translation from the Italian:

Lisa Taruschio

In acknowledging the help received in the preparation of this book, the author wishes to express his debt to the Public Relations and Documentation Department of Ministero della Difesa Aeronautica, le Service Historique de l'Armée de l'Air, the Musée de l'Air, Paris, the Union Syndicale Française des Industries Aéronautiques et Spatiales, the International Civil Aviation Organization, the Public Relations offices of U.S.A.F. and U.S. Navy, the Aviation Service of Esso Standard, the Photograph archives of Arnoldo Mondadori Publishers. Special appreciation is expressed to the members of the Public Relations offices of the Aircraft industries and Airline companies, who have contributed so much to the production of this book.

TECHNICAL DATA ON THE AIRPLANES ILLUSTRATED

The data contained in these tables has been gathered from different sources, among these: publication departments of the production factories; previously published volumes; specialized magazines; and the extraordinarily valuable technical file of the Jane's *All the World's Aircraft* which, since 1909 when it began publishing, remains the most accurate and valuable source for worldwide aircraft data.

In several instances, the figures are the closest possible estimates; data is sometimes not fully available even for relatively recent planes such as those of World War II. Quite often an official source is missing and sometimes conflicting data appears in different sources. In such cases, the data the author has selected may at times conflict with the reader's.

Notes on the headings in tables

Page
Indicates the page on which illustrations of the aircraft (here described technically) are given.

Aircraft
The names and initials of the aircraft refer to the models illustrated, for which technical data is given. For post-1950 Russian crafts, the NATO code is also given.

Builder
For aircraft built before 1950, the company's name is indicated as it was when the plane was first built. For the more recent aircraft, the present name of the company is given: for example the *Buccaneer* was built by Blackburn. Today Blackburn has become part of the Hawker-Siddeley group. The aircraft is therefore listed as the *Hawker Siddeley Buccaneer*.

Country of origin
Indicates the country where the aircraft was designed and built.

Type
The same aircraft can be built in many types: fighter, reconnaissance, attack planes, etc. Generally the basic type is indicated and is the type to which technical data refers.

Year
Generally refers to the year the basic type entered service and not necessarily to the version or series whose technical data is given and which generally are illustrated. For experimental aircraft, prototypes or other craft not yet in production, the year of the craft's first flight is given.

Engine
Horsepower is given for piston or turbine engines and thrust for jet engines. Jet power is always indicated to the point of maximum power, or with the use of the after-burning system (ab) if the engine has it.

Wing Spread
For the multiplanes with different wings or varying measurements, the length of the longest wing has been given. For variable-wing crafts, the measurements at full-wing spread is given.

Length
Total external length of the aircraft, including front and rear antennas.

Height
Total height of the aircraft with landing gear down.

Empty weight
The weight of the flight-ready aircraft without crew, fuel, freight or weapons is generally given.

Maximum takeoff weight
Maximum weight at takeoff is indicated, including all possibilities, even conceivable overweight. Under normal conditions, takeoff weight is generally less than the indicated figure.

Payload
Maximum weight for passengers or cargo is given.

Maximum speed
Highest speed of which the aircraft is capable.

Cruising speed
The most economical, that is, the speed which consumes least fuel.

Range
Unless otherwise indicated, range means the maximum distance which the aircraft can cover under optimum fuel supply and cargo conditions. Range varies according to: quantity of fuel available in relation to useful cargo; speed; cruising altitude; meteorological conditions. It is therefore a figure based on optimum conditions and is intended as indicative. For example, for fighters the maximum range generally refers to transfer flights at economic speed, while the tactical operative range is logically much shorter.

Ceiling
Refers to the maximum altitude for military aircraft and the economic altitude for commercial aircraft. For experimental planes it can also mean the maximum altitude reached during test flights.

Crew
For military aircraft the term is applied to the number of crew necessary to make the plane completely operative. For transport or passenger planes, it means the number of crew assigned to seats either in the pilot's cabin or in the passenger cabin. However, very often the number of crew may be greater, depending on the decisions of the airline itself.

Weapons
Data generally refers to the type illustrated.

THE LEGENDARY FLYING MACHINES

Page	Aircraft	Builder	Nation of origin	Year	Engine	Wing spread	
						ft	m
18	Wright Flyer	Wright Brothers	USA	1903	12 hp Wright (4 cl.)	40.4	12,29
18	Wright Flyer III	Wright Brothers	USA	1905	15-20 hp Wright (4 cl.)	40.6	12,34
19	14 Bis	Alberto Santos-Dumont	F	1906	50 hp Antoinette (8 cl.)	36.9	11,20
19	Voisin Biplane	Voisin Frères	F	1907	50 hp Antoinette (8 cl.)	32.8	9,96
20	Dunne D.5	Short Brothers	GB	1910	50 hp Green (4 cl.)	46.0	14,02
20	Safety	—	GB	1909	—	—	—
20	Coanda	Coanda	F	1910	50 hp Clerget (4 cl.)	33.1	10,08
20	Roshon	Roshon	USA	1908	—	—	—
20	Cygnet II	Aerial Experiment Ass.	USA	1908	35 hp Curtiss	52.5	15,97
21	Givaudan	Vermorel Cie	F	1908	40 hp Vermorel (8 cl.)	—	—
21	Hydravion	Henri Fabre	F	1910	50 hp Gnome (7 cl.)	45.11	13,99
21	Ellehammer IV	Jacob C. H. Ellehammer	DK	1908	30 hp Ellehammer (5 cl.)	39.4	11,99
21	Edward Rhomboidal	Edward	GB	1909	—	—	—
21	Koechlin-De Pischoff	Koechlin-De Pischoff	F	1908	12 hp Buchet	—	—
21	Miller	Franz Miller - Torino	I	1908	55 hp Miller (4 cl.)	23.0	7,01
21	Chiribiri	A. Chiribiri & C.	I	1912	60 hp Chiribiri	31.0	9,45
21	Aéroplane	Cap. Dorand	F	1908	43 hp Anzani	—	—
21	D'Équevilley	D'Équevilley	F	1909	8 hp	—	—
21	Multiplane nº 1	Horatio Phillips	GB	1904	22 hp Phillips (4 cl.)	17.9	5,41
21	Cody	Cody Factory	GB	1911	60 hp Green	43.0	13,11
21	Seddon	—	GB	1910	—	—	—
22	Vuia	Trajan Vuia	F	1906	25 hp Serpollet	28.6	8,68
22	Goupy II	Louis Blériot	F	1909	25 hp R.E.P.	20.0	6,10
22	Henri Farman III	Henri Farman	F	1909	50 hp Gnome	32.8	9,95
22	Breguet III	Breguet	F	1912	80 hp Canton Unmé (7 cl.)	44.8	13,61
23	Demoiselle 20	Alberto Santos-Dumont	F	1909	35 hp Dutheil-Chalmers (2 cl.)	16.7	5,05
23	Antoinette IV	Société Antoinette	F	1908	50 hp Antoinette (8 cl.)	42.0	12,80
24	Roe I Triplane	A. V. Roe	GB	1909	20 hp J.A.P. (4 cl.)	20.0	6,10
24	Curtiss Hydro-Aeroplane	Glenn Curtiss	USA	1911	Curtiss	26.0	7,92
24	Avro F	A. V. Roe & Co.	GB	1912	35 hp Viale (5 cl.)	28.0	8,53
24	Deperdussin Racer	Deperdussin Cie	F	1912	160 hp Gnome (14 cl.)	21.8	6,60
25	Golden Flyer	Herring-Curtiss Co.	USA	1909	50 hp Curtiss (8 cl.)	28.9	8,76
25	Benoist XIV	Benoist	USA	1914	2/100 hp Roberts	45.0	13,72
25	Blériot XI	Louis Blériot	F	1909	25 hp Anzani (3 cl.)	25.6	7,77

Abbreviations used in the table

cl.	cylinders	I	Italy
DK	Denmark	kg	kilograms
F	France	km	kilometers
ft	feet	lb	pounds
GB	Great Britain	m	meters
h	hour	ml	miles
hp	horse-power	USA	United States of America

The values expressed in the tables have been rounded off for approximation to the unit considered in order to simplify reading and reference

Length		Height		Empty weight		Max take-off weight		Speed		Crew	Notes
ft	m	ft	m	lb	kg	lb	kg	ml/h	km/h		
21.1	6,43	8.0	2,44	605	274	750	340	30	48	1	
28.0	8,53	8.0	2,44	—	—	855	388	35	56	1	
31.9	9,68	11.2	3,40	—	—	661	300	25	40	1	
39.3	11,97	11.0	3,35	1,100	500	1,320	599	34	55	1	
18.0	5,49	11.6	3,50	—	—	1,550	703	45	72	1	
—	—	—	—	—	—	—	—	—	—	1	
39.7	12,07	9.0	2,74	—	—	926	420	—	—	1	Turbines
—	—	—	—	—	—	—	—	—	—	1	
—	—	—	—	—	—	950	431	—	—	1	
19.0	5,79	—	—	—	—	—	—	—	—	1	
27.10	8,48	12.0	3,66	—	—	1,047	475	55	88	1	
—	—	—	—	286	130	—	—	42	68	1	
—	—	—	—	—	—	—	—	—	—	1	
—	—	—	—	120	54	—	—	—	—	1	
23.0	7,01	—	—	—	—	551	250	—	—	1	
24.0	7,32	—	—	772	350	—	—	103	166	1	
—	—	—	—	661	300	—	—	—	—	1	
5.2	1,57	—	—	308	140	—	—	—	—	1	
13.9	4,19	10.0	3,05	—	—	600	272	34	55	1	
38.0	11,58	13.0	3,96	—	—	1,900	862	70	113	1	Payload: 453 kg (1,000 lb) - 3 passengers
—	—	—	—	—	—	—	—	—	—	1	
9.10	2,99	10.9	3,28	—	—	531	241	—	—	1	Carbonic acid
23.0	7,01	8.0	2,44	461	209	639	290	60	97	1	Range: 2 h
39.3	11,97	11.6	3,50	990	449	1,213	550	37	60	1	
29.0	8,84	9.10	2,99	1,430	649	—	—	62	100	2	Payload: 300 kg (662 lb) - Range: 7 h
26.3	8,00	7.10	2,38	—	—	315	143	56	90	1	
37.7	11,46	9.10	2,99	992	450	1,300	590	46	75	1	
23.0	7,01	11.0	3,35	300	136	450	204	25	40	1	
—	—	—	—	—	—	—	—	50	80	1	
23.0	7,01	7.7	2,31	550	249	800	363	65	105	1	
20.0	6,10	7.6	2,28	—	—	1,350	612	130	209	1	
28.5	8,66	9.0	2,74	550	249	830	376	45	72	1	
26.0	7,92	—	—	—	—	—	—	70	113	1	2 passengers
26.3	8,00	8.6	2,59	463	210	661	300	36	58	1	

AIRCRAFT OF WORLD WAR I

Page	Aircraft	Builder	Type	Year	Engine	Wing spread ft	Wing spread m
	FRANCE						
30	Maurice Farman MF.11	Farman Frères	Rc/LB	1914	100 hp Renault	53.0	16,15
30	Dorand AR.1	Section Technique de l'Aéronautique	Rc/T	1917	190 hp Renault	43.7	13,29
30	Caudron G.IV	Caudron Frères	Rc/T	1915	2/80 hp Le Rhône (9 cl.)	56.5	17,20
31	Voisin 5	Gabriel Voisin	LB	1915	150 hp Salmson	48.4	14,73
31	Voisin 8	Gabriel Voisin	Br	1916	220 hp Peugeot	61.8	18,79
31	Henri Farman HF.20	Farman Frères	Rc/LB	1914	80 hp Gnome	44.10	13,66
31	Henri Farman HF.40	Farman Frères	Rc/LB	1916	160 hp Renault	57.10	17,62
31	Salmson 2	Société des Moteurs Salmson	Rc	1918	260 hp Salmson	38.8	11,78
31	F.B.A. C	Franco-British Aviation	AS/Rc	1915	130 hp Clerget	44.11	13,69
32	Morane-Saulnier N	Morane-Saulnier	Fr	1914	110 hp Le Rhône	27.3	8,31
32	Nieuport 11 Bébé	Établissements Nieuport	Fr	1915	80 hp Le Rhône	24.9	7,55
32	Breguet-Michelin BrM.5	Louis Breguet	Br	1915	265 hp Renault	57.9	17,60
32	Spad VII	S.P.A.D.	Fr	1916	180 hp Hispano-Suiza	25.6	7,77
32	Spad S XIII	S.P.A.D.	Fr	1917	200 hp Hispano-Suiza	26.11	8,20
32	Spad S XI	S.P.A.D.	Rc/LB	1917	215 hp Hispano-Suiza	36.10	11,22
33	Hanriot HD-1	S.A. des Appareils d'Aviation Hanriot	Fr	1917	130 hp Le Rhône	28.6	8,68
33	Nieuport 17	Établissements Nieuport	Fr	1916	110 hp Le Rhône	26.10	8,17
33	Breguet Br. 14B2	Louis Breguet	Br/Rc	1917	300 hp Renault	47.1	14,36
	GREAT BRITAIN						
34	Bristol Scout D	British & Colonial Aeroplane Co. Ltd	Rc	1915	80 hp Clerget	24.7	7,50
34	Royal Aircraft Factory B.E.12	Daimler Co. Ltd	Fr/LB	1916	150 hp R.A.F. (12 cl.)	37.0	11,28
34	Airco D.H.4	Aircraft Manufacturing Co.	Br	1917	375 hp R.R. Eagle	42.5	12,93
35	Airco D.H.2	Aircraft Manufacturing Co.	Fr	1916	100 hp Gnome Monosoupape	28.3	8,61
35	Royal Aircraft Factory F.E.2b	Various	Fr/Rc	1915	160 hp Beardmore	47.9	14,56
35	Airco D.H.5	Aircraft Manufacturing Co.	Fr	1917	110 hp Le Rhône	25.8	7,82
35	Sopwith Triplane	Sopwith Aviation Co.	Fr	1917	130 hp Clerget	26.6	8,07
35	Royal Aircraft Factory R.E.8	Various	Rc/LB	1916	150 hp R.A.F. (12 cl.)	42.7	12,98
35	Royal Aircraft Factory B.E.2c	Various	Rc	1914	90 hp R.A.F. (8 cl.)	37.0	11,28
36	Avro 504J	A.V. Roe & Co.	T	1916	100 hp Gnome Monosoupape	36.0	10,97
36	Vickers F.B.5	Vickers Ltd	Fr/Rc	1914	100 hp Gnome Monosoupape	36.6	11,12
36	Sopwith F.1 Camel	Sopwith Aviation Co.	Fr	1917	130 hp Clerget	28.0	8,53
36	Bristol F.2B	British & Colonial Aeroplane Co. Ltd	Fr	1917	275 hp R.R. Falcon III	39.3	11,97
36	Royal Aircraft Factory S.E.5a	Various	Fr	1917	200 hp Wolseley Viper	26.7	8,10
37	Short Bomber	Various	Br	1916	250 hp R.R. Eagle III	85.0	25,91
37	Handley Page 0/400	Handley Page Ltd	HB	1916	2/360 hp R.R. Eagle VIII	100.0	30,48
37	Handley Page V/1500	Handley Page Ltd	HB	1918	4/375 hp R.R. Eagle IV	126.0	38,40
37	Blackburn Kangaroo	Blackburn Aeroplane & Motor Co. Ltd	Br	1918	2/255 hp R.R. Falcon II	74.10	22,81
	RUSSIA						
38	Ilya Mourometz V	J.J. Sikorsky & R.B.V.Z.	Br	1915	4/150 hp Sunbeam	97.9	29,80
38	Anatra DS	Zavod A.A. Anatra	Rc	1916	150 hp Salmson	40.7	12,37
38	Lebed 11	V. A. Lebedev Aeronautics Ltd	Rc	1915	150 hp Salmson	43.1	13,14
	ITALY						
39	Pomilio PE	O. Pomilio & C.	Rc	1917	260 hp Fiat A-12	38.8	11,78
39	Fiat R-2	Fiat Aviazione	Rc/Br	1917	300 hp Fiat	40.5	12,32
39	Ansaldo A-1 Balilla	Giovanni Ansaldo & C.	Fr	1917	220 hp S.P.A. 6A	25.2	7,67
40	Ansaldo S.V.A.5	Giovanni Ansaldo & C.	Rc/Br	1917	220 hp S.P.A. 6A	31.0	9,45

Abbreviations used in the table

AS	anti-submarine	h	hour	m	meters
b.	bombs	HB	heavy bomber	mg.	machine-gun
Br	bomber	hp	horse-power	ml	miles
cl.	cylinders	kg	kilograms	MR	maritime reconnaissance
FB	fighter-bomber	km	kilometers	R.A.F.	Royal Aircraft Factory
Fr	fighter	LB	light bomber	Rc	reconnaissance
ft	feet	lb	pounds	T	trainer
g.	gun	LF	light fighter		

Length		Height		Empty Weight		Max take-off weight		Speed		Range	Ceiling		Crew	Armament
ft	m	ft	m	lb	kg	lb	kg	ml/h	km/h	h	ft	m		
31.0	9,45	10.5	3,18	1,360	617	2,045	928	66	106	3.45′	12,500	3.800	2	1 mg., b. (288 lb; 130 kg)
30.0	9,14	10.10	3,30	1,782	808	2,750	1.247	94	152	3.00′	18,000	5.500	2	2-3 mg., b. (180 lb; 82 kg)
23.6	7,16	8.5	2,57	1,810	821	2,915	1.322	82	132	3.30′	14,100	4.300	2	1-2 mg., b. (250 lb; 113 kg)
31.3	9,53	11.11	3,63	1,760	798	2,552	1.158	65	105	3.30′	11,500	3.500	2	1 mg., b. (132 lb; 60 kg)
36.1	11,00	11.6	3,50	2,893	1.312	4,100	1.860	82	132	4.00′	14,100	4.300	2	1-2 mg., b. (396 lb; 180 kg)
27.9	8,46	10.0	3,05	808	367	1,416	642	65	105	200 ml; 320 km	9,000	2.750	2	1 mg.
30.4	9,24	12.9	3,89	1,650	748	2,475	1.123	84	135	2.20′	16,000	4.900	2	1 mg.
27.11	8,51	9.6	2,89	1,676	760	2,798	1.269	115	185	3.00′	20,500	6.250	2	2-3 mg.
28.10	8,78	11.2	3,40	—	—	2,072	940	68	110	186 ml; 300 km	11,500	3.500	2	1 mg., b.
22.0	6,71	8.3	2,52	735	333	1,122	509	102	165	1.30′	13,100	4.000	1	1 mg.
19.0	5,79	8.0	2,44	774	351	1,133	514	97	156	2.30′	18,000	5.500	1	1 mg.
32.6	9,90	12.9	3,89	3,067	1.391	4,235	1.921	88	142	435 ml; 700 km	14,100	4.300	2	1 mg., 1 g. (37 mm), b. (640 lb; 290 kg)
20.1	6,13	7.8	2,33	1,100	500	1,550	703	119	192	2.15′	18,000	5.500	1	1 mg.
20.8	6,30	7.11	2,41	1,255	569	1,815	823	130	209	2.00′	22,300	6.800	1	2 mg.
25.5	7,75	8.6	2,59	1,485	674	2,310	1.048	109	176	2.15′	23,000	7.000	2	2-3 mg., b. (154 lb; 70 kg)
19.2	5,84	8.4	2,54	898	407	1,334	605	114	183	2.30′	23,000	7.000	1	1 mg.
18.11	5,77	8.0	2,44	825	374	1,233	559	110	177	2.00′	17,400	5.300	1	1 mg.
29.1	8,87	10.10	3,30	2,290	1.039	3,988	1.809	110	177	3.00′	19,000	5.800	2	2-3 mg., b. (660 lb; 300 kg)
20.8	6,30	8.6	2,59	760	345	1,250	567	100	161	2.00′	16,000	4.900	1	1 mg.
27.3	8,31	11.0	3,35	1,635	742	2,352	1.067	102	164	2.30′	12,500	3.800	1	1 mg.
30.8	9,34	11.8	3,55	2,387	1.083	3,472	1.575	143	230	435 ml; 700 km	22,000	6.700	2	2-4 mg., b. (460 lb; 209 kg)
25.2	7,67	9.6	2,89	943	428	1,441	654	93	150	2.45′	14,500	4.420	1	1 mg.
32.3	9,83	12.7	3,84	2,061	935	3,037	1.378	91	146	2.30′	11,000	3.350	2	2 mg.
22.0	6,71	9.1	2,77	1,010	458	1,492	677	102	164	2.45′	16,000	4.900	1	1 mg.
19.4	5,89	10.6	3,20	1,100	500	1,541	699	113	182	2.45′	20,500	6.250	1	1-2 mg.
27.10	8,48	11.4	3,45	1,803	818	2,678	1.215	102	164	4.15′	13,500	4.115	2	2-3 mg., b. (260 lb; 118 kg)
27.3	8,31	11.1	3,38	1,370	621	2,142	972	72	116	3.00′	10,000	3.050	2	2 mg., b. (224 lb; 102 kg)
29.5	8,97	10.5	3,18	1,100	500	1,800	816	82	132	3.00′	13,000	3.950	2	—
27.2	8,28	11.6	3,50	1,220	553	2,050	930	70	113	4.00′	9,000	2.750	2	1-2 mg.
18.9	5,72	8.6	2,59	929	421	1,453	659	113	182	2.30′	19,000	5.800	1	2 mg.
25.10	7,87	9.9	2,97	1,930	875	2,779	1.261	122	196	3.00′	20,000	6.100	2	2-3 mg., b. (240 lb; 109 kg)
20.11	6,38	9.6	2,89	1,387	629	1,988	902	138	222	340 ml; 550 km	19,500	5.950	1	2 mg.
45.0	13,72	15.0	4,57	—	—	6,800	3.084	77	125	6.00′	9,500	2.900	2	1 mg., b. (920 lb; 417 kg)
62.10	19,15	22.0	6,71	8,502	3.857	13,360	6.060	97	157	8.00′	8,500	2.590	4	3-5 mg., b. (1,568 lb; 710 kg)
64.0	19,51	23.0	7,01	—	—	30,000	13.608	90	146	6.00′	11,000	3.350	4	6 mg., b. (7,550 lb; 3.390 kg)
46.0	14,02	16.10	5,13	5,284	2.397	8,017	3.637	100	161	8.00′	10,500	3.200	4	2 mg., b. (1,840 lb; 832 kg)
56.1	17,10	15.6	4,72	6,950	3.153	10,130	4.595	75	121	5.00′	9,840	3.000	7	4-7 mg., b. (1,150 lb; 522 kg)
26.6	8,07	10.5	3,18	1,800	816	2,566	1.164	89	144	3.30′	14,100	4.300	2	2 mg.
26.1	7,95	—	—	1,905	864	2,678	1.215	83	134	3.00′	11,500	3.500	2	2 mg., b. (200 lb; 90 kg)
29.4	8,94	11.0	3,35	2,505	1.136	3,390	1.538	120	194	3.00′	16,400	5.000	2	2 mg.
28.8	8,73	10.10	3,30	2,690	1.220	3,690	1.674	112	180	445 ml; 716 km	—	—	2	2-3 mg.
22.5	6,84	8.3	2,52	1,823	827	1,951	885	137	220	2.00′	16,400	5.000	1	2 mg.
26.7	8,10	9.8	2,94	1,507	684	2,090	948	143	230	4.00′	22,000	6.700	1	2 mg.

AIRCRAFT OF WORLD WAR I (continued)

Page	Aircraft	Builder	Type	Year	Engine	Wing spread	
						ft	m
40	Macchi M.5	S.A. Nieuport-Macchi	Fr/MR	1917	160 hp Isotta Fraschini V-4B	39.0	11,89
40	Caproni Ca.3	Società di Aviazione Ing. Caproni	Br	1915	3/150 hp Isotta Fraschini V-4B	72.10	22,20
40	Caproni Ca.4	Società di Aviazione Ing. Caproni	Br	1917	3/270 hp Isotta Fraschini	98.1	29,90
	UNITED STATES OF AMERICA						
41	Curtiss JN-3	Curtiss Aeroplane and Motor Co.	T	1915	90 hp Curtiss OX-5	43.7	13,29
41	Standard E-1	Standard Aircraft Co.	T	1917	80 hp Le Rhône 9C	24.0	7,32
41	Thomas-Morse S-4	Thomas-Morse Aircraft Co.	T	1917	80 hp Le Rhône	26.6	8,07
42	Curtiss H-12	Curtiss Aeroplane and Motor Co.	AS/Rc	1917	2/330 hp Liberty 12	92.8	28,24
42	Curtiss N-9	Curtiss Aeroplane and Motor Co.	T	1917	100 hp Curtiss OX-6	53.4	16,25
42	Packard-Le Père LUSAC-11	Packard Motor Car Co.	Fr	1918	400 hp Liberty 12A	41.7	12,68
	GERMANY AND THE CENTRAL POWERS						
43	Etrich A-II Taube	Various	Rc/T	1910	100 hp Mercedes D I	47.1	14,36
43	Fokker E.III	Fokker Flugzeug-Werke GmbH	Fr	1915	100 hp Oberursel U.I (9 cl.)	31.2	9,50
43	Aviatik B-II	Automobil- und Aviatik-Werke A.G.	Rc	1914	120 hp Mercedes	41.0	12,50
44	Albatros D I	Albatros Werke GmbH	Fr	1916	160 hp Mercedes D III	27.10	8,48
44	Albatros D II	Various	Fr	1916	160 hp Mercedes D III	27.10	8,48
44	Albatros D III	Albatros Werke GmbH	Fr	1917	160 hp Mercedes D IIIa (6 cl.)	29.8	9,04
44	Albatros D V	Albatros Werke GmbH	Fr	1917	180 hp Mercedes D IIIa (6 cl.)	29.8	9,04
44	Albatros B II	Albatros Werke GmbH	Rc/T	1914	100 hp Mercedes (6 cl.)	42.0	12,80
44	Albatros W 4	Albatros Werke GmbH	Fr	1916	160 hp Mercedes D III (6 cl.)	31.2	9,50
44	Albatros C I	Albatros Werke GmbH	Rc	1915	150 hp Benz Bz III	42.4	12,90
44	Albatros C III	Albatros Werke GmbH	Rc	1916	160 hp Mercedes D III	38.4	11,68
44	Albatros C VII	Albatros Werke GmbH	Rc/Br	1917	200 hp Benz Bz IV (6 cl.)	41.11	12,78
44	Albatros C XII	Albatros Werke GmbH	Rc	1917	260 hp Mercedes D IVa (6 cl.)	47.2	14,38
45	Fokker Dr.I	Fokker Flugzeug-Werke GmbH	Fr	1917	110 hp Thulin/Le Rhône 9J	23.8	7,21
45	Rumpler C I	E. Rumpler Flugzeug-Werke GmbH	Rc/LB	1915	160 hp Mercedes D III	39.10	12,14
45	L.V.G. C II	Luft-Verkehrs-Gesellschaft	Rc/T	1915	160 hp Mercedes D III (6 cl.)	42.2	12,85
45	Fokker D VII	Fokker Flugzeug-Werke GmbH	Fr	1918	185 hp B.M.W. IIIa (6 cl.)	29.3	8,92
46	Lohner C I	Jakob Lohner Werke & Co.	Rc	1914	160 hp Austro-Daimler	44.2	13,46
46	Lloyd C II	Ungarische Lloyd Flugzeug A.G.	Rc/T	1915	145 hp Hiero	45.11	13,99
46	Hansa-Brandenburg D I	Phönix Flugzeug-Werke A.G.	Fr	1916	160 hp Austro-Daimler	27.11	8,51
46	Aviatik D I	Oesterreichische-Ungarische Flugzeugfabrik Aviatik	Fr	1917	200 hp Austro-Daimler	26.3	8,00
46	Hannover CL IIIa	Hannoversche Wagonfabrik A.G.	LF	1917	180 hp Argus As III (6 cl.)	38.5	11,71
46	Halberstadt CL II	Halberstädter Flugzeug-Werke GmbH	LF	1917	160 hp Mercedes D III	35.4	10,77
47	Phönix D I	Phönix Flugzeug-Werke A.G.	Fr	1917	200 hp Hiero	32.5	9,88
47	Pfalz D III	Pfalz Flugzeug-Werke GmbH	Fr	1917	160 hp Mercedes D III	30.10	9,39
47	L.F.G. Roland D VIb	Luftfahrzeug GmbH	Fr	1918	200 hp Benz Bz IIIa (6 cl.)	30.10	9,39
47	Junkers CL I	Junkers-Fokker A.G.	LF	1918	180 hp Mercedes D IIIa	39.6	12,04
47	Friedrichshafen FF 33L	Flugzeugbau Friedrichshafen GmbH	MR	1916	150 hp Benz Bz III (6 cl.)	43.8	13,31
47	Hansa-Brandenburg W 12	Hansa & Brandenburgische Flugzeug-Werke GmbH	Fr	1917	150 hp Benz Bz III (6 cl.)	36.9	11,20
48	Gotha G V	Gothaer Waggonfabrik A.G.	Br	1917	2/260 hp Mercedes D IVa (6 cl.)	77.9	23,70
48	Friedrichshafen G III	Flugzeugbau Friedrichshafen GmbH	Br	1917	2/260 hp Mercedes D IVa (6 cl.)	77.11	23,75
48	Zeppelin R VI	Zeppelin Werke Staaken	HB	1917	4/260 hp Mercedes D IVa (6 cl.)	138.5	42,19
49	L.F.G. Roland C II	Luftfahrzeug GmbH	Rc	1916	160 hp Mercedes D III (6 cl.)	33.11	10,34
49	D.F.W. C V	Deutsche Flugzeug-Werke GmbH	Rc	1916	200 hp Benz Bz IV (6 cl.)	43.7	13,29
49	A.E.G. G IV	Allgemeine Elektrizitäts Gesellschaft	Br	1916	2/260 hp Mercedes D IVa	60.2	18,34

Abbreviations used in the table

AS	anti-submarine	h	hour	m	meters
b.	bombs	HB	heavy bomber	mg.	machine-gun
Br	bomber	hp	horse-power	ml	miles
cl.	cylinders	kg	kilograms	MR	maritime reconnaissance
FB	fighter-bomber	km	kilometers	R.A.F.	Royal Aircraft Factory
Fr	fighter	LB	light bomber	Rc	reconnaissance
ft	feet	lb	pounds	T	trainer
g.	gun	LF	light fighter		

Length		Height		Empty weight		Max take-off weight		Speed		Range	Ceiling		Crew	Armament
ft	m	ft	m	lb	kg	lb	kg	ml/h	km/h	h	ft	m		
26.5	8,05	10.4	3,15	1,697	770	2,293	1.040	117	189	3.30'	19,356	5.900	1	2 mg.
35.9	10,90	12.2	3,71	5,080	2.304	8,400	3.810	85	137	3.30'	13,400	4.085	4	3-4 mg., b. (1,000 lb; 454 kg)
43.0	13,11	20.8	6,30	8,150	3.697	14,790	6.709	78	126	7.00'	9,840	3.000	4	4 mg., b. (3,197 lb; 1.450 kg)
27.4	8,33	9.10	2,99	1,580	717	2,130	966	75	121	2.15'	11,000	3.350	2	—
18.10	5,74	7.10	2,38	828	376	1,152	523	100	161	2.30'	14,800	4.510	1	—
18.6	5,64	8.1	2,47	963	437	1,373	623	100	161	—	15,000	4.570	1	1 mg.
46.0	14,02	16.9	5,11	—	—	7,989	3.624	85	137	6.00'	10,800	3.290	4	3-4 mg., b. (460 lb; 209 kg)
—	—	—	—	—	—	—	—	70	113	—	—	—	—	—
25.3	7,70	9.6	2,89	2,466	1.119	3,746	1.699	132	212	320 ml; 515 km	20,200	6.160	2	4 mg.
32.3	9,83	10.4	3,15	1,323	600	1,918	870	71	115	4.00'	9,840	3.000	2	—
23.7	7,19	7.10	2,38	878	398	1,342	609	87	141	1.30'	13,500	4.115	1	2 mg.
23.3	7,09	10.10	3,30	1,470	667	2,400	1.089	62	100	3.00'	20,000	6.100	2	—
24.3	7,40	9.6	2,89	1,423	645	1,976	896	109	176	1.30'	17,000	5.180	1	2 mg.
24.3	7,40	8.6	2,59	1,401	635	1,954	886	109	176	1.30'	17,000	5.180	1	2 mg.
24.0	7,32	9.9	2,97	1,454	660	1,949	884	109	176	2.00'	18,000	5.500	1	2 mg.
24.0	7,32	8.10	2,69	1,511	685	2,061	935	116	187	2.00'	20,500	6.250	1	2 mg.
25.0	7,62	10.4	3,15	1,591	722	2,356	1.069	66	105	4.00'	9,840	3.000	2	—
27.10	8,48	11.11	3,63	1,738	788	2,354	1.068	99	160	3.00'	9,840	3.000	1	2 mg.
25.9	7,85	10.3	3,13	1,925	873	2,618	1.188	82	132	2.30'	9,840	3.000	2	1 mg.
26.3	8,00	10.2	3,10	1,872	849	2,976	1.350	87	141	4.00'	11,100	3.380	2	1-2 mg., b. (200 lb; 90 kg)
28.6	8,68	11.9	3,58	2,176	987	3,410	1.547	106	170	3.20'	16,400	5.000	2	2 mg.
29.0	8,84	10.8	3,25	2,246	1.019	3,606	1.636	109	176	3.15'	16,400	5.000	2	2 mg.
18.11	5,77	9.8	2,94	893	405	1,290	585	103	166	1.30'	20,000	6.100	1	2 mg.
25.9	7,85	10.1	3,08	1,745	792	2,866	1.300	95	153	4.00'	16,500	5.030	2	2 mg., b. (200 lb; 90 kg)
26.7	8,10	9.7	2,92	1,859	843	3,091	1.402	81	130	4.00'	16,500	5.030	2	1-2 mg., b.
22.11	6,99	9.2	2,79	1,540	699	1,870	848	117	188	1.30'	23,000	7.000	1	2 mg.
29.3	8,92	10.8	3,25	—	—	2,998	1.360	85	137	3.00'	11,500	3.500	2	1 mg.
29.6	8,99	11.2	3,40	—	—	2,976	1.350	79	128	2.30'	9,840	3.000	2	1 mg.
20.10	6,35	9.2	2,79	1,475	669	2,024	918	116	187	2.30'	16,400	5.000	1	1 mg.
22.10	6,96	8.2	2,49	1,475	669	1,945	882	115	185	2.30'	20,400	6.220	1	2 mg.
24.10	7,57	9.2	2,79	1,577	715	2,378	1.079	103	166	3.00'	24,600	7.500	2	2 mg.
23.11	7,29	9.0	2,74	1,701	772	2,498	1.133	103	166	3.00'	16,700	5.090	2	2-3 mg., b. (110 lb; 50 kg)
21.9	6,63	9.2	2,79	1,441	654	1,771	803	112	180	3.00'	16,400	5.000	1	2 mg.
22.10	6,96	8.9	2,67	1,595	723	1,991	903	102	165	2.30'	17,000	5.180	1	2 mg.
20.9	6,33	9.2	2,79	1,450	658	1,896	860	114	183	2.00'	19,000	5.800	1	2 mg.
25.11	7,90	8.7	2,62	1,562	709	2,310	1.048	105	169	2.00'	19,685	6.000	2	3 mg.
28.11	8,81	12.10	3,91	2,021	917	3,020	1.370	85	137	5.00'	—	—	2	2 mg.
31.6	9,60	10.10	3,30	2,193	995	3,198	1.451	100	161	3.30'	16,400	5.000	2	2-3 mg.
38.11	11,86	14.1	4,30	6,028	2.734	8,745	3.967	87	140	522 ml; 840 km	21,320	6.500	3	2 mg., b. (1,100 lb; 500 kg)
42.2	12,85	12.0	3,66	5,929	2.689	8,686	3.940	88	141	5.00'	14,800	4.510	3	2-3 mg., b. (3,300 lb; 1.500 kg)
72.6	22,10	20.8	6,30	17,426	7.904	26,066	11.824	84	135	10.00'	14,170	4.320	7	4-7 mg., b. (4,408 lb; 2.000 kg)
24.8	7,52	9.6	2,89	1,681	763	2,825	1.281	103	166	4.00'	13,100	4.000	2	2 mg.
25.10	7,87	10.8	3,25	2,134	968	3,146	1.427	97	156	4.30'	16,400	5.000	2	2 mg.
32.4	9,85	12.9	3,89	5,280	2.395	8,003	3.630	103	166	4.30'	13,100	4.000	3	2 mg., b. (772 lb; 350 kg)

CIVIL AND MILITARY AIRCRAFT FROM 1918 TO 1927

Page	Aircraft	Builder	Nation of origin	Type	Year	Engine	Wing spread ft	Wing spread m	Length ft	Length m	Height ft	Height m
52	Breguet 14T	S.A. Ateliers d'Aviation Louis Breguet	F	—	1919	300 hp Renault	47.1	14,36	29.6	8,99	—	—
52	Airco D.H.4A	Aircraft Manufacturing Co. Ltd	GB	Ps	1919	350 hp R.R. Eagle VIII	42.4	12,90	30.6	9,29	11.0	3,35
52	Caproni C 60 Transaero	Caproni S.A.	I	Ps/Sp	1919	8/400 hp	98.4	29,97	76.8	23,36	30.0	9,14
53	Navy-Curtiss NC	Curtiss	USA	Sp	1919	4/400 hp Liberty (12 cl.)	126.0	38,40	68.5	20,86	24.6	7,47
53	Farman F.60 Goliath	Farman	F	Ps	1919	2/260 hp Salmson CM.9	86.10	26,46	47.0	14,33	—	—
53	Vickers Vimy IV	Vickers Ltd	GB	—	1919	2/360 hp R.R. Eagle VIII	67.0	20,42	42.8	13,00	15.3	4,65
54	Fokker F.III	Fokker	NL	Ps	1921	240 hp A.S. Puma (6 cl.)	57.9	17,60	36.4	11,07	—	—
54	A.E.G. J II	A.E.G.	D	Ps	1919	200 hp Benz Bz IV	44.2	13,46	25.11	7,90	—	—
54	Blériot Spad 46	Blériot-Aéronautique	F	—	1921	370 hp L.D. 12 Da (12 cl.)	41.6	12,65	29.8	9,04	—	—
55	Fokker T.2	Fokker	NL	Tr	1921	420 hp Liberty 12A	81.4	24,79	49.1	14,97	11.10	3,60
55	Aero A-10	Továrna Letadel Aero	CS	Ps	1924	260 hp Maybach Mb IVa	46.6	14,17	33.3	10,14	—	—
55	Douglas DWC/O-5 World Cruiser	Douglas	USA	—	1924	420 hp Liberty 12A	50.0	15,24	35.2	10,72	—	—
56	Albatros L 73	Albatros-Flugzeugwerke GmbH	D	Ps	1926	2/240 hp BMW IV	64.7	19,69	47.11	14,61	15.4	4,67
56	Lévy-Lepen	Hydravions Georges Lévy	F	Tr/Sp	1917	300 hp Renault	60.8	18,49	40.8	12,39	—	—
56	Roland II	Rohrbach-Metall-Flug-zeugbau GmbH	D	Ps	1929	3/280 hp Junkers-L5	86.3	26,29	53.9	16,38	—	—
56	Dornier Do J Wal	Costruzioni Meccaniche Aeronautiche S.A.	D/I	Ps/Sp	1922	2/360 hp R.R. Eagle IX	73.10	22,50	56.7	17,25	—	—
56	Blériot 135	Blériot-Aéronautique	F	Ps	1924	4/230 hp S. 9Ab (9 cl.)	82.0	24,99	47.5	14,46	16.2	4,93
56	Huff-Daland Petrel 31 Duster	Huff-Daland Inc.	USA	Tr	1925	400 hp Liberty	50.0	15,24	38.2	11,58	14.3	4,35
56	Douglas M-4	Douglas	USA	Tr	1927	420 hp Liberty 12A	39.8	12,09	29.7	9,02	10.3	3,13
57	Staaken 1000-PS E.4/20	Zeppelin Werke GmbH	D	Ps	1920	4/260 hp Maybach	101.8	30,98	54.1	16,49	—	—
57	Junkers F 13	Junkers	D	Ps	1919	185 hp BMW IIIa	58.3	17,76	31.6	9,60	14.9	4,50
57	Handley Page W8b	Handley Page Ltd	GB	Ps	1922	2/360 hp R.R. Eagle VIII	75.0	22,86	60.1	18,32	17.0	5,18
57	Caudron C.61bis	Avions Caudron	F	Ps	1923	3/260 hp S. CM.9 (9 cl.)	79.2	24,13	45.11	13,99	—	—
57	Cant 10ter	Cantieri Navali Triestini	I	Ps/Sp	1925	400 hp L. D.	50.2	15,29	36.7	11,15	13.4	4,06
57	Dornier Comet III	Dornier	D	Ps	1925	360 hp R.R. Eagle IX	64.3	19,59	40.4	12,29	11.4	3,45
57	Dornier Do L2 Delphin II	Dornier	D	Ps/Sp	1924	300 hp BMW IV	56.1	17,10	39.4	11,99	—	—
57	Curtiss Falcon Mailplane	Curtiss	USA	Tr	1929	435 hp Liberty 12A	38.0	11,58	27.7	8,41	10.3	3,13
57	Junkers G 24	Diversi	D	Ps	1925	3/310 hp Junkers-L5	98.1	29,90	51.6	15,69	—	—
58	De Havilland D.H.66 Hercules	De Havilland Aircraft Co. Ltd	GB	Ps	1926	3/420 hp B. Jupiter VI	79.6	24,23	55.6	16,91	18.3	5,57
58	Fokker F.VIIa	Diversi	NL	Tr	1926	400 hp G.R. Jupiter (9 cl.)	63.4	19,30	47.1	14,36	—	—
58	Potez 25A.2	Potez	F	Tr	1925	450 hp L.D. 12Eb	46.7	14,20	30.2	9,19	12.0	3,65
58	Armstrong Whitworth Argosy I	Armstrong Whitworth Aircraft Ltd	GB	Ps	1926	3/385 hp A.S. Jaguar III	90.0	27,43	64.6	19,66	19.0	5,79
59	Focke Wulf A 17a	Focke Wulf	D	Ps	1927	480 hp Si. Jupiter VI	65.7	19,99	42.6	12,95	13.1	3,99
59	Lioré et Olivier 213	Lioré et Olivier	F	Ps	1927	2/450 hp Renault 12Ja	76.10	23,41	52.4	15,95	14.1	4,30
60	Savoia Marchetti S 16ter	Società Idrovolanti Alta Italia	I	Sp	1923	450 hp I.F./L.D.	50.10	15,49	32.6	9,90	12.0	3,76
60	Ryan NYP "Spirit of St Louis"	Ryan Airlines Inc.	USA	Tr	1927	220 hp W. Whirl-wind J-5-C (9 cl.)	46.0	14,02	27.5	8,36	8.0	2,44
61	Armstrong Whitworth Siskin IIIA	Armstrong Whitworth Aircraft Ltd	GB	Fr	1925	420 hp A.S. Jaguar IV	33.2	10,11	25.4	7,72	10.2	3,10
61	Armstrong Whitworth Atlas	Armstrong Whitworth Aircraft Ltd	GB	Rc	1927	450 hp A.S. Jaguar IVC	39.6	12,04	28.6	8,68	10.6	3,20
61	Martin MB-1	Glenn L. Martin Co.	USA	Br	1918	2/400 hp Liberty 12A	71.5	21,77	44.10	13,66	14.7	4,45
61	Fokker C.V-D	Fokker	NL	Fr	1926	450 hp Hispano-Suiza	41.0	12,50	31.4	9,55	11.6	3,50
61	Nakajima Type 91	Nakajima	J	Fr	1927	450 hp Jupiter-Nakajima	36.0	10,97	23.8	7,21	9.2	2,79
61	Vought O2U Corsair	Chance Vought Co.	USA	MR	1926	450 hp P. & W. R-1340-88	34.6	10,51	24.5	7,45	10.1	3,08
61	Svenska J6 Jaktfalk	Svenska Aero Aktiebo-laget	S	Fr	1930	500 hp B. Jupiter VIIFs	29.8	9,04	23.5	7,14	11.4	3,45

Abbreviations used in the table

A.S.	Armstrong Siddeley	Fr	fighter	in	inches	ml	miles
B.	Bristol	ft	feet	J	Japan	mm	millimeters
b.	bombs	GB	Great Britain	kg	kilograms	MR	maritime reconnaissance
Br	bomber	G.R.	Gnome Rhône	km	kilometers	NL	Holland
cl.	cylinders	h	hour	lb	pounds	P.&W.	Pratt & Whitney
CS	Czechoslovakia	hp	horse-power	L.D.	Lorraine-Dietrich	Ps	passengers
D	Germany	I	Italy	m	meters	Rc	reconnaissance
F	France	I.F.	Isotta Fraschini	mg.	machine-gun	R.R.	Rolls-Royce

Empty weigh		Max take-off weight		Payload		Max speed		Cruising speed		Range		Ceiling		Crew	Passengers	Notes
lb	kg	lb	kg	lb	kg	ml/h	km/h	ml/h	km/h	ml	km	ft	m			
2,729	1.238	4,374	1.984	661	300	—	—	77	125	286	460	14,763	4.500	1	1	
—	—	3,720	1.687	—	—	121	195	—	—	300	483	—	—	1	2	
30,864	14.000	—	—	12,004	5.445	80	129	—	—	—	—	—	—	8	100	
15,100	6.849	28,500	12.928	—	—	91	146	—	—	—	—	—	—	5	—	
5,512	2.500	10,516	4.770	3,527	1.600	—	—	74	120	249	400	13,100	4.000	2	12	Figures refer to the Vimy Atlantic
6,700	3.039	13,300	6.033	—	—	100	161	—	—	2,440	3.927	10,500	3.200	2	—	
2,645	1.200	4,189	1.900	992	450	100	161	84	135	420	675	—	—	1	5	
2,425	1.100	3,572	1.620	—	—	93	150	—	—	350	565	14,763	4.500	1	1-2	
3,124	1.417	5,071	2.300	1,455	660	133	214	102	164	497	800	16,500	5.050	1	2-3	
5,622	2.550	10,759	4.880	—	—	96	155	—	—	—	—	—	—	2	—	
3,245	1.472	4,983	2.260	—	—	99	160	93	150	373	600	19,685	6.000	1	3-5	
4,268	1.936	8,827	4.004	—	—	100	161	80	129	2,200	3.540	7,000	2.135	2	—	
6,424	2.914	10,164	4.610	1,764	800	98	158	90	145	336	540	9,840	3.000	2	8	
3,197	1.450	5,401	2.450	—	—	—	—	90	145	—	—	—	—	1	1	Weights, measurements and engines changed many times over the years
10,638	4.825	16,315	7.400	2,425	1.100	133	215	110	177	808	1.300	17,550	5.350	2	10	
7,849	3.560	12,567	5.700	—	—	112	180	87	140	—	—	11,480	3.500	2	8-14	
7,095	3.218	12,126	5.500	—	—	115	185	84	135	373	600	13,780	4.200	2	10	
3,140	1.424	5,250	2.381	—	—	106	170	—	—	—	—	14,000	4.270	—	—	For use in agriculture
3,400	1.542	4,855	2.202	500	227	142	229	120	193	700	1.127	16,000	4.900	1	—	Night-flying version
13,387	6.072	18,740	8.500	—	—	143	230	131	211	745	1.200	—	—	3	12-18	
2,535	1.150	3,814	1.730	—	—	—	—	87	140	348	560	13,100	4.000	2	4	Used various engines
7,700	3.493	12,000	5.443	—	—	104	167	90	145	500	805	10,600	3.230	2	14	
6,394	2.900	10,657	4.834	1,684	764	101	163	75	121	236	380	11,500	3.500	2	8	
4,577	2.076	6,173	2.800	1,323	600	131	211	93	150	370	595	13,780	4.200	1	4	
4,564	2.070	7,099	3.220	1,764	800	105	169	96	155	652	1.050	11,500	3.500	2	6	
3,748	1.700	5,567	2.525	—	—	—	—	78	126	—	—	9,840	3.000	1	6-7	
3,179	1.442	5,110	2.318	841	381	146	235	124	200	600	965	14,000	4.270	1	—	
9,480	4.300	14,330	6.500	—	—	—	—	113	182	808	1.300	15,420	4.700	3	9	
9,060	4.110	15,600	7.076	—	—	128	206	110	177	—	—	13,000	3.950	3	7	
4,299	1.950	8,047	3.650	1,962	890	115	185	96	155	700	1.127	8,530	2.600	2	8	
2,602	1.180	4,339	1.968	—	—	137	220	106	170	311	500	—	—	1-2	—	
12,000	5.443	18,000	8.165	—	—	110	177	90	145	405	652	—	—	2	20	
5,401	2.450	8,819	4.000	—	—	125	201	104	167	497	800	14,763	4.500	2	8	
7,688	3.487	12,567	5.700	3,968	1.800	118	190	109	175	348	560	14,763	4.500	3	12	
4,079	1.850	5,732	2.600	—	—	120	194	93	150	500	805	9,840	3.000	1	4	
2,150	975	5,245	2.379	—	—	130	209	112	180	4,100	6.600	16,400	5.000	1	—	
2,061	935	3,012	1.366	—	—	156	251	—	—	—	—	27,000	8.230	1	—	Armament: 2 mg., b. (80 lb; 36 kg)
2,550	1.157	4,020	1.823	—	—	142	229	—	—	480	770	16,800	5.120	2	—	Armament: 2 mg., b. (448 lb; 137 kg)
6,702	3.040	10,225	4.638	—	—	105	169	92	148	390	630	10,300	3.140	3	—	Armament: 5 mg. (0.30 in), b. (1,040 lb; 472 kg)
3,131	1.420	4,222	1.915	—	—	200	322	—	—	—	—	—	—	2	—	Armament: 2 mg.
2,370	1.075	3,373	1.530	—	—	186	299	—	—	—	—	29,530	9.000	1	—	Armament: 2 mg. (7,7 mm)
2,342	1.062	3,635	1.649	—	—	150	241	—	—	608	980	18,700	5.700	2	—	Armament: 2 mg. (30 in)
—	—	3,241	1.470	—	—	193	311	—	—	342	550	30,500	9.300	1	—	

S.   Sweden
S.   Salmson
Si.   Siemens
Sp   seaplane
Tr   transport
USA United States of America
W.   Wright

SPORT AIRCRAFT FROM 1913 TO 1939

Page	Aircraft	Builder	Nation of origin	Type	Year	Engine	Wing spread	
							ft	m
64	Dayton-Wright R.B. Racer	Dayton-Wright Airplane Co.	USA	Rp	1920	250 hp Hall-Scott Liberty (6 cl.)	21.2	6,45
64	Verville-Packard R 1	Verville	USA	Rp	1920	638 hp Packard 1A-2025 (12 cl.)	28.2	8,58
64	Navy Curtiss R-1	Curtiss	USA	Rp	1921	405 hp Curtiss CD (12 cl.)	22.8	6,91
64	Curtiss-Cox Cactus Kitten	Curtiss	USA	Rp	1921	435 hp Curtiss C (12 cl.)	20.0	6,10
64	Army Curtiss R-6	Curtiss	USA	Rp	1922	460 hp Curtiss CD (12 cl.)	19.1	5,82
65	Verville-Sperry R-3	Verville-Sperry	USA	Rp	1924	500 hp Curtiss D-12	30.6	9,29
65	Travel Air "R" Mystery Ship	Travel Air	USA	Rp	1929	400 hp Wright-Whirlwind R-975 (9 cl.)	29.2	8,89
65	Laird Super-Solution	Matty Laird	USA	Rp	1931	535 hp Pratt & Whitney Jr R-985	21.0	6,40
65	Seversky SEV-S2	Seversky	USA	Rp	1937	1000 hp Pratt & Whitney Sr	36.0	10,97
66	Deperdussin	Armand Deperdussin	F	Sp/Rp	1913	160 hp Gnome (14 cl.)	44.3	13,49
66	Sopwith Tabloid	Sopwith	GB	Sp/Rp	1914	100 hp Gnome (9 cl.)	25.6	7,77
66	Savoia S-17	Savoia Co.	I	Sp/Rp	1919	250 hp Isotta Fraschini (6 cl.)	36.4	11,07
66	Savoia S-12	Savoia Co.	I	Sp/Rp	1920	500 hp Ansaldo V-12	43.2	13,16
66	Macchi M-7	Macchi	I	Sp/Rp	1921	250 hp Isotta Fraschini V-12	32.6	9,90
67	Supermarine Sea Lion II	Supermarine	GB	Sp/Rp	1922	450 hp Napier Lion V-12	31.10	9,70
67	Navy Curtiss R-3	Curtiss	USA	Sp/Rp	1923	465 hp Curtiss D-12 V-12	22.8	6,91
67	Army Curtiss R3C-2	Curtiss	USA	Sp/Rp	1925	619 hp Curtiss V-1400	22.0	6,71
67	Macchi M-39	Macchi	I	Sp/Rp	1926	800 hp Fiat A.S.2 V-12	30.5	9,27
67	Supermarine S-5	Supermarine	GB	Sp/Rp	1927	875 hp Napier Lion VIIB	25.6	7,77
67	Supermarine S-6	Supermarine	GB	Sp/Rp	1929	1900 hp Rolls-Royce R V-12	30.0	9,14
67	Supermarine S-6B	Supermarine	GB	Sp/Rp	1931	2600 hp Rolls-Royce R V-12	30.0	9,14
67	Macchi-Castoldi MC-72	Macchi	I	Sp/Rp	1934	2800 hp Fiat A.S.6 (24 cl.)	31.1	9,48
68	Gee-Bee Model Z Super Sportster	Granville Brothers Aircraft	USA	Rp	1931	535 hp Pratt & Whitney Wasp Jr	23.6	7,16
68	Gee-Bee Super Sporster R-1	Granville Brothers Aircraft	USA	Rp	1932	800 hp Pratt & Whitney Wasp Jr	25.0	7,62
68	Wedell-Williams	Wedell-Williams	USA	Rp	1932	550 hp Pratt & Whitney Wasp Jr	26.3	7,92
68	Howard DGA-6 "Mr Mulligan"	Howard	USA	Rp	1935	830 hp Pratt & Whitney Wasp Jr	30.6	9,29
68	Laird-Turner L-RT Meteor	Laird	USA	Rp	1939	1000 hp Pratt & Whitney Tw. Wasp Sr	25.0	7,62

Abbreviations used in the table

cl.	cylinders	km	kilometers
F	France	lb	pounds
ft	feet	m	meters
GB	Great Britain	ml	miles
h	hour	Rp	racing plane
hp	horse-power	Sp	seaplane
I	Italy	USA	United States of America
kg	kilograms		

Length		Height		Empty weight		Max take-off weight		Speed		Crew	Notes
ft	m	ft	m	lb	kg	lb	kg	ml/h	km/h		
22.8	6,91	8.0	2,44	1,400	635	1,850	839	200	322	1	
24.2	7,37	—	—	2,485	1.127	3,233	1.466	186	299	1	Winner of the Pulitzer 1920: 251,85 km/h (156.50 ml/h)
21.0	6,40	8.0	2,44	1,735	787	2,165	982	200	322	1	Winner of the Pulitzer 1921: 284,36 km/h (176.70 ml/h)
19.3	5,87	8.6	2,59	1,936	878	2,406	1.091	190	306	1	Second in the Pulitzer 1921: 277,77 km/h (170.26 ml/h)
18.10	5,74	—	—	1,615	733	2,120	962	239	385	1	Winner of the Pulitzer 1922: 331,19 km/h (205.80 ml/h)
23.5	7,14	—	—	1,955	887	2,475	1.123	220	354	1	Winner of the Pulitzer 1924: 348,76 km/h (216.72 ml/h)
20.2	6,15	8.9	2,67	1,475	669	1,940	880	209	336	1	Winner of the Nat. Air Races 1929: 313,65 km/h (194.90 ml/h)
19.6	5,94	8.0	2,44	1,385	628	1,900	862	250	402	1	Winner of the Bendix 1931: 358,93 km/h (223.04 ml/h)
25.6	7,77	9.9	2,97	3,852	1.747	6,390	2.899	305	491	1	Same as fighter Seversky P-35. Winner of the Bendix 1937, 1938, 1939
32.9	9,98	—	—	2,095	950	2,646	1.200	130	210	2	Winner of the Schneider 1913: 73,62 km/h (45.75 ml/h)
24.0	7,32	8.5	2,57	992	450	1,433	650	92	148	1	Winner of the Schneider 1914: 139,60 km/h (86.75 ml/h)
12.8	3,96	10.4	3,15	2,315	1.050	3,195	1.449	140	225	1	It was an S-13 with reduced wing spread. The Schneider of 1919, that won with an average of 200,36 km/h (124.50 ml/h), was voided
32.8	9,95	12.6	3,81	2,625	1.191	3,835	1.740	105	169	1	Winner of the Schneider 1920: 172,51 km/h (107.20 ml/h)
26.7	8,10	9.10	2,99	1,705	773	2,376	1.078	130	209	1	Winner of the Schneider 1921: 189,67 km/h (117.86 ml/h)
27.6	8,38	—	—	2,381	1.080	3,163	1.435	160	257	1	Winner of the Schneider 1922: 234,47 km/h (145.70 ml/h)
25.0	7,62	10.4	3,15	2,119	961	2,747	1.246	195	314	1	Winner of the Schneider 1923: 285,45 km/h (177.38 ml/h)
20.2	6,15	—	—	—	—	2,738	1.242	248	399	1	Winner of the Schneider 1925: 374,27 km/h (232.57 ml/h)
22.1	6,74	—	—	2,772	1.257	3,465	1.572	259	417	1	Winner of the Schneider 1926: 396,68 km/h (246.49 ml/h)
23.2	7,06	11.1	3,38	2,710	1.229	3,250	1.474	310	499	1	Winner of the Schneider 1927: 453,25 km/h (281.65 ml/h)
28.8	8,73	—	—	4,471	2.028	5,771	2.618	358	576	1	Winner of the Schneider 1929: 528,86 km/h (328.63 ml/h)
28.10	8,78	—	—	4,590	2.082	6,086	2.761	407	656	1	Winner of the Schneider 1931: 547,23 km/h (340.08 ml/h)
27.4	8,33	10.10	3,30	5,512	2.500	6,409	2.907	441	710	1	Broke the absolute seaplane speed record: 709,209 km/h (440.70 ml/h)
15.1	4,60	—	—	1,400	635	2,280	1.034	286	460	1	Winner of the Thompson 1931: 380,17 km/h (236.24 ml/h)
17.9	5,41	8.1	2,47	1,840	835	2,415	1.095	290	467	1	Winner of the Thompson 1932: 406,74 km/h (252.68 ml/h)
21.3	6,48	8.0	2,44	1,500	680	2,206	1.001	305	491	1	Winner of the Thompson 1933: 382,93 km/h (237.95 ml/h)
24.0	7,32	11.0	3,35	—	—	5,300	2.404	292	470	2	Winner of the Bendix 1935: 384,14 km/h (238.70 ml/h)
23.4	7,11	10.0	3,05	3,310	1.501	4,933	2.238	308	496	1	Winner of the Thompson 1939: 454,68 km/h (282.53 ml/h)

CIVIL AND MILITARY AIRCRAFT FROM 1927 TO 1940

Page	Aircraft	Builder	Nation of origin	Type	Year	Engine	Wing spread		Length		Height	
							ft	m	ft	m	ft	m
72	Savoia Marchetti S 55	Società Idrovolanti Alta Italia	I	Sp/Br/Ps	1925	2/700 hp Fiat A-24R (12 cl.)	79.11	24,36	54.2	16,51	16.5	5,00
72	Lockheed Vega Model 1	Lockheed Aircraft Co.	USA	Ps	1928	220 hp W. Whirlwind J-5	41.0	12,50	27.6	8,38	8.6	2,59
72	Breguet XIX Super TR "Point d'Interrogation"	Breguet	F	—	1929	650 hp H.S. V-12	60.0	18,30	35.2	10,72	13.4	4,06
72	Fokker F.VIIb-3m	Fokker	NL	Ps	1927	3/365 hp G.R. Titan Major	71.3	21,71	47.7	14,50	12.10	3,90
72	Fokker C-2 "America" (F.VIIa-3m)	Fokker	NL	Ps	1927	3/220 hp W. R-730 (9 cl.)	71.3	21,71	48.7	14,81	12.0	3,67
73	Dornier Do X	Dornier-Flugzeuge	D	Sp/Ps	1929	12/525 hp Si. Jupiter (9 cl.)	157.6	48,00	131.5	40,05	33.2	10,10
73	Ford Tri-motor "Tin Goose"	Ford-Stout	USA	Ps	1929	3/450 hp P.&W. Wasp	77.10	23,72	49.10	15,20	12.8	3,86
74	Handley Page HP 42E Hannibal	Handley Page Ltd	GB	Ps	1931	4/550 hp B. Jupiter XIF	130.0	39,62	89.9	27,36	27.0	8,23
74	Latécoère 28 III	Société Latécoère	F	Sp/Ps	1930	600 hp H.S. 12L	63.2	19,25	44.9	13,64	—	—
74	Consolidated Commodore Model 16	Consolidated Aircraft Co.	USA	Sp/Ps	1929	2/575 hp P.&W. Hornet B (9 cl.)	100.0	30,48	61.8	18,79	15.8	4,77
75	Junkers Ju 52/3m	Junkers Flugzeug und Motorenwerke A.G.	D	Ps	1932	3/525 hp BMW Hornet (9 cl.)	95.11	29,25	62.0	18,90	18.2	5,54
75	Savoia Marchetti S 64	Società Idrovolanti Alta Italia	I	Sp	1928	590 hp Fiat A.22T (12 cl.)	70.6	21,49	29.6	8,99	12.1	3,68
75	Couzinet 70 "Arc-en-Ciel"	Société des Avions René Couzinet	F	Tr	1929	3/650 hp H.S. 12Nb (12 cl.)	98.5	30,00	53.0	16,15	—	—
76	Douglas DC 2	Douglas Aircraft Co.	USA	Ps	1934	2/710 hp W. Cyclone F3 (9 cl.)	85.0	25,91	62.0	18,90	16.4	4,98
76	Douglas DC 3	Douglas Aircraft Co.	USA	Ps	1936	2/1100 hp W. Cyclone	95.6	29,11	64.6	19 b6	16.0	4,87
76	Savoia Marchetti S 73	Società Idrovolanti Alta Italia	I	Ps	1935	3/700 hp Piaggio Stella IX R.C. (9 cl.)	78.9	24,00	57.3	17,45	15.1	4,60
77	De Havilland D.H.86	De Havilland Aircraft Co. Ltd	GB	Ps	1934	4/200 hp D.H. Gipsy Six I	64.6	19,66	43.11	13,39	13.0	3,96
77	Lockheed 10A Electra	Lockheed Aircraft Co.	USA	Ps	1935	2/420 hp P.&W. Wasp Junior	55.0	16,76	38.7	11,76	10.0	3,05
77	Dewoitine D 338	Société Aéronautique Française	F	Ps	1935	3/650 hp H.S.	96.3	29,35	72.7	22,13	—	—
78	Stinson Detroiter SM-1F	Stinson Aircraft Corp.	USA	Ps	1929	300 hp W. J6 (9 cl.)	46.8	14,22	32.8	9,95	9.0	2,74
78	Boeing Monomail Model 221A	Boeing Co.	USA	Ps	1931	575 hp P.&W. Hornet B	59.2	18,03	41.2	12,55	12.6	3,81
78	Consolidated Fleetster	Consolidated Aircraft Co.	USA	Ps	1934	575 hp P.&W. Hornet B	45.0	13,72	31.9	9,68	10.2	3,10
78	Stinson Tri-motor SM-6000	Stinson Aircraft Corp.	USA	Ps	1931	3/215 hp Lycoming R-680 (9 cl.)	60.0	18,29	42.10	13,05	12.0	3,66
78	Northrop Delta	Northrop Corp.	USA	Ps	1936	775 hp W. Cyclone	47.7	14,51	33.1	10,08	9.0	2,74
79	Travel Air Model A-6000A	Travel Air	USA	Ps	1929	450 hp P.&W. Wasp	54.5	16,59	31.2	9,50	9.3	2,82
79	Curtiss Condor CO	Curtiss	USA	Ps	1930	2/600 hp Curtiss Conqueror (12 cl.)	91.8	27,94	57.6	17,53	16.3	4,96
79	Fokker F 32	Fokker Aircraft Corp. USA	USA	Ps	1930	4/575 hp P.&W. Hornet B	99.0	30,18	69.10	21,28	16.6	5,03
79	Boeing Model 40A	Boeing Co.	USA	Ps	1928	420 hp P.&W. Wasp	44.2	13,46	33.2	10,11	12.3	3,74
79	Fairchild FC-2W	Fairchild Airplane Co.	USA	Ps	1928	450 hp P.&W. Wasp (9 cl.)	50.0	15,24	31.0	9,45	9.0	2,74
79	Boeing 80A	Boeing Co.	USA	Ps	1928	3/525 hp P.&W. Hornet	80.0	24,38	56.6	17,22	15.3	4,65
79	Lockheed Orion	Lockheed Aircraft Co.	USA	Ps	1932	580 hp W. Cyclone	42.10	13,05	27.6	8,38	—	—
79	Boeing Model 247	Boeing Co.	USA	Ps	1932	2/550 hp P.&W. Wasp	74.0	22,56	51.4	15,64	15.5	4,69
79	Lockheed Model 14 "Sky Zephyr"	Lockheed Aircraft Co.	USA	Ps	1937	2/800 hp P.&W. Hornet (9 cl.)	65.6	19,96	44.2	13,46	11.5	3,48
79	Lockheed Lodestar	Lockheed Aircraft Co.	USA	Ps	1940	2/1200 hp W. Cyclone	65.6	19,96	49.10	15,20	11.1	3,38
80	Farman F 180	Farman	F	Ps	1928	2/500 hp Farman 12We (12 cl.)	85.4	26,00	59.1	18,00	—	—
80	Farman F 190	Farman	F	Ps	1928	230 hp G.R. Titan 5Ba (5 cl.)	47.3	14,40	34.3	10,45	—	—
80	Farman F 300	Farman	F	Ps	1930	3/230 hp S. 9Ab	62.8	19,08	43.9	13,35	—	—
80	Potez 62	Potez	F	Ps	1935	2/870 hp G.R. 14 Kirs (14 cl.)	73.8	22,45	56.10	17,32	—	—
80	Savoia Marchetti SM 71	Società Idrovolanti Alta Italia	I	Ps	1932	3/240 hp Walter Castor	69.7	21,20	45.11	14,00	—	—
80	ANT-9-M-17	Tupolev	SU	Ps	1932	2/680 hp M-17 (12 cl.)	77.10	23,73	55.9	17,00	16.5	5,00
80	Junkers Ju W-33 "Bremen"	Junkers Flugzeuge und Motorenwerke A.G.	D	Ps	1928	350 hp Junkers L5 (6 cl.)	58.3	17,75	34.6	10,50	11.8	3,56
80	Heinkel He 70	Enst Heinkel A.G.	D	Ps	1933	750 hp BMW VI 7,3	48.7	14,80	39.4	12,00	10.2	3,10
80	Bloch 120	Avions Marcel Bloch	F	Ps	1934	3/300 hp Lorraine Algol 9Na (9 cl.)	67.5	20,54	50.2	15,30	—	—

Abbreviations used in the table

Am	amphibian	D	Germany	G.R.	Gnome-Rhône	kg	kilograms
A.R.	Alfa Romeo	D.H.	De Havilland	h	hour	km	kilometers
A.S.	Armstrong Siddeley	Ex	experimental	HB	heavy bomber	lb	pounds
B.	Bristol	F	France	hp	horse-power	m	meters
b.	bombs	Fr	fighter	H.S.	Hispano-Suiza	mg.	machine-gun
Br	bomber	ft	feet	I	Italy	ml	miles
Cb	carrier-based	g.	gun	I.F.	Isotta Fraschini	mm	millimeters
cl.	cylinders	GB	Great Britain	in	inches	NL	Holland

Empty weight		Max take-off weight		Payload		Max speed		Cruising speed		Range		Ceiling		Crew	Passengers	Notes
lb	kg	lb	kg	lb	kg	ml/h	km/h	ml/h	km/h	ml	km	ft	m			
11,464	5.200	16,975	7.700	1,609	730	146	236	116	187	1,243	2.000	13,780	4.200	2	10-12	The first S 55 flew in 1924. It had different engines and performance
1,875	851	3,470	1.574	820	372	135	217	118	190	900	1.450	15,000	4.570	1	4	In later years the Vega had different engines and performance
4,828	2.190	14,771	6.700	—	—	142	229	—	—	5,900	9.500	21,320	6.500	2	—	
7,231	3.280	11,023	5.000	2,205	1.000	138	222	123	198	746	1.200	19,685	6.000	2	8	12 types with different engines were used
—	—	7,408	3.360	—	—	118	190	—	—	—	—	—	—	3	—	Completed Atlantic crossing on June 27, 1927
61,729	28.000	114,640	52.000	—	—	131	211	109	175	621	1.000	1,377	420	10	72	Others were equipped with Curtiss or Fiat engines
7,576	3.436	12,576	5.704	2,720	1.234	142	229	122	196	580	933	18,500	5.640	2	15-17	Figures refer to 5-AT-B model of 1929
—	—	28,000	12.701	—	—	120	193	100	161	—	—	—	—	2	24	
5,814	2.637	11,061	5.017	—	—	138	223	—	—	1,990	3.200	18,000	5.500	2	8	
10,550	4.785	17,600	7.983	2,255	1.023	128	206	108	174	1,000	1.610	11,250	3.430	3	10-18	Figures refer to first type
11,786	5.346	20,283	9.200	—	—	180	290	152	245	568	914	17,060	5.200	2	15-17	Figures refer to first type. Over 30 others are known
5,291	2.400	15,432	7.000	—	—	146	235	—	—	7,150	11.505	—	—	2	—	
16,116	7.310	37,016	16.790	1,323	600	174	280	147	236	4,225	6.800	—	—	4	—	
12,075	5.477	18,000	8.165	—	—	213	343	191	307	497	800	23,700	7.225	3	14	
17,195	7.800	24,400	11.068	—	—	212	341	174	280	540	869	—	—	2	21	Figures refer to first type
15,278	6.930	22,994	10.430	3,968	1.800	205	330	174	280	994	1.600	24,278	7.400	5	18	Maximum range is indicated. Several S 73 used G.R. engines
6,303	2.859	10,000	4.536	—	—	170	274	145	233	760	1.220	20,500	6.250	1	10	
—	—	10,500	4.763	—	—	221	356	203	327	750	1.207	20,000	6.100	2	12	
17,428	7.905	24,582	11.150	3,759	1.705	187	301	161	260	1,210	1.950	16,000	4.900	3	12-22	
2,614	1.186	4,300	1.950	874	396	132	212	113	182	680	1.095	16,000	4.900	1	5	
4,990	2.263	8,000	3.629	1,935	878	158	254	137	220	540	869	14,700	4.480	1	8	
3,439	1.560	5,900	2.676	1,325	601	175	282	148	238	625	1.006	17,500	5.335	1	6	Figures refer to Fleetster 20 of 1931
5,575	2.529	8,400	3.810	1,815	823	138	222	115	185	345	555	15,000	4.570	1	10	
4,600	2.087	7,350	3.334	—	—	219	352	200	322	1,930	3.106	23,400	7.130	2	7	
3,225	1.463	5,250	2.381	995	451	140	225	120	193	680	1.095	18,000	5.500	1	6	
11,352	5.149	17,678	8.019	2,876	1.305	139	224	120	193	550	885	17,000	5.180	2	18	
14,910	6.763	24,250	11.000	6,280	2.849	146	235	123	198	740	1.191	13,500	4.115	2	30	
3,531	1.602	6,000	2.722	1,600	726	128	206	105	169	650	1.046	14,500	4.420	1	2	
2,418	1.097	4,600	2.087	1,000	454	140	225	115	185	1,000	1.610	15,500	4.725	1	4	
10,582	4.800	17,500	7.938	—	—	138	222	125	201	460	740	14,000	4.270	2	18	
3,594	1.630	5,401	2.450	—	—	224	360	182	293	560	901	—	—	1	4	
8,400	3.810	12,650	5.737	—	—	182	293	155	249	485	781	18,400	5.610	2	10	
9,685	4.393	15,000	6.804	5,315	2.411	265	426	241	388	1,000	1.610	26,300	8.020	2	12	
11,650	5.284	17,500	7.938	—	—	253	407	215	346	1,600	2.575	23,300	7.100	3	17	
9,921	4.500	17,637	8.000	4,409	2.000	118	190	106	170	621	1.000	13,100	4.000	2	17-24	
2,041	926	3,968	1.800	1,129	512	—	—	99	160	528	850	16,896	5.150	1	4	
5,494	2.492	9,987	4.530	—	—	—	—	118	190	528	850	14,760	4.500	2	8	
10,792	4.895	16,535	7.500	3,483	1.580	—	—	174	280	621	1.000	24,600	7.500	2	14-16	
6,371	2.890	10,141	4.600	1,235	560	—	—	112	180	1,367	2.200	19,685	6.000	3	8-10	
9,700	4.400	13,669	6.200	1,786	810	147	237	109	175	621	1.000	14,760	4.500	2	9	
3,126	1.418	8,818	4.000	—	—	127	205	105	170	—	—	13,100	4.000	3	—	
5,578	2.530	7,628	3.460	882	400	224	360	190	305	621	1.000	18,370	5.600	1	4-5	Figures refer to 70G
7,937	3.600	13,228	6.000	1,764	800	—	—	143	230	—	—	20,670	6.300	3	4	

Ps   passengers
P.&W. Pratt & Whitney
Rc   reconnaissance
R.R. Rolls-Royce
S.   Salmson
Si.   Siemens
Sp   seaplane
SU   Soviet Union

TB   torpedo-bomber
Tr   transport
USA United States of America
W.   Wright

CIVIL AND MILITARY AIRCRAFT FROM 1927 TO 1940   (continued)

Page	Aircraft	Builder	Nation of origin	Type	Year	Engine	Wing spread ft	Wing spread m	Length ft	Length m	Height ft	Height m
80	Fokker F.XXXVI	Fokker	NL	Ps	1934	4/750 hp W. Cyclone	108.3	33,00	77.5	23,60	—	—
80	De Havilland D.H.91 Albatros	De Havilland Aircraft Co. Ltd	GB	Ps	1937	4/525 hp Gipsy Twelve	105.0	32,00	71.6	21,79	22.3	6,78
80	Junkers Ju 86	Junkers Flugzeug und Motorenwerke A.G.	D	Ps	1935	2/600 hp Junkers Jumo 205C	73.10	22,50	57.2	17,41	15.9	4,80
81	Junkers G.38	Junkers Flugzeug und Motorenwerke A.G.	D	Ps	1929	4/800 hp Junkers-L88 (12 cl.)	144.4	44,00	76.1	23,20	23.7	7,20
81	Wibault 283 T	Chantiers Aéronautiques Wibault-Penhoët	F	Ps	1932	3/350 hp G.R. Titan Major 7Kd	74.2	22,61	55.9	17,00	—	—
81	Armstrong Whitworth A.W.15 Atalanta	Armstrong Whitworth Aircraft Ltd	GB	Ps	1932	4/340 hp A.S. Serval III	90.0	27,43	71.6	21,79	15.0	4,57
81	Savoia Marchetti SM 74	Società Idrovolanti Alta Italia	I	Ps	1934	4/700 hp Piaggio Stella IX RC	97.5	29,70	70.1	21,37	18.0	5,49
81	Armstrong Whitworth A.W.27 Ensign	Armstrong Whitworth Aircraft Ltd	GB	Ps	1938	4/850 hp A.S. Tiger IX	123.0	37,49	114.0	34,75	23.0	7,01
82	Short S.8 Calcutta	Short Bros Ltd	GB	Sp/Ps	1928	3/540 hp B. Jupiter XIF	93.0	28,35	66.0	20,10	23.9	7,24
82	Cams 53-1	Chantiers Aéro-Maritimes de la Seine	F	Sp/Ps	1929	2/580 hp H.S. 12Lbr	66.11	20,40	48.7	14,82	—	—
82	Latécoère 300 "Croix du Sud"	Société Latécoère	F	Sp/Tr	1932	4/650 hp H.S. 12Nbr (12 cl.)	145.0	44,20	85.11	26,20	—	—
82	Blériot 5190 "Santos Dumont"	Blériot-Aéronautique	F	Sp/Tr	1933	4/650 hp H.S. 12Nbr (12 cl.)	141.1	43,00	85.3	26,00	—	—
82	Sikorsky S-42	Sikorsky	USA	Sp/Ps	1934	4/700 hp P.&W. Hornet	114.2	34,80	67.8	20,62	17.4	5,28
82	Latécoère 521 "Lieutenant de Vaisseau Paris"	Société Latécoère	F	Sp/Ps	1935	6/860 hp H.S. 12Ybrs	161.9	49,31	103.9	31,62	—	—
83	Sikorsky S-38	Sikorsky	USA	Am/Ps	1928	2/420 hp P.&W. Wasp	71.8	21,84	40.3	12,27	14.6	4,41
83	Cant 22 R.1	Cantieri Riuniti dell'Adriatico	I	Sp/Ps	1928	1/520 hp (12 cl.) Asso 500 + 2/250 hp (6 cl.) Semi Asso 200 I.F.	68.11	21,00	52.6	16,00	—	—
83	Breguet 530 Saigon	Breguet	F	Sp/Ps	1934	3/875 hp H.S. 12Ybr (12 cl.)	115.0	35,06	66.7	20,30	—	—
83	Short S 17 Kent	Short Bros Ltd	GB	Sp/Ps	1931	4/555 hp B. Jupiter XFBM	113.0	34,40	78.5	23,90	28.0	8,53
83	Savoia Marchetti SM 66	Società Idrovolanti Alta Italia	I	Sp/Ps	1932	3/750 hp Fiat A.24R (12 cl.)	108.3	33,00	54.7	16,64	16.1	4,89
83	Dornier Do R4 Super Wal II	Vàrious	D	Sp/Ps	1929	4/510 hp G.R. Jupiter	93.10	28,60	80.9	24,60	19.8	6,00
83	Macchi MC 94	Aeronautica Macchi	I	Am/Ps	1936	2/750 hp A.R. 126 R.C.10 (9 cl.)	74.9	22,79	53.1	16,17	17.10	5,45
83	Sikorsky S-43	Sikorsky	USA	Am/Ps	1936	2/750 hp P.&W. Hornet (9 cl.)	86.0	26,21	51.2	15,59	17.8	5,38
83	Macchi MC 100	Aeronautica Macchi	I	Sp/Ps	1938	3/800 hp A.R. 126 R.C.10 (9 cl.)	87.8	26,71	58.0	17,69	20.1	6,12
83	Short S 21 Maja	Short Bros Ltd	GB	Sp/Ps	1937	4/920 hp B. Pegasus XC	114.0	34,75	84.11	25,88	—	—
83	Short S 20 Mercury	Short Bros Ltd	GB	Sp/Tr	1937	4/730 hp Raper VI	73.0	22,25	51.0	15,54	—	—
84	Hawker Hart	Hawker Aircraft Ltd	GB	Br	1928	525 hp R.R. Kestrel IB (12 cl.)	37.3	11,36	29.4	8,94	10.5	3,18
84	Fiat CR 32	Fiat S.A.	I	Fr	1933	600 hp Fiat A.30 RA (12 cl.)	31.2	9,50	24.5	7,45	8.8	2,63
84	Boeing F4B-4	Boeing Co.	USA	Cb/Fr	1930	550 hp P.&W. R-1340-16	30.0	9,14	20.1	6,13	9.4	2,84
84	Grumman F3F-1	Grumman Aircraft Co.	USA	Cb/Fr	1935	700 hp P.&W. R-1535-72	28.6	8,68	21.5	6,53	9.1	2,77
84	Boeing P-26A	Boeing Co.	USA	Fr	1935	600 hp P.&W. R-1340-27	27.11	8,51	23.7	7,19	10.0	3,05
84	Vickers Vildebeest Mk III	Vickers	GB	TB	1934	635 hp B. Pegasus II M3	49.0	14,95	36.8	11,17	14.8	4,47
84	Caproni Ca 90	Società Italiana Caproni	I	HB	1929	6/1000 hp I.F. Asso (18 cl.)	114.6	34,90	88.5	26,94	35.5	10,80
84	Handley Page Heyford	Handley Page Ltd	GB	HB	1930	2/575 hp R.R. Kestrel IIIS (12 cl.)	75.0	22,86	58.0	17,68	17.6	5,33
85	Short S 23 "C"	Short Bros Ltd	GB	Sp/Ps	1936	4/920 hp B. Pegasus XC	114.0	34,75	88.0	26,82	31.9	9,68
85	Martin 130 China Clipper	Glenn L. Martin Co.	USA	Sp/Ps	1934	4/830 hp P.&W. Twin Wasp S1A4G	130.3	39,70	89.7	27,31	23.11	7,30
85	Boeing 314 Yankee Clipper	Boeing Co.	USA	Sp/Ps	1938	4/1200 hp W. GR-2600 Double Cyclone	152.0	46,33	106.0	32,31	27.7	8,41
85	Blohm & Voss HA 139B	Blohm & Voss	D	Sp/Tr	1937	4/600 hp Junkers Jumo 205C	88.7	27,00	64.0	19,50	14.9	4,50
86	ANT 20bis	Industrie di Stato	SU	Ps	1939	6/1000 hp M-100 (12 cl.)	206.8	63,00	110.0	33,52	22.11	7,00
86	ANT 14	State Industries	SU	Ps	1931	5/480 hp G.R. Jupiter 9AKK	132.7	40,40	86.11	26,48	17.9	5,40
86	ANT 25	State Industries	SU	—	1935	950 hp Mikulin M-34-R (12 cl.)	111.7	34,00	43.11	13,38	18.0	5,50
86	Nardi FN 305D	State Industries	I	Tr	1935	205 hp Fiat A.70S (7 cl.)	27.10	8,47	22.11	7,00	6.11	2,10
86	De Havilland D.H.88 Comet	De Havilland Aircraft Co. Ltd	GB	Rc	1934	2/230 hp D.H. Gipsy Six R	44.0	13,41	29.0	8,84	10.0	3,05
87	Focke Wulf F.W.200A Condor	Focke Wulf Flugzeugbau GmbH	D	Ps	1937	4/720 hp BMW 132G	107.9	32,85	78.3	23,85	19.8	6,00
87	Junkers Ju 90V2	Junkers Flugzeug und Motorenwerke A.G.	D	Ps	1937	4/830 hp BMW 132H	114.11	35,02	86.3	26,30	24.7	7,50
87	Campini N.1	Società Italiana Caproni	I	Ex	1940	900 hp I.F.	52.0	15,85	43.0	13,11	—	—

Abbreviations used in the table

Am	amphibian	D	Germany	G.R.	Gnome-Rhône	kg	kilograms
A.R.	Alfa Romeo	D.H.	De Havilland	h	hour	km	kilometers
A.S.	Armstrong Siddeley	Ex	experimental	HB	heavy bomber	lb	pounds
B.	Bristol	F	France	hp	horse-power	m	meters
b.	bombs	Fr	fighter	H.S.	Hispano-Suiza	mg.	machine-gun
Br	bomber	ft	feet	I	Italy	ml	miles
Cb	carrier-based	g.	gun	I.F.	Isotta Fraschini	mm	millimeters
cl.	cylinders	GB	Great Britain	in	inches	NL	Holland

Empty weight		Max take-off weight		Payload		Max speed		Cruising speed		Range		Ceiling		Crew	Passengers	Notes
lb	kg	lb	kg	lb	kg	ml/h	km/h	ml/h	km/h	ml	km	ft	m			
21,826	9.900	36,376	16.500	7,165	3.250	180	290	149	240	839	1.350	14,435	4.400	4	32	
21,230	9.630	29,500	13.381	—	—	225	362	210	338	1,040	1.674	17,900	5.455	4	22	
12,170	5.520	16,976	7.700	1,764	800	193	310	177	285	683	1.100	20,000	6.100	2	10	Different engines were used
32,849	14.900	52,911	24.000	20,062	9.100	140	225	112	180	2,175	3.500	21,000	6.400	7	34	
9,405	4.266	13,999	6.350	—	—	156	251	143	230	621	1.000	17,060	5.200	2	10	
13,940	6.323	21,000	9.526	—	—	156	251	130	209	400	644	—	—	2	9	
21,164	9.600	30,865	14.000	5,291	2.400	205	330	186	300	621	1.000	22,970	7.000	4	24	
32,920	14.933	49,000	22.226	—	—	205	330	170	274	800	1.290	18,000	5.500	4	40	
13,845	6.280	22,500	10.206	—	—	118	190	97	156	650	1.046	13,500	4.115	3	15	
10,362	4.700	15,212	6.900	—	—	132	212	106	170	699	1.125	14,760	4.500	2	4	
24,912	11.300	50,706	23.000	2,205	1.000	130	210	99	160	2,985	4.800	15,090	4.600	4	—	
28,109	12.750	48,502	22.000	1,323	600	—	—	118	190	1,990	3.200	—	—	8	—	
19,764	8.965	38,000	17.237	8,060	3.656	182	293	170	274	1,200	1.930	16,000	4.900	4	37	
47,355	21.480	82,453	37.400	7,496	3.400	162	261	132	213	3,600	5.800	20,670	6.300	5	30-70	
6,547	2.970	8,800	3.992	2,275	1.032	124	200	109	175	600	965	18,000	5.500	2	10	
11,023	5.000	15,432	7.000	1,389	630	—	—	87	140	373	600	11,155	3.400	2	8	
18,585	8.430	33,069	15.000	7,209	3.270	146	235	124	200	683	1.100	16,400	5.000	2	21	
20,460	9.281	32,000	14.515	—	—	137	220	105	169	450	724	19,500	5.950	4	16	
17,196	7.800	24,141	10.950	3,252	1.475	164	264	146	235	800	1.290	18,000	5.500	3	18	
21,495	9.750	30,865	14.000	—	—	130	210	118	190	930	1.500	6,560	2.000	4	18	Different engines were used
11,795	5.350	18,078	8.200	—	—	182	292	153	246	926	1.490	19,685	6.000	3	12	
12,570	5.702	19,000	8.618	—	—	194	312	169	272	803	1.292	20,000	6.100	2	15	
18,850	8.550	28,881	13.100	—	—	193	310	164	263	869	1.400	20,000	6.100	4	26	
24,745	11.224	38,000	17.237	—	—	200	322	145	233	850	1.368	20,000	6.100	3	—	
10,163	4.610	15,500	7.031	—	—	212	341	180	290	3,900	6.275	—	—	2	—	
2,530	1.148	4,554	2.066	—	—	184	295	—	—	470	756	21,320	6.500	2	—	Armament: 2 mg., b. (500 lb; 225 kg)
2,921	1.325	4,079	1.850	—	—	233	375	—	—	466	750	28,870	8.800	1	—	Armament: 2 mg. (12,7 mm), b.
1,950	885	2,750	1.247	—	—	188	303	—	—	370	595	26,900	8.200	1	—	Armament: 2 mg. (30 in)
2,691	1.221	3,847	1.745	—	—	231	372	—	—	985	1.585	27,100	8.260	1	—	Armament: 2 g. (30 in)
2,196	996	2,955	1.340	—	—	234	377	200	322	635	1.022	27,400	8.350	1	—	Armament: 2 mg. (0.50 in), b. (100 lb; 45 kg)
4,773	2.165	8,500	3.856	—	—	143	230	122	196	1,250	2.012	19,000	5.800	3	—	Armament: 2 mg., b. (1,100 lb; 499 kg)
33,069	15.000	66,139	30.000	—	—	127	204	—	—	800	1.290	14,764	4.500	8	—	Armament: 7 mg., b. (17,637 lb; 8.000 kg)
10,095	4.580	16,775	7.610	—	—	138	222	—	—	920	1.480	21,000	6.400	4	—	Armament: 3 mg., b. (3,086 lb; 1.400 kg)
23,500	10.660	40,500	18.371	—	—	200	322	165	266	760	1.220	20,000	6.100	5	24	
24,600	11.159	52,000	23.587	—	—	180	290	165	266	3,200	5.150	17,060	5.200	6	48	
50,268	22.802	82,500	37.422	—	—	193	311	183	294	3,500	5.630	13,400	4.085	10	74	
22,840	10.360	38,581	17.500	1,058	480	195	315	161	260	3,293	5.300	11,480	3.500	4	—	
—	—	102,956	46.700	—	—	186	300	171	275	1,864	3.000	22,970	7.000	9	64	
23,479	10.650	37,800	17.146	—	—	147	236	121	195	746	1.200	13,845	4.220	5	36	
9,240	4.191	24,750	11.226	—	—	149	240	103	165	9,320	15.000	22,970	7.000	3	—	
1,190	540	1,852	840	—	—	211	340	190	305	683	1.100	22,970	7.000	2	—	
2,930	1.329	5,550	2.517	—	—	237	381	220	354	2,925	4.710	19,000	5.800	2	—	
21,605	9.800	32,187	14.600	6,393	2.900	—	—	202	325	777	1.250	22,000	6.700	4	26	
31,526	14.300	52,911	24.000	8,889	4.032	217	350	199	320	1,300	2.095	18,000	5.500	4	40	
8,025	3.640	9,248	4.195	—	—	233	375	—	—	—	—	—	—	2	—	

Ps   passengers
P.&W.   Pratt & Whitney
Rc   reconnaissance
R.R.   Rolls-Royce
S.   Salmson
Si.   Siemens
Sp   seaplane
SU   Soviet Union

TB   torpedo-bomber
Tr   transport
USA   United States of America
W.   Wright

AIRCRAFT OF WORLD WAR II

Page	Aircraft	Builder	Type	Year	Engine	Wing spread		Length	
						ft	m	ft	m
	FRANCE								
90	Bloch 210	Avions Marcel Bloch	MB	1934	2/950 hp G.R. 14 N (14 cl.)	74.10	22,80	61.9	18,81
90	Farman F 222	Farman-SNCAC	HB	1936	4/970 hp G.R. 14 N (14 cl.)	118.9	36,20	70.4	21,45
90	Amiot 143	SECM-Amiot	NB	1934	2/900 hp G.R. Mistral-Major (14 cl.)	80.5	24,50	59.11	18,25
91	Breguet 691	Breguet	AB	1939	2/725 hp H.S. 14 AB (14 cl.)	50.4	15,35	31.8	9,65
91	Laté 298	Latécoère	Tr/Br/Sp	1936	880 hp H.S. (12 cl.)	50.10	15,50	41.2	12,55
91	LeO 451	Lioré et Olivier-SNCASE	MB	1937	2/1140 hp G.R. 14 N (14 cl.)	73.10	22,50	56.3	17,15
91	Breguet 521 Bizerte	Breguet	MR/Sp	1935	3/900 hp G.R. (14 cl.)	115.4	35,15	67.2	20,47
91	Bloch 174	SNCASO	Rc	1939	2/1140 hp G.R. 14 N (14 cl.)	58.9	17,90	40.1	12,22
91	Caudron C.714	Caudron	Fr	1939	450 hp Renault 12Rol (12 cl.)	29.5	8,96	27.11	8,52
92	Dewoitine D.520	SNCAM	Fr	1939	910 hp H.S. 12Y (12 cl.)	33.5	10,18	28.9	8,75
92	Bloch MB-152	SNCASO	Fr	1938	920 hp G.R. 14 N (14 cl.)	34.8	10,55	29.10	9,10
92	Morane-Saulnier M.S. 406	SNCAO	Fr	1938	860 hp H.S. 12Y (12 cl.)	34.9	10,60	26.9	8,15
92	Potez 63.11	SNCAN	Rc	1938	2/700 hp G.R. 14 M (14 cl.)	52.6	16,00	35.10	10,92
	GREAT BRITAIN								
93	De Havilland Tiger Moth II	De Havilland Aircraft Co. Ltd	Br/Tr	1932	130 hp D.H. Gipsy Major I	29.4	8,94	23.11	7,29
93	Westland Lysander Mk.I	Westland Aircraft Ltd	Li	1938	890 hp B. Mercury XII	50.0	15,24	30.6	9,29
93	Gloster Gladiator	Gloster Aircraft Co. Ltd	Fr	1936	840 hp B. Mercury IX (9 cl.)	32.3	9,83	27.5	8,36
94	Airspeed Oxford Mk.I	Airspeed Ltd	AT	1937	2/355 hp A.S. Cheetah IX	53.4	16,25	34.6	10,51
94	Avro Anson Mk.I	A.V. Roe & Co. Ltd	Rc	1936	2/350 hp A.S. Cheetah IX	56.6	17,22	42.3	12,88
94	Fairey Firefly F.R.I	Fairey Aviation Co. Ltd	Cb/Fr/Rc	1943	1730 hp R.R. Griffon IIB (12 cl.)	44.6	13,57	37.7	11,46
94	Fairey Fulmar Mk.II	Fairey Aviation Co. Ltd	Cb/Fr	1940	1300 hp R.R. Merlin 30 (12 cl.)	46.5	14,14	40.2	12,24
94	Hawker Tempest Mk.V	Hawker Aircraft Ltd	Fr/FB	1944	2200 hp Napier Sabre IIB (24 cl.)	41.0	12,50	33.8	10,26
94	Hawker Typhoon Mk.IB	Hawker Aircraft Ltd	FB	1941	2180 hp Napier Sabre IIA (24 cl.)	41.7	12,68	31.11	9,73
95	Supermarine Seafire F. Mk.III	Vickers-Armstrong Ltd	Cb/Fr	1942	1470 hp R.R. Merlin 55 (12 cl.)	36.10	11,22	30.2	9,20
95	Bristol Beaufighter Mk.X	Bristol Aeroplane Co. Ltd	NF	1940	2/1770 hp B. Hercules XVII (14 cl.)	57.10	17,62	41.8	12,70
95	Blackburn Roc	Boulton Paul Aircraft	Cb/Fr	1940	905 hp B. Perseus XII (9 cl.)	46.0	14,02	35.7	10,85
95	Boulton Paul Defiant Mk.I	Boulton Paul Aircraft	NF	1940	1030 hp R.R. Merlin III (12 cl.)	39.4	11,99	35.4	10,77
95	Bristol Beaufort Mk.I	Bristol Aeroplane Co. Ltd	TB	1939	2/1130 hp B. Taurus VI	57.10	17,62	44.7	13,59
95	Fairey Barracuda Mk.II	Fairey Aviation Co. Ltd	Cb/TB	1943	1640 hp R.R. Merlin 32	49.2	14,99	40.6	12,34
96	Supermarine Spitfire Mk.V	Supermarine Div. of Vickers-Armstrong Ltd	Fr	1941	1440 hp R.R. Merlin 45 (12 cl.)	36.10	11,22	29.11	9,12
96	Supermarine Spitfire Mk.IA	Supermarine Div. of Vickers-Armstrong Ltd	Fr	1938	1030 hp R.R. Merlin III (12 cl.)	36.10	11,22	29.11	9,12
96	Supermarine Spitfire Mk.XII	Supermarine Div. of Vickers-Armstrong Ltd	Fr	1943	1735 hp R.R. Griffon III (12 cl.)	32.7	9,92	31.10	9,70
96	Supermarine Spitfire Mk.XVI	Supermarine Div. of Vickers-Armstrong Ltd	Fr	1943	1720 hp R.R.-Packard Merlin 66 (12 cl.)	32.7	9,92	31.4	9,55
96	Supermarine Spitfire Mk.XIX	Supermarine Div. of Vickers-Armstrong Ltd	Rc	1944	2050 hp R.R. Griffon 65 (12 cl.)	36.10	11,22	32.8	9,95
96	Hawker Hurricane Mk.I	Hawker Aircraft Ltd	Fr	1937	1030 hp R.R. Merlin II (12 cl.)	40.0	12,19	31.5	9,58
96	Gloster Meteor III	Gloster Aircraft Co.	Fr	1944	2/2,000 lb (907 kg) R.R. Derwent 1 tj.	43.0	13,11	41.3	12,58
97	Fairey Battle Mk.I	Fairey Aviation Co. Ltd	LB	1937	1030 hp R.R. Merlin I	54.0	16,46	52.1	15,87
97	Fairey Swordfish Mk.I	Fairey Aviation Co. Ltd	Cb/TB	1937	690 hp B. Pegasus III M.3	45.6	13,87	35.8	10,87
97	Bristol Blenheim Mk.I	Bristol Aeroplane Co. Ltd	MB	1937	2/840 hp B. Mercury VIII (9 cl.)	56.4	17,17	39.9	12,12
97	Fairey Seafox	Fairey Aviation Co. Ltd	Rc/Sp	1937	395 hp Napier Rapier VI (16 cl.)	40.0	12,19	35.5	10,80
97	Supermarine Walrus II	Supermarine Aviation	Rc/Sp	1936	775 hp B. Pegasus VI (9 cl.)	45.10	13,97	37.7	11,46
97	Short Sunderland Mk.V	Short Bros Ltd	MR	1938	4/1200 hp P.&W. Twin Wasp R-1830	112.9	34,37	85.4	26,01
98	De Havilland B.IV Mosquito	De Havilland Aircraft Co. Ltd	LB	1941	2/1460 hp R.R. Merlin XXI (12 cl.)	54.2	16,51	40.6	12,34
98	De Havilland N.F. Mk.II Mosquito	De Havilland Aircraft Co. Ltd	NF	1942	2/1460 hp R.R. Merlin XXIII (12 cl.)	54.2	16,51	40.6	12,34
98	De Havilland F.B. Mk.VI Mosquito	De Havilland Aircraft Co. Ltd	FB	1942	2/1460 hp R.R. Merlin XXI (12 cl.)	54.2	16,51	40.6	12,34

Abbreviations used in the table

A.	Allison	BT	basic trainer	Fr	fighter	hp	horse-power
AB	attack bomber	Cb	carrier-based	ft	feet	H.S.	Hispano-Suiza
A.R.	Alfa Romeo	cl.	cylinders	g.	gun	I.F.	Isotta Fraschini
A.S.	Armstrong Siddeley	DB	dive bomber	h	hour	in	inches
AT	advanced trainer	D.B.	Daimler Benz	GA	ground attack	J.	Junkers
b.	bombs	d.c.	depth charge	G.R.	Gnome-Rhône	j.	jet
B.	Bristol	D.H.	De Havilland	HB	heavy bomber	kg	kilograms
Br	bomber	FB	fighter-bomber	HF	heavy fighter	km	kilometers

Height		Empty weight		Max take-off weight		Max speed		Cruising speed		Range		Ceiling		Crew	Armament or passengers
ft	m	lb	kg	lb	kg	ml/h	km/h	ml/h	km/h	ml	km	ft	m		
22.0	6,70	14,110	6.400	22,487	10.200	199	320	149	240	1,056	1.700	32,480	9.900	5	3 mg. (7,5 mm), b. (3,527 lb; 1.600 kg)
17.1	5,20	22,123	10.035	41,226	18.700	199	320	174	280	1,240	1.995	26,250	8.000	5	3 mg. (7,5 mm), b. (9,259 lb; 4.200 kg)
18.6	5,65	13,448	6.100	21,385	9.700	193	310	155	250	746	1.200	25,920	7.900	5	4 mg. (7,5 mm), b. (2,866 lb; 1.300 kg)
10.4	3,15	6,834	3.100	11,023	5.000	298	480	186	300	839	1.350	13,100	4.000	2	1 g. (20 mm), 4 mg. (7,5 mm), b. (880 lb; 400 kg)
17.1	5,21	6,746	3.060	10,141	4.600	180	290	152	245	497-1,367	800-2.200	21,320	6.500	2-3	3 mg. (7,5 mm), b. (1,477 lb; 670 kg)
17.2	5,23	17,229	7.815	25,133	11.400	307	495	227	365	1,428	2.300	29,530	9.000	4	1 g. (20 mm), 2 mg. (7,5 mm), b. (4,400 lb; 1.995 kg)
24.7	7,50	20,878	9.470	36,597	16.600	152	245	124	200	1,864	3.000	19,685	6.000	8	5 mg. (7,5 mm), b. (660 lb; 300 kg)
11.7	3,54	12,346	5.600	15,784	7.160	330	530	249	400	1,025	1.650	36,000	11.000	2	7 mg. (7,5 mm), b.
9.5	2,87	3,086	1.400	3,858	1.750	303	487	199	320	559	900	29,855	9.100	1	4 mg. (7,5 mm)
8.5	2,56	4,608	2.090	6,129	2.780	330	530	249	400	620	998	36,000	11.000	1	1 g. (20 mm), 4 mg. (7,5 mm)
12.11	3,95	4,376	1.985	5,710	2.590	302	485	279	450	398	640	33,000	10.000	1	4 mg. (7,5 mm) or 1 g. (20 mm), 2 mg. (7,5 mm)
9.3	2,82	4,189	1.900	5,997	2.720	302	485	249	400	497	800	30,840	9.400	1	1 g. (20 mm), 2 mg. (7,5 mm)
10.1	3,07	6,911	3.135	9,987	4.530	264	425	230	370	930	1.500	27,900	8.500	3	8 mg. (7,5 mm), b. (320 lb; 145 kg)
8.9	2,67	1,115	506	1,825	828	109	175	93	150	302	486	13,600	4.145	2	—
14.6	4,42	4,065	1.844	5,920	2.685	229	369	—	—	500	805	26,500	8.080	2	4 mg. (0.303 in)
10.4	3,15	3,476	1.577	4,750	2.155	253	407	212	341	410	660	33,000	10.000	1	4 mg. (0.303 in)
11.1	3,38	5,380	2.440	7,600	3.447	185	298	—	—	960	1.545	19,200	5.850	3	—
13.1	3,99	5,375	2.438	8,000	3.630	188	303	158	254	790	1.271	19,000	5.800	6	2 mg. (0.303 in), b. (360 lb; 163 kg)
13.7	4,13	9,750	4.423	14,020	6.360	316	509	—	—	1,070	1.720	28,000	8.535	2	4 g. (20 mm), b. (2,000 lb; 907 kg)
10.8	3,25	—	—	10,200	4.627	272	438	230	370	780	1.255	27,200	8.290	2	8 mg. (0.303 in), b. (500 lb; 227 kg)
16.1	4,90	9,250	4.196	13,500	6.125	436	702	391	629	740	1.191	36,500	11.125	1	4 g. (20 mm), b. (2,000 lb; 907 kg)
15.3	4,65	8,800	3.992	11,400	5.170	405	652	330	531	950	1.530	34,000	10.360	1	4 g. (20 mm), b. (2,000 lb; 907 kg)
11.2	3,40	5,400	2.450	7,100	3.220	352	566	310	499	465	748	33,800	10.300	1	2 g. (20 mm), 4 mg. (0.303 in), b. (500 lb; 227 kg)
15.10	4,82	15,600	7.075	25,200	11.430	320	515	249	400	1,470	2.365	26,500	8.080	2	4 g. (20 mm), 7 mg. (0.303 in), t. (2,717 lb; 1.232 kg), b. (500 lb; 227 kg)
12.1	3,68	6,121	2.776	8,800	3.992	196	315	135	217	610	982	15,200	4.630	2	4 mg. (0.303 in), b. (240 lb; 109 kg)
11.4	3,45	6,078	2.757	8,600	3.900	304	489	259	417	465	748	30,350	9.250	2	4 mg. (0.303 in)
12.5	3,79	13,107	5.945	21,228	9.630	265	426	200	322	1,600	2.575	16,500	5.050	4	4 mg. (0.303 in), t. (1,605 lb; 728 kg) or b. (1,000 lb; 454 kg)
15.5	4,69	9,350	4.241	13,910	6.310	228	367	—	—	686	1.104	16,600	5.060	3	2 mg. (0.303 in), t. (1,620 lb; 735 kg) or b., d.c. (1,800 lb; 816 kg)
11.5	3,48	5,065	2.297	6,417	2.911	374	602	322	518	1,135	1.827	37,000	11.280	1	8 mg. (0.303 in)
11.5	3,48	4,810	2.182	5,784	2.624	365	587	315	507	575	925	34,000	10.360	1	8 mg. (0.303 in)
11.0	3,35	5,600	2.540	7,400	3.557	393	632	364	586	493	793	40,000	12.200	1	2 g. (20 mm), 4 mg. (0.303 in), b. (500 lb; 227 kg)
12.7	3,84	5,800	2.631	7,500	3.402	405	652	328	528	980	1.577	42,500	12.950	1	2 g. (20 mm), 4 mg. (0.303 in)
—	—	—	—	9,000	4.082	460	740	—	—	1,550	2.495	43,000	13.100	1	Unarmed reconnaissance version
13.1	3,99	4,670	2.118	6,600	2.994	324	521	—	—	460	740	34,200	10.425	1	8 mg. (0.303 in)
13.0	3,96	8,810	3.995	13,800	6.260	493	793	—	—	1,340	2.156	44,000	13.400	1	4 g. (20 mm)
15.6	4,72	6,647	3.015	10,792	4.895	241	388	210	338	1,050	1.690	23,500	7.160	3	2 mg. (0.303 in), b. (1,000 lb; 454 kg)
12.4	3,76	4,700	2.132	7,510	3.407	138	222	—	—	546	879	19,250	5.865	2	2 mg. (0.303 in), b. (1,500 lb; 680 kg)
9.10	2,99	8,100	3.674	12,500	5.670	260	418	200	322	1,125	1.810	27,260	8.310	3	2 mg. (0.303 in), b. (1,000 lb; 454 kg)
12.1	3,68	3,805	1.726	5,420	2.459	124	200	106	170	440	708	11,000	3.350	2	1 mg. (0.303 in)
15.3	4,65	4,900	2.223	7,200	3.266	135	217	95	153	600	965	18,500	5.640	4	2 mg. (0.303 in)
32.10	10,0	37,000	16.783	65,000	29.484	213	343	—	—	2,880	4.630	19,900	6.065	13	2 g. (50 mm), 12 mg. (0.303 in), b. (2,000 lb; 907 kg)
12.6	3,81	13,400	6.078	21,462	9.735	380	612	265	426	2,040	3.283	34,000	10.360	2	b. (2,000 lb; 907 kg)
12.6	3,81	13,431	6.071	18,547	8.413	370	595	255	410	1,705	2.744	36,000	11.000	2	4 g. (20 mm)
12.6	3,81	14,344	6.506	22,258	10.096	378	608	255	410	1,855	2.985	33,000	10.000	2	4 g. (20 mm), 4 mg. (0.303 in), b. (2,000 lb; 907 kg)

LB	light bomber	mm	millimeters	Sp	seaplane
lb	pounds	MR	maritime reconnaissance	t.	torpedo
Li	liaison	NB	night bomber	TB	torpedo-bomber
LT	light transport	NF	night fighter	Tj	turbo-jet
m	meters	P.&W.	Pratt & Whitney	Tr	transport
MB	medium bomber	Rc	reconnaissance	W.	Wright
mg.	machine-gun	r.	rockets		
ml	miles	R.R.	Rolls-Royce		

AIRCRAFT OF WORLD WAR II (continued)

Page	Aircraft	Builder	Type	Year	Engine	Wing spread		Length	
						ft	m	ft	m
98	Handley Page Hampden	Handley Page Ltd	MB	1939	2/1000 hp B. Pegasus XVIII	69.2	21,08	53.7	16,33
98	Short Stirling III	Short Bros Ltd	HB	1940	4/1650 hp B. Hercules XVI	99.1	30,21	87.3	26,60
99	Vickers Wellington III	Vickers-Armstrong Ltd	MB	1938	2/1500 hp B. Hercules XI	86.2	26,26	60.10	18,54
99	Armstrong Whitworth Whitley Mk.V	Armstrong Whitworth Air. Ltd	Br	1937	2/1145 hp R.R. Merlin X	84.0	25,60	70.6	21,49
99	Avro Lancaster	A.V. Roe & Co. Ltd	HB	1942	4/1460 hp R.R. Merlin XX	102.0	31,09	69.6	21,18
99	Handley Page Halifax Mk.III	Handley Page Ltd	HB	1940	4/1615 hp B. Hercules XVI	104.2	31,75	71.7	21,82
	UNITED STATES OF AMERICA								
100	Ryan PT-20	Ryan Aeronautical Co.	BT	1940	125 hp Menasco L-365-I	30.0	9,14	21.6	6,55
100	Vultee BT-13A Valiant	Vultee Aircraft Inc.	BT	1940	450 hp P.&W. R-985-AN-1	42.0	12,80	28.10	8,78
100	North American AT-6G Texan/Harvard	North American Aviation Inc.	AT	1940	600 hp P.&W. R-1340-AN-1	42.0	12,80	29.0	8,84
101	Beech AT-11	Beech Aircraft Co.	AT	1940	2/450 hp P.&W. R-985-AN-1	47.7	14,51	34.2	10,41
101	Cessna UC-78 Bobcat	Cessna Aircraft Co.	LT	1941	2/245 hp Jacobs R-755-9	41.11	12,78	32.9	9,98
101	Bell P-63A Kingcobra	Bell Aircraft Co.	Fr/FB	1943	1325 hp A. V-1710-95 (12 cl.)	38.4	11,68	32.8	9,95
101	Republic P-43 Lancer	Republic Aviation Co.	Fr	1940	1200 hp P.&W. R-1830-47 (14 cl.)	36.0	10,97	28.6	8,68
101	Douglas A-20G Havoc	Douglas Aircraft Co.	AB	1941	2/1600 hp W. R-2600-23	61.4	18,69	48.0	14,63
101	Northrop P-61 Black Widow	Northrop Aircraft Inc.	NF	1943	2/2000 hp P.&W. R-2800-65 (18 cl.)	66.0	20,12	49.7	15,12
102	Bell P-39Q Airacobra	Bell Aircraft Co.	Fr/FB	1941	1200 hp A. V-1710-85 (12 cl.)	34.0	10,36	30.2	9,19
102	Curtiss P-40N Warhawk	Curtiss-Wright Co.	Fr	1941	1360 hp A. V-1710-81 (12 cl.)	37.4	11,38	33.4	10,16
102	Republic P-47D Thunderbolt	Republic Aviation Co.	Fr	1943	2300 hp P.&W. R-2800-59 (18 cl.)	40.9	12,42	36.1	11,00
102	Lockheed P-38E Lightning	Lockheed Aircraft Co.	Fr	1941	2/1150 hp A. V-1710-27 (12 cl.)	52.0	15,85	37.10	11,53
102	Lockheed P-38F Lightning	Lockheed Aircraft Co.	Fr	1942	2/1325 hp A. V-1710-49 (12 cl.)	52.0	15,85	37.10	11,53
102	Lockheed P-38L Droop Snoot	Lockheed Aircraft Co.	FB	1943	2/1475 hp A. V-1710-111 (12 cl.)	52.0	15,85	37.10	11,53
102	Lockheed P-38M Lightning	Lockheed Aircraft Co.	NF	1944	2/1475 hp A. V-1710-113 (12 cl.)	52.0	15,85	37.10	11,53
103	North American P-51D Mustang	North American Aviation Inc.	Fr	1942	1490 hp R.R.-Packard Merlin V-1650-7 (12 cl.)	37.0	11,28	32.3	9,83
103	North American P-51 Mustang	North American Aviation Inc.	Fr	1942	1150 hp A. V-1710-39 (12 cl.)	37.0	11,28	32.3	9,83
103	North American P-51B Mustang	North American Aviation Inc.	Fr	1942	1380 hp R.R.-Packard Merlin V-1650-3 (12 cl.)	37.0	11,28	32.3	9,83
103	North American F-6D Mustang	North American Aviation Inc.	Rc	1942	1490 hp R.R.-Packard Merlin V-1650-7 (12 cl.)	37.0	11,28	32.3	9,83
103	North American P-51H	North American Aviation Inc.	Fr	1944	1380 hp R.R.-Packard Merlin V-1650-9 (12 cl.)	37.0	11,28	33.4	10,16
103	Chance Vought F4U-1 Corsair	Various	Cb/Fr	1943	2450 hp P.&W. R-2000-8W (18 cl.)	41.0	12,50	33.4	10,16
103	Grumman F4F-4 Wildcat	Grumman Aircraft Co.	Cb/Fr	1940	1200 hp P.&W. R-1830-86 (14 cl.)	38.0	11,58	28.9	8,76
103	Grumman F6F-3 Hellcat	Grumman Aircraft Co.	Cb/Fr	1942	2000 hp P.&W. R-2800-10 (18 cl.)	42.10	13,05	33.7	10,24
104	Brewster F2A-3 Buffalo	Brewster Aeronautical Co.	Cb/Fr	1938	1200 hp W. R-1820-40 (9 cl.)	35.0	10,67	26.4	8,02
104	Curtiss SB2C-4 Helldiver	Curtiss-Wright Co.	Cb/Br	1943	1900 hp W. R-2600-20	49.9	15,17	36.8	11,17
104	Grumman TBF-1 Avenger	Grumman Aircraft Co.	TB	1942	1700 hp W. R-2600-8	54.2	16,51	40.0	12,19
104	Douglas TBD-1 Devastator	Douglas Aircraft Co.	Cb/TB	1936	900 hp P.&W. R-1830-64 (14 cl.)	50.0	15,24	35.0	10,67
104	Douglas SBD-5 Dauntless	Douglas Aircraft Co.	Cb/Br	1941	1200 hp W. R-1820-60 (9 cl.)	41.6	12,65	33.0	10,06
104	Vought SB2U-3 Vindicator	Vought-Sikorsky	Cb/Rc/Br	1937	825 hp P.&W. R-1535-02	42.0	12,80	34.0	10,36
105	Lockheed C-60A Lodestar	Lockheed Aircraft Co.	Tr	1941	2/1200 hp W. R-1820-87 (9 cl.)	65.6	19,96	49.10	15,20
105	Vultee A-35B Vengeance	Vultee Aircraft Inc.	Br	1942	1700 hp W. R-2600-13	48.0	14,63	39.9	18,12
105	Martin B-26G Marauder	Glenn L. Martin Co.	LB	1942	2/2000 hp P.&W. R-2800-43 (18 cl.)	71.0	21,64	56.1	17,10
105	Douglas A-26B Invader	Douglas Aircraft Co.	LB	1944	2/2000 hp P.&W. R-2800-27 (18 cl.)	70.0	21,34	50.0	15,24
105	Martin A-30 IV Baltimore	Glenn L. Martin Co.	MB	1941	2/1660 hp W. R-2600-19	61.4	18,69	48.6	14,78
106	North American B-25J Mitchell	North American Aviation Inc.	LB	1941	2/1700 hp W. R-2600-92	67.7	20,60	52.11	16,13
106	Consolidated B-24J Liberator	Consolidated Aircraft Co.	Br	1941	4/1200 hp P.&W. R-1830-65 (14 cl.)	110.0	33,53	67.2	20,47
106	Boeing B-17F Flying Fortress	Boeing-Douglas-Lockheed	Br	1941	4/1200 hp W. R-1820-97 (9 cl.)	103.9	31,62	74.4	22,66
106	Boeing B-29A Superfortress	Boeing-Bell-Martin	HB	1943	4/2200 hp W. R-3350-23	141.3	43,05	99.0	30,18

Abbreviations used in the table

A.	Allison	BT	basic trainer	Fr	fighter	hp	horse-power
AB	attack bomber	Cb	carrier-based	ft	feet	H.S.	Hispano-Suiza
A.R.	Alfa Romeo	cl.	cylinders	g.	gun	I.F.	Isotta Fraschini
A.S.	Armstrong Siddeley	DB	dive bomber	h	hour	in	inches
AT	advanced trainer	D.B.	Daimler Benz	GA	ground attack	J.	Junkers
b.	bombs	d.c.	depth charge	G.R.	Gnome-Rhône	j.	jet
B.	Bristol	D.H.	De Havilland	HB	heavy bomber	kg	kilograms
Br	bomber	FB	fighter-bomber	HF	heavy fighter	km	kilometers

Height		Empty weight		Max take-off weight		Max speed		Cruising speed		Range		Ceiling		Crew	Armament or passengers
ft	m	lb	kg	lb	kg	ml/h	km/h	ml/h	km/h	ml	km	ft	m		
14.11	4,55	11,780	5.343	18,756	8.508	254	409	167	269	1,885	3.034	22,700	6.920	4	4 mg. (0.303 in), b. (4,000 lb; 1.814 kg)
22.9	6,93	43,200	19.596	70,000	31.752	270	435	—	—	2,010	3.235	17,000	5.180	7-8	8 mg. (0.303 in), b. (14,000 lb; 6.350 kg)
17.5	5,31	18,556	8.417	29,500	13.381	255	410	—	—	2,200	3.540	19,000	5.800	6	8 mg. (0.303 in), b. (4,500 lb; 2.041 kg)
15.0	4,57	19,330	8.768	28,200	12.792	222	357	185	298	1,650	2.655	17,600	5.365	5	5 mg. (0.303 in), b. (7,000 lb; 3.175 kg)
20.0	6,10	36,900	16.738	70,000	31.752	287	462	210	338	1,660	2.671	24,500	7.470	7	10 mg. (0.303 in), b. (22,000 lb; 9.979 kg)
20.9	6,33	38,240	17.346	54,400	24.676	282	454	—	—	1,030	1.658	24,000	7.315	7	9 mg. (0.303 in), b. (13,000 lb; 5.897 kg)
10.1	3,08	1,100	499	1,600	726	128	206	—	—	350	565	15,000	4.570	2	—
11.6	3,50	3,375	1.531	4,496	2.039	182	293	—	—	725	1.167	21,650	6.600	2	—
11.8	3,55	4,158	1.886	5,300	2.404	208	335	—	—	750	1.205	24,200	7.375	2	2 mg. (0.30 in)
9.8	2,94	6,175	2.801	8,727	3.959	215	346	—	—	850	1.368	20,000	6.100	6	2 mg. (0.30 in), b. (1,000 lb; 454 kg)
9.11	3,02	3,500	1.588	5,700	2.586	195	314	175	282	750	1.207	22,000	6.700	1	4 passengers
12.7	3,84	6,375	2.892	10,500	4.763	408	657	378	608	450	724	43,000	13.100	1	1 g. (37 mm), 4 mg. (0.50 in), b. (500 lb; 227 kg)
14.0	4,27	5,654	2.565	7,935	3.599	349	562	280	451	800	1.290	38,000	11.580	1	2 mg. (0.50 in) + 2 mg. (0.30 in)
17.7	5,36	15,984	7.250	27,200	12.338	339	546	272	438	1,090	1.754	25,000	7.620	3	8 mg. (0.50 in), b. (2,600 lb; 1.179 kg)
14.8	4,47	22,000	9.979	29,700	13.472	366	589	—	—	2,500	4.025	33,100	10.090	3	4 g. (20 mm), 4 mg. (0.50 in), b. (1,600 lb; 726 kg)
12.5	3,79	5,645	2.561	8,300	3.765	385	620	—	—	650	1.046	35,000	10.670	1	1 g. (37 mm), 4 mg. (0.50 in), b. (500 lb; 227 kg)
12.4	3,76	6,000	2.722	8,850	4.014	378	608	288	463	730	1.175	38,000	11.580	1	6 mg. (0.50 in), b. (500 lb; 227 kg)
14.2	4,32	10,000	4.536	19,400	8.800	428	689	—	—	475	764	42,000	12.800	1	8 mg. (0.50 in), b. (2,000 lb; 907 kg)
9.10	2,99	11,880	5.389	15,482	7.023	395	636	—	—	500	805	39,000	11.890	1	1 g. (20 mm), 4 mg. (0.50 in)
9.10	2,99	12,264	5.563	18,000	8.165	395	636	305	491	500	805	39,000	11.890	1	1 g. (20 mm), 4 mg. (0.50 in)
9.10	2,99	12,800	5.806	21,600	9.798	414	666	290	467	450	724	44,000	13.400	1	1 g. (20 mm), 4 mg. (0.50 in), b. (4,000 lb; 1.814 kg)
9.10	2,99	12,800	5.806	21,600	9.798	414	666	—	—	500	805	44,000	13.400	2	1 g. (20 mm), 4 mg. (0.50 in)
12.2	3,71	7,125	3.232	11,600	5.262	437	703	362	583	950	1.530	41,900	12.770	1	6 mg. (0.50 in), b. (2,000 lb; 907 kg)
12.2	3,71	6,550	2.971	8,800	3.992	387	623	307	494	350	565	31,350	9.555	1	4 g. (20 mm)
12.2	3,71	6,985	3.168	11,800	5.352	440	708	362	583	400	644	41,800	12.750	1	4 mg. (0.50 in), b. (2,000 lb; 907 kg)
12.2	3,71	7,125	3.232	11,600	5.262	437	703	362	583	950	1.530	41,900	12.770	1	6 mg. (0.50 in)
13.8	4,16	6,585	2.987	11,054	5.014	487	784	380	612	850	1.368	41,600	12.680	1	6 mg. (0.50 in), b. (2,000 lb; 907 kg)
16.1	4,90	8,982	4.074	14,000	6.350	417	671	182	293	1,015	1.633	36,900	11.247	1	6 mg. (0.50 in)
11.10	3,60	5,785	2.624	7,952	3.607	318	512	155	249	850	1.368	34,900	10.640	1	6 mg. (0.50 in)
13.1	3,99	9,042	4.101	12,441	5.643	375	603	168	270	1,090	1.754	37,300	11.370	1	6 mg. (0.50 in)
12.0	3,66	4,732	2.146	7,159	3.247	321	517	161	259	965	1.553	33,200	10.120	1	4 mg. (0.50 in)
13.2	4,01	10,547	4.784	16,616	7.537	295	475	158	254	1,925	3.100	29,100	8.870	2	2 g. (20 mm), 2 mg. (0.30 in), b. (2,000 lb; 907 kg)
16.5	5,01	10,080	4.572	15,905	7.215	271	436	145	233	2,530	4.075	22,400	6.830	3	1 mg. (0.50 in) + 2 mg. (0.30 in), b. (1,600 lb; 726 kg)
15.1	4,60	6,182	2.804	10,194	4.624	206	332	128	206	1,000	1.610	19,700	6.005	3	2 mg. (0.30 in), t. (1,000 lb; 454 kg)
12.11	3,94	6,675	3.028	10,855	4.924	252	406	144	232	1,115	1.794	24,300	7.405	2	2 mg. (0.50 in) + 2 mg. (0.30 in), b. (2,250 lb; 1.021 kg)
10.3	3,13	5,634	2.556	9,421	4.273	243	391	152	245	1,400	2.250	23,600	7.195	2	2 mg. (0.50 in)
11.10	3,60	12,075	5.477	18,500	8.392	253	407	—	—	1,660	2.671	27,000	8.230	4	13 passengers
15.4	4,67	10,300	4.672	16,400	7.439	279	449	230	370	2,000	3.220	22,300	6.800	2	6 mg. (0.50 in), b. (2,000 lb; 907 kg)
20.4	6,20	23,800	10.796	38,200	17.328	283	455	216	348	1,100	1.770	19,800	6.050	7	11 mg. (0.50 in), b. (4,000 lb; 1.814 kg)
18.6	5,64	22,370	10.147	35,000	15.876	355	571	284	457	1,400	2.250	22,100	6.735	3	10 mg. (0.50 in), b. (4,000 lb; 1.814 kg)
17.9	5,41	—	—	23,000	10.433	302	486	—	—	1,050	1.690	24,000	7.315	4	2 mg. (0.50 in) + 4 mg. (0.303 in) + 6 mg. (0.30 in), b. (2,000 lb; 907 kg)
16.4	4,98	19,480	8.836	35,000	15.876	272	438	230	370	1,350	2.170	24,200	7.375	6	12 mg. (0.50 in), b. (4,000 lb; 1.814 kg)
18.0	5,49	36,500	16.550	65,000	29.484	290	467	215	346	2,100	3.380	28,000	8.535	10-12	10 mg. (0.50 in), b. (8,800 lb; 3.992 kg)
19.1	5,82	32,250	14.629	53,000	24.041	317	510	210	338	2,400	3.860	36,600	11.155	10	12 mg. (0.50 in) + 1 mg. (0.30 in), b. (17,600 lb; 7.983 kg)
27.9	8,46	71,360	32.369	110,000	49.896	357	575	230	370	3,250	5.230	31,850	9.710	10	1 g. (20 mm), 12 mg. (0.50 in), b. (20,000 lb; 9.072 kg)

LB	light bomber	mm	millimeters	Sp	seaplane
lb	pounds	MR	maritime reconnaissance	t.	torpedo
Li	liaison	NB	night bomber	TB	torpedo-bomber
LT	light transport	NF	night fighter	Tj	turbo-jet
m	meters	P.&W.	Pratt & Whitney	Tr	transport
MB	medium bomber	Rc	reconnaissance	W.	Wright
mg.	machine-gun	r.	rockets		
ml	miles	R.R.	Rolls-Royce		

AIRCRAFT OF WORLD WAR II (continued)

Page	Aircraft	Builder	Type	Year	Engine	Wing spread		Length	
						ft	m	ft	m
107	Douglas C-53 Skytrooper	Douglas Aircraft Co.	Tr	1941	2/1200 hp P.&W. R-1830-92 (14 cl.)	95.6	29,11	63.9	19,43
107	Curtiss C-46 Commando	Curtiss-Wright Co.	Tr	1943	2/2000 hp P.&W. R-2800-51 (18 cl.)	108.1	32,94	76.4	23,26
107	Lockheed A-29 Hudson	Lockheed Aircraft Co.	Rc	1939	2/1200 hp W. R-1820-87 (9 cl.)	65.6	19,96	44.4	13,51
107	Consolidated PBY-5 Catalina	Consolidated Aircraft Co.	MR/Sp	1936	2/1200 hp P.&W. R-1830-92 (14 cl.)	104.0	31,70	63.10	19,45
108	Piper L-4 Grasshopper	Piper Aircraft Co.	Li	1941	65 hp Continental O-170-3	35.3	10,74	22.0	6,71
108	Stinson L-5 Sentinel	Stinson Aircraft	Li	1941	185 hp Lycoming O-435-1	34.0	10,36	24.1	7,34
108	Lockheed PV-2 Harpoon	Lockheed Aircraft Co.	MB	1944	2/2000 hp P.&W. R-2800-31 (18 cl.)	74.11	22,84	52.0	15,85
108	Martin PBM-3D Mariner	Glenn L. Martin Co.	Rc/Sp	1941	2/1700 hp W. R-2600-12	118.0	35,97	80.0	24,38
108	Consolidated PB2Y-3R Coronado	Consolidated Aircraft Co.	Rc/Br/Sp	1940	4/1200 hp P.&W. R-1830-92 (14 cl.)	115.0	35,05	79.3	24,16
	SOVIET UNION								
109	Mikoyan-Gurevich MiG-3	State Industries	Fr	1941	1350 hp Mikulin AM-35A (12 cl.)	33.9	10,30	26.9	8,16
109	Mikoyan-Gurevich MiG-1	State Industries	Fr	1940	1200 hp Mikulin AM-35A (12 cl.)	33.9	10,30	26.9	8,16
109	Mikoyan-Gurevich MiG-5	State Industries	FB	1943	1600 hp Shvetsov M-82A (14 cl.)	33.9	10,30	26.0	7,92
109	Sykhoi Su-2	State Industries	LB	1940	1000 hp Shvetsov M-82 (14 cl.)	46.11	14,30	33.7	10,25
110	Lavochkin La-5	State Industries	Fr	1942	1650 hp Shvetsov M-82FN (14 cl.)	32.2	9,80	27.11	8,50
110	Lavochkin LaGG-3	State Industries	Fr	1941	1100 hp Klimov M-105P (12 cl.)	32.2	9,80	28.10	8,79
110	Lavochkin La-5FN	State Industries	Fr	1943	1700 hp Shvetsov ASh-8FN (14 cl.)	32.2	9,80	27.11	8,50
110	Lavochkin La-7	State Industries	Fr	1944	1775 hp Shvetsov ASh-8FN (14 cl.)	32.2	9,80	27.10	8,50
110	Lavochkin La-9	State Industries	Fr	1944	1850 hp ASh-82 FNV (14 cl.)	34.9	10,60	30.2	9,20
110	Polikarpov I-16 Tipo 24	State Industries	FB	1934	1000 hp Shvetsov M-62 (9 cl.)	29.6	9,00	20.1	6,13
110	Yakovlev Yak-9	State Industries	Fr	1942	1260 hp Klimov M-105PF (12 cl.)	32.10	10,00	28.1	8,55
110	Yakovlev Yak-1	State Industries	Fr	1940	1100 hp Klimov M-105PF (12 cl.)	32.10	10,00	27.10	8,48
110	Yakovlev Yak-7	State Industries	Fr	1942	1210 hp Klimov M-105PF (12 cl.)	32.10	10,00	27.10	8,48
110	Yakovlev Yak-9T	State Industries	Fr	1942	1260 hp Klimov M-105PF (12 cl.)	32.10	10,00	28.0	8,54
110	Yakovlev Yak-9P	State Industries	Fr	1945	1650 hp Klimov VK-107A (12 cl.)	32.0	9,75	26.3	8,00
111	Ilyushin Il-2 Shturmovik	State Industries	AB	1941	1600 hp Mikulin AM-38F	47.10	14,60	38.3	11,65
111	Polikarpov I-15	State Industries	Fr	1933	700 hp M-25 (W. Cyclone 9) (9 cl.)	30.0	9,15	20.8	6,30
111	Petlyakov Pe-2	State Industries	Br	1941	2/1100 hp Klimov VK-105R	56.4	17,16	41.6	12,66
111	Ilyushin Il-4	State Industries	MB	1940	2/1100 hp M-88	70.4	21,44	48.7	14,80
112	Tupolev SB-2	State Industries	MB	1936	2/990 hp M-103	70.6	21,49	41.6	12,65
112	Tupolev Tu-2	State Industries	Br	1943	2/1850 hp Shvetsov ASh-82FNV	61.0	18,60	45.3	13,80
112	Beriev MBR-2bis	State Industries	MR/Sp	1932	860 hp M-34 (12 cl.)	43.11	13,40	30.2	9,20
112	Petlyakov Pe-8	State Industries	HB	1940	4/1450 hp Mikulin AM-35A	131.0	39,94	73.9	22,47
112	Tupolev ANT-6	State Industries	Tr	1930	4/830 hp AM-34	129.7	39,50	80.5	24,50
	GERMANY								
113	Messerschmitt Bf 110C	Messerschmitt A.G.	Fr	1939	2/1100 hp D.B. 601A-1 (12 cl.)	53.4	16,25	39.7	12,07
113	Messerschmitt Me 410 A-1 Hornisse	Messerschmitt A.G.	HF	1942	2/1750 hp D.B. 603A (12 cl.)	53.8	16,35	41.0	12,50
113	Arado Ar 240C	Arado Flugzeugwerke GmbH	HF	1942	2/1750 hp D.B. 603A-2 (12 cl.)	54.5	16,60	43.9	13,35
114	Focke Wulf Fw 190 D9	Focke Wulf Flugzeugbau GmbH	Fr	1941	1776 hp J. Jumo 213A-1 (12 cl.)	34.6	10,50	33.5	10,20
114	Messerschmitt Me 163B Komet	Messerschmitt A.G.	Fr	1944	3,748 lb (1.700 kg) Walter HWK 509A-2 r.	30.8	9,35	19.2	5,85
114	Messerschmitt Me 262A Sturmvogel	Messerschmitt A.G.	Fr	1944	2/1,984 lb (900 kg) J. Jumo 004B-1 j.	40.11	12,48	34.9	10,60
114	Heinkel He 162A	Ernst Heinkel A.G.	Fr	1945	2/1,764 lb (800 kg) BMW 003E-1 tj.	23.7	7,20	29.8	9,05
114	Messerschmitt Bf 109T-2	Messerschmitt A.G.	FB	1939	1200 hp D.B. 601N (12 cl.)	36.4	11,08	28.9	8,76
114	Messerschmitt Bf 109E	Messerschmitt A.G.	Fr	1938	1100 hp D.B. 601A (12 cl.)	32.5	9,87	28.5	8,65
114	Messerschmitt Bf 109G10	Messerschmitt A.G.	Fr	1942	1475 hp D.B. 605AM (12 cl.)	32.6	9,90	29.0	8,85

Abbreviations used in the table

A.	Allison	BT	basic trainer	Fr	fighter	hp	horse-power
AB	attack bomber	Cb	carrier-based	ft	feet	H.S.	Hispano-Suiza
A.R.	Alfa Romeo	cl.	cylinders	g.	gun	I.F.	Isotta Fraschini
A.S.	Armstrong Siddeley	DB	dive bomber	h	hour	in	inches
AT	advanced trainer	D.B.	Daimler Benz	GA	ground attack	J.	Junkers
b.	bombs	d.c.	depth charge	G.R.	Gnome-Rhône	j.	jet
B.	Bristol	D.H.	De Havilland	HB	heavy bomber	kg	kilograms
Br	bomber	FB	fighter-bomber	HF	heavy fighter	km	kilometers

Height		Empty weight		Max take-off weight		Max speed		Cruising speed		Range		Ceiling		Crew	Armament or passengers
ft	m	lb	kg	lb	kg	ml/h	km/h	ml/h	km/h	ml	km	ft	m		
17.0	5,18	18,200	8.256	29,000	13.154	230	370	—	—	1,350	2.170	24,000	7.315	4	27 passengers or cargo (10,000 lb; 4.536 kg)
21.9	6,63	—	—	45,000	20.412	269	433	183	294	1,600	2.575	27,600	8.410	4	40 passengers or cargo (10,000 lb; 4.536 kg)
11.10	3,60	12,825	5.817	20,500	9.299	255	410	205	330	2,200	3.540	26,500	8.080	4	7 mg. (0.303 in), b. (1,600 lb; 726 kg)
18.6	5,64	17,526	7.950	34,000	15.422	189	304	115	185	3,000	4.830	18,100	5.520	7-9	2 mg. (0.50 in) + 2 mg. (0.30 in), b. (4,000 lb; 1.814 kg)
6.8	2,03	730	331	1,220	553	85	137	—	—	190	306	9,300	2.835	2	—
7.11	2,41	1,550	703	2,020	916	130	209	—	—	500	805	15,800	4.815	2	—
11.11	3,63	21,028	9.538	36,000	16.330	282	454	171	275	2,200	3.540	23,900	7.285	4-5	9 mg. (0.50 in), b. (6,000 lb; 2.722 kg)
27.6	8,38	32,378	14.687	58,000	26.309	198	319	—	—	2,700	4.345	16,900	5.151	9	6 mg. (0.50 in), b. (2,000 lb; 907 kg)
27.6	8,38	40,935	18.568	68,000	30.845	213	343	141	227	1,800	2.895	20,100	6.125	10	8 mg. (0.50 in), b. (12,000 lb; 5.443 kg)
11.6	3,50	—	—	7,385	3.350	398	640	—	—	776	1.250	39,370	12.000	1	1 mg. (12,7 mm) + 2 mg. (7,62 mm), b. (220 lb; 100 kg)
11.6	3,50	5,721	2.595	6,834	3.100	392	630	280	450	453	730	39,370	12.000	1	1 mg. (12,7 mm) + 2 mg. (7,62 mm)
11.6	3,50	—	—	7,055	3.200	370	595	—	—	—	—	—	—	1	4 mg. (7,62 mm), 6 r., b. (440 lb; 200 kg)
12.3	3,75	6,393	2.900	8,995	4.080	302	485	—	—	746	1.200	28,870	8.800	2	5 mg. (7,62 mm), b. (1,323 lb: 600 kg)
9.3	2,82	—	—	7,408	3.360	373	600	249	400	398	640	—	—	1	2 g. (20 mm), b. (440 lb; 200 kg)
8.10	2,69	5,776	2.620	7,055	3.200	346	556	276	446	398	640	29,530	9.000	1	1 g. (20 mm), 2 mg. (12,7 mm), b. (331 lb; 150 kg)
9.3	2,83	6,085	2.760	7,408	3.360	401	645	—	—	528	850	35,900	10.970	1	2 g. (20 mm), b. (331 lb; 150 kg)
9.2	2,79	—	—	7,496	3.400	423	680	—	—	395	635	33,300	10.150	1	3 g. (20 mm), 6 r.
9.8	2,94	—	—	—	—	429	690	311	500	1,078	1.735	36,515	11.130	1	4 g. (20 mm)
8.5	2,56	3,285	1.490	4,189	1.900	326	525	186	300	249	400	29,530	9.000	1	2 g. (20 mm), 2 mg. (7,62 mm)
8.0	2,44	6,063	2.750	7,055	3.200	364	585	292	470	565	910	36,000	11.000	1	1 g. (37 mm), 1 mg. (12,7 mm)
8.8	2,64	5,137	2.330	6,217	2.820	364	585	155	250	528	850	33,000	10.000	1	1 g. (20 mm), 2 mg. (7,62 mm)
8.0	2,44	—	—	6,636	3.010	379	610	—	—	516	830	—	—	1	1 g. (20 mm), 2 mg. (12,7 mm)
8.0	2,44	6,063	2.750	7,055	3.200	363	585	—	—	516	830	36,000	11.000	1	1 g. (37 mm), 1 mg. (12,7 mm)
—	—	5,093	2.310	7,000	3.175	416	670	298	480	889	1.430	34,000	10.360	1	1 g. (20 mm), 2 mg. (12,7 mm), b. (440 lb; 200 kg)
11.2	3,40	9,259	4.200	12,941	5.870	251	404	199	320	466	750	24,600	7.500	2	2 g. (20 mm), 1 mg. (12,7 mm) + 2 mg. (7,62 mm), b. (880 lb; 400 kg)
9.7	2,92	2,601	1.180	3,131	1.420	224	360	180	290	451	725	33,000	10.000	1	4 mg. (7,62 mm)
—	—	12,941	5.870	16,976	7.700	336	540	265	428	930	1.500	29,530	9.000	2	1 mg. (12,7 mm) + 4 mg. (7,62 mm), b. (2,200 lb; 1.000 kg)
13.9	4,20	12,103	5.490	22,046	10.000	277	445	—	—	1,616	2.600	33,000	10.000	3-4	3 mg. (7,62 mm), b. (4,398 lb; 1.995 kg)
10.8	3,25	9,436	4.280	14,330	6.500	410	660	174	280	1,400	2.250	27,900	8.500	3	4 mg. (7,62 mm), b. (1,323 lb; 600 kg)
—	—	18,210	8.260	28,219	12.800	345	555	258	415	1,555	2.500	33,000	10.000	4	2 g. (23 mm), 5 mg. (12,7 mm), b. (5,004 lb; 2.270 kg)
16.5	5,00	—	—	9,359	4.245	155	250	121	195	870	1.400	19,685	6.000	4-5	2 mg. (7,62 mm), b. (661 lb; 300 kg)
20.0	6,10	—	—	73,414	33.300	276	444	224	360	2,300	3.700	25,920	7.900	11	2 g. (20 mm), 2 mg. (12,7 mm) + 2 mg. (7,62 mm), b. (8,796 lb; 3.990 kg)
—	—	22,046	10.000	38,581	17.500	155	250	124	200	1,243	2.000	22,970	7.000	8	30 passengers
13.6	4,12	10,770	4.885	13,289	6.028	336	540	305	490	699	1.125	33,000	10.000	2-3	2 g. (20 mm), 5 mg. (7,9 mm)
14.0	4,28	16,558	7.515	21,275	9.650	388	625	367	590	1,050	1.690	33,000	10.000	2	4 g. (20 mm), 2 mg. (13 mm) + 2 mg. (7,9 mm)
12.11	3,95	18,651	8.460	25,849	11.725	454	730	—	—	1,162	1.870	34,450	10.500	2	4 g. (20 mm), 4 mg. (13 mm), b. (3,968 lb; 1.800 kg)
11.0	3,35	7,694	3.490	9,480	4.300	426	685	—	—	519	835	37,400	11.400	1	2 g. (20 mm), 2 mg. (13 mm), b. (1,102 lb; 500 kg)
9.0	2,75	4,200	1.905	9,502	4.310	597	960	—	—	8'		39,500	12.040	1	2 g. (30 mm)
12.7	3,84	9,744	4.420	14,101	6.396	541	870	—	—	652	1.050	37,565	11.450	1	4 g. (30 mm)
8.6	2,60	3,880	1.760	5,743	2.605	553	890	—	—	606	975	39,370	12.000	1	2 g. (20 mm)
8.6	2,60	4,905	2.225	6,173	2.800	357	575	329	530	568	915	34,450	10.500	1	2 g. (20 mm), 2 mg. (7,9 mm)
8.2	2,50	4,431	2.010	5,523	2.505	342	550	298	480	410	660	34,450	10.500	1	2 g. (20 mm), 2 mg. (7,9 mm)
8.2	2,50	5,886	2.670	6,945	3.150	385	620	—	—	621	1.000	37,890	11.550	1	1 g. (30 mm), 2 mg. (13 mm)

LB	light bomber	mm	millimeters	Sp	seaplane
lb	pounds	MR	maritime reconnaissance	t.	torpedo
Li	liaison	NB	night bomber	TB	torpedo-bomber
LT	light transport	NF	night fighter	Tj	turbo-jet
m	meters	P.&W.	Pratt & Whitney	Tr	transport
MB	medium bomber	Rc	reconnaissance	W.	Wright
mg.	machine-gun	r.	rockets		
ml	miles	R.R.	Rolls-Royce		

AIRCRAFT OF WORLD WAR II (continued)

Page	Aircraft	Builder	Type	Year	Engine	Wing spread		Length	
						ft	m	ft	m
115	Junkers Ju 87B-1 Stuka	Junkers Flugzeug und Motorenwerke A.G.	DB	1938	1200 hp J. Jumo 211Da (12 cl.)	45.4	13,82	36.5	11,10
115	Heinkel He 111-H	Ernst Heinkel A.G.	MB	1936	2/1350 hp J. Jumo 211F-2 (12 cl.)	74.1	22,60	53.9	16,39
115	Junkers Ju 88A-1	Junkers Flugzeug und Motorenwerke A.G.	Br	1939	2/1200 hp J. Jumo 211B-1 (12 cl.)	60.3	18,38	47.1	14,36
115	Junkers Ju 88A-15	Junkers Flugzeug und Moto-renwerke A.G.	Br	1940	2/1340 hp J. Jumo 211J-1 (12 cl.)	65.7	20,00	47.3	14,40
115	Junkers Ju 188E-1	Junkers Flugzeug und Moto-renwerke A.G.	MB	1943	2/1700 hp BMW (14 cl.)	72.2	22,00	49.0	14,95
116	Heinkel He 177A-1 Greif	Ernst Heinkel A.G.	HB	1942	2/2700 hp D.B. 606 (24 cl.)	103.2	31,44	66.11	20,40
116	Heinkel He 219A-5	Ernst Heinkel A.G.	NF	1942	2/1800 hp D.B. 603E (12 cl.)	60.8	18,50	51.0	15,55
116	Henschel Hs 123A-1	Henschel Flugzeugwerke A.G.	DB	1935	880 hp BMW 132Dc (9 cl.)	34.6	10,50	27.4	8,33
116	Dornier Do 17E-1	Dornier Werke GmbH	MB	1937	2/750 hp BMW VI 7,3 (12 cl.)	59.1	18,00	53.4	16,25
116	Dornier Do 217E-2	Dornier Werke GmbH	HB	1940	2/1580 hp BMW 801ML (14 cl.)	62.4	19,00	59.9	18,20
116	Arado Ar 234B-2 Blitz	Arado Flegzeugwerke GmbH	Br	1944	2/1,980 lb (900 kg) J. Jumo 004B tj.	46.3	14,10	41.6	12,65
117	Fieseler Fi 156C-2	Gerhard Fieseler Werke GmbH	Rc/Li	1938	240 hp Argus 10C-3 (8 cl.)	46.9	14,25	32.6	9,90
117	Junkers Ju 52/3m g5e	Junkers Flugzeug und Motorenwerke A.G.	Tr/Sp	1933	3/830 hp BMW 132T-2 (9 cl.)	95.11	29,25	62.0	18,90
117	Focke Wulf Fw 189A-2	Focke Wulf Flugzeugbau GmbH	Rc	1940	2/465 hp Argus As410A-1 (12 cl.)	60.4	18,40	39.5	12,03
117	Arado Ar 169A-3	Arado Flugzeugwerke GmbH	MR/Sp	1939	960 hp BMW 132K (9 cl.)	40.10	12,45	35.11	10,95
117	Heinkel He 115B-1	Ernst Heinkel A.G.	Rc/Sp	1939	2/970 hp BMW 132K (9 cl.)	73.1	22,28	56.9	17,30
117	Dornier Do 18G-1	Dornier Werke GmbH	MR/Sp	1936	2/880 hp J. Jumo 205D (6 cl.)	77.9	23,70	63.7	19,38
118	Focke Wulf Fw 200C-3	Focke Wulf Flugzeugbau GmbH	MR/Br	1939	4/1200 hp BMW-Bramo 323 R2 (9 cl.)	107.9	30,86	77.0	23,46
118	Blohm & Voss Bv 138C-1	Blohm & Voss	MR/Sp	1940	3/880 hp J. Jumo 205D (6 cl.)	88.4	26,92	65.1	19,85
118	Blohm & Voss Bv 222C	Blohm & Voss	MR/Sp	1940	6/1000 hp J. Jumo 207C (6 cl.)	150.11	46,00	121.5	37,00
118	Messerschmitt Me 323E Gigant	Messerschmitt A.G.	Tr	1942	6/1140 hp G.R. 14N (14 cl.)	180.9	55,00	93.6	28,50
	ITALY								
119	Reggiane Re 2001 Falco II	O.M. Reggiane S.A.	Fr	1942	1075 hp D.B.-A.R. RA 1000 R.C.41 (12 cl.)	36.1	11,00	26.11	8,20
119	Macchi MC 202 Folgore	Aeronautica Macchi S.p.A.	Fr	1941	1075 hp D.B.-A.R. RA 1000 R.C.41 (12 cl.)	34.9	10,58	29.0	8,85
119	Fiat G.55 Centauro	Fiat S.A.	Fr	1943	1475 hp D.B.-Fiat RA 1050 R.C.58 (12 cl.)	38.11	11,85	30.8	9,35
120	Breda Ba 65	Società Italiana Ernesto Breda	LB/Rc	1936	1000 hp Fiat A.80 R.C.41	39.8	12,10	31.6	9,60
120	Caproni Ca 133	Società Italiana Caproni	MB	1935	3/450 hp Piaggio P.VII C.14	69.8	21,24	50.4	15,35
120	Macchi MC 200 Saetta	Aeronautica Macchi S.p.A.	Fr	1937	870 hp Fiat A.74 R.C.38 (14 cl.)	34.9	10,58	26.11	8,19
120	Macchi MC 205 Veltro	Aeronautica Macchi S.p.A.	Fr	1943	1465 hp D.B.-Fiat RA 1050 R.C.58 (12 cl.)	34.9	10,58	29.0	8,85
120	Reggiane Re 2000 III Falco I	O.M. Reggiane S.A.	Fr	1940	1025 hp Piaggio P.XIbis R.C.40 (14 cl.)	36.1	11,00	26.3	7,99
120	Reggiane Re 2002 Ariete	O.M. Reggiane S.A.	FB	1942	1175 hp Piaggio P.XIX R.C.45 (14 cl.)	36.1	11,00	26.9	8,15
121	Reggiane Re 2005 Sagittario	O.M. Reggiane S.A.	FB	1943	1475 hp D.B.-Fiat RA 1050 R.C.58 (12 cl.)	36.1	11,00	28.8	8,73
121	S.A.I. 207	Società Aeronautica Italiana Ambrosini	Fr	1943	750 hp I.F. Delta R.C.40	29.6	9,00	26.4	8,02
121	Fiat C.R.42 Falco	Fiat S.A.	Fr	1939	840 hp Fiat A.74 R.C.38 (14 cl.)	31.10	9,70	27.1	8,26
121	Fiat G.50 Freccia	Fiat S.A.	Fr	1937	840 hp Fiat A.74 R.C.38 (14 cl.)	36.0	10,98	26.4	8,02
121	IMAM Ro 37	Industrie Meccaniche e Aero-nautiche Meridionali	Rc	1935	600 hp Fiat A.30 RA (12 cl.)	36.4	11,07	28.3	8,61
121	Caproni Ca 311M	Società Italiana Caproni	Br/Rc	1940	2/500 hp Piaggio P.VII C.35	53.1	16,19	39.8	12,09
122	Savoia Marchetti SM 79II Sparviero	S.I.A.I. Savoia Marchetti	TB	1936	3/1000 hp Piaggio P.XI R.C.40 (14 cl.)	69.7	21,20	53.2	16,20
122	Fiat BR.20M Cicogna	Fiat S.A.	MB	1936	2/1000 hp Fiat A.80 R.C.41 (18 cl.)	70.9	21,56	55.1	16,78
122	Cant Z.1007 bis Alcione	Cantieri Riuniti dell'Adriatico	MB	1940	3/1000 hp Piaggio P.XIbis R.C.40	81.4	24,80	61.0	18,60
122	Piaggio P.108B	S.A. Piaggio & C.	HB	1942	4/1500 hp Piaggio P.XII R.C.35 (18 cl.)	105.0	32,00	75.2	22,91
123	Savoia Marchetti SM 82 Canguro	S.I.A.I. Savoia Marchetti	Tr	1939	3/950 hp A.R. 128 R.C.21	97.5	29,70	74.4	22,66
123	Fiat G.12T	Fiat S.A.	Tr	1941	3/770 hp Fiat A.74 R.C.42 (14 cl.)	93.10	28,60	65.11	20,10
123	Cant Z.501 Gabbiano	Cantieri Riuniti dell'Adriatico	Rc/Sp	1935	900 hp I.F. Asso XI R2C 15 (12 cl.)	73.10	22,50	46.11	14,29
123	Cant Z.506B Airone	Cantieri Riuniti dell'Adriatico	TB/Rc/Sp	1940	3/750 hp A.R. 126 R.C.34 (9 cl.)	86.11	26,50	63.2	19,85
123	Cant Z.511	Cantieri Riuniti dell'Adriatico	Tr/Sp	1943	4/1500 hp Piaggio P.XII R.C.35 (18 cl.)	131.2	40,00	93.6	28,50

Abbreviations used in the table

A.	Allison	BT	basic trainer	Fr	fighter	hp	horse-power
AB	attack bomber	Cb	carrier-based	ft	feet	H.S.	Hispano-Suiza
A.R.	Alfa Romeo	cl.	cylinders	g.	gun	I.F.	Isotta Fraschini
A.S.	Armstrong Siddeley	DB	dive bomber	GA	ground attack	in	inches
AT	advanced trainer	D.B.	Daimler Benz	h	hour	J.	Junkers
b.	bombs	d.c.	depth charge	G.R.	Gnome-Rhône	j.	jet
B.	Bristol	D.H.	De Havilland	HB	heavy bomber	kg	kilograms
Br	bomber	FB	fighter-bomber	HF	heavy fighter	km	kilometers

Height		Empty weight		Max take-off weight		Max speed		Cruising speed		Range		Ceiling		Crew	Armament or passengers
ft	m	lb	kg	lb	kg	ml/h	km/h	ml/h	km/h	ml	km	ft	m		
13.2	4,01	6,085	2.760	9,557	4.335	239	385	174	280	370	595	26,250	8.000	2	3 mg. (7,9 mm), b. (1,102 lb; 500 kg)
13.1	4,00	19,136	8.680	30,865	14.000	252	405	211	340	1,280	2.060	27,900	8.500	5	1 g. (20 mm), 1 mg. (13 mm) + 5 mg. (7,9 mm), b. (5,501 lb; 2.495 kg)
17.5	5,32	16,976	7.700	22,840	10.360	280	450	217	350	1,056	1.700	26,250	8.000	4	5 mg. (7,9 mm), b. (3,737 lb; 1.695 kg)
15.11	4,85	21,738	9.860	30,865	14.000	280	450	230	370	1,696	2.730	26,900	8.200	3	2 mg. (7,9 mm), b. (6,614 lb; 3.000 kg)
14.7	4,45	21,738	9.860	31,989	14.510	311	500	233	375	1,209	1.945	30,660	9.345	4	1 g. (20 mm), 2 mg. (13 mm) + 2 mg. (7,9 mm), b. (6,614 lb; 3.000 kg)
21.0	6,40	39,771	18.040	66,139	30.000	317	510	267	430	3,480	5.600	22,970	7.000	5	1 g. (20 mm), 2 mg. (13 mm) + 3 mg. (7,9 mm), b. (12,346 lb; 5.600 kg)
13.6	4,11	24,692	11.200	33,731	15.300	416	670	336	540	1,243	2.000	39,600	12.070	2	6 g. (20 mm)
10.6	3,21	3,318	1.505	4,894	2.220	211	340	196	315	534	860	29,530	9.000	1	2 mg. (7,9 mm), b. (440 lb; 200 kg)
14.2	4,32	9,921	4.500	15,521	7.040	221	355	196	315	311	500	16,732	5.100	3	2 mg. (7,9 mm), b. (1,653 lb; 750 kg)
16.6	5,03	23,226	10.535	33,069	15.000	320	515	258	415	1,428	2.300	24,600	7.500	4	1 g. (15 mm), 5 mg. (7,9 mm), b. (8,818 lb; 4.000 kg)
14.1	4,30	11,464	5.200	18,541	8.410	460	740	—	—	1,013	1.630	33,000	10.000	1	2 g. (20 mm), b. (3,296 lb; 1.495 kg)
10.0	3,05	2,050	930	2,921	1.325	109	175	93	150	239	385	15,090	4.600	2	1 mg. (7,9 mm)
—	—	12,610	5.720	23,149	10.500	171	275	152	245	798	1.285	18,000	5.500	2-3	3 mg. (7,9 mm); 18 passengers
10.2	3,10	7,154	3.245	8,708	3.950	217	350	190	305	416	670	23,950	7.300	3	6 mg. (7,9 mm), b. (440 lb; 200 kg)
14.7	4,45	5,666	2.570	7,275	3.300	193	310	165	265	659	1.060	22,970	7.000	2	2 g. (20 mm), 2 mg. (7,9 mm), b. (220 lb; 100 kg)
21.8	6,60	14,749	6.690	22,928	10.400	186	300	174	280	2,082	3.350	17,060	5.200	3	2 mg. (7,9 mm), b. (2,756 lb; 1.250 kg)
17.5	5,31	13,184	5.980	23,799	10.795	165	265	143	230	2,175	3.500	13,780	4.200	4	1 g. (20 mm), 1 mg. (13 mm), b. (220 lb; 100 kg)
20.8	6,30	28,550	12.950	50,045	22.700	224	360	208	335	2,206	3.550	19,000	5.800	7-8	1 g. (20 mm), 5 mg. (7,9 mm), b. (4,630 lb; 2.100 kg)
19.4	5,90	25,948	11.770	31,967	14.500	177	285	146	235	2,669	4.295	16,400	5.000	5	2 g. (20 mm), 1 mg. (13 mm) + 1 mg. (7,9 mm), b. (661 lb; 300 kg)
35.9	10,90	67,572	30.650	101,390	45.990	242	390	214	345	3,800	6.100	23,950	7.300	11	3 g. (20 mm), 5 mg. (13 mm); 110 passengers
31.6	9,60	64,066	29.060	99,208	45.000	137	220	106	170	683	1.100	—	—	5-7	2 g. (20 mm), 7 mg. (13 mm); 130 passengers
10.3	3,12	5,501	2.495	7,231	3.280	336	540	283	455	646	1.040	39,200	11.950	1	2 mg. (12,7 mm) + 2 mg. (7,7 mm)
9.11	3,03	5,181	2.350	6,460	2.930	370	595	—	—	475	765	37,730	11.500	1	2 mg. (12,7 mm) + 2 mg. (7,7 mm)
10.3	3,13	5,941	2.695	8,157	3.700	385	620	348	560	1,025	1.650	42,650	13.000	1	3 g. (20 mm), 2 mg. (12,7 mm)
10.6	3,20	5,291	2.400	7,694	3.490	267	430	230	370	342	550	27,230	8.300	1	2 mg. (12,7 mm) + 2 mg. (7,7 mm), b. (2,205 lb; 1.000 kg)
13.1	4,00	9,237	4.190	14,738	6.685	165	265	143	230	839	1.350	18,000	5.500	3	4 mg. (7,7 mm), b. (1,102 lb; 500 kg)
11.6	3,50	4,178	1.895	5,710	2.590	311	500	283	455	354	570	29,200	8.900	1	2 mg. (12,7 mm), b. (705 lb; 320 kg)
9.11	3,03	5,941	2.695	7,981	3.620	391	630	—	—	612	985	36,910	11.250	1	1 g. (20 mm), 4 mg. (12,7 mm)
10.6	3,20	4,597	2.085	6,272	2.845	326	525	267	430	808	1.300	34,450	10.500	1	2 mg. (12,7 mm), b. (440 lb; 200 kg)
10.4	3,15	5,225	2.370	7,143	3.240	329	530	—	—	683	1.100	34,450	10.500	1	2 mg. (12,7 mm) +2 mg. (7,7 mm), b. (1,433 lb; 650 kg)
10.4	3,15	5,732	2.600	7,848	3.560	391	630	342	550	677	1.090	40,000	12.200	1	3 g. (20 mm), 2 mg. (12,7 mm), b. (1,389 lb; 630 kg)
9.5	2,87	3,858	1.750	5,324	2.415	398	640	304	490	528	850	39,370	12.000	1	2 g. (20 mm), 2 mg. (12,7 mm)
11.0	3,35	3,781	1.715	5,049	2.290	267	430	214	345	482	775	33,465	10.200	1	2 mg. (12,7 mm), b. (440 lb; 200 kg)
9.8	2,95	4,321	1.960	5,280	2.395	292	470	299	400	420	675	35,200	10.730	1	2 mg. (12,7 mm)
9.8	2,95	3,428	1.555	5,269	2.390	199	320	162	260	727	1.170	22,000	6.700	2	2 mg. (12,7 mm) + 1 mg. (7,7 mm)
10.6	3,20	8,025	3.640	11,067	5.020	217	350	186	300	1,200	1.930	19,685	6.000	3	5 mg. (7,7 mm), b. (882 lb; 400 kg)
13.6	4,10	16,755	7.600	24,912	11.300	270	435	255	410	1,243	2.000	23,000	7.000	4	3 mg. (12,7 mm) + 1 mg. (7,7 mm), b. (2,756 lb; 1.250 kg)
15.7	4,75	15,069	6.835	23,038	10.450	267	430	211	340	1,243	2.000	22,145	6.750	4	4 mg. (7,7 mm), b.(3,527 lb; 1.600 kg)
17.1	5,22	19,004	8.620	28,208	12.795	280	450	235	378	1,243	2.000	26,500	8.080	5	2 mg. (12,7 mm) + 2 mg. (7,7 mm), b. (4,409 lb; 2.000 kg)
17.0	5,19	38,107	17.285	64,904	29.440	267	430	199	320	2,479	3.990	27,900	8.500	7	8 mg. (12,7 mm), b. (7,716 lb; 3.500 kg)
18.2	5,55	26,400	11.975	39,595	17.960	199	320	—	—	2,485	4.000	20,230	6.165	4	cargo (8,796 lb; 3.990 kg)
16.1	4,91	20,459	9.280	33,003	14.970	242	389	193	310	1,428	2.300	27,900	8.500	3	22 passengers
14.6	4,42	8,466	3.840	15,543	7.050	171	275	149	240	1,490	2.400	23,000	7.000	4-5	3 mg. (7,7 mm), b. (1,400 lb; 635 kg)
24.5	7,45	19,290	8.750	28,010	12.705	217	350	202	325	1,243	2.000	26,250	8.000	5	1 mg. (12,7 mm) + 3 mg. (7,7 mm), b. (2,646 lb; 1.200 kg)
36.1	11,00	45,018	20.420	73,833	33.490	261	420	205	330	2,485	4.000	23,000	7.000	4	

LB	light bomber	mm	millimeters	Sp	seaplane
lb	pounds	MR	maritime reconnaissance	t.	torpedo
Li	liaison	NB	night bomber	TB	torpedo-bomber
LT	light transport	NF	night fighter	Tj	turbo-jet
m	meters	P.&W.	Pratt & Whitney	Tr	transport
MB	medium bomber	Rc	reconnaissance	W.	Wright
mg.	machine-gun	r.	rockets		
ml	miles	R.R.	Rolls-Royce		

AIRCRAFT OF WORLD WAR II (continued)

Page	Aircraft	Builder	Type	Year	Engine	Wing spread		Length	
						ft	m	ft	m
	JAPAN								
124	Kawanishi N1K2-J	Kawanishi Kokuki K.K.	Fr	1942	1990 hp Nakajima NK9H Homare 21 (18 cl.)	39.4	12,00	30.8	9,34
124	Kawasaki Ki-61-II	Kawasaki Kokuki Kogyo K.K.	Fr	1942	1500 hp Kawasaki Ha-140 (12 cl.)	39.4	12,00	30.1	9,16
124	Mitsubishi A5M4	Mitsubishi Jukogyo K.K.	Cb/Fr	1937	785 hp Nakajima Kotobuki 41 (9 cl.)	36.1	11,00	25.1	7,65
125	Nakajima Ki-44II	Nakajima Hikoki K.K.	Fr	1942	1450 hp Army Type 100 (14 cl.)	31.0	9,45	28.10	8,79
125	Mitsubishi J2M3	Mitsubishi Jukogyo K.K.	Fr	1942	1800 hp Mitsubishi MK4R-A Kasei 23a (14 cl.)	35.5	10,80	32.8	9,94
125	Nakajima J1N1-C	Nakajima Hikoki K.K.	Rc	1942	2/1130 hp Nakajima NK1F Sakae (14 cl.)	58.8	16,98	39.11	12,18
125	Kawasaki Ki-100	Kawasaki Kokuki Kogyo K.K.	Fr	1945	1500 hp Army Type 4 (14 cl.)	39.4	12,00	28.11	8,82
125	Mitsubishi Ki-51	Mitsubishi Jukogyo K.K.	GA	1939	900 hp Army Type 99 Model 2 (14 cl.)	39.8	12,10	30.3	9,21
125	Aichi E13A1	Aichi Kokuki K.K.	MR/Sp	1940	1080 hp Mitsubishi-Kinsei 43 (14 cl.)	47.7	14,50	37.1	11,30
126	Mitsubishi A6M3 Zero	Mitsubishi Jukogyo K.K.	Cb/Fr	1939	1100 hp Nakajima NK1F Sakae 12 (14 cl.)	36.1	11,00	29.9	9,06
126	Nakajima Ki-27	Nakajima Hikoki K.K.	Fr	1937	650 hp Army Type 97 (9 cl.)	37.1	11,31	24.8	7,53
126	Nakajima Ki-43-II	Nakajima Hikoki K.K.	Fr	1940	1150 hp Army Type 1 (14 cl.)	35.7	10,84	29.3	8,92
126	Kawasaki Ki-45 KAIc	Kawasaki Kokuki Kogyo K.K.	Fr	1942	1050 hp Army Type 1 (14 cl.)	49.3	15,02	36.1	11,00
126	Nakajima Ki-84	Nakajima Hikoki K.K.	Fr	1943	1900 hp Army Type 4 (18 cl.)	36.10	11,23	32.7	9,92
127	Aichi D3A1	Aichi Kokuki K.K.	Cb/Br	1941	1080 hp Mitsubishi-Kinsei 44 (14 cl.)	47.1	14,36	33.5	10,20
127	Yokosuka D4Y2	Dai-Juichi Kaigun Kokusho	Cb/Br/Rc	1942	1400 hp Aichi AE1P Atsuta 32 (12 cl.)	37.8	11,50	33.7	10,24
127	Mitsubishi Ki-46-II	Mitsubishi Jukogyo K.K.	Rc	1941	1050 hp Army Type 1 (14 cl.)	48.3	14,70	36.1	11,00
127	Mitsubishi G4M1	Mitsubishi Jukogyo K.K.	MB	1941	2/1530 hp Mitsubishi MK4A Kasei 11 (14 cl.)	82.0	25,00	65.7	20,00
128	Mitsubishi G3M1	Mitsubishi Jukogyo K.K.	MB	1940	2/910 hp Mitsubishi-Kinsei 3 (14 cl.)	82.0	25,00	54.0	16,45
128	Mitsubishi Ki-21-Ia	Mitsubishi Jukogyo K.K.	HB	1940	2/850 hp Army Type 97 (14 cl.)	73.10	22,50	52.6	16,00
128	Mitsubishi Ki-67	Mitsubishi Jukogyo K.K.	HB	1944	2/1900 hp Army Type 4 (18 cl.)	73.10	22,50	61.4	18,70
128	Nakajima Ki-49-II	Nakajima Hikoki K.K.	HB	1942	2/1450 hp Army Type 2 (14 cl.)	66.11	20,40	54.2	16,50
128	Kawasaki Ki-48	Kawasaki Kokuki Kogyo K.K.	LB	1940	2/950 hp Army Type 99 (14 cl.)	57.3	17,45	41.4	12,60
128	Yokosuka P1Y1	Nakajima Hikoki K.K.	HB	1943	2/1820 hp Nakajima NK9B Homare 11 (18 cl.)	65.7	20,00	49.2	15,00
129	Nakajima C6N1	Nakajima Hikoki K.K.	Cb/Rc	1943	1990 hp Nakajima NK9H Homare 21 (18 cl.)	41.0	12,50	36.1	11,00
129	Nakajima B6N2	Nakajima Hikoki K.K.	Cb/TB	1943	1850 hp Mitsubishi MK4T Kasei 25 (14 cl.)	48.11	14,90	35.7	10,86
129	Nakajima B5N2	Nakajima Hikoki K.K.	Cb/TB	1937	1000 hp Nakajima N1KB Sakae 11 (14 cl.)	50.11	15,52	33.9	10,30
129	Yokosuka E14Y1	Watanabe Tekkosho K.K.	Sp/Rc	1941	340 hp Hitashi Tempu 12 (9 cl.)	36.1	11,00	28.0	8,54
129	Kawanishi H6K4	Kawanishi Kokuki K.K.	Sp/Rc	1937	4/1000 hp Mitsubishi-Kinsei 43 (14 cl.)	131.3	40,00	84.2	25,65
129	Kawanishi H8K2	Kawanishi Kokuki K.K.	Sp/Rc	1942	4/1850 hp Mitsubishi MK4Q Kasei 22 (14 cl.)	124.8	38,00	92.4	28,13
129	Yokosuka MXY7 Ohka 22	Dai-Juichi Kaigun Kokusho	—	1944	551 lb (200 kg) Tsu-II tj.	13.6	4,12	22.7	6,88
	CZECHOSLOVAKIA								
130	Letov S 328	Letov	Rc/LB	1933	560 hp B. Pegasus II M-2 (9 cl.)	44.11	13,70	34.1	10,40
130	Avia B 534	Avia	Fr	1936	860 hp H.S.-Avia 12 Ydrs (12 cl.)	30.10	9,40	26.7	8,10
	RUMANIA								
130	I.A.R. 80	Industria Aeronautica Romana	Fr	1941	940 hp G.R.-I.A.R. 14K	32.10	10,00	26.9	8,16
	HOLLAND								
131	Fokker D.XXI	Fokker	Fr	1936	830 hp B. Mercury VIII (9 cl.)	36.1	11,0	26.10	8,18
131	Fokker G.1A	Fokker	HF	1938	2/830 hp B. Mercury VIII (9 cl.)	56.3	17,15	37.9	11,50
	AUSTRALIA								
131	CA-12 Boomerang	Commonwealth Aircraft Corp.	Fr	1943	1200 hp P.&W.-C.A.C. R-1830-S34G (14 cl.)	36.3	11,05	25.6	7,77
	POLAND								
131	P.Z.L. P-11c	Panstwove Zaklady Lotnicze	Fr	1933	645 hp B.-P.Z.L. Mercury VI S.2	35.2	10,72	24.9	7,55
131	P.Z.L. P-24f	Panstwove Zaklady Lotnicze	Fr	1934	970 hp G.R. 14 N7	35.2	10,72	24.7	7,50
131	P.Z.L. P-37B Los	Panstwove Zaklady Lotnicze	Br	1939	918 hp B.-P.Z.L. Pegasus XX	58.10	17,93	42.5	12,93

Abbreviations used in the table

A.	Allison	BT	basic trainer	Fr	fighter	hp	horse-power
AB	attack bomber	Cb	carrier-based	ft	feet	H.S.	Hispano-Suiza
A.R.	Alfa Romeo	cl.	cylinders	g.	gun	I.F.	Isotta Fraschini
A.S.	Armstrong Siddeley	DB	dive bomber	h	hour	in	inches
AT	advanced trainer	D.B.	Daimler Benz	GA	ground attack	J.	Junkers
b.	bombs	d.c.	depth charge	G.R.	Gnome-Rhône	j.	jet
B.	Bristol	D.H.	De Havilland	HB	heavy bomber	kg	kilograms
Br	bomber	FB	fighter-bomber	HF	heavy fighter	km	kilometers

Height		Empty weight		Max take-off weight		Max speed		Cruising speed		Range		Ceiling		Crew	Armament
ft	m	lb	kg	lb	kg	ml/h	km/h	ml/h	km/h	ml	km	ft	m		
13.0	3,96	5,858	2.657	10,714	4.860	370	595	230	370	1,065	1.715	35,300	10.760	1	4 g. (20 mm)
12.2	3,70	6,261	2.840	8,433	3.825	379	610	—	—	683	1.100	36,000	11.000	1	2 g. (20 mm), 2 mg. (12,7 mm)
10.9	3,27	2,681	1.216	3,684	1.671	270	435	—	—	746	1.200	32,150	9.800	1	2 mg. (7,7 mm), b. (132 lb; 60 kg)
10.8	3,25	4,643	2.106	6,598	2.993	376	605	249	400	805	1.296	36,750	11.200	1	4 g. (20 mm)
12.11	3,94	5,423	2.460	7,573	3.435	367	590	217	350	1,180	1.900	38,385	11.700	1	4 g. (20 mm)
14.11	4,56	10,697	4.852	16,594	7.527	329	530	174	280	1,678	2.700	33,800	10.300	3	1 mg. (13 mm)
12.3	3,75	5,567	2.525	7,705	3.495	360	580	249	400	870	1.400	36,000	11.000	1	2 g. (20 mm), 2 mg. (12,7 mm)
8.11	2,73	4,129	1.873	6,437	2.920	263	424	—	—	659	1.060	27,130	8.270	2	2 mg. (12,7 mm) + 1 mg. (7,7 mm), b. (451 lb; 200 kg)
24.3	7,40	5,825	2.642	8,818	4.000	233	375	137	220	1,299	2.090	28,640	8.730	3	1 mg. (7,7 mm)
11.6	3,51	3,984	1.807	5,609	2.544	339	545	230	370	1,479	2.380	36,250	11.050	1	2 g. (20 mm), 2 mg. (7,7 mm), b. (265 lb; 120 kg)
10.8	3,25	2,447	1.110	3,946	1.790	292	470	217	350	390	627	—	—	1	2 mg. (7,7 mm), b. (220 lb; 100 kg)
10.9	3,27	4,211	1.910	6,449	2.925	329	530	273	440	1,094	1.760	36,750	11.200	1	2 mg. (12,7 mm), b. (551 lb; 250 kg)
12.2	3,70	8,818	4.000	12,125	5.500	336	540	—	—	1,243	2.000	33,000	10.000	2	1 g. (37 mm) + 2 g. (20 mm)
11.1	3,38	5,864	2.660	7,965	3.613	391	630	277	445	1,053	1.695	34,450	10.500	1	2 g. (20 mm), 2 mg. (12,7 mm), b. (1,102 lb; 500 kg)
12.7	3,85	5,309	2.408	8,047	3.650	239	385	183	295	913	1.470	30,500	9.300	2	3 mg. (7,7 mm), b. (816 lb; 370 kg)
12.3	3,75	5,809	2.635	8,455	3.835	360	580	264	425	910	1.465	35,105	10.700	2	1 mg. (7,92 mm) + 2 mg. (7,7 mm), b. (1,235 lb; 560 kg)
12.9	3,88	7,194	3.263	11,133	5.050	375	604	249	400	1,305	2.100	35,531	10.830	2	1 mg. (7,7 mm)
19.8	6,00	14,991	6.800	20,944	9.500	267	430	196	315	3,750	6.035	29,000	8.840	7	1 g. (20 mm), 4 mg. (7,7 mm), b. (1,764 lb; 800 kg)
12.0	3,65	10,516	4.770	16,848	7.642	214	345	—	—	—	—	24,540	7.480	7	3 mg. (7,7 mm), b. or t. (1,764 lb; 800 kg)
14.3	4,35	10,342	4.691	16,517	7.492	268	432	—	—	930	1.500	28,215	8.600	7	3 mg. (7,7 mm), b. (2,205 lb; 1.000 kg)
25.3	7,70	19,068	8.649	30,347	13.765	378	609	249	400	2,361	3.800	31,070	9.470	6	1 g. (20 mm), 4 mg. (12,7 mm), b. (1,764 lb; 800 kg)
13.11	4,25	14,396	6.530	23,545	10.680	306	492	217	350	1,833	2.950	30,500	9.300	8	1 g. (20 mm), 6 mg. (7,7 mm), b. (2,205 lb; 1.000 kg)
12.5	3,80	8,929	4.050	13,338	6.050	298	480	217	350	1,490	2.400	31,170	9.500	4	3 mg. (7,7 mm), b. (882 lb; 400 kg)
14.1	4,30	16,017	7.265	29,762	13.500	342	550	230	370	3,337	5.370	30,840	9.400	3	2 g. (20 mm), b. (2,205 lb; 1.000 kg)
13.1	3,98	6,543	2.968	11,596	5.260	379	610	242	390	1,914	3.080	34,350	10.470	3	1 mg. (7,92 mm)
12.5	3,80	6,636	3.010	12,456	5.650	298	480	208	335	1,892	3.045	29,660	9.040	3	2 mg. (7,7 mm), b. or t. (1,764 lb; 800 kg)
12.2	3,70	5,024	2.279	9,039	4.100	236	380	162	260	1,237	1.990	27,100	8.260	3	1 mg. (7,7 mm), b. or t. (1,764 lb; 800 kg)
12.5	3,80	2,467	1.119	3,527	1.600	152	245	103	165	547	880	17,780	5.420	2	1 mg. (7,7 mm), b. (132 lb; 60 kg)
20.7	6,27	25,809	11.707	47,399	21.500	211	340	137	220	3,778	6.080	31,530	9.610	9	1 g. (20 mm), 4 mg. (7,7 mm), b. (2,205 lb; 1.000 kg)
30.0	9,15	40,521	18.380	71,650	32.500	289	465	183	295	4,443	7.150	29,035	8.850	10	5 g. (20 mm), 6 mg. (7,7 mm), b. or t. (3,527 lb; 1.600 kg)
3.9	1,15	1,202	545	3,197	1.450	277	445	—	—	81	130	—	—	1	dynamite (1,323 lb; 600 kg)
11.2	3,40	3,704	1.680	5,820	2.640	174	280	152	245	435	700	23,600	7.195	1	4 mg. (7,7 mm)
10.2	3,10	3,219	1.460	4,365	1.980	245	395	214	345	373	600	36,000	11.000	1	4 mg. (7,7 mm)
11.10	3,60	3,924	1.780	5,478	2.485	317	510	—	—	590	950	34,450	10.500	1	2 g. (20 mm), 4 mg. (7,7 mm)
9.8	2,95	3,197	1.450	4,519	2.050	286	460	239	385	608	980	31,365	9.560	1	4 mg. (7,9 mm)
11.2	3,40	7,319	3.320	10,560	4.790	295	475	—	—	945	1.520	30,500	9.300	3	9 mg. (7,9 mm), b. (661 lb; 300 kg)
11.6	3,50	5,450	2.472	7,699	3.492	295	475	—	—	932	1.500	29,000	8.840	1	2 g. (20 mm), 4 mg. (0.303 in), b. (500 lb; 227 kg)
9.4	2,85	2,524	1.145	3,957	1.795	242	390	—	—	503	810	36,000	11.000	1	4 mg. (7,7 mm), b. (110 lb; 50 kg)
8.10	2,69	—	—	4,233	1.920	267	430	—	—	497	800	34,450	10.500	1	2 g. (20 mm), 2 mg. (7,7 mm)
16.8	5,08	9,315	4.225	18,739	8.500	273	440	—	—	1,616	2.600	19,685	6.000	4	3 mg. (7,7 mm), b. (5,688 lb; 2.580 kg)

B	light bomber	mm	millimeters
	pounds	MR	maritime reconnaissance
	liaison	NB	night bomber
T	light transport	NF	night fighter
	meters	P.&W.	Pratt & Whitney
B	medium bomber	Rc	reconnaissance
g.	machine-gun	r.	rockets
	miles	R.R.	Rolls-Royce

Sp	seaplane
t.	torpedo
TB	torpedo-bomber
Tj	turbo-jet
Tr	transport
W.	Wright

CIVIL AND MILITARY AIRCRAFT: 1945 - TODAY

Page	Aircraft	Builder	Nation of origin	Type	Year	Engine	Wing spread		Length	
							ft	m	ft	m
134	Douglas DC-4	Douglas Aircraft Co.	USA	Ps	1939	4/1450 hp P.&W. R-2000-SD13G (14 cl.)	117.6	35,81	93.11	28,63
134	Douglas DC-6B	Douglas Aircraft Co.	USA	Ps	1947	4/2500 hp P.&W. R-2800-CB17 (18 cl.)	117.6	35,81	105.7	32,18
134	Douglas DC-7C Seven Seas	Douglas Aircraft Co.	USA	Ps	1954	4/3400 hp W. R-3350-18-EA tc. (18 cl.)	127.6	38,86	112.3	34,22
134	Boeing 307 Stratoliner	Boeing Co.	USA	Ps	1939	4/900 hp W. Cyclone GR-1820	107.3	32,69	74.4	22,66
135	Lockheed L-749 Constellation	Lockheed Aircraft Corp.	USA	Ps	1944	4/2500 hp W. Cyclone GR-3350-BD1 (18 cl.)	123.0	37,49	95.2	29,01
135	Lockheed L-1049E Super Constellation	Lockheed Aircraft Corp.	USA	Ps	1951	4/3250 hp W. R-3350-DA3 tc. (18 cl.)	123.0	37,49	113.7	34,62
135	Boeing 377 Stratocruiser	Boeing Co.	USA	Ps	1948	4/3500 hp P.&W. R-4360-59 Wasp (28 cl.)	141.3	43,06	110.4	33,63
136	Martin 4-0-4	Martin Co.	USA	Ps	1951	2/2400 hp P.&W. R-2800-CB16 Double Wasp (18 cl.)	93.3	28,43	74.7	22,74
136	Airspeed A.S. 57 Ambassador	Airspeed Division of D.H.	GB	Ps	1952	2/2625 hp B. Centaurus 661 (18 cl.)	115.0	35,05	82.0	24,99
136	Convair CV-240	Convair Division of General Dynamics	USA	Ps	1948	2/2400 hp P.&W. R-2800-CA18 (18 cl.)	91.9	27,97	74.8	22,76
136	Convair CV-340	Convair Division of General Dynamics	USA	Ps	1952	2/2400 hp P.&W. R-2800-CB16 (18 cl.)	105.4	32,10	79.2	24,13
136	Convair CV-440 Metropolitan	Convair Division of General Dynamics	USA	Ps	1955	2/2500 hp P.&W. R-2800-CB16/17 (18 cl.)	105.4	32,10	81.6	24,84
136	Convair CV-580	Pacific Airmotive Corp.	USA	Ps	1964	2/3750 hp A. 501-D13D tp.	105.4	32,10	79.2	24,13
136	Convair CV-600	Various	USA	Ps	1965	2/3025 hp R.R. Dart R. Da.10/1 tp.	91.9	27,97	74.8	22,76
137	Bristol 167 Brabazon	Bristol Aircraft Ltd	GB	Ps	1949	8/2500 hp B. Centaurus 20	230.0	70,10	177.0	53,95
137	Saro SR-45 Princess	Saunders-Roe Ltd	GB	Sp/Ps	1952	10/3780 hp B. Proteus Series 600 tp.	219.6	66,90	148.0	45,11
138	Vickers Viking 1B	Vickers-Armstrong Ltd	GB	Ps	1946	2/1690 hp B. Hercules 634	89.3	27,21	65.2	19,86
138	Fiat G. 212	Fiat S.p.A.	I	Ps	1947	3/1065 hp P.&W. Twin Wasp R-1830-S1C3-G (14 cl.)	96.3	29,34	75.7	23,05
138	Sud-Ouest SO-30P Bretagne	SNCASO	F	Ps	1949	2/2400 hp P.&W. R-2800-CA18	88.2	26,87	62.2	18,95
138	Sud-Est SE-161P7 Languedoc	SNCASE	F	Ps	1946	4/1220 hp P.&W. R-1830-S1C3-G	96.5	29,38	79.7	24,25
138	Vickers 953 Vanguard	Vickers-Armstrong Ltd	GB	Ps	1961	4/5545 hp R.R. Tyne RTyll 512	118.0	35,97	122.10	37,44
138	Lockheed 188 Electra	Lockheed Aircraft Corp.	USA	Ps	1959	4/3750 hp A. 501-D13A	99.0	30,18	104.6	31,85
139	Sud-Ouest SO-95 Corse	SNCASO	F	Ps	1948	2/580 hp Renault 125-02-201 (12 cl.)	59.1	18,01	40.5	12,32
139	Avro 685 York	A.V. Roe & Co. Ltd	GB	Ps	1945	4/1620 hp R.R. Merlin 502	102.0	31,09	78.6	23,92
139	Saab 90A2 Scandia	Svenska Aeroplan AB	S	Ps	1950	2/1800 hp P.&W. Twin Wasp R-2180-E1	91.10	28,00	69.11	21,30
139	Savoia Marchetti SM 95	Savoia Marchetti	I	Ps	1948	4/750 hp B. Pegasus 48	112.5	34,28	81.3	24,77
139	Avro 688 Tudor 4	A.V. Roe & Co. Ltd	GB	Ps	1948	4/1770 hp R.R. Merlin 621	120.0	36,58	85.3	25,99
139	Sud-Est SE-2010 Armagnac	SNCASE	F	Ps	1950	4/3500 hp P.&W. Wasp Major R-4360 (28 cl.)	160.7	48,95	130.0	39,63
139	Breguet 763 Provence	S.A.A. Louis Breguet	F	Ps	1953	4/2500 hp P.&W. R-2800-CB17	141.0	42,98	94.11	28,94
139	Canadair CL-44D4	Canadair Ltd	CDN	Tr	1960	4/5730 hp R.R. Tyne RTy. 12	142.3	43,36	136.8	41,65
139	Bristol 175 Britannia Series 102	Bristol Aircraft Corp.	GB	Type	1954	4/4445 hp B.S. Proteus 765 tp.	142.3	43,36	114.1	34,78
139	Tupolev Tu-114 Rossiya	State Industries	SU	Ps	1957	4/14795 Kuznetsov NK-12MV tp.	167.8	51,10	177.2	54,00
140	Vickers Viscount 708	Vickers-Armstrong Ltd	GB	Ps	1953	4/1540 hp R.R. Dart 506 tp.	93.8	28,55	81.9	24,92
140	De Havilland D.H. 106 Comet 1	De Havilland Aircraft Co. Ltd	GB	Ps	1952	4/4,450 lb (2.019 kg) D.H. Ghost 50 Mk 1 tj.	115.0	35,05	93.1	28,38
141	Sud-Aviation SE-210 Caravelle I	SNCASE	F	Ps	1959	2/10,500 lb (4.763 kg) R.R. Avon R.A.29 Mk 522 tj.	112.6	34,30	105.0	32,00
141	Boeing 707-121	Boeing Co.	USA	Ps	1958	4/13,000 lb (5.897 kg) P.&W. JT3C-6 (J57) tj.	130.10	39,87	144.6	44,04
142	Dassault MD-450 Ouragan	Générale Aéronautique Marcel Dassault	F	FB	1950	5,070 lb (2.300 kg) H.S. Neue 104B tj.	40.3	12,28	35.2	10,72
142	Mikoyan-Gurevich MiG-15	State Industries	SU	Fr	1948	5,952 lb (2.700 kg) K. VK 1 tj.	33.1	10,08	37.3	11,36
142	Saab J 29F	Svenska Aeroplan AB	S	Fr	1951	6,173 lb (2.800 kg) a.b. Sv. RM2B tj.	36.1	11,00	33.2	10,11
142	Grumman F9F-5 Panther	Grumman Aircraft Corp.	USA	Cb/Fr	1949	6,250 lb (2.835 kg) P.&W. J48-P-6A tj.	38.0	11,58	38.10	11,83
142	Northrop F-89D Scorpion	Northrop Aircraft Inc.	USA	Fr	1950	2/7,200 lb (3.266 kg) a.b. A. J35-A-35 tj.	59.8	18,18	53.10	16,40
142	Douglas F4D Skyray	Douglas Aircraft Co.	USA	Cb/Fr	1956	10,500 lb (4.763 kg) a.b. P.&W. J57-P-8B tj.	33.6	10,21	45.8	13,92
142	Gloster Javelin F(AW) Mk9	Gloster Aircraft Co.	GB	Fr	1952	2/12,300 lb (5.579 kg) a.b. A.S. Sapphire Sa. 7R tj.	52.0	15,85	56.9	17,30
142	Vought F7U Cutlass	Chance Vought Inc.	USA	Cb/Fr	1950	2/4,600 lb (2.087 kg) a.b. We. J46-WE-8A tj.	38.8	11,78	44.3	13,49
142	McDonnell F3H-2 Demon	McDonnell Aircraft Corp.	USA	Cb/Fr	1956	9,700 lb (4.400 kg) A. J71-A-2E tj.	35.4	10,77	58.11	17,96
142	Grumman F9F-6 Cougar	Grumman Aircraft Corp.	USA	Cb/Fr	1952	7,250 lb (3.289 kg) P.&W. J48-P-8 tj.	36.5	11,10	41.7	12,68

Abbreviations used in the table

A.	Allison	CDN	Canada	GB	Great Britain	K.	Klimov
a.b.	with afterburning	cl.	cylinders	G.E.	General Electric	kg	kilograms
A.S.	Armstrong Siddeley	D.H.	De Havilland	h	hour	km	kilometers
B.	Bristol	F	France	HB	heavy bomber	LB	light bomber
b.	bombs	FB	fighter-bomber	hp	horse-power	lb	pounds
Br	bomber	Fr	fighter	H.S.	Hispano-Suiza	m	meters
B.S.	Bristol Siddeley	ft	feet	I	Italy	MB	medium bomber
Cb	carrier-based	g.	gun	in	inches	ml	miles

Height		Empty weight		Max take-off weight		Payload		Max speed		Cruising speed		Range		Ceiling		Crew	Passengers or armament
ft	m	lb	kg	lb	kg	lb	kg	ml/h	km/h	ml/h	km/h	ml	km	ft	m		
27.6	8,38	40,806	18.510	73,000	33.113	21,373	9.695	280	451	219	352	4,420	7.110	22,300	6.800	5	44-86
28.5	8,66	54,148	24.561	106,000	48.082	24,565	11.143	360	579	315	507	3,000	4.830	25,000	7.620	3	54-102
31.10	9,70	72,763	33.005	143,000	64.865	31,500	14.288	405	652	345	555	4,600	7.400	25,000	7.620	5	60-115
20.9	6,33	30,310	13.749	42,000	19.051	—	—	246	396	220	354	2,390	3.850	26,200	7.985	5	33
22.5	6,84	57,000	25.855	105,000	47.628	—	—	347	558	298	480	2,500	4.025	25,000	7.620	5	44-81
24.9	7,55	73,000	33.113	150,000	68.040	—	—	370	595	327	526	3,100	4.990	25,000	7.620	6	66-192
38.3	11,66	83,500	37.876	142,500	64.638	—	—	375	603	340	547	3,000	4.830	33,000	10.000	5	55-117
28.5	8,66	29,126	13.212	44,900	20.367	—	—	312	502	280	451	1,070	1.720	30,000	9.150	3	40-52
18.10	5,74	35,377	16.047	52,500	23.814	12,250	5.557	312	502	260	418	550	885	—	—	3	47-55
26.11	8,20	30,345	13.764	41,790	18.956	9,600	4.355	347	558	270	435	1,800	2.895	30,000	9.150	3	40
28.2	8,58	32,399	14.696	47,000	21.319	—	—	314	505	284	457	2,015	3.240	30,000	9.150	3	44
28.2	8,58	33,000	14.969	49,700	22.544	14,200	6.441	309	497	289	465	1,270	2.045	30,000	9.150	3	44-52
29.1	8,87	—	—	53,200	24.132	—	—	—	—	348	560	1,620	2.610	30,000	9.150	3	44-52
26.11	8,20	26,800	12.156	45,000	20.412	—	—	—	—	315	507	1,800	2.895	30,000	9.150	3	40
50.0	15,24	159,310	72.263	290,000	131.544	—	—	—	—	250	402	5,500	8.850	—	—	6	72-80
55.9	16,99	191,000	86.638	330,000	149.688	—	—	—	—	360	579	5,270	8.480	—	—	6	200
19.6	5,94	23,250	10.546	34,000	15.422	7,240	3.284	263	423	210	338	1,700	2.735	23,750	7.240	5	24-27
—	—	24,691	11.200	38,360	17.400	7,165	3.250	—	—	186	300	1,864	3.000	24,600	7.500	3	34
19.4	5,89	29,357	13.316	44,370	20.126	9,259	4.200	303	488	272	438	851	1.370	17,400	5.300	2	30-37
16.10	5,13	33,036	14.985	51,370	23.300	8,752	3.970	—	—	211	340	621	1.000	23,620	7.200	4	33
35.0	10,67	78,575	35.641	141,000	63.958	29,000	13.154	—	—	425	684	2,340	3.765	—	—	3	76-139
32.1	9,78	57,000	25.855	116,000	52.618	21,638	9.815	448	721	405	652	3,460	5.570	27,000	8.230	5	74-99
14.1	4,30	8,863	4.020	12,346	5.600	—	—	220	354	205	330	808	1.300	—	—	2	10-13
20.0	6,10	42,040	19.069	68,000	30.845	20,000	9.072	298	480	233	375	2,700	4.345	26,000	7.925	4	18
23.3	7,09	21,958	9.960	35,275	16.000	—	—	280	450	211	340	919	1.480	24,600	7.500	5	24-36
17.3	5,25	30,865	14.000	48,502	22.000	8,717	3.954	—	—	196	315	1,243	2.000	22,300	6.800	3	20-38
20.11	6,38	49,441	22.426	80,000	36.288	—	—	282	454	210	338	4,000	6.440	27,400	8.350	2	32
—	—	99,035	44.922	170,858	77.500	38,581	17.500	329	530	282	454	3,180	5.120	22,300	6.800	4	84-160
31.8	9,65	71,079	32.241	113,758	51.600	23,906	10.844	—	—	209	336	1,423	2.290	24,000	7.315	4	107
38.7	11,76	88,872	40.312	205,000	92.988	66,128	29.996	—	—	394	634	3,050	4.910	—	—	8	—
36.8	11,17	88,000	39.917	155,000	70.308	25,000	11.340	—	—	360	579	4,580	7.370	24,000	7.315	8	92
42.0	12,80	188,274	85.400	363,762	165.000	55,116	25.000	590	949	460	740	6,215	10.000	34,120	10.400	10-15	170-200
27.9	8,46	37,918	17.200	64,500	29.257	12,250	5.557	—	—	334	538	1,450	2.335	27,500	8.380	2	47-75
28.4	8,63	—	—	105,000	47.628	12,000	5.443	—	—	490	789	1,750	2.815	35,000	10.670	4	36-44
28.8	8,72	51,588	23.400	95,901	43.500	18,453	8.370	—	—	456	734	1,150	1.850	30,000	9.150	3	64-80
41.8	12,70	112,800	51.166	247,000	112.039	52,200	23.679	—	—	585	941	3,750	6.035	36,000	11.000	4	110-189
13.0	3,96	9,127	4.140	14,991	6.800	—	—	584	940	—	—	—	—	49,210	15.000	1	4 g. (20 mm), b. (2,200 lb; 998 kg)
11.2	3,40	8,311	3.770	14,242	6.460	—	—	652	1.050	—	—	560	900	49,210	15.000	1	1 g. (37 mm) + 2 g. (23 mm), b., r.
12.3	3,74	10,141	4.600	17,640	8.000	—	—	658	1.059	—	—	1,100	1.770	50,850	15.500	1	4 g. (20 mm), 2 msl. or 24 r.
12.3	3,74	10,147	4.603	18,721	8.492	—	—	579	932	481	774	1,300	2.095	42,800	13.050	1	4 g. (20 mm)
17.7	5,36	25,194	11.428	42,241	19.161	—	—	636	1.024	523	842	1,370	2.205	49,210	15.000	2	104 r.
13.0	3,96	16,024	7.268	25,000	11.340	—	—	695	1.118	—	—	1,200	1.930	55,000	16.765	1	4 g. (20 mm), b., r., msl. (4,000 lb.; 1.814 kg)
16.0	4,87	—	—	43,165	19.580	—	—	610	982	—	—	1,370	2.205	52,000	15.850	2	4 g. (30 mm), 4 msl.
14.7	4,45	18,210	8.260	31,642	14.353	—	—	680	1.095	—	—	660	1.062	40,000	12.200	1	4 g. (20 mm), 4 msl.
14.7	4,45	22,133	10.040	33,900	15.377	—	—	647	1.041	—	—	1,370	2.205	42,650	13.000	1	4 g. (20 mm), b., r.
15.0	4,57	—	—	20,000	9.072	—	—	690	1.110	—	—	1,000	1.610	50,000	15.240	1	4 g. (20 mm), 2 b.× (1,000 lb; 454 kg)

m   millimeters
sl.   missiles
&W. Pratt & Whitney
     passengers
     rockets
c.   reconnaissance
R.   Rolls-Royce
     Sweden

Sp   Seaplane
SU   Soviet Union
Sv. Svenska
T   trainer
t.   torpedo
tc. turbo-compound
tj. turbo-jet
tp. turbo-prop

Tr   transport
USA United States of America
W.   Wright
We. Westinghouse

CIVIL AND MILITARY AIRCRAFT: 1945 - TODAY

Page	Aircraft	Builder	Nation of origin	Type	Year	Engine	Wing spread ft	Wing spread m	Length ft	Length m
142	Supermarine Scimitar	Vickers-Armstrong Ltd	GB	Cb/Fr	1958	2/11,250 lb (5.103 kg) R.R. Avon 200 tj.	37.2	11,33	55.4	16,86
142	Sud-Ouest SO-4050 Vautour	Sud-Aviation	F	FB	1958	2/7,716 lb (3.500 kg) SNECMA Atar 101E-3 tj.	49.6	15,09	54.1	16,49
142	Lockheed U-2	Lockheed Aircraft Corp.	USA	Rc	1956	17,000 lb (7.711 kg) P.&W. J57-P-13 tj.	80.0	24,38	49.7	15,12
142	North American F-100F Super Sabre	North American Aviation Inc.	USA	Fr/FB/T	1954	17,000 lb (7.711 kg) a.b. P.&W. J57-P-21A tj.	38.0	11,58	47.0	14,33
142	Douglas C-124C Globemaster II	Douglas Aircraft Co.	USA	Tr	1950	4/3800 hp P.&W. R-4360-63	174.1	53,07	130.5	39,75
143	McDonnell F2H-2D Banshee	McDonnell Aircraft Corp.	USA	Cb/Fr	1949	2/3,250 lb (1.474 kg) We. J34-WE-34 tj.	44.10	13,66	40.2	12,24
143	Douglas B-66B Destroyer	Douglas Aircraft Co.	USA	LB	1956	2/10,000 lb (4.536 kg) A. J71-A-13 tj.	72.6	22,10	75.2	22,91
143	North American B-45 Tornado	North American Aviation Inc.	USA	LB	1950	4/5,200 lb (2.359 kg) G.E. J47-GE-13/15 tj.	89.0	27,13	75.4	22,96
143	Handley Page Hastings	Handley Page Ltd	GB	Tr	1947	4/1675 hp B. Hercules 106	113.0	34,44	81.8	24,89
143	Blackburn Beverley	Blackburn Aircraft Ltd	GB	Tr	1956	4/2850 hp B. Centaurus 173 (18 cl.)	162.0	49,38	99.5	30,31
144	Northrop XB-35 Flying Wing	Northrop Corp.	USA	Br	1947	4/3000 hp P.&W. R-4360	172.0	52,43	53.0	16,15
144	Convair B-36D	Consolidated Vultee Aircraft Co.	USA	HB	1946	6/3800 hp P.&W. R-4360-53 + 4/5,200 lb (2.359 kg) G.E. J47-GE-19 tj.	230.0	70,10	162.1	49,41
145	Boeing B-47E Stratojet	Boeing Co.	USA	MB	1951	6/7,200 lb (3.266 kg) a.b. G.E. J47-GE-25 tj.	116.0	35,36	109.10	33,47
145	Martin P6M Sea Master	Martin Co.	USA	Rc	1959	4/13,000 lb (5.897 kg) a.b. A. J71 tj.	100.0	30,48	134.0	40,84
146	Lockheed P-80 Shooting Star	Lockheed Aircraft Corp.	USA	Fr	1945	4,000 lb (1.814 kg) A. J33-A-11 tj.	39.11	12,17	34.6	10,51
146	De Havilland Vampire FB5	De Havilland Aircraft Co. Ltd	GB	FB	1946	3,350 lb (1.520 kg) Goblin D.Gn.3 tj.	38.0	11,58	30.9	9,37
147	Mikoyan-Gurevich MiG-17	State Industries	SU	Fr	1954	6,989 lb (3.170 kg) a.b. K. VK-1 tj.	34.8	10,56	36.5	11,09
147	North American F-86F Sabre	North American Aviation Inc.	USA	Fr	1949	5,970 lb (2.708 kg) G.E. J47-GE-27 tj.	37.1	11,30	37.6	11,43

Abbreviations used in the table

A.	Allison	CDN	Canada	GB	Great Britain	K.	Klimov
a.b.	with afterburning	cl.	cylinders	G.E.	General Electric	kg	kilograms
A.S.	Armstrong Siddeley	D.H.	De Havilland	h	hour	km	kilometers
B.	Bristol	F	France	HB	heavy bomber	LB	light bomber
b.	bombs	FB	fighter-bomber	hp	horse-power	lb	pounds
Br.	bomber	Fr	fighter	H.S.	Hispano-Suiza	m	meters
B.S.	Bristol Siddeley	ft	feet	I	Italy	MB	medium bomber
Cb	carrier-based	g.	gun	in	inches	ml	miles

Height		Empty weight		Max take-off weight		Payload		Max speed		Cruising speed		Range		Ceiling		Crew	Passengers or armament
ft	m	lb	kg	lb	kg	lb	kg	ml/h	km/h	ml/h	km/h	ml	km	ft	m		
15.3	4,65	—	—	40,000	18.144	—	—	648	1.043	—	—	1,300	2.095	50,000	15.240	1	4 g. (30 mm), r.
14.2	4,32	22,046	10.000	33,069	15.000	—	—	680	1.095	—	—	1,600	2.575	49,210	15.000	2	4 g. (30 mm), r., b.
13.0	3,96	—	—	19,750	8.959	—	—	528	850	460	740	4,000	6.440	90,000	27.430	1	
16.0	4,87	22,300	10.115	40,000	18.144	—	—	822	1.323	536	863	1,500	2.415	50,000	15.240	2	4 g. (20 mm), b., r., msl.
48.3	14,70	101,165	45.888	185,000	83.916	56,000	25.402	304	489	272	438	1,230	1.980	22,100	6.735	5	200
14.6	4,42	11,146	5.056	23,312	10.574	—	—	532	856	501	806	1,475	2.375	44,800	13.650	1	
23.7	7,19	42,369	19.219	83,000	37.649	—	—	594	956	—	—	1,500	2.415	45,000	13.715	3	2 g. (20 mm), b.
25.2	7,67	48,903	22.182	112,952	51.235	—	—	579	932	456	734	1,910	3.075	43,200	13.170	4	2 g. (0.50 in), b. (22,000 lb; 9.979 kg)
22.6	6,86	48,427	21.966	80,000	36.288	20,311	9.213	348	560	302	486	4,250	6.840	26,500	8.080	5	50
38.5	11,71	82,100	37.241	135,000	61.236	45,000	20.412	238	383	175	282	3,690	5.940	16,000	4.900	4	94
20.0	6,10	89,560	40.624	209,000	94.802	41,200	18.688	391	629	183	294	10,000	16.100	—	—	9	20 g. (0.50 in), b. (41,200 lb; 18.698 kg)
46.8	14,22	158,843	72.051	357,500	162.162	86,000	39.010	439	706	225	362	7,500	12.070	45,200	13.780	16	12 g. (20 mm), b. (72,000 lb; 32.659 kg)
28.0	8,53	80,756	36.631	206,700	93.759	20,000	9.072	606	975	557	896	4,000	6.440	40,500	12.350	3	2 g. (20 mm), b. (20,000 lb; 9.072 kg)
31.0	9,45	—	—	160,000	72.576	30,000	13.608	600	965	—	—	3,000	4.830	40,000	12.200	4	g., b.
11.4	3,45	7,920	3.593	14,500	6.577	—	—	558	898	410	660	540	869	45,000	13.715	1	6 g. (0.50 in)
8.10	2,69	7,283	3.304	12,390	5.620	—	—	548	882	—	—	1,220	1.965	30,000	9.150	1	4 g. (20 mm), b., r. (2,000 lb; 907 kg)
11.0	3,35	9,855	4.470	15,498	7.030	—	—	630	1.014	—	—	715	1.150	57,500	17.530	1	3 g. (23 mm), b., r. (1,102 lb; 500 kg)
14.8	4,47	10,950	4.967	17,000	7.711	—	—	690	1.110	—	—	1,270	2.045	50,000	15.240	1	6 g. (0.50 in), b. (2,000 lb; 907 kg)

mm	millimeters	Sp	Seaplane	Tr	transport
msl.	missiles	SU	Soviet Union	USA	United States of America
P.&W.	Pratt & Whitney	Sv.	Svenska	W.	Wright
Ps	passengers	T	trainer	We.	Westinghouse
r.	rockets	t.	torpedo		
Rc	reconnaissance	tc.	turbo-compound		
R.R.	Rolls-Royce	tj.	turbo-jet		
S	Sweden	tp.	turbo-prop		

MILITARY AIRCRAFT: TODAY

Page	Aircraft	Builder	Nation of origin	Type	Year	Engine	Wing spread		Length	
							ft	m	ft	m
152	McDonnell Douglas F-15	McDonnell Douglas Corp.	USA	Fr	1973	40,000 lb (18.144 kg) j.	*	*	*	*
152	Grumman F-14B	Grumman Corp.	USA	Cb/Fr	1972	2/30,000 lb (13.608 kg) a. b. P.&W. JFT22 j.	64.1	19,54	61.10	18,84
153	Sepecat Jaguar A	Société Européenne de Production École de Combat et Appui Tactique	F-GB	Fr	1970	2/6,950 lb (3.153 kg) a.b. R.R. Turboméca Adour tf.	27.10	8,48	50.11	15,52
153	Saab AJ-37 Viggen	Saab-Scania Aktiebolag	S	Fr	1970	26,455 lb (12.000 kg) a.b. Sv. Flygmotor RM8 tf.	34.9	10,60	53.6	16,30
153	Saab SK-37 Viggen	Saab-Scania Aktiebolag	S	Tr	1970	26,455 lb (12.000 kg) a.b. Sv. Flygmotor RM8 tf.	34.9	10,60	53.6	16,30
154	McDonnell Douglas F-4E Phantom II	McDonnell Douglas Corp.	USA	Fr	1967	2/17,900 lb (8.119 kg) a.b. G.E. J79-GE-17 tj.	38.5	11,71	58.3	17,76
154	McDonnell Douglas F-4D Phantom II	McDonnell Douglas Corp.	USA	Fr	1965	2/17,000 lb (7.711 kg) a.b. G.E. J79-GE-15 tj.	38.5	11,71	58.3	17,76
154	McDonnell Douglas RF-4C Phantom II	McDonnell Douglas Corp.	USA	Rc	1964	2/17,000 lb (7.711 kg) a.b. G.E. J79-GE-15 tj.	38.5	11,71	62.10	19,15
154	Dassault Mirage G	Avions Marcel Dassault	F	Ex/Fr	1967	20,503 lb (9.300 kg) a.b. SNECMA TF-306E tf.	42.8	13,00	55.1	16,80
154	Dassault Mirage IIIE	Avions Marcel Dassault	F	FB	1964	13,669 lb (6.200 kg) a.b. SNECMA Atar 09C tj.	27.0	8,22	49.3	15,03
154	Dassault Milan	Avions Marcel Dassault	F	FB	1970	15,873 lb (7.200 kg) a.b. SNECMA Atar 09K 50 tj.	27.0	8,22	51.2	15,60
154	Dassault Mirage 5	Avions Marcel Dassault	F	GA	1967	13,679 lb (6.200 kg) a.b. SNECMA Atar 09C tj.	27.0	8,22	51.0	15,55
155	Lockheed F-104G Starfighter	Lockheed Aircraft Corp.	USA	Fr	1960	15,800 lb (7.167 kg) a.b. G.E. J79-GE-11A tj.	21.11	6,68	54.9	16,69
155	Lockheed TF-104G Starfighter	Lockheed Aircraft Corp.	USA	T	1962	15,800 lb (7.167 kg) a.b. G.E. J79-GE-11A tj.	21.11	6,68	54.9	16,69
155	Mikoyan Gurevich MiG-23 "Foxbat"	State Industries	SU	Fr	1965	2/24,251 lb (11.000 kg) a.b. tj.	40.0	12,20	68.11	21,00
155	Mikoyan Gurevich MiG-21PF "Fishbed D"	State Industries	SU	Fr	1960	13,118 lb (5.950 kg) a.b. R-37F tj.	24.11	7,60	55.0	16,75
155	Sukhoi Su-9 "Fishpot"	State Industries	SU	Fr	1957	22,050 lb (10.002 kg) a.b. tf.	31.0	9,45	55.0	16,75
156	General Dynamics F-111A	General Dynamics Corp.	USA	Fr	1968	2/20,000 lb (9.072 kg) a.b. P.&W. TF-30 tf.	63.0	19,20	73.6	22,40
156	VFW-Fokker VAK 191B	VFW-Fokker GmbH	D	V/Fr	1971	9,921 lb (4.500 kg) MTU RB193-12 tj. + 2/5,577 lb (2.530 kg) MTU RB. 162-81 j.	20.2	6,16	53.7	16,33
156	Yakovlev VTOL "Freehand"	State Industries	SU	Ex/V/Fr	1968	2 tj.	27.1	8,25	57.5	17,50
156	Hawker Siddeley Harrier Mk 1	Hawker Siddeley Aviation Ltd	GB	V/CIS	1969	19,000 lb (8.618 kg) R.R. Bristol Pegasus Mk.101 tf.	25.3	7,70	45.6	13,87
157	Tupolev Tu-22 "Blinder"	State Industries	SU	Br	1960	2/26,000 lb (11.794 kg) a.b. tj.	90.11	27,70	133.0	40,53
157	Boeing B-52H	Boeing Co.	USA	HB	1956	8/17,000 lb (7.711 kg) P.&W. TF33-P-3 tf.	185.0	56,38	157.7	48,03
158	Republic F-84F Thunderstreak	Republic Aviation Corp.	USA	FB	1952	7,220 lb (3.275 kg) W. J65-W-3 tj.	33.7	10,24	43.4	13,21
158	Northrop F-5A	Northrop Corp.	USA	Fr	1963	2/4,080 lb (1.851 kg) a.b. G.E. J85-GE-13 tj.	25.3	7,70	47.2	14,38
158	LTV F-8E Crusader	Ling-Temco-Vought Inc.	USA	Cb/Fr	1958	18,000 lb (8.165 kg) a.b. P.&W. J57-P-20A tj.	35.8	10,87	54.6	16,61
158	Republic F-105D Thunderchief	Republic Aviation Div. of Fairchild Hiller Corp.	USA	FB	1958	26,500 lb (12.020 kg) a.b. P.&W. J75-P-19W tj.	34.11	10,64	69.2	21,08
158	Convair F-102 Delta Dagger	Convair Div. of General Dynamics Corp.	USA	Fr	1956	17,200 lb (7.802 kg) a.b. P.&W. J57-P-23 tj.	38.1	11,61	68.4	20,83
158	Convair F-106A Delta Dart	Convair Div. of General Dynamics Corp.	USA	Fr	1959	24,500 lb (11.113 kg) a.b. P.&W. J75-P-17 tj.	38.3	11,66	70.8	21,54
158	McDonnell F-101B Voodoo	McDonnell Douglas Corp.	USA	Fr	1958	2/14,500 lb (6.577 kg) a.b. P.&W. J57-P-53 tj.	39.8	12,09	67.4	20,52
158	Northrop P530 Cobra	Northrop Corp.	USA	Fr	1975	2/15,000 lb (6.804 kg) a.b. G.E. J101-GE-100 tf.	38.0	11,58	55.0	16,76
159	BAC Lithning F. Mk.6	British Aircraft Corp. Ltd	GB	Fr	1960	2/16,300 lb (7.394 kg) a.b. R.R. Avon 302-C tj.	34.10	10,61	55.3	16,84
159	Hawker Siddeley Sea Vixen F.A.W.2	Hawker Siddeley Group Ltd	GB	Cb/Fr	1964	2/10,000 lb (4.536 kg) a.b. R.R. Avon 208 tj.	50.0	15,24	55.7	16,94
159	Dassault Super-Mystère B2	Avions Marcel Dassault	F	FB	1956	9,921 lb (4.500 kg) a.b. SNECMA Atar 101G tj.	34.6	10,51	46.1	14,05
159	Dassault Étendard IV M	Avions Marcel Dassault	F	Cb/Fr	1962	9,700 lb (4.400 kg) SNECMA Atar 8B tj.	31.6	9,60	47.3	14,41
159	Dassault Mirage F1	Avions Marcel Dassault	F	Fr	1970	15,873 lb (7.200 kg) a.b. SNECMA Atar 09K-50 tj.	27.7	8,41	49.2	15,00
159	Helwan HA-300	Helwan Air Works	RAU	Fr	1967	11,020 lb (4.999 kg) a.b. Brandner E-300 tj.	19.4	5,89	40.8	12,39
159	HAL HF-24 Marut	Hindustan Aeronautics Ltd	IND	Fr	1964	2/4,850 lb (2.200 kg) R.R. Bristol Orpheus 703 tj.	29.6	9,00	52.0	15,87
159	Mikoyan Gurevich MiG-19 "Farmer-C"	State Industries	SU	Fr	1955	2/7,200 lb (3.266 kg) a.b. K. RD-9F tj.	30.6	9,29	41.6	12,65
159	Mikoyan Gurevich MiG-21F "Fishbed-C"	State Industries	SU	Fr	1958	12,500 lb (5.670 kg) a.b. TDR R37F tj.	25.0	7,62	55.0	16,75
159	Mikoyan Gurevich MiG-21FL	Hindustan Aeronautics Ltd	IND	Fr	1960	12,500 lb (5.670 kg) a.b. TDR R37F tj.	25.0	7,62	56.0	17,07
159	Yakovlev Yak-28P "Firebar"	State Industries	SU	Fr	1967	2/13,200 lb (5.988 kg) a.b. tj.	42.6	12,95	71.0	21,65
159	Sukhoi Su-11 "Flagon-A"	State Industries	SU	Fr	1967	2/22,050 lb (10.002 kg) a.b. tj.	30.0	9,15	67.10	20,50
159	Tupolev Tu-28P "Fiddler"	State Industries	SU	Fr	1961	2/22,000 lb (9.979 kg) a.b. tj.	65.0	19,81	85.0	25,90
159	Saab J 35F Draken	Saab-Scania Aktiebolag	S	Fr	1958	17,637 lb (8.000 kg) a.b. Sv. Flygmotor Avon 300 tj.	30.10	9,40	50.4	15,35

Abbreviations used in the table

A.	Allison	BT	basic trainer	F	France	HB	heavy bomber
a.b.	with afterburning	Cb	carrier-based	FB	fighter-bomber	hp	horse-power
AS	anti-submarine	CDN	Canada	Fr	fighter	HT	heavy transport
A.S.	Armstrong Siddeley	CI	counter-insurgency	ft	feet	I	Italy
AT	advanced trainer	cl.	cylinders	g.	gun	in	inches
B.	Bristol	CIS	close support	GA	ground attack	IND	India
b.	bombs	CS	Czechoslovakia	GB	Great Britain	IP	international project
BR	Brazil	D	Germany	G.E.	General Electric	J	Japan
Br	bomber	E	Spain	GP	general purpose	j.	jet
B.S.	Bristol Siddeley	Ex	experimental	h	hour	K.	Klimov

Height		Empty weight		Max take-off weight		Max speed			Cruising speed			Range		Ceiling		Crew	Armament
ft	m	lb	kg	lb	kg	Mach	ml/h	km/h	Mach	ml/h	km/h	ml	km	ft	m		
*	*	*	*	*	*	2+	—	—	—	*	*	*	*	*	*	1	*
16.0	4,87	36,000	16.330	53,000	24.041	2+	—	—	—	—	—	1,365	2.197	59,000	18.000	2	1 mg., 10 msl.
15.3	4,64	14,780	6.704	30,865	14.000	1.7	—	—	—	—	—	775	1.247	42,650	13.000	1	2 g. (30 mm), msl., b., r. (9,920 lb; 4.500 kg)
18.4	5,60	*	*	35,274	16.000	2	—	—	—	—	—	621	1.000	*	*	1	msl., b., r., g.
18.4	5,60	*	*	35,274	16.000	2	—	—	—	—	—	621	1.000	*	*	2	msl., b., r., g.
16.3	4,96	*	*	54,600	24.767	2+	—	—	—	—	—	2,300	3.700	71,000	21.640	2	1 g. (20 mm), msl., r., b. (16,000 lb; 7.258 kg)
16.3	4,96	*	*	54,600	24.767	2+	—	—	—	—	—	2,300	3.700	62,000	18.900	2	msl., r., b. (16,000 lb; 7.258 kg)
16.3	4,96	30,000	13.600	46,500	21.092	2+	—	—	—	—	—	2,300	3.700	62,000	18.900	2	msl., r., b.
17.7	5,35	22,046	10.000	35,274	16.000	2.5	—	—	—	—	—	4,000	6.437	65,600	20.000	2	*
13.11	4,25	15,543	7.050	29,762	13.500	2.2	—	—	0.9	—	—	*	*	55,775	17.000	1	2 g. (30 mm), b., msl. (2,000 lb; 907 kg)
14.9	4,50	15,212	6.900	31,967	14.500	2.2	—	—	—	—	—	4,000	6.437	59,000	18.000	1	2 g. (30 mm), b., msl., r. (7,716 lb; 3.500 kg)
13.11	4,25	14,550	6.600	29,762	13.500	2.2	—	—	0.9	—	—	2,485	4.000	55,775	17.000	1-2	2 g. (30 mm), msl., b., r. (8,818 lb; 4.000 kg)
13.6	4,11	14,082	6.388	28,779	13.054	2.2	—	—	0.95	—	—	2,180	3.510	58,000	17.680	1	g., b., r., msl. (4,000 lb; 1.814 kg)
13.6	4,11	14,181	6.433	26,364	11.959	2.2	—	—	0.95	—	—	2,180	3.510	58,000	17.680	2	g., b., r., msl. (2,000 lb; 907 kg)
*	*	*	*	*	*	3	—	—	—	—	—	*	*	88,580	27.000	1	*
14.9	4,50	*	*	20,503	9.300	2.3	—	—	0.9	—	—	1,150	1.850	57,400	17.500	1	msl.
16.0	4,88	*	*	29,000	13.154	1.8	—	—	—	—	—	*	*	55,000	16.765	1	4 msl.
17.1	5,21	*	*	70,000	31.752	2.5	—	—	—	—	—	3,800	6.100	60,000	18.300	2	msl.
14.1	4,29	13,669	6.200	19,842	9.000	0.9	—	—	—	—	—	*	*	*	*	1	*
14.9	4,50	*	*	*	*	*	—	—	—	—	—	*	*	*	*	1	*
11.3	3,43	12,200	5.534	22,000	9.979	1.3	—	—	—	—	—	2,300	3.700	50,000	15.240	1	g., b., r. (5,000 lb; 2.268 kg)
17.0	5,18	*	*	184,970	83.902	1.4	—	—	—	—	—	1,400	2.250	60,000	18.300	5	b., msl.
40.8	12,39	*	*	488,000	221.357	0.95	—	—	—	—	—	10,000	16.100	50,000	15.240	6	4 g. (0.50 in), b., msl., r.
14.5	4,39	*	*	28,000	12.701	0.94	—	—	—	—	—	2,140	3.445	46,000	14.000	1	6 mg. (0.50 in), b., r., msl. (6,000 lb; 2.722 kg)
13.2	4,01	8,085	3.667	20,576	9.333	1.4	—	—	0.87	—	—	1,565	2.520	50,000	15.240	1	2 g. (20 mm), msl., r., b. (6,200 lb; 2.812 kg)
15.9	4,79	*	*	34,000	15.422	2	—	—	0.85	—	—	600	965	58,000	17.680	1	4 g. (20 mm), msl., r., b. (5,000 lb; 2.268 kg)
19.8	5,99	27,500	12.474	52,546	23.835	2.1	—	—	—	—	—	2,390	3.850	*	*	1	1 g. (20 mm), msl., r., b. (13,000 lb; 5.897 kg)
21.2	6,45	*	*	32,000	14.515	1.25	—	—	—	—	—	1,350	2.170	54,000	16.460	1	30 msl.
20.3	6,18	26,000	11.794	35,000	15.876	2.3	—	—	—	—	—	2,700	4.345	57,000	17.370	2	6 msl.
18.0	5,49	*	*	46,500	21.092	1.85	—	—	—	—	—	1,750	2.815	52,000	15.850	2	5 msl.
*	*	*	*	*	*	*	—	—	*	—	—	*	*	*	*	1	1 g., msl.
19.7	5,97	*	*	42,000	19.051	2	—	—	—	—	—	*	*	60,000	18.300	1	g., msl., r., b. (8,000 lb; 3.629 kg)
10.9	3,28	*	*	37,000	16.783	0.92	—	—	—	—	—	1,000	1.610	48,000	14.630	2	msl., r., b.
14.11	4,55	15,400	6.985	22,046	10.000	1.12	—	—	0.94	—	—	730	1.175	55,750	16.990	1	2 g. (30 mm), b., msl., r.
12.7	3,84	12,787	5.800	22,487	10.200	1.02	—	—	—	—	—	435	700	50,850	15.500	1	1 g. (30 mm), msl., r., b.
14.9	4,50	16,314	7.400	32,849	14.900	2.2	—	—	—	—	—	4,000	6.440	65,600	20.000	1	2 g. (30 mm), msl., b., r. (8,818 lb; 4.000 kg)
10.4	3,15	*	*	12,000	5.443	2	—	—	—	—	—	*	*	*	*	1	2 g., 2 msl.
11.10	3,60	13,658	6.195	24,250	11.000	1.02	—	—	—	—	—	420	675	46,000	14.000	1	4 g. (30 mm), b., msl., r. (4,000 lb; 1.814 kg)
13.6	4,11	12,132	5.503	22,500	10.206	1.33	—	—	—	—	—	1,365	2.195	55,775	17.000	1	3 g. (30 mm), msl., r.
14.9	4,50	*	*	18,800	8.528	2	—	—	—	—	—	1,260	2.030	*	*	1	2 g. (30 mm), msl., r.
14.9	4,50	*	*	18,800	8.528	2	—	—	—	—	—	1,260	2.030	*	*	1	2 g. (30 mm), msl., r.
12.11	3,95	*	*	35,000	15.876	1.1	—	—	—	—	—	1,200	1.930	55,000	16.765	2	msl.
*	*	*	*	*	*	2.5	—	—	—	—	—	*	*	*	*	1	msl.
20.0	6,10	*	*	100,000	45.360	1.75	—	—	—	—	—	2,000	3.220	60,000	18.300	1	msl.
12.9	3,89	*	*	33,069	15.000	2	—	—	—	—	—	2,000	3.220	*	*	1	2 g. (30 mm), msl., r., b. (10,000 lb; 4.536 kg)

kg	kilograms	mm	millimeters	Rc	reconnaissance	tf. turbo-fan
km	kilometers	mn.	mines	R.R.	Rolls-Royce	tj. turbo-jet
L.	Lycoming	MR	maritime reconnaissance	S	Sweden	tp. turbo-prop
LB	light bomber	MRo	multirole	SB	strategic bomber	Tr transport
lb	pounds	msl.	missiles	ST	STOL = short take-off and landing	USA United States of America
LT	light transport	P.&W.	Pratt & Whitney	SU	Soviet Union	V VTOL = vertical take-off and landing
m	meters	PT	primary trainer	Sv.	Svenska	W. Wright
MB	medium bomber	r.	rockets	T	trainer	We. Westinghouse
mg.	machine-gun	RA	Argentina	t.	torpedo	YU Yugoslavia
ml	miles	RAU	United Arabian Republic	tc.	turbo-compound	* not available data

MILITARY AIRCRAFT: TODAY (continued)

Page	Aircraft	Builder	Nation of origin	Type	Year	Engine	Wing spread ft	Wing spread m	Length ft	Length m
160	Handley Page Victor B.2	Handley Page Ltd	GB	MB	1961	4/17,250 lb (7.825 kg) R.R. Conway RCo.11	120.0	36,58	114.11	35,03
160	Hawker Siddeley Vulcan B.2	A.V. Roe & Co. Ltd	GB	MB	1960	4/22,000 lb (9.979 kg) B.S. Olympus 301 tj.	111.0	33,83	99.11	30,46
160	BAC Canberra B.8	English Electric Co. Ltd	GB	LB	1954	2/7,500 lb (3.402 kg) R.R. Avon 109 tj.	63.11	19,48	65.6	19,96
160	Hawker Siddeley Buccaneer S.2	Hawker Siddeley Group Ltd	GB	Cb/LB	1962	2/11,030 lb (5.003 kg) R.R. RB.168-1 Spey tf.	42.4	12,90	63.5	19,33
160	Mikoyan Gurevich MiG-? "Flogger"	State Industries	SU	LB	1968	a.b. tj.	50.0	15,24	57.0	17,37
160	Ilyushin Il-28 "Beagle"	State Industries	SU	LB	1948	2/6,040 lb (2.740 kg) K. VK-1 tj.	68.3	20,80	62.0	18,90
160	Tupolev Tu-16 "Badger"	State Industries	SU	MB	1954	2/20,950 lb (9.503 kg) Mikulin AM-3M tj.	109.11	33,50	120.0	36,58
160	Tupolev Tu-20 "Bear-A"	State Industries	SU	HB	1956	4/14795 hp Kuznetsov NK-12M tp.	163.0	49,68	150.0	45,72
160	Soko P-2 Kraguj	Preduzece Soko	YU	CIS	1968	340 hp L. GSO-480-B1A6 (6 cl.)	34.11	10,64	26.0	7,92
160	Saab 32A Lansen	Saab-Scania Aktiebolag	S	CIS	1956	9,920 lb (4.500 kg) a.b. Sv. Flygmotor RM5A tj.	42.8	13,00	49.0	14,95
160	Sukhoi Su-7B "Fitter"	State Industries	SU	GA	1956	22,046 lb (10.000 kg) a.b. TRD R31 tj.	29.3	8,93	57.0	17,37
161	Dassault Mirage IV-A	Avions Marcel Dassault	F	LB	1964	2/15,432 lb (7.000 kg) a.b. SNECMA Atar 09K tj.	38.11	11,85	77.1	23,50
161	North American OV-10A Bronco	North American Rockwell Corp.	USA	CI	1967	2/715 AiResearch T76 tp.	40.0	12,19	41.7	12,68
161	North American T-28D	North American Rockwell Corp.	USA	CI	1967	1300 hp W. R-1820-565	40.7	12,37	32.10	10,00
161	McDonnell Douglas A-4F Skyhawk	McDonnell Douglas Corp.	USA	Cb/LB	1956	9,300 lb (4.218 kg) P.&W. J52-P-8A tj.	27.6	8,38	40.3	12,27
161	Cessna A-37B	Cessna Aircraft Co.	USA	CI	1966	2/2,850 lb (1.293 kg) G.E. J85-GE-17A tj.	35.10	10,92	29.3	8,92
161	LTV A-7B Corsair II	Ling-Temco-Vought Inc.	USA	Cb/LB	1966	12,200 lb (5.534 kg) P.&W. TF-30-P-8 tf.	38.9	11,81	46.1	14,05
161	Grumman A-6A Intruder	Grumman Aircraft Corp.	USA	Cb/LB	1963	2/9,300 lb (4.218 kg) P.&W. J52-P-8A tj.	53.0	16,15	54.7	16,64
161	North American Rockwell B-1	North American Rockwell Corp.	USA	SB	1976	4/29,983 lb (13.600 kg) G.E. F-101	137.0	41,76	143.0	43,59
161	Convair B-58A Hustler	Convair Div. of General Dynamics Corp.	USA	MB	1959	4/15,600 lb (7.076 kg) a.b. G.E. J79-DE-5B tj.	56.10	17,32	96.9	29,49
162	Kawasaki P-2J	Kawasaki Jukogyo Kabushiki Kaisha	J	MR	1969	2/2850 hp G.E. T64-IHI-7C tp.	97.8	29,77	95.10	29,23
162	Shin Meiwa PS-1	Shin Meiwa Industry Co. Ltd	J	MR/AS	1970	4/2850 hp Ishikawajima-G.E. T64-IHI-10 tp.	108.9	33,14	109.11	33,50
162	Grumman S-2E Tracker	Grumman Aircraft Corp.	USA	Cb/AS	1962	2/1525 hp W. R-1820-82 WA (9 cl.)	72.7	22,13	43.6	13,26
162	Grumman OV-1B Mohawk	Grumman Aircraft Corp.	USA	RC	1962	2/1100 hp L. T53-L-15 tp.	48.0	14,63	41.0	12,50
162	Grumman E-1B Tracer	Grumman Aircraft Corp.	USA	Cb/AS	1954	2/1525 hp W. R-1820-82 WA	72.4	22,05	45.4	13,82
162	Lockheed S-3A	Lockheed Aircraft Corp.	USA	Cb/AS	1973	2/9,000 lb (4.082 kg) G.E. TF-34-2 tf.	68.8	20,93	53.4	16,25
162	Grumman Albatros UH-16B	Grumman Aircraft Corp.	USA	MR	1957	2/1425 hp W. R-1820-76A	96.8	29,46	62.10	19,15
162	Lockheed P-2H Neptune	Lockheed Aircraft Corp.	USA	MR/AS	1947	2/3500 hp W. R-3350-32W + 2/3,400 lb (1.542 kg) We. J34-WE-34 tj.	103.10	31,64	91.4	27,84
162	Lockheed P-3C Orion	Lockheed Aircraft Corp.	USA	MR/AS	1969	4/4910 hp A. T56-A-14 tp.	99.8	30,38	116.10	35,61
163	Hawker Siddeley HS 801 Nimrod	Hawker Siddeley Group Ltd	GB	MR	1969	4/11,500 lb (5.217 kg) R.R. RB.168 Spey Mk 250 tf.	114.10	35,00	126.9	38,63
163	Westland Fairey Gannet A.E.W.3	Fairey Aviation Ltd	GB	Cb/MR	1958	3875 hp B.S. Double Mamba 102 tp.	54.6	16,61	44.0	13,41
163	Hawker Siddeley Shackleton Mk.3	A.V. Roe & Co. Ltd	GB	MR	1952	4/2455 hp R.R. Griffon 57A (12 cl.)	119.10	36,52	92.6	28,19
163	Canadair CP-107 Argus	Canadair Ltd	CDN	MR	1958	4/3700 hp W. R-3350 tc.	142.3	43,36	128.3	39,09
163	Breguet Br 1050 Alizé	Breguet Aviation	F	Cb/AS	1959	1975 hp R.R. Dart R.Da.22 tp.	51.2	15,60	45.6	13,86
163	Breguet Br 1150 Atlantic	Breguet Aviation	F	MR	1965	2/6105 hp Hispano-R.R. Tyne RTy.20 Mk.21 tp.	119.1	36,30	104.2	31,75
163	Yakovlev Yak-? "Mandrake"	State Industries	SU	Rc	1962	2/8,800 lb (3.992 kg) a.b. tj.	70.6	21,50	50.0	15,25
163	Beriev Be-12 "Mail"	State Industries	SU	MR	1961	2/4000 hp Ivchenko AI-20D tp.	108.0	32,90	95.9	29,20
163	Beriev Be-10 "Mallow"	State Industries	SU	MR	1960	2/14,330 lb (6.500 kg) AL-7PB tj.	73.0	22,25	102.0	31,09
163	Myasishchev Mya-4 "Bison"	State Industries	SU	Rc	1956	4/19,180 lb (8.700 kg) Mikulin AM-3M tj.	170.0	51,82	162.0	49,38
164	Sukhoi Su-7UTI "Moujik"	State Industries	SU	AT	1966	22,000 lb (9.979 kg) a.b. tj.	29.3	8,93	57.0	17,37
164	Mikoyan Gurevich MiG-21UTI "Mongol"	State Industries	SU	AT	1956	13,120 lb (5.951 kg) R-37F tj.	24.11	7,60	55.0	16,75
164	Antonov An-14 "Clod"	State Industries	SU	GP	1965	2/300 hp Ivchenko AI-14RF (9 cl.)	72.2	21,99	37.1	11,32
164	Yakovlev Yak-12M	State Industries	SU	GP	1946	240 hp Ivchenko AI-14R (9 cl.)	41.4	12,60	29.6	8,99
164	Antonov An-2P "Colt"	State Industries	SU	GP	1948	1000 hp ASh-62 IR (9 cl.)	59.8	18,19	42.0	12,85
164	Cessna T-41A	Cessna Aircraft Co.	USA	BT	1965	150 hp L. O-320-E2D (4 cl.)	35.9	10,90	26.11	8,20
164	North American T-2 Buckeye	North American Rockwell Corp.	USA	T	1965	2/3,000 lb (1.361 kg) P.&W. J60-P-6 tj.	38.1	11,61	38.3	11,67
164	Northrop T-38A Talon	Northrop Corp.	USA	BT	1961	2/3,850 lb (1.746 kg) a.b. G.E. J85-GE-5 tj.	25.3	7,70	46.4	14,12

Abbreviations used in the table

A.	Allison	BT	basic trainer	F	France	HB	heavy bomber
a.b.	with afterburning	Cb	carrier-based	FB	fighter-bomber	hp	horse-power
AS	anti-submarine	CDN	Canada	Fr	fighter	HT	heavy transport
A.S.	Armstrong Siddeley	CI	counter-insurgency	ft	feet	I	Italy
AT	advanced trainer	cl.	cylinders	g.	gun	in	inches
B.	Bristol	CIS	close support	GA	ground attack	IND	India
b.	bombs	CS	Czechoslovakia	GB	Great Britain	IP	international project
BR	Brazil	D	Germany	G.E.	General Electric	J	Japan
Br	bomber	E	Spain	GP	general purpose	j.	jet
B.S.	Bristol Siddeley	Ex	experimental	h	hour	K.	Klimov

Height		Empty weight		Max take-off weight		Max speed			Cruising speed			Range		Ceiling		Crew	Armament or payload
ft	m	lb	kg	lb	kg	Mach	ml/h	km/h	Mach	ml/h	km/h	ml	km	ft	m		
30.1	9,17	*	*	200,000	90.720	0.95	—	—	—	—	—	2,300	3.700	60,000	18.300	5	b. (35,000 lb; 15.876 kg)
27.2	8,28	*	*	200,000	90.720	0.98	—	—	—	—	—	4,750	7.640	65,000	19.800	5	msl., b.
15.7	4,74	23,173	10.511	56,250	25.515	0.83	—	—	—	—	—	3,600	5.800	48,000	14.630	2	4 g. (20 mm), b., msl., r. (6,000 lb; 2.722 kg)
16.6	5,03	*	*	54,000	24.494	0.92	—	—	0.83	—	—	4,000	6.440	*	*	2	b. (5,000 lb; 2.268 kg)
*	*	*	*	*	*	2	—	—	—	—	—	*	*	*	*	1	*
22.0	6,70	27,400	12.429	44,000	19.958	0.81	—	—	0.65	—	—	2,200	3.540	41,000	12.500	3	4 g. (20 mm), b. (6,600 lb; 2.994 kg)
35.6	10,82	*	*	170,000	77.112	0.80	—	—	—	—	—	3,975	6.400	42,650	13.000	6	7 g. (23 mm), b., msl., r. (19,800 lb; 8.981 kg)
40.0	12,19	*	*	340,000	154.224	0.83	—	—	0.76	—	—	7,800	12.550	44,000	13.400	8	7 g. (23 mm), b. (25,000 lb; 11.340 kg)
9.10	3,00	2,491	1.130	3,580	1.624	—	183	294	—	174	280	500	805	*	*	1	2 mg. (7,7 mm), b., r.
15.3	4,65	16,398	7.438	28,660	13.000	0.9	—	—	0.8	—	—	1,000	1.610	49,210	15.000	2	4 g. (20 mm), b., r.
15.0	4,57	*	*	31,969	14.500	1.7	—	—	—	—	—	900	1.450	49,700	15.150	1	2 g. (30 mm), b., r. (7,000 lb; 3.175 kg)
18.6	5,65	31,969	14.500	69,666	31.600	2.2	—	—	1.7	—	—	1,000	1.610	65,600	20.000	2	b., msl.
15.2	4,62	6,969	3.161	14,466	6.562	—	281	452	—	—	—	1,428	2.300	*	*	2	4 mg. (0.30 in), b., r. (3,600 lb; 1.633 kg)
12.8	3,86	6,521	2.958	8,495	3.853	—	352	566	—	—	—	1,184	1.900	*	*	2	b., r.
15.0	4,57	10,000	4.536	24,500	11.113	0.9	—	—	—	—	—	2,000	3.220	49,000	14.940	1	2 g. (20 mm), b., msl., r. (7,000 lb; 3.175 kg)
8.10	2,69	5,843	2.650	14,000	6.350	—	507	816	—	489	787	1,012	1.630	41,765	12.730	2	1 mg. (7,62 mm), b., r. (5,400 lb; 2.449 kg)
16.0	4,87	18,000	8.165	42,000	19.051	0.8	—	—	—	—	—	2,820	4.540	*	*	1	1 g. (20 mm), msl., b., r. (20,000 lb; 9.072 kg)
15.7	4,74	25,684	11.650	60,626	27.500	0.9	—	—	0.8	—	—	3,225	5.190	41,660	12.700	2	b., msl. (15,000 lb; 6.804 kg)
34.0	10,36	*	*	400,000	181.440	2	—	—	0.85	—	—	6,215	10.000	*	*	6	b., msl. (50,045 lb; 22.700 kg)
31.5	9,58	*	*	163,000	73.937	2.1	—	—	0.9	—	—	2,400	3.860	60,000	18.300	3	1 g. (20 mm), msl., r., b.
29.3	8,92	42,500	19.278	75,000	34.020	—	403	649	—	250	402	2,765	4.450	30,000	9.150	12	—
31.10	9,71	51,852	23.520	86,862	39.400	—	340	547	—	196	315	2,948	4.745	29,530	9.000	10	t., b.
16.7	5,05	18,750	8.505	29,150	13.222	—	265	426	—	150	241	1,300	2.095	21,000	6.400	4	t., b., r.
12.8	3,86	11,067	5.020	19,230	8.723	—	297	478	—	207	333	1,230	1.980	30,300	9.235	2	—
16.10	5,13	21,024	9.536	26,966	12.232	—	265	426	—	180	290	1,150	1.850	22,000	6.700	4	b.
22.9	6,93	23,300	10.569	41,000	18.598	—	495	797	—	403	649	3,454	5.560	35,000	10.670	4	t., b., msl., mn., r.
25.10	7,87	22,883	10.380	37,500	17.010	—	236	380	—	150	241	3,280	5.280	21,500	6.550	4	—
29.4	8,94	47,456	21.526	75,500	34.245	—	345	555	—	207	333	2,200	3.540	22,000	6.700	10	—
33.8	10,26	61,491	27.892	142,000	64.411	—	476	766	—	230	370	2,530	4.075	28,300	8.625	12	t., b., mn., r.
29.8	9,04	*	*	*	*	0.9	—	—	—	500	805	3,728	6.000	42,650	13.000	12	t., msl., mn., b., r.
16.10	5,13	*	*	21,000	9.526	—	250	402	—	140	225	1,000	1.610	25,000	7.620	3	*
23.4	7,11	57,800	26.218	100,000	45.360	—	300	483	—	253	407	3,660	5.890	19,200	5.850	10	2 g. (20 mm), t., b., mn.
36.8	11,17	81,000	36.742	148,000	67.133	—	290	467	—	175	282	4,000	6.440	20,000	6.100	15	t., b., mn., msl. (11,800 lb; 5.352 kg)
16.5	5,00	12,566	5.700	18,078	8.200	—	292	470	—	150	240	600	965	20,000	6.100	3	t., b., msl., r., mn.
37.2	11,33	75,839	34.400	95,900	43.500	—	409	658	—	220	325	5,590	9.000	33,000	10.000	12	t., b., msl., r., mn.
*	*	*	*	21,000	9.526	—	560	901	—	—	—	2,500	4.025	70,000	21.335	1	—
22.11	7,00	*	*	65,035	29.500	—	379	610	—	199	320	2,485	4.000	*	*	5-6	*
33.0	10,06	53,000	24.040	100,000	45.360	—	560	901	—	350	565	1,500	2.415	40,000	12.200	4-5	4 g. (23 mm), b., r., mn.
50.0	15,24	*	*	352,739	160.000	—	620	998	—	520	837	7,000	11.265	*	*	5-7	7 g. (23 mm), b.
15.0	4,57	*	*	31,967	14.500	1.6	—	—	—	—	—	900	1.450	49,000	14.940	2	*
14.9	4,50	*	*	18,800	8.528	2	—	—	—	—	—	*	*	57,400	17.500	2	—
15.2	4,63	*	*	7,937	3.600	—	118	190	—	109	175	423	681	*	*	1	Payload: 1,590 lb (720 kg) or 7 passengers
10.3	3,13	2,263	1.026	3,197	1.450	—	112	180	—	79	127	475	764	13,650	4.160	1	3 passengers
13.8	4,16	7,275	3.300	11,574	5.250	—	161	259	—	124	200	1,087	1.750	16,400	5.000	3	Payload: 2,734 lb (1.240 kg) or 12 passengers
8.9	2,67	1,245	565	2,300	1.043	—	139	224	—	117	188	640	1.030	13,100	4.000	1	3 passengers
14.9	4,51	8,220	3.729	13,284	6.026	—	540	869	—	—	—	950	1.530	42,000	12.800	2	g., b., r.
12.10	3,92	7,146	3.241	12,050	5.466	1.23	—	—	0.88	—	—	1,100	1.770	53,600	16.335	2	—

kg	kilograms	mm	millimeters	Rc	reconnaissance	tf.	turbo-fan

MILITARY AIRCRAFT: TODAY (continued)

Page	Aircraft	Builder	Nation of origin	Type	Year	Engine	Wing spread ft	Wing spread m	Length ft	Length m
164	Hawker Siddeley Gnat T.1	Hawker Siddeley Group Ltd	GB	AT	1962	4,230 lb (1.919 kg) B.S. Orpheus 101 tj.	24.0	7,32	37.10	11,53
164	Hawker Siddeley Hunter T.7	Hawker Siddeley Group Ltd	GB	T	1957	7,575 lb (3.436 kg) R.R. Avon 122 tj.	33.8	10,26	48.10	14,88
164	BAC Jet Provost T.5	British Aircraft Corp. Ltd	GB	BT	1969	2,500 lb (1.134 kg) R.R. Bristol Viper 202 tj.	35.4	10,77	34.0	10,36
164	De Havilland DHC-1 Chipmunk	De Havilland Aircraft of Canada Ltd	CDN	PT	1946	145 hp B.S. Gipsy Major 8 (4 cl.)	34.4	10,46	25.5	7,75
164	Canadair CT-114 Tutor	Canadair Ltd	CDN	BT	1962	2,850 lb (1.293 kg) Orenda-G.E. Cj610-1B tj.	36.4	11,07	32.0	9,75
164	De Havilland DHC-2 Beaver	De Havilland Aircraft of Canada Ltd	CDN	GP	1948	450 hp P.&W. R-985 Wasp Junior (9 cl.)	48.0	14,63	30.4	9,24
164	HAL HJT-6 Mk.II Kiran	Hindustan Aeronautics Ltd	IND	BT	1968	2,500 lb (1.134 kg) R.R. Bristol Viper 11 tj.	35.1	10,70	34.9	10,60
164	Piaggio P-149D	Piaggio & C. S.p.A.	I	LT	1955	270 hp L. GO-480 (6 cl.)	36.6	11,12	28.11	8,80
164	Piaggio-Douglas PD-808	Industrie Aeronautiche e Meccaniche R. Piaggio S.p.A.	I	GP	1964	2/3,360 lb (1.524 kg) R.R. Bristol Viper 526 tj.	37.6	11,43	41.11	12,58
164	Aerfer-Aermacchi AM-3C	Aerfer-Aeronautica Macchi S.p.A.	I	GP	1970	340 hp Piaggio-L. GSO-480-B1B6 (6 cl.)	38.6	11,73	28.8	8,73
164	Aérospatiale CM 170 Super Magister	Société Nationale Industrielle Aérospatiale	F	T	1962	2/1,050 lb (476 kg) Turboméca Marboré	37.5	11,40	33.0	10,06
164	Morane-Saulnier MS 760 Paris	Aéroplanes Morane-Saulnier	F	GP	1958	2/880 lb (399 kg) Turboméca Marboré II	33.3	10,15	33.0	10,05
164	Nord 3202	Nord-Aviation	F	BT	1959	260 hp Potez 4-D 34B (4 cl.)	31.2	9,50	26.8	8,12
164	Holste MH-1521M Broussard	Max Holste, Société des Avions	F	GP	1953	450 hp P.&W. R-985-AN Wasp	45.1	13,75	28.3	8,60
164	Neiva Regente C-42	Sociedade Construtora Aeronáutica Neiva, Ltda	BR	GP	1965	210 hp Continental IO-360 D (4 cl.)	29.11	9,13	23.1	7,04
164	IA 50 Guarani II	Fábrica Militar de Aviones	RA	GP	1963	2/930 hp Turboméca Bastan VI-A tp.	64.1	19,53	48.9	14,86
164	Dinfia IA 35 Huanquero	Dirección Nacional de Fabricaciones e Investigaciones Aeronáuticas	RA	AT	1954	2/620 hp IA 19R El Indio (9 cl.)	64.3	19,60	45.10	13,98
165	Mikoyan Gurevich MiG-15UTI "Midget"	State Industries	SU	AT	1950	5,952 lb (2.700 kg) K. RD-45FA tj.	35.5	10,80	36.1	11,00
165	Yakovlev Yak-18A	State Industries	SU	T	1947	260 hp Ivchenko AI-14R (9 cl.)	34.9	10,60	28.0	8,53
165	Aero L-29 Delfin "Maya"	Aero Vodochody Národní Podnik	CS	T	1962	1,960 lb (889 kg) M-701c 500 tj.	33.9	10,29	35.5	10,81
165	Aero L-39	Aero Vodochody Národní Podnik	CS	T	1971	3,307 lb (1.500 kg) Walter Titan tf.	29.11	9,11	39.9	12,11
165	Cessna O-2A	Cessna Aircraft Co.	USA	GP	1966	2/210 hp Continental TSIO-360-A (6 cl.)	38.2	11,63	29.10	9,09
165	Helio U-10 Super Courier	Helio Aircraft Co.	USA	GP	1959	295 hp L. GO-480-G1D6 (6 cl.)	39.0	11,89	31.0	9,45
165	Beagle Basset CC Mk.1	Beagle Aircraft Ltd	GB	GP	1964	2/310 hp R.R.-Continental GIO-470-A (6 cl.)	45.9	13,95	33.3	10,14
165	Fuji T1A	Fuji Jukogyo Kabushiki Kaisha	J	T	1959	4,000 lb (1.814 kg) B.S. Orpheus 805 tj.	34.6	10,50	39.9	12,12
165	Mitsubishi MU-2S	Mitsubishi Jukogyo Kabushiki Kaisha	J	GP	1964	2/705 hp AiResearch TPE 331-1-151A tp.	39.2	11,95	38.10	11,84
165	Aero 3	State Industries	YU	PT	1958	185 hp L. (6 cl.)	36.1	11,00	28.2	8,58
165	Soko G2-A Galeb	Preduzece Soko	YU	BT	1963	2,500 lb (1.134 kg) R.R. Bristol Viper 11 Mk 22-6 tj.	34.4	10,47	33.11	10,34
165	Saab SK 60	Saab-Scania Aktiebolag	S	BT	1965	2/1,640 lb (744 kg) Turboméca Aubisque tj.	31.2	9,50	34.6	10,50
165	Hispano HA-200E Super Saeta	La Hispano-Aviación S.A.	E	AT	1960	2/1,058 lb (480 kg) Turboméca Harboré VI tj.	34.2	10,42	29.5	8,97
165	Dassault-Breguet-Dornier "Alpha Jet"	Dassault-Breguet-Dornier	F-D	T	1973	2/2,300 lb (1.043 kg) SNECMA-Turboméca Larzac tf.	27.7	8,41	39.5	10,02
165	Dornier Do 27A	Dornier-Werke GmbH	D	GP	1956	340 hp L. GSO-480-B1B6 (6 cl.)	39.4	12,00	31.6	9,60
166	De Havilland DHC-3 Otter	De Havilland Aircraft of Canada Ltd	CDN	LT	1952	600 hp P.&W. R-1340-S1 H1-G	58.0	17,68	41.10	12,75
166	De Havilland DHC-4 Sr 300 Twin Otter	De Havilland Aircraft of Canada Ltd	CDN	ST/LT	1966	2/652 hp P.&W. PT6A-27 tp.	65.0	19,81	51.9	15,77
166	De Havilland DHC-4A Caribou	De Havilland Aircraft of Canada Ltd	CDN	ST/Tr	1958	2/1450 hp P.&W. R-2000-7M2 (14 cl.)	95.7	29,14	72.7	22,13
166	De Havilland DHC-5 (CC-115) Buffalo	De Havilland Aircraft of Canada Ltd	CDN	ST/Tr	1965	2/3055 hp G.E. CT64-820-1 tp.	96.0	29,26	79.0	24,08
166	Fiat G222	Fiat S.p.A.	I	Tr	1970	2/3400 hp G.E. T64-P-4C tp.	94.2	28,70	74.5	22,70
166	Namc XC-1A	Nihon Kokuki Seizo Kabushiki Kaisha	J	Tr	1970	2/14,495 lb (6.575 kg) P.&W. JT8D-9 tf.	101.9	31,00	95.2	29,00
166	Breguet Br 941	Breguet-Aviation	F	ST/Tr	1967	4/1500 hp Turboméca Turmo	76.9	23,40	77.11	23,75
166	Nord 2501 Noratlas	Nord-Aviation	F	Tr	1952	2/2040 hp SNECMA Hercules 738 (14 cl.)	106.7	32,50	72.0	21,96
166	Transall C-160	Arbeitsgemeinschaft Transall	F-D	Tr	1968	2/6100 hp R.R. Tyne RTy.20 Mk.22 tp.	131.3	40,01	106.3	32,40
167	Hawker Siddeley Argosy C.1	Whitworth Gloster Aircraft Ltd of H.S. Group	GB	Tr	1961	4/2470 hp R.R. Dart RDa.8 Mk.101 tp.	115.0	35,05	89.0	27,13
167	Scottish Aviation Twin Pioneer	Scottish Aviation Ltd	GB	ST/LT	1956	2/640 hp Alvis Leonides 531/8B	76.6	23,31	45.3	13,80
167	Short Belfast C.1	Short Bros & Harland Ltd	GB	HT	1966	4/5730 hp R.R. Tyne RTy-12 tp.	158.9	48,39	136.5	41,58
167	Ilyushin Il-14 "Crate"	State Industries	SU	Tr	1953	2/1900 hp Shvetsov ASh-82T-7	104.0	31,70	69.10	21,28

Abbreviations used in the table

A.	Allison	BT	basic trainer	F	France	HB	heavy bomber
a.b.	with afterburning	Cb	carrier-based	FB	fighter-bomber	hp	horse-power
AS	anti-submarine	CDN	Canada	Fr	fighter	HT	heavy transport
A.S.	Armstrong Siddeley	CI	counter-insurgency	ft	feet	I	Italy
AT	advanced trainer	cl.	cylinders	g.	gun	in	inches
B.	Bristol	CIS	close support	GA	ground attack	IND	India
b.	bombs	CS	Czechoslovakia	GB	Great Britain	IP	international project
BR	Brazil	D	Germany	G.E.	General Electric	J	Japan
Br	bomber	E	Spain	GP	general purpose	j.	jet
B.S.	Bristol Siddeley	Ex	experimental	h	hour	K.	Klimov

Height		Empty weight		Max take-off weight		Max speed			Cruising speed			Range		Ceiling		Crew	Armament or payload
ft	m	lb	kg	lb	kg	Mach	ml/h	km/h	Mach	ml/h	km/h	ml	km	ft	m		
10.6	3,20	5,560	2.522	8,985	4.076	0.95	—	—	—	—	—	1,180	1.900	48,000	14.630	2	msl., b., g.
13.2	4,01	13,270	6.019	24,000	10.886	—	660	1.062	—	—	—	1,840	2.960	49,500	15.090	2	1 g. (30 mm)
10.2	3,10	*	*	9,200	4.173	—	440	708	—	—	—	900	1.450	36,750	11.200	2	—
7.0	2,13	1,425	646	2,014	914	—	138	222	—	119	192	280	451	14,800	4.510	2	—
9.4	2,84	4,840	2.195	7,348	3.333	—	486	782	—	356	573	1,210	1.950	44,500	13.570	2	mg., b., r.
9.0	2,74	3,000	1.361	5,100	2.313	—	160	257	—	143	230	750	1.207	18,000	5.500	1	7 passengers
11.11	3,63	5,362	2.432	8,660	3.928	—	446	718	—	—	—	600	965	*	*	2	—
9.6	2,90	1,160	526	3,704	1.680	—	189	304	—	165	266	680	1.095	19,800	6.050	1	4 passengers
15.9	4,80	10,648	4.830	18,000	8.165	—	529	851	—	449	723	1,270	2.045	45,000	13.715	1	Payload: 1,600 lb (726 kg) or 9 passengers
9.0	2,75	2,381	1.080	3,748	1.700	—	173	278	—	153	246	615	990	27,550	8.400	1	3 passengers
9.2	2,80	5,093	2.310	7,187	3.260	—	451	726	—	—	—	870	1.400	39,370	12.000	2	2 mg. (7,5 mm), b., r., msl.
8.6	2,60	4,280	1.941	7,650	3.470	—	345	555	—	—	—	930	1.500	33,000	10.000	1	3 passengers
9.3	2,82	1,896	860	2,690	1.220	—	161	259	—	121	195	560	901	—	—	2	—
9.2	2,80	3,637	1.650	5,953	2.700	—	161	259	—	143	230	745	1.200	17,500	5.335	1	5 passengers
9.7	2,93	1,410	640	2,293	1.040	—	139	224	—	132	212	562	904	11,800	3.600	1	3 passengers
19.1	5,81	8,650	3.924	16,204	7.350	—	310	500	—	280	451	1,600	2.575	41,000	12.500	2	Payload: 3,307 lb (1.500 kg) or 15 passengers
15.5	4,70	7,700	3.493	12,540	5.688	—	225	362	—	200	322	975	1.569	21,000	6.400	8	*
12.10	3,90	*	*	11,905	5.400	—	631	1.015	—	—	—	422	679	*	*	2	*
11.0	3,35	2,138	970	2,866	1.300	—	161	259	—	133	214	465	748	13,100	4.000	2	—
10.3	3,13	5,027	2.280	7,804	3.540	—	407	655	—	—	—	555	893	36,000	11.000	2	b., r.
14.4	4,38	6,283	2.850	8,378	3.800	—	454	731	—	—	—	930	1.500	37,225	11.350	2	—
9.4	2,84	2,850	1.293	4,630	2.100	—	230	370	—	173	278	1,550	2.495	29,300	8.930	2	2 passengers
8.10	2,69	2,080	943	4,420	2.005	—	167	269	—	150	241	1,380	2.220	20,500	6.250	1	5 passengers
11.4	3,45	4,620	2.096	7,500	3.402	—	210	338	—	185	298	509	819	17,500	5.335	1	6 passengers
13.3	4,03	5,335	2.420	10,670	4.840	—	485	781	—	397	639	780	1.255	*	*	2	1 mg. (0.5 in), msl., r., b.
13.8	4,17	6,563	2.977	10,053	4.560	—	326	525	—	300	483	1,555	2.500	27,000	8.230	2	10 passengers
11.9	3,58	*	*	2,646	1.200	—	143	230	—	112	180	422	679	14,100	4.300	2	—
10.9	3,28	5,775	2.620	7,690	3.488	—	505	813	—	453	729	770	1.240	39,370	12.000	2	2 mg. (0.50 in), b., r.
8.10	2,70	5,534	2.510	8,930	4.051	—	478	769	—	438	705	1,106	1.780	44,300	13.500	2	g., r., b. (1,543 lb; 700 kg)
9.4	2,85	4,453	2.020	7,937	3.600	—	429	690	—	360	579	930	1.500	42,650	13.000	2	g., r., b.
*	*	*	*	9,920	4.500	1	—	—	—	*	*	1,243	2.000	*	*	2	—
11.6	3,50	2,162	985	3,461	1.570	—	155	250	—	127	205	540	870	18,000	5.500	1	4 passengers
12.7	3,84	4,168	1.891	8,000	3.629	—	160	257	—	138	222	960	1.545	18,800	5.730	2	10 passengers
18.7	5,67	7,000	3.175	12,500	5.670	—	210	338	—	—	—	745	1.200	26,700	8.140	2	20 passengers
31.9	9,68	18,260	8.283	31,300	14.198	—	216	348	—	182	293	1,307	2.103	24,800	7.560	2	Payload: 8,740 lb (3.965 kg) or 32 passengers
28.8	8,73	23,154	10.505	41,000	18.598	—	271	436	—	208	335	2,170	3.490	30,000	9.150	3	Payload: 13,843 lb (6.279 kg) or 41 passengers
32.2	9,80	28,000	12.700	58,422	26.500	—	323	520	—	249	400	3,107	5.000	29,530	9.000	4	Payload: 19,842 lb (9.000 kg) or 44 passengers
32.10	10,00	50,706	23.000	85,980	39.000	—	507	816	—	438	705	2,073	3.336	39,370	12.000	5	Payload: 17,637 lb (8.000 kg) or 60 passengers
31.8	9,65	32,408	14.700	58,420	26.500	—	280	450	—	248	400	1,925	3.100	31,170	9.500	3	Payload: 22,046 lb (10.000 kg) or 57 passengers
19.8	6,00	28,825	13.075	50,706	23.000	—	273	440	—	201	324	1,555	2.500	24,600	7.500	4	Payload: 18,000 lb (8.165 kg) or 45 passengers
38.3	11,65	63,400	28.758	108,250	49.102	—	333	536	—	306	492	2,832	4.558	27,900	8.500	4	Payload: 35,272 lb (16.000 kg) or 93 passengers
27.0	8,23	58,000	26.309	105,000	47.628	—	—	—	—	269	433	3,250	5.230	18,000	5.500	4	Payload: 29,000 lb (13.154 kg) or 69 passengers
12.3	3,74	10,200	4.267	14,600	6.623	—	165	266	—	140	225	733	1.180	20,000	6.100	1	Payload: 4,000 lb (1.814 kg) or 16 passengers
47.0	14,33	127,000	57.607	230,000	104.328	—	310	499	—	336	540	5,300	8.530	30,000	9.150	5	Payload: 78,000 lb (35.481 kg) or 150 passengers
25.11	7,90	26,400	11.975	38,000	17.237	—	247	397	—	200	322	2,000	3.220	22,970	7.000	2	26 passengers

kg	kilograms	mm	millimeters	Rc	reconnaissance	tf. turbo-fan
km	kilometers	mn.	mines	R.R.	Rolls-Royce	tj. turbo-jet
L.	Lycoming	MR	maritime reconnaissance	S	Sweden	tp. turbo-prop
LB	light bomber	MRo	multirole	SB	strategic bomber	Tr transport
lb	pounds	msl.	missiles	ST	STOL = short take-off and landing	USA United States of America
LT	light transport	P.&W.	Pratt & Whitney	SU	Soviet Union	V VTOL = vertical take-off and landing
m	meters	PT	primary trainer	Sv.	Svenska	W. Wright
MB	medium bomber	r.	rockets	T	trainer	We. Westinghouse
mg.	machine-gun	RA	Argentina	t.	torpedo	YU Yugoslavia
ml	miles	RAU	United Arabian Republic	tc.	turbo-compound	* not available data

MILITARY AIRCRAFT: TODAY (continued)

Page	Aircraft	Builder	Nation of origin	Type	Year	Engine	Wing spread		Length	
							ft	m	ft	m
167	Antonov An-24 "Coke"	State Industries	SU	Tr	1961	2/2500 hp Ivchenko AI-24 tp.	95.9	29,20	77.3	23,53
167	Antonov An-12 "Cub"	State Industries	SU	Tr	1960	4/4015 hp Ivchenko AI-20 tp.	124.8	38,00	121.3	36,95
167	Fairchild C-123 Provider	Fairchild Engine and Airplane Corp.	USA	Tr	1955	2/2500 hp P.&W. R-2800-99	110.0	33,53	76.3	23,24
167	Lockheed C-130B Hercules	Lockheed Aircraft Corp.	USA	Tr	1954	4/4050 hp A. T56-A-7A tp.	132.7	40,41	97.9	29,80
167	Fairchild C-119G Flying Boxcar	Fairchild Engine and Airplane Corp.	USA	Tr	1946	2/3500 hp P.&W. R-4360-20	109.3	33,30	86.6	26,36
167	Lockheed C-141A Starlifter	Lockheed Aircraft Corp.	USA	Tr	1963	4/21,000 lb (9.526 kg) P.&W. TF33-P-7 tf.	160.1	48,80	145.0	44,20
167	McDonnell Douglas C-133B Cargomaster	McDonnell Douglas Corp.	USA	Tr	1957	4/7500 hp P.&W. T34-P-9W tp.	179.8	54,76	157.6	48,00
168	Cavalier F-51D Mustang	Cavalier Aircraft Corp.	USA	CI	1967	1490 hp Packard-R.R. Merlin V-1650-7	37.0	11,28	32.3	9,83
168	Cavalier Turbo Mustang III	Cavalier Aircraft Corp.	USA	CI	1970	1740 hp R.R. Dart Mk.510 tp.	37.0	11,28	36.9	11,20
168	Fiat G91Y	Fiat S.p.A.	I	FB/Rc	1968	2/4,079 lb (1.850 kg) a.b. G.E. J85-GE-13A tj.	29.7	9,01	38.3	11,67
169	Lockheed SR-71A	Lockheed Aircraft Corp.	USA	Rc	1966	2/32,500 lb (14.744 kg) P.&W. JT11D-20B tf.	55.7	16,94	107.5	32,74
169	Lockheed YO-3A	Lockheed Aircraft Corp.	USA	Rc	1971	210 hp Continental (6 cl.)	*	*	*	*
169	North American RA-5C Vigilante	North American Rockwell Corp.	USA	Cb/MR	1958	2/17,859 lb (8.101 kg) a.b. G.E. J79-GE-10 tj.	53.0	16,15	75.10	23,11
169	Grumman E-2B Hawkeye	Grumman Corp.	USA	Cb/Rc	1961	2/4050 hp A. T56-A-8/8A tp.	80.7	24,56	56.4	17,17
170	Aermacchi M.B. 326GB	Aeronautica Macchi S.p.A.	I	BT	1967	3,410 lb (1.547 kg) R.R. Bristol Viper 20 Mk.540 tj.	35.7	10,85	34.11	10,65
170	Panavia 200 Panther	Panavia Aircraft GmbH	IP	MRo	1973	2/14,500 lb (6.577 kg) a.b. R.R.-MTU RB.199-34R tf.	44.4	13,50	54.2	16,50
171	Lockheed C-5A Galaxy	Lockheed Aircraft Corp.	USA	HT	1971	4/41,000 lb (18.598 kg) G.E. TF-39-GE-1 tf.	222.8	67,87	247.10	75,54
171	Antonov An-22 "Cock"	State Industries	SU	HT	1967	4/15000 hp Kuznetsov NK-12MA tp.	211.4	64,40	189.7	57,80

Abbreviations used in the table

A.	Allison	BT	basic trainer	F	France	HB	heavy bomber
a.b.	with afterburning	Cb	carrier-based	FB	fighter-bomber	hp	horse-power
AS	anti-submarine	CDN	Canada	Fr	fighter	HT	heavy transport
A.S.	Armstrong Siddeley	CI	counter-insurgency	ft	feet	I	Italy
AT	advanced trainer	cl.	cylinders	g.	gun	in	inches
B.	Bristol	CIS	close support	GA	ground attack	IND	India
b.	bombs	CS	Czechoslovakia	GB	Great Britain	IP	international project
BR	Brazil	D	Germany	G.E.	General Electric	J	Japan
Br	bomber	E	Spain	GP	general purpose	j.	jet
B.S.	Bristol Siddeley	Ex	experimental	h	hour	K.	Klimov

Height		Empty weight		Max take-off weight		Max speed			Cruising speed			Range		Ceiling		Crew	Armament or payload
ft	m	lb	kg	lb	kg	Mach	ml/h	km/h	Mach	ml/h	km/h	ml	km	ft	m		
27.3	8,32	28,108	12.750	42,330	19.201	—	317	510	—	295	475	1,280	2.060	29,855	9.100	4	Payload: 8,819 lb (4.000 kg) or 44 passengers
32.2	9,80	*	*	134,482	61.000	—	444	715	—	342	550	2,112	3.400	*	*	5	Payload: 32,000 lb (14.515 kg) or 100 passengers
34.1	3,39	31,380	14.234	60,000	27.216	—	253	407	—	186	299	1,470	2.365	29,000	8.840	2	61 passengers
38.3	11,66	69,300	31.434	135,000	61.236	—	376	605	—	368	592	3,830	6.165	30,000	9.150	5	Payload: 35,700 lb (16.194 kg) or 92 passengers
26.3	8,00	39,982	18.136	74,400	33.748	—	296	476	—	200	322	2,280	3.670	21,200	6.460	4	Payload: 30,000 lb (13.608 kg) or 62 passengers
39.3	11,97	136,118	61.743	318,000	144.245	—	570	917	—	558	898	4,200	6.760	40,000	12.200	4	Payload: 86,210 lb (39.105 kg) or 154 passengers
48.3	14,70	120,363	54.597	300,000	136.080	—	347	558	—	310	499	4,360	7.015	20,100	6.125	4	Payload: 90,000 lb (40.824 kg) or 200 passengers
13.4	4,06	*	*	13,700	6.214	—	430	692	—	—	—	800	1.290	*	*	2	6 mg. (0.50 in), b., r., msl. (2,500 lb; 1.134 kg)
14.11	4,54	7,396	3.355	14,000	6.350	—	541	871	—	—	—	2,300	3.700	*	*	1-2	6 mg. (0.50 in), b., r., msl. (3,000 lb; 1.361 kg)
14.6	4,43	8,598	3.900	19,180	8.700	0,95	—	—	—	—	—	2,175	3.500	41,000	12.500	1	2 g. (30 mm), msl., r., b. (4,000 lb; 1.814 kg)
18.6	5,64	*	*	77,160	35.000	3	—	—	—	—	—	*	*	98,425	30.000	2	
*	*	*	*	*	*	*	*	*	*	*	*	*	*	*	*	2	—
19.5	5,92	52,470	23.800	80,000	36.288	2	—	—	0.83	—	—	2,995	4.820	63,975	19.500	2	t., msl., r., b.
18.4	5,60	36,063	16.358	49,638	22.516	—	368	592	—	315	507	1,905	3.066	31,700	9.660	5	
12.2	3,72	5,920	2.685	11,500	5.216	—	539	867	—	495	797	403	649	47,000	14.325	2	g., msl., r., b.
*	*	*	*	35,274	16.000	2.2	—	—	*	*	*	*	*	*	*	1-2	*
65.1	19,84	325,244	147.531	764,000	346.550	—	571	919	—	537	864	6,500	10.460	34,000	10.360	5	Payload: 265,000 lb (120.204 kg) or 345 passengers
41.1	12,53	251,327	114.000	551,155	250.000	—	460	740	—	—	—	6,800	10.950	33,000	10.060	6	Payload: 176,370 lb (80.000 kg)

g	kilograms	mm	millimeters	Rc	reconnaissance	tf.	turbo-fan
m	kilometers	mn.	mines	R.R.	Rolls-Royce	tj.	turbo-jet
	Lycoming	MR	maritime reconnaissance	S	Sweden	tp.	turbo-prop
LB	light bomber	MRo	multirole	SB	strategic bomber	Tr	transport
b	pounds	msl.	missiles	ST	STOL = short take-off and landing	USA	United States of America
T	light transport	P.&W.	Pratt & Whitney	SU	Soviet Union	V	VTOL = vertical take-off and landing
	meters	PT	primary trainer	Sv.	Svenska	W.	Wright
MB	medium bomber	r.	rockets	T	trainer	We.	Westinghouse
ng.	machine-gun	RA	Argentina	t.	torpedo	YU	Yugoslavia
nl	miles	RAU	United Arabian Republic	tc.	turbo-compound	*	not available data

CIVIL AIRCRAFT: TODAY

Page	Aircraft	Builder	Nation of origin	Type	Year	Engine	Wing spread ft	Wing spread m	Length ft	Length m
176	Concorde	British Air Corp.-Aéro-spatiale	GB-F	Ss/Ps	1969	4/38,400 lb (17.418 kg) a.b. R.R.-SNECMA Olympus 593 tj.	84.0	25,60	203.9	62,10
177	Boeing 2707-300 SST	Boeing Co.	USA	Ss/Ps	?	4/68,600 lb (31.117 kg) G.E. GE4/J5P tj.	141.8	43,18	286.8	87,37
177	Tupolev Tu-144 "Charger"	State Industries	SU	Ss/Ps	1968	4/28,660 lb (13.000 kg) Kuznetsov NK-144	88.7	27,00	196.10	60,00
178	Boeing 707-320C	Boeing Co.	USA	Ps	1963	4/18,000 lb (8.165 kg) P.&W. JT3D-3B tf.	145.9	44,43	152.11	46,61
178	Boeing 707-120B	Boeing Co.	USA	Ps	1960	4/18,000 lb (8.165 kg) P.&W. JT3D-3 tf.	130.10	39,87	144.6	44,04
178	Boeing 720B	Boeing Co.	USA	Ps	1960	4/17,000 lb (7.711 kg) P.&W. JT3D-1 tf.	130.10	39,87	136.2	41,50
178	BAC VC10	British Aircraft Corp.	GB	Ps	1963	4/21,000 lb (9.526 kg) R.R. Conway RCo.42 Mk.540 tj.	146.2	44,55	158.8	48,36
178	BAC Super VC10	British Aircraft Corp.	GB	Ps	1965	4/21,800 lb (9.888 kg) R.R. Conway RCo.43 tf.	146.2	44,55	171.8	52,32
179	Douglas DC-8 Super 61	McDonnell Douglas Corp.	USA	Ps	1967	4/18,000 lb (8.165 kg) P.&W. JT3D-3B tf.	142.5	43,41	187.5	57,13
179	Douglas DC-8 Super 63	McDonnell Douglas Corp.	USA	Ps	1967	4/19,000 lb (8.618 kg) P.&W. JT3D-7 tf.	148.5	45,24	187.5	57,13
179	Douglas DC-8 Super 62	McDonnell Douglas Corp.	USA	Ps	1967	4/18,000 lb (8.165 kg) P.&W. JT3D-3B tf.	148.5	45,24	157.5	47,98
179	Douglas DC-8 Sr 40	McDonnell Douglas Corp.	USA	Ps	1959	4/17,800 lb (8.074 kg) R.R. Conway RCo.12 tj. (1)	142.5	43,41	150.6	45,87
179	Ilyushin Il-62 "Classic"	State Industries	SU	Ps	1967	4/23,149 lb (10.500 kg) Kuznetsov NK-8-4 tf.	142.1	43,30	174.3	53,12
180	Boeing 747B	Boeing Co.	USA	Ps	1970	4/43,500 lb (19.732 kg) P.&W. JT9D-3 tf.	195.8	59,64	231.4	70,51
180	Lockheed L-1011 Tristar	Lockheed Aircraft Corp.	USA	Ps	1971	3/40,600 lb (18.416 kg) R.R. RB.211-22-02 tf.	155.4	47,34	177.8	54,15
181	Airbus A-300B	Airbus Industries	F-D	Ps	1973	2/51,000 lb (23.134 kg) R.R. RB.211-52 tf.	147.1	44,84	167.2	50,96
181	Douglas DC-10 Sr 10	McDonnell Douglas Corp.	USA	Ps	1971	3/40,000 lb (18.144 kg) G.E. CF6-6 tf.	155.4	47,34	181.5	55,30
182	Boeing 727-100	Boeing Co.	USA	Ps	1963	3/14,000 lb (6.350 kg) P.&W. JT8D-7 tf.	108.0	32,92	133.2	40,59
182	Boeing 727-200	Boeing Co.	USA	Ps	1967	3/14,000 lb (6.350 kg) P.&W. JT8D-7 tf.	108.0	32,92	153.2	46,68
183	Tupolev Tu-154 "Careless"	State Industries	SU	Ps	1971	3/20,944 lb (9.500 kg) Kuznetsov NK-8-2 tf.	123.2	37,55	157.2	47,90
183	Hawker Siddeley Trident 1	Hawker Siddeley Group	GB	Ps	1964	3/9,850 lb (4.468 kg) R.R. RB.163/1 Mk.505/5 Spey tf.	89.10	27,38	114.9	34,98
183	Hawker Siddeley Trident Three	Hawker Siddeley Group	GB	Ps	1970	3/11,930 lb (5.411 kg) R.R. RB.162 Spey tf.	98.0	29,87	131.2	39,98
184	Douglas DC-9 Sr 30	McDonnell Douglas Corp.	USA	Ps	1966	2/14,000 lb (6.350 kg) P.&W. JT8D-7 tf.	93.5	28,48	119.3	36,35
184	Douglas DC-9 Sr 40	McDonnell Douglas Corp.	USA	Ps	1968	2/14,500 lb (6.577 kg) P.&W. JT8D-9 tf.	93.5	28,48	125.7	38,28
184	Douglas DC-9 Sr 10	McDonnell Douglas Corp.	USA	Ps	1965	2/12,250 lb (5.557 kg) P.&W. JT8D-5 tf.	89.5	27,26	104.5	31,82
184	Aérospatiale SE 210 Caravelle (Sr 12)	Aérospatiale	F	Ps	1970	2/14,500 lb (6.577 kg) P.&W. JT8D-7 tf.	112.6	34,30	118.11	36,24
184	BAC One-Eleven Sr 200	British Aircraft Corp.	GB	Ps	1965	2/10,330 lb (4.686 kg) R.R. Mk.506 Spey 25 tf.	88.6	26,97	93.6	28,50
184	BAC One-Eleven Sr 500	British Aircraft Corp.	GB	Ps	1968	2/12,500 lb (5.670 kg) R.R. Mk.521 DW Spey tf.	93.6	28,50	107.4	32,71
184	BAC Three-Eleven	British Aircraft Corp.	GB	Ps	?	2/40,600 lb (18.416 kg) R.R. RB.211-22-02 tf.	*	*	*	*
185	Tupolev Tu-134A "Crusty"	State Industries	SU	Ps	1967	2/14,991 lb (6.800 kg) Soloviev D-30 tf.	95.2	29,00	121.9	37,10
185	Tupolev Tu-124V "Cookpot"	State Industries	SU	Ps	1961	2/11,905 lb (5.400 kg) Soloviev D-20P tf.	83.10	25,55	100.4	30,58
185	Dassault Mercure	Avions Marcel Dassault	F	Ps	1973	2/15,498 lb (7.030 kg) P.&W. JT8D-15 tf.	100.3	30,55	111.7	34,00
185	Boeing 737-200	Boeing Co.	USA	Ps	1967	2/14,500 lb (6.577 kg) P.&W. JT8D-9 tf.	93.0	28,35	100.0	30,48
185	Boeing 737-100	Boeing Co.	USA	Ps	1967	2/14,000 lb (6.350 kg) P.&W. JT8D-7 tf.	93.0	28,35	94.0	28,65
186	Short SC.7 Skyvan Sr 3	Short Bros & Harland Ltd	GB	LT/Ps	1967	2/715 hp Garret AiResearch TPE 331-201 tp.	64.11	19,79	40.1	12,22
186	IAI-101 Arava	Israel Aircraft Industries Ltd	IL	ST/LT/Ps	1970	2/715 hp P.&W. PT6A-27 tp.	68.6	20,88	42.7	12,99
186	L-410 Turbolet	Let Národní Podnik	CS	ST/LT/Ps	1971	2/730 hp M-601 tp.	56.1	17,10	44.8	13,61
186	Handley Page H.P. 137 Jetstream	Handley Page Ltd	GB	LT/Ps	1966	2/850 hp Turboméca Astazou XIV tp.	52.0	15,85	47.1	14,37
186	Beriev Be-30 "Cuff"	State Industries	SU	LT/Ps	1970	2/950 hp Glushenkov TVD-10 tp.	55.9	17,00	51.6	15,70
186	Potez 841	Potez Aéronautique	F	LT/Ps	1964	4/588 hp P.&W. PT6A-6 tp.	64.4	19,60	52.1	15,89
186	Swearingen SA-226TC Metro	Swearingen Aircraft	USA	LT/Ps	1971	2/840 hp AiResearch TPE 331-3U-303 tp.	46.3	14,10	59.4	18,08
186	Aérospatiale N 262	Aérospatiale	F	LT/Ps	1967	2/1130 hp Turboméca Bastan VIIA tp.	71.10	21,90	63.3	19,28
186	De Havilland DHC-7	De Havilland Aircraft of Canada Ltd	CDN	ST/Ps	1973	4/1035 hp P.&W. PT6A-50 tp.	93.0	28,35	80.4	24,48
187	Yakovlev Yak-40 "Codling"	State Industries	SU	Ps	1967	2/3307 lb (1.500 kg) Ivchenko AI-25 tf.	82.0	25,00	66.10	20,36
187	VFW-Fokker VFW 614	VFW-Fokker GmbH	D	Ps	1973	2/7,518 lb (3.410 kg) R.R.-SNECMA M45H tf.	70.6	21,50	67.7	20,60
187	Fokker F-28 Mk 1000 Fellowship	Fokker-VFW NV	NL	Ps	1969	2/9,850 lb (4.468 kg) R.R. RB.183-2 Spey Mk.515-15 tf.	77.4	23,58	89.11	27,40
187	Hawker Siddeley 748 Sr 1	Hawker Siddeley Group	GB	Ps	1962	2/1600 hp R.R. Dart R.Da.6 Mk.514 tp.	98.6	30,02	67.0	20,42
187	Handley Page H.P.R. 7 Herald	Handley Page Ltd	GB	Ps	1960	2/1910 hp R.R. Dart Mk. 527 tp.	94.9	28,88	75.6	23,01
187	Ilyushin Il-18E "Coot"	State Industries	SU	Ps	1959	4/4250 hp Ivchenko AI-20M tp.	122.8	37,40	117.9	35,90
187	Convair 990 Coronado	Convair Division of General Dynamics	USA	Ps	1960	4/16,100 lb (7.303 kg) G.E. CJ-805-23B tf.	120.0	36,58	139.5	42,50

Abbreviations used in the table

A.	Allison	ft	feet	J	Japan	ml	miles
a.b.	with afterburning	GB	Great Britain	kg	kilograms	NL	Holland
CDN	Canada	G.E.	General Electric	km.	kilometers	P.&W.	Pratt & Whitney
CH	Switzerland	GP	general purpose	L.	Lycoming	Ps	passengers
cl.	cylinders	h	hour	LA	light aviation	R.R.	Rolls-Royce
CS	Czechoslovakia	hp	horse-power	lb	pounds	S	Sweden
D	Germany	I	Italy	LT	light transport	Ss	supersonic
F	France	IL	Israel	m	meters	ST	STOL = short take-off and landing

Height		Empty weight		Max take-off weight		Payload		Max speedx			Cruising speed			Range		Ceiling		Crew	Passengers
ft	m	lb	kg	lb	kg	lb	kg	Mach	ml/h	km/h	Mach	ml/h	km/h	ml	km	ft	m		
49.10	12,15	169,000	76.658	385,000	174.636	28,000	12.701	2.2	1,450	2.335	2.05	—	—	4,020	6.470	65,000	19.800	4	144
50.1	15,27	*	*	635,000	288.036	*	*	2.7	—	—	*	*	*	6,000	9.656	70,000	21.335	6	250-321
37.0	11,27	*	*	330,693	150.000	*	*	2.35	1,550	2.495	*	*	*	4,040	6.500	65,000	19.800	6-8	121
42.5	12,93	138,323	62.743	333,600	151.321	83,996	38.101	—	600	965	—	550	885	3,925 *	6.317 *	38,500	11.735	6	215
42.0	12,80	123,151	55.861	257,000	116.575	46,849	21.251	—	618	995	—	557	896	4,235 *	6.815 *	42,000	12.800	6	181
42.0	12,80	109,580	49.705	229,000	103.874	34,264	15.542	—	622	1.001	—	541	871	4,200 *	6.760 *	40,000	12.200	6	140
39.6	12,04	146,979	66.670	314,000	142.430	38,532	17.478	—	568	914	—	550	885	5,040 *	8.110 *	42,000	12.800	5	135
39.6	12,04	158,594	71.938	335,000	151.956	50,406	22.864	—	581	935	—	550	885	4,720 *	7.600 *	42,000	12.800	5	174
42.5	12,93	148,897	67.540	325,000	147.420	66,665	30.239	—	—	—	—	600	965	3,750 *	6.035 *	30,000	9.150	5	259
42.5	12,93	153,749	69.741	350,000	158.760	67,735	30.725	—	—	—	—	600	965	4,500 *	7.240 *	30,000	9.150	5	259
42.5	12,93	141,903	64.367	335,000	151.956	47,335	21.471	—	—	—	—	600	965	6,000 *	9.655 *	30,000	9.150	5	189
42.4	12,90	124,369	56.414	310,000	140.616	36,500	16.556	—	—	—	—	593	954	5,430	8.740	30,000	9.150	5	144-173
40.6	12,35	149,473	67.800	347,228	157.500	50,706	23.000	—	—	—	—	560	901	4,160 *	6.700 *	39,370	12.000	5	186
63.5	19,33	361,216	163.848	775,000	351.540	165,284	74.973	—	680	980	—	—	—	6,620 *	10.655 *	45,000	13.715	10	374-490
55.4	16,86	225,491	102.283	409,000	185.522	87,811	39.831	—	583	938	—	—	—	3,287 *	5.290 *	35,000	10.670	13	345
54.4	16,56	181,824	82.474	291,010	132.000	58,478	26.525	—	582	937	—	—	—	1,404	2.260	40,000	12.200	4	261
58.1	17,71	230,323	104.475	410,000	185.976	80,435	36.485	—	—	—	—	600	965	2,500	4.025	39,370	12.000	6	270-345
34.0	10,36	89,000	40.370	142,000	64.411	22,000	9.979	—	630	1.014	—	570	917	1,900 *	3.058 *	37,400	11.400	3	131
34.0	10,36	98,000	44.453	172,000	78.019	40,000	18.144	—	630	1.014	—	568	914	1,290 *	2.076 *	35,200	10.730	3	163
37.5	11,40	95,901	43.500	198,416	90.000	35,274	16.000	—	605	974	—	528	850	1,565 *	2.520 *	39,370	12.000	5	158
27.0	8,23	67,732	30.723	107,000	48.535	22,000	9.979	—	606	975	—	585	941	1,170	1.880	32,000	9.750	3	103
28.3	8,61	83,104	37.696	150,000	68.040	32,396	14.695	—	601	967	—	533	858	1,094 *	1.761 *	33,000	10.000	3	179
27.6	8,38	52,935	24.011	98,000	44.453	26,156	11.864	—	—	—	—	565	909	1,484	2.388	30,000	9.150	3	115
28.0	8,53	55,690	25.261	114,000	51.710	34,195	15.511	—	—	—	—	561	903	1,192	1.920	30,000	9.150	3	125
27.6	8,38	45,300	20.548	77,700	35.245	18,050	8.187	—	—	—	—	561	903	995	1.601	25,000	7.620	3	90
29.7	9,01	70,107	31.800	123,459	56.000	29,101	13.200	—	—	—	—	503	810	1,000 *	1.610 *	35,000	10.670	3	128
24.6	7,47	46,405	21.049	79,000	35.834	17,595	7.981	—	548	882	—	507	816	875 *	1.410 *	35,000	10.670	2	89
24.6	7,47	54,807	24.860	99,650	45.201	26,193	11.881	—	548	882	—	507	816	1,140 *	1.835 *	35,000	10.670	2	119
*	*	*	*	270,000	122.472	*	*	—	580	933	—	—	—	2,000	3.220	*	*	4	220
29.7	9,02	63,934	29.000	103,617	47.000	18,001	8.165	—	540	869	—	466	750	1,490 *	2.400 *	39,370	12.000	2	80
26.6	8,08	49,604	22.500	83,776	38.000	13,228	6.000	—	540	869	—	497	800	760 *	1.220 *	33,000	10.000	2	56
37.3	11,36	56,383	25.575	114,640	52.000	36,509	16.560	—	—	—	—	576	927	446 *	718 *	22,000	6.700	2	155
37.0	11,28	58,607	26.584	109,000	49.442	29,393	13.333	—	586	943	—	568	914	2,135 *	3.436 *	30,000	9.150	2	125
37.0	11,28	56,893	25.807	100,500	45.587	28,107	12.749	—	—	—	—	570	917	1,840 *	2.960 *	30,000	9.150	2	115
15.1	4,60	8,100	3.674	12,500	5.670	4,600	2.087	—	201	323	—	173	278	665	1.070	22,500	6.860	1	19
17.1	5,20	7,789	3.533	12,500	5.670	4,410	2.000	—	217	349	—	209	336	867	1.395	28,550	8.700	1	20
18.0	5,50	6,180	2.803	11,245	5.100	4,085	1.853	—	229	369	—	205	330	707	1.138	25,500	7.770	1	17
17.5	5,31	8,450	3.833	12,500	5.670	3,330	1.510	—	306	492	—	250	402	1,900	3.058	30,000	9.150	3	18
17.11	5,46	*	*	12,919	5.860	3,307	1.500	—	298	480	—	285	459	372 *	599 *	*	*	2	14
17.9	5,40	12,015	5.450	20,944	9.500	5,512	2.500	—	311	500	—	282	454	1,060 *	1.706 *	20,000	6.100	2	24
16.8	5,08	7,000	3.175	12,500	5.670	*	*	—	—	—	—	310	499	345 *	555 *	25,000	7.620	2	20
20.4	6,21	15,286	6.934	23,369	10.600	6,834	3.100	—	260	418	—	247	397	650 *	1.046 *	26,250	8.000	2	29
26.3	8,00	*	*	38,500	17.464	9,600	4.355	—	—	—	—	276	444	530 *	853 *	27,000	8.230	3	48
21.4	6,50	20,602	9.345	30,203	13.700	6,151	2.790	—	373	600	—	342	550	621 *	1.000 *	—	—	2	33
25.9	7,84	26,896	12.200	41,006	18.600	8,598	3.900	—	457	735	—	449	723	391 *	629 *	24,925	7.600	3	44
27.9	8,47	34,502	15.650	63,008	28.580	14,506	6.580	—	528	850	—	427	687	1,266 *	2.037 *	30,000	9.150	2	65
24.10	7,57	23,467	10.645	38,000	17.237	10,133	4.596	—	294	473	—	317	510	1,210 *	1.950 *	24,500	7.470	3	52
24.1	7,34	25,320	11.485	43,000	19.505	11,680	5.298	—	—	—	—	272	438	1,095 *	1.762 *	26,700	8.140	2	56
33.4	10,17	76,346	34.630	134,923	61.200	29,762	13.500	—	419	674	—	388	624	1,990 *	3.200 *	33,000	10.000	5	122
39.6	12,04	120,560	54.686	244,200	110.769	26,440	11.993	—	—	—	—	625	1.006	3,920	6.308	41,000	12.500	5	121

SU   Soviet Union
turbo-fan
turbo-jet
turbo-prop
transport
USA United States of America
max useful cargo
not available data

CIVIL AIRCRAFT: TODAY (continued)

Page	Aircraft	Builder	Nation of origin	Type	Year	Engine	Wing spread ft	Wing spread m	Length ft	Length m
187	Lockheed 1329 Jetstar	Lockheed Aircraft Corp.	USA	LT/Ps	1961	4/3,300 lb (1.497 kg) P.&W. JT12A-8 tj.	54.5	16,59	60.5	18,42
187	MBB HFB 320 Hansa	Messerschmitt-Bölkow-Blohm GmbH	D	LT/Ps	1966	2/3,100 lb (1.406 kg) G.E. CJ610-9 tj.	47.6	14,49	54.6	16,61
187	IAI Commodore Jet 1123	Israel Aircraft Industries Ltd	IL	LT/Ps	1971	2/3,100 lb (1.406 kg) G.E. CJ610-9 tj.	43.3	13,19	52.3	15,93
187	Learjet 24D	Gates Learjet Corp.	USA	LT/Ps	1966	2/2,950 lb (1.338 kg) G.E. CJ610-6 tj.	35.7	10,85	43.3	13,19
187	Cessna 500 Citation	Cessna Aircraft Co.	USA	LT/Ps	1971	2/2,200 lb (998 kg) P.&W. JT15D-1 tf.	43.8	13,32	44.1	13,44
187	Aérospatiale SN 600 Corvette	Aérospatiale	F	LT/Ps	1971	2/2,200 lb (998 kg) P.&W. JT15D-1 tf.	42.0	12,80	42.0	12,80
188	Fokker F.27 Friendship	Fokker-VFW NV	NL	Ps	1958	2/2050 hp R.R. Dart 532-7 tp.	95.2	29,00	77.3	23,56
188	Namc YS-11 Sr 200	Nihon Kokuki Seizo Kabushiki Kaisha	J	Ps	1964	2/3060 hp R.R. Dart Mk.542-10K tp.	105.0	32,00	86.3	26,30
189	Aero Spacelines Guppy-201	Aero Spacelines Inc.	USA	Tr	1971	4/4680 hp A. 501-D22C tp.	156.8	47,75	143.10	43,84
189	Canadair CL-215	Canadair Ltd	CDN	GP	1969	2/2100 hp P.&W. R-2800-83AM2AH (18 cl.)	93.10	28,60	65.0	19,81
190	Moravan Zlin Z526F	Moravan Národní Podnik	CS	LA	1947	180 hp Avia M 137 (6 cl.)	34.9	10,60	26.3	8,00
190	Robin DR 221 Dauphin	Avions Pierre Robin	F	LA	1967	115 hp L. O-235-C2A (4 cl.)	28.8	8,72	22.11	7,00
190	Socata MS 893 Rallye Commodore	Soc. de Constr. d'Avions de Tour. et d'Affaires	F	LA	1961	180 hp L. O-360-A2A (6 cl.)	31.6	9,60	23.5	7,13
190	Socata ST 60 Rallye 7-300	Soc. de Constr. d'Avions de Tour. et d'Affaires	F	LA	1970	300 hp L. IO-540-K (6 cl.)	36.1	11,00	28.9	8,75
190	Dornier Do 28 D-1 Skyservant	Dornier A.G.	D	ST/LT/Ps	1967	2/380 hp L. IGSO-540 (6 cl.)	50.10	15,50	38.1	11,60
190	SAN Jodel D.140E Mousquetaire IV	Société Aéronautique Normande	F	LA	1958	180 hp L. O-360-A2A (4 cl.)	33.8	10,27	25.8	7,82
190	Piaggio P. 166C	Ind. Aeronaut. e Mecc. R. Piaggio S.p.A.	I	LT/Ps	1958	2/380 hp L. IGSO-540-AIC (6 cl.)	47.0	14,33	39.0	11,90
190	Pilatus PC-6 Porter	Pilatus Flugzeugwerke A.G.	CH	ST/GP	1960	500 hp L. TIO-720-C1A (6 cl.)	49.8	15,13	33.5	10,20
190	Britten-Norman BN-2A Islander	Britten-Norman Sales Ltd	GB	LT/Ps	1967	2/260 hp L. O-540-E4C5 (6 cl.)	49.0	14,95	35.8	10,87
190	Beechcraft B55 Baron	Beech Aircraft Corp.	USA	LA	1960	2/260 hp Continental IO-470-L (6 cl.)	37.10	11,53	27.0	8,23
190	Beechcraft A60 Duke	Beech Aircraft Corp.	USA	LA	1968	2/380 hp L. TIO-541-E1A4 (6 cl.)	39.3	11,97	33.10	10,31
190	Beechcraft B80 Queen Air	Beech Aircraft Corp.	USA	LT/Ps	1962	2/380 hp L. IGSO-540-A1D (6 cl.)	50.4	15,34	35.6	10,82
190	Beechcraft B90 King Air	Beech Aircraft Corp.	USA	LT/Ps	1966	2/550 hp P.&W. PT6A-20 tp.	50.3	15,32	36.6	11,12
190	Beechcraft 99A Airliner	Beech Aircraft Corp.	USA	LT/Ps	1968	2/680 hp P.&W. PT6A-27 tp.	45.11	14,00	44.6	13,57
190	Cessna T210 Turbo-System Centurion	Cessna Aircraft Co.	USA	LA	1966	285 hp Continental TSIO-520-C tp.	36.9	11,20	28.3	8,61
190	Cessna 207 Skywagon	Cessna Aircraft Co.	USA	LT/Ps	1970	300 hp Continental IO-520-F (6 cl.)	35.10	10,92	31.9	9,68
190	Cessna 414	Cessna Aircraft Co.	USA	LT/Ps	1970	2/310 hp Continental TSIO-520-J (6 cl.)	39.10	12,15	33.9	10,29
190	Aero Commander Hawk Commander	North American Rockwell Corp.	USA	LT/Ps	1966	2/605 hp AiResearch TPE331-43BL tp.	44.1	13,44	43.0	13,11
190	Piper PA-23-250 Aztec D	Piper Aircraft Corp.	USA	LT/Ps	1961	2/250 hp L. IO-540-C4B5 (6 cl.)	37.2	11,33	30.3	9,22
190	Piper PA-32-260 Cherokee Six C	Piper Aircraft Corp.	USA	LT/Ps	1965	260 hp L. O-540-E (6 cl.)	32.9	9,98	27.9	8,45
190	Piper PA-31-300 Navajo	Piper Aircraft Corp.	USA	LT/Ps	1967	2/300 hp L. IO-540-M (6 cl.)	40.8	12,39	32.7	9,92
191	Wassmer WA-51 Pacific	Wassmer-Aviation S.A.	F	LA	1971	150 hp L. O-320-E2A (4 cl.)	30.10	9,40	23.5	7,15
191	Ambrosini NF 15	Soc. Aeronautica Ital. Ing. A. Ambrosini & C.	I	LA	1969	300 hp Continental IO-520-F (6 cl.)	32.6	9,90	24.7	7,50
191	SIAI-Marchetti S.208	SIAI-Marchetti S.p.A.	I	LA	1968	260 hp L. O-540-E4A5 (6 cl.)	35.7	10,86	26.3	8,00
191	SIAI-Marchetti S.210	SIAI-Marchetti S.p.A.	I	LA	1971	2/200 hp L. TIO-360-A tp.	38.2	11,63	28.4	8,63
191	MFI-15A	AB Malmö Flygindustri	S	LA	1970	160 hp L. IO-320-B20 (4 cl.)	28.7	8,70	22.1	6,75
191	Mooney Mark 22	Mooney Aircraft Corp.	USA	LA	1967	310 hp L. TIO-541-A1A (6 cl.)	35.0	10,67	27.0	8,23
191	Beechcraft Bonanza A36	Beech Aircraft Corp.	USA	LT/Ps	1968	285 hp Continental IO-520-B (6 cl.)	32.10	10,00	26.4	8,02
191	Beechcraft Musketeer Super R	Beech Aircraft Corp.	USA	LA	1962	200 hp L. IO-360-A2B	32.9	9,98	25.0	7,62
191	Cessna A-150K Aerobat	Cessna Aircraft Co.	USA	LA	1958	100 hp Continental O-200-A (4 cl.)	33.2	10,11	23.9	7,24
191	Cessna T310Q Skynight	Cessna Aircraft Co.	USA	LT/Ps	1957	2/285 hp Continental TSIO-520-B tp.	36.11	11,25	29.6	8,99
191	Aero Commander Lark Commander	North American Rockwell Corp.	USA	LA	1968	180 hp L. O-360-A2F (4 cl.)	35.0	10,67	27.2	8,28
191	Piper PA-18 Super Cub 150	Piper Aircraft Corp.	USA	LA	1951	150 hp L. O-320 (4 cl.)	35.2	10,72	22.7	6,89
191	Piper Turbo Comanche C	Piper Aircraft Corp.	USA	LA	1970	260 hp L. IO-540 (6 cl.)	36.0	10,97	25.0	7,62
191	Piper PA-39 Twin Comanche C/R	Piper Aircraft Corp.	USA	LA	1970	2/160 hp L. IO-320-C1A tp.	36.0	10,97	25.2	7,67
192	Dassault Mystère 20/Falcon 20	Avions Marcel Dassault	F	LT/Ps	1964	2/4,250 lb (1.928 kg) G.E. CF700-2D tf.	53.6	16,30	56.3	17,15
192	Dassault Falcon 10	Avions Marcel Dassault	F	LT/Ps	1970	2/3,230 lb (1.465 kg) AiResearch TFE-731-2 tf.	43.0	13,11	44.11	13,69
192	Hawker Siddeley 125	Hawker Siddeley Group (De Havilland)	GB	LT/Ps	1964	2/3,360 lb (1.524 kg) R.R. Bristol Viper 522 tj.	47.0	14,33	47.5	14,46
193	North American Rockwell Sabreliner Sr 60	North American Rockwell Corp.	USA	LT/Ps	1961	2/3,300 lb (1.497 kg) P.&W. JT12A-8 tj.	44.5	13,54	48.4	14,73
193	Grumman Gulfstream II	Grumman Corp.	USA	LT/Ps	1966	2/11,400 lb (5.171 kg) R.R. Spey Mk.511-8 tf.	68.10	20,98	79.11	24,36

Abbreviations used in the table

A.	Allison	ft	feet	J	Japan	ml	miles
a.b.	with afterburning	GB	Great Britain	kg	kilograms	NL	Holland
CDN	Canada	G.E.	General Electric	km	kilometers	P.&W.	Pratt & Whitney
CH	Switzerland	GP	general purpose	L.	Lycoming	Ps	passengers
cl.	cylinders	h	hour	LA	light aviation	R.R.	Rolls-Royce
CS	Czechoslovakia	hp	horse-power	lb	pounds	S	Sweden
D	Germany	I	Italy	LT	light transport	Ss	supersonic
F	France	IL	Israel	m	meters	ST	STOL = short take-off and landin

Height		Empty weight		Max take-off weight		Payload		Max speed			Cruising speed			Range		Ceiling		Crew	Passengers
ft	m	lb	kg	lb	kg	lb	kg	Mach	ml/h	km/h	Mach	ml/h	km/h	ml	km	ft	m		
20.5	6,23	22,074	10.013	42,000	19.051	2,926	1.327	—	570	917	—	507	816	2,120	3.410	37,400	11.400	2	10
16.2	4,93	11,960	5.425	20,283	9.200	3,913	1.775	—	513	826	—	420	675	1,472	2.370	40,000	12.200	2	12
15.9	4,81	11,070	5.021	20,500	9.298	—	—	—	—	—	—	541	871	1,450	2.335	45,000	13.715	2	10
12.7	3,84	6,851	3.108	13,500	6.124	2,762	1.253	—	545	877	—	481	774	1,960	3.154	45,000	13.715	2	6
14.3	4,35	5,408	2.453	10,350	4.695	*	*	—	—	—	—	400	644	1,320	2.124	38,400	11.704	2	5
14.4	4,37	7,297	3.310	12,500	5.670	2,493	1.131	—	466	750	—	391	630	760 *	1.220 *	39,900	12.160	2	13
27.11	8,50	24,868	11.280	43,497	19.730	12,628	5.728	—	—	—	—	295	475	1,227	1.972	28,500	8.690	2	48
29.5	8,98	33,942	15.396	54,013	24.500	14,559	6.604	—	291	468	—	281	452	680	1.095	22,900	6.980	2	60
45.10	13,97	101,075	45.848	170,000	77.112	52,925	24.007	—	—	—	—	280	451	*	*	*	*	3	—
29.5	8,97	27,000	12.247	36,000	16.330	6,850	3.107	—	—	—	—	—	—	390 *	628*	—	—	2	19
6.9	2,06	1,466	665	2,150	975	—	—	—	154	248	—	133	214	295	475	19,000	5.800	2	—
6.1	1,85	1,047	475	1,852	840	—	—	—	146	235	—	127	205	565	910	12,800	3.900	1	3
9.2	2,80	1,224	555	2,315	1.050	—	—	—	—	—	—	140	225	621	1.000	12,800	3.900	1	4
9.2	2,80	1,962	890	3,946	1.790	—	—	—	186	300	—	174	280	930	1.500	16,400	5.000	1	6
12.10	3,90	4,775	2.166	8,047	3.650	—	—	—	199	320	—	143	230	1,125	1.810	24,300	7.405	2	12
6.9	2,05	1,367	620	2,646	1.200	—	—	—	158	255	—	149	240	870	1.400	16,400	5.000	1	4
16.5	5,00	5,820	2.640	8,708	3.950	2,205	1.000	—	245	394	—	176	283	726	1.170	27,000	8.230	2	10
10.6	3,20	2,840	1.288	5,512	2.500	—	—	—	149	240	—	124	200	838	1.350	32,000	9.750	1	6
13.8	4,16	3,550	1.610	6,300	2.858	—	—	—	170	274	—	153	246	425 *	684 *	14,600	4.450	1	10
9.7	2,92	3,073	1.394	5,100	2.313	—	—	—	236	380	—	195	314	1,225	1.971	19,685	6.000	1	4
12.4	3,76	4,175	1.894	6,775	3.073	—	—	—	286	460	—	252	406	1,027	1.653	30,800	9.387	1	5
14.2	4,33	5,060	2.295	8,800	3.992	—	—	—	248	399	—	183	294	1,560	2.510	26,800	8.170	1	5-10
14.8	4,47	5,685	2.579	9,650	4.377	—	—	—	270	435	—	256	412	1,466	2.360	27,200	8.290	2	8
14.4	4,37	5,780	2.622	10,400	4.717	—	—	—	254	409	—	252	406	375 *	603*	8,100	2.470	2	15
9.8	2,94	2,180	989	3,800	1.724	—	—	—	219	352	—	175	282	1,065	1.715	28,500	8.690	1	5
9.7	2,92	1,880	853	3,800	1.724	—	—	—	168	270	—	158	254	585	941	13,300	4.054	1	6
11.10	3,60	4,039	1.832	6,350	2.880	—	—	—	272	438	—	252	406	1,389	2.235	30,100	9.175	1	6
14.6	4,42	5,647	2.561	9,400	4.264	—	—	—	290	467	—	278	447	1,294	2.080	25,600	7.800	1	7
10.4	3,15	3,006	1.364	5,200	2.359	—	—	—	216	348	—	204	328	1,210	1.950	21,100	6.430	1	5
7.11	2,41	1,688	766	3,400	1.542	—	—	—	168	270	—	160	257	570	917	13,000	3.960	1	5
13.0	3,96	3,744	1.698	6,200	2.812	—	—	—	213	343	—	197	317	1,275	2.050	16,600	5.060	1	8
—	—	1,320	600	2,249	1.020	—	—	—	—	—	—	161	260	621	1.000	—	—	1	3
9.2	2,80	1,949	884	2,998	1.360	—	—	—	202	325	—	194	312	1,229	1.978	—	—	1	4
9.6	2,89	1,720	780	2,976	1.350	—	—	—	—	—	—	187	300	746	1.200	19,685	6.000	1	4
15.5	4,70	2,271	1.030	4,079	1.850	—	—	—	211	340	—	195	314	1,180	1.900	26,570	8.100	1	5
8.6	2,60	1,153	523	1,929	875	—	—	—	—	—	—	141	226	500	805	14,500	4.420	1	1
9.10	2,99	2,440	1.107	3,680	1.669	—	—	—	256	412	—	—	—	1,493	2.403	24,000	7.315	1	4
8.5	2,57	2,023	918	3,600	1.633	—	—	—	195	314	—	167	269	980	1.577	16,000	4.900	1	5
8.3	2,52	1,625	737	2,750	1.247	—	—	—	162	261	—	140	225	657	1.057	15,000	4.570	1	3
8.7	2,62	1,030	467	1,600	726	—	—	—	115	185	—	90	145	555	893	12,650	3.856	1	1
9.11	3,02	3,292	1.493	5,500	2.495	—	—	—	274	441	—	183	294	1,929	3.105	28,200	8.595	1	5
10.1	3,08	1,532	695	2,475	1.123	—	—	—	—	—	—	132	212	560	901	11,100	3.385	1	3
6.8	2,03	930	422	1,750	794	—	—	—	115	185	—	105	169	460	740	19,000	5.800	1	1
7.6	2,28	1,894	859	3,200	1.452	—	—	—	242	389	—	209	336	975	1.569	25,000	7.620	1	3
8.2	2,49	2,384	1.081	3,725	1.690	—	—	—	246	396	—	207	333	1,670	2.688	20,000	6.100	1	3
17.5	5,32	15,609	7.080	27,337	12.400	3,042	1.380	—	536	862	—	466	750	2,200	3.540	42,000	12.800	2	8-10
14.3	4,35	9,709	4.404	16,136	7.319	1,329	603	—	—	—	—	559	900	2,095	3.370	45,200	13.780	2	7
16.6	5,03	11,275	5.114	23,300	10.569	1,890	857	—	510	821	—	450	724	1,940	3.120	41,000	12.500	2	7
16.0	4,87	10,600	4.808	20,000	9.072	2,764	1.254	—	563	906	—	497	800	2,000	3.220	45,000	13.715	2	10
24.6	7,47	—	—	57,500	26.082	—	—	—	585	941	—	565	909	3,460	5.570	43,000	13.100	3	19

U   Soviet Union
     turbo-fan
     turbo-jet
     turbo-prop
     transport
SA   United States of America
     max useful cargo
     not available data

VTOL CRAFT AND HELICOPTERS

Page	Aircraft	Builder	Nation of origin	Type	Year	Engine	Ø of the rotor		Length	
							ft	m	ft	m
196	Gyroplane N° 1	Breguet-Richet	F	H	1907	45 hp Antoinette	26.3	8,00	—	—
196	Sikorsky I Helicopter	Sikorsky	Russia	H	1909	25 hp Anzani	15.0 16.6	4,57 5,03	—	—
196	Helicopter by Cornu	Paul Cornu	F	H	1907	24 hp Antoinette	19.8	5,99	20.4	6,20
197	Helicopter by Ellehammer	Jacob Christian Ellehammer	DK	H	1912	36 hp Ellehammer (6 cl.)	24.6	7,47	—	—
197	Pescara N° 2	Raul Pateras Pescara	E	H	1924	180 hp H.S.	23.8	7,21	—	—
197	Oemichen N° 2	Étienne Oemichen	F	H	1922	120 hp Le Rhône	24.11 21.0	7,60 6,40	—	—
198	Cierva C-6A	Juan de la Cierva	E	Ag	1924	110 hp Le Rhône 9JA	36.0	10,97	34.4	10,46
198	Cierva C-8L-11	A.V. Roe	GB	Ag	1928	180 hp A.S. Lynx	39.7	12,06	36.0	10,97
198	Gyroplane Laboratoire	Louis Breguet-René Dorand	F	H	1936	350 hp H.S. 9Q	53.10	16,40	29.6	9,00
199	Vought-Sikorsky VS-300	Vought-Sikorsky Div. of United Aircraft Corp.	USA	H	1940	100 hp Franklin	30.0	9,14	28.0	8,53
199	Vought-Sikorsky R-4 (VS-316)	Vought-Sikorsky Div. of United Aircraft Corp.	USA	H	1944	185 hp Warner R-550-I	38.0	11,58	48.1	14,65
199	Focke FA-61	Focke-Achgelis GmbH	D	H	1936	160 hp Bramo SH 14A	23.0	7,01	23.11	7,29
200	Bell 47G-2	Bell Aircraft Corp.	USA	H/MP	1946	200 hp L. VO-435-A1A	35.1	10,69	31.7	9,63
200	Hiller H-23D Raven	Hiller Aircraft Co.	USA	H/MP	1946	250 hp L. VO-435-A1C	35.5	10,80	27.8	8,43
200	Sikorsky CH-37A (S-56)	Sikorsky Aircraft Div. of United Aircraft Corp.	USA	H/TA	1955	2/2100 hp P.&W. R-2800	72.0	21,95	82.10	25,24
200	Sikorsky UH-34D (S-58)	Sikorsky Aircraft Div. of United Aircraft Corp.	USA	H/MP	1955	1525 hp W. R-1820	56.0	17,07	46.9	14,25
200	Sikorsky HH-3E (S-61)	Sikorsky Aircraft Div. of United Aircraft Corp.	USA	H/Tr	1961	2/1500 hp G.E. T58-GE-5 tu.	62.0	18,90	57.3	17,45
201	Bell AH-1J Seacobra	Bell Helicopter Co.	USA	H/Co	1967	1800 hp P.&W. T400-CP-400 tu.	44.0	13,41	44.7	13,59
201	Lockheed AH-56A Cheyenne	Lockheed Aircraft Co.	USA	H/Co	1967	3435 hp G.E. T64-GE-16 tu.	50.4	15,34	54.8	16,66
201	Boeing-Vertol CH-47C Chinook	Boeing Co.	USA	H/Tr	1964	2/3750 hp L. T55-L-II tu.	60.0	18,29	51.0	15,54
202	Hughes Model 500	Hughes Tool Co.	USA	H/Ps	1965	317 hp A. T63-A-5A tu.	26.4	8,02	23.0	7,01
202	Dornier Do 132	Dornier A.G.	D	H/Ps	1971	720 hp P.&W. PT6G-20	35.1	10,70	24.7	7,50
202	Bölkow Bo-105	Bölkow GmbH	D	H/Ps	1967	2/350 hp MAN 6022-701-A3 tu.	32.1	9,80	27.11	8,50
202	Agusta A-106	Costruzioni Aeronautiche G. Agusta S.p.A.	I	H/AS	1966	330 hp Turboméca-Agusta	31.2	9,50	28.7	8,70
202	Fairchild Hiller FH-1100	Fairchild Hiller Corp.	USA	H/MP	1966	317 hp A. 250-C18 tu.	35.4	10,79	29.9	9,08
202	Westland Scout	Westland Aircraft Ltd	GB	H/MP	1961	685 hp R.R. Bristol Nimbus tu.	32.3	9,83	30.4	9,24
202	Kamov Ka-25K "Hormone"	State Industries	SU	H/MP	1967	2/900 hp Glushenkov tu.	51.8	15,74	32.3	9,83
202	Kaman UH-2A	Kaman Aerospace Corp.	USA	H/AS	1962	1250 hp G.E. T58-GE-8B tu.	44.0	13,41	52.2	15,90
202	Westland WG 13N Lynx	Westland Aircraft Ltd	GB	H/AS	1971	2/900 hp R.R. BS.360-07-26 tu.	42.0	12,80	38.3	11,66
202	Bell UH-1L Iroquois	Bell Helicopter Co.	USA	H/MP	1960	1400 L. T53-L-13 tu.	44.0	13,41	38.5	11,71
202	Westland Wessex 60	Westland Aircraft Ltd	GB	H/Ps	1966	2/1350 hp B.S. Gnome	56.0	17,07	48.4	14,74
202	Aérospatiale-Westland SA-300 Puma	Aérospatiale	F	H/Tr	1969	2/1320 Turboméca Turmo IIIC4 tu.	49.2	15,00	46.1	14,06
202	Mil Mi-8 "Hip"	State Industries	SU	H/Ps	1962	2/1500 hp Isotov TB-2-117A tu.	69.10	21,29	60.1	18,31
202	Aérospatiale SA-321G Super Frelon	Aérospatiale	F	H/MP	1963	3/1550 Turboméca Turmo IIIC6 tu.	62.0	18,90	63.8	19,40
202	Agusta A-101G	Costruzioni Aeronautiche G. Agusta S.p.A.	I	H/MP	1965	3/1400 R.R. Bristol Gnome H.1400 tu.	66.11	20,40	66.3	20,19
202	Sikorsky CH-53D (S-65)	Sikorsky Aircraft Div. of United Aircraft Corp.	USA	H/As	1965	2/3695 hp G.E. T-64-GE-412 tu.	72.3	22,03	67.2	20,47
202	Sikorsky CH-54 (S-64) Skycrane	Sikorsky Aircraft Div. of United Aircraft Corp.	USA	H/Tr	1964	2/4500 hp P.&W. JFTD12-4A tu.	72.0	21,95	70.3	21,42
203	Aérospatiale-Westland SA-341 Gazelle	Aérospatiale	F	H/MP	1968	600 hp Turboméca Astazou IIIN tu.	34.6	10,50	31.3	9,52
203	Aérospatiale SA-318C Alouette II Astazou	Aérospatiale	F	H/MP	1961	530 hp Turboméca Astazou IIA tu.	33.5	10,20	32.0	9,75
203	Bell OH-58A Kiowa	Bell Helicopter Co.	USA	H/MP	1967	317 hp A. T63-A-700 tu.	35.4	10,77	32.3	9,83
203	Aérospatiale SA-316B Alouette III	Aérospatiale	F	H/MP	1960	870 hp Turboméca Artouste IIIB tu.	36.2	11,02	32.11	10,03
203	Bell UH-1N	Bell Helicopter Co.	USA	H/MP	1969	1800 hp P.&W. PT6T-3 Twin-Pac tu.	48.2	14,69	42.10	13,07
203	Mil Mi-4 "Hound"	State Industries	SU	H/MP	1953	1700 hp ASh-82V (18 cl.)	68.11	21,00	55.1	16,80
203	Mil Mi-6 "Hook"	State Industries	SU	H/Tr	1957	2/5500 hp Soloviev D-25V tu.	114.10	35,00	108.10	33,18
203	Mil Mi-10 "Harke"	State Industries	SU	H/Tr	1961	2/5500 hp Soloviev D-25V tu.	114.10	35,00	107.10	32,86
204	McDonnell XV-1 (Model 82)	McDonnell Aircraft Corp.	USA	H/Ex	1954	550 hp Continental R-975-19	—	—	30.0	9,14
204	Convair XFY-1 Pogo	Convair Division of General Dynamics	USA	H/Ex	1954	A. T40 tp.	—	—	—	—

Abbreviations used in the table

A.	Allison	Co	combat	GB	Great Britain	kg	kilograms
Ag	autogiro	D	Germany	G.E.	General Electric	km	kilometers
AS	anti-submarine	DK	Denmark	H	helicopter	L.	Lycoming
As	assault	E	Spain	h	hour	lb	pounds
A.S.	Armstrong Siddeley	Ex	experimental	hp	horse-power	m	meters
B.S.	Bristol Siddeley	F	France	H.S.	Hispano-Suiza	mg.	machine-gun
CDN	Canada	ft	feet	I	Italy	ml	miles
cl.	cylinders	g.	gun	j.	jet	mm	millimeters

Height		Empty weight		Max take-off weight		Max speed		Cruising speed		Range		Ceiling		Crew	Passengers	Notes
ft	m	lb	kg	lb	kg	ml/h	km/h	ml/h	km/h	ml	km	ft	m			
—	—	1,102	500	1,274	578	—	—	—	—	—	—	—	—	1	—	
—	—	—	—	—	—	—	—	—	—	—	—	—	—	1	—	
—	—	420	191	573	260	—	—	—	—	—	—	—	—	1	—	
—	—	—	—	—	—	—	—	—	—	—	—	—	—	1	—	
—	—	1,874	850	—	—	8	13	—	—	—	—	—	—	1	—	
—	—	1,764	800	—	—	—	—	—	—	—	—	—	—	1	—	
—	—	1,490	676	—	—	—	—	—	—	—	—	—	—	1	—	
14.9	4,50	1,750	794	2,440	1.107	100	161	20	32	255	410	—	—	1	—	
14.7	4,45	3,153	1.430	4,475	2.030	60	97	—	—	45	72	—	—	1	—	
10.0	3,05	—	—	1,150	522	—	—	40	64	75	121	—	—	1	—	
12.1	3,68	—	—	2,540	1.152	—	—	65	105	200	322	8,000	2.440	2	—	
8.10	2,70	—	—	2,101	953	—	—	62	100	142	229	7,907	2.410	1	—	
9.5	2,87	1,564	709	2,450	1.111	100	161	89	143	238	383	12,620	3.850	1	2	
9.8	2,94	1,773	804	2,700	1.225	95	153	82	132	197	317	13,200	4.025	1	2	
22.0	6,71	20,690	9.385	31,000	14.062	130	209	115	185	200	322	8,700	2.650	3	33	
15.11	4,84	7,646	3.468	13,600	6.169	122	196	97	156	247	397	12,000	3.660	2	18	
18.1	5,51	13,255	6.012	22,050	10.002	162	261	144	232	465	748	11,100	3.385	2	30	
13.8	4,16	—	—	10,000	4.536	207	333	—	—	359	578	10,550	3.215	2	—	Armament: g. (20 mm), r.
13.8	4,16	11,725	5.318	22,000	9.979	253	407	242	389	875	1.408	26,000	7.925	2	—	Armament: g. (30 mm), mg. (7,62 mm), msl., r.
18.7	5,67	20,378	9.243	39,200	17.781	178	286	160	257	350	565	10,200	3.110	2	33	Payload: 13,450 lb (6.101 kg)
8.1	2,47	1,086	493	2,550	1.157	152	245	138	222	377	607	14,400	4.390	1	5	
9.2	2,80	1,488	675	3,637	1.650	142	229	137	220	275	443	—	—	1	4	
9.6	2,90	2,359	1.070	4,409	2.000	155	249	140	225	279	449	19,685	6.000	1	3	
8.2	2,50	1,520	690	3,086	1.400	110	177	105	169	460	740	—	—	1	—	Armament: 2 t.
9.3	2,83	1,396	633	2,750	1.247	127	204	122	196	348	560	14,200	4.330	1	4	
8.11	2,72	3,232	1.466	5,300	2.404	131	211	122	196	315	507	17,000	5.180	1	4	
17.7	5,36	9,700	4.400	16,094	7.300	137	220	120	193	405	652	11,500	3.500	2	12	Payload: 4,409 lb (2.000 kg)
13.6	4,11	6,216	2.820	10,000	4.536	162	261	152	245	670	1.078	17,400	5.300	2	11	
11.3	3,43	7,487	3.396	8,784	3.984	184	296	159	256	150	241	—	—	2	12	Armament: 2 t.
12.7	3,84	5,921	2.686	9,500	4.309	161	259	—	—	317	510	10,200	3.110	2	8	
14.5	4,40	8,657	3.927	13,600	6.169	133	214	121	195	334	538	10,000	3.050	2	10	Developed from the Sikorsky S-58
13.8	4,18	7,562	3.430	14,110	6.400	174	280	165	266	390	630	15,750	4.800	2	16	
18.4	5,60	16,352	7.417	26,455	12.000	155	249	140	225	264	425	14,760	4.500	3	28	Payload: 8,818 lb (4.000 kg)
21.10	6,66	14,639	6.640	27,558	12.500	149	240	143	230	572	920	11,480	3.500	2	37	
21.6	6,56	15,102	6.850	28,440	12.900	150	241	135	217	250	402	15,090	4.600	2	36	
17.1	5,21	23,485	10.653	42,000	19.051	196	315	173	278	257	414	21,000	6.400	3	64	
18.7	5,67	19,234	8.725	42,000	19.051	127	204	109	175	253	407	13,000	3.960	3	—	Payload: 20,000 lb (9.072 kg)
10.4	3,16	1,873	850	3,748	1.700	165	266	149	240	403	650	16,732	5.100	2	3	
9.0	2,75	1,962	890	3,638	11.650	127	204	112	180	447	720	10,830	3.300	1	4	
9.6	2,89	1,583	718	3,000	1.361	138	222	117	188	356	573	19,000	5.800	2	2	Armament: mg. (7,62 mm)
9.10	3,00	2,447	1.110	4,850	2.200	131	211	112	180	335	539	10,660	3.250	1	6	
14.4	4,39	6,119	2.776	10,000	4.536	121	195	—	—	296	476	11,500	3.500	1	14	
17.0	5,18	8,488	3.850	17,196	7.800	130	209	99	159	250	402	18,000	5.500	3	16	Payload: 3,835 lb (1.740 kg)
32.4	9,86	60,054	27.240	93,696	42.500	186	299	155	249	621	1.000	14,760	4.500	5	65	Payload: 26,450 lb (12.000 kg)
32.6	9,90	59,525	27.000	95,791	43.450	137	220	112	180	397	640	9,840	3.000	3	28	Payload: 33,070 lb (15.000 kg)
10.0	3,05	—	—	—	—	—	—	—	—	—	—	—	—	1	3	
—	—	—	—	—	—	—	—	—	—	—	—	—	—	1	—	

MP   multi-purpose
nsl.   missiles
P.&W. Pratt & Whitney
s   passengers
      rockets
R.R.   Rolls-Royce
U   Soviet Union
      torpedo

TA   attack transport
tj.   turbo-jet
tp.   turbo-prop
Tr   transport
tu.   turbine
USA   United States of America
W.   Wright

VTOL CRAFT AND HELICOPTERS (continued)

Page	Aircraft	Builder	Nation of origin	Type	Year	Engine	Ø of the rotor		Length	
							ft	m	ft	m
204	Bell XV-3 (Model 200)	Bell Helicopter Co.	USA	H/Ex	1955	450 hp P.&W. R-985	25.0	7,62	30.0	9,14
204	SNECMA C-450-01 Coléoptère	Société Nationale d'Étude et de Construction de Moteurs d'Aviation	F	H/Ex	1959	8,155 lb (3.700 kg) SNECMA Atar 101E.V tj.	—	—	26.4	8,02
204	Fairey Rotodyne	Fairey Aviation Ltd	GB	H/Ex	1957	2/5250 hp R.R. Tyne tu.	104.0	31,70	64.6	19,66
204	Bell VTOL ATV	Bell Aircraft Corp.	USA	H/Ex	1953	2/1,000 lb (454 kg) Fairchild J44 tj.	26.0	7,93	21.0	6,40
204	Rolls-Royce TMR Flying Bedstead	Rolls-Royce Ltd	GB	H/Ex	1953	2/R.R. Neue j.	—	—	—	—
204	Vertol VZ-2A (Model 76)	Vertol Aircraft Corp.	USA	H/Ex	1957	L. YT-53-L-1 tu.	24.11	7,60	26.5	8,05
205	Lockheed XFV-1	Lockheed Aircraft Co.	USA	H/Ex	1954	A. T40 tp.	—	—	—	—
205	Ryan X-13 Vertijet	Ryan Aeronautical Co.	USA	H/Ex	1955	R.R. Avon tj.	21.0	6,40	24.0	7,32
205	Short SC-1	Short Bros & Harland Ltd	GB	H/Ex	1957	5/R.R. RB.108 tj.	23.6	7,16	24.5	7,45
205	Bell X-14	Bell Helicopter Co.	USA	H/Ex	1956	2/1,750 lb (795 kg) A.S. Viper ASV 8 J	34.0	10,36	25.0	7,62
205	Hiller X-18	Hiller Aircraft Co.	USA	H/Ex	1959	2/5850 hp A. T40-A-14 tu.	48.0	14,63	63.0	19,20
205	Ryan VZ-3RY (Model 92)	Ryan Aeronautical Co.	USA	H/Ex	1958	1000 hp L. T53-L-1 tu.	23.5	7,14	27.8	8,43
205	Vought-Hiller-Ryan XC-142	Vought-Hiller-Ryan	USA	H/Ex	1964	4/G.E. T64-GE-1 tu.	67.6	20,57	58.1	17,71
205	Bell D-188A	Bell Helicopter Co.	USA	H/Ex	1960	—	—	—	—	—
205	Dassault III-V-001 Balzac	Générale Aéronautique Marcel Dassault	F	H/Ex	1965	4,400 lb (1.995 kg) B.S. Orpheus; 8/2,160 lb (980 kg) R.R. RB. 108	27.0	8,22	43.10	13,35
205	Ryan XV-5B	Ryan Aeronautical Co.	USA	H/Ex	1964	2/2,658 lb (1.205 kg) G.E. J85-GE-5 tj.	29.10	9,09	44.6	13,57
205	Aérospatiale N-500	Aérospatiale	F	H/Ex	1967	2/317 hp A. 250-C18 tu.	20.1	6,14	21.7	6,58
206	PiAC 16H-3J Pathfinder	Piasecki Aircraft Corp.	USA	H/Tr	1972	2/690 hp P.&W. PT6B-16 tu.	44.3	13,49	42.9	13,03
207	Bell X-22A (Model D2127)	Bell Aerospace Co.	USA	H/Ex	1966	4/1250 hp G.E. YT58-GE-8D tu.	39.3	11,97	39.7	12,07
207	Canadair CL-84-1	Canadair Ltd	CDN	H/Ex	1970	2/1500 L. T53 tu.	33.4	10,16	47.3	14,41
207	Dornier Do 31E3	Dornier A.G.	D	H/Ex	1967	2/15,500 lb (7.000 kg) R.R. Bristol Pegasus 5-2 tj.; 8/4,400 lb (2.000 kg) R.R. RB.162-4D tj.	59.3	18,06	68.6	20,88

SUPERSONIC EXPERIMENTAL AIRCRAFT

Page	Aircraft	Builder	Nation of origin	Type	Year	Engine	Wing spread	
							ft	m
210	Bell X-1A	Bell Aircraft Corp.	USA	Ss	1946	6,000 lb (2.722 kg) Reaction Motors E6000-C4 r.	28.0	8,53
210	Bell X-2	Bell Aircraft Corp.	USA	Ss	1953	Curtiss-Wright r.	—	—
210	Bell X-5	Bell Aircraft Corp.	USA	Ss	1951	4,900 lb (2.680 kg) A. J35-A-17 tj.	32.9	9,98
210	Douglas X-3 Stiletto	Douglas Aircraft Co.	USA	Ss	1952	—	22.8	6,91
211	North American X-15	North American Aviation Inc.	USA	Ss	1959	70,000 lb (31.750 kg) Reaction Motors XLR-99 r.	22.0	6,71
211	North American XB-70A Valkyrie	North American Aviation Inc.	USA	Ss	1964	6/31,000 lb (14.060 kg) a.b. G.E. J93-GE-3 tj.-GE-3 tj.	105.0	32,00
212	Martin Marietta X-24A	Martin Marietta Corp.	USA	Ss	1967	8,000 lb (3.625 kg) Thiokol XLR-24A tr.	13.8	4,16
212	Northrop/NASA M2-F3	Northrop Corp.	USA	Ss	1965	8,000 lb (3.630 kg) Thiokol XLR11 tr.	9.7	2,92
212	Northrop/NASA HL-10	Northrop Corp.	USA	Ss	1966	8,000 lb (3.630 kg) Thiokol XLR11 tr.	15.1	4,60

Abbreviations used in the tables

A.	Allison	ft	feet	km	kilometers	tj.	turbo-jet
a.b.	with afterburning	GB	Great Britain	L.	Lycoming	tp.	turbo-prop
A.S.	Armstrong Siddeley	G.E.	General Electric	lb	pounds	Tr	transport
B.S.	Bristol Siddeley	H	helicopter	m	meters	tr.	turbo-rocket
CDN	Canada	h	hour	ml	miles	tu.	turbine
D	Germany	hp	horse-power	P.&W.	Pratt & Whitney	Ss	experimental supersonic
Ex	experimental	j.	jet	r.	rockets	USA	United States of America
F	France	kg	kilograms	R.R.	Rolls-Royce		

Height		Empty weight		Max take-off weight		Max speed		Cruising speed		Range		Ceiling		Crew	Passengers	Notes
ft	m	lb	kg	lb	kg	ml/h	km/h	ml/h	km/h	ml	km	ft	m			
13.6	4,11	3,600	1.633	4,800	2.177	175	282	—	—	—	—	12,000	3.660	1	3	Wing spread: 30.0 ft (9,14 m)
—	—	—	—	6,614	3.000	500	805	—	—	—	—	9,840	3.000	1	—	
23.2	7,06	—	—	50,000	22.680	—	—	201	323	650	1.046	—	—	2	70	Wing spread: 56.6 ft (17,22 m)
—	—	2,000	907	—	—	—	—	—	—	—	—	—	—	1	—	
—	—	—	—	—	—	—	—	—	—	—	—	—	—	1	—	
10.0	3,05	2,500	1.134	3,200	1.452	—	—	—	—	—	—	—	—	1	—	
—	—	—	—	—	—	—	—	—	—	—	—	—	—	1	—	
15.0	4,57	—	—	—	—	—	—	—	—	—	—	—	—	1	—	
10.8	3,25	—	—	—	—	—	—	—	—	—	—	—	—	1	—	
8.0	2,44	—	—	3,500	1.588	160	257	—	—	—	—	—	—	2	—	
24.7	7,50	—	—	33,000	14.969	250	402	—	—	—	—	—	—	2	—	
10.8	3,25	—	—	2,600	1.179	—	—	—	—	—	—	—	—	2	—	
26.1	7,95	22,595	10.249	42,500	19.278	—	—	—	—	—	—	—	—	2	32	Payload: 8,000 lb (3.630 kg)
—	—	—	—	—	—	—	—	—	—	—	—	—	—	1	—	
14.9	4,50	14,330	6.500	—	—	—	—	—	—	—	—	—	—	1	—	
14.9	4,50	7,541	3.421	12,300	5.579	547	880	345	555	1,000	1.610	40,000	12.200	2	—	
10.2	3,10	—	—	2,756	1.250	217	350	—	—	—	—	—	—	1	—	
12.3	3,75	5,925	2.688	9,600	4.355	190	306	—	—	850	1.368	—	—	1	14	
20.8	6,30	16,274	7.382	18,016	8.172	316	509	213	343	445	716	15,000	4.570	2	—	
14.3	4,35	8,437	3.827	12,600	5.715	321	517	309	497	421	678	—	—	2	12	
28.0	8,53	49,604	22.500	60,627	27.500	404	650	—	—	—	—	34,450	10.500	2	36	

Length		Height		Empty weight		Max take-off weight		Max speed		Cruising speed		Range		Ceiling		Crew
ft	m	ft	m	lb	kg	lb	kg	ml/h	km/h	ml/h	km/h	ml	km	ft	m.	
35.7	10,85	10.8	3,25	—	—	—	—	1,650	2.655	—	—	—	—	90,000	27.430	1
—	—	—	—	—	—	—	—	—	—	—	—	—	—	—	—	1
32.4	9,85	12.0	3,66	—	—	10,000	4.540	—	—	—	—	—	—	—	—	1
66.9	20,34	12.6	3,81	—	—	—	—	—	—	—	—	—	—	—	—	1
50.0	15,24	13.6	4,11	12,971	5.884	31,276	14.187	4,105	6.606	—	—	—	—	314,750	95.935	1
185.0	56,38	30.0	9,14	—	—	525,000	238.140	1,980	3.186	—	—	7,500	12.070	80,000	24.400	4
24.6	7,47	10.4	3,15	6,000	2.722	11,000	4.990	—	—	—	—	—	—	—	—	1
22.2	6,76	8.10	2,69	—	—	9,400	4.264	—	—	—	—	—	—	—	—	1
22.2	6,76	11.5	3,48	—	—	9,400	4.264	—	—	—	—	—	—	—	—	1

CIVIL AIRCRAFT NATIONALITY AND REGISTRATION MARKS

Afghanistan	YA	Guatemala	TG	Nicaragua	AN
Algeria	7T	Guinea	3X	Niger	5U
Argentina	LV, LQ	Guyana	8R	Nigeria	5N
Australia	VH			Norway	LN
Austria	OE	Haiti	HH		
		Holland	PH	Pakistan	AP
Barbados	8A	Dutch Antilles	PJ	Panama	HP
Belgium	OO	Surinam	PZ	Paraguay	ZP
Bolivia	CP	Honduras	HR	Peru	OB
Brazil	PP, PT	Hungary	HA	Philippines	PI
Bulgaria	LZ			Poland	SP
Burma	XY, XZ	Iceland	TF	Portugal	CS, CR
Burundi	9U	India	VT		
		Indonesia	PK	Rumania	YR
Cambodia	XU	West Irian	PK	Rwanda	9XR
Cameroon	TJ	Iran	EP		
Canada	CF	Iraq	YI	Saudi Arabia	HZ
Central African		Ireland	EI, EJ	Senegal	6V, 6W
Republic	TL	Israel	4X	Sierra Leone	9L
Ceylon	4R	Italy	I	Singapore	9V
Chad	TT	Ivory Coast	TU	Somaliland	6OS
Chile	CC			South Africa	ZS, ZT, ZU
China	B	Jamaica	6Y	Spain	EC
Colombia	HK	Japan	JA	Sudan	ST
Congo (Brazzaville)	TN	Jordan	JY	Sweden	SE
Congo (Kinshasa)	9Q			Switzerland	HB
Costa Rica	TI	Kenya	5Y	Syria	YK
Cuba	CU	Korea, Republic of	HL		
Cyprus	5B	Kuwait	9K	Tanzania,	
Czechoslovakia	OK			United Republic of	5H
		Laos	XW	Thailand	HS
Dahomey	TY	Lebanon	OD	Togo	5V
Denmark	OY	Lesotho	7P	Trinidad and Tobago	9Y
Dominican, Republic	HI	Liberia	EL	Tunisia	TS
		Libya	5A	Turkey	TC
Ecuador	HC	Liechtenstein	HB		
El Salvador	YS	Luxembourg	LX	Uganda	5X
Ethiopia	ET			United Arab Republic	SU
		Malagasy, Republic	5R	United States of America	N
Finland	OH	Malawi	7QY	Upper Volta	XT
France	F	Malaysia	9M	Uruguay	CX
		Mali	TZ		
Gabon	TR	Malta	9H	Venezuela	YV
Germany, Federal		Mauritius	5T	Vietnam, Republic of	XV
Republic	D	Mexico	XA, XB, XC		
Ghana	9G	Monaco	3A	Western Samoa	5W
Great Britain	G	Morocco	CN		
Colonies and Pro-				Yemen	4W
tectorates	VP, VQ, VR	Nepal	9N	Yugoslavia	YU
Greece	SX	New Zealand	ZK, ZL, ZM	Zambia	9J

CHRONOLOGY OF WORLD WAR II

To better understand the determining role that airplanes played in the Second World War, the author has deemed it necessary to present a concise chronology which covers the historical period from 1936 to 1945.

Background

1936

June 18—Civil war breaks out in Spain. Armed forces revolt in Spanish Morocco against the Madrid government. The revolt is headed by General Franco, who crosses the Strait of Gibraltar with his troops.

July 30—A national government is formed at Burgos. Italy and Germany intervene in support of Franco while France and the U.S.S.R. support the Republican government.

September 30—General Franco is proclaimed head of the national government of Spain.

November 6—Franco begins his march on Madrid. The Republican government moves to Valencia.

November 18—Italy and Germany recognize the Franco regime.

1937

May 31—During the Spanish Civil War, following the attack of the Russian Air Force on the battleship *Deutschland*, German warships bomb Almeria.

1938

March 11—Hitler annexes Austria *(Anschluss).*

September 29—Hitler, Mussolini, Chamberlain, and Daladier meet for the Munich conference. Czechoslovakia forced to evacuate its territory on the German border.

October 1—Germans march into Sudetenland without meeting Czech resistance.

October 6—Slovakia becomes an independent nation.

December—Following various ups and downs in the Spanish Civil War, Franco launches his final offensive. The major Italian and German aerial contributions are: *CR 32* and *SM 79* for Italy; *Ju 87, He 111, Hs 123A, Do 17* (which made up the Condor Legion) for Germany.

1939

January 26—Barcelona occupied by Franco's troops.

February 27—England and France recognize Franco's government.

March 15—Nazi Germany meets no resistance in occupying Bohemia and Moravia, turning them into German protectorates.

March 23—Lithuania surrenders the Memel territory to Germany.

March 26—Poland refuses to yield the Danzig Corridor to Hitler's Germany.

March 28—Franco's troops enter Madrid.

March 31—British and French guarantee Poland's integrity.

April 1—End of the Spanish Civil War. The U.S. recognizes Franco's government.

April 7—Italian troops occupy Albania.

April 12—Albanian National Assembly ratifies the alliance between Albania and Italy.

May 22—Military alliance between Italy and Germany: "The Steel Pact."

August 23—German-Russian agreement signed in Moscow.

The War

1939

September 1—German troops invade Poland. 1000 bombers and 1500 German fighters attack Poland's main cities.

September 2—Mussolini declares Italy's nonbelligerance.

September 3—England and France declare war against Germany.

September 5—Roosevelt declares neutrality.

September 6—First German air raid on England.

September 17—Russian troops invade Eastern Poland. British aircraft carrier *Courageous* sunk by a German submarine.

September 18—Warsaw besieged by German troops.

September 24—U.S. approves "cash and carry" policy (permits trade with warring nations). Among the most important items exported: *Martin A-30, Bell P-39, Curtiss P-40* and *North American P-51.*

September 27—Warsaw surrenders. War ends in Poland.

September 28—Russian-German alliance establishes the division of Poland.

October 5—Hitler enters Warsaw.

October 14—A German submarine sinks the English battleship *Royal Oak* on the Scapa Flow Naval base.

November 30—Russian troops attack Finland and bomb Helsinki.

December 14—Naval battle between the mini battleship *Graf Spee* and three British cruisers near Montevideo. The battle ends (on the seventeenth) with the sinking of the German ship. The hunt is carried out with the valuable aid of 2 *Fairey Seafoxes,* standard equipment on British ships.

1940

January 12—First German air raid on London.

March 12—Finland signs peace treaty with Russia and gives up part of Karelian Isthmus and other territory.

March 18—Hitler and Mussolini meet at the Brenner Pass.

April 9—German occupation of Denmark, which surrenders without a fight. The invasion of Norway, which strongly resisted the advancing German troops (with the support of 1300 airplanes, 300 of them transports).

April 13—German troops land at Narvik. German torpedo bombers sunk in the Narvik fiord by a British Naval squadron while German troops drive back the British.

May 5—King Haakon VII of Norway flees to England.

May 10—German troops invade Holland, Belgium and Luxembourg with massive Luftwaffe support. Dutch air resistance, consisting of a few *Fokker D.XXI*'s and *G.1A*'s, is crushed in a matter of days.

May 11—Chamberlain resigns. Churchill takes his place.

May 13—German troops occupy Liège.

May 14—Rotterdam bombed by German planes.

May 15—Holland surrenders. The Dutch Queen flees to England.

May 17—Brussels occupied by German troops.

May 26—German troops occupy Calais.

May 28—The Belgian Army surrenders. King Leopold III remains in Belgium as a German prisoner.

May 29—Ostend and Lille occupied by German troops.

Beginning in June—German sub warfare against Allied convoys intensifies (the "Battle of the Atlantic").

June 4—German troops occupy Dunkirk which had been evacuated by the British, whose 338,000 men (including some French divisions) were able to cross the Channel. The first *Boulton Paul Defiants* appear in the skies.

June 5—The Germans attack on the Somme, which falls on June 7.

June 10—Italy enters the War against France and England. Last resistance of Norwegian forces breaks.

June 11—Malta bombed for the first time by Italian planes. The defense of the island is in the hands of only 3 British planes: three *Gladiators,* christened *Faith, Hope* and *Charity.*

June 14—German troops enter Paris. The French government flees to Bordeaux.

June 16—Marshal Pétain, forced to seek an armistice, forms a new government.

June 18—From London, General de Gaulle proclaims continued French resistance and forms the provisional Free French Government.

June 22—Franco-German armistice signed in the Compiègne forest. Three-fifths of French territory including the entire Atlantic Coast, occupied by the Germans.

June 24—Armistice between France and Italy signed in Rome. The Pétain government estabishes headquarters in Vichy.

June 26—Rumania forced to hand over Bessarabia to Russia.

July 3—The British destroy France's strongest Naval squadron anchored at Oran so that it would not fall into German hands. Petain and Laval's Vichy government severs diplomatic relations with Great Britain.

July 4—Italian troops enter Anglo-Egyptian Sudan.

July 9—Naval battle of Punta Stilo between an English and an Italian squadron. The outcome is doubtful. Italian air force land-based squadrons and British *Swordfish* torpedo bombers based on the aircraft carrier *Eagle* participate.

July 16—Hitler, having vainly hoped to reach an agreement with Great Britain after the fall of France, orders preparations for the invasion of the British Isles (operation "Sea Lion"). He assigns the German Air Force the task of destroying the R.A.F. and the "Battle of Britain" begins.

August 6-19—Italian troops led by Duke Amedeo D'Aosta, Viceroy of Abyssinia, occupy British Somaliland. Beginning August 13—Massive German air raids (with 1300 bombers and 900 fighters) on Great Britain, particularly on London, begin. The German Air Force is nevertheless unsuccessful in weakening R.A.F. resistance (made up mainly of *Hurricane* and *Spitfire* squadrons) and suffers heavy losses (about 1730 planes shot down, among which many *Stukas*).

August 13—Italian troops in Cirenaica commanded by General Graziani begin the Egyptian offensive, occupying Salum and (August 17) Sidi Barrâni.

August 25—Massive British bombing attacks carried out mainly by *Hampdens* begin over Berlin.

August 30—Germany guarantees Rumanian boundary.

September 3—The U.S. delivers 50 torpedo-boat destroyers to England in exchange for Naval bases in Central America.

September 27—German-Italian-Japanese Axis formed.

October 7—German troops invade Rumania.

October 12—Project "Sea Lion" is declared inoperative, implicit admission that the "Battle of Britain" has been lost.

October 19—Italian bombers attack oil wells in the Bahrein islands.

October 23—Fruitless meeting between Hitler and Franco at Hendaye. Spain refuses to let German troops cross her territory, obstructing the attack on Gibraltar.

October 24—Hitler meets Marshal Pétain and Laval at Montoire but fails to obtain an alliance with Germany.

October 28—Mussolini and Hitler meet in Florence. Italian ultimatum to Greece, which refuses to abandon its policy of neutrality. Italian troops in Albania invade Greek territory.

October 29—British troops land in Greece.

November 11—English air attacks (a group of *Fairey Swordfish* taking off from the carrier *Illustrious*) on an Italian Naval squadron based at Taranto. Three Italian battleships badly damaged.

November 12-13—Unproductive Hitler-Molotov meeting in Berlin.

November 14—German air strikes against England resume with a massive attack on Coventry.

November 27—British aircraft bomb Cologne. Air-naval battle of Cape Teulada between an Italian and a British squadron. *SM 79* and *Cant Z.1007* bombers take part, escorted by *CR42* fighters on the Italian side, and British *Swordfish* torpedo bombers which take off from the carrier *Ark Royal*.

December 9—British counteroffensive against Italian troops in Egypt. The Italians forced to evacuate Sidi Barrâni.

December 17—Italian troops also forced to abandon Salum.

December 29—German aircraft attack London, dropping incendiary bombs.

1941

January 22—Italian retreat from Tobruk.

February 6—British occupy Bengazi.

March 1—Bulgaria joins the Axis.

March 27—Military revolt in Belgrade. The government is entrusted to young King Peter II.

March 28—Naval battle at Gaudo, Italian squadrons force a British formation to retreat. Later it is attacked south of Cape Matapan by *Fairey Swordfish* torpedo bombers and by British heavy artillery. Three cruisers are sunk.

March 31—Italian troops and German troops in Africa under General Rommel's command begin a new offensive in Cirenaica.

April 2—Asmara abandoned by Italians.

April 4—Bengazi reoccupied by Italo-German troops.

April 5—Italians retreat from Addis Ababa. Yugoslavia and Russia sign a pact.

April 6—German troops invade Yugoslavia and Greece.

April 10—Croatia becomes an independent nation.

April 12—Germans take over Belgrade.

April 17—Yugoslavia surrenders.

April 21—Germans force Greece to sign a surrender.

April 24—British troops abandon Greece.

April 27—German troops enter Athens.

May 5—Haile Selassie, Emperor of Ethiopia, returns to Addis Ababa.

May 18—Italian garrison at Amba Alagi, under the command of the Duke of Aosta, surrenders.

May 20—The island of Crete occupied by German troops tranported by *Junkers Ju 52/3m*'s.

May 24—German battleship *Bismarck* sinks British cruiser *Hood,* in a battle south of Greenland.

May 27—The *Bismarck,* cornered by British Naval and air forces and attacked by *Swordfish* torpedo bombers, is sunk in the Atlantic.

June 22—Hitler, convinced that Russian policy in the Balkans and Finland is contrary to German interests, launches an attack on Russia, "Operation Barbarossa," without giving an ultimatum. Germany's allies in the war against Russia are Italy, Rumania, Hungary and Finland.

June 24—German troops occupy Brest Litovsk and Vilna.

July 12—Russian-British pact signed for a joint effort against Germany.

July 13—Germans break through the "Stalin Line."

July 16—Fall of Smolensk. The U.S. occupies Iceland.

July 31—German troops surround Leningrad from the South.

August 8—Berlin bombed by Russian *Ilyushin Il-4.*

August 14—Churchill and Roosevelt sign the "Atlantic Charter."

August 25—British and Russian troops enter Iran.

August 28—German troops entirely occupy the Baltic States, reaching Tallinn.

September 10—Kiev is surrounded. The Germans occupy the Donets Basin, but the Soviet resistance continues.

September 19—Kiev falls.

October 2-16—German troops surround Bryansk and Vyazma and attempt to reach Moscow, forcing the Soviet government to evacuate to Kuibyshev (October 16). Rumanian troops conquer Odessa.

October 24—Kharkov is occupied by the Germans.

November 7—Massive British air attack on Berlin with 400 R.A.F. bombers.

November 14—British carrier *Ark Royal* sunk by a German *U-81* submarine near Gibraltar.

November 15—A new German attack on Moscow stopped by Soviet troops.

November 18—Beginning of British counteroffensive in Libya.

November 25—The British carrier *Barham* sunk by a German submarine at Salum.

November 27—Gondar, last bulwark of Italian resistance in Ethiopia, falls.

266

December 7—Japanese surprise attack on the American Naval base at Pearl Harbor, Hawaii, with 423 aircraft (among which 144 *Nakajima B5N2* bombers and 126 *Aichi D3A1*'s) which take-off from 6 aircraft carriers. Five American battleships and 2 cruisers sunk.

December 8—The U.S. and Great Britain declare war on Japan.

December 10—Japan invades the Philippines; the British battleships *Prince of Wales* and *Repulse* are sunk by *Mitsubishi G3M1*'s off the coast of Malaya. Japanese land at Guam.

December 11—Italy and Germany declare war on the U.S.

December 14—Germans fail in their advance on Moscow and suffer heavy losses.

December 17—Italo-German retreat in Libya.

December 19—Hitler takes over supreme command of the German Army.

December 24—Bengazi occupied by the British.

December 25—Japan forces Hong Kong to surrender.

1942

January 2—Japanese win Manila and Cavite.

January 21—Italian-German counteroffensive in Cirenaica.

January 22—Brazil declares war on Germany.

January 29—Bengazi reoccupied by Italian and German troops.

February 6—Italians and Germans reach Ain-el-Gazala.

February 15–16—Japanese reach Singapore, land in Java and occupy Jakarta.

March 7—The Burmese capital, Rangoon, surrenders to the Japanese, who land on Sumatra the same day.

March 17—General MacArthur takes command of U.S. air and naval forces in the Southwestern Pacific.

April 10—British drop the first 7055 pounds of bombs on Essen.

April 18—Tokyo attacked by American aircraft (*B-25J Mitchell*'s), which take off from an aircraft carrier, commanded by Jimmy Doolittle.

May 4–8—The "Battle for the Coral Sea" begins. Americans lose the carrier *Lexington* but block the Japanese advance in the Pacific. Losses: 66 American aircraft out of 144 and 80 Japanese planes out of 180.

May 6—American base at Corregidor, Manila Bay, falls.

May 26—Italian-German offensive under General Rommel's command breaks British resistance in Cirenaica.

May 31—1000 British bombers (*Hampdens* and *Wellingtons*) drop over 3,086,500 pounds of explosives on Cologne.

June 3—The U.S. declares war on Rumania, Bulgaria and Hungary.

June 4–7—The "Battle of Midway." Although the Americans lose the carrier *Yorktown* and many planes, by sinking 4 of the chief Japanese carriers they gain the upper hand in the Pacific.

June 21–30—The British, surrounded at Tobruk, surrender to the Italians and Germans. Rommel's offensive ends at El Alamein.

July 2—Sebastopol falls to German and Rumanian troops.

July 4—First American air strikes over Continental Europe.

July 23—Rostov occupied by German and Rumanian troops.

August 7—Americans land on Guadalcanal (Solomon Islands).

August 8—Air and Naval battle in the Solomons. Americans and Australians against Japanese forces.

August 10—German troops reach the oil fields of Maikop and Piatigorsk north of the Caucasus.

August 12—Churchill visits Stalin in Moscow.

August 23–24—German offensive against Stalingrad. Russian defense is supported by *Lavochkin La-5* and *Yakovlev Yak-9*s.

August 28—Russian air attack on Berlin.

October 23—British, under General Montgomery's command, break through the Italo-German front at El Alamein and drive Rommel's troops back to Cirenaica.

End of October—Stalingrad is almost completely occupied by the German 6th Army under the command of General Von Paulus.

November 8—American troops under the command of General Eisenhower land in Morocco and Algeria.

November 11—German troops invade previously unoccupied French territory except for Toulon.

November 13–14—Another air-naval battle at Guadalcanal between American and Japanese forces, with heavy losses on both sides.

November 20—British troops reoccupy Bengazi.

November 22—Following the Russian offensive on the Don, the German 6th Army is surrounded in Stalingrad. The Luftwaffe attempts to set up an air corridor with *Fw200 Condors* to supply the besieged troops.

November 27—Toulon falls to the Germans. The French Naval Squadron anchored at the base is sunk.

November 28—American planes bomb Bangkok.

December 19—Italian attack craft (better known as "Pigs") sink the British battleships *Queen Elizabeth* and *Valiant* at Alexandria.

1943

January 6—German troops retreat from Caucasus and, later, from the Don.

January 14–16—The Casablanca conference. Roosevelt

and Churchill agree to accept only an unconditional surrender from the Axis.

January 18—The siege of Leningrad ends. It lasted 16 months.

January 23—Tripoli is occupied by British forces.

January 27—First American bombing raid on German territory.

February 2—The German 6th Army surrenders at Stalingrad.

February 8—The Japanese evacuate Guadalcanal.

February 16—Kharkov falls back into Russian hands.

April 18—An American *Lockheed P-38E Lightning* shoots down a bomber carrying Admiral Yamamoto, Commander of the Japanese fleet, the man who conceived the attack on Pearl Harbor.

May 7—Anglo-American troops enter Tunis.

May 12—The last German-Italian troops leave Africa.

May 17—A group of *Avro Lancasters* boldly bombs the Moehne and Eder dams which collapse causing heavy floods.

May 24—After many unsuccessful attempts, Admiral Doenitz puts a stop to German submarine warfare against Allied convoys in the Atlantic.

June 11–12—The islands of Pantelleria and Lampedusa are occupied by the Allies.

June 30—First American landing in New Guinea.

July 5—Last American offensive on the Eastern front begins in the Kursk Region.

July 10—Anglo-American landing in Southern Sicily.

July 15—Russian counteroffensive at Orel drives back last German attacks.

July 19—Mussolini and Hitler meet at Feltre. Rome is bombed by American airplanes.

July 22—Palermo falls to the Allies.

July 24–August 3—Heavy air raids on Hamburg. Entire sections of the city are completely destroyed.

July 25—Mussolini is driven from power and arrested. The fascist regime collapses. Badoglio is in charge of the new Italian government.

August 3–17—Italian and German troops evacuate Sicily.

August 11–24—Churchill-Roosevelt conference at Quebec.

August 17—German base of Peenemünde, where secret military experiments were being carried out *(V2)*, is bombed.

August 18—Sicily is occupied by the Allies.

August 19—Allied landing at Dieppe is driven back by the Germans.

September 3—A secret armistice between Italy and the Allies is signed at Cassibile, near Syracuse. Allied troops land at Reggio Calabria.

September 7—The retreating Germans entrench on the other side of the Dnieper.

September 8—The armistice between Italy and the Allies is made public.

September 9—U.S. 5th Army lands near Salerno. The Italian fleet moves from La Spezia to Malta. During the voyage the battleship *Roma* is sunk by German *Do 217* bombers. Germans disarm Italian troops in Central and Northern Italy.

September 10—Rome is garrisoned by German troops. King Victor Emanuel II and Badoglio flee.

September 12—Mussolini is prisoner of the new Italian government at Campo Imperatore (Gran Sasso). Skorzeny, an SS Major, frees Mussolini and brings him to Germany.

September 20—Bari is occupied by the British.

September 23—Mussolini establishes and is proclaimed head of the Socialist Republic of Italy in Northern Italy, which is still under German control.

September 25—Russian troops reach Smolensk.

October 1—Naples is freed from German occupation.

October 5—Germans abandon Sardinia and Corsica.

October 8—Russian troops cross the Dnieper.

October 13—The Badoglio government declares war on Germany.

End of October—Allies break through the new German front on the Volturno. German troops retreat to the Cassino-Ortona line.

November 6—Russian troops reoccupy Kiev.

November 18—The R.A.F. begins systematic air raids on Berlin.

November 20–25—American invasion of the Gilbert islands.

November 22–26—Roosevelt, Churchill and Chiang Kai-shek meet for the Cairo conference.

November 23—King Peter II is deposed by Tito, leader of the Yugoslav partisan resistance against the Germans, who proclaims the "People's Republic of Yugoslavia."

November 26—Eisenhower is named Commander in Chief of Anglo-American landing forces in Europe.

November 28—Stalin, Churchill and Roosevelt meet for the Teheran conference.

1944

January 22—Anglo-American troops land at Anzio-Nettuno. Their advance is blocked by German troops.

January 30—American offensive in the Marshall Islands.

February 15—Monte Cassino Abbey is destroyed by Allied artillery fire. The "Battle of Cassino" begins (it will last until May 17).

March 2—Japanese abandon Manila.

March 5—In order to cover their retreat, the Germans damage dams in Holland, causing widespread floods.

March 26—In its advance, the Russian Army overruns the Rumanian frontier.

April 30—The Crimea is liberated.

May 14-17—Allied troops break through the German front in Central Italy ("Gustav Line") and occupy Cassino on the seventeenth.

June 4—Anglo-American troops enter Rome, which has been evacuated by the Germans.

June 6—Allies land on the coast of Normandy between Cherbourg and Caen, protected by 11,000 aircraft (among which are 2500 fighter planes and 1500 bombers); 2395 transport planes land 3 airborne divisions.

June 9—Russian offensive against Finland begins.

June 13—The new German flying bombs *(V1)* fall on London for the first time. Others will follow, an average of 200 a day totaling about 8000 by September. Anti-aircraft artillery shot down 1886; 1847 shot down by fighter planes.

June 19-20—Air-Naval battle (many American *F6F-3 Hellcat*s participate) in the Philippine Sea, which results in the sinking of 3 Japanese carriers and 400 planes.

June 22—Soviet Army resumes its offensive on the Eastern front.

July 9—British occupy Caen.

July 18—The *Messerschmitt 262,* the first German jet-fighter plane, enters action.

July 20—The plot to murder Hitler in his German headquarters, organized by Colonel Von Stauffenberg, fails. Soon after Hitler and Mussolini will meet in the same place.

July 29—Turkey severs diplomatic relations with Germany.

July 31—Americans break through German lines at Avranches in Normandy.

August 11—British enter Florence.

August 15—Anglo-American landing on the French coast between Toulon and Nice.

August 20—American troops reach the outskirts of Paris.

August 23—A coup d'état takes place in Rumania. King Michael orders that all resistance to Russian troops cease.

August 25—General de Gaulle's Free French troops enter Paris, fighting the retreating Germans. Rumania declares war on Germany.

September 2—British attack on the "Gothic Line" (Viareggio-Rimini).

September 4—Finland severs relations with Germany and asks Russia for an armistice.

September 8—The first of the new and perfected *V2* flying bombs fall on London. Altogether, more than 1000 were launched. Bulgaria declares war on Germany and asks the Soviet government for an armistice.

September 12—Having crossed the borders of Belgium and Holland, the Allies head for Aquisgranum.

September 17—The largest paratrooper and airborne-troop operation takes place (3 divisions: the British 1st and the American 82nd and 101st) at Eindhoven and Nijmegen in Holland, behind German lines.

September 22—Russians occupy the Estonian capital of Tallinn.

October 4—Allies occupy Greece.

October 9—End of the Dumbarton Oaks conference. The United Nations Organization will replace the League of Nations.

October 10-13—Air-naval battle between American and Japanese at Formosa.

October 13—Riga falls to the Russians.

October 14—British enter Athens.

October 19—Japanese *Kamikaze* in *Mitsubishi A6M3 Zero* and *Ki-51* are used for the first time.

October 20—Belgrade is occupied by Russian troops.

October 22—American troops occupy Aquisgranum.

October 24-26—Air and Naval battle at Leyte. The Japanese attempt to stop American troops from landing in the Philippines is unsuccessful. Americans begin to win back the islands.

October 28—Armistice between the Allies and Bulgaria.

November 2—Germans evacuate Belgium.

November 7—Roosevelt is reelected President of the United States.

November 11—Churchill and de Gaulle meet in Paris.

November 12—British *Avro Lancasters* sink the battleship *Tirpitz* in the fiord of Tromsö.

November 24—Allies occupy Strasbourg. Air attack (*Boeing B-29*s) on Tokyo.

December 16—German counteroffensive, which will last about a month, begins in the Ardennes.

December 29—Russians take Budapest.

December 30—Hungary declares war on Germany.

1945

January 1—Last massive German bomber attack on Allied lines. 200 out of 800 aircraft will not return.

January 12—Russians launch an offensive against Baranovichi (Galicia) and break through the German front in Poland.

January 17—Germans abandon Warsaw.

January 20—Russian troops reach Cracow. Russian-Hungarian armistice is signed.

February 3—Massive Allied air attack on Berlin with 959 *B-17*'s.

February 4-11—Stalin, Roosevelt and Churchill meet for the Yalta conference.

February 11—Breslau surrounded by the Russians.

February 13—Russian occupation of Budapest.

February 13-14—Massive R.A.F. attack on Dresden (1400 bombers) which is almost entirely destroyed (about 200,000 victims).

February 19—American landing on Iwo Jima.

February 22—Allies strike a massive offensive, with 9000 aircraft, on key communication centers in Germany, Austria and Italy.

March 3—Finland declares war on Germany.

March 7—American troops enter Cologne.

March 9—Tokyo is bombed by 334 American *Superfortresses,* which destroy ¼ of the city.

March 17-29—Americans cross the Remagen bridge on the Rhine and advance on the entire front towards the center of Germany, conquering Frankfurt. At the same time the coal fields of the Saar are occupied.

April 1—American troops land on Okinawa.

April 9—Allied offensive to liberate Northern Italy from German occupation begins.

April 12—Roosevelt dies. Truman succeeds him as President of the United States.

April 13-16—Russian occupation of Vienna. On the sixteenth, final Russian offensive against Berlin begins.

April 19—Americans reach Leipzig.

April 21—German troops evacuate Bologna. Collapse of German resistance in Northern Italy.

April 23—U.S. 5th Army crosses the Po river.

April 25—Russian and American troops meet at Torgau on the Elbe.

April 26—Berlin is surrounded by Russian troops. Milan is liberated.

April 28—While attempting to flee to Switzerland, Mussolini is captured by Italian partisans at Dongo and shot at Giulino di Mezzegre on Lake Como.

April 29—Armistice signed at Caserta between the Allies and the German troops still on Italian territory.

April 30—Hitler's suicide in Berlin. Admiral Doenitz succeeds him as Commander in Chief of German armed forces. Munich is occupied by the Americans.

May 1—Yugoslav troops, under Tito's command, occupy Trieste and Istria.

May 2—The defenders of Berlin surrender to the Russians.

May 3—British troops, under Lord Mountbatten's command, occupy Burma and reach Rangoon after a tough offensive which began in India.

May 4—German Army on the Western front surrenders to British Marshal Montgomery, near Lüneburg.

May 7-9—Germans sign an unconditional surrender to the Allies at Reims and, on the ninth, in Berlin, to the Russians.

July 17-August 2—Truman, Stalin and Churchill meet for the Potsdam conference. East Germany is assigned to the U.S.S.R. (Northern part of Eastern Prussia) and to Poland (up to the Oder-Neisse Line).

July 22—The Paris peace conference begins. Peace treaties with Italy, Finland, Hungary, Rumania and Bulgaria are drawn up.

August 6—An American *B-29* drops the first atom bomb on Hiroshima.

August 9—Another *B-29* drops the second atom bomb on Nagasaki.

August 15—Japan's unconditional surrender.

September 2—Japanese surrender signed on the American battleship *Missouri.*

BIBLIOGRAPHY

Books

C. Dollfus - H. Bouche, *Histoire de l'aéronautique*, Paris, L'Illustration, 1932.

Luigi Mancini, *Grande enciclopedia aeronautica*, Milano, Edizioni Aeronautica, 1936.

Jean Mermoz, *Mes vols*, Paris, Flammarion, 1937.

Igor I. Sikorsky, *The Story of the Winged-S*, London, Robert Hale Ltd., 1939.

René Cornille, *La guerre aérienne*, Paris, Les Editions de France, 1942.

Frank Cunningham, *Sky Master, The Story of Donald Douglas*, Philadelphia, Dorrance and Co., 1943.

J. Hébrard, *Vingt-cinq années d'aviation militaire (1920-1945)*, voll. I, II, Paris, Editions Albin Michel, 1946.

Voyenno-Vozdushnye Sily SSSR, 1918-1948, Moscow, Voenizdat, 1948.
Mosca, Voenizdat, 1948.

Raymond Saladin, *Les temps héroïques de l'aviation*, Paris, Editions Arcadiennes, 1949.

Giuseppe Santoro, *L'aeronautica italiana nella seconda guerra mondiale*, vol. I, Roma, Editore Danesi, 1950.

José Goma, *Historia de la aeronáutica española*, Madrid, Gráficas Huerfanos Ejército del Aire, 1950.

I primi voli .di guerra nel mondo, edited by Ufficio Storico dell'Aeronautica Militare, Roma, 1951.

Gene Gurney, *The War in the Air*, Los Angeles, Floyd Clymer, 1952.

Adolf Galland, *Die Ersten und die Letzten*, Darmstadt, Schneekluth Verlag, 1953.

General View of Japanese Military Aircraft in the Pacific War, Tokio, Aireview, Kantosha Co. Ltd., 1953.

Charles Lindbergh, *The Spirit of St. Louis*, New York, Scribner, 1953.

Lloyd Morris - Kendall Smith, *Ceiling Unlimited: The Story of American Aviation from Kitty Hawk to Supersonics*, New York, Macmillan Co., 1953.

J. Hébrard, *L'aviation des origines à nos jours*, Paris, Robert Laffont, 1954.

D. M. Desoutter, *All about Aircraft*, London, Faber & Faber Ltd., 1955.

John W. Underwood, *The World's Famous Racing Aircraft*, Los Angeles, Floyd Clymer, 1955.

Rodolfo Gentile, *Storia delle operazioni aeree nella Seconda Guerra Mondiale (1939-1945)*, Roma, Editrice Ali, 2nd edition, 1956.,

Bruce Robertson, *Aircraft Camouflage and Markings 1907-1954*, Letchworth, Herts, Harleyford Publications Ltd., 1956.

Henrique Dumont Villaves, *Foto-história de Santos Dumont 1898-1910*, São Paulo, Comp. Melhoramentos de São Paulo, 1956.

Henrique Dumont Villaves, *Santos-Dumont, Il Padre dell'aviazione* (Italian edition), São Paulo, Comp. Melhoramentos de São Paulo, 1956.

William Green, *Famous Fighters of the Second World War*, voll. I, II, London, Macdonald & Co. (Publishers) Ltd., 1957-62.

Giuseppe Santoro, *L'aeronautica italiana nella Seconda Guerra Mondiale*, vol. II, Milano, Edizioni Esse, 1957.

German Military Aircraft in the Second World War, Tokio, Aireview, Kantosha Co. Ltd., 1958.

Tadashi Nozawa, *Encyclopedia of Japanese Aircraft 1900-1945*, 5 voll., Tokio, Shuppan-Kyodo, 1958-66.

Charles Wilson - William Reader, *Men and Machines - A History of D. Napier & Son, Engineers, Ltd., 1808-1958*, London, Weidenfeld and Nicolson, 1958.

William Green, *Famous Bombers of the Second World War*, voll. I, II, London, Macdonald & Co. (Publishers) Ltd., 1959-60.

A. J. Jackson, *British Civil Aircraft 1919-59*, voll. I, II, London, Putnam & Co. Ltd., 1959-60.

Peter Lewis, *Squadron Histories: RFC, RNAS, & RAF since 1912*, London, Putnam & Co. Ltd., 1959.

Arch Whitehouse, *The Years of the Sky Kings*, Garden City, N.Y., Doubleday & Co., 1959.

Charles H. Gibbs-Smith, *The Aeroplane: An Historical Survey of its Origins and Development*, London, Science Museum, Her Majesty's Stationery Office, 1960.

William Green, *War Planes of the Second World War*, voll. I-X, London, Macdonald & Co. (Publishers) Ltd., 1960-68.

W. M. Lamberton, *Fighter Aircrafts of the 1914-1918 War*, Letchworth, Herts, Harleyford Publications Ltd., 1960.

Henry R. Palmer Jr., *This was Air Travel*, Superior Publishing Company, 1960.

Piaggio & C., *75 anni di attività*, Genova, Piaggio & C., 1960.

John W. R. Taylor, *Warplanes of the World*, London, Ian Allan Ltd., 1960.

Ray Wagner, *American Combat Planes*, Garden City, N.Y., Doubleday & Co., 1960-68.

Arch Whitehouse, *The Years of the War Birds*, Garden City, N.Y., Doubleday & Co., 1960.

Peter W. Brooks, *The Modern Airliner*, London, Putnam & Co. Ltd., 1961.

Francis K. Mason, *Hawker Aircraft since 1920*, London, Putnam & Co. Ltd., 1961.

Fokker - The Man and the Aircraft, Letchworth, Herts, Harleyford Publications Ltd., 1961.

United States Army and Air Force Fighters 1916-1961, Letchworth, Herts, Harleyford Publications Ltd., 1961.

Derek Wood - Derek Dempster, *The Narrow Margin, The Definitive Story of the Battle of Britain*, London, Arrow Books Ltd., 1961.

Joseph P. Juptner, *U.S. Civil Aircrafts*, voll. I-IV, Fallbrook, California, Aero Publishers Inc., 1962-67.

W. M. Lamberton, *Reconnaissance & Bomber Aircraft of the 1914-1918 War*, Letchworth, Herts, Harleyford Publications Ltd., 1962.

G. Bignozzi - B. Catalanotto, *Storia degli aerei d'Italia*, Roma, Editrice Cielo, 1962.

Maynard Crosby, *Flight Plan for Tomorrow. The Douglas Story: A Condensed History*, Santa Monica, Douglas Aircraft Co., 1962.

272

Peter Gray - Owen Thetford, *German Aircraft of the First World War*, London, Putnam & Co. Ltd., 1962.

A. J. Jackson, *De Havilland Aircraft*, London, Putnam & Co. Ltd., 1962.

Robert A. Kilmarx, *A History of Soviet Air Power*, London, Faber & Faber, 1962.

Asher Lee, *The Soviet Air Force*, New York, The John Day Co. Inc., 1962.

Peter Lewis, *British Aircraft 1909-14*, London, Putnam & Co. Ltd., 1962.

Paul R. Matt, *U.S. Navy & Marine Corps Fighters 1918-62*, Letchworth, Herts, Harleyford Publications Ltd., 1962.

Kenneth Munson, *Aircraft of World War II*, London, Ian Allan Ltd., 1962.

John Stroud, *Annals of British and Commonwealth Air Transport*, London, Putnam & Co. Ltd., 1962.

John Stroud, *Soviet Transport Aircraft since 1945*, London, Putnam & Co. Ltd., 1962.

F. G. Swanborough, *Turbine-Engined Airlines of the World*, London, Temple Press Book Ltd., 1962.

John W. R. Taylor, *Aircraft Annual*, London, Ian Allan Ltd., 1962.

Owen Thetford, *Aircraft of the Royal Air Force since 1918*, London, Putnam & Co. Ltd., 3rd edition, 1962.

Owen Thetford, *British Naval Aircraft Since 1912*, London, Putnam & Co. Ltd., 1962.

The American Heritage History of Flight, New York, American Heritage Publ. Co. Inc., 1962.

Über den Wolken, München, Sudwest-Verlag, 1962.

Rosario Abate - Giulio Lazzati, *I velivoli Macchi dal 1912 al 1963*, Milano, Ali nel Tempo, 1963.

Charles H. Gibbs-Smith, *The Wright Brothers*, London, Science Museum, Her Majesty's Stationery Office, 1963.

Kenneth Munson, *Aircraft the World Over*, London, Ian Allan Ltd., 1963.

Seventy Fighters of the II World War, Tokio, Aireview, Kantosha Co. Ltd., 1963.

Robert T. Smith, *Classic Biplanes*, New York, Sports Car Press Ltd., 1963.

Gordon Swanborough - Peter M. Bowers, *United States Military Aircraft since 1909*, London, Putnam & Co. Ltd., 1963.

Jonathan Thompson, *Italian Civil and Military Aircraft 1930-45*, Fallbrook, California, Aero Publishers Inc., 1963.

Don C. Wigton, *From Jenny to Jet*, New York, Bonanza Books, 1963.

R. E. G. Davis, *A History of the World's Airlines*, London, Oxford University Press, 1964.

Leu Morgan - R. P. Shannon, *The Planes the Aces Flew*, New York, Arco Publishing Co. Inc., 1964.

Douglas H. Robinson, *LZ 129 Hindenburg*, Dallas, Morgan Aviation Books, 1964.

F. G. Swanborough, *Vertical Flight Aircraft of the World*, Fallbrook, California, Aero Publishers Inc., 1964.

58 Bombers of the II World War, Tokio, Aireview, Kantosha Co. Ltd., 1965.

J. M. Bruce, *War Planes of the First World War: Fighters*, voll. I-III, London, Macdonald & Co. (Publishers) Ltd., 1965-69.

Roger A. Caras, *Wings of Gold. The Story of the U.S. Naval Aviation*, Philadelphia, Lippincott Co., 1965.

Thomas R. Funderburk, *The Fighters: Men and Machines of the First Air War*, New York, Grosset & Dunlap, 1965.

Paul E. Garber, *The National Aeronautical Collections*, Washington, D.C., Smithsonian Institution, National Air Museum, 10th edition, 1965.

Charles H. Gibbs-Smith, *The World's First Aeroplane Flights*, London, Science Museum, Her Majesty's Stationery Office, 1965.

William Green - Gerald Pollinger, *The Aircraft of the World*, London, Macdonald & Co. (Publishers) Ltd., 3rd edition, 1965.

Historical Aviation Album, voll. I-VIII, Temple City, California, Paul R. Matt, 1965-70.

Hugo Hooftman, *Russian Aircraft*, Fallbrook, California, Aero Publishers Inc., 1965.

A. J. Jackson, *Avro Aircraft since 1908*, London, Putnam & Co. Ltd., 1965.

A. R. Weyl, *Fokker: The Creative Years*, London, Putnam & Co. Ltd., 1965.

60 Attack / Reconnaissance Aircraft of the II World War, Tokio, Aireview, Kantosha Co. Ltd., 1966.

Peter M. Bowers, *Boeing Aircraft since 1916*, London, Putnam & Co. Ltd., 1966.

G. R. Duval, *British Flying-Boats and Amphibians 1909-1952*, London, Putnam & Co. Ltd., 1966.

Charles H. Gibbs-Smith, *A Directory and Nomenclature of the First Aeroplanes 1809 to 1909*, London, Science Museum, Her Majesty's Stationery Office, 1966.

Charles H. Gibbs-Smith, *Aeronautics, 1: Early Flying up to the Reims Meeting*, London, Science Museum, Her Majesty's Stationery Office, 1966.

Charles H. Gibbs-Smith, *The Invention of the Aeroplane 1799-1909*, London, Faber & Faber Ltd., 1966.

Lloyd S. Jones, *U.S. Bombers B-1, B-70*, Fallbrook, California, Aero Publishers Inc., 1966.

G. W. B. Lacey, *Aeronautics, 2: Flying since 1913*, London, Science Museum, Her Majesty's Stationery Office, 1966.

Philip J. R. Moyes, *Bombers Squadrons of the R.A.F.*, London, Macdonald & Co. (Publishers) Ltd., 1966.

Kenneth Munson, *Bombers, Patrol and Transport Aircraft*, London, Blandford Press Ltd., 1966.

Kenneth Munson, *Fighters, Attack and Training Aircraft*, London, Blandford Press Ltd., 1966.

Kenneth Munson, *Warplanes of Yesteryear*, London, Ian Allan Ltd., 1966.

W. T. O'Dea, *Aeronautica*, London, Science Museum, Her Majesty's Stationery Office, 1966.

Page Shamburger, *Classic Monoplanes*, New York, Sports Car Press Ltd., 1966.

John Stroud, *European Transport Aircraft since 1910*, London, Putnam & Co. Ltd., 1966.

W. J. Tuck, *Power to Fly*, London, Science Museum, Her Majesty's Stationery Office, 1966.

Kenneth Munson, *Civil Airlines since 1946*, London, Blandford Press Ltd., 1967.

Kenneth Munson, *Private Aircraft since 1946*, London, Blandford Press Ltd., 1967.

C. H. Barnes, *Shorts Aircraft since 1900*, London, Putnam & Co. Ltd., 1967.

Thomas E. Doll, *U.S. Navy Markings W. W. II - Pacific Theater*, Sun Valley, Aeronautica John W. Caler, 1967.

Charles H. Gibbs-Smith, *A Brief History of Flying*, London, Science Museum, Her Majesty's Stationery Office, 1967.

Charles H. Gibbs-Smith, *Leonardo Da Vinci's Aeronautics*, London, Science Museum, Her Majesty's Stationery Office, 1967.

William Green, *The World Guide to Combat Planes*, voll. I, II, Garden City, N.Y., Doubleday & Co., 1967.

John Killen, *The Luftwaffe, A History*, London, Frederick Muller Ltd., 1967.

Reed Kinert, *Racing Planes and Air Races*, voll. I-IV, Fallbrook, California, Aero Publishers Inc., 1967-68.

J. V. Mizrahi, *Dive and Torpedo Bombers*, Northridge, California, Sentry Book, 1967.

Kenneth Munson, *Civil Aircraft of Yesteryear*, London, Ian Allan Ltd., 1967.

Heinz J. Nowarra, *Die Sowjetischen Flugzeuge 1941-1966*, München, J. F. Lehmanus Verlag, 1967.

Edmond Petit, *Histoire mondiale de l'aviation*, Paris, Librairie Hachette, 1967.

Harald Penrose, *British Aviation: The Pioneer Years*, London, Putnam & Co. Ltd., 1967.

Karl Ries Jr., *Markierungen und Tarnanstriche der Luftwaffe in 2. Weltkrieg*, voll. I-III, Mainz, Verlag Dieter Hoffmann, 1967.

Bruce Robertson, *Aircraft Markings of the World 1912-1967*, Letchworth, Herts, Harleyford Publications Ltd., 1967.

Kenn C. Rust, *The Ninth Air Force in World War II*, Fallbrook, California, Aero Publishers Inc., 1967.

John W. R. Taylor, *Aircraft, Aircraft*, London, The Hamlyn Publishing Group Ltd., 1967.

André Achard - Jack Tribot-Laspierre, *Répertoire des Aéronefs de construction française pour la période 1890-1967*, Paris, Doc. Air Espace, Centre de Documentation de l'Armement, 1968.

Heimer Emde - Carlo Demand, *Conquerors of the Air*, Lausanne, Edita S.A., 1968.

Uve Feist - René J. Francillon, *Luftwaffe in World War II*, Fallbrook, California, Aero Publishers Inc., 1968.

René J. Francillon, *American Fighters of World War II*, Windsor, Hylton Lacy, 1968.

Charles Gablehouse, *Helicopters and Autogyros*, London, Frederick Muller Ltd., 1968.

Charles H. Gibbs-Smith, *Sir George Cayley 1773-1857*, London, Science Museum, Her Majesty's Stationery Office, 1968.

A. J. Jackson, *Blackburn Aircraft since 1909*, London, Putnam & Co. Ltd., 1968.

Douglas J. Ingells, *Tin Goose, The Fabulous Ford Trimotor*, Fallbrook, California, Aero Publishers Inc., 1968.

Ronald Miller - Davis Sawers, *The Technical Development of Modern Aviation*, London, Routledge & Kegan Paul, 1968.

E. Moreau-Berillon, *L'aviation française 1914-1940, Ses escadrilles - Ses Insignes*, voll. I-VIII, Paris, E. Moreau-Berillon.

Philip J. R. Moyes, *Royal Air Force Bombers of World War II*, voll. I, II, Windsor, Hylton Lacy, 1968.

Kenneth Munson, *Aircraft of World War I*, London, Ian Allan Ltd., 1968.

Kenneth Munson, *Bombers, Patrol and Reconnaissance Aircraft, 1914-1919*, London, Blandford Press Ltd., 1968.

Kenneth Munson, *Fighters, Attack and Training Aircraft, 1914-1919*, London, Blandford Press Ltd., 1968.

Kenneth Munson, *Helicopters and other Rotorcraft since 1907*, London, Blandford Press Ltd., 1968.

Heinz J. Nowarra, *Eisernes Kreuz und Balkenkreuz*, Mainz, Verlag Dieter Hoffmann, 1968.

Alfred Price, *German Air Force Bombers of World War II*, voll. I, II, Windsor, Hylton Lacy, 1968-69.

John B. Rae, *Climb to Greatness. The American Aircraft Industry, 1920-1960*, Cambridge, USA, Massachusetts Institute of Technology Press, 1968.

Page Schamburger - Joe Christy, *Command the Horizon*, New York, A. S. Barnes and Co., 1968.

Heinz A. F. Schmidt, *Historische Flugzeuge*, voll. I, II, Stuttgart, Motorbuch-Verlag, 1968-70.

Robert Scharff - Walter S. Taylor, *Over Land and Sea: Glenn A. Curtiss*, New York, David McKay Co. Inc., 1968.

G. R. Simonson, *The History of the American Aircraft Industry (Anthology)*, Cambridge, USA, Massachusetts Institute of Technology Press, 1968.

Gordon Swanborough - Peter M. Bowers, *United States Navy Aircraft since 1911*, London, Putnam & Co. Ltd., 1968.

John W. R. Taylor, *Aircraft Sixty Nine*, London, Ian Allan Ltd., 1968.

John W. R. Taylor, *Civil Aircraft of the World*, London, Ian Allan Ltd., 1968.

John W. R. Taylor, *Helicopters and Vtol Aircraft*, Garden City, N.Y., Doubleday & Co., 1968.

John W. R. Taylor, *Pictorial History of the RAF*, voll. I, II, London, Ian Allan Ltd., 1968.

Lowell Thomas - Lowell Thomas Jr., *Famous First Flights that changed History*, Garden City, N.Y., Doubleday & Co., 1968.

Donald W. Thorpe, *Japanese Army Air Force Camouflage and Markings World War II*, Fallbrook, California, Aero Publishers Inc., 1968.

Martin C. Windrow, *German Air Force Fighters of World War Two*, voll. I, II, Windsor, Hylton Lacy, 1968-69.

Aircam "Specials" Series, voll. I-VII, Canterbury, Osprey Publications Ltd., 1969-71.

Aircam Aviation Series, voll. I-XVIII, Canterbury, Osprey Publications Ltd., 1969-71.

Jane's 1909-1969: 100 Significant Aircraft, London, Jane's All the World's Aircraft Publishing Co. Ltd., 1969.

C. F. Andrews, *Vickers Aircraft since 1908*, London, Putnam & Co. Ltd., 1969.

Michael J. F. Bowyer, *Fighting Colours: RAF Fighter Camouflage and Markings 1937-1969*, London, Patrick Stephens, 1969.

Ulrich Keller, *Propellerflugzeuge im Dienste des Schweizerischen Fluglinienverkehrs 1919-1968*, Basel und Stuttgart, Birkhäuser Verlag, 1969.

John Killen, *A History of Marine Aviation*, London, Frederick Muller Ltd., 1969.

Francis K. Mason, *British Fighters of World War II*, Windsor, Hylton Lacy, 1969.

J. V. Mizrahi, *Carrier Fighters*, voll. I, II, Northridge, California, Sentry Book, 1969.

Kenneth Munson, *Bombers, Patrol and Transport Aircraft, 1939-45*, London, Blandford Press Ltd., 1969.

Kenneth Munson, *Fighters, Attack and Training Aircraft, 1939-45*, London, Blandford Press Ltd., 1969.

Kenneth Munson, *Pioneer Aircraft 1903-1914*, London, Blandford Press Ltd., 1969.

Houston Peterson, *See Them Flying*, New York, Richard W. Baron Publishing Co. Inc., 1969.

Harald Penrose, *British Aviation: The Great War and Armistice*, London, Putnam & Co. Ltd., 1969.

John W. R. Taylor - Philip J. R. Moyes, *Pictorial History of the R.A.F.*, voll. I, II, London, Ian Allan Ltd., 1969.

John W. R. Taylor, *Combat Aircraft of the World*, London, George Reinbird Ltd., 1969.

Don Vorderman, *The Great Air Races*, Garden City, N.Y., Doubleday & Co., 1969.

R. J. Francillon, *Japanese Aircraft of the Pacific War*, London, Putnam & Co. Ltd., 1970.

Roger A. Freeman, *The Mighty Eighth - A History of the U.S. 8th Army Air Force*, London, Macdonald & Co. (Publishers) Ltd., 1970.

William Green, *Warplanes of the Third Reich*, London, Macdonald & Co. (Publishers) Ltd., 1970.

International Academy of Astronautics, *Astronautical Multilingual Dictionary*, Praha, Academia - Amsterdam, Elsevier, P.C., 1970.

Paul Lambermont - Anthony Pirie, *Helicopters and Autogyros of the World*, London, Cassel & Co. Ltd., revised edition, 1970.

Francis K. Mason - Martin C. Windrow, *Air Facts and Feats*, London, Guinness Superlatives Ltd., 1970.

Kenneth Munson, *Fighters between the Wars 1919-39*, London, Blandford Press Ltd., 1970.

John Rawlings, *Fighter Squadrons of the R.A.F.*, London, Macdonald & Co. (Publishers) Ltd., 1970.

Carlo Rossi Fantonetti, *Le grandi battaglie aeree della seconda guerra mondiale*, Milano, Arnoldo Mondadori Editore, 1970.

The Lore of Flight, Gothenburg, Tre Tryckare Cagner & Co., 1970.

The Military Balance 1970-1971, London, The Institute for Strategic Studies, 1970.

Derek N. James, *Gloster Aircraft since 1917*, London, Putnam & Co. Ltd., 1971.

H. F. King, *The World's Fighters*, London, The Bodley Head Ltd., 1971.

Peter Lewis, *British Racing and Record-Breaking Aircraft*, London, Putnam & Co. Ltd., 1971.

John Stroud, *The World's Airlines*, London, The Bodley Head Ltd., 1971.

Dornier-Flugzeuge, München, Luftfahrt-Verlag, Walter Zuerl, s.d.

G. W. Haddow - P. M. Grosz, *The German Giants*, London, Putnam & Co. Ltd., s.d.

Hugo Hooftman, *Alles over de Fokker Friendship*, Amsterdam, L. J. Veen's Uitgeversmij N.V., s.d.

Messerschmitt-Flugzeuge, München, Luftfahrt-Verlag, Walter Zuerl, s.d.

Truman C. Weaver, *62 Rare Racing Planes*, New York, Arenar Publications, s.d.

Periodicals

"Air Classic", Canoga Park, Challange Publications, Inc.

"Aircraft Illustrated", Shefferton, Ian Allan Ltd.

"Air Pictorial", London, Air League.

"Air Progress", New York, The Condé Nast Publications, Inc.

"Ala Rotante", Roma, Costruzioni Aeronautiche Giovanni Agusta S.p.A.

"Aviation Magazine International", Paris, Union de Presse Européenne.

"Aviation Week & Space Technology", New York, McGraw-Hill.

"Aviazione di Linea Aeronautica e Spazio", Roma.

"Camouflage & Markings", London, Ducimus Books Ltd.

"Cross & Cockade", Leicester, Society of World War I Aero Historians.

"Der Flieger", Postfach, Luftfahrt-Verlag, Walter Zuerl.

"Esso Air World", New York, Esso International Inc.

"Flight International", London, IPC Business Press Ltd.

"Flug Revue - Flugwelt", Stuttgart, Vereinigte Motor-Verlage GmbH.

"Flying Review International", London, Haymarket Press Ltd.

"Icare, Revue de l'Aviation Française", Orly.

"Interavia", Genève, Interavia S.A.

"Interconair Aviazione Marina", Genova, Interconair S.A.

"Koku-Fan", Tokio, Bunrin-do Co. Ltd.

"I primi cinquant'anni dell'aviazione italiana", Roma, Rivista Aeronautica.

"L'Album du Fanatique de l'Aviation", Paris, Editions Larivière.

"Profile", Windsor, Profile Publications Ltd.

"The Aeroplane", London.

Annuals

"Aerospace Facts and Figures", Aerospace Industries Association of America Inc. - Aviation Week & Space Technology, New York, McGraw-Hill Publication.

"Jane's All The World's Aircraft", London, Sampson Low, Merston & Co. Ltd., from 1909.

"The Aerospace Year Book", Washington, D.C., Book Inc., from 1922.

INDEX

284

INDEX BY NATION OF AIRCRAFT ILLUSTRATED